TENNESSEE
GENEALOGICAL RECORDS:

Records of Early Settlers
From State and County Archives

By
EDYTHE RUCKER WHITLEY

Baltimore
GENEALOGICAL PUBLISHING CO., INC.
1981

Copyright © 1980
Genealogical Publishing Co., Inc.
Baltimore, Maryland
All Rights Reserved
Second Printing: Baltimore, 1981
Library of Congress Catalogue Card Number 79-67871
International Standard Book Number 0-8063-0873-7
Made in the United States of America

FOREWORD

DYTHE R. WHITLEY'S *Tennessee Genealogical Records* brings together in one volume many documents copied from records either at the State Archives in Nashville or at over twenty county courthouses. Originally compiled in the 1930s, in a series of eleven pamphlets, this valuable material has never before been available to the general public. It is here presented in a totally restructured form, and is now in easy reach of the researcher.

The Revolutionary warrants, original grants, and certificates of survey are helpful not only in establishing Revolutionary service, but in locating elusive emigrants from North Carolina and Virginia. In the case of the warrants, many heirs are named in the notes concerning sales of the original warrants.

While the many petitions printed herein do not provide vital statistics, they do place individuals in a particular place at a definite time and tell something of the interests and concerns of the communities in which the signers lived. The abstracts of pension reports are helpful in tracing migrations of various individuals.

In addition to notes on the formation and boundaries of many of the early counties, Mrs. Whitley has gathered together a voluminous collection of will abstracts, tombstone inscriptions, deed abstracts, court minutes, and marriage bonds. The latter not only show the name of the prospective bride and groom, but often give the name of a male relative.

In transcribing Mrs. Whitley's work, every effort has been made to copy the names exactly as they were printed in the original pamphlets, including the spelling of various names. Even the name Benjamine *(sic)* has been transcribed as it appeared in the pamphlets.

ROBERT BARNES

TABLE OF CONTENTS

REVOLUTIONARY WARRANTS

All the original papers which have been abstracted and published in this section are from loose papers which were located
by the compiler in the State Archives in the nineteen-thirties,
stored in unclassified and unindexed boxes. All the papers were
cleaned and read thoroughly, with the vital items in each abstracted. The papers have now been refiled and some have been
laminated for preservation. They are in the State Archives
Division of the Tennessee State Library and Archives, Nashville.
Tennessee.

No. 645. Heirs of John Atkinson, a private, 228 acres. Issued
9 October 1820 by William Hill, Secty. of State, N.C. There
were two John Atkinsons in the army. One enlisted 24 April 1776
under Capt. White of the 6th Regt., for 2½ years, and served until Nov. 1778. For his services Warrant no. 645 was issued.
  The other John Atkinson enlisted 26 May 1777 under Capt.
Vanoy of the 10th Regt. for 3 years. This man was made a musician, June 1778 and a private again in Sept. 1778. On proof
being given that he died in service without heirs, the commissioners ordered Warrant # 794 be issued to the Trustees of the University of North Carolina.
  John Atkinson of Warrant 645 drew up a power of attorney on
28 July 1808 while living in Person or Orange Co., N.C. The
file contains several affidavits referring to John Atkinson of
Caswell Co., N.C. He is said to have died in 1822.

No. 663. Heirs of David Allen, 640 acres. Allen was a private
in the N. C. Continental Line. The land was granted and surveyed
from lands reserved for officers and soldiers of the said line,
by Act of N. C. General Assembly issued 27 March 1821.
  Deed dated 24 August 1808 states that Champion Allen of
Granville Co., N.C., lawful heir of David and Samuel Allen, both
of whom lived in Granville Co., and both of whom died in the
Rev. War, sells the above grant to Westwood A. Jones of Wake Co.,
N.C. Champion Allen seems to have been the eldest son of the
family. Mary Carvinner of Granville Co., N.C., in an affidavit
made 1821 stated that David Allen and his son Samuel Allen both
enlisted as soldiers in foot troops under Capt. Turner for two
years and six months and marched south and that they both died
between Savannah and Sunsbury, and neither ever returned to
their families.

No. 1013. Heirs of John Allen, lieutenant in N. C. Line. The
warrant was granted under Act of 1819 pertaining to military
lands and grants. John Whitehead and James Jones of Carteret
Co., N.C., stated that John Allen was a lieutenant in Capt. Caswell's Co., 5th Regt. of N.C. Line, and that Benjamin Allen was
his only true and lawful heir.

No. 3143. Heirs of Stephen Arthur, private in the N.C. Cont.
Line. 640 acres of land, assigned to Richard Barbour. Land was
in Sumner Co., on the south side of Caney fork of the Cumberland
River, in the Caney Fork Valley. 14 Sept. 1797.

No. 2038. Isaac Abbott, private in N.C. Cont. Line. 640 acres
assigned by Abbott, of Tennessee Co., N.C., to Rachel Hays on
12 May 1795. Land was on the north side of the Cumberland River
about one mile from Thomas Fletcher's. on the westfork of Red
River. Land was surveyed for Rachel Hays on 1 Nov. 1892 (sic).

No. 2343. John Artest, private in N.C. Line. Grant for his
services in the Cont. Line marked VOID. Grant was assigned to
George Henry Barger by Artest. 274 acres in Sumner Co. on Little Cedar and Ground Lick, near Capt. William Martin's northeast
corner. 28 Oct. 1792.

No. 4569. Lincoln Amey, private in N.C. Cont. Line. 9 Feb. 1797.
228 acres, later assigned by Amey to William Tinnon on 14 Feb.
(year not shown). Tinnon assigned it Joseph Doris on 1 March
1797, who then assigned it to James Haynes on 2 Aug. 1803.

No. 4568. John Amey, private in N.C. Cont. Line. 228 acres,
surveyed by Col. Martin Armstrong on 9 Feb. 1797, and assigned
to Sterling Brewer on 23 Feb. 1797. Brewer assigned it on 5
June 1797 to Thomas Johnson, who assigned it to Wm. Wills on 19
Feb. 1803.

No. 4566. Willis Anderson, private in N.C. Cont. Line of the
Rev. War. Col. Martin Armstrong surveyed the 640 acres on 9
Feb. 1797. Jeffrey Anderson assigned it to Sterling Brewer,
who on 4 March 1797 assigned it to William Tyrrell. In July
1807 Jno. Boyd, sheriff of Davidson Co., sold the land to satisfy a claim of William T. Lewis against William Tyrrell. This
sale was made to John P. McConnell. A note on the warrant states
that John Madarias, late captain in the Rev. War, knew Willis
Anderson a soldier in the N. C. Line.

No. 241. Frederick Alberty, ensign in the N.C. Line. 731 acres
for his services on 10 Dec. 1813, assigned to John Spencer on 25
Feb. 1818.

No. 664. Heirs of Samuel Allen, private in the N.C. Cont. Line.
27 March 1821, tract of land for his services. 18 April 1821,
Champion Allen assigned it to Allen Wilkins, who on 19 April
1821 assigned it to George Bradfield, who assigned it to Gern-
don Harralson on 12 Oct. 1821.

No. 1012. Heirs of Jonathan Allen, private in the line of this
state in the Rev. War. 640 acres on 10 Sept. 1821. Benjamin
Allen assigned land to John Roberts on 14 Sept. 1821. Roberts
assigned it on 21 Dec. 1821 to James Hart, who on 19 Dec. 1821
assigned it to James Welbourn. On 15 Jan. 1822 Welbourn assigned
it to Col. Newton Cannon.

No. 160. Heirs of John Ames, a private in the N.C. Cont. Line.
LO June 1808 640 acres granted for his services.

No. 151. John Lawson Arthur, sergeant in the N.C. Cont. Line.
428 acres granted 16 Dec. 1807. On reverse is statement that
on 12 May 1808, in Greene Co., N.C., Arthur assigned the warrant to Charles Carr and James Porter.

No. 135. Lanier Adams, private in N.C. Cont. Line. 640 acres
issued to his heirs on 19 Dec . 1806. William Adams, lawful

heir of Lanier Adams, assigned the warrant to Daffarn Davis.

No. 415. Heirs of Absolom Austin, private in N.C. Cont. Line. 640 acres surveted 14 Aug. 1820 and assigned by Mose Austin to Peter Williams on 26 Aug. 1820.

No. 542. Heirs of Richard Arkinson, private in N.C. Cont. Line, were issued a tract of land on 4 Sept. 1820.

No. 393. Heirs of John Adams, sergeant in the N.C. Cont. Line, were issued 1000 acres of land on 3 Aug. 1820. Attached statement of James Adams that on 18 June 1820 while living in Washington Co., N.C., he assigned the warrant to Darling Cherry of Martin Co., N.C. (Bounty Land).

No. 3702. Heirs of Simon Albright, 640 acres within the lands referred by law for the officers and soldiers of the N.C. Cont. Line. 1 Dec. 1789.

No. 4565. Heirs of John Augustus, private in N.C. Cont. Line. 640 acres issued 9 Feb. 1797. The heirs assigned it to Sterling Brewer who on 20 Feb. 1797 assigned it to William Tyrrell.

No. 4561. Jeffrey Arden, issued 228 acres of land from that reserved for officers and soldiers of the N.C. Cont. Line, on 9 Feb. 1797. Arden assigned it to Sterling Brewer on 24 Feb. 1797. Brewer assigned it to Morgan Brewer.

No. 4371. Heirs of Thomas Avent, private. 640 acres within the limits of land reserved by law for officers and soldiers of the N.C. Line, on 17 Dec. 1786. Assigned to Sterling Brewer on 7 Feb. 1797. Brewer assigned the land to Thomas Molloy.

No. 4318. John Jo. Alston, William Chy. Alston, and Aaron Davis Alston, heirs of William Alston, dec., a lieutenant-colonel in the N.C. Line. Issued 1646 acres of land within the limits of lands reserved by law for officers and soldiers of the Cont. Line. 14 Dec. 1796. Land assigned to Willis Alston by said heirs of William Alston on 22 April 1808.

No. 314. John Armstrong. William Maclin, Secretary of State for Tennessee authorized to lay off 111 acres of land on any unappropriated lands for David Winchester. This warrant issued from a grant to James Winchester and George Winchester for 200 acres of No. 171 bearing date 9 Jan. 1794. This warrant dated 26 May 1803. On the back was written: Nashville, 25 July 1807, "Invalid." J. Winchester was President of the Board of Commissioners for West Tennessee. This file contains a paper showing the following transfers appearing on the back of the original. Warrant No. 1722 required to lay off for John King, Sr., 1200 acres of land on Field's Creek on the **north** side of Cumberland Mountain. Surveyed by John Armstrong on 8 May 1797. Issued 16 April 1786. Thomas King assigned the land by Jno. King. Thomas assigned the land to Abraham Riston on 9 May 1787. On 9 May 1787, Riston assigned land to Jos. Dickson, who assigned the land to Wm. Meredith on 11 March 1790. Across the back is written "Invalid."
    No. 1027. 5000 acres to Micajah Thomas; marked "Invalid." Appears to have been assigned to Elijah Boddie who was not satisfied.
    No. 68. John Buchanan, for 100 acres, on Nov. 1802. Same warrant appears to have been rejected.
    No. 315. David Winchester has a warrant for 2 acres from a grant issued to James and George Winchester for 200 acres.
    No. 171. 9 Jan. 1794, obtained by virtue of a service right

20 May 1803; signed by William Maclin, and marked "Invalid."
No. 2278. By John Armstrong, Esq., Entry Officer of Claims
for the Welfare Lands, to William Polk, Esq., surveyor requiring
the survey for John Withrow, on east fork of the Buffaloe River
which empties into Duck River on the south side, 30 Nov. 1784.
James Withrow stated on 30 May 1807 that John Withrow was his
son. Marked "Invalid."
     Jesse Franklin on 19 May 1807 claimed 1000 acres of land
lying on Rock Creek, adjoining the lands of John Sevier, entered
in the office of John Armstrong, and that same had been paid
for. Marked "Invalid."
     There is a copy of warrant no. 5237 for 274 acres entered
on 16 July 1800 to George Smith, assignee of Boaz Finley on the
waters of Indian Creek between Indian Creek and Hurricane Creek.
Isaac Walton, locator. Same transferred to Isaac Walton on 12
May 1801 by G. Smith.
     No. 5231, 640 acres entered 16 July 1800 to George Smith,
originally assignee of Richard Slocig on Indian Creek. Transferred to Isaac Walton on 12 May 1801.
     (These various claims appear to have been overlapping and
there was considerable dissatisfaction in regard to their survey - Ed.)

No. 4048. Heirs of Samuel Arnold, private, for 640 acres for
his services in the N.C. Cont. Line. 1 Dec. 1796. Wake Co.,
N.C., Phil Hodges, administrator to the heirs of Samuel Arnold,
dec., to sell said warrant to Henry Farley Wade, 16 Dec. 1796.
Wade sold the same to Mathew Brooks on 23 Dec. 1796.

No. 3647. Heirs of John Atkins, soldier in the Rev. War. 640
acres within the lands reserved for officers and soldiers of the
N.C. Cont. Line. 10 Dec. 1788. At various times the land was
assigned to Allen Brewer, John Ferguson, Haden Wells, and Thomas Clinton.

No. 3161. Heirs of Charles Adams, private in the N.C. Cont.
Line, 640 acres granted by Martin Armstrong. Issued 19 Dec.
1785. On 22 Aug. 1796 Nicholas Adams, heir-at-law, assigned the
warrant to William Lytle, who assigned it to W. P. Anderson on
30 Dec. 1808.

No. 2289. Heirs of Levi Alexander, private in N.C. Cont. Line,
640 acres, issued 28 Sept. 1785.

No. 1844. Heirs of Elijah Abbott, private in N.C. Cont. Line.
Abbott was dec. 14 June 1785.

No. 1959. 640 acres surveyed for William Arthur who was wounded in the N.C. Line. The land was taken from that reserved for
officers and soldiers of the N.C. Line. 10 Aug. 1785, land assigned to John Smith. Wake Co., N.C., Jesse Tharp, Joseph Marcom and Abraham Wagerty (?) made oath that they knew William
Arthur did sign the transfer. 30 Dec. 1796.

No. 3500. Balitha Anderson, private in N.C. Cont. Line of Rev.
War, granted 640 acres on 8 Feb. 178(?). 6 June 1786 Anderson
assigned land to Thomas Hickman who assigned it to Ambrose Maul-
ding on 9 Oct. 1786.

No. 300. Martin Armstrong granted land 24 July 1797 by Act for
relief of officers and soldiers of the N.C. Cont. Line. Armstrong assigned 100 acres to John Donelson in Davidson Co. at
Tatum and Wiggins' northeast corner adjoining the land of James
Robertson.

No. 4.   Martin Armstrong granted 560 acres in Davidson Co., 8
Oct. 1787.   Land assigned to Landon Clark.

No. 3953.   Heirs of Zadock Beasley, private in the N.C. Cont.
Line of Rev. War granted 640 acres on 30 Sept. 1785.   John
Beasley, heir of Zadock Beasley, transferred land to Richard
Fenner on 10 Dec. 1785.   J. W. Bell(?) witnessed.   Fenner transferred it to Capt. Thomas Evans.   On 9 Feb. 1795 Isaac McCannan,
heir-at-law of Major Thomas Evans, dec., transferred the land
to Alexander McCall.   Martin Armstrong witnessed.

No. 694.   James Ballard, soldier in the N.C. Line, granted 640
acres surveyed and granted Nancy Sheppard in Davidson Co., Tenn.,
said Nancy having been assigned Ballard's warrant.   James Ballard
and John and Josiah Ballard, heirs of James Ballard, assigned
the warrant to Nancy Sheppard.   This grant vacated cert. no.
3530, heirs of Hardy Murfree, in 1836.   On 5 Nov. 1806 Robert B.
Castleman, register of Davidson Co., granted # 694 and 691 conveyed by deed by O. Smith and wife Nancy Smith to Hardy Murfree.

No. 2535.   Baily (Bally) Benson, private in the N.C. Cont. Line
of the Rev. War, granted 640 acres in Sumner Co. on Salt River
of Caney Fork on 10 Dec. 1795.   Assigned to William King.

No. 2988.   Heirs of Moses Braxton, private in N.C. Cont. Line of
the Rev. War, granted 640 acres on 30 Sept. 1785.   Assigned to
James Linn.

No. 85.   Emannuel Brown, private in N.C. Cont. Line of the Rev.
War.   Issued 21 Dec. 1803.   Transferred to George Smith with
Joseph Hambough and Reuben Searcy as witnesses.   Jacob Mercer
transferred it to Seth Malery with Thomas Harney and Arm. Stuart
Stubblefield as witnesses.   Malich Brown, heir of Emmanuel Brown,
appointed to Jacob Mercer attorney to sell the bounty.

No. 47.   John Barrow, private in the N.C. Cont. Line of the Rev.
War, issued 3 Dec. 1801.   Barrow assigned it to Joseph Wilson
and Wilson assigned it to Thomas Young.   Young assigned it to
Miram Ray, who in 1806 assigned 228 acres to Lazarth Tilley.

No. 1218.   Heirs of Richard Barneycastle, private, 458 acres of
land for his services in N.C. Cont. Line.   Issued 31 Dec. 1824.

No. 87.   Thomas Belsiah, Rev. soldier, granted 640 acres.   Thomas Belsire, private in N.C. Cont. Line.   Issued 22 Dec. 1803.
He sold the warrant to Nathan Williams on 31 Aug. 1804, Thomas
Colmance a witness as were Luke Pendergast, Andrew McClary, Ane
mar Deans, Jr.   On 31 Aug. 1804 Williams assigned it to William
Adams, who assigned it to Wm. L. Webb on 24 Sept. 1804, and Webb
assigned it to John Kimbrough on 12 Dec. 1804.

No. 498.   Heirs of John Brown, private in the N.C. Cont. Line,
granted 640 acres on 28 Aug. 1820.

No. 4026.   Willis Bares, private in N.C. Cont. Line, granted
640 acres on 25 Nov. 1796.   Transferred at Camden, N.C., to
William Lurry (or Surry), Jr., James Elder and Michael Elder
witnesses.   Land transferred to James Elder on 22 Aug. 1797.

No. 1929.   Heirs of Thomas Blanat, corporal, dec., in N.C. Cont.
Line, granted 1000 acres on 27 July 1785.

No. 2409.   Jerem'h Banks, private, granted 640 acres from land
for officers and soldiers of the Rev. War, on 30 Sept. 1785.
Same transferred to Thos. Butcher in 1785 and transferred by
Butcher to Thomas Smith in 1787.

No. 2411. Heirs of David Baswell, private in N.C. Cont. Line.
640 acres, issued 30 Sept. 1785.

No. 3594. William Boswell, sergeant, for services in Cont. Line.
1000 acres. Boswell assigned the land to Sarah Decrow (?) of
Perq's Co., N. C., who assigned it to William Williams on 4 June
1793. In May 1796 Nathaniel Williams of Perquimons Co., N.C.,
brother and only heir of William Williams, assigned the land to
Hardy Murfree.

No, 717, Military land warrant. Capt. John Baker, for service
in Rev. War. Certificate of survey dated 25 Nov. 1798.

No. 3569. Joseph Bailey, sergeant in Cont. Line in Rev. War;
570 acres.

No. 501. James Barfield, private in N.C. Cont. Line; 342 acres.

No. 1989. Heirs of Arthur Branch, private in N.C. Cont. Line;
640 acres, issued 16 Aug. 1785. Arthur Branch died a soldier
in the N.C. Line, and his heir, Thomas Branch, transferred the
warrant to William Faircloth on 20 Aug. 1785. 8 Oct. 1785,
Faircloth assigned the land to William Purkins, who assigned it
to Daniel Welbourn in Dec. 1785.

No. 1990. Heirs of Mark Bouge, private in N.C. Cont. Line; 640
acres of land. Isaac Holdman of Sumner Co., Tenn., in 1804 made
oath he knew Mark Bogue as a soldier in the 3rd Regt. of N.C. in
Capt. Coles' Co. Bogue was at the battles of Brandywine and
Germantown. Bogue assigned the warrant to John Price in July
1785, and Price transferred it to James Cole Mountflowrence.

No. 3124. Heirs of Jacob Bennett, 640 acres of land. Jacob
was a private in the N.C. Cont. Line. Issued 13 Dec. 1785 and
assigned in 1810 to Allen Brown (Montgomery Co., Tenn., sheriff's
sale). Jacob Bennett mustered as a private in Jarvis' Co., N.C.
Line on 8 Sept. 1777, for an indefinite term. Wm. Douglass of
Davidson Co., stated on 7 Feb. 1811 that he knew Charles Brisner,
Wm. Peete, Peter Guan, and Jacob Bennett, and that they served
faithfully to the end of the war.

No. 2988. Heirs of Moses Branton, Rev. soldier in N.C. Line;
640 acres entered 2 Oct. 1786. Archibald Lytle bought the warrant from Branton, which adjoined John Blackmore's preemption on
the east and Thomas Murray's preemption on the west in 1807.

Thomas Brandon, Rev. soldier. See Joseph Hanna, both in one
warrant.

No. 1808. Heirs of Jonathan Baker; 640 acres issued 20 May 1793
for Baker's services as a private in the N.C. Line The heirs assigned the land to Samuel Sanford.

No. 1948. William Buck, private in N.C. Line; granted 9 Dec.
1783. Land, in Davidson Co., Tenn., was granted to John Overton.

No. 6406. John G. Blount, soldier in the N.C. Line; 1600 acres,
transferred to Capt. John Allen.

No. 4736. Sylvanus Barton, private in N.C. Cont. Line; 320
acres in Sumner Co., Tenn.

No. 4737. Peter Blackstone, served 3½ years. Also received
Warrant no. 4734. 320 acres of land, issued 13 Feb. 1797, and
assigned to Robert Stothart.

No. 1528.   Richard Bradley, private in N.C. Line; granted 274
acres and assigned it on   19 March 1796 6o James Dickson, Sr.,
and James Dickson, Jr., of Duplin Co., N.C.   On 23 March 1798
the two Dicksons assigned to to William Dickson.

No. 20774.   Reading Blount, Major in the N.C. Line. The Register of Rutherford Co., Tenn., certified this was a true copy of
the grant in his office. 18 Feb. 1819, Sam'l R. Rucker, Robert
H. Dyer, and Blackman Coleman, by cert. no. 2237, for 200 acres
of land had land adjoining Reading Blount's 4800 acres.   Entry
made in name of R. H. Dyer for 10 acres.

No. 4526.   Reese Brewer, private in N.C. Cont. Line; issued 24
Dec. 1796, for 320 acres of land.

No. 851.   Allen Brewer, 6 Sept. 1797, by virtue of military
warrant. Located 31 Aug. 1797. Brewer was assignee of Abel
Moslander for 2560 acres in Davidson Co., about four miles above
the mouth of Harpeth River.

No. 2835.   Heirs of Absolom Burriss, private in N.C. Line; 640
acres; 30 Sept. 1785.

No. 232.   Solomon Bibby, served three years in Col. Summers'
Regt. of N.C. Line (attested 5 Nov. 1801 by J. W. Carver, Capt.
of the 7th Regt., Daniel Jones, Capt., and Ck. J. Devony, J. P.)
Bibby received 274 acres on 27 Oct. 1783 within lands reserved
for officers and soldiers of the N.C. Cont. Line.   Thomas Brick-
ell, clerk of Franklin, N.C., also mentioned.

No. 3301.   William Burk, private in N.C. Cont. Line; 228 acres;
7 Jan. 1786.   Burk assigned the land to John Lynch or his heirs,
on 18 Feb. 1786. 20 Feb. 1786, Lynch assigned it to Charles
Parker, who assigned it back to Lynch on 27 Feb. 1786.   The same
day Lynch assigned it to Jno. Walfersberger, who on 6 May 1786
assigned it to Joseph Williams.   Witnesses to these assignments
were Micael Delone, Abraham Potter, Daniel Hunt, and Robert
Williams.

No. 3302.   Giles Bruce, private; 228 acres for service in N.C.
Line, 7 Jan. 1786.   On 17 Feb. 1786 Bruce assigned the warrant
to John Lynch and Micael Delone. Lynch assigned it to Charles
Parker on 20 Feb. 1786, John Lanchester and Forrester Phillips
were witnesses. Parker reassigned it on 27 Feb. 1786 and the
same day Lynch reassigned to John Wolfersbarger, who on 6 May
1786 assigned it to Joseph Williams.   Witnesses were Robert
Williams, Daniel Hunt, and Abraham Potter.

No. 2445.   Heirs of Joshua Ballard, private in N.C. Line; 640
acres; 30 Sept. 1785.   On 1 Sept. 1785 the Ballard heirs assigned
the warrant to John Ford, with John S. Keaton as witness.   On
31 May 1794 by virtue of an attachment against John Ford by
Martin Armstrong, the warrant was sold at auction by Arthur
Tate, who by his attorney transferred the warrant to John Given
on 20 March 1807.

No. 3333.   Heirs of Archibald Beckham; 640 acres for his services
in the N.C. Cont. Line; 7 Jan. 1786.   On 12 Jan. 1786, John
Beckham, heir-at-law to Archibald Beckham, assigned the warrant
to Charles Marshall, with John Evans a witness.

No. 2408.   Heirs of Michael Braner, private in the N.C. Line.
9 Nov. 1785.   Joshua Braner, heir of Michael Braner, assigned
the warrant to Thomas Smith, with Thos. Bathen (M) a witness.
26 Aug. 1798, Smith assigned the warrant to James McCasety,

who assigned it to Thomas Molloy on 17 Nov. 1798. Daniel Ross, devisee of Molloy, assigned it to Joseph Perrine, with Morgan Brown a witness. 27 Nov. 1805, assigned to Francis Perrine, Thomas Perrine, and William Perrine, with a request that a grant be made in their name. W. C. Jamison a witness.

No. 659. Laurence Byrum, private in N.C. Line; 228 acres, issued 21 Feb. 1821. On 19 Aug. 1821 Byrum assigned the warrant to Allen Wilkins, who on 17 Oct. 1821, assigned the warrant to William Brasfield. Absalom Long and Solomon Jones, witnesses.

No. 614. Heirs of John Boyce; 640 acres for services as a private in N.C. Line. 18 Oct. 1808.

No. 192. Heirs of Charles Bryley, private in N.C. Cont. Line, dec.; 640 acres issued 9 Dec. 1809. On 16 Dec. 1811, James Hearns, attorney for Bryley's heirs, all of Edgecomb Co., N.C., conveyed the warrant to Nathaniel Taylor; D. Givins a witness.

No. 309. Heirs of James Butler, private; 640 acres within the limits of land reserved for officers and soldiers of the N.C. Cont. Line; 23 Feb. 1820.Marked "Valid 1820." John Butler of Bertie Co., N.C., heir of James Butler, transferred the warrant to Darling Cherry on 26 Aug. 1820. William Harrelle and Reuben Horson (?) were witnesses. Jethro Butler of Bertie Co., N.C., heir of James Butler, a continental soldier, conveyed the same to Darling Cherry on 16 April 1820, with Laurence Cherry and Ann Scott as witnesses.

No. 4050. Heirs of David Brown. Military warrant for 640 acres in name of heirs of Dugald Carmical, dated 1 Dec. 1796 (Warrant No. 4049), appears to be the same grant. Robert King stated that in about Jan. 1799 Peter Casso of Raleigh, N.C., gave King warrants 4049 and 4050, for purposes of laying them out, but not having done so, King returned them to Casso, om 13 May 1807 before Sampson Williamsof Blount Co., Tenn.
    Another paper states that Peter Casso gave the warrant to King to be laid out for the benefit of one of his (Casso's) daughters, Henrietta King. 5 June 1807, Peter Casso appeared before J. A. Parker, justice of Davidson Co., and deposed as to the above grant.

No. 4039. Benjamin Ballard, private in N.C. Line; 278 acres; 26 Nov. 1796. Ballard assigned the warrant to R. D. Barry on 12 April 1801, and Barry assigned the warrant to Roger B. Sappington. Benjamin Ballard was a soldier in the Regular Troops, with Capt. John Pugh Williams for 2½ years, and served 12 months when he became incapable of service. Sworn before James Cryerm, J. P. of Sumner Co.

No. 4025. Heirs of Jacob Bray, private in N.C. Line; issued 25 Nov. 1796. In 1796 Bray conveyed the same to William Surry, Jr., all of Camden Co., N.C. Peter Harney, witness. Robertson Co., Tenn., Surry transferred the same to Joseph Phillips on 20 Jan. 1803, with John Phillips a witness, who appeared before James Byrn, justice of peace for Davidson Co., on 21 Nov. 1808.

No. 4027. Heirs of Isaac Burguss, private in N.C. Line; 640 acres; 22 Nov. 1796. In 1796 Hezekiah Burguss of Camden Co., N.C., made the warrant over to William Surry, Jr., with Richard Smith a witness.

No. 6855. George Beard, assignee of George Martin, recorded 19 April 1815. Willie Blount signed cert. no. 1805, in Bedford Co., in second district on waters of the Wartrace Fork of Duck River.

No. 123. Jno. Bradbury. Warrant no. 49, requiring that 100 acres be laid off for Elijah Chism (Chisum) because of grant no. 733 dated 20 July for 640 acres; 22 Oct. 1802. Wm. Maclin. The within warrant is rejected; 24 Aug. 1807. Elijah Chism assigned his right to John Bradbury, with Nancy Chism a witness. Entry file is marked "Invalid."

No. 122 (47). John Bradbury, assignee of Elijah Chism; same as above.

No. 215. Heirs of John Boyd, private in N.C. Cont. Line; 640 acres granted 1 Oct. 1811. James Boyd, heir of John Boyd, assigned the warrant to Reuben B. Jones; Thomas Patridge witness.

No. 126. John Butler, private in N.C. Cont. Line; issued 20 Dec. 1805. John Butler of Bertie Co., N.C., assigned the warrant to William White. 11 Feb. 1806; John Johnston a witness.

No. 12. William Bradley, Guard Right. (File is in bad condition).

No. 5800. Heirs of Jesse Bond, private in N.C. Cont. Line; 640 acres of land; issued 16 Dec. 1797; marked "Invalid." May 1796, Bond assigned the warrant to William Hardin; Charles Burks a witness. 20 Nov. 1807, Hardin assigned the warrant to Armstead Blivens who assigned it to George Pain in Nov. 1807, Elizabeth Cameron a witness. 1 April 1814, Pain assigned it to John Glass, James Neale a witness. 4 May 1814, Glass assigned the warrant to Asshal Romax or Bomax.

No. 1000. Byrd Braswell, private; 228 acres (bad condition); assigned 18 May 1797 to John Tate by Bird Brazill or Byrd Braswell of Sumner Co., Tenn.

No. not given. Solomon Bibby, Franklin Co., N.C., was in the Cont. service of the U. S. for three years to clear a class. 16 June 1802, witnessed by John Munick and Thos. Sherrad, all of Franklin Co., N.C.

No. 1015. Baxter Boling, private in the N.C. Line; 640 acres issued 14 Sept. 1821.

No. 661. James Blackwell, sergeant in the N. C. Cont. Line; 357 acres; issued 21 Feb. 1821; assigned to William Person on 9 March 1822, Thos. Person and John Knight witnesses.

No. 301. Heirs of Job Bright, corporal in the N.C. Line; 522 acres being balance of land due him as a corporal, warrant no. 283 having been issued for 428 acres. Issued 23 Dec. 1819; assigned by Frances Davis and Frederick Davis as heirs of Job Bright, to Darling Cherry, witnessed by Laurence Cherry and Samuel Keeter. Darling Cherry assigned the same to William Hill on 23 Dec. 1819. Marked "Valid 1820."

No. 322. Heirs of James Bennett, private in the Line; 640 acres, issued 9 June 1820. 2 Sept. 1820 warrant assigned to Joseph Seurluck.

No. 571. Heirs of Thomas Brees, private in the N.C. Cont. Line, 274 acres; issued 9 Sept. 1820. Jeremiah Watson paid Rhoda Berney or Berry, formerly Rhoda Brees, only heir of Thomas Brees or Rees, dec., Sept. 1820, witnessed by Peter Pillitieu and Ferdinand Pittetine(?). Watson assigned the warrant to James F. Taylor.

No. 571. Heirs of Amos Berry, private in the N.C. Cont. Line; 640 acres issued 9 Sept. 1820. Same day, Rhoda Berry, the only heir of Amos Berry, dec., assigned the warrant to Jeremiah Watson, who assigned it to James F. Taylor.

No. 295. Gideon Downey or Bonney, corporal in the N.C. Cont. Line; 428 acres, issued 27 Nov. 1819. Jonathan Bonney of Currituck Co., N.C., one of the heirs of Gideon Bonney, assigned the warrant to Darling Cherry on 30 Nov. 1819. Daniel Cherry and Laurence Cherry were witnesses.

No. 4030. Heirs of Hardy Brogdon, private in the N.C. Line; 640 acres; issued Nov. 1796. Brogdon assigned the warrant to Thomas E. Summer on 3 May 1803, in presence of Danl. Naulx or Vaulx. Vaulx (sic) assigned the warrant to Robert McLemore on 16 Nov. 1803. Wm. Christmas and S. Green witnesses.

No. 3438. James Bidger, private in the N.C. Cont. Line, 640 acres, issued 20 Jan. 1786 This warrant was transferred to Thomas Smith; James Lanier a witness. Smith transferred it to Elijah Robertson on 28 Dec. 1786; John Rice, wit. Robertson conveyed it to Phillip Phillips and Michael Campbell, 26 July 1790, wit. by G. C. Mountflorence.

No. 1234. Richard Bullock, heir of Joshua Bullock, a lieutenant in N.C. Cont. Line, issued 10 Sept. 1827. Notation that Benja. Siles lives in Bedford Co., 15 miles from Shelbyville. Lae (?) F. Gooch and Thomas Gooch, executors of Rowland Gooch, dec., promise to pay $280.06 as soon as it can be collected.

No. 3595. Joseph Brown, private in the N.C. Cont. Line; issued 27 June 1788; assigned to Charles Wallwoode in July 1790. Wallwoodeassigned the same to Edward Harris in 1796. On 31 Aug. 1798 Edward Harris of Newbern Town, N. C., assigned the same to Robert Weakley, Willie Blount a wit. Weakley assigned it to William Scott, Sr., with J. Childree as wit.

No. 576. Joseph Brown; 100 acres issued 17 Nov. 1790 (28 March 1805) Grant no. 832 by virtue of 50 shilling entry, marked "Invalid." Also no. 30, Joseph Brown, 140 acres. 28 Sept. 1802. Notation states that Frank Allison entered 37 acres in no. 131, Robert Mitchell entered 40 acres in no. 133, and Joseph Brown entered 63 acres in no. 158, signed Joseph Britten, entry taker.

No. 4349. Henry Boyles, private in the N.C. Cont. Line, 274 acres, issued 17 Dec. 1796. Boyles assigned it to Nathaniel Jones and witnesses were Abz. Swagerty, Jesse Sheisp (?) and James Marcom. Nathaniel Jones of Wake Co., N.C., assigned it to Jesse Sharp, Joseph Marcom, and Abraham Swagerty.

No. 3993. Robert Barge, private in N.C. Cont. Line, 640 acres; 25 Nov. 1796; marked "Invalid." Barge assigned the warrant to Joseph Semlock on Dec. 1796. The warrant was transferred to Thomas Shute; John Irwin a witness.

No. 4351. Heirs of Joseph Babb, private in the N.C. Cont. Line; 640 acres, issued 17 Dec. 1796. Jan. 1797, John Babb, heir of Joseph Babb, assigned the warrant to Thomas Molloy, and on 21 April 1797 Molloy assigned it to Robert Weakley. Abraham Swagerty, Jesse Sharp, and Jas. Marcum, all of Wake Co., N.C., wit. the transfer before Nathaniel Jones, J. P., on 30 Dec. 1796.

No. 4350. Richard Bean, private in N.C. Cont. Line; issued 17 Dec. 1796; assigned to Edward Settle, and acknowledged in Wake Co., N.C., before Nathaniel Jones.

No. 4368. Heirs of Samuel Blackwood, private in N.C. Cont. Line;
640 acres, issued 17 Dec. 1796. John Blackwood, heir of Samuel
Blackwood, issued the warrant to Stockley Donelson and William
Tyrrel in Wake Co., N.C., before Nath'l Jones, a J. P. In 1818
the same land was sold to Jacob McGavock. File contains other
transfers.

No. 240. Heirs of John Ballard, private in the N.C. Cont. Line;
640 acres, issued 11 Nov. 1814. John Ballard of Martin Co., N.C.,
only heir to John Ballard, dec., who was a private in the N.C.
Line, transfers the warrant to Jesse Cherry of same county. J.
W. Hassell and Jonathan Jolley witnessed it.

No. 4384. Heirs of John Bruce, private in the N.C. Cont. Line;
640 acres issued 20 Dec. 1796. Stephen Bruce, heir of John
Bruce, transferred to William Dickson on 2 Feb. 1797; John Bruce
and Sarah Bruce witnessed. 10 April 1797. Dickson transferred
the warrant to Wm. Jonathan, with Andrew Soddy a witness.

No. 4369. Heirs of James Burnes, Jr., private in the N.C. Cont.
Line; 640 acres; issued 17 Dec. 1796. May 1797, John Burnes,
heir of James Burnes, Jr., transferred the warrant to Thomas
Molloy; witnessed by Jesse Sharp, Joseph Marcom, in Wake Co.,
N.C., before Nathaniel Jones, a J. P., on 30 Dec. 1796.

No. 4367. Heirs of William Blair, private in the N.C. Cont.
Line; 640 acres; issued 17 Dec. 1796. Same was transferred to
Sterling Brewer in Jan. 1797, by John Blair; David Strayhorn
and James Little, witnesses. This warrant was later transferred
to Thomas Molloy.

No. 1014. Heirs of Isaac Bratcher, private in the N.C. Cont.
Line; 640 acres; issued 10 Sept. 1821. Transferred 26 Sept. 1821
to Robert Read by Umphrey Brackin (sic) as having a right to same,
in Carteret Co., N.C.; acknowledged Nov. 1821.

No. 3163. Heirs of Lewis Beard, private in the N.C. Cont. Line;
640 acres issued at Newbern, 19 Dec. 1785, and transferred to
William Lytle, Jr., in Oct. 1797, by Abraham Beard, heir of Lewis
Beard. This transfer was witnessed by John Jones, 30 Dec. 1808.
Lytle transferred it to W. P. Anderson.

No. 3162. Heirs of Henry Baldwin, private in the N.C. Cont.
Line; 640 acres; issued 19 Dec. 1785. 18 July 1797, Henry Baldwin, heir at law of Henry Baldwin, transferred the warrant to
William Lytle, Jr.; Green Young a witness. 30 Dec. 1808, Lytle
transferred it to William P. Anderson.

No. 3274. Heirs of Francis Burke, private in the N.C. Cont.
Line, dec.; issued 24 Nov. 1785, and assigned to Edward Harris
in Aug. 1786.

No. 3216. William Barber, private in the N.C. Cont. Line; 640
acres; issued 21 Dec. 1785.

No. 3254. William Brumley, private in N.C. Cont. Line, issued
24 Dec. 1785, and transferred to John Whitaker on 24 Dec. 1785;
F. Boon a witness.

No. 4576. John Burhsall or Burshaw, private in the N.C. Cont.
Line; issued 9 Feb. 1797. Transferred to Sterling Brewer (John
Enright a witness), and transferred by Brewer to William Tyrrell
on 4 March 1797 (W. Lackey and William Lytle witnesses.).

No. 4573. James Brock, private in the N.C. Cont. Line; 640
acres, issued 9 Feb. 1797; transferred to William Searey on 23
Oct. 1803, and later to Samuel Mitchell.

No. 4571.   Isaiah Bledsoe, private in N.C. Cont. Line; 640
acres; 9 Feb. 1797.   Sterling Brewer purch. this warrant, John
Enright and William Reed witnesses.   Brewer assigned it to William Tyrrell, W. Lackey and Wm. Lytle witnesses.   In 1807 Wm.
Tyrrel and Wm. P. Lewis had legal transaction in Davidson Co.

No. 4579.   Henry Blatkston (sic); fifer in the N.C. Cont. Line;
1000 acres, issued 9 Feb. 1797. Transferred to Sterling Brewer;
James Cannady and Wm. Smith witnesses.   20 Feb. 1797, transferred to William Tyrrell, Wm. Lackey and Wm. Lytle, witnesses.
Warrant mentioned in legal transaction in Davidson Co., April
1800.

No. 4578.   John Bumberdie, private in N.C. Cont. Line; 640 acres,
issued 9 Feb. 1797, and transferred to Wm. Nash on 12 Feb., with
Wm. Reed and Jas. Marcum, witnesses.   Wm. Nash testified in Davidson Co., Tenn., on 24 March 1808.

No. 4580.   John Bustenton, private in N.C. Cont. Line; 640 acres;
issued 9 Feb. 1797.   Transferred to Samson Williams, 17 Feb.
1797, Abram Swargthy(?) and Robert Brown, witnesses.

No. 4750.   Heirs of Charles Bresher, private in the N.C. Cont.
Line; 640 acres, issued Feb. 1797.   Transferred to Sterling
Brewer by Obediah Bresher, James Horton and Wm. Smith, witnesses.
Brewer transferred it to Wm. Tyrrell, Wm. Lackey and Wm. Lytle,
witnesses.   Procedure by sheriff of Davidson Co., 1807.

No. 4480.   Joseph Brown, private in N.C. Cont. Line; 274 acres;
22 Dec. 1796.   Transferred to Stockley Donelson on 29 Dec. 1796,
Stephen Shumate, witness.   Jan. 1797, Donelson assigned it to
Abner Pillow, Simon Bugg a witness.

No. 4478.   Thomas Bootle, private in N.C. Cont. Line; 274 acres;
issued 22 Dec. 1796.   Attached slip states that Thomas Bootle
served three years in the service of his state, 11 Dec. 1796,
John Medearis, Capt.   Jan. 1797 warrant was transferred to
Stockley Donelson, James Smith a witness.   25 Jan. 1797, Donelson transferred the same to Thomas Dillon, John Wilson a witness.   Dillon transferred same to James Patten on 23 July 1802,
Wm. A. Gibson, witness.   April 1805, Patten endorsed it to John
Neely, Phebe Patten a witness.   Dec. 1805, Neely transferred it
to William Grayson, Wm. Berry a witness.   Grayson transferred
it to Larkin Riggers (Wiggers), Jno. Sterling a witness.

No. 4479.   Caleb Berry, private in the Cont. Line; 274 acres;
issued 22 Dec. 1796.   Transferred to Stockley Donelson in 1797.
Transferred to   James (surname not given - R. B.) Feb. 1797.
James Cannon transferred to Robert Muir, 1787 (1797? - R. B.).
Muir transferred the same to Robert Stothart, who made it over
to David Affick.   24 March 1807.

No. 4458.   Zachariah Bond, private in N.C. Cont. Line; 228
acres; issued 22 Dec. 1796.   Transferred to Redmond D. Barry
in 1797, and assigned by him to Edward Given in 1789 (sic;
1799? - R. B.) who assigned it over to John Givin.

No. 4403.   Jesse Benton, sergeant in the N.C. Cont. Line; 357
acres within the lands reserved for officers and soldiers of the
Cont. Line; issued 22 Dec. 1796.   Transferred to William Lytle
in 1798, Thomas Taylor a witness.

No. 4388.   Abner Bottle, private in the N.C. Cont. Line; 312
acres; issued 20 Dec. 1796.   21 Dec. 1798, David Fowler transferred it to Redmond D. Barry, who transferred it to Edward
Givin on 13 Aug. 1798.

No. 4538. John Brantley, private in the N.C. Cont. Line; 228 acres; issued 24 Dec. 1796. Attached statement says that John Brantley late a soldier in the Cont. Line for two and a half years, transfers the warrant to William Jackson, on 10 Jan. 1797, Micajah Bridgers or Bridgus a witness with William Bridgus. Feb. 1797, Jackson assigned the same to Reddick Bridgers, Dinton Mann a witness. Reddick Bridgers transferred it to Edward Givin on 24 June 1800.

No. 407. Heirs of James Bowen, a private in the N.C. Cont. Line; 274 acres; issued 11 Aug. 1820.

No. 4370. Heirs of James Barr, a private in the N.C. Cont. Line; 640 acres; issued 17 Dec. 1796. Samuel Barr, heir to James Barr, transferred to Allen Brewer in Wake Co., N.C., before Nathaniel Jones, J. P., on 30 Dec. 1796. Papers state that on 18 July 1797 this land was surveyed for William Tyrrell, assignee of James Barr's heirs, opposite Turner's Creek of Harpeth River, in Davidson Co. G. Bradley, Capt., stated on 9 Dec. 1796 that James Barr was a soldier in the Cont. Line and died in the service thereof.

No. 4527. James Bigsby, private in N.C. Cont. Line; 640 acres; issued 24 Dec. 1796. Transferred to Thomas Johnston on 13 Feb. 1797. James Bigby served under Capt. John Mahary. This land was in Sumner Co. on the waters of White Oak Creek and Barren River.

No. 1668. Samuel Barton, assignee of Ignatius Beak, heirs, a private in the N.C. Cont. Line; 640 acres in Sumner Co. on Barton's Creek; issued 1793. There is a deed where same was transferred by sheriff's sale in Sumner Co., 1833, to satisfy a claim of John Irwin against Samuel Barton at April Court, the warrant having been transferred to Irwin.

No. 1836. Heirs of Joseph Bailey, private in the N.C. Cont. Line; issued 14 June 1785, within the limits of land reserved for officers and soldiers of the N.C. Cont. Line. Warrant was transferred to John Boyd in Oct. 1785, and Boyd transferred it to John Nichols on 18 Oct. 1785. In Feb. 1786 Nichols transferred it to Edwin Hickman, who on 3 Feb. 1786 made it over to Wikoff T. (?) Clark, Robert Nelson a witness.

No. 1873. Heirs of William Blake, sergeant in the N.C. Line; 1000 acres within the limits of land reserved for officers and soldiers of the N.C. Cont. Line; issued 1 July 1785. John Blake, heir of William Blake made the land over to Thomas Donoho, James Blake a witness.

No. not given. "These may certify that James Burns, Jr., was a soldier in the State of N. C. Cont. Line and died in the service thereof, Given under my hand this 9th of Decr. 1796. G. Bradley, Capt."

No. 218. Thomas Brannon, private in the N.C. Line,; 274 acres within the limits of land reserved for officers and soldiers of the land reserved for officers and soldiers of the N. C. Cont. Line; issued 21 Oct. 1783, and transferred to John C. McLemore on 14 Jan. 1797. Robert Brown and James Canady witnessed.

No. 216. Heirs of Robert Brown, private in the N. C. Line; 274 acres within the limits of lands reserved for officers and soldiers of the N. C. Cont. Line; issued 30 Nov. 1811. Brown transferred it to Nathaniel Taylor; Thos. Outlaw, Wm. A. Carter and D. Givin, witnesses.

No. 2247. Simon Baker, private in the N.C. Line; 640 acres of land for his services (Record is a grant and in bad condition).

No. 1998. John Gray Blount; 640 acres, Davidson Co., marked "Void." Grant was issued to James Broadstreet a private in the N.C. Line. Assigned to John Gray and Thomas Blount, on west fork of Stones River, being on Capt. Rumsey's line. Grant dated 7 May 1793. Grant was registered in Rutherford Co., Tenn., Book C, pp. 9-10, on 20 May 1807, and signed by John Dickson, Register of Rutherford Co., and by Joseph Herndon, county clerk, 30 July 1807.Grant was vacated. John Doak made affidavit about Grant no. 1935. Doak was deputy surveyor of William Christmas, the principal surveyor of 1st district. Doak's statement was in regard to confusion of two grants, and was dated 30 July 1807.

No. 3533. Isaac Bloodgood, fifer in the N.C. Line; 428 acres within the limits of lands reserved for officers and soldiers of the Cont. Line; issued 15 Feb. 1786. 26 March 1786, transferred to John McNees. In Sept. 1787, Bloodgood again transferred the warrant to Joseph Brock, who in Oct. 1787 transferred it to Anthony Foster, who in Dec. 1787 made it over to Elijah Ruth, with Lewis Ford a witness.

No. 396. Heirs of William Boomer, a private in the N.C. State Line; 274 acres within the limits of land reserved for officers and soldiers of the N.C. Cont. Line; issued 3 Aug. 1820. A transfer dated 20 July 1820, stated that Isaac Sawyer, Henry and Nella Gibbs, Thomas Harris, and Tabby Harris of Hide Co., N.C., the only heir of William Boomer, a Cont. soldier in the Rev. War in the N.C. Line, sell the warrant to Laurence Cherry, William Harrell, Peledey Harris and Francis Harper witnesses.

No. 342. Heirs of Jeremiah Beaman, private in the N.C. Line; 640 acres within the limits of land reserved for officers and soldiers of the N.C. Line; issued 1 July 1820. 8 Oct. 1819, Martha Bennett, formerly Martha Beamon of Wake Co., N.C., heir at law of Jeremiah Beaman a Cont. soldier of the Rev. War, sells the warrant to Daniel Cherry. Bennett Jones, Sally Jones, and Sally Flowers a witness.

No. 417. Heirs of Mich'l Brinkley, a private in the N.C. Line; 185 acres; issued 15 Aug. 1820.

No. 300. Heirs of James Bundy, private in the N.C. Cont. Line; 91 acres within the limits of land reserved for officers and soldiers of the said state; issued 23 Dec. 1819. Josiah Bundy of Pitt Co., N.C., transferred the warrant issued to his father, James Bundy, to Darling Cherry on 18 Nov. 1819, John Smith and James Evans witnesses. Cherry transferred the warrant to James Welborn on 24 Dec. 1819.

No. 404. Heirs of Levi Branton, private in the N.C. state line; 640 acres; issued 11 Aug. 1820.

No. 400. Heirs of Mich'l Bull, private in the line of this state; 640 acres; issued 5 Aug. 1820. Stephen Bull, brother and heir at law of Michael Bull in Franklin Co., N.C.

No. 283. Job Bright, corporal in the N.C. Cont. Line of the Rev.; 428 acres for his services; issued 24 Aug. 1819. 26 June 1819, Frederick Davis and Francis Davis, proper heirs of Job Bright, transferred the warrant to Darling Cherry, who made the warrant over to William Hill, who transferred it to Gen. Calvin Jones in March 1820.

No. 726. The present trustees of the University of North Carolina, for the services of Christopher Brannon, a sergeant in the
Rev. War; 1000 acres; issued 4 August 1821. William Polk, attorney for the University, transfers the same to Thomas Henderson
in 1821, and Henderson transferred it to William A. Tharp.

No. 358. Heirs of William Barler, private in the N.C. Cont.
Line; 640 acres; issued 17 July 1820. Barler's heirs, a Mr.
Kendal, William and John Barler, and Gardner White the husband
of Sally Barler, transferred the warrant to Jesse Gill in July
1822.

No. 774. The present trustees of the University of N.C., for
the services of David Burnett, a private in the N.C. Cont. Line;
640 acres; issued 8 Aug. 1821.

No. 481. Heirs of James Boyatt, private in N.C. Cont. Line; 640
acres; issued 21 Aug. 1820. In Aug. 1820, Solomon Boyatt, only
heir of James Boyatt, transferred the warrant to Darling Cherry.

No. 188. Robert Cowan, sergeant in the N.C. Cont. Line; 428
acres; issued 29 Nov. 1809. 5 Nov. 1810, Ephraium Cowan, only
heir at law of Robert Cowan, transferred it to James Douglass.

No. 2447. Heirs of Abraham Cowan, private in the N.C. Line; 640
acres. Col. Martin Armstrong was ordered to lay off the land
within the limits of land reserved for officers and soldiers
of the said land. Issued 30 Sept. 1785.

No. 362. Heirs of Butler Cowall, ensign in the N.C. Line; 2560
acres; issued 22 July 1820. The heirs of Butler Cowell (son
Henry G.; James Eborn husband of Elizabeth Eborn; Elizabeth Cowell relict of William Cowell a son; Benjamin Slade husband of
Lucintia Slade, dau. of William Cowell, and granddau. of Butler;
and Mary Cowell, dau. of son William), all of Beaufort Co., N.C.,
transferred the warrant to Calvin Jones of Raleigh, N.C., in
right of their heirship and the provisions of the will of William
Cowell. Other heirs were Elizabeth Cowell, widow and relict of
Aisley Cowell, James Cowell, and Sally Cowell, children of Benjamin Cowell, dec., who was a son of Butler Cowall. This was acknowledged in Johnston Co., N.C., on 17 July 1820.

No. 391. Heirs of Hillery Cason, a corporal in the N.C. Cont.
Line; 1000 acres; issued 3 Aug. 1820. Certificate dated 18 July
1820 stated that James Cason and Milberry Cason, the only children and heirs of Hillery Cason, transferred the warrant to Darling Cherry.

No. 379. Heirs of William Carbon, private in the N.C. state
line of the Cont. Line; issued 29 July 1820. Stephen Brooks of
Pitt Co., N.C., one of the heirs of the said William Carbon,
transferred the warrant to Roderick Cherry pn 15 July 1820,
Ephraium Brooks a witness. Roderick Cherry made the warrant
over to Eli Cherry on 12 Aug. 1820.

No. 494. James Carter, a private in the N.C. Cont. Line; 274
acres; issued 28 Aug. 1820. Carter, of Warren Co., N.C., made
the warrant over to Calvin Jones of Raleigh in Aug. 1820.

No. 378. Heirs of James Carbon, private in the N.C. Cont. Line;
366 acres; issued 29 July 1820. Ephraium and Stephen Brooks of
Pitt Co., N.C., transferred the warrant to Roderick Cherry in
July 1820.

No. 1522. William Casell, Grant "in consideration of service
performed by William Caswell;" warrant no. 158 dated 22 Oct.

1783 and entered on 2 Sept. 1807 by no. 466, there was granted
to William Caswell and his heirs 640 acres in Bedford Co., in
the 2nd dist., 4th range, 7th section on Alexander's Creek, next
to Joseph Dickson's grant of 5000 acres.

No. 347. Heirs of Jacob Clarke, private in the N.C. Line; 336
acres within the limits of land reserved for officers and soldiers of the N.C. Cont. Line; issued 10 July 1820. Isaac Clark
of Lenoir Co., N.C., true and lawful heir of Jacob Clarke, conveyed to Toderick Cherry, 1 July 1820.

No. 377. Heirs of Jacob Clarke, private in the N.C. Line; 640
acres of land within the limits reserved for officers and soldiers of the N.C. Cont. Line; issued 29 July 1820. Isaac Clark
of Lenoir Co. transferred the warrant to Roderick Cherry on 12
Aug. 1820.

No. 620. Cornelious Callayhan, private in the N.C. Line; 274
acres; issued 22 April 1784.

No. 185.   Also no. 793. Heirs of Amos Carl or Cail, private
in the N.C. Cont. Line; 640 acres; issued 22 April 1809. On 25
April 1809 Scaley Cale of Martin Co., N.C., heir of Amos Cale,
dec., conveyed the warrant to Daniel Cherry.

No. 1999. Jno. G. and Thomas Blount are assigned this grant, 1
Aug. 1798 issued to William Crow a private in the N.C. Cont. Line
for his services. Based on Warrant no. 1546, dated 14 Jan. 1786.

No. not given. John Collins, soldier in the N.C. Cont. Line,
enlisted for the duration of the war. Statement signed 23 Nov.
1797. 20 Jan. 1798 John Collins assigned the warrant to Jno.
Hague, who on 25 Jan. 1798 assigned it to Samuel Crocket.

No. 654. Heirs of William Chronicle, capt. in the N.C. Cont.
Line; 3800 acres; issued 23 Nov. 1820. James McKee of Lincoln
Co., N.C., the only heir and legal representative of Capt. Wm.
Chronicle, assigned said warrant to Robert Henry on 23 Nov.
1820.

No. 3328. Heirs of Thompson Chapman, private in the N.C. Cont.
Line; 640 acres; issued 7 Jan. 1786.   Granted by Martin Armstrong. 24 Aug. 1790, it was certified that the land was duly
sold having been taken by an attachment at the suit of John Conrod and sold to him in Surry Co., N.C.

No. 3336. Samuel Chappell, private in the N.C. Cont. Line; issued 7 Jan. 1786. On 8 Feb. 1786 Chappell assigned the warrant
to John Marshall. 25 Feb. 1800, Dixon Marshall, heir at law of
John Marshall assigned the warrant to Jessey Powel, who made it
over to John Lancaster on 2 Nov. 1801. Lancaster assigned it to
William Henderson in Jan. 1805. Henderson assigned it to James
Henderson in June 1805.

No. 274. James Cocks, heir of Robert Cocks, sergeant in the N.C.
Line; 1000 acres of land within the limits of land reserved for
officers and soldiers of the N.C. Line; issued 15 Dec. 1818.
In 1818, James Cocks, son of Robert, transferred the warrant to
Daniel Cherry.

No. 115. Heirs of Joseph Cox, private in the N.C. Cont. Line;
640 acres of land; issued 18 Dec. 1804. Daniel Cox of Beaufort
Co., N.C., son and heir of Joseph Cox, sold the warrant to James
Hern (?) who transferred it Joseph Terry.

No. 121. Heirs of John Cooper, corporal in the N.C. Cont. Line; 1000 acres; issued 28 Nov. 1805. Jordan Cooper, heir of John Cooper, transferred same to John Brown and James Welbourn in 1805.

No. 688. Heirs of William Cooper,, lieutenant in the N.C. State Line; issued 21 July 1821. Elisha Ham made oath before Amos Jones, J. P., Franklin Co., N. C., that William Cooper was a lieutenant in the N. C. Cont. Line, and that Cooper marched away in the said army and never returned , and said Ham understood that Cooper was killed while in the service, was unmarried, and left one brother, Robert Cooper, who now lives in Franklin Co., N. C.; 14 July 1821. Robert Cooper, only lawful heir of William Cooper, transferred the warrant to Andes Jones; 1821.

No. 166. James Cronister, private in the N.C. Cont. Line; 640 acres; issued 25 Nov. 1808.

No. 163. Heirs of James Carmady, private in the N.C. Cont. Line; 640 acres of land within the limits of land reserved for officers and soldiers of the N.C. Cont. Line; issued 17 Sept. 1808. Elizabeth Hanes, only heir of James Carmady, dec., assigned the warrant to Reuben P. Jones, who assigned it to Frederick B. Nelson on 23 Sept. 1813. In the same month Nelson assigned it to John C. McLemore.

No. 124. Thomas Creecy, on account of a balance due for the services performed by William Luppencute, musician in the N. C. Line; 360 acres; issued 14 Dec. 1805. In Jan. 1806 Creecy assigned the warrant to William Clemens, who assigned it to Thomas N. Clark.

No. 1036. John Cotants, a soldier in the N.C. Cont. Line. Jeesey Cherry, administrator of John Cotants (Concante), endorses the warrant to William Cherry to have surveyed, 2 July 1796. On 2 July 1796 William Cherry assigned it to Samuel Barton, Thomas King and Noah Lilley, witnesses. 13 Aug. 1796, Samuel Barton assigned the warrant to James Saunders. 29 Sept. 1807, James Saunders assigned the warrant to William Davidson, with John Lowery, Daniel Griffin, and Johncon Lowery, Joseph Cummins (?) and Robert Cooper, witnesses. (Paper is in very bad condition).

No. 384. Heirs of Thomas Caswell, corporal, 428 acres within the limits of land reserved for officers and soldiers of the N.C. Cont. Line; issued 3 Aug. 1820. Uriah Caswell, one of the heirs of soldier Thomas Caswell, transferred the warrant to Lawrence Cherry. Milley Bateman, another heir of Thomas Caswell, also transferred her right to the warrant to Lawrence Cherry.

No. 670. Heirs of Hugh Curren, private; 640 acres; issued 27 March 1821. 5 July 1822, Benjamine Hester of Granville Co., N. C., made oath that he knew Hugh Curren, Sr., and Elisha Curren, who enlisted as a soldier in the Troop of Horse under Capt. John Sickerson or Dickerson for two years and six months in the N.C. Cont. Line, and served in the same until they both died in the Rev. War, and Hester further stated that Hugh Curren is the only rightful male heir to the deceased Hugh and Elijah Curren.

No. 582. Heirs of William Campbell, corporal in the N.C. Line; land within the limits of that reserved for officers and soldiers in the Cont. Line; issued 12 Sept. 1820. On 13 Sept. 1820 William Campbell of Beaufort Co., N.C., only true and lawful heir of continental soldier William Campbell, conveyed the warrant to George Brown.

No. 689. Heirs of John Carney, private; 640 acres. Carney was a soldier in the N C Cont. Line in the Rev. War; issued 21 July

1821. Transferred to John Bartholomew on 24 July 1821 and then
to Jacob Bartholomew on 27 Sept. 1821. In June 1821 John and
Frederick Carney of Beaufort Co., N.C., transferred the warrant
to Calvin Jones. On 28 June 1821 Henry Harding of Beaufort Co.,
N.C., made oath before Israel Harding, J. P., that he was a soldier in the Cont. Line and that he knew John Carney, a soldier in
Capt. Sharp's Co., and that they were in the same company. He
also stated that John Carney was taken sick and carried to the
hospital in Camden, S.C., where Carney died in 1781. Harding
testified that Carney was married and left two children now living, John and Frederick Carney both of Cravens Co.

No. 304. William Cooper, private in the N.C. Line; 228 acres
within the limits of land reserved for officers and soldiers of
the Cont. Line; 23 Feb. 1820. Jonathan Cooper of Bertie Co.,
N.C., only heir of said Cooper, transferred the warrant to Laurence Cherry.

No. 496. Heirs of Giles Carter, private in the N.C. Cont. Line;
366 acres; issued 28 Aug. 1820. Ricks Carter, nephew and only
heir of Giles Carter, transferred the warrant to Calvin Jones
for $200.00, on 15 Aug. 1820.

No. 545. Heirs of Thomas Champion, private; 228 acres; within
the limits of lands reserved for officers and soldiers of the
N.C. Line; issued 4 Sept. 1820.

No. 392. Heirs of Cannon Cason, private; 640 acres within the
limits of lands reserved for officers and soldiers of the N.C.
Cont. Line; issued 3 Aug. 1820. Tanner Cason and Milbery Cason,
of Currituck Co., N.C., and heirs of Cannon Cason, transferred
the warrant to Darling Cherry of Martin Co., N.C.

No. 552. Heirs of Solomon Carpenter; ensign; 2560 acres within
the limits of lands reserved for officers and soldiers of the
Cont. Line. Samuel Carpenter and Benjamine Carpenter, heirs of
Solomon Carpenter, transferred the warrant to Richard Smith of
Wake Co., N.C.

No. 355. Heirs of Alxander Coles, corporal; 360 acres of land
within the limits of that reserved for officers and soldiers
of the N.C. Line; 14 July 1820. On 24 Aug. 1820 James McAfee in
right of his wife Polly, and Polly McAfee in her own right,
Jesse Barret (Barnett) in right of his wife Sally and Sally
Burnett in her own right (said Polly and Sally being the daughters and only heirs of Alxander Cole, dec.)assigned the warrant
to Robert Henry. In 1820 John Jarrett, J. P. of Duncombe Co.,
N.C., made oath he knew the above two daughters of Alxander
Cole.

No. 421. Heirs of David Carter, corporal; 360 acres within the
limits of land reserved for officers and soldiers of the Cont.
Line; 19 Aug. 1820. Thomas Carter, uncle and only heir of said
David Carter, said Thomas living in Nash Co., N.C., sold the
warrant to Calvin Jones on 3 Aug. 1820. John Bartholomew appeared before Joel King and Robert H. Wynne, justices for Franklin Co.,, and swore he saw Thomas Carter sign the above conveyance; Aug. 1820.

No. not given. Benjamine Coffield, late an adjutant in the 6th
Regt. of the N.C. Cont. Line. Oct. 1821, Jesse Martin made oath
before John Walton, J. P. for Gates Co., N. C., that he waited
on the aforesaid Coffield, who "had his guts let out by an officer at Cross Creek, and he hoped to carry him (Coffield) to a
small town close by after it was done, and he was discharged."

No. 717. Heirs of Jonathan Cahoon, private; 640 acres within the limits of land reserved for officers and soldiers of the N.C. Cont. Line; issued 3 Aug. 1821.

No. 671. Heirs of Elisha Curron, private; 640 acres of land within the limits of lands reserved for officers and soldiers of the Cont. Line; issued 17 March 1821. Transferred to Allen Wilkins.

No. 153. Heirs of Henry Cheshire, non-commissioned officer in the N.C. Line; 428 acres of land within the limits of that reserved for officers and soldiers of the N.C. Cont. Line; issued Dec. 1807.

No. 169. James Calley, private in the N.C. Line; 274 acres; grant issued 6 Dec. 1808.

No. 899. Shadrack Cummins, private in the N.C. Cont. Line; 640 acres within the limits of land reserves for officers and soldiers of the said line; issued 19 May 1784.

No. 634. Laughlin Campbell, sergeant in the artillery in the N.C. Lines (in both state and Cont.); issued 23 April 1784.

No. 640. William Campbell, private in the N.C. Cont. Line; 640 acres; issued 23 April 1781. Sept. 1796, the warrant was transferred to James Dougherty and Thomas McCrory, with John Doherty a witness.

No. 3054. Joshua Curtis, ensign in the N.C. Cont. Line; issued 26 Nov. 1785. 12 Nov. 1810, Joshua Curtis files an affidavit in Davidson Co., Tenn., stating that the warrant was for 741 acres.

No. 796. Joseph Case, private in the N.C. Cont. Line; 274 acres within the limits of land reserved for officers and soldiers of the N.C. Cont. Line; issued 4 May 1784.

No. 878. Heirs of James Craft, private; 228 acres within the limits of land reserved for officers and soldiers of the N.C. Line; issued 5 Sept. 1821. 20 Sept. 1821, transferred to William G. Hadnott by Mary Craft, Sopha Eubanks, Isaac Eubanks, Nancy Eubanks, and Elisha Eubanks. In 1821 these heirs of James Craft made William G. Hadnott their attorney to sell the warrant. File contains considerable data on the Rev. service of James Craft.

No. 1484. Elijah Cotton, private in the N.C. Cont. Line; 274 acres; issued 20 Dec. 1784. Ephraium Cotton assigned the warrant to David Davis, and Sarah Davis transferred the warrant to Oliver Williams in 1806. Jesse Cobb held the right some time in 1784. In July 1806 the heirs of David Davis (A. Pearce, Mary Pearce, John Page, Levy Page, Sam Wilson, Martha Wilson, Leonard Wood, and Sally Wood) assigned the warrant to Sarah Davis.

No. 4384. Heirs of Oliver Carmach; 640 acres for his services in the Cont. Line; issued at Raleigh on 20 Dec. 1796. In Feb. 1797 transferred to Willia Dickson, with William Rollins a witness. Land was located on 11 May 1797 in Mero District on Red River in Robertson Co., adjoining Daniel Flannery's line.

No. 128. William Caswell, capt. in the N.C. Cont. Line; 1280 acres within the limits of land reserved for officers and soldiers of the said line; issued 22 Oct. 1783.

No. 211. Francis Coops, private in the N.C. State Line; 274 acres
within the limits of land reserved for officers and soldiers of
the Cont. Line; issued 15 Dec. 1810. 26 Jan. 1811, John Anderson, the lawful and sole heir of Francis Coops, transferred the
warrant to James Hearn, with Thomas Edwards a witness. In Feb.
1811 James Hearn transferred it to Arthur Dew who in Jan. 1812
assigned it to Joseph Tarver, with William White, Jr., as a witness.

No. 555. Levi Cotton, private in the N.C. Cont. Line. Location
of grant. N.C. Warrant no. 902. No. location 1077. On Goose
Creek beginning at Charles Dixon's west boundary and running as
the law directs; issued 15 Sept. 1787.

No. 3610. Jones Co., N.C., May Term 1800. Dudley Cahoon, heir
at law of Jonathan Cahoon, a fifer in the N.C. Line, acknowledged
he had assigned warrant no. 3610 to Edward Whitely, Joseph Hill,
Esq., and Daniel Komegy. Warrant for 1000 acres within the
lands reserved for officers and soldiers of the N.C. Line in the
name of Jonathan Cahoon, dated 1788. Dudley Cahoon assigned the
warrant to Wm. Gardner who later assigned it to George Ellis;
the assignments are returned. Same transferred to Mr. Abraham
Kerngy. Transferred by Edward Whitely in 1795. Abraham Kongy
transferred it to Basil Kongy in 1802.

No. 960. Heirs of James Carpenter; 640 acres. Carpenter was a
private in the N.C. Cont. Line. Issued 6 Sept. 1821. In Sept.
1821 the heirs of James Carpenter (Sarah Carpenter, widow, Benjamine Williams, Milley Williams, Claracy Carpenter, Sally Carpenter, and Elizabeth Carpenter) transferred the warrant to William A. Tharpe   Philip Adams made oath in Wake Co., N.C., on 5
June 1821, that James Carpenter was in the Rev. War; that they
lived in the same family; that Carpenter enlisted for three
years in the regular army under Pink Eaton in Halifax Co.; that
Adams always understood that Carpenter served his time with great
credit; that Carpenter returned home and married and had three
children all of whom died without issue and then Carpenter married again and died some few years ago leaving a widow and several children in the neighborhood where Adams now lives.

No. 202. Heirs of Daniel Cherry, private in the N.C. Cont. Line;
640 acres out of lands reserved for officers and soldiers of the
N.C. Cont. Line; issued 31 March 1810.

No. 218. James Campbell, captain in the N.C. Cont. Line; 1780
acres from military lands by Act of General Assembly of 18 Dec.
1811; issued 20 Dec. 1811.

No. 879. Heirs of Stephen Craft, private in the N.C. Cont. Line;
228 acres; issued 6 Sept. 1821. Archibald Craft transferred the
warrant to William G. Hadnott who on 3 Nov. 1821 assigned it to
Joseph Pearce.   Craft, heir at law of Stephen Craft, had made
Hadnott his attorney to sell the warrant. Stephen Craft, father
of Archibald, was a private in the Donohoes Co. of the 6th Regt.
and served two and a half years in the N.C. Cont. Line. Thomas
Prescot and Jeremiah Watson were witnesses to the transfer.

No. 336. Heirs of Jacob Conner, private in the N.C. Cont. Line;
640 acres within the lands reserved for officers and soldiers
of the N.C. Cont. Line; issued 25 June 1820.

No. 356. Heirs of Nathaniel Cooper, private in the N.C. Cont.
Line; 640 acres of land within the limits of land reserved for
officers and soldiers of the N. C. Cont. Line; issued 14 July
1820.

No. 335. Heirs of John Conner, private in the N.C. Cont. Line; 640 acres within the limits of land reserved for officers and soldiers of the N.C. Line; issued 23 June 1820.

No. 327. Heirs of John Cooper, private in the N.C. Cont. Line; 640 acres within the limits of land resrved for officers and soldiers of the said line; issued 30 May 1820.

No. 574. Heirs of John Cardy, private in the N.C. Cont. Line; 640 acres within the limits of land reserved for officers and soldiers of the Cont. Line; issued 9 Sept. 1820. On the same day, Ellender Puwood, sister and only heir at law of John Cardy, dec. assigned the warrant to John Roberts, with James Roberts and John Miller, witnesses. On 11 Sept. 1820 Roberts assigned the warrant to Richard Smith.

No. 556. Heirs of Benjamin Cummins, private; 640 acres within the limits of land reserved for officers and soldiers of the Cont. Line; issued 9 Sept. 1820.

No. 1562. Heirs of Benjamin Commer (or Conner), private in the N.C. Cont. Line; 640 acres; issued 23 Feb. 1785. 19 Jan. 1785 in Hertford Co., N.C., James Conner, brother of Benjamin Conner, authorized Hardy Murfree to receive the grant for 640 acres; Jonathan Pope and Wm. Murfree, Jr., witnesses.

No. 1895. Heirs of Hack Cee, private; 640 acres; issued 15 July 1785, and assigned to Oliver Tuton on 27 Feb. 1786 with James Corbitt a witness. An attached paper states that Charles Robertson, dec., was in possession of the land in 1807. The transfer was signed by C. Robertson, Susanna Robertso, and Jno. Davis.

No. 3276. Heirs of Abner Cole, private in the N.C. Cont. Line; 640 acres; issued 26 Dec. 1785. 28 Dec. 1790, Joseph Cole of Perquimans Co., N.C., heir at law of Abner Cole, dec., assigned the warrant to William Richards of the same county. In 1795 Pollu Richards assigned the warrant to Charles Smallwood, Esq., who transferred the same to William Tyrrell in 1796. Tyrrell assigned the warrant to William Bass in 1797, and in 1799 the same warrant was transferred by William B. Cheatham by his attorney John Cheatham.

No. 2637. Heirs of Simon Carson, private in the N.C. Cont. Line; 640 acres; issued 30 Sept. 1785. In 1785 Isaac Carson assigned it to Thomas Smith and Smith assigned it to Elijah Robertson.

No. 2995. Heirs of George Cooke, a corporal in the N.C. Cont. Line; 1000 acres; issued 30 Sept. 1785. In 1785 Abraham Cooke assigned the warrant to John and James Bonner. Henry Bonner transferred the same to John and James Bonner. Phillip Phillips and Micahel Campbell assigned the warrant to George Cook.

No. 2978. Heirs of John Colchester, private in the N.C. Cont. Line; 640 acres; issued 27 Dec. 1803. In 1788 William Colchester, heir of John Colchester, assigned the same to Mann Phillips.

No. 3144. Heirs of Alexander Cherry, private in the N.C. Cont. Line; 640 acres; issued Dec. 1785.

No. 4717. William Crow, private in the N.C. Cont. Line; 228 acres; issued 15 Feb. 1797. File contains a letter from Hugh Crawford, Sumner Co., Tenn., 1808 relative to this warrant, and a statement from Joshua Scott of Livingston Co., Ky., in 1808.

This land was at Bledsoes Lick in Sumner Co., and Joshua Scott
made his statement before Samuel C. Duff, J. P. of Livingstone
Co., Ky.

No. 4428. Heirs of Walter Dickson, private in the N.C Cont.
Line; 640 acres within the limits of land reserved for officers
and soldiers of the Cont. Line; issued 22 Dec. 1796. On the back
of this warrant it states that on 3 Sept. 1797 John Wright, Jr.,
attorney and administrator of Robert Webb transferred the warrant
to James Roney (Boney or Rooney). In Nov. 1797 Roney transferred
the warrant to Ambrose Mauldin, who in Nov. 1799 made it over to
Joshua Cate; later assigned to John Gwinn.

No. 4354. Cornelius Dean, private in the N.C. Cont. Line; 274
acres; issued 17 Dec. 1796, and later transferred to William
Hall.

No. 296. Joseph Dickson, private in the N.C. Cont. Line; 640
acres; issued 2 Dec. 1819, and transferred to Robert Henry on
26 April 1820.

No. 118. Nimrod Dawson. (No. 58). "Invalid."

No. 117. Nimrod Dawson. "Invalid."

No. 165. Josiah Danforth, no. 950, 600 acres from any unappropriated lands, under the rules, regulations and restrictions as
by law directed. This warrant was issued from a grant to Stockley Donelson for 100,000 acres of land, no. 204 dated 6 Jan.
1795; by virtue of a ten pound warrant issued 27 Sept. 1805.

No. 202. James Davis; 100 acres of land on any unappropriated
lands, under the rules, regulations, and restrictions as by law
directed. This warrant issued from a grant to Robert Nelson
for 640 acres of no. 379, dated 15 Sept. 1787, obtained by virtue of a military warrant. Issued 12 May 1808. 18 July 1803
assigned to John Harris, with Frederick Leek a witness. In
1803, same was tranferred to David Dobbins, with Jno. Childress
as a witness.

No. 3489. Henry Drewry, private in the N.C. State Line; 228
acres within the limits of lands reserved by law for the officers and soldiers of the Cont. Line; issued 2 Feb. 1786. The
same month it was transferred to Daniel Anderson, with John
Marshall a witness.

No. 106. Henry Dyke; 50 acres; transferred by Dyke to George
Gordon or Gordan.

No. 115. Nimrod Dawson; no. 55. L00 acres "Invalid."

No. 116. Nimrod Dawson, "Invalid."

No. 2337. Jno. G. and Thomas Blount, 640 acres on account of
the services of John Darden, private in the N. C. Cont. Line.
The land was located on the Harpeth River in Davidson Co., on 3
August 1798.

No. 3146. Rd. Barbour; 365 acres. Richard Barbour was the assignee of Frederick Davis, a private in the N.C. Cont. Line,
Sept. 1797.

No. 4446. Heirs of John Daniel; 640 acres. Daniel was a private in the N.C. Cont. Line. Issued 22 Dec. 1796. On 22 Aug.
1797 Daniel assigned the warrant to Joseph Ming, with Benj. S.

Simp, witness. 19 Nov. 1798, Joseph Ming assigned same to Stephen Merigno, with Hardy Rundle a witness.

No. 4485. Hugh Davis, private in the N.C. Cont. Line; 640 acres
within the limits of land reserved for soldiers and officers of
the N.C. Cont. Line; issued 22 Dec. 1796. 20 Feb. 1797 the warrant was transferred to Abner Pillow, with John Moore a witness.

No. 389. Heirs of Francis DeLong, a musician in the state line:
1000 acres of land within the limits reserved for soldiers and
officers of the Cont. Line; issued 3 Aug. 1820. On 13 July 1820
Henry Delong, Meriam Delong, Simon Delong, Jesse Delong, Ann De-
long, Pennina Delong, and Margaret Delong of Pasteotank Co., N.C.,
the only heirs of their father Mark Delong who was the only heir
of Francis Delong a continental soldier, all transferred the warrant to Darling Cherry of Martin Co., N.C. Eli Cherry, Nathan
Delong and Mark S. (A or E) Delong were witnesses.

No.4555. Jeremiah Doxey, private in the N. C. Line; 228 acres
within the limits reserved for officers and soldiers of the N.C.
Cont. Line; issued 7 Feb. 1797. On 16 Feb. the warrant was
transferred to Andrew Coussar, with William Horton and James
Marcum or Marcom as witnesses.

No. 492. Heirs of Jehu Davis, an ensign; 2560 acres within the
limits of land reserved for officers and soldiers of the state
Cont. Line; issued 25 Aug. 1820.

No. 637. Heirs of William Dennis, private in the N.C. Cont. Line;
640 acres; issued 15 Sept. 1820.

No. 328. Heirs of Hugh Donnelly, private in the N.C. Cont. Line;
640 acres; issued 30 May 1820.

No. 105. Philip Dean, private in the N.C. Cont. Line; 640 acres;
issued 11 Dec. 1804. John Wooten and Shad Wootin, attorneys for
Nathan Dean who was heir of Philip Dean, dec., assigned the warrant to Archable McMillin on 24 Jan. 1801.

No. 133. Heirs of John Durham, musician in the N.C. Cont. Line;
1000 acres; issued 18 Dec. 1806. On 16 Feb. 1807 Thomas Sutton
and his wife Milley (who was sister and only heir of John Durham)
transferred the warrant to John Gray Blount. The Suttons were of
Beaufort Co., N.C.

No. 104. Sterling Dean, private in the N.C. Cont. Line; 640
acres; issued 11 Dec. 1804. Shadrick Wooten and John Wooten certify they had signed over their rights to the warrant to Nathaniel
Davis, 9 April 1805. Abraham Hunter, George Wiggins and Grays
Westbrook, witnesses.

No. 167. John Dean, private in the N.C. Cont. Line; issued 5
Jan. 1808.   On 30 Nov. 1808 William Dean, brother and heir at
law of said John Dean, transferred the warrant to Robert W. Goodman of Raleigh.

No. 193. William Dennis, private in the N.C. Cont. Line; 228
acres within the limits reserved for officers and soldiers of
the N.C. Cont. Line; issued 9 Dec. 1809. The same was transferred to Benjamine Batts by Asa Dennis, heir of William Dennis,
4 Jan. 1812, James Hearn and Jeremiah Batts were witnesses. 12
May 1818 Benjamine Batts transferred same to William C. Powell,
with Richard Powell as witness.

No. 171. Elijah Duncan, private in the N.C. Cont. Line; 274
acres within the limits reserved for officers and soldiers of

of the N.C. Cont. Line; issued 22 Oct. 1783. On 1 Dec. 1783
Duncan transferred the same to James Sanders. In July 1784 James
Sanders assigned it to Denas Condra, James Shaw a witness.

No. 152. Heirs of James Dodrill, non-commissioned officer in
the N.C. Line; 1000 acres; issued 16 Dec. 1807.

No. 147. Joseph Davidson, private in the N.C. Cont. Line; is-
sued 6 April 1807. On 24 May 1807 William Stephenson, agent for
Joseph Davidson, transferred the warrant to Newton Cannon, with
Merion Sanderson and Jonathan Floyd as witnesses.

No. 143. Henry Dundalon (Dundalow) heirs. Henry Dundalow was a
corporal in the N.C. Cont. Line. 428 acres issued for his services on 19 Dec. 1806.In April 1807 Lemuel Hosea of Perquimans
Co.,N.C., and wife Sarah who was the only heir of Henry Dundalow,
transferred the warrant to Daniel Cherry.

No. 142. Elisha Dotson; also no. 868. On 26 Oct. 1809 Elisha
Dotson appeared before Enun Cameron, J. P. of Williamson Co.,
Tenn., and deposed that he made an entry in Adair's office for
300 acres at the mouth of Crockett's Creek, to run up the river
for compliment for which entry he paid the purchase money and
office fees, and never applied for nor received any warrant,
etc.

No. 880. Geirge Dismukes, private; 228 acres within the limits
reserved for officers and soldiers of the Cont. Line; issued
5 Sept. 1821.

No. 686. Heirs of Joab Douge, drummer, balance of 726 acres;
issued 19 July 1821. Caleb Dozer assigned the same to Joseph
L. (or S.) Jones on 7 March 1822, with Miles Gregory and William
Jones as witnesses.

No. 2414. William Darnald, private in the N.C. Cont. Line; 640
acres; issued 30 Sept. 1783. In Nov. 1785, Darnald assigned the
warrant to Thomas Smith, with Thos. Butcher as a witness. On
16 April 1798 Smith assigned the warrant to James H. (or N.)
Caffety, who on 17 Nov. 1798 assigned it to John Court.
      William Darnall of Caswell Co. made oath before Davis Gooch
and Nanah Williams, acting justices of the said county, that
he never sold, made over, or conveyed his right to warrant 2414
drawn by Capt. Joshua Davis on 30 Sept. 1785 to any person nor
ever received any compensation for same. He received the warrant for his service in the Cont. Army, and got a discharge.
The statement was made on 25 Aug. 1804. In Aug. 1804 Darnall
assigned the warrant to John Kimbrough of Rutherford Co., Tenn.,
David Gooch a witness.

No. 2972. Heirs of Martin Douglas, sergeant in the N.C. Cont.
Line; 1000 acres within the limits of land reserved for officers
and soldiers of the N.C. Cont. Line; issued 27 Dec. 1803. Mann
Phillips, assignee of the heirs of Martin Douglas, entered 1000
acres in the Barrens on the trace from McFadens to the mouth of
Red River, 4 Nov. 1788, George Bell signed. On 25 May 1805
Phillips transferred the same to Thomas Dillon, with George
Keeling, Thos. White, and Alexander Lester as witnesses. On 20
Oct. 1805 Dillon transferred the same to Thomas N. Clarke, with
Can (?) Moore, witness.

No. 1886. William Deacon, private in the N.C. Cont. Line; 182
acres: issued 11 July 1785.

No. 1188. John Dickson: 640 acres in Tennessee County, for the
bravery and zeal of John Dillar, a private in the said line of

N.C. The 640 acres were granted to John Dickson as assignee of said Dillar, and were located on both sides of the Cumberland River, on eastern branch of the upper fork of Barton's Creek, and adjoining Edward Dickson's north boundary and Claborn Ivey's east boundary. Samuel Blair and James Russell witnessed the transfer.

No. 194. Jeremiah Dixon, private in the N.C. Cont. Line; 274 acres; issued 19 Dec. 1809. 15 Jan. 1810 Jeremiah Dixon of Richmond Co., transferred the same to Rufus Johnson, who on 1 March 1810 assigned it to Isaac Lanier. On 10 June 1810 Lanier assigned it to Benjamine Edwards.

No. 3167. Heirs of Zach. Davis, private in the N.C. Cont. Line; 640 acres within the limits of land reserved for officers and soldiers of the N.C. Cont. Line; issued 19 Dec. 1785.

No. 3228. Heirs of Abner Dennis, dec., private in the N.C. Cont. Line; 640 acres; issued 23 Dec. 1785.

No. 1967. Granville Davies (Davis), private in the N.C. Cont. Line; issued 10 Aug. 1785. On 6 April 1797 Benjamine Davis, as attorney for Granville Davis, assigned the same to Thomas Perror, William Bullock a witness. At that time Thomas Perror, Esq., lived in Granville Co., N.C. On 22 Feb. 1806 Perron (sic) assigned it to William P. Little, with Thomas Dillon a witness.

No. 3045. Heirs of Thomas Dring, private in the N.C. Cont. Line; issued 25 Nov. 1785. On 26 Jan. 1786, James Dring of Craven Co., N.C., only brother and sole heir of Thomas Dring, dec., transferred the warrant to Stephen Slade of Craven Co.

No. 1098. Ethelred Dance, ensign in the N.C. Cont. Line; 914 acres; issued 11 April 1823. On 26 Jan. 1825 Henry Dance for Ethelred Dance, assigned the same to William Barron, with R. M. McClroy a witness. Samuel H. Nelm, clerk of Perry Co., Alabama, court certified that Ransom McClroy or McElroy acknowledged the deed before him.

No. 3000. Benjamine Davison, private in the N.C. Cont. Line; 274 acres within the limits of land resrved for officers and soldiers of the N.C. Cont. Line; issued 30 Sept. 1785. Benjamine Davison assigned the same to John and James Bonner. Henry Bonner, as executor of the last will and testament of James Bonner, dec., survivor and devisee of John Bonner, dec., assigned the same to Edward Harris.

No. 2997. Isaac Dines, private in the N.C. Cont. Line; issued 30 Sept. 1785, and assigned in Oct. 1785 to John and James Bonner. Henry Bonner assigned it to Edward Harris. Henry Bonner was the executor of the last will and testament of James Bonner, dec., survivor and devisee of John Bonner.

No. 2976. Heirs of Ephraium Daniel, private in the N.C. Cont. Line; 640 acres; issued 27 Dec. 1803. Mann Phillips as assignee of the heirs of George Daniel, entered 640 acres on 17 June 1786 lying on a small branch of Blooming Grove, to join an entry of Robert Nelson's.

No. 2981. Heirs of Elias Dobson, private in the N.C. Cont. Line; 640 acres within the limits of land reserved for officers and soldiers of the N.C. Cont. Line; issued 27 Dec. 1803. Mann Phillips, assignee of the heirs of Elias Dobson, entered 640 acres on the north side of Robert Nelson's 640 acre entry of 1786. Phillips assigned it to Thomas Dillon in 1805. Dillon assigned it to someone else.

No. 365. Heirs of John Downs, sergeant; 1000 acres; issued 24
July 1820. Bartholomew Bowers and Louis D. Wilson purchased the
same from the heirs of John Downs, dec.; i.e., Willie Downs and
Rebecca Price, with Stephen Lee and Charleton Clemons witnesses.

No. 2800. Heirs of Jesse Davis, private in the N.C. Cont. Line;
640 acres; issued 13 Dec. 1802. The same was transferred to
Armstead Stubblefield in May 1805 by heirs of Jesse Davis, Henry
W. Lawson, with William Thompson and George Stubblefield as wit-
nesses. There are three signatures, almost obliterated: (?)
Davis, Wile Davis, and (?)inney Gast(?).

No. 2911. Heirs of Hugh Dundeloe, private in the N.C. Cont. Line;
issued 30 Sept. 1785. On 12 May 1785, John Dundalo assigned the
same to John Sheppard. On 11 Aug. 1806 John Sheppard, James Sheppard, and Reading Sheppard assigned the same to Stephen Mongomery
or Montgomery, with Andrew Love as a witness. On 2 May 1807 S.
Montgomery assigned it to Andrew Love.

No. 100. Asa Davis, private in the N.C. Cont. Line; 640 acres;
issued 30 Nov. 1804. In Sept. 1805, David Davis, only lawful heir
of said Asa Davis, sold the same to John Garrowon. In 1806 Lydia
Garowan, widow and only heir of John Garowan assigned it to James
Roulston, with James Ewing a witness.

No. 210. Heirs of William Deal, private in the N.C. Cont. Line;
640 acres; issued 30 Nov. 1810. William Deal of Chowan Co., heir
at law of William Deal, dec., a private in the N.C. Cont. Line,
transferred it to Jesse Cherry in 1811, with Sam Skinner and Dem-
sey Skinner as witnesses.

No. 205. Heirs of Roger Drapper, private in the N.C. Cont. Line;
640 acres; issued 2 Oct. 1810. In 1810 Nathaniel Louis (?), heir
of R. Draper, assigned it to Reuben P. Jones.

No. 1049. Robert Dean, private in the N.C. Cont. Line; 640 acres;
issued May 1784. In Nov. 1795, Henry Nowlin, a legal heir, assigned the warrant to William Gill.

No. 1495. George Davis, private in the N.C. Cont. Line; 228
acres; issued Nov. 1784.

No. 4739. Heirs of Sterling Devaney, private in the N.C. Cont.
Line; 640 acres; issued Feb. 1797. The land was in Mero District,
Sumner Co., on Barren River; surveyed to Robert Stothard.

No. 1524. Ezekial Dennis, private in the N.C. Cont. Line; issued
Jan. 1785, and assigned to David Davis, Wm. Davis, and Gideon
Pillow.

No. 1811. Samuel Lanford, assignee of Jesse Dewet who was a private in the N.C. Cont. Line; 640 acres in Sumner Co., in 1793.

No. 669. Heirs of John Dickson, a captain in the N.C. Cont. Line;
1371 acres; issued 27 March 1821. John Dickson assigned it to
Harvey Smith in 1821, and Smith assigned it to Allen Wilkins in
the same year. Wilkins assigned it to David Goodloe.

No. 1380. Davidson Co., Tenn/ Lands adjoining James Dickson
and Joseph Grimes, and James Dickson, Jr.; issued 26 May 1807.

No. 128. Francis Mayberry (Maybury), 100 acres of land on any
unappropriated lands under the rules, regulations and restrictions
as by law directed. This warrant issued from a grant of Thomas
King for 100 acres, no. 431, dated 29 July 1793. Signed 11 July
1803 by William Maclin. Aug. 1803 assigned to John Dale, with
James Boyd a witness.

No. 4556. Joshua Dillon, private in the N.C. Cont. Line; issued
9 Feb. 1797. John Medeares, capt., Joshua Hadley, capt., and
G. Bradley, capt., all stated that Joshua Dillon served two and
a half years in Capt. McRees Co.

No. 5069. Heirs of Elleck Dawson, corporal in the N.C. State
Line; 1000 acres within the limits of land reserved for officers
and soldiers of the Cont. Line; issued 6 Dec. 1797.

No. 1725. Samuel Barton; 640 acres; issued 20 May 1793 to Samuel
Barton, assignee of John Duffey, private in the N. C. Cont. Line.
10 July 1800 Reuben Cage, sheriff of Sumner Co., Tenn., deeded
this warrant to John Irwin of the same county. The land was on
Barton's Creek, Sumner Co., Tenn.

No. 3460. George Dealer, private in the N.C. Cont. Line; 274
acres; issued 26 Feb. 1796.

No. 3915. Benjamine Dorton, private in the N.C. State and Cont.
Lines; 228 acres; issued 5 Dec. 1795.

No. no. given. Jehu Dimery of Liberty Co., S. C., late of Bla-
den Co., N.C., transferred a military land warrant to Benjamine
Fitzrandolph, Jr., of Bladen Co., N.C., in the presence of John
Dimery and John Brown of Zah.

No. 4339. Heirs of John Davis, a private in the N.C. Cont. Line;
640 acres; issued 16 Dec. 1797. On 20 June 1797 Matthew Davis
transferred the warrant to Jobe Smith who assigned it to William
Patterson on 25 Aug. 1797. John Patterson and Jonathan Gullick
witnessed the transfer. In July 1803 Patterson assigned it to
Benjamin Clark.

No. 4353. Heirs of Elven Denneston, private in the N.C. Cont.
Line; 640 acres within the limits reserved for officers and soldiers of the Cont. Line; issued 17 Dec. 1796. To satisfy a
judgement obtained by Charles I. Lover against William Tyrrell
in the Superior Court in Smith Co., Tenn., on 13 May 1807.
John Denneston, heir of Eleven Denneston, assigned the warrant
to William Tyrrell and Wm. Lytle, with Abra. Sewagerty, Jesse
Sharp, and James Marcorm or Marcorn witnesses. In 1818 H. Tatum
assigned this warrant to Jesse Blackfam.

No. 3901. Jehu Dimery...(only a small piece of this record was
found; in bad condition).

No. 5160. Heirs of Joel Dawes, private; 640 acres of land within
the limits reserved for officers and soldiers of the N.C. Cont.
Line; issued 8 Dec. 1797. This warrant was transferred several
times. In 1799 it was transferred to Thomas Dillon who in Oct.
1804 made it over to Moses Fisk.

No. 507. Heirs of John Evans, private; 640 acres within the
limits reserved for officers and soldiers of the N.C. Cont. Line;
issued 29 Aug. 1820.

No. 1538. Nathan Ewell, private; 223 acres; issued 5 Feb. 1785.
Richard Robberd (?) transferred the warrant to William Kornegy
on 9 Feb. 1785, with Philip Shields a witness.

No. 1219. Heirs of Joseph Elkins, corporal; 360 acres within
the limits reserved for officers and soldiers of the Cont. Line;
issued 6 Jan. 1825. Shadrack Elkins, only heir of said Joseph
Elkins assigned the warrant to Jacob Harder on on 28 June 1826,
with Moses Thompson and George Riddle, witnesses.

No. 2100.   Robert Ecart, private in the N.C. Cont. Line; 297
acres.

No. 881.   Ely Eli, captain in the Rev. War, died in the service
of the U. S. without issue or heirs, and whose real estate thus
became escheated, and belongs to the Trustees of the University
of North Carolina. Warrant issued 5 Sept. 1821. On the back of
the warrant, Willis Reaves, executor of ANdes Jones, dec., the
purchaser and agent from Eliza W. Eley, the only heir of aforesaid Ely Eli, transferred the right, title, and interest of
the within warrant to Richard Smith, on 23 Dec. 1822.

No. 3555.   Jacob Eason, private in the N.C. Line; issued 27 May
1787.   In Dec. 1789 the warrant was transferred to Robert Ewing
who on 15 March 1790 made it over to Hugh McWilliams, with Reuben Ewing a witness.

No. 4488.   Andrew Ellison, private in the N.C. Cont Line; 274
acres; issued 22 Dec. 1796. On 27 Dec. 1796, Ellison transferred
the warrant to Stockley Donelson, with John McFarlin a witness.
Donelson assigned it to Joshua Hadley on 2 Jan. 1797, with Mark
Cole a witness.   Hadley assigned it to Wilson Cage on 22 April
1797.

No. 1842.   Abner Everidge, private in the N.C. Cont. Line; 640
acres; issued 14 June 1785.   William T. Lewis of Surry Co., N.
C., purchased the warrant on 7 Feb. 1785, with Parks King and
Michael Bacon as witnesses.   William Armstrong, captain in the
regular U. S. Army, during the Revolution in North Carolina,
appeared before Andrew Campbell, J. P., of Hawkins Co., Tenn.,
and stated that Abner Everidge was a soldier in his company,
was taken sick and got leave to go home, and that after peace
a. Mr. Williem Terrell Lewis produced an order for a land grant
for him.   Statements, etc., 2 July 1808.

No. 3130.   David Edward, private in the N.C. Line; issued 10
June 1826.

No. not given.   James Edwards, Mathew Edwards, Martha Edwards,
Rebecca Edwards, Charles Edwards, and Temperance Edwards of
Northampton Co., N.C., all heirs of John Edwards, a corporal
in the Revolutionary War, for $125.00 paid by Andes Jones
of Nash Co., N. C., on 5 Jan. 1822 (evidently transferred the
warrant to Jones - R. B.).   William Daugherty was a witness.
22 Jan. 1822 Andes Jones transferred the warrant to the Trustees of the University of North Carolina.

No. 156.   Suckey Enloe, legatee of John Enloe, dec., who was a
captain in the N.C. Cont. Line, was issued a warrant on 22 Oct.
1785.   On 25 Dec. 1785. The warrant was transferred to Thomas
Person.

No. 489.   John Ellis, private in the N.C. Cont. Line; 228 acres;
issued 23 Aug. 1820. Transferred to Thomas Henderson, Jr., on 29
Aug. 1820.

No. 660.   Pumfret Edwards, a private in the N.C. Cont. Line;
228 acres; issued 21 Feb. ;821, and transferred to George Brasfield Esq., on 18 June 1821, with David Clements as a witness.
Brasfield transferred it to Joseph Lynn on 19 Oct. 1821, with
Willie Brasfield a witness.

No. 648.   Charles Ellums, private in the N.C. Line; 228 acres
within the limits reserved by law for officers and soldiers of
the Cont. Line; issued 24 Oct. 1820.

No. 957. Heirs of Mathew Everett, private; 640 acres within the
limits of land reserved for officers and soldiers in the N. C.
Cont. Line; issued 6 Sept. 1821. On 10 Sept. 1821 James Everett
transferred the warrant to William A. Tharpe.   On 30 June 1821
Richard Standly testified that Mathew Everett was an enlisted
soldier under Capt. Lytle for twelve months, and that he died
in service between Charleston (Charlestown) and Little York.
Mathew left three brothers: William, the eldest, who left Wake
Co., N.C., with a woman named Viney London many years ago; James,
the second brother; and Zachariah, the youngest.

No. 375. Heirs of John Eager, private; 274 acres of land for
services in the N. C. Cont. Line; issued 28 July 1820.

No. 876. Heirs of James Eslick, private in the line of this
state; 640 acres of land; issued 5 Sept. 1821. James Eslick, Jr.,
went before justices in Willoughby Precinct, Carteret Co., N. C,
and testified that he knew his uncle, James Eslick, who served
in the Cont. Line, and that the said James Eslick died in Feb.
1778 while in the service. James Eslick left a brother Francis
Eslick, father of said deponent, who claimed to be the heir of
the soldier. On 24 Aug. 1822 the warrant was transferred to John
C. McLemore and Jesse Blackfar, after Eslick had assigned it on
23 Feb. 1822 to Jonathan Hibbs.

No. 360. Heirs of Moses Eastus, private; 640 acres for services
in the N. C. Cont. Line; issued 19 July 1820.

No. 142. Ezekial England; a 50 shilling warrant dated 3 Nov.
1803.

No. 35. Jacob Eaterley; marked "Invalid;" issued 28 Oct. 1803;
Eaterley sold it to George Gordon on 30 Aug. 1804.

No. 567. Heirs of Thomas Evans, private in the N. C. Cont. Line;
640 acres. On 12 Sept. 1820, Elizabeth Banttett (Bantlett), the
heir at law of Thomas Evans, dec., sold the warrant to Jonathan
Hibbs.

No. 4309. Heirs of Nicholas Flynn, private in the N. C. Cont.
Line; 640 acres of land within the limits reserved for officers
and soldiers of the Cont. Line; issued 14 Dec. 1796. The warrant was assigned to Stockley Donelson on 10 Nov. 1796. In Dec.
1796 Donelson assigned the warrant to James M. Lewis, who then
assigned it to Thomas Hickman, with William Hickman as a witness.

No. 4308. Robert Flinn, private in the N. C. Cont. Line; 640
acres of land within the limits of land reserved for officers
and soldiers of the N. C. Cont. Line; issued 14 Dec. 1796. The
said Robert Flinn assigned the warrant to Stockley Donelson who
made it over to Geo. B. Curtis, who assigned it to James Marshall
in 1802.

No. 116. James Falconer, sergeant in the N. C. Cont. Line; 428
acres within the limits of land reserved for officers and soldiers of the N. C. Cont. Line; issued 29 March 1805. John Webb,
attorney for J. Falconer, transferred the warrant to Benjamine
Broschell or Brackett, with Melton Younge a witness. B. Brackett
assigned the same to John Rutherford in 1805, with E. P. Chambers
a witness.

No. 649. William Foster, private in the N. C. Cont. Line; 640
acres within the limits reserved for officers and soldiers of the
N. C. Line; issued 27 Oct. 1820. The warrant was assigned to
Alexander B. Bradford in 1826.

No. 3169.   Heirs of John Farrille, private in the N. C. Cont. Line; 640 acres within the limits reserved for officers and soldiers of the N. C. Cont. Line; issued 19 Dec. 1785. The warrant was transferred to William Lytle in March 1796, with P. Casso a witness.

No. 129.   Heirs of Ambrose Franklin, private in the N. C. Cont. Line; 412 acres; issued 16 April 1806, and assigned to John McGee in June 1806.

No. 128.   Heirs of Charles Franklin, private in the N. C. Cont. Line; 412 acres within the limits of land reserved for officers and soldiers of the N. C. Cont. Line; issued 16 April 1806. In Dec. 1806 Sarah Boon, lawful heir, transferred the warrant to Darrell Young, with Henry Exum as a witness.

No. 2018 (or 3108).   Luke Lamb Ferrell, Esq., lieutenant, within the lines of this state; 2560 acres within the limits of land reserved for officers and soldiers of the N. C. Cont. Line; issued 8 Dec. 1785. In 1802 Luke Lamb, heir of Luke Lamb Ferrell, and admin. of the dec. Ferrell, transferred the warrant to John Swain. Swean transferred the warrant to Armstead Stubblefield in 1803.

No. 2848.   Heirs of William Fillgon, private in the N. C. Cont. Line; 640 acres within the limits of land reserved for officers and soldiers of the N. C. Cont. Line; issued 30 Sept. 1785. In Aug. 1785 the warrant was assigned to John Sheppard. James Sheppard and Reading Sheppard, heirs of John Sheppard, transferred the warrant to Stephen Montgomery in 1806, and Montgomery made it over to Andrew Love in 1807.

No. 2802.   Heirs of Samuel Flemin, private in the N. C. Cont. Line; issued 30 Sept. 1785, and assigned to George Augustus Sugg in Oct. 1785.

No. 660.   John Franks, private in the line of this state; 640 acres for services in the N. C. Cont. Line; issued 23 April 1784. The same was sold to Edward Butler, 158 acres.

No. 3343.   Timothy Fields, private in the N. C. Cont. Line; 274 acres within the limits reserved for officers and soldiers of the N. C. Cont. Line; issued 7 Jan. 1786. In 1798 James Fields, heir of Timothy Fields, assigned the warran to James Arbuthnot, who in 1796 (sic) transferred the warrant to John McClellan who assigned it to Charles McClung.

No. 2450.   Heirs of John Fones, dec., private in the line of the said state; 640 acres within the limits reserved for officers and soldiers of the N. C. Cont. Line; issued 30 Sept. 1785. In Oct. 1805 Aaron Fones transferred the warrant to Benjamine McCulloch. Fones appears to be the heir of John Fones, but the fact is not expressly stated. In 1792 the warrant was transferred by McCulloch to John Lancaster, by direction of Robert Hayes. Geo. M. Deadrick was a witness.

No. 3495.   Jarrell Fitchjarrell, private in the N. C. Cont. Line; 640 acres within the limits reserved for officers and soldiers of the N. C. Cont. Line; issued 8 Feb. 1786, and transferred in that month to Nathaniel Taylor. Taylor transferred it to John C. Hamilton, who then made it over to John Glover.

No. 4599.   Heirs of Lewis Fields, private in the N. C. Cont. Line; 640 acres within the limits of land reserved for officers and soldiers of the N. C. Cont. Line; issued 9 Feb. 1797. John Fields, heir at law of Lewis Fields assigned the warrant to Hezekiah Woodward and John Ward, with George Sims a witness.

No. 3598. Heirs of Thomas Flynear, private in the N. C. Cont.
Line; 640 acres; issued 9 Feb. 1797. Jonathan Flynear transferred the warrant to Stockley Donelson on 13 Feb. 1799. Jonathan described himself as Thomas' heir. A. Bromley was a witness. On 23 Feb. 1797 Donelson assigned the same to James Cowan
who assigned it to Robert Searcey on 13 April 1804, with Thomas
Dillon a witness. Searcey assigned it to James Huling.

No. 4424. Henry Ferguson, a military grant (Warrant is in poor
condition and does not show rank). The warrant was transferred
to William and Gideon Pillow in Wake Co., N. C.

No. 46. Heirs of Robert Forbus, private in the N. C. Cont.
Line; 640 acres within the limits reserved for officers and soldiers of the N. C. Cont. Line; issued 30 Nov. 1801.

No. 920. Aquilla Sugg, dec. A grant for the services of private Joshua Fowler of the N. C. Line; 640 acres granted to said
Sugg (See certificate no. 3644). Issued to H. H. Sugg; interference with grant no. 2125.

No. 173. George Farragut; by virtue of a fifty shilling warrant;
assigned to Charles McClung in May 1803.

No. 3960. A petition was sent to the General Assembly of Tennessee for the purpose of examining the warrant of Moses Fisk.

No. 1936. Micajah Fullington, private in the N. C. Cont. Line;
issued 27 July 1785.

No. not given. John Fisher; power of attorney to N. Ewing, recorded in Book 4, p. 329, on 9 Dec. 1803. Nathan Ewing of Davidson Co., Tenn., being possessed of a military land warrant for
274 acres, numbered 50, issued to James Fisher, now dec., the
19th of Dec. 1801 for services performed by the said James Fisher
as a soldier in the N. C. Cont. Line. John Fisher of Currituck
Co.; N. C. brother and heir at law of the said James Fisher,
granted the power of attorney to Nathan Ewing to sell the warrant.

No. 4425. Isham Ferguson, private; 640 acres for his services
in the N. C. Cont. Line; issued 22 Dec. 1796, and assigned to
William Tyrrell. The land was located in Davidson Co., on Dog
Creek, a branch of Harpeth River.

No. 3926. Malachi Fike. The heirs of James Fike were granted
640 acres for James' services as a private in the line of this
state; issued 8 Dec. 1795.

No. 4677. Sampson Ferrell (or Terrell), private; 640 acres; issued 9 (?) 1797. The same was transferred to Sterling Brewer,
who transferred it to William Tyrrell on 4 March 1797. Jno. Allen, sheriff of Stewart Co., Tenn., assigned the same to Bennet
Searcy on entry made in Military Land Office on 27 March 1797
for 640 acres in the name of William Tyrrell, assignee of Sampson Tyrrell heirs.

No. 50. This file is in bad condition and incomplete. There is
no full copy of the warrant. Same transferred 13 Sept. 1802 by
Renchett McDaniels to Nathan Ewing in Davidson Co., and was assigned to John Buchanan and Moses Ridley on 21 May 1816, Thomas
Childress a witness. This warrant was issued to James Fisher;
274 acres for his revolutionary services.

No. 177. Moses Fisk, assignee, marked "Invalid." No. 1011. Survey for Hugh Dunlap, 100 acres of land on any unappropriated

under the rules, regulations and restrictions as by law directed.
The warrant was issued from a grant to Hugh Dunlap for 500 acres,
of no. 263, dated 7 March 1796, obtained by virtue of fifty
shilling warrant.

No. 4424. Henry Ferguson, private; 640 acres for his services
in the N. C. Cont. Line; land located in Davidson Co.

No. 869. Heirs of Thomas Ferrell; 640 acres; for services as a
private in the N. C. Line; issued 23 Aug. 1821, and transferred
on the same date by Veazey Ferrell to George Brasfield, who on
6 Oct. 1821, assigned the same to Thos Wynns.

No. 337. Heirs of William Flury, sergeant, 1000 acres for services in the N. C. Cont. Line; issued 23 June 1820.

No. 510. Heirs of James Fikes, sergeant; 1000 acres within the
limits of lands reserved for officers and soldiers of the N. C.
Cont. Line; issued 30 Aug. 1820, and transferred on 31 Aug. 1820
by Nathan Fike to Joseph Hurbork (?), Zach. Harman a witness.

No. 359. Heirs of Timothy Fields, private; 640 acres within the
limits of land reserved for officers and soldiers of the N. C.
Cont. Line; issued 17 July 1820. John G. Field, heir at law of
the within named Timothy Fields, authorized Joseph N. Seawell to
locate and obtain a grant for the warrant, 1 Aug. 1820.

No. 3947. A. Foster; 200 acres; a military warrant.

No. 4426. James Ginn, private in the N. C. Cont. Line; 640
acres within the limits of land reserved for officers and soldiers of the N.C. Line; issued 22 Dec. 1796. John Hunter, attorney for James Ginn, on 22 Feb. 1797 assigned the warrant to Samuel French, witnessed by (?) Shelton, Jonathan Church, and Moses
Vincent, 7 Sept. 1797. Samuel French of Pittsylvania Co., Va.,
transferred same to Alexander Joyce, with Adam Tate and Geo.
Adams as witnesses.

No. 4415. Oliver Gresham, private in the N. C. Cont. Line; 228
acres; issued 22 Dec. 1796. On 1 March 1797 Gresham transferred
the warrant to Redmond Dillon Barry, who assigned it to Edward
Gwin on 13 Aug. 1798.

No. 4531. Elisha Garland, private in the N. C. Cont. Line; 228
acres within the limits of land reserved for officers and soldiers of the N. C. Cont. Line; issued 24 Dec. 1796. The warrant
was assigned to Jonathan Frier Robertson on 30 July 1802, with
Jno. Davis a witness.

No. 4532. John Garland, private; 228 acres of land; issued 24
Dec. 1796, and transferred to James Robertson.

No. 1902. David Gunn, private in the N. C. Cont. Line; issued
15 July 1785, and transferred to James Cole Mountflorence on 20
Aug. 1788, with Robert King a witness.

No. 4378. Heirs of Lewis Guttrege, private in the N. C. Cont.
Line; 640 acres within the limits reserved for officers and soldiers of the Cont. Line; issued 20 Dec. 1796.

No. 4377. Matthew Guttrige, private in the N. C. Cont. Line;
640 acres; issued 20 Dec. 1796.

No. 318. Heirs of Thomas Gibson, ensign in the N. C. Cont. Line;
within the limits of land reserved for officers and soldiers of
the said line; issued 15 May 1820. Thomas J. Davis of New Hano-

ver Co., N. C., sold the warrant to Calvin Jones of N. C. in 1820, H. Potter a witness.

No. 130. Heirs of Isaac Gumbs, a private in the N. C. Cont. Line; 640 acres within the limits reserved for officers and soldiers of the Cont. Line; issued 2 Dec. 1806.

No. 687. Heirs of William Green, lieutenant; 2560 acres for services in N. C. Line; issued 21 July 1821.

No. 1046. John Grimmage (Grummage), private in the N. C. Cont. Line; 640 acres; issued 26 May 1784, and transferred to Wm. Lytle in May 1785.

No. 1041. Alexander Gill, private in the N. C. Cont. Line; issued 26 May 1784, and assigned to Allen Brewer.

No. 125. Heirs of Ambrose Goslin, private in the N. C. Cont. Line; 640 acres within the limits of land reserved for officers and soldiers of the Cont. Line; issued 18 Dec. 1805.

No. 2377; Grant no. 1823. Samuel Sanford assignee of David Ginn, private in the N. C. Cont. Line; 640 acres in Sumner Co.,on the head of the eastern branch of Roaring River; 20 May 1793.

No. 2287. Granted to John Marr, assignee of Isaac Griffin, a private in the N. C. Cont. Line; 640 acres in Sumner Co. on the south side of Big Barren River, on the south creek that the Virginia Line crosses that empties into Barren River; May 1793.

No. 165. Isaac Griffith; sergeant in the N. C. Cont. Line; 428 acres within the limits of land reserved for officers and soldiers of the Cont. Line; issued 22 Nov. 1808. The same was transferred to William Horne on 1 Jan. 1784, with Samuel Lockhart a witness. William Horne of Northampton Co., N. C., transferred to Elias Troost of Halifax Co., the warrant on 19 May 1807, with Anson Jeffreys a witness.

No. 536. Heirs of Edward Griffith, sergeant in the N. C. Cont. Line; 1000 acres within the limits of land reserved for officers and soldiers of the N. C. Cont. Line; issued 4 Sept. 1820. Elizabeth Artis, of Edgecomb Co., N. C., only true and lawful heir of Edward Griffith, dec., sold the warrant to Dempsey Bryan and his heirs on 18 Aug. 1820. In Sept. 1820 Bryan sold it to Louis D. Wilson.

No. 1819, Samuel Sanford, assignee of Simon Grimes, a private in the N. C. Cont. Line; 640 acres in Sumner Co., on the eastern branch of Roaring River; issued 20 May 1793.

No. 1042. Jacob Gerrard, private in the N. C. Cont. Line; 640 acres. 26 May 1784. He transferred the same to Stockley Donelson, who assigned it to William Tyrrell, who then made it over to Stephen Hills, on 10 Dec. 1796. On 4 Dec. 1795 (sic) Hills assigned it to David Henley.

No. 2461. No. 257. Granted to Nicholas Gibbs, assignee of Martin Armstrong, from lands reserved for officers and soldiers of the N. C. Cont. Line; issued 7 March 1796.

No. 250. James Garret, a continental soldier in the last American war with Great Britain. Pursuant to an act 10 Dec. 1813 the heirs of James Garrett were granted 640 acres within the limits reserved for officers and soldiers; issued 11 Nov. 1814. Thomas Garret of Martin Co., N. C., heir of James Garret, transferred the warrant to Darling Cherry on 29 Nov. 1814, Jesse Cherry a witness.

No. 3672. Heirs of Jno. Gardner, private in the N. C. Cont.
Line; 640 acres within the limits of land reserved for officers
and soldiers of the N. C. Cont. Line; issued 10 Dec. 1788. On
10 April 1789 Mary Gardner transferred the warrant to Thomas Edwards and Jno. Peyton, with Thomas Broomley.

No. 4609. David Gilston, private in the line of this state;
640 acres of land within the limits reserved for officers and
soldiers of the N. C. Cont. Line; issued 9 Feb. 1797. Gilston
assigned the warrant to George Buckhammon. with Walter Patrick
a witness. Charles I. Love owned the warrant in 1803.

No. 4608. James Gilston, private in the N. C. Cont. Line; 228
acres within the limits reserved for officers and soldiers of
theN. C. Cont. Line; issued 9 Feb. 1797. This was transferred
to Sterling Brewer on 14 Feb., with William Reed a witness.
In July 1797 Brewer assigned the warrant to Ezekiel Norris, with
William Lytle, Jr., as a witness. In Aug. 1797 Norris transferred
the warrant to William Armstrong, with William Armstrong, Sr., a
witness.

No. 3640. William Guin (Guion, Gueon, Guinn), private in the
N. C. Cont. Line; 274 acres; issued 12 Dec. 1788. Transferred
to Stockley Donelson and William Tyrrell on 1 June 1792. They
assigned it to James Adair and Sterling Brewer witnessed the
transfer. In May 1797 Adair assigned it to Samuel Donnel.

No. 3597. Heirs of Willis Gregory, in the N. C. Cont. Line; 640
acres within the limits of land reserved for officers and soldiers
of the Cont. Line; issued 27 June 1788. On 28 July 1796 James
Gregory, heir of William Gregory, transferred the warrant.

No. 4017. Thomas Garrot, sergeant in the N. C. Cont. Line of
the Rev. War; 489 acres of land within the limits reserved for
officers and soldiers of the N. C. Cont. Line; issued 25 Nov.
1796. Thomas Garrot of Currituck Co., N. C., transferred the
warrant to Samuel Tillett of the same place, with Isaac Tarlis-
ton as a witness.

No. 436. Joshua Hadley, assignee of Dempsey Gardner who was a
private in the Cont. Line of this state; 274 acres on the north
side of Cumberland River, about two miles above Roaring River;
15 Sept. 1787. Thomas Hickman the original surveyor of this
land made a statement, Davidson Co., Tenn.

No. 187. Rabon Gibbs, heir at law to John Gibbs, private in the
N. C. Cont. Line; land within the limits of land reserved for
officers and soldiers of the N. C. Cont. Line; issued 23 Oct.
1783.

No. 4319. Jones Glover, private in the N. C. Cont. Line; 228
acres within the limits of land reserved for soldiers of the
Cont. Line; issued 13 Dec. 1796. On 30 Dec. 1800 Jones Glover
assigned the warrant to Daniel Mason, with Wm. Dancey a witness.
In 1801 Mason assigned the warrant to Howell Tatum, with Thos.
Vaughan a witness.

No. 4536. David Glover, private in the N. C. Cont. Line; 640
acres within the limits of land reserved for officers and soldiers of the Cont. Line; issued 24 Dec. 1796. John Hunter, attorney for David Glover, assigned the warrant to Robert Young
and Frederick Stump.

No. 4630. Benjamine Glover, private in the N. C. Cont. Line;
640 acres; issued Dec. 1796, and assigned to Daniel Mason in 1797
with N. Goe a witness.

No. 1935. Thos. Greer, a soldier in the Rev. War; 2500 acres; issued Nov. 1784. (The document is in very poor condition).

No. 178. Thomas Grimes, assignee of Francis Mayberry. This warrant was issued from a grant to Thomas King; 1000 acres of land. This warrant was for 150 acres. King's grant, no. 431, issued 29 July 1793 by virtue of a ten pound warrant. On 19 Nov. 1803 Mayberry assigned the warrant to Nathaniel and Thomas Grimes, with James Wilson a witness.

No. 34. George Gordon. In 1802 Gordon assigned it to Blackburn Jones, and it was transferred to Andrew Culwell in Nov. 1802. In 1803 Culwell transferred the same to James Russell, with S. Grewer a witness.

No. 28. This is a list of grant numbers which are marked "Invalid" and issued to Allen T. Gilliland.

No. 4665. John Gouch a private in the N. C. Cont. Line; 640 acres within the limits reserved for officers and soldiers of the Cont. Line; issued 11 Feb. 1797. This warrant was assigned to William Tyrrell in 1797, and witnessed by John Odwers, John King, and D. Delk, Jr. The land was in Davidson Co., Tenn.

No. not given. Solomon Gay was granted land for service in the Rev. War (the original warrant is missing). On 4 Sept. 1821 Solomon Gay of Northampton Co., N. C., for $80.00 transferred the warrant to Andes Jones of Nash Co., N. C. Wm. Daugherty was a witness.

No. 100. Jos. Grayson. Warrant no. 1017, Arthur Crozier for 100 acres marked "Invalid," the land having been laid off within the unappropriated lands under the rules, regulations and restrictions as by law directed, for 600 acres. No. 356 dated 29 July 1793 obtained by virtue of a fifty shilling warrant, and assigned to Joseph Grayson in 1806.

No. 1017. Heirs of Solomon Gay, private; 640 acres for his services in the N. C. Cont. Line; issued 20 Sept. 1821. The warrant was assigned to Robert Blick by Andes Jones. Blick assigned it to Thomas Cobb, Thomas Scott, and Benjamine S. King, executors of Jehu Scott, dec.

No. 509. Heirs of Alex'r Gilliland, private in the N. C. Cont. Line; 640 acres within the limits reserved for officers and soldiers of the N. C. Cont. Line; issued 30 Aug. 1820.

No. 568. Heirs of John Guard, private in the N. C. Cont. Line; 640 acres within the limits of land reserved for officers and soldiers of the Cont. Line; issued 9 Sept. 1820. Sary Guard and Susanna Guard, heirs at law of John Guard, sold the warrant to Jonathan Hibbs in Sept. 1820, with David F. Sennis and Wilkins Hibbs were witnesses.

No. 638. Heirs of John Grinnage or Grimmage, private in the N. C. Cont. Line; 640 acres; issued 15 Sept. 1820. Hardy Grinnage, legal heir of John Grinnage, dec., sold the same in Sept. 1820, with Geo. Denton and Abraham Wallace as witnesses. Josiah Hall of Smith Co., Tenn., made oath that the transfer was made out in the handwriting of Abner Masson, now dec., in 1820.

No. 653. Samuel Goodman, corporal; 375 acres for his services in the Cont. Line; issued 18 Nov. 1820.

No. 312. Heirs of Robert Gregory, private; 640 acres within the limits of land reserved for the officers and soldiers of the

N. C. Cont. Line; issued 23 Feb. 1820. Gideon Gregory of Currituck Co., N. C., one of the heirs of said Robert Gregory, transferred the warrant to Lawrence Cherry in 1820, witnessed by Phillip Gregory, Lovey Gregory, and Isham Anderson.

No. 3016. Francis Graves; grant in Sumner Co., Tenn., in 1796.
(This record is almost obliterated).

No. 1825. Jacob Grayson, soldier of the Revolutionary War; warrant to Samuel Sanford. Davidson Co.

No. 3599. Heirs of Thomas Hendricks, private; 640 acres. Solomon Hendrix, son of Thomas, and heir at law of Thomas Hendrix,
dec., transferred his right and title in the warrant to Sarah
Decrow of Perquimans Co.,on 3 Aig. 1789. Joseph Hendrickes and
James Lessley were witnesses. On 4 June 1793 Sarah Decrow of
Perquimans Co., transferred the warrant to William Williams, in
the presence of Wm. Wheaton.

No. 3999. Heirs of Timothy Hardcastle; 640 acres; 25 Nov. 1796;
in Bladen Co., N. C. Wm. Hardcastle assigned the warrant to
Daniel McAllester of the same county and state, the land due
to William's brother Timothy Hardcastle, dec., in consideration
of the latter's services under command of Capt. Daniel Williams,
on 30 Aug. 1796. Charles McAlester witnessed the transfer along
with Benjamine Adams, and J. Lewis. On 30 Aug. 1796 Mrs. Elizabeth Hardcastle signed her rights away and stated that William
Hardcastle was her only surviving son and lawful brother to
Timothy Hardcastle.

Nos. 451 and 102. Nathaniel Hughes; 316 acres. The warrant was
issued to William Ross on 16 Sept. 1803. Hughes was a private
in the N. C. Cont. Line. The land was in Davidson Co. on Sinking Creek, a branch of Red River that empties in on the west side
of the west fork of the said river. 7 March 1786.

Nos. 1098 and 2031. Matthew Hearon; 640 acres for services as
a private in the Cont. Line of this State. On 9 Dec. 1786, Sarah
Hearon, the widow of Matthew Hearon, transferred the same to Dan_
iel Quilling who on 7 March 1787 assigned it to John Pickens
(or Pickins), with Geo. West a witness. On 15 Nov. 1787 Pickens
assigned it to Stephen Slade.

No. 1764. Isaac Hutson, grant for services of John Nichols.
Hutson was a private in the N. C. Line and received 640 acres in
Davidson Co. on Weakley's Creek, a west fork of Barton's Creek
on 13 May 1789. Tennessee County Reg. Office, Book A, folio
140; 31 Dec. 1793; Hugh Lewis, Registrar.

No. 3235. John Hughs, a sergeant; 428 acres; issued 23 Dec.
1785. The same was transferred to Martin Armstrong who assigned
it to Robert King and Joseph Cobb on 24 Aug. 1797 in the presence
of William King. On 8 April 1805 Robert King assigned it to
James Hamilton, witnessed by Edm'd Waller.

No. 238. Heirs of Ezekiel Habbit, drummer; 1000 acres; issued
25 Aug. 1813. On 4 Sept. 1813 Elizabeth Hogan of Beaufort Co.,
N. C., the only heir of her father Ezekiel Habit, dec., transferred the warrant to Daniel Cherry.

No. 217. Heirs of Benjamine Hinson, dec.; 640 acres; issued 17
Dec. 1811. James Hinson of Martin Co., N. C., heir of Benj.
Hinson, dec.; 5 May 1812. Laurence Cherry and Wm. Anderson
were witnesses.

No. 4020. William Herrington, a private; 274 acres; issued 25

Nov. 1796. Isaac Herrington of Camden Co., N. C., legal representative of said William Herrington, assigned the warrant to Letty Harney (or Selby Marney). S. Marney sold the same to Geo. Chandler on 3 Aug. 1797, with Richard Lawson a witness. Chandler assigned the warrant to Sam'l Marsh on 17 Oct. 1797. To Matthew Brown.

No. 199. Samuel Hail, private; 640 acres; issued 2 Jan. 1810. Joshua Hail sold the warrant to Daniel Cherry on 23 Feb. 1810.

No. 174. Heirs of Delany Hale, private in the N. C. Cont. Line; 640 acres; issued 19 Dec. 1808.

No. 75. Joseph Hopkins; 100 acres. Warrant was issued from a grant in the name of Ephraim Payton for 200 acres of no. 205, dated 27 Feb. 1796, obtained in consideration of services of Martin Armstrong, surveyor of lands allotted officers and soldiers of the N. C. Cont. Line; 25 Nov. 1802.

No. 3591. Heirs of Samuel Horton, private; 640 acres; 27 June 1788. On 16 July 1796, John Horton, Sr., transferred it to Charles Smallwood, who on 7 Aug. 1796 transferred it to James L. White, who on 9 Sept. 1797 assigned it to Wm. Nash, with Wm. Tait and Wm. Black as witnesses.

No. 1509. Frederick Harper, dec.., private; 640 acres; 20 Jan. 1785. The same was transferred on 10 Nov. 1785 by Graham Gossett to Daniel Sutherland.

No. 3601. Samuel Hart, private; 274 acres; issued 9 Aug. 1788. The same was transferred to James Hamble of Georgia on 31 Dec. 1790. Hamble (transferred to - R. B.) Alex'r Patton on 5 Nov. 1796, with Isaac Patten a witness.

No. 3173. Heirs of Roger Hilton, private; 640 acres; issued 19 Dec. 1785. David, Hilton, heir of Roger, transferred the same to William Lytle on 11 June 1797, with Thophilus Hunter a witness.

No. 955 (4955). Heirs of John Hathaway, private; 640 acres; issued 6 Sept. 1821. On 9 June 1821 Wm. Robbins of Nash Co., N. C., soldier in the N. C. Cont. Line, deposed he knew John Hathaway who died in winter quarters at Valley Forge, leaving one brother David Hathaway now also dead. David had one son named John, living in Pitt Co., N. C.

No. 369 (2182). Heirs of William Harrison, a private; 640 acres; issued 24 July 1820. Thomas Swindle and Barbary Swindle, formerly Barbary Harrison, only heirs of William Harrison, dec., a private in the N. C. Line, assigned the warrant to Abner Wasson on 28 Aug. 1820.

No. 388 (2114). Heirs of Thomas Hatson (Huston) a sergeant; 1000 acres; issued 23 June 1820.

No. 581 (3401). James Huggins, a private; 640 acres; issued 11 Sept. 1820.

No. 325 (2722). Jacob Hoover, private; 185 acres; issued 25 May 1820.

No. 403 (2718). Heirs of Thomas Hardy, private; 228 acres; issued 10 Aug. 1820.

No. 206 (1280). Jesse Hutchins, peivate; 274 acres; issued 6 December 1815.

No. 257 (3318). Heirs of William Herbert, sergeant; 1000 acres; issued 27 Nov. 1816. James Butler and wife Margaret assigned the warrant to John Roberts and his heirs and assigns on 2 Sept. 1817. On 6 Jan. 1819 the warrant was assigned to Geo. Read, with Rob't Read a witness. George Read assigned it to John Roberts, Rob't Read again a witness. On 11 Sept. 1820 Roberts assigned it to Richard Smith of Raleigh, N. C., with Jno. M. Brasfield and Jesse Williams as witnesses.

No. 133 (171). George Farragut; 50 acres. This warrant was issued from a grant for 380 acres of no. 171 dated 8 April 1794, obtained by virtue of a fifty shilling warrant dated 2 May 1803. It was assigned to Charles McClung on 4 May 1803, and McClung transferred it to John Hickey on 9 Feb. 1805.

No. 97 (340). David Haley; 153 acres. This warrant was issued from a grant to Landon Carter for 500 acres, no. 611, dated 12 July 1794 by virtue of a fifty shilling warrant dated 6 June 1803. Registered 29 June 1807. Signed Archibald Roane, Pres. of Board of Commissioners, for East. Tennessee.

No. 574. Daniel Harget, devisee of David Miller, dec., a soldier; 640 acres.

No. not given. John Hathaway of Pitt Co., N. C., for $50.00 sold to Calvin Jones of Wake Co., N. C., the land John Hathaway received for his military service in the N. C. Cont. Line, 4 June 1821.

No. 188. Samuel Hollis made oath before Hardy S. Bryan, Justice of   Peace for Robertson Co., Tenn., on 20 Dec. 1809 that his father James Hollis, dec., had several claims for lands in Washington Co. for lands entered in Carter's office, and that James Hollis moved from that place after said office was opened, to Cumberland, and never returned. James Hollis has been dead for about 15 years last April, and that Samuel was young when his father left Washington, and he (Samuel) cannot recollect about the aforesaid entry.

No. 4018. Isaac Herrington, private in the N. C. Cont. Line; 274 acres; issued 25 Nov. 1796. Isaac Herrington of Camden Co., N. C., assigned the same to William Lurry, Jr., of the same county on 9 Feb. 1797. Wm. Lurry of Sumner Co., Tenn., assigned the same to Manoah Taylor on 6 Nov. 1803.

No. 171. Heirs of John Hern, private in the N. C. Cont. Line; issued 9 Dec. 1808. Mary Hern of Edgecomb Co., N. C., transferred the same to Daniel Cherry on 22 Dec. 1808, in the presence of Christmon Winam (?), Micajah Windom, and Jesse Florin. The warrant was signed Mary Hearn.

No. 186. Nicholas Hilderman, private in the N. C. Cont. Line; 640 acres; issued 21 Nov. 1809. On 10 March 1810 the same was assigned to Andrew Derr in the presence of Millington Abernathey and Jas. Bleckley.

No. 247. John Hawks, a private in the N. C. Cont. Line; issued 29 Sept. 1814. Mary Sandy of Cravin Co., N. C., only heir of John Hawks, assigned the warrant to Reuben P. Jones on 4 Oct. 1811, with Elizabeth Charlott a witness.

No. not given. William Hays and Elisha Hays of Gates Co., N. C., to Calvin Jones of Wake Co., N. C., transferred a warrant or claim to land to which James Hays a lieutenant was entitled for military service in the N. C. Cont. Line; John Gatling and Andes Jones were witnesses.

No. 1578. John Holley; 100 acres of land in Washington Co., N. C., joining Holley's line, running up to and including the cabin where John Loveday. Two dates: 26 Sept. 1779, and 12 Oct. 1796. J. Carter, E. T.

No. not given. Jones Hays of Hertford Co., N. C., on 22 Feb. 1822, deeded to James Freeman of Bute Co., N. C., a military warrant that Hays became heir to for the service of his father, James Hays, a lieutenant in Capt. Dawson's Co., in the 7th Regt. of the N. C. Line. David Atkins and Will. Miers were witnesses. Solomon White deposed he was personally acquainted with James Hays, a lieutenant in the 7th Regt. of the N. C. Line, and that James Hays married Winniefried Jones of Hertford Co., N. C., and had by her several children, all of whom died except Jones Hays, now living in Hertford Co., the only heir of Samuel Hays. Deposition made 23 Feb. 1822 before Joseph F. Dickinson, clerk of the county court. George H. Bond and Irvin Jenkins witnessed the deposition.

No. 2925. Heirs of Joel Hobbs, private in N. C. Cont. Line; 640 acres; issued 30 Sept. 1785. John Sheppard purchased it from Jacob Hobbs on 3 May 1785. Sheppard assigned it to William King who assigned it to Sterling Brewer on 7 Feb. 1797, with John Horton and Daniel King, witnesses. Brewer assigned it to Samuel Thornton and William Downes.

No. 1964. Anthony Hart; 9 Nov. 1802. On 17 May 1802 Susanna Hart of Davidson Co., Tenn., executrix of the last will and testament of Anthony Hart, dec., according to the will of the dec. sold land in Smith Co., on Caney Fork River on the mouth of Indian Creek, to Thomas Hickman. Date 20 May 1793 is given.

No. 2927. Heirs of Moses Hobbs, private in the N. C. Cont. Line; 640 acres; issued 30 Sept. 1785.

No. 2926. Heirs of Timothy Hunter, private; 640 acres; issued 30 Sept. 1785. On 25 July 1785 James Hunter sold the same to John Sheppard. On 11 Aug. 1806 Reading Sheppard, heir of John Sheppard sold the same to Stephen Montgomery. James Sheppard, heir of John Sheppard, also signed.

No. 3093. William Humphries, private in the N. C. Cont. Line; 640 acres; issued 6 Dec. 1785. The warrant was transferred to S. Donelson and Wm. Tyrrell, who assigned it to Francis Nash. Rutherford Co., N. C. Wm. Humphries of Spartanburgh Co., S. C., appointed Samuel Sevan of Rutherford Co., attorney to sell, act, and demand of Wm. Skiner, Esq., all rights entitled to for services as a soldier in the Cont. Line under the command of Col. Thos. Polk for two and a half years in 1777-1778. Dated 29 Sept. 1792.

No. 3137. Heirs of John Hartley, fifer in the N. C. Cont. Line; 1000 acres; issued 14 Dec. 1785. Joseph Hartley made oath in Beaufort Co., N. C., that John Hartley his brother died in the army of the U. S. during the war with Great Britain without leaving any issue and that Joseph is the eldest brother of the said John. The deposition was witnessed by J. G. Blount, C. Offidant (or Olifant) and Branfort Cannly (?). Joseph Hartley assigned the same to Edward Harris.
Warrant no. 1648 was issued to Thomas Hartley, heir of John Hartley, dec., a private. John Hartley was mustered as a private and died in 1778. "Of course warrant no. 1648 is good and this warrant (no. 3137?) is not good unless better proof is made."

No. 537. Heirs of Peter Higgins, a private in the N. C. Cont. Line; 640 acres; issued 4 Sept. 1820. Elizabeth Higgins signed the warrant away on 5 Sept. 1820 to Bartholomue Bowers and Stephen Higgins of Edgecomb Co., N. C., the only true and lawful heir of Peter Higgins a Cont. soldier in the Rev. War, in the presence of Riddick Barnes and Eli Anderson. Bowers assigned the same to James W. Wilson on 4 Sept. 1820. On 19 Oct. 1820 the same was assigned to Louis D. Wilson.

No. 488. Betsy Jones formerly Betsy Hockaday, and Worrick Hockaday, heirs of William Hockaday, private in the N. C. Line; 640 acres (no date shown).

Grant no. 1506. John Henly; 640 acres on south side of Red River adjoining Martin Armstrong's Middle Corner adjoining Parson Boyd's claim, 4 Jan. 1792. This grant was vacated for 338 and 3/4 acres, certificates having been issued for that amount to the grantee (see nos. 2202 and 2203). 1 May 1822, Tennessee County.

No. 2805. Heirs of Thomas Harwood, private in the N. C. Cont. Line; issued 30 Sept. 1785, and assigned to Sterling Brewer on 3 Oct. 1785, and then assigned by Brewer to Thomas Molloy. On 1 Aug. 1785 James Harrowood endorsed the warrant to William Harrowood.

No. 437. Heirs of Reuben Hamm, private in the N. C. Line; 640 acres; issued 26 Nov. 1796.

No. 249. Laurence Hare, a lieutenant in the N. C. Line. A grant of 914 acres in Davidson Co., on both sides of Cedar Creek, adjoining Col. Murphey's, was made to Hardy Murphy, assignee of the said John Laurence Hare. Warrant no. 115, located 5 July 1784.

No. 264. Heirs of Isaac Hardy, a lieutenant of the N. C. Cont. Line; 1097 acres; issued 10 Dec. 1817. Abraham Hardee of Pitt Co., N. C., sole heir to Isaac Hardy, dec., a lieutenant in the Rev. War, assigned the grant to William Hill on 24 Nov. 1808, with John Phillips and Richard Evans as witnessed.

No. 265. Heirs of Wm. Henson, private; 640 acres; issued 18 Dec. 1817. James Hinson, the proper owner of the warrant assigned it to Darling Cherry on 2 Feb. 1818. Cherry assigned it to James Vaulx on Nov. 1818. Eli Cherry, attorney for his brother Darling Cherry, signed the transfer.

No. 870. Heirs of Zachariah Hampton, private; 640 acres; issued 23 Aug. 1821. John Hampton transferred the same to John Terrell on 11 Sept. 1821, witnessed by Wilbourn F. Hampton and William Clement. John Washington deposed before Richard Sneed, a justice of the peace for Granville Co., N. C., that he was well acquainted with Zachariah Hampton, reported to have died of wounds received from the enemy at the Hughtaugh (Eutaw - R. B.) Battle in the Revolutionary War. John Hampton is the oldest son and rightful heir of said Zachariah, dec. 20 July 1821.

No. 159. Capt. John Herritage, captain in the N. C. Line; 1280 acres; issued 22 Oct. 1783. William H. Bryan, one of the heirs at law of John Herritage, dec., for himself and for James Bryan, the other heir, all right and title to Thomas Shute, his heirs and assigns, assigned all land granted said Herritage. The transfer was dated 31 Aug. 1808, Isaac Shute a witness.

No. 574. John Cocke, attorney, sheriff of Montgomery Co., Tenn., by virtue of two executions or orders of sale to John Saunders from sheriff of said county; to make lands of Daniel Harogate the sum of $13.60 to satisfy judgement.

No. 6. James Hibbett. Guard right. John Tate and Henry Rutherford made oath that James Hibbett served as one of the Guards
for the line in 1782; sworn 22 Jan. 1807. Hibbett was discharged
12 March 1784.

No. 21 (2444). Heirs of Lazarous Heart, private; 640 acres; issued 30 Sept. 1785. On 1 Oct. 1785 John Heart, heir of Lazerous
Heart, transferred the warrant to Thomas Smith, who endorsed it
to Martin Armstrong, whose attorney, Alexander McCall, made it
over to Christopher Alles.

No. 690. Heirs of Abraham Harding, private; 640 acres; issued
21 July 1821. On 15 Sept. 1821 John Bartholomew transferred
the warrant to Jacob Bartholomew. On 28 June 1821 Israel Harding of Beaufort Co., N. C., for $10.00, transferred his right
and claim to land due to Abraham Harding to John Bartholomew
of FRanklin Co., N. C.

No. 376. Heirs of John Harrell, private in the N. C. Line; 228
acres; issued 29 July 1820. Lewis Harrill of Greene Co., N. C.,
only lawful heir of John Harrell, a continental soldier, transferred the warrant to Roderick Cherry. Cherry transferred it to
Eli Cherry on 12 Aug. 1820, with Wm. Bell, Wm. Anderson, and
Laurence Cherry as witnesses.

No. 980. Joshua Harvey; 640 acres; issued 22 May 1784. Jno. H.
Bryan, agent, transferred the warrant to Thos. Henderson.

No. 3538, Robert Howell, private; 274 acres; issued 15 Feb.
1786. On 7 Sept. 1789, Robert Howell assigned the same to
Stockley Donelson who transferred it to William Donelson on 25
Aug. 1795.

No. 4399. Heirs of David Hatfield, private; 640 acres. Richard
Hatfield, Sr., heir of David, assigned the warrant on 24 Aug.
1797 at Perquimans Co., N. C., to Thomas B. Littlejohn, who made
it over to Wm. Shute.

No. 3511. Heirs of Zachariah Hughs; 640 acres; issued 8 Feb.
1786. Ben Harrison made it over to Robert Hooks, Esq., on 9
Feb. 1786.

No. 4562. Adam Hampton; 228 acres; 9 Feb. 1797. It was assigned
to Sterling Brewer on 12 Feb. 1797, with William Reed and Jesse
Sharp as witnesses. On 7 April 1797 Brewer assigned the warrant
to Peter Johnson, who transferred it to Abner Pillow on 3 Aug.
1804, with Geo. W. Payne and A. Mathes as witnesses.

No. 3128. Thomas Hickman; 640 acres on 14 Sept. 1797, the land
having been issued to Simon Sumhley (?), a private in the N. C.
Line. The land was located on the waters of Big Barron, Caney
Creek, in Sumner Co., on 22 Sept. 1797.

No. 690. John Laughinghouse of Pitt Co., N. C., made oath before
Bryan Grimes, Justice of the Peace, that he, John Laughinghouse,
was a soldier in the N. C. Cont. Line, and that he knew Abraham
Harding who enlisted and served in the said line, and that Harding was taken sick at Santee Hills and carried to a hospital in
Camden, S. C., where he died. Abraham Harding was never married
and left a brother Israel Harding who in 1821 was living in Beaufort Co., N. C. Sworn on 17 June 1821 (See no. 690 above).

No. 1917. James Hays; 640 acres in Sumner Co., in 1796. David
Humphries was a private in the N. C. Line. Land was on Cedar
Lick Creek.

No. 329. Heirs of Thomas Hill, corporal; 357 acres; 30 May 1820.

No. 5198. Heirs of Benj. Hill, private; 640 acres; 9 Dec. 1797. Richard Hill assigned the warrant to William Lytle on 10 Dec. 1797.

No. 544. John Hill, lieutenant; 2560 acres; issued 20 April 1784.

No. 685. Heirs of Jesse Harris, private; 640 acres; issued 23 May 1821. John Harris assigned it to John Jenkins on 6 June 1821. No. 146. Heirs of Jesse Harris, a private; on 10 Feb. 1807 the warrant was transferred to O. P. Nicholson, with Edward Harris and John Nicholson as witnesses. Samuel Bailey made oath on 11 May 1821 in Wake Co., N. C., before William Reavis, a Justice of the Peace, that he was acquainted with Abner Harris and Jesse Harris, who enlisted in the Cont. Line, and that they were sons of William Harris, dec., and that John Harris of Cheatham Co., Tenn., and was a brother and rightful heir of Abner and Jesse Harris.

No. 311. Heirs of Henry Hanners, private; 640 acres; issued 23 Feb. 1820. Thomas Hanners, George White, Frankey White, Joel Ethridge and Elizabeth Ethridge, part of the heirs of Henry Hanners, a continental soldier, sold the warrant to Laurence Cherry on 10 March 1820, with Isham Anderson and Malbourn Kilgro as witnesses.

No. 954. James Hayes. James Brown of Gates Co., N. C., made oath on 22 Aug. 1821 before Henry Gilliam, J. P., that previous to and during the Rev. War he knew well a James Hayes who entered the N. C. army as a lieutenant and marched to the north where he died, as the deponent was informed by a soldier of the army, as well as from a common report of his friends and connections, and adding the circimstances of his never having returned from the said army. James Hayes was not married and left an only brother named Jacob Hayes who married and is now dead and leaving by marriage only two sons, William Hayes and Elisha Hayes, both now living in Gates Co. The heirs of James Hayes, lieutenant, were issued 2560 acres. The grant was transferred by Calvin Jones to James Kimball.

No. 162. Jacob Holly, private; 640 acres; issued 19 July 1808. Jacob Holly transferred the warrant to William Phips or Ships in Wake Co., on 20 Feb. 1812, with Paty Head a witness. The same was transferred to Thomas Jones on 30 March 1812, with Holloway Kee. a witness.

No. 331 and 431. Thomas King, 1000 acres in Hawkins Co., on the north side of Clinch Mountains, adjoining Thos. Morrison, issued 29 July 1793. Certificate was issued 29 Aug. 1814. Francis Mayberry, on 29 Aug. 1814, made oath that he had searched for a tract of land granted by N. C. to Thos. King for 1000 acres on 29 July 1793 and no. 431 and was unable to find the same and that he knew of no other claimant to the said land; that James King was one of the chain carriers and thet he does not know where James King is living, if he is still alive.
    Robert Patterson of Grainger Co., on 10 Sept. 1807 made oath before Charles Hutcheson, J. P. for the said county, and stated that he believed that in 1787 he was called by Thomas King a chain carrier on the head waters of Flat Creek, and they made and marked a corner, they did not run any line on the said survey, and now they cannot find any corner of the same.
    Joseph Cobb made oath on 16 Aug. 1814 before Thomas Henderson, J. P. for Crainger Co., Tenn., that he made a search for a tract of land no. 431 for 1000 acres granted Thos. King by

N. C. and was unable to identify same, 10 April 1800. Thos.
King of Hawkins Co., deeded the land to Francis Mayberry of
Knox Co., Tenn. The land was in Grainger Co. on the waters of
Flat Creek. Thomas Jackson and Joseph Gentry were witnesses.
Another deed dated 7 April 1798 was between William Henshaw of
Jefferson Co., Tenn., and Stephen Stafford of Grainger, with
NathanielPeters and Elihu Swain as witnesses. A plat showed the
interference of grants 131 and 133 and 2497. On 15 April 1807
a certificate showed Francis Mayberry's military warrant no.
3803 was issued to the heirs of James Horseford for 640 acres;
signed Robert Searcy, clerk of commission for West Tenn. No.
2497 for bravery of James Horseford, private, granted to Francis
Mayberry, 640 acres in Eastern District. Registered in Campbell
Co., Tenn., on 20 Sept. 1809, Book A, page 100.

No. not given. Thos. Harrowood, a revolutionary soldier. See
Petition of Executors of Thomas Mallory in Davidson Co., Tenn.,
in 1807.

No. not given. Henry Hicks, private; 300 acres; 14 April 1792.
Hicks served in a battalion of troops raised pursuant to an
Act of our General Assembly for protection of the inhabitants of
Davidson Co. for the first half year's pay; land west from the
Cumberland Mountains.

No. 4756. John Hawthorn, private; 274 acres; issued 27 Feb.
1797. The warrant was assigned to Robert King on 17 Oct. 1797.
William Lackey for Robert King assigned it to John Brown (?) on
5 June 1803. John Brown (?) assigned it to Nathaniel Steele on
17 Nov. 1825.

No. not given. Roger Herndon, a revolutionary soldier. See
petition of executors of Thomas Mallory in Davidson Co., Tenn.,
in 1807.

James Hawkins (or Hawkins Hames), revolutionary soldier. See
Secretary State papers, Archives, Legislative Papers and petitions
where Hawkins stated he served at the surrender of Cornwallis.

No. 4620. James Hanley, private; 228 acres; 9 Feb. 1797. The
warrant was assigned to Sterling Brewer on 18 Feb. 1797.

No. 4619. Heirs of Roger Herndon, private; 640 acres; issued 9
Feb. 1797. William Herndon assigned the warrant to Sterling
Brewer, with John Enright a witness. Brewer assigned the war-
rant to Thomas Molloy.

No. 4621. Benj. Holley, private; 640 acres; 10 Feb. 1797. Jacob
Holley, oldest brother and heir of Benjamin Holly, transferred
the warrant to Thomas Hunt on 4 April 1799. Charles Collier and
Hardy Hunt were witnesses. Proved in Sumner Co., Tenn.

No. 4618. Heirs of Hardy Hunt, private; 640 acres; issued 9
Feb. 1797. John Hunt, an heir, assigned it to Sterling Brewer,
with Robert Brown and Jno. Enright were witnesses. Brewer assigned the warrant to Wm. Tyrrell.

No. 3467. Heirs of Charles Holland, private; 640 acres; issued
agreeable to provisions of 26th section of Land Laws of 1807.
A duplicate of the original of 2 Feb. 1786. Davidson Co., Tenn.,
Hayden Wells made oath.

No. 507. James Hawkins, a private; 640 acres; issued 2 April
1784.

No. 4610. Heirs of William Hodges, private; 640 acres; issued 9 Feb. 1797. Timothy Hodges assigned the warrant to Sterling Brewer who assigned it to Thomas Malloy on 26 Nov. 1797.

No. 2664. (Warrant incomplete). Stockley Donelson transferred it to Wm. Donelson, 10 Nov. 1795.

No. 3924. Heirs of Conrod Halfaker, private; 640 acres; issued 8 Dec. 1795.

No. 4612. Heirs of Thomas Hair, private; 640 acres; issued 9 Feb. 1797. James Hair assigned the warrant to Sterling Brewer, with James Horton a witness. Brewer assigned the land to William Tyrrell, 4 March 1797.

No. 508. Hardy Hawkins, private; 274 acres; 2 April 1784.

No. 4615. Heirs of Charles Hughlet, private; 640 acres; 9 Feb. 1797. John Allen, sheriff of Stewart Co., sold to Beunch Searcy the grant for $5.00, in 1810. Daniel Hughlett sold the warrant to Sterling Brewer.

No. 4616. Heirs of Carter Harter, private; 640 acres; issued 9 Feb. 1797. Zebulon Harlord (?) as heir sold it to Sterling Brewer who sold it to William Tyrrell on 4 March 1797, and later sold by the sheriff of Stewart Co., Tenn.

No. 4617. Heirs of William Harper, Jr.; 640 acres; issued 9 Feb. 1797. Nimrod Harper sold it to Sterling Brewer, with Robert Brown witness. In June 1810 the land was sold by the sheriff of Stewart Co., Tenn.

No. 3922. Harot Hadley; 640 acres in the Middle District. Hadley was assignee of the heirs of Leonard Kellon, private. The warrant was issued 8 Dec. 1795. George Kellen, an heir, assigned it to Joshua Hadley, who on 21 Nov. 1797 assigned it to Harrott Hadley.

No. 4355. John C. Hogan, private; 228 acres; issued 17 Dec. 1796. Hogan assigned the warrant to Benjamine Williams.

No. 4755. Micajah Henry, private; 320 acres; 27 Feb. 1797. The warrant was assigned to Robert King.

No. 5073. Heirs of Dabiel Honycut, private; 640 acres; issued 5 Dec. 1797.

No. 4535. Albert Hendricks, private; 640 acres; issued 24 Dec. 1796. John Hunter, attorney for Albert Hendricks, transferred the warrant to John McGee on 31 Dec. 1796.

No. 4489. George Howard, private; 274 acres; 22 Dec. 1796. The warrant was assigned to Thomas Harvey on 26 Dec. 1796, with Henry Herring a witness.

No. 4457. Morgan Hart, corporal; 1000 acres; 22 Dec. 1796. The warrant was assigned to Sampson Williams on 27 Jan. 1797, with Abram Hunter a witness.

No. 4401. Abemelech Howell, drum major; 1000 acres; 22 Dec. 1796. Howell assigned the warrant to John Smith on 24 Dec. 1796, with Thomas Hunter a witness.

No. 4600. Tubill Hall, private; 274 acres; 9 Feb. 1797. On 16 March 1798 Futreller Hall assigned it to William Lofton of Montgomery Co., N. C.

No. not given. Joseph Hanna and Thomas Brandon, privates in
Guard to the Commissioners appointed by the State of N. C. in
178-(?) for laying off lands allotted the officers and soldiers
of the N. C. Cont. Line.

No. 3130. Thomas Hickman; 640 acres in Sumner Co., Tenn., granted for services of Robert Williams, a private, on 22 Sept. 1797.

No. 334. Heirs of Robert Howe, a major general; 16,000 acres;
19 May 1820.

No. 3601. Located 7 March 1797. Benjamin Jossling, assignee of
Alexander Patten, issued originally of Samuel Hart, 274 acres of
land in Davidson Co., on the first creek on the east side of
Harpeth (River) below Joneses Creek, one and half miles above
the mouth; survey dated 5 Sept. 1797.

Nos. 691 and 3531. Nancy Sheppard, 640 acres; 11 July 1788.
(See no. 930 for evidence). Holladay Hathcock, private in the
N. C. Cont. Line, assignee of Nancy Sheppard; 640 acres on
Cycamore (Sycamore?) in Davidson Co.

No. not given. John Hart of Northampton Co., N. C., a soldier
in the N. C. Line of Cont. Army in the Rev. War, deposed that
before the war he well knew John Edwards, who enlisted in the
said line for and during the war; that he was a corporal in
Child's Company and that the said Edwards through the inclemency
of the weather was taken sick with a combination of complaints
so far that he was deemed unfit for service and returned home
to Northampton where the said Edwards died leaving by marriage
six children, to wit: James Edwards, Mathew Edwards, Martha Edwards, Rebecca Edwards, Charles Edwards, and Temperance Edwards,
all of whom live in Northampton Co., and who J. H. believes are
the only living and remaining heirs at law of said John Edwards.
Deposition dated 5 Sept. 1821.

No. 3699. Henry Hos Story, private in the N. C. Cont. Line; 182
acres; 1 Dec. 1789. John Story, heir of Henry H. Story, on 5
March 1802, assigned the warrant to William Hughlett. William
Chapman was a witness.

No. 314. Joseph Hudler, private; 366 acres; 30 March 1820. David Hudler assigned the same to Calvin Jones on 30 March 1820.

No. 313. Heirs of Lem'l Hudler, private; 366 acres; 30 March
1820. Kenan Hudler, only heir at law of Lem'l Hudler, dec.,
late a soldier in the Rev. War, assigned the warrant to Calvin
Jones of Raleigh the military warrant on 13 March 1820.

No. 1931. John Ingram, a sergeant; 797 acres; issued 27 July
1785.

No. 319. Heirs of Joseph Inglish, musician in the line of this
state; 360 acres within the limits of land preserved by law for
the officers and soldiers of the Cont. Line; issued 22 May 1820.
William Inglish of Pitt Co., N. C., only lawful heir of Joseph
Inglish, transferred the grant to Roderick Cherry on 11 Aug.
1820.

No. 3174. Heirs of James Ingram, private in the N. C. Cont.
Line; 640 acres; issued 19 Dec. 1785.

No. 4622. Heirs of Daniel Icalentine, a private in the N. C.
Cont. Line of the Rev. War; 640 acres; issued 9 Feb. 1797. William Carter, heir of Daniel Icalentine, transferred the warrant

to Sterling Brewer, John Enright and Wm. Smith witnesses. Sterling Brewer assigned it to William Tyrrell on 4 March 1797.

No. 4492. Crawford Johnston, private; 640 acres of land within the limits of land reserved by law for the officers and soldiers of the Cont. Line; issued 22 Dec. 1796. The same was assigned to Stockley Donelson on 1 Jan. 1797. On 24 Feb. 1797 Donelson assigned the warrant to Thomas Dillon, with James Williams a witness. Dillon assigned the same to Gen. James Robertson on 6 Aug. 1802.

No. 196. Noah James, corporal in the line of this state; 428 acres; issued 19 Dec. 1809. Same was assigned on 22 Dec. 1811 by Nathaniel Lay, by William Mercer, attorney for Noah James.

No. 195. Heirs of Jacob Jackson, private in the N. C. Line; 640 acres; issued 19 Dec. 1809.

No. 179. Heirs of Charles Jones, private in the line of this state; 640 acres; issued 19 Dec. 1808. Benjamine Jones of N. C., only heir to Charles Jones, dec., in the war, to Darling Cherry on 13 March 1810.

No. 4628. Lebulon Johnston, private; 224 acres within the limits of land reserved by law for the officers and soldiers of the Cont. Line of this state; observing directions of the Act of Assembly in such cases made and provided; issued 9 Feb. 1794. The warrant was assigned to Samuel Barton, with James Latham and Henry Rigs, witnesses. Later the warrant was transferred to Wm. Lytle on 14 Feb. 1797.

No. 3029. Located 23 Dec. 1796 and surveyed for Thomas Johnson, assignee of Charles Walden; 640 acres in Robertson Co., on the Sulpher Fork.

No. 161. Darlin Jones; marked "Invalid."

No. 657. Thomas Jennins, corporal; 113 acres within the limits of land reserved by law for the officers and soldiers of the Cont. Line; issued 15 Jan. 1821, and assigned to Calvin Jones on 16 Jan. 1821.

No. 579. William Jackson, 102 acres on Grant no. 653 of 274 acres; issued 8 Dec. 1787. The warrant was transferred to James McMurtry on 20 May 1807, witnessed by William Montgomery.

No. 1935. Ambrose Jacobus, private, assignee of John Baker; 640 acres in Sumner Co. on the west side of Caney Fork on the head waters of Hickman Creek; issued 17 May 1793.

No. 152. Samuel Johnson; marked "Invalid." No. 24, Joseph Duncan, 200 acres, 1890 (sic). "Rejected claim;" assigned to Archibald Roane.

No. 2073, grant. Abraham Jacobs, private in the N. C. Cont. Line of the Revolution; 640 acres on Round Lick Creek, Sumner Co., adjoining Benjamine Mills; assigned to Anthony Head Bledsoe, assignee of Abraham Jacobs, on 20 May 1793. James Blakemore, Deputy to William Christmas, surveyor of the aforesaid district, certified he had surveyed for John Rock and William L. Bledsoe a tract of land in Smith Co. originally granted to Anthony H. Bledsoe by no. 2073; dated 20 May 1793. Attached paper states "Davidson Co., 13 Nov. 1788. Martin Armstrong and Anthony Crutcher assignee of John Forde, 2560 acres, in Davidson Co., Thompson's Creek, etc., etc." Grant marked "Void."

No. 149. Thos. Johnson, assignee. Warrant issued from a grant
to George Gordon for 720 acres. The grant was dated 28 Aug.
1795 obtained by virtue of a fifty shilling grant.

No. 3219. Joshua Jacobs, private in the N. C. Cont. Line; 640
acres; issued 21 Dec. 1785. Jacobs transferred the warrant to
Walter Braly, witnessed by Jesse Latham and Joseph Keach. Braly
endorsed the warrant to Robert Hunter, with Thos. Henderson and
David Hartt as witnesses. Hunter endorsed it to Walter Braly,
with Jno. Braly, Jr., a witness. Walter Braly transferred it to
William Hart in the presence of William Topp. Hart endorsed it
to John Gillespie with And'w Hart as a witness. John Gillespie
by his attorney Simon Gillespie assigned it to Ansheled (?)
Woods in presence of Wm. Goodloe.

No. 3517. Menoah Jolly, private in the N. C. Cont. Line; 274
acres; issued 8 Feb. 1786. The same was transferred to Thos.
Bulcher on 10 Feb. 1786, witnessed by John Greenfield. Butcher
or Bulcher transferred it to Jesse Read in the presence of Anth'y
Hart, and Read assigned it to James Hall in the presence of Thos.
Hickman.

No. not given. George Jameson appeared before Lonez Griffin,
J. P. of Monroe Co., Tenn., on 22 Aug. 1824, and declared that
he (Jameson) had served in the Army of the United States in the
Rev. War for two years and nine months during which time he was
severely wounded, and that he had never applied nor drawn any
compensation from the government.

No. not given. William Jones, revolutionary soldier. See Petitions to the Legislature, 1824, Claibourne Co., filed under the
Secretary of State Files in the Archives.

No. 1472. Thomas Johnston, private, for services in the N. C.
Cont. Line; issued 17 Dec. 1802, and assigned to William Fulton.
Land is in Smith Co., Tenn., located Sept. 1785, and consisted
of 274 acres on the Cumberland River.

No. 2738. Heirs of Jeremiah Jordan, private in the N. C. Cont.
Line; 640 acres; issued 30 Sept. 1785. Isaac Jordan, heir of
Jeremiah Jordan assigned the same to Thomas Butcher on 3 Oct.
1785, witnessed by Robert Noble. Butcher transferred the same
to John Ford on 11 Feb. 1786 in the presence of James Tatum. On
31 May 1794 the warrant was sold at public auction to Arthur
Tate to satisfy an attachment obtained against John Ford by Martin Armstrong.

No. 49. Thomas Johnston, private; 274 acres of land, agreeable
to an Act or Resolution of the General Assembly passed the 1st
of Dec. 1801; issued 16 Dec. 1801.

No. 386. Heirs of Brinson Jones, a corporal in the line of this
state; 360 acres within the limits of land reserved by law for
the officers and soldiers of the Cont. Line; issued 3 Aug. 1820.
Lawrence Cherry purchased the warrant from Thomas Jones, Silas
A. Jones, Reuben Farrow, Rebecca Farrow, and Permelia Lee Brook
of Hide Co.,N. C., heirs of Brinson Jones, revolutionary soldier, on 17 July 1820, with William Harrell and Benjamin Neal as
witnesses. On 19 July 1820 Solomon Jennett and Pembroke Jennett
of Hide Co., N. C., heirs of Brinson Jones, acknowledged the
sale, with William Harrell and Nathan Jennett as witnesses.

No. 490. Matthew Joyner, private in the N. C. Cont. Line; 185
acres; issued 23 Aug. 1820.

No. 2666. Heirs of Lewis Joyner, private in the N. C. Cont. Line; 640 acres; issued Feb. 1795. On 4 Dec. 1795 Joshua Hadley transferred the warrant to John Brevard, with Basil Gaither as a witness.

No. 230. Heirs of Jonathan Jackson; 640 acres within the limits reserved by law for soldiers and officers of the N. C. Cont. Line; issued 2 June 1813. Samuel Reasons and his wife Louisa Reasons, the only heir of Jonathan Jackson, dec., transferred the warrant to Daniel Cherry on 9 Jan. 1814, with Darling Cherry a witness.

No. 511. Heirs of Thomas Jennings, corporal in the N. C. Cont. Line; 428 acres; issued 31 Aug. 1820.

No. 4400. Heirs of Singleton Jones, a private; 640 acres for his services in the N. C. Cont. Line; issued 22 Dec. 1796, and transferred on 26 Aug. 1797 to Thomas B. Littlejohn.

No. 4436. Heirs of Benj. G. Jeffries, sergeant in the N. C. Cont. Line; 1000 acres within the limits allotted the soldiers and officers of the said line; issued 22 Dec. 1796. On 24 June 1807 Robert McConnell transferred the same to William Searcy. McConnell had obtained the warrant on 22 Jan. 1797 from Reuben Jeffries, heir of Benjamine G. Jeffries, with Richard Howell and John Jones as witnesses. The land was in Mero Dist., Sumner Co.

No. 1869. Asa Jenkins, private in the N. C. Cont. Line; issued 26 June 1785, and assigned on 22 Feb. 1786 to Thomas White. Halifax, 19 Sept. 1785, same assigned to Edm'd Gamble, witnessed by Wm. Wootten. (It is not clear whether the grantee on 22 Feb. 1785 was named Thomas White or Thomas White Halifax - R. B.)

No. 67. Willis Johnson; 182 acres; issued 27 Nov. 1816, and assigned to H. W. Watson on 22 Dec. 1828, with G. A. Ivion (?) a witness.

No. 653. William Jackson, private in the N. C. Cont. Line; 274 acres located in Davidson Co., on the east side of Big Harpeth, adjoining the land of Alexander Nelson; issued 8 Dec. 1787.

No. 4522. Phillip Jones, private in the N. C. Cont. Line; 274 acres; issued 22 Dec. 1796.

No. 3959. Heirs of Isaac Jessap, private in the N. C. Cont. Line; 640 acres; issued 23 Feb. 1796. Jon Jessap, heir of Isaac Jessap, on 17 Jan. 1797 transferred the same to Stockley Donelson, with Abr. Swagerty as a witness. On 21 March 1803 Donelson assigned the same to Charles L. Love, with William Tyrrell as a witness.

No. 4623. Heirs of David James, a private; 640 acres; issued 9 Feb. 1797, and transferred by Roger James to Sterling Brewer in the presence of John Enright. Brewer assigned it to Thomas Malloy in the presence of Wm. Lackey and Wm. Lytle.

No. not given. Winn Jones, a revolutionary soldier. See the petition of executors of Thomas Mallory in Davidson Co., 1807.

No. 3935. Heirs of Solomon Jones, private in the N. C. Cont. Line; 640 acres; issued 8 Dec. 1795. Simon Jones, heir of Solomon Jones on 10 June 1796 assigned the same to Joshua Hadley, with Samuel Bruce a witness. Hadley assigned it to Gen. James Robertson in the presence of Robert Searcy.

No. 658. Heirs of Thomas Jennings, private; 274 acres for service in the N. C. Cont. Line; issued 15 Jan. 1821, and assigned to Wilson Sanderlin on 16 Jan. 1821 by Calvin Jones.

No. 321. Heirs of Solomon Johnson, a private; 640 acres for service in the N. C. Cont. Line; issued 22 May 1820. Stephen Johnston (sic) of Onslow Co., N. C., only heir of Solomon Johnson (sic), transferred the warrant to Laurence Cherry on 30 March 1820 in the presence of High Standley and William Harrell.

No. 3029. Located 23 Dec. 1796; surveyed for Thomas Johnson, assignee of Charles Watson, 640 acres in Robertson Co., on Sulpher Fork.

No. 1101. Heirs of John Jarvis, captain; 1920 acres for his services in the N. C. Line; issued 15 Aug. 1823.

No. 110. Jonathan Jones, corporal; 427 acres of land for his services in the N. C. Cont. Line; issued 17 Dec. 1804. On 1 Jan. 1805 in Camden Co., Griffith Jones transferred the warrant to Jacob Mercer in the presence of Amas Lovett and Nancy Tamplin. On 6 June 1806, in Sumner Co., Tenn., Mercer transferred the same to Jno. White, witnessed by Armstreat Stubblefield and Clement Stubblefield. Attached papers state that Griffith Jones was the son and heir of Jonathan Jones a continental soldier in the last war; 1807. Halifax Co., N. C.: Jonathan Jones, formerly a soldier in the 7th N. C. Regt., transferred on 8 Jan. 1778 to Capt. Tillman Dixon's Co. of the 1st N. C. Regt. and served in the said companies for the term of three years and was discharged. His occupation was farmer, and he had gray eyes and fair complexion, was 23 years old, and five feet, six inches high; 31 Jan. 1780.

No. not given. Thomas Jarvis, John Jarvis, Nancy Ballance, widow, and Elizabeth Jarvis, only heirs and representatives of Capt. John Jarvis, dec., a captain in the N. C. Cont. Line, to whom a military land warrant has or will be issued for all lands sue him as captain. The heirs transferred to Nelson Sanderlin the warrant for land in Tennessee, witnessed by Isaac Bapter and Jeremiah Ethreidge. Certified in Currituck Co., N. C., 1823.

No. 99. Jonathan Kimmey, private in the N. C. Cont. Line; 251 acres issued 21 Nov. 1804. David Carter, attorney for Peter L. C. Williams, lawful heir to the said Kimmey, transferred the same to Armstead Stubblefield, with Clement Stubblefield and Benj. Ingram as witnesses; 1 March 1805.

No. 4023. Heirs of Joab Kennedy, private; 640 acres in N. C. reserved for officers and soldiers of the N. C. Cont. Line; issued 25 Nov. 1796. Camden Co., S. C.: James Kennedy transferred to William Surry, Jr., the warrant; 1796, witnessed by Lemu'l Surry. On 7 Sept. 1797 Surry transferred it to John Young, in the presence of Robert Searcy. An attached note states that John Kennedy enlisted and served three years from 1 March 1777, but died before his term expired.

No. 4022. James Kennedy, private; issued 25 Nov. 1796. James Kennedy transferred 640 acres to William Surry in Camden Co., S. C. Lemu'l Surry a witness.

No. 4021. Heirs of Robert Kennedy or Kenady; 640 acres. He was a private in the N. C. Cont. Line. The warrant was issued 25 Nov. 1796. James Kennedy transferred it to Wm. Surry, Jr., in Camden Co., in 1796, and Surry made it over to Francis Nash on 11 11 Sept. 1796 in the presence of William Lytle. An attached

document stated: Camden Co., N. C., James Kennedy, admr. of
Robert Kennedy, Sr., sold the warrant to William Surry, Jr.
Robert Kennedy, Sr., died as a soldier in the service of the U.
S.; 12 July 1796. Robert Kennedy enlisted as a soldier under
me for three years, from 1 March 1777, but he died before the
term was expired. Signed Thos. Bressie (?), captain.

No. 3773. Benjamine Kennedy, sergeant; 600 acres; issued 21
Dec. 1792. Attached document states: Martin Co., N. C.: Ruth
Kennedy, Tempy Kennedy, Cullin Kennedy, and Nancy Kennedy, the
only heirs of Benjamine Kennedy, transferred the warrant to
Jeremiah Cherry on 15 Sept. 1806, with Reuben Ross and Darling
Cherry as witnesses.

No. 626. John Kennedy, Jr., entered a preemption for 640 acres
of land lying on a creek of Obed's River; located 18 Nov. 1784.

No. 4630. John Kinnon, private in the N. C. Cont. Line; 640 a-
cres; issued 9 Feb. 1797, and assigned to Sterling Brewer, with
Jesse Sharp as a witness. Brewer assigned this warrant to Hayden Wells.

No. 102. Heirs of Jacob Kean, private in the N. C. Cont. Line;
640 acres; issued 7 Dec. 1804. Simpson Co., N. C.: Cornelius
Autry and Wm. Kean, as heirs of Jacob Kean, sold the warrant
to Daniel Wheaten, merchant, of Fayetteville, the warrant due
to the heirs of the dec. Jacob Kean; 10 June 1796. Theophilus
Autry and Dal. M. Keen (?) were witnesses.

No. 159. William Kearsey, private in the N. C. Cont. Line; 640
acres; same issued 12 April 1808.

No. 2809. Heirs of Richard King, private in the N. C. Cont. Line;
640 acres; issued 30 Sept. 1785; and transferred by Stephen King,
heir of Richard King on 1 Oct. 1785 to Thomas Rucker or Butcher,
with John Derum a witness. On 26 May 1813 it was assigned to
Anthony Hart.

No. 190. Heirs of James King; private in the N. C. Cont. Line;
640 acres; issued 6 Dec. 1809 . Harmon King, the only heir to
the within mentioned military land warrant, transferred it to
Isham Cherry, 320 acres, on 4 Jan. 1810 before Peter May and
John D. Roach. Cherry assigned the same to Isaac Lanier.

No. 2979. Heirs of Epaphrotihis King, private in the N. C. Cont.
Line; 640 acres; issued 27 Dec. 1803. The same was assigned to
Mann Phillips, who then made it over to Thomas Dillon.

No. 3573. William Knott, lieutenant in the N. C. Cont. Line;
1882 acres; issued 24 Oct. 1787.

No. 3018. Joseph Kelley, private in the N. C. Cont. Line; 30
Sept. 1785; later assigned to Jno. Jas. (?) Bonner, 1785.

No. 3635. Heirs of John Keith, transferred. A warrant for his
services as a private in the line of this state for 640 acres;
issued 12 Dec. 1786. The land was to be laid out from the lands
reserved for officers and soldiers of the N. C. Line. William
Keith assigned it to Wm. Terrell and Stockley Donelson, who then
assigned it to Sampson Williams on 1 Aug. 1796. A. McCoy a witness.

No. 975. 2560 acres of land for the use and benefit of the
President and Trustees of the University of N. C., on behalf of
the services of lieutenant Caleb Keen. 6 Sept. 1821.

No. 833. Jacob Kittle, private in the N. C. Cont. Line; issued
16 Aug. 1821 to the President, Trustees of the University of N.
C. for the services of Kittle.

No. 962. Patrick Kelly; 640 acres issued to the President and
Trustees of the University of N. C.

No. 482. Heirs of Robert Kilpatrick; musician; 1000 acres;
transferred on 29 Aug. 1820 by Martha Kilpatrick of Nash Co.,
N. C., to Geo. Bowers.

No. 713. Joseph Kees, private in the N. C. Cont. Line; 228 acres.

No. 556. Heirs of John Kail, private; 228 acres; transferred by
Cealey and Gracy Kail of Martin Co., N. C., to Laurence Cherry.

Petition to the House of Represntatives of Tennessee by citizens
of Green County: Peter Green, now 82, and his aged wife and two
orphan children constitute his family. He served in the Revolution, and is asking for himself and his family. The petition
was signed by many inhabitants of Green Co., Tenn.

No. 4431. William Kerby, private; 274 acres; issued 22 Dec.
1796. John Kirby, heir of William Kirby, transferred the warrant
to John McGee on 17 June 1797.

No. 953. Heirs of John Lynch, lieutenant; 2560 acres; issued 6
Sept. 1821. William Lynch of Edgecomb Co., N. C., sold the warrant to Calvin Jones of Wake Co., N. C., on 11 Aug. 1821, with
Jno. H. Bailey and Andes Jones as witnesses. Gates Co., N. C.:
James Brown appeared before Henry Gilliam, J. P. , and deposed he
well knew John Linch who entered the N. C. Line of the Cont.
Army as a lieutenant, and that the said John Linch died unmarried
but leaving one brother named Henry who died leaving two children,
one daughter who died unmarried, and a son William Linch now living in Halifax Co.

No. 959. Heirs of Thomas Lynch, private in N. C. Cont. Line; 640
acres; issued in 1821.

No. 414. John Love. This is a William Maclin warrant for 50
acres, and was issued from a grant to Stockley Donelson for 5000
acres. No. 1359 dated 28 Aug. 1795 obtained by virtue of a ten
pound warrant. Given under date of 20 Aug. 1803. John Love
transferred the same to John White in 1805.

No. 1016. Heirs of Josiah Lillie, corporal; 1000 acres; issued
20 Sept. 1821. Edith Lillie of Perquimans Co., N. C., sold it to
Andes Jones of Nash Co., N. C., and she had obtained it as heir
of Josiah Lillie. Transfer dated 7 Sept. 1821, and witnessed by
Wm. Daughtry. Andes Jones assigned it to Robert Blick on 16 Oct.
1821. Blick assigned it to Thomas Cobb, Thomas Scott, and Benjamine S. King, executors of Jehu Scott, dec.

No. 261. Philip Logan; 640 acres of land within the limits reserved for officers and soldiers of the N. C. Cont. Line; issued
6 Sept. 1817. Baldwin Co., Ga.: Philip Logan transferred the same
to John Davis of Warren Co., Tenn., in June 1818, with William
Kelly, Wm. Montgomery, and R. Trotter as witnesses. In 1818 John
Davis assigned it to Samuel Hurber in the presence of Alexander
Hill and Elijah Harbean (?).

No. 498. Heirs of John Long; ensign; 1097 acres; issued in 1820.

No. 339. Heirs of Emeuel Luton, corporal; 1000 acres; issued in
1820.

No. 239. Heirs of Henry Loyd, private; 640 acres; issued in Aug. 1813. Judah Brayley, formerly Judah Loyd of Martin Co., N. C., only heir of Henry Loyd, dec., a soldier in the Cont. Line, transferred the warrant to Daniel Cherry in 1813 in the presence of Amy Counsell and Cullen Wood.

No. 152. Thomas Loyd, heir of Leonard Loyd who was a private in the Line and died while in service; 640 acres of land; issued 22 Oct. 1783.

No. 154. Heirs of Thomas Laughinghouse, a private in the N. C. Cont. Line; issued 17 Dec. 1807. Beaufort Co., N. C.: Andrew Laughinghouse, Richard Laughinghouse, John Laughinghouse, Thomas Laughinhouse, John Crummer and Esther Crummer, heirs at law of Thomas Laughinghouse, dec., who was a soldier in the Revolutionary War, assigned the warrant to John Gray Blount in Feb. 1808.

No. 320. Heirs of John Luts, a corporal; 1000 acres; issued 22 May 1820. Jehu Taylor and Zilpha Taylor of Carteret Co., N. C., only heirs to John Luts who was a continental soldier in the N. C. Line, sold to Laurence Cherry the warrant in March 1820, with William Hassell or Harrell and Lydia Hatchet or Hatcher as witnesses.

No. 200. Heirs of Burrel Loyd, private; 640 acres; issued 20 Jan. 1810. Judah Brayboy, formerly Judah Loyd, the only heir of Burrel Loyd who was dec. in the war, transferred unto Daniel Cherry a military land warrant for 640 acres. Amy Counsel and Cullen Wood were witnesses. Transfer was dated March 1810.

No. 3592. George Lee, private, 274 acres; issued 27 June 1788. Perquimans Co., N. C.: Nathaniel Williams, brother and only heir of William Williams, dec., hereby transferred the warrant to Jesse Williams. The warrant was granted to George Lee who sold it to William Richards who conveyed it to Sarah Decrow, and by the said Sarah Decrow conveyed to William Williams, now dec. The transfer was dated 1796 and witnessed by Joseph Harvey and John Metcalf. In 1801 Jesse Williams, Sr., conveyed it to Jesse Williams, Jr., with Jno. Baker a witness. The conveyance is dated from Wayne Co., N. C., and signed George Lowe, but the warrant is styled Lee and bears date 1890 (sic) and witnessed by Solomon Roberts.

No. 4494. Thomas Love, private; 274 acres; issued 22 Dec. 1796, and transferred on 25 Jan. 1797 to William Askew in the presence of John Stevens.

No. 4631. Heirs of Thomas Lenoir, Sr., a private in the N. C. Cont. Line; 640 acres; issued 9 Feb. 1797, and transferred on 11 Feb. 1797 by Henry Lenoir, heir at law, to John Ward and Hezekiah Woodward, with Jesse Sharp and Joseph Marcum as witnesses. Elsewhere it appears that John Ward and Benjamine Clack purchased the warrant and William Lytle and Jno. Boyd received some of the payment therefor.

No. 4632. Heirs of Thomas Lenoir, Jr., private; 640 acres; issued 9 Feb. 1797. Moses Lenoir, heir of said Thomas, endorsed the warrant to Sterling Brewer on 10 Feb. 1797, with William Cantrell and Jas. Marcom as witnesses.

No. 1845. Hugh Lettrice, lieutenant in the N. C. Cont. Line; 2260 acres; issued 12 June 1787. The land was located in Davidson Co., on the west branches of Big Harpeth River, beginning at John Donelson's corner...1793.

No. 1965. Artiminsia Wilmouth entered and obtained a grant for

10 acres based on a military warrant issued to the heirs of Andrew Lytle, a sergeant; no. 5112; dated 6 Dec. 1797.

No. 1993. Heirs of John Langston, private; 640 acres; issued 16 Aug. 1785. Joseph Langston, heir of John Langston, dec., endorsed the warrant to William Farrelton or Faircloth on 20 Aug. 1785. William Faircloth endorsed it to John McNees on 26 Aug. 1785, and McNees assigned it to James Cole Mountflorence dated Halifax, 26 Sept. 1785. (Part of the paper is missing.) It appears that Mountflorence assigned it to Richard Finner.

No. 3146. John Laffman, private; 274 acres; issued 16 Dec. 1785. John Luffman assigned it to John Marshall in June 1786, with Joles (Isles) Simmons a witness. On 12 Aug. 1786 Marshall assigned it to James Molloy, with S. Benton a witness.

No. 4636. Jonathan Lynn, private in the N. C. Cont. Line; 640 acres; Feb. 1797; Cornelius Lynn transferred it to Sterling Brewer with Robert Born and William Read as witnesses. Brewer assigned it to Hayden Wells and John Given. In Aug. 1797 John Given released his claim to Hayden Wells. The land was located on Middle Fork of east fork of Yellow Creek. The last transfer was witnessed by Benj. Wells and Lem'l. Sugg.

No. 4633. Heirs of John Looker, private in the N. C. Cont. Line; issued 9 Feb. 1797. James Looker, heir of John Looker, assigned it to Sterling Brown, with Robert Brown and William Reed as witnesses. The land was located in Sumner Co. It was assigned by Brewer to Thomas Johnson on 1 June 1797, with Wm. Lytle a witness.

No. 3175. Heirs of Jera. Litteral, private in the N. C. Cont. Line; 640 acres; issued 19 Dec. 1785. Moses Litteral, heir of Jera. Litteral, sold the warrant to William Lytle on 14 May 1797 with William Feimone a witness.

No. 4637. Heirs of Jonas Little, private in the N. C. Cont. Line; 640 acres; issued 1797. George Little assigned it to Sterling Brewer in 1797 with Robert Brown and William Reed as witnesses. Brewer assigned it to Robert Searcy, who assigned it to John Watson in 1797.

No. 219. Heirs of William Lee, musician in the N. C. Cont. Line; issued 11 May 1812. David Ward and Sarah Ward, formerly Sarah Lee, the only heir of William Lee, sold Daniel Cherry the warrant on 25 May 1812 with Laurence Cherry a witness. Docktron Lee and William Lee of Beaufort Co., N. C., lawful heirs to their uncle William Lee, dec. in the last war, sold to Daniel Cherry in 1812. William Pate, Enoch Garrets, Frederick Waters, John Ross, and Wm. Hornly(?) signed.

No. 1901. Morgan Lewis, private in the N. C. Line; issued 15 July 1785. Aaron Lewis assigned it to Oliver Tuton on 27 Feb. 1786, with James Corbitt, witness. Tuton assigned it to Thomas Shute and John Harding on 14 July 1806, wigned by William Tuton, heir of Oliver Tuton. John Q. Talbot was a witness.

No. 888. Francis (?)aro, non-commissioned officer; 1000 acres; issued 19 May 1784 and transferred to Allen Ramsey in July 1784.

No. 4560. John Lightfoot, private in the N. C. Cont. Line; 228 acres of land; 9 Feb. 1797. Lightfoot sold it to Sterling Brewer in 1797, and Brewer assigned it to John Donelson in March 1797.

No. 4559. Timothy Lessinby, private in the N. C. Cont. Line;
228 acres; issued 9 Feb. 1797. The same was transferred to Sterling Brewer on 21 Feb. 1797, witnessed by Wm. Pullen and Richard
Howell. Brewer assigned the warrant to Morgan Brown.

No. 4495. Walter Linsey, private in the N. C. Cont. Line; 274
acres; issued 22 Dec. 1796. Walter Linsey assigned it to Stockley Donelson on 10 Jan. 1797, witnessed by Peter Morse. Donelson
in turn assigned it to James Coman (or Cowan) on 23 Feb. 1797.
James Cowan transferred it to Garret Fitzgerald on 27 Feb. 1797,
with James Thompson a witness.

No. 4463. Heirs of Richard Laughlin, a fifer in the N. C. Cont.
Line; 1000 acres; issued 22 Dec. 1796. James Laughlin assigned
it to Redmond Dillon Barry on 7 May 1797 in the presence of Joseph
Adams. Barry transferred it to Benjamine Cooper and Jacob Adams
on 23 Feb. 1802, with Wm. Morrison as a witness. Cooper and
Adams made it over to Ay Alexander, with Abram Britton and John
Wright as witnesses.

No. 4419. Heirs of Frederick Lucy, private; 640 acres; issued
22 Dec. 1796. In Aug. 1797 Burwell Lucy assigned it to Daniel
Mason, witnessed by Seth Peebles, Alex'r Love, and N. Gee.

No. 4374. Heirs of John Larremore; 640 acres of land for services in the N. C. Cont. Line; issued 22 Dec. 1796. John Larremore, heir, transferred the warrant to Jonathan Robinson on 9
Jan. 1797, witnessed by William Porter. Jonathan F. Robertson
transferred one half the value of the warrant to John Davis on
4 Nov. 1797.

No. 4357. Zebulon Laurence, private in the N. C. Line; 320
acres; issued 17 Dec. 1796. This was assigned to Benjamine Williams.

No. 4372. John Lovey, private in the N. C. Line; 640 acres; issued 20 Dec. 1796. A notation says: "Hereby relinquish my
whole title assignee to Beleny Laucius whom I purchased of Jesse
Mitchell, D. Hall." Hall also made this notation: Wake Co., 1
March 1797: I do hereby relinquish my whole right and Boling
Loveys of the within claim unto James Mitchell as witness my
hand (signed) D. Hall, witnessed by Jesse Mitchell. James Mitchell of Wake Co., N. C., on 3 June 1797 assigned to Ralph Williams
in the presence of Jno. Terrell. Ralph Williams of Person Co.,
N. C., assigned it to Daniel Farmer on 20 June 1797 in the presence of Wm. Jeffreys. Farmer assigned it to Wm. Cocke as surety
for the payment of $21.00 in Person Co., N. C., on 5 March 1799.

No. 548. Heirs of Wm. Lewis, musician; 427 acres; issued Sept.
1820.

No. 541. Heirs of Lewis Leigh, sergeant; 1000 acres for services
in the N. C. Line; issued 20 Sept. 1820.

Bo. 380. Heirs of Wm. Lewis, lieutenant in the N. C. Cont. Line;
823 acres; issued 31 July 1820.

No. 1181. William Terril Lewis; a tract of land containing 600
acres on the north side of Tennessee including the mouth of a
creek some distance below the mouth of Clinch River up and down
the river, etc.; 27 Dec. 1787. This entry was transferred to
Joseph Porter. Stockley Donelson, for Wm. Terril Lewis, assigned
it to William Terrell.

645. Francis Lewis, private in the N. C. Cont. Line; 640
s; issued 23 April 1784.

No. 2859. Heirs of Joshua Laurnce, private; issued 30 Sept. 1785. On 2 June 1785 James Laurence assigned it to John Sheppard. James J. Reading Sheppard, heir of John Sheppard, transferred it to Stephen Montgomery for two shillings of Virginia money per acre on 11 Aug. 1806, witnessed by Andrew Love.

No. 550. Heirs of Richard Lawson, private; 640 acres; issued 4 Sept. 1820. Andrew Lawson of Warren Co., N. C., only heir at law of Richard Lawson, assigned it to Andes Jones of Franklin Co., N. C., on Aug. 1820 in the presence of Wm. Pike.

No. 91. Heirs of Alloway Longford, lieutenant; 2560 acres; issued 7 May 1804. James McMains, heir at law of Alloway Longford, dec., assigned the warrant to John Taylor on 1 April 1805., witnessed by C. Campbell, J. P., and A. B. Bruce, J. P. A certificate states that Alloway Longford served in the Cont. Army in the last war under Capt. McMiece and died in the service, as witness our hand at New Bern 23 May 1803 (signed) James Cammen, Capt. Richard Harget, capt. in the 8th N. C. Regt., and Levi Dawson, lt. col. of the 8th N. C. Regt.
   Certificate from Craven Co., N. C., that Francis Southharp and John Sems, Esqrs., who are subscribing witnesses to the annexed deed from Sarah McMains to John Taylor are Acting Justices of the Peace for Craven Co., etc. May 1805: Sally McMains, wife of James McMains, and formerly widow of Alloway Longford, dec., sold to John Taylor of Hillsborough, N. C., the warrant and same due by husband, James McMains, May 1804.
   The will of Alloway Longford dated 8 Feb. 1782 and proved in Craven Co., N. C., appointed Thomas Evans, shoemaker in New Bern, and testator's wife Sarah Longford as executors. Wife Sarah is to have two negroes, boy George and girl Nann and her increase forever, a Dark bay mare and her increase, and all household furniture, dated 8 Feb. 1782. Shad Fullshue and Elias Justice witnessed the will.
   Lovey Ellsworth and Fanny Parks made an affidavit that they were present in Newbern when James McMains a tailor by trade, and Sally Langford, widow of Alloway Langford, were joined together as man and wife by Joseph Lunch, Esq., on 16 Jan. 1783.
   Notation from the Secretary's Office, 9 Dec. 1803: This certifies that Alloway Langford stands mustered on 8 Feb. 1777 as an Ensign, Remarked "Lt. 1 Aug. 1777, omitted Jan. 1778" and that no warrant has been issued for and in that name. (Signed) Will White.

No. 3296. Daniel Wheaton, assignee of William Laramore, a private in the N. C. Cont. Line; 640 acres in Tenn. County on west fork of Barretts Creek, adjoining William Bitts northwest corner; Dec. 1797. The same was proved in Stewart Co., Tenn., in 1816.
   A deed of 15 Feb. 1816 between Thomas Buckingham, sheriff of Stewart Co., Tenn., and John C. McLemore, Jesse Blackforn and Burnet Searcey. The sheriff conveyed to McLemore, Blackforn and Searcey a tract of land granted to Daniel Wheaton by grant no. 3296, warrant no. 4323 on the west fork of Barretts Creek, 1815. At Dover on Thursday, 10 Feb. 1814, present William Outlaw, Ephraium B. Davidson and Yancey Thornton, Esqrs., state that Daniel Wheaton failed to give in his taxable property for the year 1815, and that he was granted a tract of land which he did not report.

No. 3145. Richard Barbour, assignee of William Leppencute, a private in the N. C. Cont. Line; 640 acres in the Eastern District, 1797.

No. 136. Heirs of Joel Murst, revolutionary soldier; 640 acres (The rest of the warrant is missing.).

No. 2372. James Moore, a soldier in the N. C. Line; 12,000 acres.
He states he was a brigadier general in the said war. This land
was in the Harpeth River Valley in Davidson Co., and adjoined
the land of James Robertson.

No. 68. Jacob Mowra, private in the N. C. Cont. Line; issued
13 Dec. 1802. Andrew Bostian and Frederick ·Mowry, only heirs of
Jacob Mowry, sold the warrant to G. Rutherford on 28 April 1806,
witnessed by Andrew Bostian, Jr., and Jacob Bostain (Bostian?).

No. 851. Heirs of Abel Mossander, lieutenant; 2560 acres; issued May 1784. In 1797 this was assigned to William T. Lewis
and later to Allen Brewer who obtained it in 1787 from Nathan
Markland, administrator, granted him in Wake Co., N. C., on the
estate of Abel Moslander. William Douglas of Davidson Co., Tenn.,
in 1811 made oath before John Childress, a J. P., that he was a
soldier in the late revolutionary war and that he served in the
N. C. Line, part of the time as lieutenant, and that he knew
Isaiah Bledsoe who was also a soldier in the same line and that
he never heard that the said Bledsoe deserted the service. Howel
Tatum of Davidson Co., Tenn. in 1811 made oath that he was of
full age and that he knew Abel Masslander a lieutenant in the
Fourth N. C. Regt., commanded by Col. Thomas Polk, and that
Masslander died at the Valley Forge on the Schuylkill River
between 1 Jan. 1778 and 18 May 1778.

No. 4376. Heirs of Peter Mercer; 540 acres; issued Dec. 1796.
William Mercer, the heir, transferred it to Joshua Hadley in
1796 in the presence of William Moor. Hadley transferred the
warrant to John Overton on 20 Nov. 1797 in the presnece of John
Payton. This land was located and surveyed for Overton and was
between the south connential (sic) line and the Indian Boundary
Line on the west side of the maineast fork of the west fork of
Stones River.

No. 447. Heirs of Solomon Melbern, sergeant; 1000 acres; issued
22 Dec. 1796. Notation on back: Solomon Maulbon mustered as a
sergeant and was entitled to 1000 acres of land, but another
warrant besides this one has been issued in the same name and
for the same quantity; no. 517; for a grant had not been issued.

Nos. 3290 and 3291. Both to Hardy Murfree by the General Assembly of N. S.; 28 Dec. 1785. An attached note says that the above
warrants were put in the Commissioner's Office for the benefit
of Hardy Murfree should he have occasion to call for them, but
if he does not have occasion for them he will relinquish his
right to them to the State. Nashville, 29 May 1807.

No. 136. Heirs of Joel Merrett, private in the N. C. Cont. Line;
issued 19 Dec. 1806.

No. 3368. John Mabry, private; 228 acres; issued 7 Jan. 1786,
and assigned to John Marshall, with Evan Shell a witness.

No. 3367. Gary or Cary Mabry, private in the N. C. Cont. Line;
228 acres; issued 7 Jan. 1786. Gray Mabry transferred the same
to John Marshall on 8 Feb. 1786, witnessed by John Shell. Dixon
Marshal on 21 Feb. 1800 assigned it to William Williams, with
William Powel a witness. Dixon Marshall signed as heir to John
Marshall, dec. William Williams on 11 March 1801, assigned it
Daniel Hylton, who on 1 Nov. 1820 assigned it to Benjamine Cooper, with Wm. Mading a witness. Cooper assigned it to John Rice
on 18 Nov., 1803, with Wm. Mading a witness. Rice made it over
to William Engles in June 1809. Benjamine Cooper located 228
acres of land in Smith Co., on the main fork of clear fork

of Smith's Fork to join George Smith's upper tract, 2 Nov. 1802.
Smith Co., Tenn.: William Madin made oath before John Looney,
J. P. of said county, that he was by and heard Benjamine Cooper
sell John Rice a land warrant, etc. Mading also certified that
John Rice gave William Tuglish (English?) authority to get the
land warrant as he went to Georgia. George Little of Smith Co.
certified that he heard Rice sell the warrant in 1809. Thomas
Harvey on 18 Oct. 1796 made a transfer to James Watson, with Samuel Scott as witness. Watson assigned the same to John Morgan
in Oct. 1796 with Jeremiah Watson as a witness.

No. 245. Heirs of James Milligan, lieutenant, dec.; 2560 acres
of land; issued 8 Oct. 1814. Joseph Milligan transferred the
same to Briu McGarner who assigned it to David W. Moore, with
John McKinney a witness.

No. 3956. David Manifee, private in the N. C. Cont. Line; 274
acres; issued 23 Feb. 1796. The same was assigned to Philip
Raiford on 12 April 1796, with Richard Howell and Will Terrell
as witnesses. Raiford on 14 April 1796 assigned the warrant to
James Roberts, with Will Tyrrell as witness. A certificate
that John Mannifee for two and a half years a soldier served
the aforesaid time as a sergeant; signed Joshua Hadley, captain, on 22 Oct. 1795.

No. 3958. Heirs of James McParish, sergeant; 1000 acres; issued
23 Feb. 1796. Zebular McParish and Nathaniel McParish, heirs of
James McParish, transferred the same to Thomas Johnston and
William Tyrrell on 2 March 1796, witnessed by Richard Howell and
Wm. Davidson. Thomas Johnson on April 1818 transferred his in-
terest to Jesse Blackforn (Blackford).

No. 3925. Heirs of Stephen Moglin, private in the N. C. Line;
640 acres; issued 8 Dec. 1795. Stephen Maglin assigned it to
Joshua Hadley on 7 May 1796, witnessed by John Moore.

No. 4031. Jonathan Melton or Mellon, private; 228 acres of land.
Onslow Co., N. C.: Jonathan Melton of said county conveyed a
military warrant to Charles Hendry on 3 Feb. 1796, witnessed by
James Foy. Hendry sold it to Duncan Stewart on 2 Jan. 1797 with
Charles Stewart a witness.

No. 3361. Samuel Murray, private; 274 acres; issued 7 Jan. 1786.
Samuel Murray endorsed the warrant to John Marshall on 8 Feb.
1786 in the presence of David Rods. Dixon Marshall, heir at law
of John Marshall and agent and attorney for Charles, William,
and Matthew Marshall, sold the same to William Haywood in March
1803. Haywood assigned it to Henry E. Kearney in August 1803.

No. 3360. John Marcer, private; 228 acres; issued 7 Jan. 1786.
This warrant was transferred to John Marshall on 19 Feb. 1786.
Dixon Marshall, heir of John Marshall, assigned the same to William Dickson on Jan. 1798, with Frank Nash and Thos. (illegible)
as witnesses.

No. 3365. Heirs of Joseph Mendinhall, private; 640 acres of
land; issued 7 Jan. 1786. William Mendehall, heir at law of
Joseph Mendenall, assigned it to William Marshall in Feb. 1786
witnessed by Joseph Hall. Marshall in turn assigned it to Stephen
Sneed in 1799 with John Washington as a witness. In 1801 Stephen
Sneed assigned it to William Russell.

No. 4358. Heirs of Richard E. Murfree, private; 640 acres; issued 17 Dec. 1796. By virtue of a writ to me directed issued
at the instance of James Eastern against William Tyrrell. Sheriff's sale to Jacob McGavock by James Malloy, sheriff of Stewart

Co., Tenn., 1818. Same was assigned to William Tyrrell and Jesse Spaight in the presence of J. H. Wilson (?) and David Jones, Sr.

No. 2386. Heirs of George Martin, a private; 640 acres; issued 30 Sept. 1785, and transferred by Phillip Martin, the heir, to Thomas Butcher on 4 Oct. 1785, witnessed by John Wans.

No. 2482. Ezekiel Medlin, private in the said line; 640 acres; granted to Joseph Beard, assignee of the heirs of said Medlin. The land was located in Hawkins Co. on the north side of Clinch Ricer south of Walnut Ridge west side of the path that leads from German Creek to Powels Valley, a place known by the name of Big Spring, at the end of Powel's Mountain; 1794.

No. 965. Issued 6 Sept. 1821 to the President and Trustees, etc., of the University of North Carolina, for the services of Jerome McMullin, a private. William Polk, agent and attorney for the President and Trustees, transferred the same to Thomas Henderson, Jr., in Oct. 1821. Henderson assigned it to John Jenkins in the same month.

No. 891. Henry Miller; 1000 acres for his services as a private; issued 19 May 1784. Henry Miller of New Hanover Co., N. C., transferred the warrant to William Bludworth of Tenn., in 1822, with Jo. H. Lamb, and Roger P. Larkins, witnesses. Samuel Buexton and David Jones, Justices of the Peace for New Hanover Co., witnessed the deed. N. Williams certified that Henry Miller was a sergeant in the War. Wm. Bludworth of Humphries Co., Tenn., petitioned the Assembly of Tennessee. The file also contains a letter to Huling and Fitzgerald, Esqrs., dated 12 Oct. 1828, Huntington.

No. 1961. Heirs of Richard Minshew, private; 640 acres; issued 10 Aug. 1785. Wm. Micher, or Minshew, heir of Richard, transferred it to Thomas Molloy on 20 June 1797, witnessed by Abra. Swagerty, Jesse Sharp, and James Marcome.

No. 5945, John Moseley, private; 274 acres; issued 26 Feb. 1796. An Johnson and Moseley on 23 March 1796 transferred the same to James Watson, witnessed by Benj. Hillutin (?) and B. R. Smith. Watson assigned it to Armstead Stubblefield in Aug. 1796, witnessed by Jonathan Boone. In the same year Stubblefield assigned it to Thomas Harvey and James Watson. On 6 Oct. 1796 Thomas Harvey transferred his share to James Watson, with Agness Cornly a witness. There is also a transfer by Watson to Thomas Harvey on 6 Oct. 1796, Sarah Watson a witness.

No. 2936. Heirs of Jonathan Miller, private; 640 acres; issued 30 Sept. 1785. Solomon Miller, heir of said Jonathan Miller, endorsed it to Thomas Dillon on 9 Oct. 1785, witnessed by Andr. Newman. Thomas Dillon, on 24 March 1804 sold it to Charles Stewart pf Montgomery Co., witnessed by John Stewart. In April 1804 Stewart assigned it to John Harvey.

No. 2746. Heirs of Drury Morgan, private in the N. C. Cont. Line; 640 acres; issued 30 Sept. 1785. Joel Morgan, heir of Drewry Morgan, endorsed it to Matthew Barrow in 1785.

No. 506. (Most of Warrant missing). Hannah McNeese and Mary McNeese, heirs of John McNeese, assigned the within warrant to Sampson Williams. William Tyrrell witnessed.

No. 4039. (Most of Warrant missing). Duncan Stewart transferred the warrant to Arthur Hasson on 8 Match 1797, witnessed by Samuel Eliot.

No. 155. Jonathan McJilton.   G. Bradley, captain, certified
that Jonathan McJilton was formerly a private soldier in the
N. C. Cont. Line, and that he served truly and faithfully for
a term of two and a half years and was regularly discharged.
Dated 9 Nov. 1796.

No. 290. Isaac Lindsey; 186 acres; based on a warrant for
Isaac Lindsey for 400 acres, no. 154, dated 1 Dec. 1794, by an
Act for raising troops for the protection of the Inhabitants of
Davidson County." Given 23 May 1803. (This warrant was found
filed woth the M's).

No. not given. Solomon Mitchell, revolutionary soldier. See
Legislative Petitions to the Secretary of State, Sumner and
Robertson Counties, Box 51. See also Legislative Petitions,
1829, Sumner Co.

No. 1958. Heirs of Peter Melone, private in the N. C. Line;
issued 10 Aug. 1785. Arthur Melone, heir to Peter Melone, assigned it to William Lytle, witnessed by Abra. Swagerty, Jesse
Sharp, and James Marcom.

No. 2174. Wm. Burgess, 274 acres as assignee of one Mains, a
private in the N. C. Cont. Line. The land was located in Sumner Co. on the Middle Fork of Goose Creek, 20 May 1793.

No. 3273. James Morgan, private, 274 acres within the limits
of land reserved for officers and soldiers of the N. C. Cont.
Line; issued 24 Dec. 1785.

No. 101. Heirs of Shadrack Morris, private; 640 acres; issued
5 Dec. 1804.

No. 263. Heirs of Wm. Moseley, private; 640 acres; issued 10
Dec. 1817.

No. 4036. Heirs of Thomas Murry, private; 640 acres of land;
issued 26 Nov. 1796. On 14 Jan. 1798 the heirs of Thomas Murry
assigned the warrant to Joseph Williams; signed Morgan Murry,
witnessed by Wm. Christian (or Christmus) and Isaac Collins,
Jr. On 16 March 1799 the same warrant was assigned to William
Christ, as witnessed by Y. Horton (probably Thornton). Franklin
Co., Sept. 1800: William Christmas appeared in court and made
oath that Morgan Murry assigned the warrant to him. Yancey
Thornton also made oath that he saw Joseph Williams make the
above assignment to the said William Christmus.

No. 4439. Shadrack Medlin, 228 acres. Notation that Shadrack
Medlin is mustered for two and a half years and absented him-
self without leave. Medlin was a private in the N. C. Line.
The warrant was issued 22 Dec. 1796, and transferred to Robert
Young on 1 June 1797, witnessed by Jos. William and Magin (or
Norgin) Williams. Robert Young transferred it to Mark Cooke in
March 1815.

No. 1097. Heirs of Joel Martin, private; 640 acres; Feb. 1823.
Martin Co., N. C.: Thomas G. Brick of Plmo., N. C. sold the
warrant to Laurence Cherry in 1824. John Martin of Washington
Co., N. C. sold the warrant to Charles Oden, Jr., of Beaufort
Co., N. C. John Martin was the true and lawful heir of Joel
Martin a soldier in the N. C. revolutionary line. Aug. 1823.
Hosea Gaylord and Langley Nippy(?) witnesses.

No. 1181. Nathaniel Medlock, private; 640 acres; 1824 to the
Trustees, etc.

No. 1180.   Mas. Minson, private; 640 acres; 1824 to the trustees, etc.

No. 1173.   David McDonel, private; 640 acres granted to the trustees, etc.

No. 1171.   Arthur Mitchell, private; 640 acres granted to the trustees, etc.

No. 1172.   Barnabas McAltree, private; issued 17 Feb. 1824, to the trustees.

No. 1174.   John McNulty, private; 640 acres; issued 17 Feb. 1824 to the trustees, etc.

No. 1175.   Bryan Maddin, a private; 640 acres for services in the N. C. Cont. Line, issued 17 Feb. 1824 to the trustees, etc.

No. 1176.   Daniel McKinley, a sergeant, balance of 360 acres; issued 17 Feb. 1824 to the trustees, etc.

No. 1177.   Robert McRennells, an ensign, 2560 acres; issued 1824 to the trustees, etc.

No. 1178.   Joseph McGraves, private; 640 acres; issued 1824to the trustees, etc.

No. 485.   Heirs of Wm. Muchlerby, private; 640 acres; issued 22 Aug. 1820.

No. 1179.   Bethro Mitchell, private; 640 acres; issued 1824 to the trustees, etc.

No. 554.   John Morplis, an ensign, 2560 acres; issued 6 Sept. 1820.   This was assigned to Alexander Morphis on 8 Sept. 1820, witnessed by Thomas Parham and John Thompson.

No. 512.   Joseph McCuller, a sergeant; 360 acres of land in those reserved for officers and soldiers of the N. C. Cont. Line; issued 1 Sept. 1820.

No. 647.   Alex'r McCorkle, a revolutionary soldier. (Part of the warrant is missing). The land was located on Duck River; issued 10 July 1784. William McCorkle assigned it to Sam. McCorkle on 28 Nov. 1810, witnessed by Richard B. McCorkle.

No. 410.   Heirs of John Morgan, musician; 1000 acres; issued 11 Aug. 1820.

No. 557.   Heirs of Abraham Mexico, private; 640 acres; issued 7 Sept. 1820.

No. not given.   John Marr, assignee of Isaac Griffin, private in the N. C. Cont. Line; 2687 acres in Sumner Co. on the south side of Big Barron River on the south creek that the Virginia line crosses that empties unto Barron River runs west. Dated 20 May 1793; signed by Richard Dobbs Spaight.

No. 3142.   William Mahains, a private; 274 acres; issued by James Glasgow at New Bern, 16 Dec. 1785. Mahains delivered the warrant to Howell Tatum on 23 Jan. 1786 witnessed by John Williams. Tatum transferred it to Joshua Hadley in 1786 and Hadley assigned it to Josiah Fort in Nov. 1794, in Robertson Co., Tenn., on Elk River on a bluff near Cave Spring.

No. 4359. Richard McGraves, a private in the N. C. Cont. Line;
640 acres; 17 Dec. 1796. Assigned to Allen Brewer with Reuben
Goodloe and Ch. Goodloe, witnesses. Brewer assigned the warrant
to William Tyrrell, witnessed by James Chisholm, Nathan Markland
and Bennet Rogers. J. G. Bradley a captain certified that Richard McGraves served three years in the war. 22 Feb. 1796.

No. 148. Heirs of John McCaleb, private in the N. C. Cont.
Line; 30 Nov. 1807.

No. 2949. John Casey was granted 640 acres for the services of
Alexander McCulloch, a revolutionary soldier, land on Duck River
in Davidson Co.; 20 July 1796.

No. 108. Heirs of James McGown, private in the N. C. Cont. Line;
640 acres; 17 Dec. 1804. William McGowne, lawful heir of James
McGown, assigned the warrant to Abel Hutson on 30 Sept. 1805,
witnessed by L. Jarvis. Abel Hutson assigned the warrant to
James Raulton in 1806, and James Ewing was a witness. David
Greene also mentioned.

No. 4119. Andrew McDaniell, private in the N. C. Cont. Line;
a grant. Solomon P. Goodrick and Sterling Wheaton, assignees
of the heirs of McDaniell, had 640 acres in Davidson Co., between
Marrowbone and Sycamore Creek, in 1797.

No. 3177. Heirs of Henry McClancey, private in the N. C. Cont.
Line; 640 acres; 19 Dec. 1785, assigned by Nicholas McClancey,
Sr., to Wm. Lytle, with Moses Hutson a witness.

No. 3086. Heirs of Daniel McDaniel, a private, dec.; 5 Dec.
1785. John McDaniel assigned it to John Armstrong.

No. 397. James McCrory, an ensign in the N. C. Cont. Line;
2560 acres; issued 4 Aug. 1820.

No. 326. Heirs of John McKay, private in the N. C. Cont. Line;
640 acres; 30 May 1820. Thomas Tomlinson, Jas. A. Harrison,
Alsey Austin and Amos Johnson of Johnson Co., N. C., heirs of
John McKay, and Ambrose Ingram, guardian of Mary Tomlinson,
heir at law of McKay, sold the warrant to Calvin Jones, May
1820.

No. 2937. Heirs of Stephen McDaniel, private in the N. C. Cont.
Line; 30 Sept. 1783. The warrant was endorsed to Thomas Dillon
by Isaac McDowel on 3 Oct. 1785. Jacob Sirgrove witnessed the
transaction. Dillon assigned it to William Robinson of Jackson
Co. on 20 June 1803, with Hy McKinney a witness.

No. 39. Nathan McClure, Guard Right. "Invalid." John McClure
for himself and Robert McClure, heirs of Nathan McClure, sold
the warrant to James Robertson on 25 Jan. 1805. Thomas Stuart
was a witness. Dan Smith appears to have found the warrant on
17 May 1807 and turned it over to the proper authorities. Nathan McClure's entry was dated 30 March 1784, Davidson Co., no.
377, and states that Nathan McClure, a soldier in the Guards;
320 acres of land on the Harpeth River about two miles above
the mouth of Turneys Creek, beginning about one quarter mile
below the Spring running up the river on both sides. Nathan
McClure was a soldier in the commissioner's guard.

No. 4328. Benjamine McFarland, private; 274 acres; 10 Dec. 1796.
On 31 May 1797 John Hunter, attorney for Benjamine McFarland,
transferred the warrant to Rob, Allenm with Willis Rogers and
Thomas Seawell.

No. 3927. Heirs of Duncan McBridge, private in the N. C. Cont. Line; 640 acres; issued 8 Dec. 1795. Bladen Co., N. C.: Archibald McBridge, heir of Duncan McBridge, transferred the warrant to Samuel Eliot of the same county and state; John Wicker and Duncan McKeithen, witnesses.

No. 3948. Heirs of Reuben McCarmach, private in the N. C. Cont. Line; 640 acres; issued 23 Feb. 1796. John McCorne, heir, assigned it to Stockley Donelson on 17 Jan. 1797. Donelson assigned it to Thomas Hickman on 10 Jan. 1801, with Will Tyrrell a witness.

No. 4496. Jeremiah McMullin, private in the N. C. Cont. Line; 274 acres; 22 Dec. 1796. The warrant was transferred to Joshua Hadley on 18 July 1797 and transferred to Wright Taylor on 18 July 1797. Mark Cole witnessed the first transfer and D. Stewwart witnessed the second. On 28 Sept. 1797 Wright Taylor made it over to Benjamine Clarke and John Ward, with J. Armstrong as a witness. No. 1071. State of N. C.: John Medaris, captain, certifies that Jeremiah McMullin was a soldier in the late Cont. Line of the state and served in the line for three years; 18 Dec. 1796.

No. 4498. D. McCloud, a private in the N. C. Cont. Line; 274 acres; 22 Dec. 1796. Daniel McCloud transferred the same to William Askew on 14 Jan. 1797, with William Brice a witness.

No. 4015. Malcorn (Malcolm?) McSwain, private in the N. C. Cont. Line; 640 acres; 25 Nov. 1796. Bladen Co., N.C.: Malcolm McSwain transferred the warrant to Samuel Eliot on 12 April 1796, in the presence of Good Bethed(?).

No. 3624. James McCalop, private in the N. C. Cont. Line; 274 acres; 19 Dec. 1804. (The following item may pertain to this.)

No. not given. 17 April 1805 Arthur Addams, lawful heir of said Arthur Albertson for $50.00, transferred the warrant to William Alberson. Signed by Arthur Addams and Benjamine Addams, with John Holdins and John Boyet. On 10 Jan. 1806 William Alberson assigned the warrant to James McCalop, with Fred Grady and Benety West.

No. 128. Thomas McCrory; 38 acres. The warrant was issued from a grant to Thomas McCrory for 640 acres of no. 733, dated 10 July 1788.

No. 187. Chas. McLung; 1000 acres; 18 May 1789. Grant no. 504; ten pound warrant. The same was assigned to Charles McLung by Thomas Jackson on 7 April 1803, with J. Cocke and Wm. Mcaclin as witnesses.

No. 184. Robert McNut; no. 464; 200 acres based on grant no. 190; 20 Sept. 1787, a fifty shilling warrant.

No. 188. Charles McClung; no. 163; Thomas Jackson; 100 acres; based on grant no. 237 to George Brooks for 200 acres on 10 Nov. 1784; a fifty shilling grant. Thomas Jackson assigned it to Charles McClung on April 1803. Nathaniel B. Markland was a witness.

No. 374. Heirs of Philip McConnell, private in the N. C. Cont. Line; 640 acres; 27 July 1820.

No. 3592. Heirs of Arthur McRery, private in the N. C. Cont. Line; 640 acres; 23 Jan. 1796. Nancy McRery and Nathan McRery assigned it to Edward Veal, with R. Ricgards and Wm. McLenister as witnesses. On 13 Dec. 1796 Edward Veal assigned it to Samuel Barton, with Jesse Sharp and Wm. Kennaday as witnesses. Barton assigned it to Margaret Barton on 19 March 1797, with Samuel Barton, Jr., a witness.

No. not given. David McNabb, captain in the South Carolina Cont. Line under Gen. Marion. See his petition of 1823 from Carter Co., asking for reimbursement of money paid to Armstrong's office for which he received nothing in compensation.

No. not given. Lazarus McCurdy, revolutionary soldier. See petition of executors of Thomas Mallory, 1807, Davidson Co. petitions.

No. not given. Clement McDaniel, revolutionary soldier. See Legislative Petitions 1819, Secretary of State File.

No. 550. Robert Nelson, 68 acres. Based on a warrant issued from a grant to Joseph Brock for 640 acres, no. 24, dated 8 October 1787. Nelson transferred it to David Smith on 19 Feb. 1805, witnessed by Jno. H. Hyde.

No. 874. Heirs of Thomas Needham, a sergeant in the Revolutionary War from N. C.; 1000 acres; issued 5 Sept. 1821, and transferred to William G. Hudnott on 17 Sept. 1821; signed Mathias Gallop and Mary Gallop, witnessed by Thomas Prescout. The same was transferred to Zepheniah Howland and Joseph Midget on 20 Sept. 1821. In Jan. 1822 Midget assigned it to Phillip Miller.

No. 636. Heirs of Thos. Nixon, Sr., a captain in the N. C. Cont. Line; 3840 acres; 15 Sept. 1820.

No. 1120. John Nelson; 5000 acres. The warrant was assigned to Samuel Nelson on 18 Jan. 1784. John Nelson assigned it to William Preston Anderson in Jan. 1802. John Nelson was a resident of Montgomery Co., Tenn. The land was on Clear Creek. The witnesses were B. G. Pollack and Richard Manley.

No. 348. Heirs of Arthur Nelson, private in the N. C. Cont. Line; 640 acres; 10 July 1820. John Nelson of Craven Co., N. C., only heir to Arthur Nelson, a continental soldier, assigned the warrant to Roderick Cherry on 14 July 1820. Turner Nelson and Harmon Jinkins were witnesses. Roderick Cherry assigned it to Eli Cherry on 12 Aug. 1820.

No. 364. Heirs of John Neill, private in the N. C. Cont. Line; 640 acres; 22 July 1820. John Neil and Cudbirth Neil, sons and heirs at law of John Neil, who was once a soldier in Capt. Turner's Co., assigned the warrant to Calvin Jones on 8 July 1820. The grantors were living in Warren Co., N. C.

No. 4413. Heirs of Henry Nightshead, private in the N. C. Cont. Line; 640 acres; issued 22 Dec. 1796. The warrant was assigned to Redmond Dillon Barry o 29 Aug. 1797.

No. 4409. Sanders Nesbet, private; 640 acres; issued 22 Dec. 1796 and sold to Redmond Dillon Barry on 21 May 1797, and then assigned to Edward Given on 13 Aug. 1798.

No. 4537. William Norriss, a private in the N. C. Cont. Line; 640 acres; issued 24 Dec. 1796, and assigned on the same day to Wm. Lytle, with Willis Rogers a witness. Signed by John Hunter, attorney. It was transferred to James Frayor on 20 Feb. 1797.

No. 4317. Heirs of Edward Neeken, private in the N. C. Cont. Line; 640 acres; 14 Dec. 1796. Reuben Davis as heir of Edward Neeker or Nockers transferred the warrant. Richard Nickers was also an heir of Edward Nickers a private in the Cont. service of the U. S., 11 March 1797.

No. 1622. Aron Newman, private in the N. C. Cont. Line; 640 acres in Tenn. County, 1805. (1792)

No. 4413. Zeal of Henry Nightsteade, private in the N. C. Cont. Line. Marmaduke Bell, Henry C (?) and Robert Joyner, heirs of Bythell Bell, were to have 640 acres laid off and surveyed on 29 March 1819. A letter in this file dated 14 Dec. 1824, Shelby-ville, addressed to Dr. Robert Church and signed S. R. Rucker, regarding relief of the heirs of Bythen Bell.

No. 3013. Stephen Newton, a private in the N. C. Cont. Line; 30 Sept. 1785. The same was assigned to Thomas Dillon on 4 Oct. 1785, witnessed by John Wavse (?). Dillon transferred it to Thomas Hutchinson on 21 June 1802.

No. 653. Michael Nash, private in the N. C. Cont. Line; 23 April 1784.

No. 111. James Nicols, private in the N. C. Cont. Line; 228 acres; 17 Dec. 1804.

No. 144. James Norsworthy, a sergeant in the N. C. Cont. Line; 22 Dec. 1806.

No. 134. Heirs of Noah Vandiford (probably is Nandiford), a private in the N. C. Cont. Line; 640 acres; issued 19 Dec. 1806. Richard Davis, attorney for John Vandiford, transferred the war-rant to William Hulme of Wilkes Co., N. C., 21 Dec. 1806. On 29 Jan. 1807 Hulme transferred the same to John McGimpsey of Burke Co., N. C., with J. Coleman and Tilman Wlaton as witnesses.

No. not given. Peter Oringer, Rev. soldier, mentioned in a pe-tition; in Legislative papers of the executors Thomas Maccary, Davidson Co., 1807.

No. 138 (grant). Wm. Terrell and Jno. Payne; 1000 acres as as-signee of Martin Armstrong, surveyor of lands allotted to offi-cers and soldiers of the N. C. Cont. Line. The land was in the Middle District. 4 Feb. 1795.

No. 411. Heirs of Jesse Prichard, sergeant in the N. C. Cont. Line; 572 acres of land within the limits of land reserved by law for officers and soldiers of the Line; 11 Aug. 1820.

No. 4004. James Parker, private in the N. C. Cont. Line; 228 acres; 25 Nov. 1796. New Hanover Co., N. C., 4 March 1796: Major McRee of the N. C. Line of the late army certified that James Parker of Duplin Co. enlisted under him on the Cont. ser-vice in the N. C. Line and that he served two and a half years.

No. 4043. Heirs of John Phipps, private in the N. C. Cont. Line; 640 acres; 25 Nov. 1796. The same was assigned to John Overton on 9 Dec. 1796. Overton transferred it to Abraham Murray and Joel Parrish, with Wm. Christmas a witness.

No. 3916. Drury Parham, private in the N. C. Cont. Line; 228 acres; 5 Dec. 1795. The same was assigned to Stockley Donelson and Will'm Terrell on 5 Dec. 1795. Joseph Stewart, attorney for Drury Parham, signed the transfer witnessed by Robert Young.

These two men assigned the warrant to Edward Simmins on 10 April 1796, with Wm. Lytle a witness.

No. 3923. Heirs of Abner Pasmore, private in the N. C. Cont. Line; 640 acres; 8 Dec. 1795. George Passmore assigned it to Joshua Hadley on 20 Dec. 1795, with John Moore a witness. Hadley assigned the same to Lee Sullivan on 23 Oct. 1797, with Stephen Brown a witness.

No. 3944. Heirs of Gideon Petit, private in the N. C. Cont. Line; 640 acres; dated 22 Feb. 1796. John Walk or Walsh, heir of said Petit, assigned the warrant to James Easton on 16 March 1796, with Daniel McLean a witness. Easton assigned the warrant to John Boyd, Jr., on 14 Sept. 1796, with James C. Graham and Wm. Rogers as witnesses. J. Boyd, Jr., transferred the same to Thomas Edmondson and Jonathan Phillips on 25 Oct. 1796.

No. 4661. Heirs of William Peete, private in the N. C. Cont. Line; 640 acres; 9 Feb. 1797. William Peete, Jr., heir, transferred the warrant to Sterling Brewer, with Jesse Sharp and Wm. Smith as witnesses. Brewer assigned itto Wm. Tyrrell on 4 March 1797, with Wm. Lackey witness. Certificate on warrant dated 4 March 1797 , sheriff of Davidson Co., July 1807, by instance of Wm. T. Lewis against William Tyrrell. Lewis, through bid of Jno. P. McConnell, obtained the same for $26.00. Signed John Boyd, sheriff of Davidson Co.

No. 4366. Harman Peelle, private in the N. C. Cont. Line; 640 acres; 17 Dec. 1796. Transferred to Benjamine Williams.

No. 4422. Heirs of William Poor, private in the N. C. Cont. Line; 640 acres; 22 Dec. 1796. The same was assigned to Wm. Tyrrell on 28 April 1797; Allen Brewer, attorney for John Hunter, witnessed by Samuel Clenning. The land was surveyed and located in Davidson Co. on the west fork of Turners Creek on the Harpeth River. 21 Dec. 1796: certificate that William Poor served as a continental soldier in the N. C. Line during the late war between America and Great Britain and that he died in the service before his term expired for which he enlisted, it being for the term of 3 years. Signed, John Medearis, captain.

No. 4564. Dempsey Pervenes, private in the N. C. Cont. Line; 228 acres; 9 Feb. 1797. The same was assigned to Thomas Molloy and witnessed by William Read and Jesse Sharp.

No. 4563. Silas Prindle, private in the N. C. Cont. Line; 228 acres; 9 Feb. 1797. The same was assigned to Sterling Brewer on 13 Feb. 1797. Richard Howell and John Parlin were witnesses.

No. 4502. Andrew Phillips, private in the N. C. Cont. Line; 274 acres; 22 Dec. 1796. The warrant was transferred to William Askew on 25 Feb. 1797, with Hugh Lanier a witness.

No. 3217. Heirs of Stephen Paul, private in the N. C. Cont. Line; 640 acres; 17 Dec. 1785 (duplicate warrant). On the back it states that the original warrant, proven by affidavit of Hayden Wells, to have been assigned to William Tyrrell and Wm. T. Lewis. Davidson Co., Tenn.: Wm. T. Lewis appeared before Joseph Coleman, J. P., in 1805. Hayden Wells appeared before Thos. A. Claiborne and made oath.

No. 237. Heirs of John Portress, private in the N. C. Cont. Line; 640 acres; 25 Aug. 1813. Littlebury (Littleberry) Protros and Perciller Protros and Della Protros, the proper owners of the warrant, assigned it to Darling Cherry on 29 Aug. 1813, with Levi Harrell a witness.

No. 3267. Emanuel Paratree, private in the N. C. Cont. Line, deceased; 640 acres; 24 Dec. 1785. Nathaniel Williams assigned it to Nathan Goodwin on 8 April 1787. Survey dated 14 Oct. 1797 located the land on the waters of Barretts Creek in Montgomery Co., adjoining John Manns lower tract.

No. 3178. Heirs of John Parrott, private in the N. C. Cont. Line; 640 acres; 17 Dec. 1785. It was assigned to William Christmas on 23 April 1798, witnessed by Corlean Juchey, Hardy Hunt, and Cullan Jones.

No. 506. Benjamine Powell, private in the N. C. Cont. Line; 640 acres; 2 April 1784. Pitt Co., N. C.: Benjamine Powell sold the warrant to John McRees on 6 April 1784. In July 1802 S. Williams assigned the warrant to Christopher Buller.

No. 3370. Heirs of John Purnong(?), private in the N. C. Cont. Line. 640 acres; 7 Jan. 1786. Jacob Punang, heir at law of John Purnang, assigned the warrant to John Morthall on 9 Feb. 1786, with Hennery Davis a witness.

No. 2977. Heirs of Stephen Perkins, private in the N. C. Cont. Line; 640 acres; 27 Dec. 1803. Mann Phillips was assignee of Perkins' heirs. On 17 Nov. 1788 the land was located below the mouth of Plumb Creek of Round Lick Creek.

No. 3017. Jesse Pritchard, sergeant in the N. C. Cont. Line; 423 acres; 8 Dec. 1785. Maxy Pritchard was a private in the N. C. Cont. Line; assigned the warrant to Reuben Davis on 25 Feb. 1797, with David Foster and D'd Davis witnesses.

No. 2944. Heirs of William Putnall (Putnell), private in the N. C. Cont. Line; 640 acres; 30 Sept. 1785.

No. 2943. Stephen Philips, private in the N. C. Cont. Line; 640 acres; 30 Sept. 1785.

No. 2942. Heirs of Zedekiah Perkins, private in the N. C. Cont. Line; 640 acres; 30 Sept. 1785. Joseph Perkins, heir of Zadock Perkins, transferred the same to John Markland on 19 Jan. 1786. John Markland transferred it on 22 July 1796. The survey shows the land was in Montgomery Co., Tenn.

No. 2431. Peter Pointer or Poiner, private in the N. C. Cont. Line; 640 acres; 30 Sept. 1785, was transferred to Thos. Smith on 2 Nov. 1795. Smith assigned it to James McCaffety on 16 April 1798, and McCaffety to John Coatt on 17 Nov. 1798. Coatt assigned it to Edmund Jennings on 21 Dec. 1802.

No. 176. Caleb Powers, private in the N. C. Cont. Line. 274 acres within the limits of land reserved by law for the officers and soldiers of the Cont. Line; issued 19 Dec. 1808. Caleb Powers assigned it to Darling Cherry on 11 April 1809.

No. 290. Heirs of Thomas Petejohn, corporal in the Cont. Line of this state. Laid off for the heirs of Thomas Petejohn 1000 acres within the limits of land reserved for officers and soldiers of the N. C. Line, on 27 Nov. 1819. John Pettejohn of Chowan Co., N. C., the only heir of his brother, Thomas, dec., a corporal, dec. in the old war as a continental soldier in the N. C. Line, transferred the warrant to Daniel Cherry on 9 Dec. 1819, with Laurence Cherry and Jonathan Houghton as witnesses.

No. 157. William Payford, musician in the N. C. Cont. Line; 360 acres; 22 Dec. 1807. The warrant was assigned to William Hill

and Mack Hardin on 7 May 1808, with William Mayab and Mishuk Barrett as witnesses.

No. 3275. Thomas Pettejohn, soldier. John Pettejohn, only heir
and brother of said Thomas, a private and was deceased. The
warrant was delivered to Lemuel Creasey who sold the warrant to
Edward Houghton and said Houghton was going to the State of Tennessee and sold the warrant to Isaac Bateman of Chowan Co., N.C.
on 2 Nov. 1819, with Jonathan Houghton a witness. The warrant
was issued at New Bern on 24 Dec. 1785.

No. 3226. **Heirs of John Patterson**, private; 640 acres; issued
23 Dec. 1785 at New Bern. Patterson was deceased.

No. 183. Jacob Purce or Pearce, or Pierce, a private in the N.
C. Cont. Line; 640 acres; issued 22 April 1809. Luke Parker and
wife Ann Parker, the only heirs of Jacob Pierce, a continental
soldier in the last war, transferred the warrant to Daniel Cherry,
on 19 Dec. 1809, with Darling Cherry a witness.

No. 178. Heirs of Reuben Pierce, private in the N. C. Cont.
Line; 640 acres; issued 19 Dec. 1808. William Pierce, Jr., of
Pitt Co., N. C., only heir of Reuben Pierce, transferred the
warrant to Samuel Whealley, Sr., of Martin Co., N. C., on 6 Jan.
1809, with Samuel Whitely, Jr., and Samuel Cherry as witnesses.
Samuel Whitely transferred the warrant to Daniel Cherry on 8
March 1810, with Pierce Whitely and Jesse Cherry as witnesses.

No. 158. Heirs of Theophilus Pearce, private in the N. C. Cont.
Line; 640 acres; dated 15 Feb. 1808. Elijah Pierce, only heir
of Theophilus Pearce, does transfer the warrant to Durean
Gameron.

No. not given. Benjamine Patrick, revolutionary soldier of N.
C. Martha Patrick of Nash Co., N. C., sold the warrant to Cal-
vin Jones of Wake Co. The warrant was issued for the sevice of
Benjamine Patrick, a musician. 21 Dec. 1821. Cordal Hunter,
Mose (?) Mapssenburg and Andes Jones were witnesses. Halifax
Co., N. C.: Joseph Masingill deposed that he served in the
Cont. Army in the Revolution and that he knew Benjamine Patrick,
a fifer of the said line. Patrick died while in the said army,
leaving a widow and a daughter. The widow is now dead, having
but one child, a daughter named Betsy Patrick who never married,
but Betsy had out of wedlock an only child, a daughter, born in
1800, and that she is known by the name of Martha Patrick; 16
Aug. 1821

No. 672. Heirs of John Perkison, a sergeant; 428 acres within
the limits of land reserved for officers and soldiers of the
N. C. Cont. Line; 27 March 1821. Joseph and Polly Perkerson
transferred the within warrant to John Terrelle on 26 April 1821,
witnessed by Allen Wilkins. Granville Co., N.C., Joseph J. Perkerson and Polly S. Perkerson, heirs and representatives of their
father, John Perkerson, dec., late of Granville Co., overseer of
Samuel Parker some 16 or 17 years ago. George Brasfield was
appointed attorney.

No. 683. Heirs of William Pipkin, a private in the N. C. Cont.
Line; 640 acres; 23 May 1821. John Pipkin transferred the warrant to John Terrell on 20 Sept. 1821, with Susannah Brantley
and James Spence as witnesses. Wayne Co., N. C.: Ezekiel Holeman made oath that he was acquainted with William Pipkin, dec.,
a soldier in the Revolutionary War in the Cont. Line, and is
reported to have enlisted under the command of Capt. Mills of
the 10th N. C. Regt., and served until he died near Charleston,
S. C. The deponent stated he was a soldier at the same time

and that he understood that Pipkin died without lawful issue, leaving as heir at law his oldest brother, John Pipkin.

No. 583. William Peoples, a private in the N. C. Cont. Line; 228 acres of land within the limits reserved for officers and soldiers of the Cont. Line; 12 Sept. 1820.   George Bowers purchased from William Peoples of Pitt Co., N..C., who was a continental soldier in the Revolutionary War in the N. C. Line, on 13 Sept. 1820, with Thos. Southerland and Samuel Merril as witnesses.

No. 655. Joshua Potts, captain in the N. C. Cont. Line; 3840 acres; 21 Dec. 1820.

No. 103. Heirs of Henry Phillips, private in the N. C. Cont. Line; 640 acres; 7 Dec. 1804. Johnston Co., N. C.: to Mr. Martin Armstrong: you are required to lay off for Mr. Daniel Wheatin the land warrant for the heirs of Henry Philips, dec., for his services in the Army in the late war in behalf of his services in the army in the late war; 27 May 1796. Benj. Lanhon, witness.

No. 118. John Patterson, private; 274 acres reserved by law for the officers and soldiers of the N. C. Cont. Line; 28 Aug. 1805.

No. 3998. Heirs of Daniel Poe, private in the N. C. Cont. Line; 640 acres; 25 Nov. 1796. The same was assigned to James Robinson on 27 Dec. 1796, by John Poe, heir, with Peter Jones a witness. On 12 July 1797, James Robertson assigned the same to John Davis and Jonathan F. Robertson. Certificate states that Daniel Poe was a three year soldier in Capt. James Company, and died at Charleston in the service; 19 Sept. 1794; signed, Joshua Hadley, captain.

No. 3188. Heirs of Joshua Perry, a private in the N. C. Cont. Line; 640 acres; 19 Dec. 1785. John Perry, heir at law, transferred the warrant to William Lytle, Jr., on 19 May 1796, with Henry Hart a witness. William Lytle, Jr., assigned it to W. P. ANderson on 30 Dec. 1808.

No. 349. Heirs of Joseph Phillips, private in the N. C. Cont. Line; 10 July 1820. Curtis Phillips, of Pitt Co., N. C., only true and lawful heir of Joseph Phillips, a continental soldier in the N. C. Line, transferred the warrant to Roderick Cherry on 11 July 1820, with Harmon Jinkins and Pherefe Phillips as witnesses. Roderick Cherry assigned it to Eli Cherry, with Wm. H. Bell, Wm. Anderson and Laurence Cherry as witnesses.

No. 640. Thomas Poore, private; 640 acres; 15 Sept. 1820.

No. 414. John Polson, corporal; balance of 128 acres; 11 Aug. 1820.

No. 343. Heirs of Wm. Pearce; 640 acres; 1 July 1820. Luke Parker and wife Ann Parker, formerly Ann Pierce of Bertie Co., N. C., transferred the warrant to Daniel Cherry on 17 Nov. 1818, with William Turner, Wm. Parker, and Esther Parker witnesses.

No. 877. Heirs of Pearson Peal, sergeant in the N. C. Rev. War; 328 acres; 5 Sept. 1821. The same was transferred to William G. Hadnett on 17 Sept. 1821; signed by Henery Barnes, Polly Barns, Jonathan Scarborough and Betheney Scarborough. Wm. G. Hudnett assigned the same to Joseph Power on 3 Nov. 1821. The transfer mentioned Carteret Co., N. C., and Currituck Co., N. C.

No. 186. Wm. Pursley, "Invalid," no. 522. James Campbell, 100 acres by virtue of a ten # warrant. Grant no. 873 on 17 Nov. 1790. 1 Sept. 1807 the warrant ejudicated (sic).

No. 185. Wm. Pursley; "Invalid," no. 518. James Campbell a ten # warrant based on grant to James Campbell no. 813, for 600 acres; dated 17 Nov. 1790.

No. 2870. Heirs of Isaac Perry, private in the N. C. Cont. Line; 640 acres; issued 30 Sept. 1785. Jacob Perry transferred the warrant to Thomas Dillon on 16 Oct. 1782.

No. 2869. Heirs of John Persey, a private in the N. C. Cont. Line; 640 acres; 30 Sept. 1785. Peter Persey endorsed the same to Moses Fisk on 9 Oct. 1785, with Hardy Wlsch (sic) as a witness.

No. 2868. Heirs of Isaac Pelt, private in the N. C. Cont. Line; 640 acres; 30 Sept. 1785. Joseph Pelt, heir of Isaac Pelt, transferred it to John Markland on 20 Oct. 1786, with David Jones a witness. J. Markland assigned it to Joseph Hopkins on 8 July 1786, with Hardy Askew a witness.

No. 577. Jesse Potts, a captain in the N. C. Cont. Line; 3840 acres; issued 9 Sept. 1820.

No. 1001. Heirs of Benjamine Pendleton, private in the N. C. Cont. Line; 640 acres; 10 Sept. 1821. Frances Pendleton assigned the warrant to James Hart on 1 Dec. 1821, with John N. O. Jackson a witness. On 24 Dec. 1821 James Hart assigned it to Gen. James Wellborn, with William Hill a witness. Wellborn transferred his interest to Col. Newton Cannon on 15 June 1822.

No. 1904. John Phillips, a private in the N. C. Cont. Line; 15 July 1785. It was assigned to Oliver Tuton on 27 Feb. 1786, signed by Levi Phillips and witnessed by James Corbitt. Jas., heir of Oliver Tuton, assigned it to Richard Mitchell on 10 July 1804; signed Wm. Tuton, witnessed by Robert Searcy.

No. 2758. Heirs of Randel Putnam, private; 640 acres; for his services in the N. C. Cont. Line; 30 Sept. 1785. John Putnam, heir of Randel Putnam, dec., transferred it to John Hannah on 20 Oct. 1785, witnessed by Thos. Barrow. John Hammon assigned it to John Dickson on 12 Dec. 1795, with Alex'n Deak a witness. Notation that "The above transfers are not legal." John Dickson assigned it to James Dickson and Hayden Wells of Duplin Co., N. C., 20 Nov. 1792, witnessed by Archelcus Wells.

No. 2871. Heirs of Benjamine Pender, private in the N. C. Cont. Line; 640 acres; 30 Sept. 1785. Joel Pender, heir, endorsed the warrant to Spencer Griffin on 16 Oct. 1785, with Stephen Rutherford a witness. Spencer Griffin assigned it to Andrew Peddy or Reddy on 26 March 1805, with David Abernathy a witness.

No. 1009. Thomas Quinn, private; 274 acres; 10 Sept. 1821. The same was transferred to John Roberts in Sept. 1821. Roberts assigned it to Henry Seawell, Esq.

No. 662. Heirs of Eleanor (Eleazer? - R. B.) Quinby or Guimby, private; 274 acres; 21 Feb. 1821. Bertie Co., N. C., William Evans made oath that he was personally acquainted with Eleazer Quinby and that he died leaving no wife nor children, but had one brother by the name of Jesse who died having one son by the name of William Quimby who is the heir of the aforesaid Elezer Quinby, a soldier in the 10th Regt. of the N. C. Line. Hertford Co., N. C., 1821: William Quinby made oath that he was the heir at law of Eleazer Quinby, late a private in Capt. Shepards Co. in the 10th N. C. Regt., and appointed James Turner his attorney for the sale of the warrant.

No. 4029. Heirs of Joseph Richards, private in the N. C. Cont.
Line; 3 Feb. 1806. The same was assigned to Thomas E. Sumner
on 19 March 1806, witnessed by Wm. Fawn. Sumner made oath before
William Christmas that the 640 acres granted to Robert Winn on
the warrant of Richards and heirs appear to overlap the survey
of other lands; 1807.

No. 4042. Heirs of David Rogers, a private in the N. C. Cont.
Line of the American Revolution; 640 acres; issued 25 Nov. 1796.
John Rogers assigned it to John Overton on 9 Dec. 1796, with
Thomas Nenon as a witness. Overton assigned it to Abraham Murray
in July 1807.

No. 3475. Heirs of Samuel Rose, private in the N. C. Cont. Line;
640 acres; issued 26 Feb. 1786. John Rose assigned it to James
Lanier on 8 Feb. 1787 in the presence of David Saunt. James
Lanier assigned it to Laurence Croutzman on 17 July 1788.

No. 4668. Abraham Ruth, private in the N. C. Cont. Line; 320
acres; issued 9 Feb. 1797. Abram Ruth assigned it to Nathan
Brown on 15 Feb. 1797, with James Tulloch and Richard Howells
as witnesses.

No. 3914. Heirs of Caleb Roper (or Raper), private; 640 acres;
issued 2 Dec. 1795. Caleb Raper enlisted in the N. C. Cont.
service for three years or during the war and died in the war.
Certificate by H. Murfree, late army, 2 Dec. 1795. John Roper,
heir of Caleb Rober, by R. H. Daniel transferred the same to
William Bagard and George West on 21 Sept. 1803, with D'd. Enloe
and Henry Stark, witnesses. On 8 July 1806 William Bagard assigned the warrant to George West, witnessed by Robert Searcy.

No. 4666. Heirs of Laurence Racos (or Raws), private in the
N. C. Cont. Line; 640 acres; issued 9 Feb. 1797. On 5 Jan. 1797
the same was transferred to Sterling Brewer by James Racos or
Raws, with Daniel Davidson a witness. Brewer assigned it to
Thomas Molloy.

No. 4669. Heirs of Abraham Rickey, private; 640 acres; issued
9 Feb. 1797. Sterling Richey transferred the same to Sterling
Brewer, who assigned it to Robert Stothars, who assigned it to
John Buchanan on 25 Dec. 1797, in the presence of Thomas McCrory.

No. 4303. Johnston Reynolds, a private; 640 acres; issued 14
Dec. 1796. He transferred the same to Stockley Donelson, who
made it over to David Moore.

No. 4312. Samuel Reaves, private in the N. C. Cont. Line; 228
acres; issued 14 Dec. 1796. Reaves transferred it to Isaac
Hicks, who assigned it to Solomon P. Goodrich on June 1797, with
Aaron Sugg as witness. Goodrick transferred it to Edward Pride
with F. Crenshaw as witness in June 1797. Pride in turn sold
it to Isaac McCattum in April 1801, with Zachariah Smith as a
witness.

No. 4326. John Reardon, private in the N. C. Cont. Line; 274
acres; issued 16 Dec. 1796. John Hunter, attorney, transferred
it to Robert Young on 3 May 1797, with Willis Rogers and Jos.
Seawell as witnesses. On 17 Aug. 1798 Young assigned it to
Cohen Reed by Frederick Stump, with C. Stump, C. Ryburn, and
Frederick Fisher as witnesses. (The Whitley manuscript states
John Hunter was attorney for John Hunter - R. B.)

No. 547. Heirs of John Robinson, private in the N. C. Cont.
Line; issued 4 Sept. 1820.

No. 310. John Rogers, private in the N. C. Cont. Line of the American Revolution; 640 acres; issued 23 Feb. 1820. The same was transferred by John Rodgers on 22 Jan. 1828 to Laurence Cherry. Rodgers describes himself as a resident of Perquimans Co., N. C., and states he was a continental soldier. Wm. Wood, Isham Anderson, and John G. Wood were witnesses.

No. 363. Heirs of John Ratley, private in the N. C. Cont. Line; 640 acres; issued 22 July 1820. John Batcheler, Frances Ratley, Mathew Ratley, and Molly Ratley, all of Nash Co., N. C., heirs of John Ratley, sold the warrant to Calvin Jones on 21 June 1820.

No. 419. Heirs of Thomas Rice, sergeant in the N. C. Cont. Line; 1000 acres; issued 16 Aug. 1820. Francis Rice of Warren Co., N. C., in right of heir of Thomas Rice, sergeant, sold the warrant to Calvin Jones on 12 Aug. 1820.

No. 399. Heirs of William Russell, private in the N. C. Cont. Line of the Rev. War; issued 5 Aug. 1820. Luke Russell of Craven Co., N. C., sold the warrant to Calvin Jones. Luke Russell was the rightful heir of said William. The transfer, dated 10 July 1820, was witnessed by Geo. Lane and Wm. McKinney.

No. 2876. Andrew Russell, private in the N. C. Cont. Line; issued 30 Sept. 1785. Richard Russell, heir of Andrew Russell, sold the same to Thomas Dillon on 18 Oct. 1782, with Jesse Sapitter(?) a witness. Dillon sold it to Beal Bosley in May 1803, with Daniel Wheaton as a witness. Bosley sold it to Thomas Shute in May 1803, with John Hill a witness.

No. 3286. Heirs of Henry Rhodes, private in the line of this state; 640 acres; issued 20 Dec. 1806.

No. 2288. James Roach, a private in the N. C. Cont. Line; 502 acres; issued 28 Sept. 1785. On 27 Oct. 1800 James Roach assigned his right to William Roach, with Jos. Turrentine a witness.

No. 3285. Heirs of William Rhoades, dec., a sergeant; 1000 acres; 28 Dec. 1785.

No. 3997. Heirs of Timothy Randle, private in the N. C. Cont. Line; 640 acres; issued 25 Nov. 1796.

No. 2694. John Rice, private in the N. C. Cont. Line; 640 acres issued to William Flemming, assignee of Rice, 1793. The land was located in Sumner Co., on Cumberland River, adjoining the land of Daniel Smith. (This is a copy of the grant.)

No. 3600. John Roggerson, private in the N. C. Cont. Line; 360 acres; issued 27 June 1788. Perquimans Co., N. C., 12 May 1796: the same was assigned to Charles Smallwood, with John Wood a witness.

No. 3625. Thomas Rutherford, private in the line of this state; 640 acres; issued Dec. 1785. Davidson Co., Tenn.: Thomas Rutherford appeared before Stephen Cantrell, J. P., and made oath that he never transferred the warrant to anyone.

No. not given. William Richards of Perquimans Co., received a warrant as per the provisions for officers and soldiers of the N. C. Cont. Line. Patrick Burk of Chowan Co., N. C., sold the same to William Richards on 2 Dec. 1790, land in Davidson Co., no. 3274, witnessed by Benjamin Coffield. Polly Richards assigned the same to Charles Smallwood on 28 July 1796.

No. 872. Franklin Co., N. C.: John Bartholomew went before Amos Jones, J. P., and made oath that he was acquainted with Moses Reed who enlisted in the N. C. Cont. Line in the Revolutionary War, under Capt. Soleman for three years, and served in the North until he died near the white plains (Bartholomew believes) in the year 1779. He further said that Burrell Reed is the rightful heir of the said Moses Reed, dec.; 13 June 1821.

No. 128. Heirs of William Rollen, dec., a private who died in the line of this state; 640 acres; 22 Oct. 1783.

No. 305. James Reynolds, private in the N. C. Cont. Line; 274 acres; 23 Feb. 1820. James Runneld transferred the same to Daniel Cherry on 13 Nov. 1819, with Laurence Cherry a witness.

No. 131. Heirs of Adam Raby, private in the N. C. Cont. Line; 640 acres; 12 Dec. 1806.

No. 240. Heirs of Joseph Reed, sergeant; 1000 acres of land for his services in the N. C. Cont. Line; 25 Aug. 1813. Thomas Breckett, the proper owner of the military land warrant, signed it over to Darling Cherry on 12 Feb. 1813, witnessed by Laurence Cherry and James Outlaw.

No. 872. Heirs of Moses Reed, private in the N. C. Cont. Line; 630 acres; issued 23 Aug. 1821. John Bartholomew transferred the same to Jacob Carthlamen on 27 Sept. 1821.

No. 182. Heirs of Thomas Ramage, private in the N. C. Line; 640 acres; issued 4 April 1809. Montgomery Co., N.C.: George Ramage, heir at law of Thomas Ramage who died in the American War, makes the within warrant for 640 acres to Rufus Johnson on 7 July 1809. On 1 March 1810 Johnson assigned the same to Isaac Lenoir.

No. 180. John Rice, lieutenant in the N. C. Line; 731 acres; 19 Dec. 1808. The same was assigned to Peter Toel on 6 Jan. 1809, witnessed by Millnovde (?) and John Robinson.

No. 177. John Riggs, private in the N. C. Cont. Line; 274 acres; issued 19 Dec. 1808.

No. 1453. Sanders Rogers entitled to enter and obtain a grant for 114 acres of land within this state in lieu of so much of a military warrant issued to the heirs of Daniel Forbush, a private, dated 8 June 1793 for 1200 acres. March 1817, the same was assigned to Thomas B. Smith, 16 Aug. 1820, and Smith assigned it to Thomas Allexander on 20 Sept. 1820.

No. 406. Heirs of James Reed, a private in the N. C. Cont. Line; 274 acres; 1820.

No. 4347. Heirs of Godfrey Rolen, private in the N. C. Cont. Line; 640 acres; issued 17 Dec. 1796. Godfrey Bolin (sic) was a soldier in the company of Selby Hanney, lieut.-col., Joseph Freebye, captain. It is stated that Rolin died in the service, having enlisyed for three years in a company in the 10th N. C. Regt. Certified 2 March 1793.

No. 4362. Heirs of Ebenezer Reed, private in the N. C. Cont. Line; 640 acres; 17 Dec. 1796. The same was assigned to William Tyrrell by Allen Brewer, witnessed by Nathan Markland and Bennet Rogers. Allen Brewer had purchased it from John Reed, heir of Ebenezer Reed, with David King and Jn. Horton as witnesses.

No. 4437. Heirs of Joseph Thompson Rogers, sergeant, 1000 acres; 22 Dec. 1796. Michael Rogers, heir of Joseph Thompson Rogers, transferred it to William Lytle, 1796.

No. 4507. William Reed, private; 640 acres; 22 Dec. 1796. The same was assigned to Stockley Donelson on 1 Jan. 1797, with Jacob Durnsides as witness. Donelson assigned it to Abner Pillow on 2 Jan. 1797, John Stephens a witness.

No. 4506. Peter Ruff, a private in the N. C. Cont. Line; 274 acres; issued 22 Dec. 1796.

No. 4504. Jacob Robeson, private; 274 acres; issued 22 Dec. 1796. Robeson transferred the same to Stockley Donelson on 25 Dec. 1796, with John Williams a witness. Donelson assigned it to William Askew on 2 Jan. 1797, with Samuel Jones a witness.

No. 4503. Patrick Ryan, a private; 274 acres; issued 22 Dec. 1796. This was transferred to William Askew on 26 Dec. 1796, with John Stone a witness.

No. 4508. John Rice, a private; 274 acres; issued 22 Dec. 1796. John Rice transferred the same to Stockley Donelson in Dec. 1796. Donelson assigned it to Abner Pillow.

No. 4510. Roger Rice, private in the N. C. Cont. Line; 274 acres. Roger Rice assigned it to Stockley Donelson on 27 Dec. 1796, with Peter Strong a witness. Donelson made the warrant over to Abner Pillow on 2 Jan. 1797, with Mark Cole a witness.

No. 4521. Heirs of John Rowlance, private in the N, C. Cont. Line; issued 17 Dec. 1796. The same was transferred to Allen Brewer and witnessed by Alex'r. Duny(?). A certificate by Capt. Bradley and H. Murfree, lieut.-col. of the N. C. Cont. Line, stated that he died in the service, and that John Rowlance was a soldier in the said war. The land was in Davidson Co.

No. 4544. Joseph Randolph, private in the N. C. Cont. Line; 228 acres; issued 9 Feb. 1797. The same was transferred to Joshua Hadley on 22 Feb. 1797, with Mark Stephens a witness. Hadley assigned it to Edmond Jennings on 14 Oct. 1797, with William Sullivan a witness.

No. 1556. Lewis Rodes, revolutionary soldier; 640 acres. Samuel Barton, assignee of Lewis Rodes; 640 acres in Sumner Co. on the headwaters of Jening Fork of Round Lick Creek. A deed dated 10 July 1800 between Reuben Cage, sheriff of Sumner Co., and John Irwin of Tennessee County. 1833.

No. 1729. John Ralph, revolutionary soldier, private in the N. C. Cont. Line. The same was assigned to Joshua Hadley. The land was in Davidson Co.

No. 3113. Joshua Rinehart, private; 640 acres; issued 8 Dec. 1785. The same was assigned to Stockley Donelson and W. Terrelle, witnessed by David Hains and Charles Hodge. Donelson assigned it to Thomas Crutcher in Sept. 1797, witnessed by Allen Brewer.

No. 3375. Joseph Roberts, private in the N. C. Cont. Line; 228 acres; issued 7 Jan. 1786. John Roberts assigned it to Ambrose Moulder in Aug. 1786, in the presence of John Pown. Moulder assigned it to Edwin Hickman and Hickman in turn transferred it to Garner Boone in March 1790, with T. C. Mountflorence a witness.

No. 2873. Heirs of Thomas Reddick, private in the N. C. Cont.
Line; 640 acres; issued 30 Sept. 1785. Henry Raimer witnessed.
In 1804 it was transferred to to Capt. John Mury, with Francis
Branch a witness. John Murry transferred it to Francis McKay
in 1805.

No. 450. William Ross; 150 acres, by virtue of a military
warrant, issued 14 Aug. 1786.

No. 449. William Ross; 211 acres; warrant no. 265, dated 14
Aug. 1786.

No. 1011. Heirs of Joseph Runnells, corporal; 1000 acres; issued 10 Sept. 1821. On 10 Sept. 1821 Syntha Runnals transferred
the same to John Roberts, with D. Dauphin and James Dauphin as
witnesses. Roberts assigned it to Jonathan Hibbs on 2 July
1822 in the presence of Jno. Hibbs and Wilkins Hibbs.

No. 340. Heirs of Thomas Ryan, musician; 356 acres; issued 23
June 1820.

No. 793. Heirs of John Rochel, captain; 1600 acres; issued 16
Aug. 1821.

No. 1007. Heirs of Lewis Richards, private; 640 acres; issued
10 Sept. 1821. Joanah C. Richards assigned the same to James
Hart on 21 Oct. 1821. Hart transferred the same to Gen. James
Wellbourn on 19 Dec. 1821, and Wellborn assigned it to Col.
Newton Cannon on 15 Jan. 1822.

No. 580. Heirs of Charles Rhodes, sergeant; 356 acres; issued
11 Sept. 1820. Elizabeth Rhodes transferred the same to Joseph
H. Bryan on 9 Oct. 1820, with Robert C. Watson and J. Sumner as
witnesses.

No. 958. Heirs of Jeptha Rice, ensign; 2560 acres; issued 6
Sept. 1821.

No. 575. William Rogers, a private; 274 acres; issued 9 Sept.
1820. William Rogers of Carteret Co., N. C., assigned the same
to John Roberts on 9 Sept. 1821, with James Roberts and John
Miller (or Milles) as witnesses. Jno. Roberts endorsed it to
Richard Smith of Raleigh, N. C., on 11 Sept. 1820, with Jesse
Williams and John M. Brasfield as witnesses.

No. 227. James Read, Esq., a captain in the N. C. Cont. Line;
3840 acres; 25 Oct. 1783. (This is a duplicate.) Warrant no.
2399 dated 7 Jan. 1794, transferred to Wm. P. Anderson on 7 Jan.
1810, signed by Robert Searcy, commissioner of West Tennessee.

No. 2. Certificate. Captain Looney states that William Reasons
was a soldier in the company of Moses Looney, a Captain of the
Guard to Griffith Rutherford, Absalom Tatum, James Robertson,
Archibald Lytle, and Anthony Bledsoe, Commissioners for ascertaining the bounds of the military reservation in 1784. Looney
states that Looney was in his company when in service in the
State of North Carolina as a guard; 2 Oct. 1805. Griffith Rutherford and James Robertson, commissioners appointed by the state
of N. C. to lay off the lands for officers and soldiers of the
Cont. Line of said state, certified that William Reasons did
serve as a private in the guard of said state in Capt. Moses
Luney's Company, and is entitled to 150 acres; dated 12 April
1804.

No. 791. Thomas Roberson, private in the N. C. Line; 228 acres;
4 May 1784. In Aug. 1797 John Taylor, by his attorney Will

Tyrrell sold the same to Allen Brewer, with Nathan Markland and
Barnet Rogers a witness. John Taylor, Sr., of Orange Co., N. C.,
for natural love and affection he had towards his son John Taylor, Jr., transferred the warrant to him in 1805.

No. 2874. Heirs of John Rainer, private in the N. C. Cont. Line;
640 acres; issued 30 Sept. 1785. Richard Rainer transferred the
same to Thomas Dillon on 7 Oct. 1785, with Jacob Winkles (or
Winkler) a witness. Dillon transferred the warrant to Jonathan
Magness on 13 July 1803.

No. 655. James Roz, a fifer, in the artillery of N. C. Cont.
Line; 1000 acres; 23 April 1784.

No. 637. Maliche Russell, private in the N. C. Cont. Line; 640
acres; issued 23 April 1784. Craven Co., N. C.: a certificate
stated that Russell was a private in the Artillery of the Cont.
Army of the U. S. in N. C. under Capt. John Vance for and in
consideration of 35 pounds paid by William Blackledge, Russell
sold the warrant to Blackledge, witnessed by Wm. Cox and Geo.
Lane. Blackledge assigned the warrant to Edward Harris of the
same place on 23 Jan. 1802.

No. 2955. Heirs of Timothy Rich, private in the N. C. Cont.
Line; 640 acres; issued 30 Sept. 1785. This warrant was en-
dorsed to Robert Hays on 8 Oct. 1785, with John Wilson a witness.
On 20 July 1796 Hays assigned it to Thomas Hickman, with Daniel
James a witness.

No. 2374. Heirs of Peter Rains, private in the N. C. Line; 640
acres; issued 30 Sept. 1785. On 9 Nov. 1804 John Hamilton transferred the same to James Russell, with Jas. Erwin as a witness.
James Russell assigned the same to James Lovell on 18 Dec. 1805
with Thos. Hickman a witness.

No. 502. Ephraim Rogers, a private; 27 acres; issued 2 April
1784. Abraham Rogers transferred one-half of the warrant to
Martin Armstrong in consideration of his having the same located
and surveyed, on 7 May 1802. Cha. Boiles witnessed the transfer.

No. 2685. Heirs of Elijah Revill, private in the N. C. Cont.
Line; 640 acres; issued 30 Sept. 1785. The land was located in
the Mero District of Davidson Co. on the south side of the Cumberland River, on Big Harpeth River. By virtue of a power of
attorney under the hand and seal of Benjamine McCulloch, He.
Tatum transferred the same to George Walker, by direction of
Robert Hays the warrant no. 2685 issued in the name of the heirs
of Elijah Reville in Nov. 1792.

No. 3034. Howell Rowell, private in the N. C. line of the Rev.
War; 228 acres; issued 30 Sept. 1785. On 7 Nov. 1785 Howell
Rowell of the state of Georgia and Howell Tatum of the state of
N. C. Tatum obtained the warrant, and the transfer was witnessed
by Jonathan Mawbry and Cary Whitaker. Tatum assigned the same
to Jos. Hadley on 2 May 1786, with Benj Easley witness. Hadley
transferred the same to Edwin Hickman on 22 July 1786.

No. 3191 Grant. James Robertson, assignee of the heirs of Jeremiah Banks, a Revolutionary soldier, warrant no. 2409, for 64
acres on both sides of Cane Creek, a fork of Elk River, adjoining
the heirs of Michael Ward, in Williamson Co. in the second district, third section and third range. Surveyed 1808.

No. not given. Alexander Reed deposed "respecting my service right
how I have missed obtaining land for it. Gen. Robertson as to
locate and survey my land allowed one for my service as a chain

cerrier when he went down the river on the Mississippi, surveying and when he and his surveyor, Henry Rutherford, Esq., both
returned, Gen. Robertson told me that he had done it and likewise
he had surveyed a 600 acres by virtue of a Treasury warrant of
that quantity. I purchased of a Mr. Kuykendall he told me himself he had run off one of the tracts and Henry Rutherford the
other. Some time after Mr. Rutherford met me in Nashville and
told me that money was wanting to clear the expenses and likewise the certificate I had from the commissioners. I gave him
my certificate, but I told him if Gen. Robertson would furnish
him with sufficient money I would settle with him for the same
as the General owed me for schooling his children being at school
with me at Nashville then. I heard no more bur before Esq. Rutherford returned from the Settlement I received a patent for my
600 acres Treasury warrant, but no account of my service right.
When Rutherford came here I asked him about my service right,
he told me several times he did not know nor remember anything
of it, although I expected surely the grant for my service right
would come the same time the grant for the Treasury warrant
because Henry Rutherford's name is to the Plat that is with the
patent of the Treasury Warrant which I have now in my possession
and recorded in this county; likewise I have not sold, (or) gave
away...said service right to any person whatsoever. (Signed)
Alexander Reed. Sworn before Thos. A. Claiborne on 19 July 1806.

Major John Buchanan came before Thos. Claiborne and certified that Alexander Reed served a tour of duty as a chain carrier the second time the boundary line for continental officers
and soldiers was run, under the direction of Gen. Robertson, Gen.
Rutherford and Major Tatum, commissioners. Sworn to on 19 July
1806. James Mulherrin also certified to the above certificate.

No. 9. Elijah Roberson, quartermaster of the guard appointed
to the commissioners to lay off the lands granted the Cont.
Line; 625 acres on Duck River at the mouth of Beaver Creek, Jan.
1786. James Mulherrin made oath in Davidson Co., 1808, that he
attended the commissioners appointed run the southern boundary
line in the military reservation of the state of N. C., 1784,
and that Elijah Robertson also attended.

No. 219. Powell Riggins (Riggens), private; 274 acres; issued
25 Oct. 1783. Orange Co., N. C., Powel Rigins sold it to William
Bryan of Craven Co., on 2 June 1784, witnessed by Arch. Lytle.

No. 3183. Heirs of Moses Richardson, private in the N. C. Cont.
Line; 640 acres; issued 19 Dec. 1785.

No. 3218. Charles Rice (Rue), private in the N. C. Cont. Line;
640 acres; 21 Dec. 1785. George Jordon or Jordan purchased the
warrant from Southey Rue (Rice), lawful heir to the above Charles
Rue (Rice) on 13 Nov. 1805, with David Carter, Arthur Goold, and
Ralph Dodd.

No. 3103. Heirs of John Ralph, private; 640 acres; issued 8 Dec.
1785. Mary Ralph, lawful heir of John Ralph, transferred the
same to Col. Selby Harney in 1786, who transferred it to Joshua
Hadley in April 1786, witnessed by Jno. Ford.

No. 1488. James Roberts, a private; 274 acres; issued 5 Feb.
1785, endorsed to William Kornegy, with request that Richard
Robberds or his deputy, make the survey in the name of William
Kornegy on 9 Feb. 1785, signed by Richard Robberds, and witnessed by Phillip Shrille.

No. 1818. Jesse Row, private in the N. C. Cont. Line; 640 acres,
assigned to Samuel Lanford in May 1793, and located on the south
side of Cumberland River on Smith's Fork of the waters of Caney

Fork, adjoining a tract of Rurner Williams on the East.

No. 539. Heirs of Henry Robertson, musician; 360 acres; issued 4 Sept. 1820. Peter Robertson of Edgecomb Co., N. C., only true and lawful heir of Henry Robertson, dec., a continental soldier in the Revolutionary War, transferred the warrant to one Wilson, in Sept. 1820, with D. Bryan and John D. Ward as witnesses. Wilson assigned his right and title to Louis D. Wilson in Oct. 1820.

No. 1815. Survey for James Robertson, son of John, a private who died in the line of this state; 640 acres; 11 June 1785, David Robertson, heir to James Robertson, assigned it to an unnamed person in 1796.

No. 551. Heirs of Samuel Roberts, musician; 1000 acres; issued 4 Sept. 1820. John Roberts of the County of Northampton in N. C., sold to Nades Jones of Franklin Co., N. C., the warrant for lands due Samuel Roberts, in Aug. 1820, with William Pike as a witness.

No. not given. Reuben Roberts, a revolutionary soldier. See Legislative Petitions for Warren Co., Tenn., 1827.

No. not given. Hezekiah Rice, a revolutionary soldier. See Legislative Petition of Secretary of State, file 1851-2, Sumner Co., Tenn. Joseph H. Rice made oath that in the year 1847 he was in possession of a land warrant for 3840 acres which Hezekiah Rice, captain in the Revolutionary War, received. The said Hezekiah Rice was the grandfather of Joseph H. Rice. This warrant was in the hands of R. J. Meigs, Senator, in 1847, to have compensation given in money.

No. 137. Heirs of George Rochel, private; 640 acres; issued 19 Dec. 1806. Also no. 138, for the heirs of Stokes Rochel, private 640 acres; issued 19 Dec. 1806.
Mary Simmons of Hartford Co., N. C., sold to Hardy Murfree of the same county one fourth part of the land warrants to which she was entitled, being one of the heirs of George Rochel and Stokes Rochel, dec., for their services in the N. C. Cont. Line and died in the same.
Celia Rochel of Northampton Co., N. C., sold her share of the same to Hardy Murfree of Hertford Co., N. C. Melichia Taylor and Wineford Taylor of Hertford Co., N. C., and John Morris and wife Elizabeth of Northampton Co., N. C., sold their shares to Hardy Murfree, in 1807.

No. 1934. George Summins; 640 acres; 20 May 1793. Thomas Smithly, private in the N. C. Cont. Line. The land was located in Sumner Co., on the south side of Cumberland River on Lick Creek, about three miles from the mouth. Warrant no. 3325.

No. 4638. Heirs of Roger Sentor, private; 640 acres; 9 Feb. 1797. Willis Sentor sold it to Sterling Brewer on 18 Feb. 1797, witnessed by Robert Brown and William Reed. Brewer assigned the same to Thomas Johnson on 1 June 1797.

No. 44. Evan Shelby, one of the commissioner's guard; 1200 acres; registered 10 March 1788. The land was in Davidson Co., on Stewart's Creek adjoining the lands of Moses Shelby, northeast corner. Surveyed for said Shelby on 9 June 1785, by John Buchanan, D. S., in consequence of warrant no. 241, entered 6 Feb. 1784 in Rutherford Co.

No. 157. Gen. Jethro Sumner, a brigadier-general in the N. C. Line; 12,000 acres; issued 27 April 1793. The land was located in Davidson Co., on Big Harpeth River, Arrington Creek, Stuart's Creek, and Mill Creek. The land was surveyed on 20 Nov. 1786 by Thomas Molloy, D. S., Military Warrant no. 166, located 29 Oct. 1784. Platted.

No. 3031. Grant in Davidson Co. William Tyrrell, assignee of John Gee, heir of James Gee; 3840 acres including 320 acres belonging to John Buchanan on Mill Creek and Stuart's Creek, joining Gen. Sumner's, adjoining John Foreman's and Thos. Cotton's lines. Warrant no. 38. Located 1 June 1785, and grant dated 10 April 1797.

No. 426. James Strange, private; 274 acres; 22 Jan. 1784. James Strange assigned it to George Briscoe on 3 April 1796, with Wm. Pulleem and Richard Howell as witnesses. Briscoe assigned it to Charles McIntosh on 14 June 1796.

No. 409. Martin Strickler or Strickland, private; 228 acres; 16 Jan. 1784. Martin Striclen assigned same to John Ferguson on 5 June 1796, with Robert Brown and James Canady. John Ferguson endorsed it to John Gray Blount in May 1796.

No. 386. John Sillunaver, private; 640 acres; 13 Dec. 1783. On 17 June 1796 it was assigned to James Bevar or Brewer.

No. 390. John Skees or Skeen, private; 20 Dec. 1783. It was sold by John Cocke, sheriff of Montgomery Co., Tenn., on 30 Aug. 1806. John Skeen sold it to Joseph Woolfolk who transferred it to Frances Lofton and sold in the name of said Lofton. John Skeen was a resident of Dobbs Co., N. C.

No. 255. Heirs of Colwell Stuart; issued 19 Aug. 1815 within the lands reserved for officers and soldiers of the Cont. Line; 640 acres.

No. 1625. Heirs of George Stewart granted 1000 acres to Wm. Maclin by warrant no. 3563. The file also contains Grant no. 18 to Thomas Cumstock on 8 Aug. 1787 for the service right of Martin Armstrong.

No. 344. John Sugg, private; 274 acres; 27 Nov. 1783. The warrant was sold by the sheriff of Montgomery Co., Tenn., on 20 May 1807, and transferred to Nicholas Conrod and Archibald Mahon. The land was located on Richland Creek at the mouth of Spring Creek.

No. 492. Lieut. Stephen Slade; 2560 acres; 22 March 1784.

No. 1778. Bryant Whitfield; 365 acres; 20 May 1793, as an assignee of Hugh Stephenson, private in the N. C. Cont. Line; in Davidson Co., above Stones Lick Creek.

No. 1613. Grant to heirs of William Simmons, private in the N. C. Cont. Line; 640 acres, assigned to William Sheppard, and located in Tennessee Co. on the north side of Cumberland Co., about three miles below Clarksville, adjoining William Maclin, no. 3563. 23 Feb. 1793.

No. 223. Heirs of Nathan Scott, a revolutionary soldier; 640 acres; 25 Dec. 1812. John Scott, the proper heir to the warrant, assigned it to Isham Cherry on 25 Dec. 1812. Isham Cherry assigned it to Samuel Dewes on 28 Dec. 1813.

No. 2233. Heirs of Samuel Shute, a private; 640 acres; 12 Sept. 1785. Isaac Shute sold it to Beal Bosley on 24 Jan. 1807. The

file also names Archibald Lytle and the heirs of Samuel Shutes.
The land was located on the waters of the fifth creek that the
Virginia line crosses to the east of Red River, being the waters
of Big Barren; entered 20 Nov. 1792.

No. 2042. Warrant no. 1052 dated 17 Dec. 1802 for the services
of John Sullivan to the State of North Carolina. It was granted
to William Marchbanks, assignee of William Luton who was an assignee of the said Jno. Sullivan. The land was in Overton Co.,
3rd District on Turkey Creek.

No. 203. To Samuel Barton, assignee of Lieut. Thomas Smith, in
Sumner Co. Thos. Smith was a lieutenant in a battalion of troops
for protection of Davidson Co., on the south side of the Cumberland River on 6 Dec. 1797. Certified in Wilson Co.

No. 2032. Heirs of George Swagot, private; 26 Aug. 1785. James
Swagot, heir of George Swagot, dec., transferred it on 31 Aug.
1785 to Nathaniel Lofetton, who on 26 Sept. 1785 transferred it
to James Cole Mountflourence, who endorsed it to William Wickoff,
Jr., in 1791. The land was on the east fork of Yellow Creek.

No. 894. James Sisk, private; 640 acres; issued 19 May 1784.
Thomas Buckingham, sheriff of Stewart Co., sold it to Jesse
Blackfan in Nov. 1814. The land lay on the waters of first
creek on the south side of Cumberland River below the Cross
Creek about three miles from the said river.

No. 38. Lott Stroud, private; 9 March 1801; transferred to Gabriel Jones by Mark Stroud. Jones sold it to Mordecai Mendenhall.

No. 5018. Heirs of Daniel Smith, private; 640 acres; 1 Dec.
1797. Samuel Bostick and Nancy Bostick, heirs of Daniel Smith,
sold the same to Nath'l Looney on 23 Feb. 1799. Nath'l Loonas
of Onslow Co., N. C., sold the land to Thomas Dillehunty in 1801.
Nancy Bostick, only heir of her father Daniel Smith, sold. Joseph Rhodes is also named in the file.

No. 4798. Heirs of William Smith, private; 640 acres; 24 Nov.
1797. The same was assigned to John Stroud and Pomfritt Herndon,
both of Orange Co., N. C., on 9 Jan. 1798; signed James Smith,
and witnessed by Anderson Stroud and Isham Thrift. John Stroud
and Pomfrett Herndon sold the warrant to Marshall Stroud on 2
April 1798, with Henry Johnson a witness.

No. 1376. John Smith, private; died in the service of the Line
of this state; 640 acres; 11 Nov. 1784. John Niblett, sheriff
of Montgomery Co., sold the same in 1816.

No. 3886. Job Smith, a sergeant; 355 acres; 18 Nov. 1795. Jobe
Smith sold the same to John Gray Blount on 19 Nov. 1795.

No. 3760. William Smith, private; 274 acres; 18 Aug. 1792. It
was endorsed to Henry Gray, Esq., on 25 Aug. 1790, D. E. Outlaw,
a witness. Gray sold the same to Thomas Rogers, with Isaac White
a witness. Thomas Rodgers sold the same to Sam'l Camchs (?) on
16 April 1796. Sam Camick sold it to Edmond Jennings on 9 Feb.
1797.

No. not given. Reuben Smith, private; 640 acres; 14 April 1792;
also 400 acres for service as a private in the battalion of
troops for protection of Davidson Co., as provided by law; for
the first half year's pay.

No. 220. Heirs of Adam Scott, private; 640 acres; 19 Dec. 1812.
John SCott sold it to Sham (Isham?) Cherry on 19 Dec. 1812.

No. 5006. Heirs of Willis Sawyers, private; 640 acres; 24 Nov.
1797. Orange Co., N. C.: 15 Aug. 1806: Willis Sawyers sold the
warrant to James McVey who sold the same to Henry Pickard and
Pickard and others wishing the grant to come out in his name and
mentioned the subject when he left in the country, etc. The
warrant was purchased from John Empson, heir of Willis Sawyer,
dec. John Empson sold the same to Francis McKinnie on 6 Feb.
1798, with Daniel Turrentine a witness. A bond for John Emson
as heir of Willis Sawyer, dec., of Camden Co., on 24 Nov. 1797
is in the file. Frances McKenney sold the same to James McVey
on 4 Feb. 1799 and McVey sold to Henry Pickard in the same year.

No. 4764. William Scott, private; 228 acres; 27 Feb. 1797.
William Scott had two and a half years service; also Isaiah Vick
for three years service. Wm. Binford and Jas.(?) Saunders are
mentioned. Jas. White assigned it to John Young on 12 Sept.
1797. Stockley Donelson, attorney for William Scott, sold to
James L. White, 11 July 1797. John Young sold to Thomas Smith
on 28 Sept. 1797.

No. 4732. Ceasar Santee, private; 640 acres; 24 Feb. 1797.
James Cummins, assignee, sold the same to Thomas Hickman on 20
Nov. 1801. Ceasar Santee sold the warrant to James Cummins on
8 July 1799, with L. Seth Peebles and Turner Harris as witnesses.

No. 854. Jno. Storey, heir of Caleb Story, a private; 640 acres;
14 May 1784. Thomas Scott sold it to Marmaduke Scott on 13 Feb.
1787.

No. 3020. Levi Sanderlin, private in the Rev. War; issued to Wm.
Burgiss and again to the heirs of John Prevatt, a sergeant in
the Rev. War; 1824.

No. 1767. James Southerland, private in the Revolutionary War;
granted to Charles Gerrard, assignee of James Southerland, on
the south side of the Cumberland River, Tennessee Co. Registered
in Stewart Co., Book A, p. 113, on 31 May 1807.

No. 5021. Levi Sanderline, private; 640 acres; 6 Dec. 1797.

No. 1972. Jacob Sitgraves, private; 640 acres; 14 Aug. 1785.
Murry Co., Tenn.: Jacob Segraves, Sr., of lawful age, appeared
before William Edmundson and William Fly, both Justices of the
said county, and deposed that he enlisted in the N. C. Cont.
Line when he was about 16, and was enlisted by a man named Rush
or Bush at Harrisburg in Granville Co., and was returned to Capt.
Goodman's Co., then marched towards Charleston, S. C., and on the
way was engaged in battle at Utaw Springs, where Capt. Goodman
was killed with many of his men, among whom were Thomas Sanders
and Hutson Ray, who he knew very well. Then he was transferred
to Capt. Roades Co., First Regt., and there continued until the
end of the war, and was discharged by Capt. Roads at Camblin in
South Carolina. He received monthly pay from a gentleman named
Briton Sanders at Hillsborough some years after the end of the
war, in two certificates. This Mr. Sanders he knew very well
before the war in Wake Co., and for some years after, and that
Mr. Sanders stated he was entitled to 640 acres of land besides
what he had already received. Jacob Hardin of Sumner Co., Tenn.,
was his attorney. Deposition filed 6 Nov. 1824. It was signed
by Wm. Edmondson, J. P., Wm. Fly, J. P., William Kursey, Joshua
Williams, Robert W. Hamilton, Robert Oakley, and James Hope.

No. 678. Anthony Hart, granted 640 acres as assignee of John
Sillers, private in the Cont. Line. The land was in Davidson
Co., on the south side of the Cumberland River, adjoining Capt.
Farns survey on Elk Creek; 8 Dec. 1787.

No. 134. Littleberry Stem, private in the said line; land was assigned to Nathaniel Holley, Montgomery Co., Tenn., on 30 Dec. 1794.

No. 166. Thomas Standfield; 147 acres for services in the Revolutionary War; 8 April 1803. It was assigned to Henry Farnsworth, then to James Temple.

No. 5022. James Snell, private; 274 acres; 6 Dec. 1797.

No. 2453. James Sanders, private in the N. C. Line; 228 acres in Sumner Co., on Tuckey Creek, above Bledsoe Lick, adjoining a line of William Branch and William Morrison.

No. 3876. Heirs of Henry Stepp, private; 640 acres; dated 2 Nov. 1795. Peter Step, the heir, transferred it to Joshua Handley on 10 Nov. 1795, with David Hand a witness. Joshua Hadley assigned it to Robert Barnet on 21 May 1796, with Howell Tatum a witness.

No. 3883. Isaac Sanderlin, private; 640 acres; issued 14 Nov. 1795. It was transferred to William Sutheron on 29 Sept. 1802. Diveton Sanderlin transferred it to Lee Sullivan on 14 Dec. 1801 (evidently after) Isaac Sanderlin transferred it to Devotion Sanderlin., with John Chandley a witness. 16 March 1798. Devotion Sanderlin assigned it to Benjamine Hide on 3 July 1799.

No. 3817. Boston Splendor, private; 640 acres; 28 May 1794. Wm. Boren assigned it to James Karr, with Bazel Brown and William Dorris as witnesses on 6 Dec. 1796. Wm. Camp (sic) assigned it to Abishar Camp on 4 Nov. 1796 (sic). Jas. Karr assigned it to Solomon Squire. Boston Splinder assigned it to Henry Hoke on 20 June 1894 (1794?). Hoke made it over to Robert McAfee on 11 July 1796. Wm. Born (Bown) transferred it to James Karr on 14 Jan. 1801.

No. 1754. James Robertson, grant, on 21 March 1794 for the zeal and bravery of Isaac Shockley, private in the N. C. Cont. Line; 640 acres in Davidson Co.

No. 3792. Heirs of James Simmeral, sergeant; 1000 acres; 15 Nov. 1793.

No. 729. Thomas Thompson, assignee of John Stepps, private in the N. C. Cont. Line; 640 acres in Davidson Co., above Stoners Lick Creek, east side of Stones River; 11 July 1788.

No. 6678. Levi Sanderline, for services performed by the said Sanderline to N. C. Warrant no. 1021, dated 6 Dec. 1797 and entered 2 Sept. 1807 by no. 608 for 540 acres, part of warrant lying in White Co., in the first district on the waters of Caney Fork.

No. not given. Davidson Co., 6 June 1807: William Slade, a lieutenant in the First Regt. of the N. C. Cont. Line, made oath that he served in the first, second, and fourth regiments of the Cont. Line of the said state from the month of September 1775 to the month of February 1780 during which time he was well acquainted with the officers of the said line, and during the time he never heard of a commissioned officer by the name of Gray, and was with a party of troops of said line who were detached to Georgia in 1776.

No. 5203. John Stickley, private in the N. C. Cont. Line; 9 Dec. 1797, assigned to Benjamine Black.

Solesbury, Benjamine, private; 228 acres; 24 Feb. 1797. Benjamine Solesbury in Nash Co., deposed that he was a soldier in the N. C. Cont. Line for a term of two years and a half. He sold the grant to Reddick Bridges on 18 Feb. 1797, with Elias Boon and John Parker. Bridges sold it to Edward Given on 24 June 1800. No. 4731.

No. 5204. Moses Stickley, private in the N. C. Line; 640 acres; 9 Dec. 1797, and assigned to Benjamin Blacklan.

No. 5225. Charles Sprat, private; 288 acres; 9 Dec. 1797, and assigned to Wm. P. Anderson, by Redd D. Barry, who received it from Sprat.

No. 3810. Heirs of Charles Shaddock, private in the N. C. Line; 640 acres; 7 Jan. 1794. Mary Shaddock on 22 Oct. 1796 assigned it to Elijah Philips, with John Blake and Charles Boston as witnesses. On 25 Feb. 1796 (sic) Philips assigned it to Nathan Arnett. 12 Nov. 1796, John Bullard and Christopher Bullard, witnesses: Luke Baugor and Abraham Woodward sold the same to Mr. Mathew Brooks, the warrant was issued to Charles Shaddock, dec., who was a continental soldier, Stockes Co., N.C. Mary Shaddock made oath on 23 Oct. 1796, before John Blake, a J. P., for the said county that her son, Charles Shaddock, is dead, and that she knows of no other heir in line but herself, and that she was in need of selling the warrant. 23 Oct. 1796. 6 Jan. 1794, application of Matthew Brooks, Esq., of Stokes Co., N. C. Charles Shaddock's service was ceryified by Capt. Joshua Hadley on 6 Jan. 1794; also Joseph T. Rhodes, Major, U. S. Army, was named in the file.

No. 5231. Rich'd Slocey, private; 9 Dec. 1797. Richard Stockley assigned it to Redd. D. Barry. Barry transferred it to George Smith, Esq., on 17 Oct. 1799, with Roger B. Sappington a witness. Geo. Smith assigned the same to Isaac Walton on 12 May 1801, with Wm. Searcy a witness.

No. 5228. Reuben Stockley, corporal; 1000 acres; 9 Dec. 1797. It was assigned to R. D. Barry who transferred it to Wm. Nash on 10 Oct. 1800.

No. 5242. Heirs of Absalom Sallinger; 640 acres; 11 Dec. 1797. Stephen Salenger assigned the same to Evin S. Kennon on 5 May 1805, with John Skinner as witness. Skinner (sic) transferred it to John Skinner on 13 Nov. 1805.

No. 5261. Sam'l Smithson, private; 12 Dec. 1797. Samuel Smithson of Camden, N. C., transferred the grant to Enock Morriset on 6 Jan. 1798, with Selby Marney a witness.

No. 5256. Heirs of James Stephenson, a sergeant; 1000 acres; 13 Dec. 1797. On 22 Dec. 1799 Jere. Miller assigned it to Henry Rowan, Charles Spurrill on 21 Dec. 1799 (had transferred it) to Jeremiah Miller.

No. 4701. Heirs of Julian Sumner, private; 14 Feb. 1797. Thomas Sumner, heir at law of Julius Sumner, sold the same to Garnet Fitzgerald on 20 Feb. 1797. ·In Feb. 1783 (sic) the same was assigned to Peronis Wheldeon(?).

No. 4493. Elisha Tredwell, rpivate in the N. C. Cont. Line; 274 acres; issued 22 Dec. 1796. The same was assigned to William Askew on 10 Jan. 1797, witnessed by John Smith.

No. 1926. Heirs of Solo. Thrift, private in the N. C. Cont. Line; 640 acres; issued 27 July 1785. On the back is a transfer which states on 29 May 1807 that Abraham Thrift was heir to his brother Solomon Thrift, dec., in the N. C. Cont. Line. The transfer was marked "Invalid," because Solomon Thrift had a son now of full age who had sold the warrant to William White, who purchased it in 1795 soon after the son came of age. Lenoir Co., N. C.: William Thrift of Jones Co., N. C., only son and heir of Solomon Thrift, dec., who was a private soldier in the Revolutionary War, who resided in Caswell Co. at the time of his enlistment.

No. 4533, Edward Tulford (or Tilford), private in the N. C. Cont. Line in the Rev. War; 640 acres; 24 Dec. 1796. The same was assigned to James Easton and William Tyrrell on 28 April 1797 by John Hunter, attorney, with Allen Brewer, Jos. Seawell, Samuel Clanney as witnesses. The land was located in Davidson Co. on Turner's Creek of Harpeth Creek.

No. 394. Heirs of Christopher Tow, a private in the line of this state; 640 acres; issued 3 Aug. 1820. Joseph Tow, of Perquimans Co., sold the land warrant which was due to his father, Christopher Tow, dec., a continental soldier, to Darling Cherry of Martin Co., N. C., on 11 July 1820. Frederick Saunders and Eli Cherry were witnesses.

No. 533, Heirs of Abraham Tyson, private in the N. C. Cont. Line; 640 acres; issued 2 Sept. 1820.

No. 2120. Heirs of Samuel Thompson. This is a different kind of warrant. "I, David M'Gavock, Register of West Tennessee in pursuance of an Act of the General Assembly of the State of Tennessee, passed on 23 Nov. 1809, entitled "An Act to Authorise the Division of Warrants and Certificates of Land," do hereby certify that the heirs of Samuel Thompson are entitled to enter and obtain a grant for 93 acres of land within this state, in lieu of so much of a Military Warrant issued to the heirs of Samuel Thompson, and dated 18 Aug. 1794. No. 897 for 640 acres." Dated 4 Dec. 1817 at Nashville.

This warrant was transferred to Thomas B. Smith on 15 Aug. 1820, and Smith transferred it to Anthony Stewart on 20 Sept. 1820. This is marked "Invalid."

No. 1923. William Thurston, a private in the N. C. Cont. Line of the Rev. War; issued 26 July 1785. Edgecombe Co., N. C., Wm. Rhurston transferred the same to David Collins on 6 Jan. 1795. John J. Mann witnessed the transfer. Bertie Co., N. C.: David Collins assigned the same to James Byrm. The same was assigned to Red D. Barry on 15 Nov. 1796. Thomas Shelon or Skelon was a witness.

No. 5. John Tates, Guard Right. Henry Rutherford, on 22 Jan. 1807, made an oath that John Tate served as chain bearer or marker in ascertaining the Military bounds in the year of 1784; 400 acres.

No. 1872. James Tison, private in the N. C. Cont. Line of the Rev. War; issued 1 July 1785. Transferred by James Tison of Pitt Co., N. C., to Major Reading Blount on 2 July 1785, with Jesse Randolph as a witness. On 17 Jan. 1786 Blount transferred the same to John Foard. By virtue of an attachment obtained by Col. John Armstrong against Capt. John Ford, said warrant was transferred to John Armstrong, Jr., on 3 Aug. 1793, by William Hughlett, sheriff.

No. 956. G. Bradley and John Medearis, captains in the N. C. Cont. Line, certify that Sampson Terrell served as a continental soldier during the war and was discharged. Signed 8 Aug. 1796. See also Sampson Ferrell.

No. 416. Jonathan Trickle, soldier in the Continental Line of N. C., who died in the service, under Geo. Brady, Capt. The statement was dated 5 Dec. 1796.

No. 1840. Heirs of Gen. Joseph McDowell, assignee of William Tucker, private in the N. C. Cont. Line of the Rev. War; issued 3 Dec. 1801.

No. 215. "The bearer, William Taylor, who enlisted in the 7th Regt. of the N. C. Cont. Troops, hath faithfully served the space of three years and hath drawn his wages and clothing, in full, in consequence of his service. He is accordingly discharged the 7 Feb. 1782, by Jethro Sumner, Brig.-Gen. of the Cont. Army." Also in the file is no. 141. Wm. Taylor was a soldier in the N. C. Cont. Line of the Rev. War. G. Bradley, captain.

No. 109. Heirs of Willis Thompson, private in the line of this State; 640 acres; issued 17 Dec. 1804.

No.2885. Heirs of William Todd, private in the N. C. Cont. Line of the Rev. War; 640 acres; issued 30 Sept. 1785. It has been transferred to Thomas Dillon in 1785, witnessed by Jacob Ellit. Dillon transferred it to Uriah Anderson in the presence of James Jones. Anderson transferred it to Sampson Williams on 6 May 1806, in the presence of Obediah Pinson.

No. 4678. Alexander Trayner, private in the N. C. Cont. Line; 640 acres; issued 3 Feb. 1797. The warrant was transferred to Sterling Brewer, who assigned it to William Tyrrell.

No. 3157. Ross Thomas, private in the line of N. C. Cont. Line; issued 16 Dec. 1785.

No. 3383. Heirs of Luke Turner, private in the N. C. Cont. Line; 640 acres; issued 7 Jan. 1786. Jacob Turner, heir at law to Luke Turner, assigned it to John Marshall, on 14 Feb. 1786, in the presence of Henry Tolar. Dixon Marshal, heir at law to John Marshall, transferred the same to Wm. Person on 4 Nov. 1801, in the presence of O. Fitts.

No. 871. Heirs of James Tann, a private in the N. C. Cont. Line; 640 acres; issued 23 Aug. 1821. It was transferred by Hannah Tann to John Terrell in Sept. 1821 in the presence of Nath'l Duncan or Dunn and Joseph Terrill. An attached paper states: Nash Co., N. C.: Jesse Boothe made oath that he knew James Tann who enlisted in the Rev. War in the N. C. Cont. Line and that Hannah Tann was the daughter of Jesse Tann, dec., who was the rightful heir of James Tann on 20 June 1821.

No. 647. Heirs of Robert Turner, lieutenant in the N. C. Cont. Line of the Rev. War; 640 acres; issued 10 Oct. 1820.

No. 189. Fred'k Threat, private in the N. C. Cont. Line; 228 acres; issued 6 Dec. 1809. The same was transferred to Isham Cherry on 4 Jan. 1810 in the presence of Wm. B. Lucy and Paton Lucy. Isham Cherry transferred the same to William Yarborough on 15 Feb. 1810 in the presence of Reuben White and A. Lockhart.

No. 120. Heirs of James Todd, private in the N. C. Cont. Line of the Rev. War; 640 acres; issued 28 Nov. 1805. Joseph H. Bryan transferred it to Daniel Cherry, with Pete Rascoe and William Burlingham as witnesses.

No. 5286. Henry Terrel, a private in the N. C. Cont. Line; 228 acres; issued 15 Dec. 1797. The same was transferred to William Lytle, Jr., on 15 May 1798 in the presence of Thomas Hunt.

No. 4676. Heirs of Jca. Thorn, private in the N. C. Cont. Line; 640 acres; issued 9 Feb. 1797. Abner Thorn, heir of Jca. Thorn, transferred the same to Sterling Brewer in 1797, witnessed by Rob't Brown and Wm. Smith. Brewer transferred the same to Thomas Molloy.

No. 3168. Heirs of Henry Terrell, private in the N. C. Cont. Line of the Rev. War; 640 acres; issued 19 Dec. 1785. Solomon Terrell, heir of Henry Terrell, transferred the same to William Lytle, Jr., on 13 July 1797, witnessed by Britten Saunders.

No. 3189. Heirs of Oliver Terry, private in the N. C. Cont. Line; 640 acres; issued 19 Dec. 1785. Rheuber Terry, heir of Oliver Terry, transferred the same to William Lytle, Jr., in 1797 in the presence of Henry Cummins.

No. 694. Heirs of Benjamin Taylor, corporal in the N. C. Cont. Line; 1000 acres; issued 24 July 1821. Mary Moore of Lenoir Co., N. C., true and lawful heir of Benjamin Taylor, a continental soldier, transferred the same to Darling Cherry on 10 May 1821, in the presence of John Moore and Sally Clarke.

No. 623. Sam'l Tarbarra, private in the N. C. Line of the Rev. War; 640 acres; issued 14 Sept. 1820.

No. 1004. Heirs of William Toby, private in the N. C. Cont. Line; 640 acres; issued 10 Sept. 1821. Nancy Toby on 21 Sept. 182(?) in the presence of John R. C. Jackson, assigned the title John Roberts, and on the same day Roberts transferred it to James Hart. On 15 June 1822 Hart assigned the same to Gen. James Welborn. It was later transferred to Newton Cannon.

No. 354, Heirs of Aaron Taylor, musician in the N. C. Cont. Line; 1000 acres; issued 14 July 1820.

No. 578. Heirs of John Tesley, private in the N. C. Cont. Line; 640 acres; issued 11 Sept. 1820.

No. 258. Heirs of John Tate, private in the N. C. Cont. Line; 640 acres; issued 20 Feb. 1817. William Tate, heir of John Tate, dec., assigned the same to his son Turner Tate on 20 Feb. 1817.

No. 3652. James Tubbs, assignee of Robert and Thomas Anderson. Certificate no. 83, 6 Sept. 1808. The land was located in Smith Co. in the first district on the waters of Smiths Fork, adjoining said Tubbs Line. The grant was issued by Willie Blount on 12 Jan. 1836.

No. 1882. Jason Thompson, assignee of William Rowland, in lieu of military service performed by Wm. Rowland to the state of N. C. Warrant no. 31, dated 20 Dec. 1800, and entered 22 Sept. 1807 by no. 589. The land was located in Bedford Co., Tenn., in the Second District; 240 acres, Second Range and Fifth Section on the waters of Duck River, a small creek called Rock Creek, adjoining Thos. Sorrel.

No. 1018. Heirs of Caleb Taylor, private; 640 acres in the Line of this state; issued 20 Sept. 1821. Andis Jones assigned the same to Robert Blick on 16 Oct. 1821. Robert Blick assigned the warrant to Thomas Cobb, Thomas Scott, and Benjamin S. King, executors of Jehu Scott, dec. John Taylor of Northampton Co., N.C.,

deeded the lands or warrant claimed by Caleb Taylor, to Andes
Jones on 5 Sept. 1821.

No. 1027. Micajah Thomas, revolutionary soldier; issued 25 June
1784. Micajah Thomas late of Nash Co., and agent John Slaton
are named in the file.

No. 111. William Teer, pruvate in the N. C. Cont. Line; 640
acres in Davidson Co., on the south side of the Cumberland River;
issued 7 March 1786, and assigned to William Buxton. James Douglas was granted 640 acres on the north side of Cumberland River
and joining an entry of 1000 acres of Stephen Cantrell on the
north. Douglas granted (the land) to Wm. Buxton, assignee of
Sarah Tilly or Lilly, heir of John Tilly or Lilly, a soldier in
the N. C. Cont. Line, on 28 July 1787. This latter certificate
was signed in Sumner Co., Tenn.

No. 80. Heirs of Bishop Tharp, private in the N. C. Cont. Line;
640 acres; issued 19 Dec. 1803.

No. 4709. Jonas Tolley, private in the N. C. Cont. Line; 640
acres; issued 14 Feb. 1797. The warrant was endorsed to Sterling Brewer on 19 Feb. 1797, with Jesse Sharo and Joseph Marcom
as witnesses. The land was in Sumner Co., Tenn., Mero District,
located on the waters of White Oak Creek and Indian Creek.
Jonas Talley or Tolley served in the N. C. Cont. Line during the
Rev. War and was discharged at the end of the war. Certified
14 July 1796 by G. Bradley, Capt., and John Medearis, Capt.

No. 4710. Thomas Tolley or Talley, a private; 640 acres for
services in the N. C. Cont. Line; issued 14 Feb. 1797. The warrant was assigned to Sterling Brewer, with Joseph Marcom and
Jesse Sharp as witnesses. G. Bradley, capt., and John Medearis
capt., certified that Thomas Tally or Tolly served as a soldier
in the N. C. Cont. Line during the war. The land was located in
Sumner Co., Tenn., on Mero Dist., on the eastern branch of
Stones River.

No. 4046. Andrew Thompson, private in the Cont. Line; 274 acres;
issued 29 Nov. 1796. The warrant was assigned to James Montgomery.

No. 4757. Aaron Terrell, private in the N. C. Cont. Line; 320
acres; issued 27 Feb. 1797. The warrant was transferred to
Robert King and Mos. Looney, by power of attorney.

No. 4675. Heirs of Thos. Charles Todd, private in the N. C.
Cont. Line; 640 acres; issued 9 Feb. 1797. Thomas Todd, Jr.,
heir, transferred the warrant to Sterling Brewer, with James
Cannady and Wm. Smith as witnesses. Brewer assigned it to Thomas Molloy.

No. 4306. Samson Turner, private in the N. C. Cont. Line; 312
acres; issued 14 Dec. 1796. James Turner transferred it to Stockley Donelson who on 17 Jan. 1797 transferred it to Joseph Engel-
man, who in turn assigned it to John Kimble on 28 Aug. 1808.

No. 4341. William Taylor, private in the N. C. Cont. Line; 274
acres; issued 17 Dec. 1796. On 15 Nov. 1796 Solomon Carter made
oath in Duplin Co., N. C., that he was in company with William
Taylor on Cape Fare (Fear?) River near Rockfish Creek under the
command of Gen. Moore, a few days before Gen. Caswell defeated
the Toreys at Moore's Creek, and that he saw the said Taylor
enlist himself in the Continental Service and receive the money.
(He) says he thought he enlisted himself for three years but

Taylor told him later that he had enlisted himself during the war. James Outlaw, J. P., took the above deposition. James Taylor, son and heir of William Taylor, assigned the warrant to Frederick Barfield on 1 Aug. 1796, with Isaac Oliver and Thos. Hicks. On 16 Nov. 1796 Sarah McCillen, sister of the said William Taylor, appeared and made oath that James Taylor was the lawful heir of her brother William Taylor, and that James Taylor was the only child of William.

No. 4343. Lewis Tilley, private in the N. C. Cont. Line; 274 acres; issued 17 Dec. 1796. The original warrant was assigned to Elisha Cheek. Joseph Phillips made oath that he sold and transferred a military warrant to Elisha Cheek that was issued to Lewis Tilly. The sale was dated 9 Feb. 1809, witnessed by James Crabtree.

No. 4359. William Tyrrell, assignee of the heirs of Richard McGraves; 640 acres of land lying in Davidson Co., on the waters of Harpeth River.

No. 4379. Heirs of John Trapp, private; 640 acres; 22 Dec. 1796.

No. 4420. Heirs of Goodwin Thompson, private; 640 acres; issued 22 Dec. 1796.

No. 4567. Heirs of John Anthony, private; 640 acres; issued 9 Feb. 1797. Theophilus Anthony, heir of John Anthony, transferred the warrant to (Brewer?), with James Horton and William Smith as witnesses. Brewer transferred the same to William Tyrrell.

No. 3071. Thomas Hickman, assignee of Nathaniel Linwick; 1040 acres in Sumner Co., Tenn., on Round Lick Creek and Smith's Fork of Caney Fork; issued 19 July 1797.

No. 1832. Martin Titus, private in the N. C. Cont. Line; 640 acres of land in Sumner Co., on the waters of Caney Fork; issued 20 May 1793.

No. 3144. Nimrod Terrell, drummer, in the N. C. Cont. Line; 1000 acres in Sumner Co., on Flat Creek, a branch of Mim's Fork of Caney Fork; assigned to Richard Barbour on 14 Nov. 1811.

No. 36. Heirs of John Tesley, private, dec.; 640 acres; issued 3 March 1801. On 19 July 1801 the warrant was assigned to Robert Macklen by James Moss, with Atkins McLemore and L. B. Williams as witnesses. On 27 Aug. 1801 McLemore (sic) assigned it to James Trousdale, Jr., in the presence of Nath'l McLemore. On 5 Jan. 1802 Trousdale transferred it to John Orr in the presence of Jas. Sanders. On 13 July 1802 Orr assigned it to Moore Stevenson, who on 29 Dec. 1806 assigned it to John Rhea with Philip Koonce as witness.

No. 48. Heirs of John Turner, quarter-master in the line of this state; 2560 acres; issued 4 Dec. 1801.

No. 35. Daniel Toller (Foller?), private; 264 acres; issued 2 Jan. 1801, and transferred to William Crathers; signed by Danel fooller (sic), in the presence of Jesse Hearick and Aron Bell, Jr.

No. 370. Heirs of John Turner, private in the N. C. Cont. Line; 24 July 1820. Benj. Turnner (sic) only and legal heir of John Turner. Ransome H. Byrn and Felix W. Henry witnesses. The same was assigned to John P. Thomas who assigned it to John C. McLemore on 23 Sept. 1820.

No. 3502. Drewry Tadlock, private; 640 acres; issued 8 Feb.
1786. It was transferred to William Fort in Feb. 1786.

No. 350. Heirs of Joseph Taylor, private; 228 acres; issued
10 July 1820. Morgan Moore, of Lenoir Co., N. C., only true
and lawful heirs (sic) to Joseph Taylor who was a continental
soldier in the Rev. War, transferred the warrant to Rodrick
Cherry on 1 July 1820, with John Oxley and Harmon Jinkins as
witnesses. On 12 Aug. 1820 Roderick Cherry assigned the same to
Eli Cherry, with Wm. W. Bell, Wm. Anderson, and Laurence Cherry
as witnesses.

No. 351. Heirs of James Taylor, corporal in the N. C. Cont.
Line; 154 acres; issued 10 July 1820. Morgan Moore of Lenoir
Co., N. C., only true and lawful heir of James Taylor, a continental soldier in the N. C. Line, assigned the warrant to Roderick Cherry, on 14 July 1820.

No. not given. Thos. C. Todd, revolutionary soldier. See the
petition of executors of Thos. Mallory (Mollory?) in Davidson
Co., 1807.

No. 5032. Grant no. 208. Elijah Trapp; 50 acres in Robertson
Co.; assigned to Thos. Huey. Leonard P. Cheatham made an oath
regarding the grant and warrant.

No. 2439. Jno. Upton, private in the N. C. Cont. Line; issued
30 Sept. 1783. The warrant was assigned to Thos. Smith in 1785
in the presence of Thos. Butcher. Smith assigned it to James
McCafsety (sic) or McCafferty or McCassisty, on 17 Nov. 1798.
McCafferty assigned it to Howel Tatum.

No. 4448. Riely (Rieley) Vickers, private in the N. C. Cont.
Line; 228 acres; issued 22 Dec. 1796. Riley Vickers was a soldier in the N. C. Cont. Line and served as such for two and a
half years. Signed G. Bradly, capt., on 1 Dec. 1796.

No. 1925. David Vance, lieutenant in the N. C. Cont. Line; issued 26 July 1785. The same was assigned to William White on 22
Dec. 1785 in the presence of Samuel Buds.

No. 1871. Heirs of Danl. Vinters, a private in the N. C. Cont.
Line; issued 1 July 1785.

No. 3260. Heirs of Malachal Valentine, private, dec., in the
N. C. Cont. Line; 640 acres; issued 24 Dec. 1785, and trans-
ferred by Joseph Dorbes(?) for the heirs of Malicha Volintine.
Joseph Ferebe of Currituck Co., N. C., to Thos. Hofler of Gates
Co., N. C., transferred the warrant in 1786. William Walton
transferred it in 1788 to Thomas Payton in the presence of Thos.
Caruthers.

No. 1228. Heirs of Malachi Venters, private in the N. C. Cont.
Line; 640 acres; issued 1 July 1825.

No. 4765. Isaiah Vick, private; 274 acres; 27 July 1797. On
11 July 1797, Stockley Donelson, for Isaiah Vick, assignee of
James L. White (sic). J. S. (or L.) White, on 20 Oct. 1797,
assigned it to James Elder and Robert McConnell.

No. 5233. Heirs of Abraham Visor, private; 640 acres; issued
9 Dec. 1797. Jo. Visor, heir of A. Visor, assigned same to
Redd. D. Barry. On 4 June 1799 Barry assigned it to Js. Gwin.

No. 846. Robert Verner, lieutenant; 1280 acres. Duplicate
warrant 29 Dec. 1803.

No. 269. Heirs of Moses Venters, private; 274 acres; 21 Jan.
1818. Moses Venters of Pasquotank Co., N. C., sold the same to
William Walton of Hertford Co., N.C., the land in Davidson Co.,
on 26 March 1784. Ann Walton and Sarah Bowers were witnesses.

No. 403. William Vance, corporal; 6 Jan. 1784.

No. 3554. William Water or Watts, private; 640 acres. William
Waters stood mustered for three years and died in the service,
of the N. C. Cont. Line; issued 22 Dec. 1786. George Walker of
Knox assigned the warrant to Thomas Dillon of Davidson Co., on
25 Aug. 1804, in the presence of Jesse Walker, John Watters, and
Alley Watters, son and heirs (sic) of Wm. Watters. William Watters appointed George Walker of Burke Co., N. C., his attorney
to sell the warrant, in Oct. 1796. (The paper is in very bad
condition.)

No. 1911. Heirs of Francis Ward, a private in the N. C. Cont.
Line; 640 acres; issued 15 July 1785. The same was assigned to
George Sugg on 6 Jan. 1788 by Joshua Ward in the presence of
John Durham. Sugg transferred it to George Walker in Jan. 1791.
In May 1796 Walker transferred it to George A. Sugg who then as-
signed it to Samuel or Lemuel Sugg in 1797. In 1807 Lem. Sugg
transferred it to Andrew Shanklin (in?) Wood Forest, 9 Feb. 1807.

No. 2967. Heirs of Michael Ward, private in the N. C. Cont.
Line; 640 acres; issued 30 Sept. 1785. John Ward on 25 April 1785
transferred it to John Sheppard, who with James Sheppard assigned
it to Stephen Montgomery on 11 Aug. 1806.

No. 8190. Heirs of Garrot Watts, sergeant in the N. C. Cont.
Line; 1000 acres; issued 19 Dec. 1785. The same was transferred
to William Lytle on 18 May 1797 by Lazarus Watts, heir, in the
presence of Rumfrett Nolan.

No. 2481. Heirs of Abolam Wallace, private, dec., in the N. C.
Cont. Line of the Rev. War; issued 30 Sept. 1785. The same was
assigned to Col. Joseph McDowell on 3 Oct. 1785 by James Wallace
in the presence of David Pugh.

No. 1037. Dudley Williams, in the N. C. Cont. Line; 640 acres;
issued 21 May 1784. Jno. Williams, heir at law, of Dudley Williams, assigned the warrant to William Tyrrell, with Jesse Sharp
and James Marcom as witnesses.

No. 544. Heirs of Caleb Woodward, private in the N. C. Cont.
Line; issued 4 Sept. 1820.

No. not given. A. Walke, revolutionary soldier. See Legislative Petition, Smith Co., 1825.

No. not given. Wm. Wilkens, revolutionary soldier. See petition
of the executors of Thos. Mallory in 1807, Davidson Co.

No. not given. Jullian Williamson, revolutionary soldier. See
Legislative Petition, Smith Co., 1825.

No. not given. A. Walker, revolutionary soldier. See Legislative Petition, Smith Co., 1825.

(The files contain several single small pieces of paper with
just notations. No number of grant or warrant number are shown
on them - E. R. W.)

No. 1189. Abraham Wise, private; 674 acres; assigned 17 Dec.
1791 to Robert Nelson. The land was in Tennessee County on a

a creek called Blooming Grove that empties into the north side of the Cumberland River, about twelve miles below Clarksville.

No. 573. Heirs of Andrew Watts, a private in the N. C. Cont. Line; 366 acres; issued 9 Sept. 1820. Samuel Hall and Patience Hall, only heirs of Andrew Watts, dec., assigned the same to John Roberts on 9 Sept. 1820, with James Roberts and John Millis or Willis as witnesses.

No. 576. Charles Williamson, private in the N. C. Cont. Line; 274 acres; issued 9 Sept. 1820. Williamson, by John Jarrett, his attorney, transferred the same to Robert Henry on 22 Sept. 1820.

No. 692. George William private in the N. C. Cont. Line; 640 acres; issued 24 July 1821. George Willis, of Pitt Co., N. C., transferred the same to Roderick Cherry in 1821, with Samuel Allbritton and Josiah Griffin as witnesses. Cherry assigned the same to William Coleman of Edgecomb Co., N. C., in 1821 with Stapleton Powell and Daniel Hopkins as witnesses.

No. 508. Heirs of William Webster, private in the N. C. Cont. Line; 640 acres, assigned to Joseph Peurlick(?).

No. 346. Heirs of Robert Walsh, a private in the N. C. Cont. Line of the Rev. War; 640 acres; issued 8 July 1820. Transferred by Eli Hill, Anna Walsh, and Charles Pingle, heirs of Robert Walsh, dec., to Jonathan Hibbs on 18 July 1820, with Church Bell, Wikkins Hibbs and Jos. C. Bell as witnesses.

No. not given. Jesse Waughmocks, private in the N. C. Cont. Line; 640 acres in Sumner Co., on Roaring River; to his heirs, who assigned it to Samuel Sanford on 20 May 1793.

No. 535. Heirs of Willis Wills, private in the N. C. Cont. Line; 640 acres; issued 4 Sept. 1820. Polly Cotton of Edgecombe Co., N. C., only legal heir of said Wills, transferred the warrant to Dempsey Bryan and Louis D. Wilson on 5 Sept. 1820, with William Savidge and James Bradley as witnesses.

No. 367. Heirs of Joshua Wilkins, private in the N. C. Cont. Line; 640 acres; issued 24 July 1820. Louis D. Wilson bought the same from Benjamin Wilkins of Edgecombe Co., N. C., only true heir of Joshua Wilkins, dec. soldier of the N. C. Cont. Line, on 16 Aug. 1820, with Henry Bryan and Robert Bryan as witnesses.

No. 3913. Heirs of Will'm Winuoright, private; 640 acres; issued 28 Nov. 1795.

No. 3960. Heirs of James R. Whitney, private in the N. C. Cont. Line; 640 acres. The warrant was transferred by John Whitney, the heir, to Stockley Donelson.

No. 4019. Heirs of Levi Write, a private; 640 acres. Sarah White (sic), widow and heir at law of Levi Write, transferred the same to Geo. Chandler on 3 Aug. 1797, signed by Silbey Narncey and witnessed by Richard Lawson. Chandler assigned it to Samuel Marsh, who on 16 Oct. 1797 assigned it to Mathew Brown. (The paper definitely states Levi Write and Sarah White - E. R. W.)

No. 630. James Wall, lieutenant in the Artillery of the N. C. Cont. Line; 260 acres; issued 24 April 1784.

No. 3040. James Wiggins, private in the N. C. Cont. Line; 640 acres; issued 20 Nov. 1785. It was assigned to John G. Blount on 12 May 1796 by John and Mary Tayler, with William Orr as a witness. Beaufort Co., N. C. Jacob James made oath that Mary Taylor, wife of John Taylor, who signed the transfer was the only child of James Wiggins who was a soldier in the N. C. Cont. Line. Sworn before Wm. Farris, J. P. John G. Blount assigned the warrant to James Roberts on 1 Sept. 1798.

No. not given. Certificate that Hardy Murfree's Grant no. 249 takes 122 acres from Grant no. 2356 in the name of David Wilson for 640 acres. Wilson Co., 1807.

No. 954. Solomon Waters, private in the N. C. Cont. Line; 640 acres; issued 19 May 1784.

No. 1981. John Womble, private in the N. C. Cont. Line; 640 acres in Davidson Co. on West Harpeth, adjoining the lands of Anthony Newman on the east and Absalom Tatum on the north, 1793. John Crawford made an oath on 12 Aug. 1808 in Davidson Co., Tenn., before Christopher Stump, J. P.

No. 393. James Willoughby enlisted as a soldier in the N. C. Cont. Line during the war, and died in service. Signed G. Bradley, capt., 14 May 1796.

No. 4679. Heirs of Abso. Miller; private; 640 acres; issued 9 Feb. 1797. The file contains a deed between Robert Hays, Marshal for the District of Tennessee, and William P. Anderson and Randale McGavock.

No. 3191. Heirs of John Wisdom, private in the N. C. Cont. Line; 640 acres; issued 19 Dec. 1785. Joseph Wisdom, heir at law of John Wisdom, transferred the warrant to William Lytle, Jr., on 14 Nov. 1797. Miles Horton was a witness.

No. 3192. Heirs of Garrot Whitelock, private in the N. C. Cont. Line; 640 acres; issued 19 Dec. 1785. Anson Co., N. C.: Henry Whitelock, heir at law to Garrot Whitlock, transferred the warrant to William Lytle, Jr., on 21 Nov. 1797, with Moses Hooper, Sr., as a witness. On 30 Dec. 1808 Lytle transferred the same to W. P. Anderson.

No. 3194. Heirs of James Wright, private; 640 acres; issued 19 Dec. 1785. James Wright, Jr., heir of James Wright, dec., transferred the warrant to William Lytle on 17 Dec. 1797, with Anson Boyles a witness.

No. 5284. Heirs of William Walker, private; 640 acres; issued 15 Dec. 1797. The same was assigned to E. Davison on 29 Dec. 1801, by Jno. Walker, Jr.

No. 538. Heirs of Wm. Wooten (Wooton), private; 640 acres; issued 4 Sept. 1820. William Wootton, only true and lawful heir of William Wooton of Wayne Co., N. C., transferred the same to Bartholomew Bowers on 5 Sept. 1820, with Bartley Deans and Dempsey Deans as witnesses.

No. 584. Robert Walker, Jr., a John Armstrong grant, entry officer of Claims for the Western Lands; 1800 acres in Green Co., on Duck River, beginning where the soldiers' west Boundary line crosses the said river the last time, etc.; issued 10 July 1784. 1 Oct. 1814, Robert Walker, Jr., assigned the warrant to Thomas Wright, who in March 1819 assigned it to William Wright in the presence of Wm. Cash.

No. 4429. Heirs of Bennit Woodard, private; 640 acres; issued
22 Dec. 1796. It was transferred to Robert Wiles on 17 Jan.
1797; to John Porter on 24 Dec. 1796; to Stockley Donelson on
17 Jan. 1796; to Samuel Shaw on 26 March 1801.

No. 4558. Stephen Wyron, private; 228 acres; issued 9 Feb. 1797.
It was assigned to James Frazer or Frazor on 14 Feb. 1797, with
Jas. Erwin and Jesse Sharp as witnesses. On 1 June 1806 James
Frazer assigned it to William Montgomery with Peter Looney a
witness.

No. 4534. Alfred Wilson, private; 228 acres; issued 24 Dec.
1796. John Hunter, attorney for Alfred Wilson, transferred the
same to Lemuel Sugg on 28 April 1797, with Allen Brewer, Ro.
Seawell and Samuel Clonney as witnesses. This warrant transferred to John Davidson on 12 Oct. 1800.

No. 4523. William Wilson, private; 274 acres; issued 22 Dec.
1796. Wayne Co., N. C. The warrant was transferred to John
Barfield in Oct. 1796, with Barnaby McKinnie a witness.

No. 4519. Thomas Wright, private; 274 acres; issued 22 Dec.
1796. The warrant was assigned to Stockley Donelson on 10 Jan.
1797, with Walter Lincy a witness. Donelson assigned the same
to James Cannon in 1797, and Cannon transferred it to James
Easton in 1797, with James Thompson a witness. Easton transferred the warrant to William Richard in 1806.

No. 4432. Nehemiah Williams, private; 228 acres; issued 22 Dec.
1796. It was assigned to William Christmas on 2 Sept. 1797. The
transfer was acknowledged in March 1802 in Franklin Co., N.C.
Hickman Williams deposed that Nehemiah Williams was a continental soldier in the N. C. Line, and served two and a half years.
Franklin Co., N. C.; Certificate that Nehemiah Williams and Zebulon Hicks were enlisted for the term of two and a half years
in Capt. Jacob Turner's Co., the 3rd N. C. Regt., from Franklin
Co., and that both served their time faithfully. Signed, Daniel
Jones, First Lieutenant of the Regt.

No. 4404. William Wiggins, sergeant; 350 acres; issued 22 Dec.
1796. Wiggins transferred the same to Arch'd Lytle on 21 June
1798, with James Meabane as a witness.

No. 4364. Abraham Watts, a private; 375 acres; issued 17 Dec.
1796. Geo. Bradley, captain in the 3rd N. C. Regt., certified
that Watts served as a soldier for four years, and was discharged.
The warrant was transferred to Wm. Tyrrell, with Norman Jones and
Danl Ross, Sr., as witnesses.

No. 4520. Andrew Watts, private; 274 acres; issued 22 Dec. 1796.
It was assigned to J. Easton on 2 Jan. 1797. Easton assigned it
to George Bell on 14 Aug. 1800 in the presence of Sam'l A. Love
Bell assigned it to William Christmas on 20 Sept. 1800, with Wm.
Searcy as a witness. Christmas transferred it in 1809 to W. P.
Anderson.

No. 4421. Hickman Williams, private; 228 acres; issued 22 Dec.
1796. The warrant was assigned to Joseph Williams on 12 March
1799, with William Christmas as witness. On 8 Feb. 1800 Joseph
Williams assigned it to Yancey Thornton. On 29 Nov. 1802 Yancey
Thornton assigned it to Edward Suttler (Settles), with John
Thornton as a witness. John Bartholomew made oath that Hickman
Williams and Nehemiah Williams were in the N. C. Line, in Capt.
Jacob Turner's Co., and served two and a half years. This was
sworn to in Franklin Co., N. C. Daniel Jones, First Lieut. of

of the Regt. went before the court in March 1801 and swore that Hickman Williams was a continental soldier for two and a half years in Capt. Jacob Turner's Co., and that he served his time faithfully.

No. 3177. Heirs of William Whitton, private; 640 acres; issued 19 Dec. 1785. Moses Whotton, heir of Wm. Whittom, transferred the same to William Lytle on 18 Nov. 1797, with John Bright as a witness. Wm. Lytle, Jr., transferred it to W. P. Anderson on 30 Dec. 1808.

No. 3196. Heirs of Thomas Waters, a private; 640 acres; issued 19 Dec. 1785. Henry Watters, heir of Thomas Waters, transferred the warrant to William Lytle on 17 Nov. 1797, with John Garrett as a witness. Lytle transferred it to W. P. Anderson on 30 Dec. 1808.

No. 3029. Charles Warldon, private; 640 acres; issued 20 Sept. 1785. It was assigned to Thomas Johnson, in 1785, with Mark Marer as a witness. Johnson assigned it to Robert McConnel in 1796, with Jno. Overton as a witness.

No. 4365. Heirs of Matthew Wallace, Jr., private; 640 acres; issued 17 Dec. 1796. Joseph Wallace, heir of Matthew Wallce, assigned it to Sterling Brewer on 4 Jan. 1797, with David Ray and Roger Griffin, Sr., as witnesses. Brewer assigned it to Edward Lucas.

No. not given. Heirs of John Wall. Joseph Wall, heir of John Wall, of Beaufort Co., N. C., sold to Calvin Jones of Wake Co., N. C., his interest in a land warrant in right of John Wall, on 27 June 1821, with Andes Jones a witness.

No. 691. Heirs of John Wall, private; 640 acres; issued 21 July 1821. It was assigned by Calvin Jones to John Bartholomew, who assigned it to James Bartholomew. John Wall was a revolutionary soldier.

No. 546. Heirs of Lewis Willeford, private; 640 acres; 4 Sept. 1820.

No. 543. Heirs of John Woodward, private; 640 acres; 4 Sept. 1820.

No. 3195. Heirs of Thomas Watts, sergeant; 1000 acres; issued 19 Dec. 1795. Josiah Watts, heir of Thomas Watts, assigned the same to William Lytle on 14 May 1797, with Jas. Austin a witness.

No. 9112. Redmond D. Barry, Smith Co., Military Warrant of Frederick Winstead of N. C. Warrant no. 5212, dated 9 Dec. 1797. Granted to Barry. The land was on Snow Creek.

No. 1850. Heirs of James Wagner, private; 640 acres. Duplicate warrant. Issued 15 June 1785.

No. 3059. Capt. William Williams, captain in the N. C. Cont. Line; 3840 acres; issued 30 Nov. 1785. In Orange Co., N. C., John Armstrong, the Collector, conveyed to Wm. Tyrrelle and Wm. Lytle, Jr., both of Knox Co., Tenn., on 13 Aug. 1796.

No. 701. Richard Ward, sergeant; 1000 acres; issued 1 Aug. 1821 to the President and Trustees, etc. William Polk, attorney of the President and Trustees of the University of N. C., transferred the warrant to Thomas Henderson on 4 Oct. 1821 On the same day Henderson assigned the warrant to Allen Wilkins. The said Wilkins assigned the same to Thomas Jones on 30 Oct. 1821.

Thomas Jones assigned it to Samuel Polk on the 8th of November 1821.

No. 114. Heirs of Miles Watson, private; 640 acres; issued 18 Dec. 1804.

No. 763. Heirs of James Wallace, lieutenant in the N. C. Cont. Line; 2560 acres; issued 5 Aug. 1821.

No. 3229. Heirs of Francis West, private, dec.; 640 acres; issued 23 Dec. 1785. Henry I. West, heir of Francis West, dec., transferred the warrant to Thomas Dillon, on 23 Jan. 1804, with Luke Stanard as a witness. Dillon assigned the same to Thomas N. Clark on 16 Sept. 1806.

No. 388. Heirs of Willis Wickes (or Vicker), sergeant; 357 acres; issued 3 Aug. 1820. Mordecai Beasley and wife Sally of Currituck Co., N. C., sold the warrant to Darling Cherry of Martin Co., N. C., the said warrant being due to their father Willis Vickers (or Vicker), a soldier of the Revolution, in N. C., on 21 July 1820.

No. 956. Heirs of Thomas Williams, private; 640 acres; issued 6 Sept. 1821. Henry Gilliam, J. P. of Gates Co., N. C., took a deposition from one James Brown who said he knew Thomas Williams who enlisted in the N. C. Cont. Line, and who was killed at the Battle of Monmouth. Williams was never married and left one brother, Warner Williams, who was married and left one son named William Williams. The deposition was dated 21 Aug. 1821.

No. 201. Heirs of Prince O. Wright, private; 640 acres; 2 Jan. 1810. Winnifred Orange, only heir to her uncle Prince Orange Wright, soldier in the Revolution, dec., conveyed the same to Daniel Cherry on 25 Jan. 1810, with Holly Wiggins a witness.

No. 395. Lemuel Whorton, private; 274 acres; issued 3 Aug. 1820. Samuel or Lemuel Wharton of Pasquotank Co., N. C., sold to Darling Cherry of Martin Co., N. C., his right and title to the land warrant due to his father Lemuel Whorton, a continental soldier, dec., on 27 July 1820.

No. 497. Heirs of Moses Wallis, private; 640 acres; issued 28 Aug. 1820. John Wallis, only son and heir at law of Moses Wallis, of Halifax Co., N. C., transferred the warrant (grantee's name not given), on 8 Aug. 1820. William Pike was a witness.

No. 416. Heirs of Sion Williams, private; 640 acres; 15 Aug. 1820.

No. 361. John Wilson, private; 640 acres; issued 21 July 1820.

No. 418. Heirs of John Wallace, private; 640 acres.

No. 298. William Ward, heir of Thomas Ward, private; 228 acres; issued 7 Dec. 1819. William Ward of Robeson Co., N. C., assigned the warrant issued to his father Thomas Ward, for service in the Revolution, to Kenneth Black of the same county on 10 Dec. 1819. Black assigned it to James Willborn, with Thomas Love and Wm. Hill as witnesses.

No. 114. Sampson Williams, assignee of 100 acres granted to Nimrod Dodson, and assigned 6 June 1805 by Elijah Chisum to said Williams, with Nath'l. Evans a witness.

No. 5041. Wy. Williams, warrant no. 1282, granted to Willoughby Williams.

No. 353. Heirs of William Wren, a corporal; 726 acres; issued 14 July 1820.

No. 203. Heirs of James White, private; 640 acres; issued 31 March 1810. Luke White of Bertie Co., N. C., only heir to his brother, James White, dec., in the land war, conveyed the warrant to Daniel Cherry on 18 Feb. 1810, with James Thompson and Mary Freeman as witnesses.

No. 197. Heirs of John White, private; 640 acres; issued 23 Dec. 1809. Jacob Mercer, attorney for Esaw Snow, Wm. Snow, and Caleb Williams, heirs at law for John White, assigned the warrant to Armstead Stubblefield on 5 Feb. 1810, with A. Henderson and William Exum as witnesses.

No. 184. Heirs of John White, private; 640 acres; issued 22 April 1809. Luke White, heir of John White, dec. in the last war, asssigned the warrant to Daniel Cherry of Wilson Co., Tenn., (issued?) 2 March 1812, with James White and Isaac White as witnesses.

No. 3385. Heirs of Jesse White, private; 640 acres; issued 7 Jan. 1786. Henry White assigned it to Moses Shelby, who transferred it to Capt. Francis Graves or Groves on 17 Jan. 1796, and Graves assigned it to George Briscoe on 6 June 1796, with Thos. Johnson and Shadrack Nye as witnesses.

No. 324. Heirs of Paul White, a private; 640 acres; issued 22 May 1820. Luke White of Bertie Co., N. C., only heir to his brother Paul White who died in the old war, assigned the warrant to Daniel Cherry on 23 Oct. 1819, with Josiah White, J. White, Lawrence Cherry, and Ceney White as witnesses.

No. 1000. Heirs of Joseph White, Sr., private; 274 acres; issued 10 Sept. 1821. Samuel White assigned the same to James Hart on 2 Oct. 1821. On 19 Dec. 1821, Hart assigned the same to Gen. James Willbourn, who assigned it to Col. Newton Cannon in Jan. 1822.

No. 107. Heirs of William White, ensign; 2560 acres; issued 12 Dec. 1804.

No. 642. Heirs of Benjamin White, a private; 640 acres; issued 16 Sept. 1820.

No. not given. John Wynburn made oath before Roderick B. Gray, J. P. for Northampton Co., N. C., that he (Wynburn) was a soldier in the Continental Line and that he well knew John Edwards a corporal. Edwards is now deceased leaving the following children: James Edwards, Mathew Edwards, Martha Edwards, Rebecca Edwards, Charles Edwards, and Temperance Edwards, believed to be the only children of and heirs of John Edwards. The deposition was dated 5 Sept. 1821.

No. not given. John Walker appeared before Nathan Biffle, a J. P. for Wayne Co., Tenn., and deposed that he served as a quarter-master sergeant in the Revolutionary War; deposition dated 26 July 1818. Wm. Basnett, clerk of county Court of Pleas and Quarter, certify in regard to Nathan Biffle. Elizabeth Walker of Hickman Co., Tenn., appointed Thomas Hiter her lawful agent to transact matters pertaining to a warrant for the service of one John Walker, a private; 21 Sept. 1819. Signed by Elizabeth Walker, admr. of John Walker, dec., and witnessed by Henry Mayberry and Hannah C. Mayberry.

No. 4680. Heirs of Uriah Wills (Wells?), private; 640 acres;

issued 9 Feb. 1797. James Wells, heir of Uriah Wells, assigned the warrant to Sterling Brewer, who transferred it to Hayden Wells on 4 March 1797.

No. 4028. Zebedee Williams, private; 640 acres; issued 25 Nov. 1796. Wm. Surry, attorney for Zeb. Williams, assigned the warrant to John White, with Ben Rawlings and John Buchanan as witnesses.

No. 3633. Sam'l Wheeler, private; 228 acres; issued 12 Dec. 1788. The same was transferred to Stockley Donelson and Wm. Terrell on 10 Oct. 1789. They assigned the same to James Adair who made it over to Wm. Lytle, on 18 Jan. 1797. Lytle assigned it to Wm. Cage on 17 April 1797, with Wilson Cage a witness.

No. 123. Heirs of Matthew Whitehead, pruvate; 640 acres; issued 12 Dec. 1805.

No. 112. Heirs of Charles Whitehurst; 640 acres; issued 18 Dec. 1804. Gideon and Henry Whitehurst of Pasquotank Co., N. C., and John and Christopher Whitehurst of Camden Co., N. C., sons and heirs of Charles Whitehurst who served as a soldier in the N. C. Cont. Line, assigned the warrant to Rencher McDaniel on 28 Oct. 1797. John Whyte of Williamson Co., Tenn., to Rencher McDonneel on 19 March 1805, with Willis Cherry a witness.

No. 132. Heirs of Jacob Wharton, private; 640 acres; issued 12 Dec. 1806.

No. 156. Heirs of Charles Williams, private in the N. C. Cont. Line; 640 acres; issued 17 Dec. 1807. Theophilus Williams, heir of Charles Williams, assigned the warrant to Wm. Alberson on 1 Jan. 1809, with D. Gilpson and Jesse Ellison as witnesses.

No. 1999. Wm. A. Robertson, Rutherford Co., assignee of William Whitton, a soldier in the Revolution. The land was on Overall Creek.

No. 3599. Jesse Williams of Perquimans Co., N. C. Nathaniel Williams, only heir and brother of William Williams, dec., made a transfer of the warrant to the said Jesse Williams. The warrant was dated 1788, granted the heirs of Thos. Hendrick and by Solomon Hendrick, the heir, conveyed to Sarah Decrow and by her conveyed to William Williams, dec., on 7 May 1796.

No. 3198. Heirs of Micajah Woodward, sergeant; 1000 acres; issued 19 Dec. 1785. Abemmalick Woodward, heir at law, assigned the warrant to Wm. Lytle on 17 May 1797, with Obediah Wainwright as a witness.

No. 3199. Heirs of Thomas Whitehead, private; 640 acres; issued 19 Dec. 1785. John Whitehead, the heir, assigned it to Wm. Lytle, with John Taylor a witness. Lytle assigned it to Wm. P. Anderson.

No. 127. Heirs of Absolom Wiggins. private; 640 acres; issued 14 Feb. 1806. Rachel Wiggins, lawful wife of and sole heir of Absalom Wiggins transferred it to James Hearn on 21 Feb. 1806, with Zachariah Hart as witness. Hearn transferred it to Walter McDaniel in Oct. 1806, with James McDaniel a witness.

No. 4035. Heirs of Isaac Young, private; 640 acres; issued 25 Nov. 1896 (1796?). John Young of Bladen Co., N. C., assigned the warrant issued to his brother, Isaac Young, dec., to Alexr. Strahan in 1796, with Donald Baun a witness. Alexander Strahan transferred it to Duncan Stewart on 2 Jan. 1797, with Charles

Stewart as witness. D. Stewart assigned it to Gen. James Robertson on 12 April 1797, with Raiford Crumpler a witness. Gen.
Robertson made it over to Jonathan Robertson on 15 Jan. 1801,
with Joseph Woodward a witness.

No. 1554. Edward Yarborough, captain; 3840 acres of land on the
south side of Cumberland River on Second Creek below Obed's
River about four or five miles from the Cumberland River. The
warrant was registered on 22 May 1807 in Jackson Co., Tenn.,
Book A, paged 321 and 322. Abner Henley Register of the county.
Davidson Co., Tenn.: Edmund Jennings made oath on 12 May 1807
that he was called upon to show a tract of land, warrant no.
167, issued by N. C. to Edward Yarborough, surveyed by Robert
Harp, and that at the request of Lassfield Leonard, he made a
careful search and found no such survey.

No. 5297. John Young, corporal; 359 acres; 15 Dec. 1797.

No. 5210. Heirs of Jonas Yarbey, private; 640 acres; issued 9
Dec. 1797. It was assigned by Thomas Yarbey to R. D. Barry on
10 Nov. 1799, with Samuel H. Love as a witness.

No. 5167. Heirs of James Young, private; 640 acres; issued 8
Dec. 1797. Robert Young, heir at law, assigned the same to
William Lytle, Jr., on 14 Oct. 1798, with Humphrey Lindsey as
a witness.

No. 42. Heirs of James Yarborough, private; 640 acres; issued
1 Oct. 1801.

No. 22. John Yates, Tennessee County, 16 Aug. 1791. Military
Warrant no. 22, located 13 Sept. 1784, surveyed for John McCoy
Alston, assignee of Thomas Kilgore, assignee originally of
John Yates; 640 acres on Red River. John Yates was a soldier
in the N. C. Line. The grant was dated 17 Oct. 1783.

No. 2136. Will York, private in the N. C. Line; 533 acres in
Sumner Co., on a corner of Lazarus Jones' land, was granted to
Tilghman Dixon, assignee of Will York.

No. 4430. James Yoes, private; 274 acres; issued 22 Dec. 1796.

ORIGINAL GRANTS

These loose papers were filed alphabetically in the Tennessee State Archives in Nashville.

Anderson, John, of Mero District, Davidson Co.; by virtue of a military warrant from North Carolina, no. 3736 located on 2 Nov. 1795, surveyed for William Nash, assignee of John Anderson, 640 acres of land on the east side of Stones River on the east fork of the first creek above Stone Lick Creek, adjoining his own survey on the south and Suggs' on the east. John Anderson was a private in the N. C. Cont. Line. Grant no. 2776.

Asbet (or Asbot), James, private N. C. Grant no. 1111 made 17 Feb. 1824, location not stated.

Andrews, Peter, a private in the battalion of troops raised pursuant to an Act of the General Assembly for the protection of inhabitants of Davidson Co.; 400 acres as full for second half of year's pay. 14 April 1792. Grant no. 3850 N. C.

Ammon, Vaun, of Sampson Co., N. C., heir of Jordon Ammon, sold to Charles Stewart a military land grant or warrant signed 30 July 1795. Jordan Ammon died a prisoner with the British troops after the capture of Charestown, S. C. He was in the late Cont. Line in S. C.

Avery, James, N. C. Warrant no. 3832 for 228 acres of land to James Avery within the limits of land reserved for officers and soldiers of the N. C. Cont. Line; 4 Feb. 1795. The land was transferred to William Nilson on 9 Feb. 1795.

Alldridge, Joseph, private in the N. C. Cont. Line; 274 acres; 21 Nov. 1795. N. C. Warrant no. 3892 or 3992.

Aikins, Gideon, a non-commissioned officer in the N. C. Line; 1000 acres; 11 Nov. 1784. He was from Beaufort Co., N. C., and sold the warrant to Joseph Wilson Kidd of the same county and state. N. C. Warrant no. 887.

Askew, Coleman, fifer in the N. C. Line; 1000 acres to his heirs on 9 Dec. 1797. N. C. Warrant no. 5182.

Askew, Phillip, private in the N. C. Line; 640 acres; 14 Dec. 1797. The same was assigned to Capt. Wm. Faun on 17 Dec. 1797. Faun assigned it to Thomas E. Sumner on 3 April 1798. N. C. Warrant no. 5263.

Askew, Serg, private in the N. C. Line; 640 acres; 14 Dec. 1797. The same was assigned to Jesse Williams on 17 Dec. 1797. N. C. Warrant no. 5264.

Askew, Hardy, private in the Battalion of Troops raised pursuant to an Act of the General Assembly for protection of Davidson Co.; 400 acres in full payment of his second half year's pay; 10 Jan. 1794. Another grant for 400 acres was in full for his first half year's pay.

Alexander, William, private in the N. C. Cont. Line; 168 acres in Sumner Co. on the north side of the Cumberland River. N. C. Grant no. 2350. The same was assigned to David Wilson on 20 May 1793.

Armstrong, William, captain in the N. C. Cont. Line; 3840 acres in Davidson Co.; surveyed 21 July 1785. N. C. Grant no. 25.

Alexander, Benjamine, private in the N. C. Cont. Line; 274 acres; issued 6 Dec. 1797. N. C. Warrant no. 5023.

Anolle (or Snelle), James, private in the line of this state; 274 acres; 6 Dec. 1797. N. C. Warrant no. 5022.

Arnold, David, for his military services to the said state. Warrant no. 3115, Grant no. 228, entered 25 Nov. 1789; 274 acres in the state of Tennessee. The same was assigned to John Darden. The land was in Tennessee Co., on the Cumberland River. 14 F(eb.) 1808.

Alberty, Frederick, ensign; 1098 acres in the limits of land reserved for the officers and soldiers of the Cont. Line of this state; 23 Jan. 1818. N. C. Warrant no. 271.

Alford, William. Warrant no. 376, N. C., 3 March 1791; (located) surveyed for William Alford, assignee of Nathaniel Wooten (or Wooting) 640 acres of land on the fourth large creek that empties into the Tennessee River above the mouth of Duck River on the south side. Nathaniel Wooten was heir of Christopher Wooten, dec.

Anglea, Cornelius, private in the N. C. Line; 640 acres; issued 12 Feb. 1784. Duplicate Warrant no. 440, N. C. Aaron Anglea made oath that his brother Cornelius Anglin or Anglea was a soldier in the N. C. Cont. Line of N. C. and died in service, leaving a sister and the deponent. 16 April 1819.

Atkins, Thomas. N. C. Warrant no. 355. Elisha Davis, assignee of Thomas Atkins; 274 acres in Sumner Co., on Round Creek; 1784.

Arnold, Arthur, private in the N. C. Line; 640 acres; 22 March 1784. N. C. Warrant no. 493.

Name not given. N. C. Grant no. 203. Ten pounds for every 100 acres. James Woods Lackey was granted 1500 acres in the Eastern District on Little River of the waters of the Holston River, 1811 (This was probably in Blount Co.).

Badwell, Zadock, non-commissioned officer in the N. C. Cont. Lineof N. C.; 1000 acres in Tennessee Co.; 20 May 1793; N. C. Warrant no. 1992. Assigned to Joseph Dixon.

Name not given. N. C. no. 1193, to William Cockran; 640 acres on Cumberland River on the upper fork of Barton's Creek; 30 Nov. 1790. Land in Dickson Co., adjoining Joseph Dickson.

Beck, George; N. C. no. 4797. Survey for the heirs of George
Beck, a private in the N. C. Line; 640 acres. Warrant signed
24 Nov. 1797. George Beck, son and heir of George Beck who died
in the war and was a soldier, sold the land to Richard Cook
in 1804. The land was in Dickson Co., on Roarin River. The same
land was sold in 1804 for taxes, costs, charges, etc.

Book, Joseph, private in the N. C. Line; 228 acres; signed 30
Nov. 1797. N. C. Warrant no. 5011. In 1799 the same was assigned to Joshua Wise of Murfreesboro, N. C. The same was assigned to William Outlaw by Thos. Davis, guardian of the orphans
of Joshua Wise, dec., in 1805.

Brown, William, a private in the Cont. Line; 228 acres; signed
2 Dec. 1797. In 1798 Gabriel Bailey, constable of Pasquetank
Co., N. C., sold by virtue of the execution of the estate of
William Brown, dec., the within land to James Newby in June
1798. In 1802 James Newby of Camden Co., N. C., transferred the
land to William Surry of the same place. In April 1803 Surry
conveyed it to John King, and in 1804 John King assigned it to
James King. In June 1804 James King assigned it to John Shannon.
N. C. Warrant no. 5013.

Barker, Joseph, private in the N. C. Cont. Line; 640 acres; signed
2 Dec. 1797. John Barker was heir of said Joseph. N. C. no.
5017.

Baxster (Baxter), Thomas, private in the N. C. Line; 640 acres.
The land was assigned to Sampson Williams, and was in Davidson
Co., on Mill Creek and Stuarts Creek. The original grant was
burned in the storehouse of Black and Williams on 19 Dec. 1795.
By 1807 the land appeared to have been vacated. N. C. no. 2317.

Brown, David Evan; N. C. no. 227. On 14 Dec. 1812, 228 acres
were surveyed for Brown within the limits of the lands reserved
for officers and soldiers of the N. C. Cont. Line; signed 23
March 1813. The land was assigned to Daniel Ross of Davidson
Co., Tenn., on 16 Sept. 1814.

Brown, Thomas, a private in the Cont. Line; 640 acres within the
limits of land reserved for officers and soldiers of the N. C.
Cont. Line on 4 Sept. 1817. N. C. Warrant no. 260.

Burke, James, private in the Cont. Line; 640 acres of land in
the limits of land reserved for officers and soldiers of the
Cont. Line; 28 Oct. 1783. The same was assigned to Major William
Hughlett on 1792.

Boren, Jacob, sergeant in the N. C. Cont. Line; 1000 acres to
the heirs of said Jacob Boren on 21 Jan. 1818. Maxilian Boren,
the lawful heir of Jacob Bowren, dec., of Currituck Co., N. C.,
sold the land to William Walton on 26 Jan. 1786. The land was
in Davidson Co., N. C.

Bullock, Moses, of the line of this state, dec. N. C. Warrant
no. 464 to his heirs; 23 Feb. 1784. John and James Bonner,
assignee of Moses Bullock, held the land on Obey's River. In
1792 the land was sold for taxes to Wilson Cage.

Butler, Charles, private in the N. C. Line. N. C. Warrant no.
381 (duplicate) for 640 acres; signed 27 Dec. 1803 in view of
the original deed dated 13 Dec. 1783.

Berry, Solomon, sergeant in the N. C. Cont. Line; N. C. Warrant
no. 359; signed 7 Dec. 1783 and assigned to Thomas Stubblefield.

Bunton, James, private in the N. C. Cont. Line; 640 acres in the Middle District of Obey's River; 31 Jan. 1795. Assigned to Willoughby Williams by Thos. Bunton, heir of James Bunton.

Bloxam, Lovereign, private in the N. C. Cont. Line; 274 acres; 1 April 1784. N. C. Warrant no. 499.

Brawmun, David, private in the N. C. Cont. Line. The grant was to James C. Graham, assignee of the heirs of said Brawmun; 640 acres in Tennessee Co., on Red River. Survey no. 4065, dated 14 Sept. 1797. N. C. Grant no. 3149. The land is in Hawkins Co.

Brevard, Joel, captain in the state line in the Revolutionary War; 3840 acres; signed 1 July 1825. Warrant no. 1230.

Bryan, Benjamine, ensign in the N. C. Line; 2560 acres of land on 1 July 1825. Warrant no. 1229.

Bryan, John, private in the N. C. Line; 640 acres; 1 July 1825. N. C. Warrant no. 1223.

Hooser, Jacob; warrant no. 3532, located Jan. 1789. Assignee of Thomas Smith of Thomas McClain of Samuel Brooks, a private; 274 acres. 1792.

Bass, Esau, private in the Cont. Line. N. C. Warrant no. 1531 for 274 acres in Davidson Co., on Stones River. 1793.

Beasley, John, corporal in the N. C. Cont. Line; 428 acres; 24 Aug. 1819. N. C. Warrant no. 282.

Bombardey, John, soldier; N. C. Warrant no. 4678. Mero District, Sumner Co., 1797: William Nash, assignee of John Bombardey; 640 acres of land on both sides of Fowling Creek on the Eastern Branch of Stones River.

Blair, Samuel, private in the battalion of troops raised by Act of the General Assembly for the protection of the inhabitants of Davidson Co.; 400 acres in full for his second half year's pay. 10 Jan. 1794.

Blanchard, Jas., private. No. 5259; 640 acres to the heirs of Jas. Blanchard; dated 12 Dec. 1797 at Raleigh.

Burguss (Burgiss), Peter, private; No. 5260, for 640 acres; dated 12 Dec. 1797 at Raleigh.

Bowmans, Norris, private; 640 acres. No. 5239, dated 9 Dec. 1797 at Raleigh.

Bunch, Jno., private. No. 5172 for heirs of said Bunch; dated 9 Dec. 1797 at Raleigh.

Beasley, Hardy, private. No. 4734 dated 12 Feb. 1797 at Raleigh.

Bright, Charles, non-commissioned officer. No. 886 for 1000 acres, dated 19 May 1784.

Breece, Thos., private. No. 3779 for 300 acres, dated 26 Dec. 1792, at Raleigh.

Butcher, John, private. No. 4735 for 265 acres, dated 12 Feb. 1797 at Raleigh.

Barcoe, John. Bo. 840 for 365 acres in Mero District, Sumner Co., lying on Dixon's Creek; dated 19 Dec. 1792.

Ballentine, Alex., sergeant;1000 acres; 15 Nov. 1793. No. 3787. Assigned to John Sevier.

Bell, George, private in the N. C. Line; 640 acres; 15 Nov. 1793 to his heirs. No. 3788.

Baker, Norris, a private; 640 acres; 14 April 1794. No. 3817.

Brazel, John, musician; 1000 acres; 26 Octo. 1801 at Raleigh. No. 43.

Brown, Dumon, private; 640 acres; 25 Nov. 1795 at Raleigh. No. 3896. Transferred to Joshua Hadley on 20 Jan. 1796.

Barnet, James, private in the Cont. Line; 274 acres in Tennessee County, just below Deers Island, assigned to Jesse Benton on 20 May 1793. No. 1865.

Bonner, Wm., corporal in the line; 1000 acres; 8 Aug. 1797 at Raleigh. No. 4769.

Bell, Joab, prvate; 640 acres within the limits of land reserved for officers and soldiers in the continental line of this state; 8 Sept. 1823 at Raleigh. No. 1103. Grant was pursuant to a resolution of the General Assembly passed 31 Dec. 1822.

Bell, Reuben D., private; 274 acres; 6 Dec. 1797 at Raleigh. No. 5040.

Brown, Micajah. No. 1104. To the Surveyor of Military Lands: Pursuant to a resolution of the General Assembly of this state, passed 31 Dec. 1822, you are required to lay off and survey for the heirs of Micajah Brown 640 acres within the limits of land reserved for officers and soldiers in the continental line of this state. 8 Sept. 1823, Raleigh.

Bullock, Joshua, lieutenant; 888 acres of land within the limits reserved for officers and soldiers of the continental line of this state. No. 1234, dated 17 Feb. 1843, for the heirs of said Bullock.

Bullock, Daniel, lieutenant; 2560 acres of land for the Trustees of the University of N. C., within the limits of land reserved by law for the officers and soldiers of the continental line of the said state, it being for the services of Daniel Bullock. No. 1115. Dated 17 Feb. 1824 at Raleigh.

Bullock, John. No. 461. Order to lay off and survey for John Bullock, a private in the line of this state, 228 acres of land within the limits of land reserved by law for the officers and soldiers of the continental line. Dated 23 Feb. 1784 at Fairfield.

Name not given. No. 1116. Dated 17 Feb. 1824 at Raleigh.

Brown, Samuel, private; 640 acres; dated 17 Feb. 1824 at Raleigh. No. 1117.

Bany, Lyon, private; 640 acres; 7 Feb. 1824 to be laid off within the limits of land reserved by law for the officers and soldiers of the continental line of this state. No. 1118.

Blurton, Edward, private; Secretary of State William Hill to the Surveyor of Military Lands: pursuant to a resolution of the General Assembly dated 10 Dec. 1823, you are required to lay off 640 acres of land for the Trustees of the University of

North Carolina, within the limits of land reserved by law for the officers and soldiers of the continental line of the said state, for the services of Edward Blurton. Dated 17 Feb. 1824. No. 1114.

Barnes, William, private; 640 acres. No. 1113. Same as above.

Brandon, William, private; 640 acres. No.1112. Same as above.

Beeney, Joseph, private; 640 acres. No. 1119. Same as above.

Brown, Richard, private in the N. C. Cont. Line; 274 acres. Col. Martin Armstrong ordered to lay out the land within the limits of land reserved for officers and soldiers of the N. C. Cont. Line. Dated 31 Jan. 1785 at Newbern. J. Glasgow. No. 1528.

Beck, William. Pursuant to an act of the General Assembly entitled an Act for the relief of officers and soldiers of the Continental Line and in consideration of the signal bravery and zeal of William Beck, a private in the said line, John Overton, assignee of said Beck, is granted 640 acres of land in Davidson Co., Tenn. 17 May 1793. No. 1948.

Blount, John Gray, and Thomas Blount. No. 914. William Maclin, Sec. of the State of Tennessee orders any lawful surveyor in the said state to survey and lay off for Lewis Claipier 100 acres of land. This warrant was issued from a grant to John Gray Blount and Thos. Blount for 95,000 acres of land, of no. 517, dated 26 April 1794, obtained by virtue of a ten pound warrant. Dated 7 Aug. 1785.
John Gray Blount and Thomas Blount were also granted nos. 900, 901, 902, 903, 904, 905, 906, 907, 909, 910, 912, 913, 915, 916, 917, and 918.
All the above to John Gray Blount and Thos. Blount are tied in one package and marked "Invalid."

Cage, Edward. No. 363. William Maclin, Secretary of State, directs any lawful surveyor in the said state to lay out 50 acres for Edward Cage. The warrant was issued from a grant to David Shelby for 400 acres of No. 160, dated 26 March 1795, and obtained by virtue of a warrant issuedpursuant to an act entitled "An Act for raising troops for the protection of the inhabitants of Davidson County." Dated 12 July 1803.

Cage, Edward; 50 acres. No. 364; same as above.

Clark, Joseph. By order of William Maclin, Secretary of State for Tennessee, lay off for Elijah Chisum 50 acres of land on any unappropriated land. This warrant issued from a grant in the name of Elijah Chisum for 640 acres of no. 733, dated 20 July, 21st year of our independence, obtained by virtue of a fifty shilling warrant. Dated 22 Oct. 1802; Knoxville. No. 125; Clark was an assignee. Invalid. No. 46

Crozier, A. No. 182. Assignee, Invalid No. 1010. Wm. Maclin, Secretary of State, orders to have laid off for Samuel Crawford 110 acres of land on any unappropriated lands. This warrant issued from a grant to John Long for 600 acres of no. 356, dated 29 July 1893(1803? - R. B.), obtained by virtue of a fifty shilling warrant. Dated 5 Oct. 1805.

Cook, James. No. 946, same as above. To Josiah Danforth, 500 acres from a grant to Stokely Donelson for 100,000 acres of land of No. 204. Dated 6 Jan. 1795. Ten pound warrant. Given 27 Sept. 1805. No. 167. James Cook, assignee, invalid.

Cook, James. No. 163. Assignee. Invalid. No. 937. Wm. Maclin Secretary of State of Tennessee authorized to lay off for Josiah Danforth 200 acres, same as above, from grant to Stockley Donelson for 100,000 acres of No. 204. 6 Jan. 1795. Ten lbs. warrant. Given 27 Sept. 1805.

Copeland, Joseph. No. 499. State of N. C. Jno. Armstrong required to lay off for Devereaux Guilliam, 640 acres. Given 25 June 1784. Signed, Jno. Armstrong, E. T. No. 652 to the heirs of Joseph Copeland, 31 Aug. 1818.

Chapman, Benj. No. 6701. Grant from Tenn. Assignee of Jno. McIver; 15 acres in Robertson Co., dated at Nashville, 6 March 1815. Gov. Willie Blount.

Cantrell, Simon. No. 4009. Their heirs of Simon Cantrell to have 640 acres. James Glasgow, Esq., Secretary of State, to Col. Martin Armstrong: You are hereby required to lay out and survey for the heirs of Simon Cantrell, a private in the Cont. Line of this state, 640 acres of land within the limits of land allotted to the officers and soldiers in the said line; dated 25 Nov. 1796 at Raleigh.

Collins, Thomas, private in the N. C. Cont. Line; 640 acres. The heirs of Thomas Collins. No. 4002. Same conditions as above.

Carmical, Dugald, private; 640 acres. Heirs of Dugald Carmical. 1 Dec. 1796. Same as above. No. 4049.

Carney, Henry, private; 180 acres, at Fayette on 1 Dec. 1796. No. 3705. Same conditions as above.

Carney, Jacob, private; 182 acres; 1 Dec. 1796 at Fayette. No. 3706.

Carray, Samuel, private; 274 acres; 15 Feb. 1786, at Fairfield. No. 3537.

Campbell, James, revolutionary soldier; 65 acres; 14 March 1786. No. 2075.

Cathey, George. No. 35; 320 acres; 22 Dec. 1818; same as above.

Cypert, Robert. Original Claim. Memorial for the relief of Robert Cypert or Sypert, revolutionary soldier. 4 Sept. 1824.

Clay, John, private; 640 acres; 19 Dec. 1785, for the heirs of John Clay. No. 3166.

> NOTE: The following are listed from papers in the files in this list but are all the same line of considerations and I have extracted them as briefly as possible. E. W.

Coram, John, private; 640 acres for the heirs of John Coram; 19 Dec. 1785 at Newbern. No. 3165.

Collins, Sampson, private; 274 acres. No. 3245.

Culbreth, Daniel, private; 640 acres; 9 Feb. 1797 at Raleigh. No. 4501.

Craig, James, private; 640 acres for his heirs; 23 Dec. 1785 at Newbern. No. 3224.

Culbreath, Daniel, private; 640 acres; 9 Feb. 1797 at Raleigh. No. 4502.

Cyle, Robert. No. 4584 for 640 acres; 9 Feb. 1797 at Raleigh.

Child, Francis, Rev. soldier in the Cont. Line; 13 March 1786. Warrant no. 34.

Carrigan, Jno., private; 274 acres; 14 Dec. 1796 at Raleigh. No. 4304.

Carrigan, Abraham. No. 4305 for 312 acres; 14 Dec. 1796 at Raleigh.

Comer, Jacob. No. 4322 for 274 acres; 15 April 1806.

Carson, Thomas. No. 4327 for 274 acres; 31 May 1797.

Cartwright, Timothy. No. 3918 for 640 acres; 19 Aug. 1797.

Carrington, William, private; 228 acres; 9 Feb. 1797 at Raleigh. No. 4593.

Cary, Andrew, private; 640 acres to the heirs of Andrew Cary. No. 4505.

Carter, Simon, private; 640 acres; 9 Feb. 1797 at Raleigh. No. 4503.

Cope, Richard, private; 228 acres; 9 Feb. 1797 at Raleigh. No. 4540.

Carbon, Wm., private; 274 acres; 22 Dec. 1796 at Raleigh. No. 4484.

Crabtree, Campbell, private; 320 acres for 17 Dec. 1796. No. 4352.

Carbon, William, private; 274 acres; 22 Dec. 1796 at Raleigh. No. 4404.

Cates, Mathias, private; 640 acres; at 22 Dec. 1796 at Raleigh. No. 4305.

Cooksey, Hezekiah; 640 acres for the heirs of Hezekiah Cooksey; 17 Dec. 1796 at Raleigh. No. 4344.

Cooksey, Thomas; 640 acres for the heirs of Thos. Cooksey; 17 Dec. 1796 at Raleigh. No. 4345.

Clarke, Downham, private; 400 acres; 14 April 1792 at Hillsborough. No. 31.

Cherry, Job, Revolutionary soldier in Sumner Co., private; 640 acres. 27 Dec. 1808. No. 317.

Chalk, William, private; 640 acres, 1795, military warrant; 12 Nov. 1795. No. 3070.

Charlton, William; 2560 acres (Military) 1795 for the heirs of William Charlton. No. 3836.

Capps, William. No. 3895. 274 acres; military; 1795.

Cummins, John; 640 acres for the heirs of John Cummins; military; 1795. No. 3790.

Cole, Alex. No. 3767. 640 acres to heirs of Alex Cole. Military; 1792.

Corbett, John, private; 640 acres; 24 April 1705. No. 1702.

Carmichael, Maurice. No. 2624. 5000 acres; 25 May 1784.

Cornwall, Francis, private; 274 acres; 27 Feb. 1797, at Raleigh. No. 4762.

Cole, Melchiah, private; 640 acres; 9 Dec. 1797, at Raleigh, to the heirs of Melchiah Cole. No. 5175.

Cotter, Alexander, private; 640 acres; 9 Dec. 1797 at Raleigh. Military. No. 5174.

Carson, Sam'l, drummer; 1000 acres to his heirs. No. 5181.

Cheek, James, sergeant; 1000 acres to his heirs. No. 5183.

Cheek, John, private; 640 acres to his heirs. No. 5184.

Carney, Patrick, private; 640 acres. No. 5191.

Cotgrove, Jonas, private; 640 acres. No. 5192.

Carr, Isaiah, private; 640 acres. No. 5193.

Condy, Roger, private; 274 acres. No. 5221.

Cooper, William; 640 acres to his heirs. No. 5267. Military Grant no. 1797.

Conner, John, private; 274 acres; 5 Dec. 1797 at Raleigh. No. 5200.

Corbin, William; 640 acres to his heirs; military; 1797. No. 4711.

Coleson, James; 274 acres; military; 1797. No. 4713.

Campbell, Angus; 274 acres; military; 1797. No. 4712.

Carrold, Hardy; 220 acres; military; 1797. No. 4715.

Childress, John, private in the Revolution; 14 April 1792 at Hillsborough. No. 2

Covington, John, private; 400 acres; 14 April (year not given); Hillsborough. No. 48.

Clarke, Downham, private; 400 acres; April 1792 at Hillsborough. No. not given.

Cove, William, private; 640 acres to the heirs of Wm. Cove; 11 Sept. 1820 at Raleigh. No. 579.

Cook, Frederick. No. 2742. William Tyrrell. 640 acres sold to Cook, 1830.

Carmicals, Douglas, revolutionary soldier; 640 acres; 1808 at Knoxville. No. 487.

Chamberlain, Henry, revolutionary soldier; 640 acres; military; 1795. No. 2388.

Cleghorn, Shubal, private; 640 acres to his heirs; 1807 at Nashville. No. 4130.

Chance, Stephen, private; 365 acres; 19 March 1784 at Fairfield. No. 492.

Cooley, Samuel, surgeon; 1428 acres; 6 Jan. 1784 at Fairfield. No. 397.

Chalton, William, private; 274 acres; 13 Dec. 1783, at Fairfield. No. 379.

Clark, James, private; 274 acres. No. 378.

Copeland, Job, private; 640 acres to his heirs; 27 Nov. 1817 at Raleigh. No. 262.

Cole, A., died in the line; 640 acres to his heirs; 28 Oct. 1783. No. 284.

Carey, Andrew, sergeant; 1000 acres to his heirs; 29 June 1815 at Raleigh. No. 254.

Corbett, James, corporal; 572 acres to his heirs; 26 Dec. 1814 at Raleigh. No. 253.

Cox, William, private; 640 acres; 15 March 1813 at Raleigh. No. 225.

Capehearts, John. No. 2492. (Paper illeigible - E. W.)

Curling, Sampson, private; 640 acres; 6 Dec. 1797, at Raleigh. No. 5019.

Cox, Jesse, private; 274 acres; 29 Nov. 1797 at Raleigh. No. 5010.

Canfield (or Banfield), Silas; 640 acres to his heirs; 24 Nov. 1797 at Raleigh. No. 5001.

Carter, Jacob, private; 274 acres; 24 Nov. 1797 at Raleigh. No. 4795.

Cooley, Jeffrey, private; 274 acres; 24 Nov. 1797 at Raleigh. No. 4789.

Cornelius, William, matross of the line; 640 acres; 17 Feb. 1824 at Raleigh. No. 1217.

Cox, Edward, private; 640 acres; 25 Nov. 1797 at Raleigh. No. 5007.

Coats, John, private; 640 acres to his heirs; 5 Dec. 1797 at Raleigh. No. 5044.

Cameron, John, private; 640 acres to his heirs; 26 Aug. 1785. No. 2035.

Cornelius, Isaac, fifer; 640 acres to his heirs; 9 Sept. 1785. No. 2116.

Crawley, David, sergeant; 1000 acres to trustees, etc.; 17 Feb. 1824, at Raleigh. No. 1121.

Charleton, George, private; 640 acres to the trustees, etc.; 17 Feb. 1824, at Raleigh. No. 1122.

Carey, John, private; 640 acres to the trustees, etc.; no date. No. 1120.

Carpenter, Benjamine, revolutionary soldier; 428 acres; 14 July 1820. No. 357.

Campbell, William, corporal; 1000 acres; 21 Aug. 1820 at Raleigh. No. 440.

Cherry, Daniel. No. 858. 50 acres. This warrant was obtained from a grant to Samuel Barton for 320 acres of land, of no. 113, obtained by virtue of a Guard right. 20 July 1805.

Cartwright, Timothy, private; 640 acres to his heirs; 5 Dec. 1795, at Raleigh. No. 3918.

Cooper, Jeremiah, private; 640 acres to his heirs; 11 Feb. 1814. No. 234.

Collin, Joseph, drummer; 428 acres; 28 Nov. 1795 at Raleigh. No. 3908.

Chisum, James, private; 640 acres; 23 Feb. 1796 at Raleigh. No. 3954.

Clayton, Moses, private; 640 acres to his heirs. No. 3950.

Cage, Wilson. No. 76. 50 acres. This warrant is issued from a grant in the name of Edward Douglass for 400 acres of no. 174; 6 Dec. 1802.

Curtis, George B. No. 102. 100 acres. This warrant is issued from a grant to Stockley Donelson and Wm. Tyrrell for 640 acres of no. 2550; 22 Jan. 1803.

Dew, Leonard. No. 5230. 640 acres. Military service. 1797.

Duncan, Alexander, private; 274 acres; 12 Dec. 1797 at Raleigh. No. 5245.

Davis, Leonard. No. 3064. Grant of 640 acres in Sumner Co.; 19 July 1797.

Dukemore, Marina, private; 640 acres to the trustees, etc.; 17 Feb. 1824, at Raleigh. No. 1127.

De'ell, Wm., private; 640 acres. No. 1126.

Docan, John, private; 640 acres. No. 1125.

Dawson, Henry, captain; 3840 acres. No. 1123.

Davey, James, private; 640 acres. No. 1128.

Dobbin, Hugh, lieutenant; 2560 acres. No. 1124.

Drury, John, private; 640 acres in Davidson Co.; 7 March 1786. No. 106.

Driver (or Drive), James, private; 640 acres to his heirs; 14 Feb. 1797 at Raleigh. No. 4694.

Dupree, Mail, private; 640 acres to his heirs. No. 4693.

Davis, Sam'l, private; 278 acres; 20 Oct. 1819. No. not given.

Deen, Sterling, private; 640 acres; 20 May 1793, at Newbern. No. 2006.

Dobbins, William, Guard right; 250 acres; 1793 (void). No. 392.

Dauson, Levi, rank not shown; 2125 acres; 1 Aug. 1796. No. 3338.

Discern, Francis, private; 640 acres to his heirs; April 1794 at Hillsborough. No. 3814.

Douglas, James, private; 640 acres to his heirs; 15 Nov. 1793. No. 3794.

Day, Peter, private; 640 acres; 9 Dec. 1797 at Raleigh. No. 5207.

Dobb, Simpson, private; 640 acres to his heirs; 9 Dec. 1797, at Raleigh. No. 5200.

Dawney, Nehemeah, private; 228 acres; 27 Feb. 1797, at Raleigh. No. 4760.

Davis, Elisha, private; 365 acres; 12 May 1784 at Hillsboro. No. 838.

Darden, Noah, sergeant; 1000 acres; 9 Dec. 1797, at Raleigh. No. 523.

Dixon, John, sergeant; 1000 acres; 15 Nov. 1793. No. 3789.

Douglas, Malcolm, fifer; 428 acres; 9 Dec. 1797 at Raleigh. No. 5240.

Donalson, James, private in battalion of troops; 400 acres; 10 Jan. 1794 at Fayette. No. not given.

Dalton, William, trumpeteer; 460 acres; 10 Jan. 1794, at Fayette. No. not given.

Dunham, Joseph, private; 400 acres; 10 Jan. 1794, at Fayette. No. not given.

Dailey, Charles. G-ant of 274 acres in Sumner Co.; 1780. No. 599.

Darnold, Henry, captain; 1849 acres in Robertson Co.; 1801. No. 3378.

Dykes, John, private; 640 acres in Davidson Co.; 26 Aug. 1833. No. 635.

Demedicis, Capt. No. 2521 for 1872 acres; Davidson Co., 1795.

Drewry (Drury), John, private; 640 acres in Davidson Co.; 7 March 1786. No. 106.

Drake, Jonathan; private; 640 acres in Sumner Co.; 22 Feb. 1795. No. 1701.

Dan, Malici, private; 640 acres in Davidson Co.; 18 May 1789. No. 1016.

Danley, Abraham, private; 640 acres in Sumner Co.; March 1782. No. 1213.

Dempsey, Squire, private; 640 acres; 11 Nov. 1814. No. 251.

Davie, William, private; 278 acres; 27 Nov. 1783 at Fairfield. No. 331.

Dobey, Nath'l, private; 220 acres; 21 Oct. 1783. No. 39.

Dawson, Isaac, private; 274 acres; 31 Dec. 1793 at Newbern. No. 2427.

Dunn, Nicholas, private; 640 acres; 3 Dec. 1797. No. 5029.

Dowday, George, private; 640 acres; 24 Nov. 1797 at Raleigh. No. 5000.

Dinkins, Theophilus, heirs of; 640 acres; 24 Nov. 1797, at Raleigh. No. 4892.

Dean, Philip. No. 1812. (Fragment of record).

Drake, John; 640 acres; 15 July 1807. No. not given.

Elliot, John, private; 365 acres; 12 Feb. 1784, at Fairfield. No. 437.

Edwards, John, private; 400 acres; 14 April 1792, at Hillsborough. No. not given.

Ellis, Levi, private; 400 acres; 14 April 1792, at Hillsborough. No. not given.

Evans, Thomas, Major Commandant; 1840 acres; 14 April 1792 at Hillsborough. No. not given.

Edward, John, private; 400 acres; 14 April 1792 at Hillsborough. No. not given.

Edwards, John, quarter master sergeant; 640 acres; 14 April 1792 at Hillsborough. No. not given.

Echols, Joel, private; 400 acres; 10 Jan. 1794 at Fayette. No. not given. Another grant for 400 acres, same date; no. not given.

Etheride, Isaac, private; 640 acres; 12 Dec. 1797, at Raleigh. No. not given.

Ellis, Charles, private; 274 acres; 13 Feb. 1797 at Raleigh. No. 4740.

Edminston, Samuel, private; 640 acres; 13 Dec. 1797, at Raleigh. No. 5288.

Eppes, John, private; 274 acres; 20 Sept. 1792 at Glasgow. No. 3762.

Eppes, William, private; 274 acres; 21 Nov. 1795. No. 3892.

Elliott, John, private; 320 acres; 27 April 1793 at Newbern. No. 115.

Edwards, Benjamin, private; 640 acres; 17 Feb. 1824 at Raleigh. No. 1129.

Edwards, Lemuel, private; 640 acres; 17 Feb. 1824. No. 1130.

Evans, Thomas, private; 640 acres; April 1797. No. 2996.

Empson, Jno., private; 640 acres; 10 April 1797. No. 3034.

Eburn, John, private; 640 acres; 22 April 1807 at Raleigh. No. 617.

Fly, Charles, private; 640 acres; 17 Feb. 1824 to the Trustees, etc. No. 1136.

Ferril, James, private; 274 acres; 24 Nov. 1797. No. 4793.

Faulks, Joseph, private; 640 acres; 27 Oct. 1783. No. 268.

Fenton, Caleb, private; 640 acres to his heirs; 6 Dec. 1797. No. 5026.

Fenton, Thomas, private; 640 acres to his heirs; 6 Dec. 1797. No. 5025.

Freeland, Jacob, private; 640 acres to his heirs; 30 Sept. 1785. No. 2290.

Foster, Burwell, private; 640 acres; 31 Jan. 1795. No. 2394.

Fitzer, Jacob, private; 400 acres; 14 April 1792. No. not given.

Foster, Joshua, private; 400 acres; 14 April. 1792. No. not given.

Ferrel, Clement, private; 640 acres; 16 Nov. 1790. No. 1258.

Freeman, Isaac, private; 640 acres to his heirs; 9 Dec. 1797. No. 5236,

Finley, Boaz, private; 274 acres; 9 Dec. 1797. No. 5237.

Fisher, John, private; 274 acres; 9 Dec. 1797. No. 5224.

Frost, Andrew, private; 640 acres; 9 Dec. 1797. No. 5220.

Frost, Daniel, private; 640 acres; 9 Dec. 1797. No. 5217.

Harman (?), Peter, private; 365 acres; 9 Dec. 1797. No. 5214.

Flinthorn, John; 640 acres to his heirs; 9 Dec. 1797. No. 5186.

Flinthorn, Robert; 640 acres to his heirs; 9 Dec. 1797. No. 5105.

Flood, Edward, private; 640 acres to his heirs; 1797. No. 5171.

Fisk, George, private; 640 acres to his heirs; 15 Dec. 1797. No. 5209.

Fitzherbert, Theophilus, private; 274 acres; 27 Feb. 1797. No. 4761.

Falconer, James, private; 428 acres in Humphreys Co.; 20 Jan. 1814. No. 5294.

Flemming, Thomas, private; 640 acres to his heirs; 15 Nov. 1793. No. 3795.

Frost, William, private; 620 acres; 20 May 1793. No. 1879.

Foreman, Caleb, lieutenant; 2560 acres; 17 Feb. 1824. No. 1131.

Fillips (Phillips), Joseph, private; 640 acres to the trustees, etc.; 17 Feb. 1824. No. 1132.

Fearless, Elisha, private; 640 acres; 17 Feb. 1824. No. 1134.

Fall (or Fail), Thomas, private; 640 acres; 17 Feb. 1824. This was granted to the trustees. No. 1133.

Fearle, Ansol, private; 640 acres to the trustees; 17 Feb. 1824. No. 1135.

Glaughan, Daniel, private; 640 acres to the trustees; 17 Feb. 1824. No. 1139.

Griffis, Allen, private; 640 acres to the trustees; 17 Feb. 1824. No. 1137.

Garnes, Gab'l, private; 640 acres to the trustees; 17 Feb. 1824. No. 1124.

Ginew, William, private; 640 acres to the trustees; 17 Feb. 1824. No. 1134.

Gerrell, William, private; 640 acres to the trustees; 17 Feb. 1824. No. 1142.

Grandy, Odeb'h, private; 640 acres to the trustees; 17 Feb. 1824. No. 1141.

Garland, Humphrey, private; 640 acres to the trustees; 1824. No. 1140.

Guy, William, private; 640 acres to his heirs; 5 Dec. 1797. No. 5035.

Glenn, Tobias, musician; 1000 acres; to the trustees; 17 Feb. 1824. No. 1138.

Goodins, Christopher, captain; 3840 acres; 19 May 1784. No. 959.

Grimes, Anthony, private; 640 acres; 16 Nov. 1790. No. 1292.

Gray, Henry, non-commissioned officer; 1000 acres in Sumner Co. No. 2779.

Garrett, Anthony, private; 640 acres; 15 July 1794. No. 3819.

Graddy, Reubin, private; 640 acres to his heirs; 5 June 1794 at Glasgow. No. 3817.

Gee, William, private; 228 acres; 21 Oct. 1783. No. 40.

Grant, David, private; 640 acres; 16 Sept. 1792. No. 3761.

Gamewill, William, private; 640 acres; June 1792. No. 3754.

Garland, Humphrey, private; 228 acres; 12 May 1784. No. 868.

Graham, Martin, private; 274 acres; 21 July 1797. No. 4759.

Gee, James, captain; 3840 acres; 10 April 1797. No. 3031.

Grinage, John, private; 640 acres (torn off). No. 620.

Gammel, Robert, private; 640 acres to the heirs; 9 Dec. 1797. No. 5173.

Gilston, Davis, corporal; 1000 acres; 9 Dec. 1797. No. 5180.

Gerry, James, private; 274 acres; 9 Dec. 1797. No. 5216.

Grigle, Charles, private; 640 acres; 9 Dec. 1797. No. 5229.

Gibson, Jonathan, private; 640 acres; 11 Dec. 1797. No. 5246.

Good, John, private; 228 acres; 15 Feb. 1797. No. 4717.

Griffis, Samuel, private; 400 acres; 10 Jan. 1794. No. not given.

Gunn, John, non-commissioned officer; 1000 acres; 20 May 1793. No. 2239.

Gordon, Ephraim, private; 400 acres; 14 April 1792. No. not given.

Guilford, Jeremiah, private; 400 acres; 14 April 1792. No. not given.

Gogum, John, Revolutionary soldier; 640 acres in White Co.; 1807. No. 2966.

Gafford, William, private; 640 acres in Davidson Co.; 1807. No. 2748.

Gray, George; captain; 3840 acres in Davidson (Co.?) to his heirs; 1807. No. 1816.

Garner, Aaron, Revolutionary Soldier; 640 acres in Davidson Co.; 1790. No. 1199.

Guan, Peter; 640 acres. No. 4140.

Gudler (or Hudler), Joseph, Sr., private; 278 acres; 9 March 1784. No. 482.

Gray, William, private; 278 acres; 9 March 1784. No. 484.

Grigory, Honey, private; 274 acres; 23 Feb. 1784. No. 470.

Guy, William, private; 640 acres to his heirs. No. 3035.

Haynes, John; 5000 acres; 14 Dec. 1797. No. 1507.

Hay, Isaac, private; 365 acres; 17 March 1784. No. 490.

Humphreys, Daniel, private; 6 Jan. 1784. No. 400.

Ryan, Patrick, sergeant; 1000 acres; 10 Nov. 1783. No. 301.

Hutson, Isaac, sergeant; 357 acres; Nov. 1783. No. 307.

Hogg, Thomas, major; 4800 acres; 10 Nov. 1783. No. 293.

Hicks, Zebulon, private; 24 Nov. 1797. No. 5002.

Harris, Sherrod, private; 228 acres; 24 Nov. 1797. No. 4794.

Hanbery, William, private; 640 acres; 14 Feb. 1797. No. 4698.

Hamm, William, private; 640 acres to his heirs; 1800. No. 2100.

Henley, William, private; 640 acres to his heirs; 1 Sept. 1785. No. 2009.

Hull, Jackson, Revolutionary Soldier; 100 acres in Bertie Co., N. C.; 1805. No. not given.

Hall, David, Revolutionary soldier; 428 acres; 6 Dec. 1786. No. 4129.

Hart, Samuel, private; 640 acres; 17 Feb. 1824. No. 1150.

Howington, William, private; 640 acres; 17 Feb. 1824. No. 1151.

Hide, Samuel, private; 640 acres; 17 Feb. 1824. No. 1152.

Hussar, Francis, private; 640 acres; 17 Feb. 1824. No. 1133 or 1153.

Hassle, Stephen, private; 640 acres; 17 Feb. 1824. No. 1154.

Hern, Howell, private; 640 acres; 17 Feb. 1824. No. 1155.

Hewell, Caleb, private; 640 acres; 17 Feb. 1824. No. 1156.

Hardy, Joseph, private; 640 acres; 17 Feb. 1824. No. 1157.

Harvey, Absolom, private; 640 acres; 17 Feb. 1824. No. 1158.

Holt, Thomas, private; 640 acres; 17 Feb. 1824. No. 1145.

Hollenbeck, John, private; 640 acres; 17 Feb. 1824. No. 1148.

Huggin, Jeff, private; 640 acres; 17 Feb. 1824. No. 1149.

Holland, Reason, private; 640 acres; 17 Feb. 1824. No. 1147.

Howell, James, private; 640 acres; 12 Sept. 1785. No. 2187.

Hubbard, Warburton, sergeant; 1000 acres; 12 Sept. 1785. No. 2130.

Haden, Bainard, dec., private; 640 acres; 12 Sept. 1785. No. 2129.

Harrison, James, sergeant, dec.; 1000 acres to his heirs; 3 March 1801. No. 37.

Harris, Hardy, Revolutionary Soldier; 640 acres in Sumner Co.; 1807. No. 2472.

Holland, Thomas, private; 274 acres; 13 Feb. 1797. No. 4742.

Hooper, Enos, private; 274 acres; 12 Feb. 1797 at Raleigh. No. 4733.

Hill, Benjamine, private; 640 acres; 9 Dec. 1797 at Raleigh. No. 5198.

Harper, Reading, private; 640 acres; 9 Dec. 1797. No. 5176.

Hunter, Cherry, corporal; 428 acres; 9 Dec. 1797 at Raleigh. No. 5209.

Hicks, Micajah, private; 228 acres; 12 Dec. 1797 at Raleigh. No. 5260.

Henuter, James, private; 400 acres; 10 Jan. 1794, at Fayette. No. not given.

Hunter, James, private; 400 acres; 10 Jan. 1794, at Fayette. No. not given.

Hunter, John, captain; 1260 acres; 10 Jan. 1794, at Fayette. No. not given.

Hendricks, Joseph, private; 400 acres; 10 Jan. 1794, at Fayette. No. not given.

Hadley, Joshua, captain; 1280 acres; 14 April, 1792, at Hillsborough. No. not given.

Herndon, Drury, private; 640 acres; 16 Dec. 1797, at Raleigh. No. 5296.

Haley, Joseph, rank not given; 640 acres; 16 Dec. 1797 at Raleigh. No. 5294.

Heron, Henry, private; 640 acres; 14 Feb. 1797 at Raleigh. No. 4697.

Hill, Jno., lieutenant; 2560 acres; 20 April 1784 at Hillsborough. No. 544.

Hislip, Hindal, private; 640 acres; 23 April 1784 at Hillsborough. No. 638.

Houston, William, private; 640 acres; 15 Nov. 1793, at Hillsborough. No. 3796.

Williams, William, private; 274 acres; 20 Dec. 1793 at Fayette. No. 3800.

Hyas, Southy, private; 640 acres; 1 Jan. 1794 at Fayette. No. 3805.

Haynes, William, private; 640 acres; 29 April 1801, at Raleigh. No. 39.

Davis, Moses, private; 640 acres; 15 Nov. 1793. No. 3797.

Hogan, James, brig.-general; 12,000 acres; 14 March 1786. No. not given.

Hearn, George, private; 640 acres in Sumner Co.; date not given. No. 1746.

Hicks, William, private; 640 acres; 1794. No. 2415.

Harrison, Patrick, private; 640 acres in Davidson Co.; 17 Dec. 1794. No. 154.

Hicks, Robert, private; 640 acres; July 1797, at Raleigh. No. 3082.

Hays, John, private; 640 acres; 5 Sept. 1784, at Fairfield. No. 1178.

Hair, James, private; 640 acres; 14 Jan. 1792 at Newbern. No. not given.

Hodgton, Alvery, lieutenant and adjutant; 2560 acres; 17 Feb. 1824. No. 1146.

Johnston, Harrel, private; 640 acres; 11 July 1788 at Fairfield. No. 776.

Jacob, John, lieutenant; 2560 acres; 17 Feb. 1824 at Raleigh. No. 1159.

Juniper, Richard, private; 640 acres; 17 Feb. 1824 at Raleigh. No. 116.

Jones, Robert, private; 640 acres; 17 Feb. 1824 at Raleigh. No. 1160.

Jones, Aaron, private; 640 acres; 12 Sept. 1785, at Fairfield. No. 2202.

James, John, private; 640 acres; 12 Sept. 1785, at Fairfield. No. 2200.

Jarvis, Thomas, rank not given; 1000 acres; 5 Dec. 1797 at Raleigh. No. 5036.

James, David, rank not given; 588¼ acres; 6 Feb. 1837 at Nashville. No. 4547.

Johnson, Reubin, private; 640 acres; 2 Nov. 1797 at Raleigh. No. 3877.

Jackson, Edmond, private; 640 acres; 2 Nov. 1797 at Raleigh. No. 3824.

Jenkins, Lewis, private; 274 acres; 19 Nov. 1795 at Raleigh. No. 3890.

Johnson, David, private; 640 acres; 1793 at Raleigh. No. 3793.

Johnston, James, private; 640 acres; 1 Nov. 1792 at Glasgow. No. 3766.

Johnston, George, private; 640 acres; 23 April 1785 at Fairfield. No. 1768.

Jackson, Charles, private; 640 acres; 15 Dec. 1797 at Raleigh. No. 5290.

Johnston, Abel, private; 320 acres; 13 Feb. 1797 at Raleigh. No. 4743.

Jones, Coleman, private; 640 acres; 9 Dec. 1797 at Raleigh. No. 5202.

Jones, Julian, private; 640 acres; 9 Dec. 1797 at Raleigh. No. 5197.

Jacobs, Peter, private; 640 acres; 20 Dec. 1793 at Raleigh. No. 2126.

Jefferson, Josel, private; 640 acres; date not given, at Raleigh. No. 2449.

Johnston, Richard, sergeant; 428 acres; 22 March 1784 at Fairfield. No. 494.

Jones, William, private; 274 acres; 4 Dec. 1783. No. 362.

Joyner, Benj., private; 640 acres; 27 Oct. 1783. No. 257.

Jackson, William, private; 274 acres; 27 Nov. 1783 at Fairfield. No. 320.

Jones, Frederick, private; 640 acres; 13 Jan. 1792 at Raleigh. No. 2733.

Johnston, Marlen, private; 640 acres; 6 Dec. 1797 at Raleigh. No. 5028.

Jones, Thomas, private; 640 acres; 2 Dec. 1797 at Raleigh. No. 5016.

Johnston, Benjamin, private; 228 acres; 24 Nov. 1797, at Raleigh. No. 5004.

Jenney, Abel, sergeant; 1000 acres; 9 Feb. 1797, at Raleigh. No. 4625.

Jones, Winn, private; 640 acres; 9 Feb. 1797 at Raleigh. No. 4627.

King, William, private; 640 acres. No. 3818.

Knight, Reuben, fifer; 357 acres; 1795. No. 3809 (?).

Kilpatrick, Hugh, private; 274 acres; 15 Feb. 1797, at Raleigh. No. 4723.

Kingsmiller, Robert, private; 640 acres; 15 Feb. 1797, at Raleigh. No. 4703.

Knell, William, private; 640 acres; Feb. 1797, at Raleigh. No. 4704.

Kirkpatrick, Hugh, private; 400 acres; 10 Jan. 1794, at Fayette. No. 7

Kirkpatrick, Hugh, private; 400 acres; 10 Jan. 1794, at Fayette. No. 41.

Kirby, William, private; 400 acres; 14 April 1792. No. not given.

Kink, William, private; 640 acres; 6 Feb. 1823, at Raleigh. No. 1084.

Kuykendall, Benj., private; 274 acres; 16 April 1791. No. 402.

Keel, Hardy, sergeant; 428 acres; 2 Dec. 1797 at Raleigh. No. 5015.

Kenny, Thomas, private; 640 acres; 17 Feb. 1824, at Raleigh. No. 1163.

Lutzell, Jno., lieutenant-colonel; 5760 acres at Raleigh; 17 Feb. 1824. No. 1164.

Lee, Bryan, private; 640 acres; 17 Feb. 1824, at Raleigh. No. 1166.

Lewis, Elishaj private; 640 acres; 17 Feb. 1824, at Raleigh. No. 1165.

Labiel, Francis, private; 640 acres; 17 Feb. 1824. No. 1167. Also no. 1168.

Lawrence, Nathaniel, lieutenant; 2560 acres; 20 Aug. 1785, at Fairfield. No. 2020.

Leighton, Wm., private; 640 acres; 16 March 1795 at Raleigh. No. 3839.

Lane, Jonathan, private; 640 acres; 16 Aug. 1794 at Glasgow. No. 3820.

Lusk, William, private; 640 acres; 15 Nov. 1793. No. 3891.

Lacey, John, ensign; 853 acres; 25 Dec. 1792 at Newbern. No. 3778.

Law, Richard, private; 274 acres; 24 Dec. 1792, at Newbern. No. 3772.

Lewis, William, musician; 427 acres. No. 468.

Lutteral, James, private; 640 acres; 8 Dec. 1797, at Raleigh. No. 5168.

Lard, Lemon, private; 640 acres; 9 Dec. 1797, at Raleigh. No. 5215.

Lemar, Gallant, private; 400 acres; 14 April 1792, at Hillsborough. No. not given.

Little, Charles, private; 600 acres; 10 Jan. 1794, at Fayette. No. not given.

Larremore, Marmaduke, private; 640 acres; 20 Dec. 1795, at Raleigh. No. 2519.

Loomas, Jonathan, doctor; 3942 acres; 14 March 1786. No. 59.

Lilly, John, private; 640 acres; 5 April 1833, at Nashville. No. 332.

Lansciter, Shadrick, lieutenant; 731 acres; 6 Jan. 1784, at Fairfield.

Lawless, Matthew, private; 640 acres; 15 Sept. 1787. No. 485.

Loyd, Abemelech, private; 640 acres; 9 Feb. 1797, at Raleigh. No. 4639.

Lewis, Joshua, sergeant; 1000 acres; 6 Dec. 1797, at Raleigh. No. 5027.

Lawyer, Willis, private; 640 acres; 4 Nov. 1797, at Raleigh. No. 5006.

Lock, John, private; 228 acres; 24 Nov. 1797, at Raleigh. No. 4793.

McCabe, Joshua, private; 640 acres; 6 Dec. 1796, at Raleigh. No. 4126.

Massey, John, private; 228 acres; 31 Dec. 1806, at Raleigh. No. 145.

Turner, Titus Jennings, private; 640 acres; 1 July 1825, at Raleigh. No. 1220.

Waller, Nath'l, private; 640 acres; 1 July 1825 at Raleigh. No. 1221.

Olphin, William, private; 640 acres; 1 July 1825, at Raleigh. No. 1222.

McCormack, John, private; 640 acres; 20 July 1796, at Raleigh. No. 2741.

McDowell, John, private; 640 acres; 15 Sept. 1787. No. 561.

Mackey, James, private; 640 acres; 24 Dec. 1805, at Raleigh. No. not given.

McGuire, Dilud, private; 640 acres; 13 Nov. 1784, at Raleigh. No. 1393.

Mills, Jacob, private; 400 acres. 14 April 1792, at Hillsborough. No. not given.

Middleton, Samuel, private; 1000 acres; 1793, issued at Newbern. No. 2074.

McLean, William, sergeant; 2560 acres; 15 July 1792. No. 1546.

Morrison, James, private; 640 acres; 10 Jan. 1794, at Fayette. No. not given.

Martin, Archibald, private; 400 acres; 10 Jan. 1794, at Fayette. No. not given.

Massey, Joseph, private; 640 acres; 15 Dec. 1797, at Raleigh. No. not given.

McGown, John, private; 640 acres; 15 Dec. 1797, at Raleigh. No. 5257.

Murray, William, sergeant; 428 acres; 17 Dec. 1797, at Raleigh. No. 5241.

Mayor, or Mayo, James, corporal; 428 acres; 9 Dec. 1797, at Raleigh. No. 5208.

Mason, Christopher, private; 640 acres; 12 Feb. 1797, at Raleigh. No. 4745.

Morrison, John, private; 640 acres; 23 April 1785, at Fairfield. No. 1779.

McAllister, Joseph, private; 274 acres; 18 May 1784, at Hillsborough. No. 881.

McArthur, Alexander, private; 274 acres; 18 Jan. 1794, at Fayetteville. No. 3812.

Morgan, Morris, private; 640 acres; 21 Oct. 1783, issued at Hillsborough. No. 618.

Martin, Miles, private; 640 acres; 25 Nov. 1795 at Raleigh. No. 3900.

Morrison, Duncan, private; 640 acres; 16 March 1795 at Raleigh. No. 3842.

McDonald, Archibald, private; 640 acres; 16 March 1795, at Raleigh. No. 3843.

Malpus, Henry, private; 640 acres; 12 Oct. 1795, at Raleigh. No. 1366.

Morpus, John, private; 640 acres; 12 Oct. 1795, at Raleigh. No. 3871.

McCracken, John, private; 640 acres; 6 Feb. 1797, at Raleigh. No. 4651.

Mebanr (sic), Alexander, private; 640 acres; 10 Dec. 1790, at Fayetteville. No. 1206.

Morris, John, private; 640 acres; 23 Feb. 1793. No. 1579.

McElay, James, private; 400 acres; 14 April. 1792, at Hillsborough. No. not given.

McClurdy, Lazarus, private; 640 acres; 9 Feb. 1797, at Raleigh. No. 4649.

Melner, Samuel, private; 640 acres; 9 Feb. 1797, at Raleigh. No. 4650.

Medum, John, private; 640 acres; 17 Feb. 1824. No. 1170.

McGibbon, Neal, private; 640 acres; 17 Feb. 1824 at Raleigh. No. 1169.

MacQuillin, William, private; 640 acres; 14 Sept. 1797, at Raleigh. No. 3173.

Mitchell, Joseph, private; 274 acres; 7 March 1786. No. 197.

Maclin, Jerome, captain; 3840 acres; 22 Jan. 1823, at Raleigh. No. 1076.

Meeks, William, private; 228 acres; 20 Aug. 1785. No. 2018.

Middlestaff, Zachariah, private; 640 acres; 5 Dec. 1797, at Raleigh. No. 5037.

Moore, Sampson, private; 320 acres; 9 Feb. 1797, at Raleigh. No. 4646.

Marshall, Silas, private; 640 acres; 9 Feb. 1797, at Raleigh. No. 4645.

Nelson, Arthur, private; 640 acres; 15 March 1813, at Raleigh. No. 226.

Nelson, Jesse, private; 640 acres; issued 22 Jan. 1784, at Fairfield. No. 428.

Nelson, William, private; 640 acres; date not given. No. 427.

Nusom, Ethelred, private; 640 acres; 6 Oct. 1796. No. 441.

McNees, Jno., private; 640 acres; 10 Dec. 1790. No. 1276.

Hogg, Thomas, private; 640 acres; 3 March 1790. No. 1323.

Norris, Moses, fifer; 1000 acres; 9 Dec. 1797, at Raleigh. No. 5235.

Normley, Job, private; 640 acres; 9 Dec. 1797, at Raleigh. No. 5213.

Newsom, William, private; 640 acres. No. 5189.

Nail, Nicholas, private; 640 acres; 9 Dec. 1797, at Raleigh.
No. 5177.

Nail, Matthew, private; 640 acres; 9 Dec. 1797, at Raleigh. No.
5170.

Norton, Winney, private; 640 acres; 1 July 1801, at Raleigh.
No. 41.

Newman, Reuben, private; 640 acres; 31 Aug. 1795, at Raleigh.
No. 3849.

Orange, William, private; 640 acres; issued at Kinston. No.
369.

Owens, Stephen, second lieutenant; 1097 acres; 16 Jan. 1794, at
Fayette. No. 3813.

O'Neal, Arch, private; 640 acres; 8 Dec. 1787. No. 665.

Olefer, Neal, private; 640 acres; 14 Feb. 1797, at Raleigh. No.
4709.

Outlaw, Jesse, private; 342 acres; 9 Dec. 1797, at Raleigh. No.
5219.

Odam, Harman, private; 640 acres; 9 Dec. 1797, at Raleigh. No.
5206.

Outlaw, Moses, private; 640 acres; 9 Dec. 1797, at Raleigh. No.
5218.

Overton, Joab, private; 640 acres; issued 8 June 1792 at Glasgow. No. 3752.

Ord, John, private; 640 acres; 12 Feb. 1797 at Raleigh. No.
4746.

Overton, Jerry, private; 274 acres; 26 May 1800. No. 5205.

O'Brion, Samuel, private; 640 acres; 9 Dec. 1797, at Raleigh.
No. 5190.

Overton, James, private; 365 acres; 13 July 1784. No. 835.

Patterson, Hugh, private; 640 acres. No. 2489.

Page, William, private; 400 acres; 14 April 1793, at Hillsborough.
No. not given.

Powell, Francis, private; 640 acres; 15 Dec. 1804, at Raleigh.
No. 1782.

Prescott, Francis, private; 640 acres. No. 2957.

Palmore, John, private; 640 acres; 1787. No. 505.

Phillips, Mark, private; 640 acres; 1787. No. 651.

Pearcy, Nemiah, private; 640 acres; 11 July 1788. No. 709.

Perry, David, private; 400 acres; 14 April 1792, at Hillsborough. No. 47.

Phillips, Oswald, private; 640 acres; 10 Jan. 1794, at Fayette.
No. 38.

Page, Abraham, private; 640 acres; 20 May 1833. No. 2149.

Perkison, Beverly, private; 640 acres; issued 24 April 1785 at Fairfield. No. 1725.

Powell, Nicholas, private; 640 acres. No. 1781.

Powell, Moses, private; 640 acres. No. 1783.

Parish, Johnston, private; 640 acres; issued 16 Dec. 1797 at Raleigh. No. 5295.

Parish, Booker, private; 640 acres; issued 16 Dec. 1797 at Raleigh. No. 5297.

Peters, Barnard, private; 640 acres; issued 16 Feb. 1797 at Raleigh. No. 4750.

Pittis, James, private; 274 acres; issued 15 Feb. 1797, at Raleigh. No. 4720.

Privitt, William, private; 228 acres; issued 1797 at Raleigh. No. 4727,

Potter, Daniel, private; 220 acres; issued 15 Feb. 1797, at Raleigh. No. 4725.

Pembroke, Jno., private; 640 acres; 1797. No. 5222.

Phillips, Craven, private; 640 acres; issued 9 Dec. 1797 at Raleigh. No. 5195.

Pottor, John, sergeant; 1000 acres; issued 9 Dec. 1797 at Raleigh. No. 5223.

Previll, Lacy, private; 640 acres; issued 9 Dec. 1797 at Raleigh. No. 5227.

Pettyshall, Joshua, sergeant; 1000 acres; issued 14 Dec. 1797 at Raleigh. No. 5278.

Perryshall, Thomas, private; 640 acres; issued 14 Dec. 1797 at Raleigh. No. 5258.

Parr, Isiah, sergeant; 154 acres; 1825 at Raleigh. No. 1226.

Parker, William, sergeant; 1000 acres; 1825. No. 1227.

Phelps, Rador, sergeant; 1000 acres; 19 May 1784. No. 434.

Phelps, James, sergeant; 1000 acres; 19 May 1784. No. 435.

Parr, Noah, private; 640 acres; 6 Jan. 1784 at Fairfield. No. 412.

Parr, Caleb, private; 274 acres; 6 Dec. 1797 at Raleigh. No. 5024.

Parish, Ab, private; 640 acres. No. 5003.

Peters, Abraham, private; 640 acres; 1785 at Raleigh. No. 2221.

Pully, Benjamine, private; 640 acres; 1785 at Raleigh. No. 2215.

Pewat, John, sergeant; 1000 acres; 1824. No. 3020.

Moore, Joseph, private; 130 acres; 1810. No. 1920.

Robertson, Gardiner, private; 640 acres; 12 Sept. 1785, at Fairfield. No. 2223.

Roger, Jesse, private; 640 acres; 12 Sept. 1785 at Fairfield. No. 2228.

Ronn, Jesse, private; 640 acres; 12 Sept. 1785 at Fairfield. No. 2229.

Ralston, Robert, captain; 1097 acres; 14 March 1786. No. 17.

Rabourn, George, private; 274 acres; 20 May 1801, at Raleigh. No. 40.

Robeson, Edward, sergeant; 1000 acres; 25 Jan. 1795 at Raleigh. No. 3826.

Reynolds, John, private; 228 acres; 26 Dec. 1792, issued at Newbern. No. 3780.

Rogers, Stephen, private; 356 acres; 26 Dec. 1792 at Newbern. No. 3775.

Ryals, Joseph, private; 640 acres; 26 Dec. 1792 at Newbern. No. 3758.

Rankin, John, private; 320 acres; 14 Feb. 1797 at Raleigh. No. 4696.

Ross, Johnston, private; 640 acres; 9 Dec. 1797 at Raleigh. No. 5169.

Roundtree, Andrew, private; 640 acres; 18 Jan. 1798 at Raleigh. No. 5179.

Ross, Elijah, private; 640 acres; 9 Dec. 1797 at Raleigh. No. 5178.

Resors (Kersors), Richard, sergeant; 428 acres; 9 Dec. 1797 at Raleigh. No. 5232.

Ross, James, private; 220 acres; 12 Dec. 1797 at Raleigh. No. 5243.

Rasco, Teagle, private; 640 acres; 12 Dec. 1797 at Raleigh. No. 5255.

Richardson, Alexander, private; 640 acres; 12 Dec. 1797 at Raleigh. No. 5272.

Robertson, Jacob, private; 640 acres; 1807. No. 1322.

Rukels, Reason, private; 274 acres; 24 Nov. 1797 at Raleigh. No. 4796.

Russwurm, John S., private; 1825 acres; 15 Feb. 1841. No. 1479.

Reel, James, private; 640 acres; 1785. No. 2156.

Robertson, Lewie, private; 640 acres; 1785. No. 2222.

Ring, Aaron, private; 640 acres; 1785. No. 2267.

Read, James, captain; 3840 acres; 25 Oct. 1783, at Hillsborough. No. 227.

Ramsey, Henry, Guard.

Whitiker, Josiah; filed with R.

Richards, Jonathan, private; 274 acres. No. 419.

Ridley, William, private; 400 acres; 14 April 1793 issued at Hillsborough. No. not given.

Rains, Jno., Guard; 400 acres; 1784. No. 45.

Reaves, Benjamine; private; 640 acres. No. 1264.

Roase, William, private; 428 acres; May 1793. No. 2046.

Ramey, Peter, sergeant; 1000 acres; 23 Oct. 1793 at Hillsborough. No. 272.

Reynolds, George, sergeant; 1000 acres; 15 Dec. 1783 at Hillsborough. No. 384.

Rountree, Reuben, lieutenant; 1144 acres; 10 July 1784. No. not given.

Robins, James, private; 274 acres; 6 Jan. 1784 at Fairfield. No. 402.

Scott, William, private; 228 acres; 27 Feb. 1797 at Raleigh. No. 4764.

Lantee, Ceaset, private; 640 acres; July 1799. No. 4732. (Filed under letter R.)

Storey, Caleb, private; 640 acres; 14 May 1784 at Hillsboro. No. 854.

Scott, Thomas, private; 388 acres; 20 April 1784 at Hillsboro. No. 533.

Stem, Littleberry, private; 187 acres, at Hillsboro. No. 134.

Hart, Anthony, private; 640 acres; 1787. No. 678.

Smith, John, private; 640 acres; 1784. No. 1376.

Southerland, James, private; 274 acres; 1807. No. 1767.

Smith, William, private; 274 acres; issued 10 Aug. 1792 at Glasgow. No. 3760.

Simmeral, James, sergeant; 1000 acres; 15 Nov. 1793. No. 3792.

Shaddock, Charles, private; 640 acres; 7 Jan. 1794 at Fayetteville. No. 3810.

Splendo, Boston, private; 640 acres; 1796. No. 3817.

Sanderlin, Isaac, private; 640 acres; 1795. No. 3883.

Stepp, Henry, private; 640 acres; 2 Nov. 1795 at Raleigh. No. 3876.

Smith, Job, sergeant; 355 acres; 10 Nov. 1795 at Raleigh. No. 3886.

Sitgraves, Jacob; 1785. No. 1972.

Smith, William, private; 640 acres; 24 Nov. 1797 at Raleigh. No. 4798.

Sanderling, Levi, private; 640 acres; 17 May 1800. No. 5021.

Scott, Adam, private; 640 acres; 19 Dec. 1812 at Raleigh. No. 220.

Smith, Daniel, private; 640 acres; 1 Dec. 1797. No. 5018.

Smitkly, Thomas, private; 640 acres; 20 May 1793. No. 1934.

Senton, Roger, private; 640 acres; 9 Feb. 1797, at Raleigh. No. 4630.

Shelby, Evan, private; 1200 acres; 8 Oct. 1787 at Raleigh. No. 44.

Sumner, Jethro, general; 12,000 acres; 27 April 1793. No. 157.

Strange, James; 274 acres; 22 Jan. 1784 at Fairfield. No. 426.

Strickler, Martin, private; 228 acres; 22 Jan. 1784. No. 409. (Issued at Fairfield.)

Sullinaver, John, private; 640 acres; 13 Dec. 1783 at Fairfield. No. 386.

Skeen, John, private; 640 acres; 30 Aug. 1806. No. 390.

Stuart, Colwell, private; 640 acres; 19 Aug. 1815 at Raleigh. No. 255.

Stewart, George; 5 Aug. 1785. No. 1625.

Sugg, John, private; 274 acres; 27 Nov. 1783 at Fairfield. No. 344.

Slade, Stephen, lieutenant; 2500 acres; 22 March 1784 at Fairfield. No. 492.

Sumner, Jethro, brig.-gen.; 12,000 acres; 27 April 1793. No. 157.

Stephenson, Hugh, private; 365 acres; 8 Aug. 1833 at Nashville. No. 1778.

Stepp, Joseph, private; 640 acres; 11 July 1788. No. 729.

Sheppard, William, private; 640 acres; 23 Feb. 1793. No. 1613.

Smith, Thomas, lieutenant; 1000 acres; 1797. No. 203.

Sullivan, John; 78 acres in Overton Co.; 1810. No. 2042.

Shute, Samuel, private; 640 acres; 12 Sept. 1785. No. 2233.

Scott, Nathan, private; 640 acres; 7 Jan. 1814. No. 223.

Sanderlin, Levi; no. 3020.

Swagot, Geo., private; 640 acres; 1785. No. 2032.

Sisk, James, private; 640 acres; issued 19 May 1784 at Hillsborough. No. 894.

Strom, Scott, private; 228 acres. No. 38.

Shockley, Isaac, private; 640 acres; 29 Aug. 1792. No. 1754.

Sanders, Jos., private; 228 acres. No. 2453.

Sanderlin, Levi, private; 640 acres in White Co., Tenn.; 1807.
No. 6678.

Smith, Reubin, private; 1792. No. 400.

Sumner, Julian, private; 640 acres; 1797. No. 4701.

Smithson, Sam'l, private; 640 acres; 1797. No. 5261.

Timbrel, John, private; 640 acres; 17 Feb. 1824 at Raleigh. No.
1205.

Taylor, John, musician; 1000 acres; 17 Feb. 1824 at Raleigh.
No. 1206.

Taylor, James, private; 640 acres; 17 Feb. 1824 at Raleigh. No.
1207.

Tharp, Bishop, private; 640 acres; 17 Feb. 1824 at Raleigh. No.
1208.

Terrell, John, private; 640 acres; 17 Feb. 1824 at Raleigh. No.
1211.

Tracey, John, private; 640 acres; 17 Feb. 1824 at Raleigh. No.
1210.

Troy, James, private; 640 acres; 17 Feb. 1824 at Raleigh. No.
1209.

Tankesley, William, private; 640 acres; 17 Feb. 1824 at Raleigh.
No. 1212.

Trapp, Elijah, musician; 1000 acres; 5 Dec. 1797. No. 5032.

Tosel, Robert, private; 640 acres; 2 Jan. 1784. No. 393.

Taylor, William, private; 274 acres. No. 469.

Twigg (Trigg), Daniel, musician; 428 acres; 1825. No. 1231.

Thomas, Philip, private; 640 acres; 1825. No. 1225.

Tucker, Woody, private; 640 acres; 1825. No. 1224.

Taylor, Philip, captain; 24 acres; 1 July 1825 at Raleigh. No.
12321.

Thomas, John, ensign; 1280 acres; 1825. No. 1233.

Topp, Roger, general; 1791. No. not given.

Thompson, John, private; 400 acres; 1792. No. 12.

Tulley, Abel, private; 640 acres; 1797. No. 4700.

Teal, Jacob, private; 640 acres; 1797. No. 3870.

Tucker, Richard, private; 640 acres; 15 Aug. 1823. No. 1102.

Thompson, Ezekiel, private; 274 acres; 1797. No. 5038.

Trickle, Jonathan, private; 26 acres. No. 1615.

Trautham, Martin, private; 640 acres; 17 Feb. 1824 at Raleigh. No. 1204.

Vick, Isaiah, private; 274 acres; 27 Feb. 1797 at Raleigh. No. 4765.

Visor, Abraham, private; 640 acres; 1797 at Raleigh. No. 5233.

Verner, Robert, lieutenant; 1280 acres; 29 Dec. 1803 at Raleigh. No. 846.

Vance, William, corporal; 228 acres; 6 Jan. 1784 at Fairfield. No. 403.

Woods, Arch'd; no rank given; no acreage. No. 3821.

Worsley, Bryan, private; 365 acres; 1793 at Raleigh. No. 3882.

Warner, John, private; 320 acres; 19 Nov. 1795 at Raleigh. No. 3887.

Whitley, Ham, private; 228 acres; 20 May 1793 at Newbern. No. not given.

White, John, private; 228 acres; 7 March 1786. No. 165.

Williams, Theophilus, ensign; 1096 acres; 6 Dec. 1792 at Newbern. No. 3771.

Walsby, Charles, private; 274 acres; 29 July 1797 at Raleigh. No. 4762.

Wells, Jacob, private; 640 acres; 12 Sept. 1785 at Fairfield. No. 2246.

Wilkerson, Rich'd, private; 640 acres; 10 Dec. 1797 at Raleigh. No. 5166.

Wilhite, Richard, private; 640 acres; 9 Dec. 1797 at Raleigh. No. 5196.

Wimstead, Fred'k, private; 392 acres; 9 Dec. 1797. No. 5212.

Wiggins, Arthur, private; 228 acres; 15 Feb. 1797 at Raleigh. No. 4720.

Woodward, David, private; 274 acres; 15 Feb. 1797 at Raleigh. No. 4718.

Walker, Elijah, private; 400 acres; 10 Jan. 1794 at Fayette. No. 6.

Wright, Hezekiah, private; 400 acres; 10 Jan. 1794, at Fayette. No. not given.

Walker, Daniel, private; 400 acres; 14 April 1792 at Hillsborough. No. not given.

Williams, Samuel, private; 640 acres. No. 792.

Jones, Allen; 1000 acres; issued 30 May 1793 at Newbern. No. not given.

Williams, Benjamine, captain; 1828 acres; 6 Jan. 1784, at Fair-field. No. 411.

Wyatt, John, sergeant; 1000 acres; 21 Jan. 1818 at Raleigh. No. 268.

Williams, Elisha, private; 274 acres; 9 Nov. 1783 at Fairfield. No. 292.

Williams, William, private; 228 acres; 24 Nov. 1797 at Raleigh. No. 4799.

Williamson, Rober (sic), private; 640 acres; 17 Feb. 1824 at Raleigh. No. 1216.

Wiley, Stephen, private; 640 acres; 17 Feb. 1824 at Raleigh. No. 1215.

Willis, Augusta, sergeant; 1000 acres; 17 Feb. 1824 at Raleigh. No. 1214.

Walton, Richard, private; 640 acres; 17 Feb. 1824 at Raleigh. No. 1213.

Wilkenson, Reuben, lieutenant; 2560 acres; 17 Dec. 1819 at Raleigh. No. 1349.

Williams, Jesse, private; 640 acres; 18 May 1807 at Raleigh. No. 3385.

Wills, John, private; 640 acres; 1820. No. 195.

Williams, Theophilus, private; 640 acres; 7 March 1786 at Kinston. No. 154.

Whitaker, Burton, private. No. 172.

Weeks, Theophilus, private; 640 acres. No. 1226.

Wilson, Francis, private; 640 acres. No. 4193.

York, Will; 533 acres; issued 29 May 1795 at Newbern. No. 2136.

Yates, John, private; 640 acres; 16 June 1808 at Raleigh. No. 22.

Yarbrough, James, private; 640 acres; 1 Oct. 1801, at Raleigh. No. 42.

Young, James, private; 640 acres; 1797. No. 5167.

Yarby, Jonas, private; 640 acres; 9 Dec. 1797 at Raleigh. No. 5210.

Young, John, corporal; 357 acres; 15 Dec. 1797 at Raleigh. No. 5279.

LEGISLATIVE PAPERS AND PETITIONS

Many of these petitions deal with divorce and with legitimization of children. Others are petitions from inhabitants of various counties. All were found in the Tennessee State Archives, often in numbered boxes. If the box number is known it is given.

Petition to the Honourable the General Assembly of the State of Tennessee. The exact date is not known, but was around the time that Tennessee was made a state and the time that lands were acquired from the Cherokee Indians (c.July 1796). The petition reads in full:

We the undersigned citizens of that tract of country lately acquired from the Cherokee Tribe of Indians and its vicinity, as well with a view to promote Publick good as individual interest, beg leave to represent to your honourable body, what we believe to be the true situation of the aforesaid tract of land, and what will be the result if the cause now contemplated should be forward relative to the sales.

The whole of the good lands in this tract of country (the river land excepted) is situate in narrows, vallies running from northeast to southwest or nearly betwixt the rivers, Little Tennessee and Highawassee, each of which vallies are separated by large uninhabitable Ridges unfit for cultivation and when the Township and Sectional lines are applied to it, it so cuts and divides the land fit for cultivation as to render it of very little value.

(We) would therefore suggest to your honourable body that propriety of changing the present course and opening an office to receive entries for land in such quantities as your wisdom may direct, which course we varily believe would inhance the value of the land and promote the interest of individuals in which event we do believe, it would be honest and correct, to allow the settlers a preperance (sic) of entry or compensation for hisimprovement. (We) would further suggest that by raising the price of good land you would be enabled to reduce the price of poor land, provided it would average at two dollars per acre, and by this means would sell Thousands of acres that would never have sold for two dollars and we think the revenue arising from the tax of poor land thus sold at a reduced price would be an object worthy the attention of this honourable assembly and we as in duty bound Shall pray, etc.
(Signed):

Samuel Vance	Miller Isbell
John Vance	John Sheets
John Black	William Isbell
Alexander Caughern	Benjamin McDowl
A. M. D. Cowan	William Stodam
Samuel Gould	Adam Davis

Jerry Pilmon
James Robinson
Wm. Robinson
J. L. Tullock
Micajah Turner
Wm. White
Joseph Welcin
Hevin Marrer
Edward Hart
Daniel Duggan
Minte Dolloway
Waldcon Mead
Thomas Blaire
James Reagan
William M. Stephenson
Joseph Halaway
William Bain
John Gould
John Rider
Jonathan Kuykendall
William Cordull
Jason Isbell
Nathaniel White
George Wethers
John Stephens
William Vanon
Levy Stephens
John Cordill
Roberts Mitchell
John Rider, Jr.
John White
Martin Webb
John Cleaton
Mitchell White
William White
Archer Muse
Robert Claton
Eliza Claton
Binn Noel
Jesse Neal
Akerny Brannon
John Blair
Wm. White
John Batey
John Wear
Iconge Holoway
Benjamin Nicheson
E. N. Cain

Henry Sheets
James White
Sam Looney
James Gherml(e)y
William Z. Weldon
Joseph Stephenson
George Snider
Joshua Stephens
Thos. Morison
N. White
J. N. Davidson
D. Bain
James Mason
James Edington
Joseph Edington
Elaxender Hamentree
H. Hamentree
Joseph Hamentree
Joseph Blair
Eliza Beard
Samuel White
William Blair
Elexander Hugg
James Beard
Stephen Beard
Milton Morison
Austin Rider
John Beaty
John Beaty
Francis Bradley
Robert Rhea
Jeremiah Hatfield
John Daugherty
Bartley Causin
James Alley
Willy Linallen
Josiah Hart
Benjamin Brown
Timothy Chadwick
Edward Brannon
John Muse
John Ruff
John Pitman
John L. White
Hill Thompson
Jacob Holoway
A. Orr
S. White

- * -

Extracts from Legislative Papers

1799 - Box 2. Patsy Chisholm, wife of John Chisholm, 1796.
Deposition of Pleasant M. Miller, 1799. Knox Co., Tenn., before
Joseph Greer, J. P.   This was a divorce proceeding.

1799 - Box 1.   7 Dec. 1798: Petition of Mark Noble for divorce
from Caty Elliott. Robertson Co., Tenn. William Noble's
affidavit. Mark Noble and Caty Elliott were married 13 Dec.
1792 and they had two children, born by 1798.

Box 1. Petition of Thomas and Mary Buzby for divorce. 28 Dec.
1798.

Box 9. 1813. Thomas Wright in 1784 entered a petition for 250 acres for services rendered in running the Indian Line in 1784.

Box 10. 1812-1813. Israel Standefer petitions regarding the changing of the name of his two illegitimate children, Polly Hasler, born to Evie Hasler, and James Stewart, born to Katherine Stewart.

Box 10. Pension Papers of Christopher Hains or Haines of Va. W. 8896. Allen Co., Ky., on 15 Oct. 1832 in open court, the said Hains, aged 72, stated he entered service as a regular soldier in June or July of 1777 under Capt. Samuel Gilkerson in Frederick Co., Va., and was discharged in the spring of 1779. He went to Rockingham Co., Va., to live with his mother and his step-father, David Maunger. In 1780 he was drafted as a militia man for three months and served under Capt. John Rush. In 1781 he was again drafted and served under Capt. John Rogan for three months. He was in no battles. After the war, he moved to Russell Co., Va., and then to Kentucky. He was born in Winchester, Va., in 1760, on June 8.
    Washington Co., Tenn.: On 29 Sept. 1832, George Hains swore he knew Christopher Hains enlisted for two years. Tabitha Hains aged 87, deposed she was the widow of Christopher Haines, who died 9 September 1846. They were married on 14 July 1772.

Box 8. 1809. Petition of John Halburton asking that his illegitimate child, now known as Patsy Paul, be given his name.

Box 8. 1809. Petition of Vance Greer, attorney for the heirs of Andrew Greer, dec., asking that they be given the right to appeal to the courts on a decision of the Commissioners of East Tennessee as to lands granted. 28 Oct. 1809.

Box 8. 1809. Petition of Agnes Thompson, asking for a divorce. 21 Sept. 1809. She married William Thompson. Agy Thompson of Montgomery Co., Va., made a statement on 22 Jan. 1803 that she married William Thompson c.1783, and lived with him, and they had children. James Medford made a statement from Knox Co., Tenn., that William Thompson was in Jackson Co., Tenn., in 1803. Thompson owned property.

Box 9. 1809. Bedford Co., Tenn.: petition to legislature from Rebeccah Barker, asking for a divorce from Alexander B. Barker, who has absconded for two years. She had a child.

Box 8. 1809. Petition of John Allison, 15 Sept. 1809. Certificate that John Allison served as a private soldier in the N. C. Cont. Line, a nine month man under the command of Col. Archibald Lytle; 1809, and the same is signed by Will Lytle, late captain in the Revolutionary War.

Box 8. 1809. Petition of John and Jane McCutcheon, asking for a divorce. 25 Sept. 1809, Claiborne Co., Tenn.

Box 5. 1801. The House of Representatives appoints the following persons Justices of the Peace for Davidson Co.: John Anderson, Joseph Coleman, Alexander Ewing, Robert Weakley, William Nash and James Rucker.

Martin Adams of Davidson Co. asks for divorce from his wife Martha. 1812. Box not given.

Hugh Kennedy of Knox Co. asks for divorce from his wife Eleanor Walker, 1812. Box not given.

Sarah Watkins from Robertson Co. asks for divorce from her husband John Watkins, 1812. Box not given.

William Roper asks for divorce from his wife Polly, 1812. They were married on 29 April 1792. In 1794 she visited her father in South Carolina. About twelve months later she returned to her husband in his home in Va. Early in 1806 Roper moved to Tennessee and his wife left him in 1810. Box not given.

Elizabeth Woods, divorce from John Woods, 1812. They were wed on 8 Jan. 1807. She was formerly Elizabeth Compass, Sullivan Co. Tenn. Box not given.

Patsy Berry of Maury Co. asks for divorce from Francis Berry, her husband, 1812. She was formerly Patsy Sellers or Sellars. Francis Berry had married a widow Hamilton of Smith Co., Tenn. Robert Sellars deposed pertaining to Berry and wife. Elijah Hunter of Williamson Co. confirmed Robert Sellars' statement. Francis Berry had a wife in Pulaski Co., Ky., before this time. Box not given.

Thomas Anderson, admr. of David (Davis) King of Sumner Co., regarding land. Sally King, widow and legatee of Davis King. 1813. Box not given.

Chloe Hendry of Greene Co., asks for divorce from William Hendry in 1813. Hendry was formerly of Washington Co., Tenn., and he married again. Box not given.

Rebecah Stuart of Rutherford Co. asks for divorce from Wm. Stuart, 1813. They were married 14 years ago and they lived together until December 1810. Sworn to in Greene Co., Tenn. Box not given.

Denson Fields of Ocerton Co., asks for divorce, 1813. About five years ago he married Rachel Petty, with whom he lived about three months. Box not given.

Daniel Tredway of Hawkins Co. asks for divorce. He lived in Jefferson Co., Tenn., also. In Feb. 1806 he married Rebeccah Eaton. In 1809 he entered the service of the U. S. against his wife's desire. He lived in camp for almost twelve months. He and his wife had children, and parted in 1812. Benjamin Davis is mentioned. Rachel Eaton of Hawkins Co., Tenn., made an affidavit. Box not given.

Nancy Reese of Bedford Co., Tenn., asks for divorce from Jesse Reese, 1813. Nancy Reese wife of Jesse Reese of Laurens Dist., S. C., is removing to Tennessee with her brother, Jonathan York, and her mother. Box not given.

John Anderson of Carter Co., petitions for legalizing his son, 1813. He married Margaret Christy and had a son Isaac Christy and several other children. Box not given.

James Doherty petitions to have his daughter Eliza Davis have her name changed to Eliza Campbell Doherty, 1813. The file contains papers pertaining to James Doherty's marriage. Box not given.

James G. Raulston petitions to be allowed to sell certain lots in Knoxville, and grants that he may educate himself and other minor heirs of George Raulston, 1813. Box not given.

Eliza Ortts petitions for a divorce from Frederick Ortts, 1813. They were married 2 July 1805 and he divorced her that Nov.

Box 16. John Strain and John Campbell, admr's of David Robertson, 1815. Robertson died in 1792 and his estate settlement went before the legislature.

Box 16. J. Youngblood of Rutherford Co., Tenn., petitions to have his name given to his illegitimate children, 1815. A child aged six years born to Pheby McMillon was named James Maddison McMillin, and had his name changed to James Maddison Youngblood and made a legal heir.

Box 16. Josiah Shipp petitions that four children be given his name, 1815. Mary McClannahan has four children; namely, Felix G., Marciller, Eliza, and Bartly McClannahan, and Josiah wants their name changed from McClannahan to Shipp.

Box 19. Prudence Sanders, wife of James Sanders of Maury Co., Tenn. William Williams and Mathew Williams his wife make affidavits regarding, 1817.

Box 19. James Patterson petitions for divorce from wife, 1817, in Stewart Co., Tenn. They were married in Oct. 1797 and her name was Jenney Massey. William James went to Missouri Terr. James Latimer made an affidavit in Humphreys Co., Tenn. John Brighan, J. P. for Stewart Co., named. Solomon Grice of Stewart Co. made affidavit. Henry Edwards of Stewart Co. also made his affidavit. 1817.

Box 19. Margery Barber, relict and executrix of Joseph Barber, dec., late of Orange Co., N. C., petitions pertaining to purchase of military lands, 1797. 1817.

Box 19. David Spear petitions that he be issued a military warrant, Davidson Co., Tenn. Howell Tatum, a captain in the 1st N. C. Regt. in the Revolutionary War deposed that he knew said Spear to have been a soldier or non-commissioned officer in the 2nd Regt. of N. C. in the spring of 1776 until after the fall of Charlestown in May 1780, at which time both Spear and Tatum were both captured.

Box 22. Martha A. R. Jones divorce from Alexander W. Jones, 1819, Davidson Co., Tenn. They were married 19 Dec. 1816. Her father was John Cockrill, Sr., of Davidson Co., Tenn.

Box 22. Polly T. Depriest divorce from Charles C. Depriest, 1819. They were married in Williamson Co., Tenn., 13 Nov. 1817.

Box 22. William Knott and Mary Davis, divorce, 1819. She married Jesse Davis about 1791 in Granville Co., N. C., and is now a citizen of Bedford Co., Tenn. They had eleven children. The petitioner's father died in 1799. Property is involved.

Box 22. Robert Moore of Rutherford Co., married Sarah Haile in 1810, and has a family in Rutherford Co.. He petitions for a divorce. 1819.

Box 83. Allen S. Haley of Roane Co., Tenn., petitions to adopt Margaret A. Cash, a ten year old female, his daughter by a woman who is now married to another man.

Box 83. Petition from Sumner Co., 1833. Elizabeth Harper, divorce. Noah Cotton says he has natural children by Elizabeth Harper, named Sophia, Harriott N., Zelda, John M., James L., Tabitha, Mary(?), and Alexander T. Harper, and he asks that they be legalized and their name changed to Cotton. The said Elizabeth had a child Nancy by her husband Joseph Harper, who abandoned her about 20 years ago.

Box 83. Bedford Co., Tenn. Franklin M. Brown petitions for divorce. He married Polly Anthony of Bedford Co. in Jan. 1826. Four months later she bore a child whose father was her cousin Alfred Anthony.

Box 83. 16 Sept. 1833. Jean Cantrell petitions for a divorce from her husband, Lewis Cantrell.

Box 83. 1833. Elizabeth Kesee petitions to sell the land of her deceased husband, Charles Kesee, who died about the end of Nov. 1832, leaving his widow and four children, three of whom are daughters.

Box 83. Rebecca Kelly petitions for divorce. Formerly Rebecca Hamilton, she married Jesse Kelly in 1806, and had two children. 27 Aug. 1833.

Box 83. Stewart Co., Tenn. Briggs Barker asks for divorce from his wife Elizabeth. They were married 17 Sept. 1818 in Stewart Co., and now live in Humphreys Co., Tenn.

Box 83. 1833. Perry Co., Tenn. Sarah Raymond petitions for divorce. Burrell Benton of Perry Co. let his daughter Sarah marry David B. Raymond. She is or was about 16 years of age, and had two children.

Box 83. 1835, Claiborne Co. Sally Hopson petitions for divorce. About 20 years ago she married Harrod Hopson and had 12 children. About three years ago he left her.

1833. Opinion of Judge N. Green, in the case of F. A. Ross vs. Cobbs. Frederick A. Ross vs. Pharaoh B. Cobb and others. The plaintiffs below claim under John and Catherine Blair who in 1809 were infants, and orphans without a guardian. Joseph Cobb, their step-father, made several lands in controversy for seven years. Action in Circuit Court of Fentress Co., Tenn.; Feb. Term of 1833.

Box 82. 1827. Ann Swisher petitions for divorce from Michael Swisher. 22 Oct. 1827.

Box 82. 1829. Jacob Haun petitions to legalize William Dixon Cusuan and Alfred Cobb, Haun's illegitimate sons, and he asks that their names be changed to William Dixon and Alfred Carter Haun.

Box 82. 1829. Joseph Sloss petitions to be divorced from his wife, Sally Sloss. Rutherford Co., Tenn.

Box 82. John Hale petitions for divorce in 1827. In April 1822 he married Anna Brown, who left him in April 15, 1827, and went with George Pasinger.

Box 82. 1827. Joel Chambers petitions for divorce. He married Margaret Hull on 8 March 1826. She left him in 1826. 20 Aug. 1827.

Box 82. 1827. Mary Harris petitions for divorce from Richard C. Harris.

Box 82. Monroe Co., Tenn., 1825. Mary Silvidge petitions for divorce on 22 Sept. 1825. She left her husband in 1818.

Box 82. March 1827. Willie Tilly of Sumner Co. on 23 Oct. 1829 asked the legislature to allow him to adopt a child of Jessy

Ragon's, aged 8 months. The mother died and the father has deserted the child. Said Tilly and his wife have no children.

Box 82. Nancy Cooper, formerly Nancy Jones, has been married to William Cooper for four or five years. Her petition, dated 7 Sept. 1823 is signed by a number of citizens:

Nancy Cooper	Stephens Jones
Jno. W. Howell	John Davy
Samuel Davis	Jones Davis
Richard Jones	William Mann
Nathan McCoggin	David Wade
John Davis	Robert Davis
Joseph Howell	Leml. B. Lisenley
Francis Baker	John Barnett
Joab Barnett	Samuel Jordan
Edward Wade	James Bramill
Robert Searcy	William Tramill
Saml Haggard	

Box 82. 1823. McMinn Co. Rhebe (Phebe?) Campbell asks for lands. She states her husband died in the summer of 1821 from a rattlesnake bite while trying to locate lands, and his family is left without support. He left a large family of children, all of whom appear to have been minors at the time.

The following were extracted from an old book on Hamilton District Territory of the United States of America south of the Ohio, and filed at the Tennessee State Archives, Nashville.

p. 1.   Bill of James Turman, complainant against John Gardin, defendant, regarding land in Greene Co., Tenn., 1791.

p. 5.   Bill of James Turman, complainant, against Thomas Keeny, respondent, regarding sale of paper money. James Turman is going northwest, 1792.

p. 10. James Turman, complainant vs. Frederick Mayberry, respondent, Sept. 1792. Turman purchased a steer from Mayberry. Hamilton was attorney for the complainant, and A. Roan was attorney for the respondent.

p. 14. Sarah Kearns enters a bill of complaint against John Kearns, whom she married about 26 years ago. They lived together until Sept. 1794 when he turned her out. A. Roan was her attorney. Case dismissed.

p. 15. Court of Equity. Benjamine Mony Wallace complainant in 1791. Obligation to Robert Duglas. Wm. Small seems to have received money from Money Wallace for Robert Duglas and failed to delivered the same.

p. 19. James Gibson, 1795, suit regarding a tract of land on French Broad River, which he improved in 1782.

p. 21. John Sevier and Adam M-ek, executors of the last will and testament of Isaac Taylor, dec., to a bill of complaint of James Gibson. 1795.

p. 24. Richard Brumlee entered a bill of complaint against John Hodge, in 1795, regarding a note of 1792.

p. 27. Thomas Arthor vs. John Fryer and Wm. Nelson regarding land on Flat Creek south of French Broad.

p. 37. Bill of complaint, Amos Bird vs. Jacob Vanhouser; regarding a mulatto slave; 1795.

p. 38. Complaint of Ruth Gist vs. Joseph Teans, 1795, concerning a horse.

p. 40. Complaint of Ruth Gist against Stephen Duncan.

p. 42. Complaint of Wm. McNeal against Charles O'Neal, 1795, concerning certain lots in Knoxville.

p. 45. Wm. Boyd, orator (petitioner), in 1792 contracted and bargained with Abner Witt over a tract of land.

p. 49. John McClellan, complainant, vs. Edward McFarland, defendant.

Box 82. To the Honorable the General Assembly of the State of
Tennessee. 1819, Davidson Co. The undersigned citizens of
Tennessee beg leave to represent to the Legislature that, owing
to the law passed at the last session, authorizing the notes of
the Nashville and State Bank to be received in payment for all
debts due for taxes and to individuals, it has by this preference,
caused the notes of the Farmers and Mechanics Bank of Nashville
to depreciate and thereby many persons have been seriously in-
jured, and the community deprived of a portion of its circulating
emduim (sic), which, at this time of embarrassment is very
interesting to them. It has generally been believed and admitted
by all who have known the situation of this Bank, that its capa-
city to redeem its notes in circulation, is equal to any of the
banks of this state; and we consider it entirely safe and solvent.
We therefore pray, that owing to the great pecuniary distress,
and as an act of justice to this institution that the legislature
will grant it the same privileges and immunities as are granted
to other banks, whose notes have been made currently law; and
we will as in duty bound ever pray. 15 June 1820. Signed by:

Th. Claiborne
Geo. B. McNeill
T. A. Bedford
Samuel B. Marshall
Nich. Campbell
John B. West
A. G. Goodlet
West and Bradford
E. S. Hall
Richmond and Flint
D. A. Dunham (or Durham)
Crockett and Adams
F. W. H. Fletcher
R. W. Armstrong
Was. L. Hannim
Alex Somerville and Co.
Nathan Ewing
Francis Linch
Jas. Grizzard
Berryhill and McKee
Reuben Pauper(?)
Jno. Aborn
Martin Smith
Robert W. Briggs
Jno. P. Erwin
Isaiah Cassey
Wm. Faulkner
Stephen Cantrell
Wm. Rutherford
Hy. Terrass
R. L. Anderson
F. Whiteside
Braddock Richmond
M. Barrone
Edmund Lanier
John Decker
Z. W. Hash
Saml Seay
Duncan Robertson
Jas. Condon
Jos. and R. O. Woods
John McNairy
J. Smith
Solomon Clark

Wm. Quarles
R. A. McNairy
I. N. Roane
Robertson and Casey
Th. J. Read
Wm. Carroll
Thos. Johnson
Geo. W. Martin
Thos. Hickman
John Price
W. H. Guinn
Arch'd McNeill
Will Lytle
Geo. Bell
Jno. H. Oloput
Jas. Lockhart
J. Blackfan
Thos. Deadrick
Lewis Joslin
Robt. W. Guine
Ben W. Bedford
Jas. J. Gill
Wm. Compton
James Stewart and Co.
James McGavock
W. Bosworth
James H. Foster
Thos. Shackelford
F. B. Foggs
Peter Douglas
J. S. Kingsbury
N. B. Pryor
Roger B. Sappington
W. Campbell
Jno. B. Craighead
C. Cooper
Robert Woods
Wm. Donelson
Gordon Z. Walker
R. White (Whyte)
J. B. Houston
Thomas Talbot
Alfred Balch
Will White

Box 82. 1831. Washington Co. Petition asking that Elias Jones, a free man of color, aged 77 years, be allowed to prove his accounts. Signed by the following citizens of Washington Co.:

A. E. Jackson
James S. Johnston
John Ryland
William P. Christen, Jr.
James McAlister
Adam Mitchell
Ezra Pevie (?)
John S. Waddell
W. Williams
John S. King
John Bricker
Wm. C. Nelson
Orville P. Nelson
A. W. Brabson
B. Brown
John N. Douk
Washington Witten(?)
George W. Coffman
Thomas I. Wilson
Iavo K. Brown
John M. Clark
Jacob Brown
Reuben Rogers
Rich'd Belle
Thos. Burress
Joseph Rogers
Isaac Henley
William Treadway
Jon Leslie
Alfred Coyban
William Sikes
Jonathan G. Haynes
Robert Foore
Aaron Jones
Andrew Jones
George Freeman
Joseph Boothe
Wm. Conyan, Sr.
Frederick Staens
Hudson Lyterate
John Matthews
Jonathan H. Collom
Phillip McCray
Elijah Euelean

James A. Mitchell
Thomas O. Roberts
Wm. K. Blair
Wm. Gilleyland
Robert McLin
W. Mitchell
John McCray
Thos. J. Brown
D. C. Hunter
Skelton Taylor
Peter Hicks
Henry McCray
G. L. Daker
Ewing McClure
J. Humphreys
A. W. Carter
David Odell
John Lening
Henry McCray
Wm. Wilson
Reuben Boyles
John Patton
Lisburn Blackburn
Roth Blair
Adam Broyles
Isaac Broyles
Laurne (?) Ufferd
John C. Phields
David C. Woods
Alexander Bates
Danl L. Bayles
Adam May
Morris Hartsell
Jessee Wyett
Isaac Hartsell
Jacob Hartsell
Daniel Huffins
Anthony Hartsell
William Chester
James H. Jones
John P. Chester
Addison Treadway
John Coppengen
Joseph Hickey

Box 75. Petition of sundry citizens of Washington County praying an alteration of certain civil districts; 24 Oct. 1837. Signed by the following:

Wm. Tredway
Allen Jungle (Ingle)
John P. Hattringe
Sarah McIntire
Jerrel Chandler
T. J. Wilson
Hugh Carloway
Joseph Chandler
John Masters
Jesse Clark
John Brickers
Joshua Bill (or Hill)
Solte Wales
Wm. R. Presley
Edward Baker

Andrew Jones
Jesse Williams
Jacob Temple
Bless Hensley
Zachariah Wells
James Dean
Daniel Roberts
Henry Williams
Henderson Henley
Jeremiah Hill (or Bill)
Lilban Eashbarger
William McCloud
Reuben Bill
Hy Bogles
J. M. Welser

Isaac P. Galy
A. D. Taylor
Davis Butler
Christian F. Galy (?)
John Chandler
John Hunt
Hart Duncan
Isaac Taylor
Samuel Warden
Wm. Clark
Martin Chander
Franklin Durham
D. T. Polson
William Hensley
Allen Underwood
A. E. Jackson
James Saunders
Elijah Crawley
Charles Embree
Pleasant Hensley
Robert Tredway
Joseph West
Henry Boldman
Richard Bell
Ira Bricker
Welcom Stephen
John Haulston
Calvin Hoss
J. M. Brumet
William Roulston
William Gillegland
P. McCray
Saml. G. Boyles
G. W. Tilford
B. S. West
Daniel Deakins
Elijah Shannon
William Nelson
John P. Chester
H. L. Brown
Albert G. Bayles
Martin H. Bayles
Isaac Henley
T. Hickey
John Humphreys
Isaac T. Humphreys
John Ingle, Jr.
John McMulkin
James H. Brezeley
John Jugle (Ingle)
Jacob Click
Joseph Boyd
F. G. Slemons
These names were sent in
by T. J. Wilson on 6 Oct.
1837. Some names were
added after the paper was
signed.

Elihu Baker
Bird Brown
H. Cloyde
Fielding Justes
J. W. Wilson
Larkin Chandler
William Slage (Slagle)
J. B. Clark
Benjamine Hensley
Edmundson Casey
J. Hottsinger
James C. Brumet
Barnet Casey
Andrew Scrays
Abraham Martin
Samuel Patrick
Elijah Embro
Green B. Chandler
William Duncan
Chas. W. Hunt
Miles Irwin
Hugh Bill
Samuel Beard
Wm. Irvin
William Hensley
Danl. L. Bayles
James Brumet
Mitchell Raulston
Adam May
Addison Treadway
Joseph Howel
John Beaver
Huston Literall
Jordan Literall
Levi Thacker
Frederick Starns
Abraham Starns
Robert Taylor
Benjamine Kidd
James Kean
William Brewer
J. Gibson
J. H. Bell
Wm. Carrol
A. Jones
Elijah H. Shipley
William Hickey
Henry Hickey
Jersey Snuhl(?)
Jon Leslie
O. S. Embree
Thomas Hanley

Box 82. Legislative Papers, Tenn. State Archives. Petition
asking for a survey by the United States of the Railroad from
Paint Rock on N. C. Line to Knoxville in conformity with a resolution adopted at Ashville, 3 Sept. 1831. Sevier Co., Tenn.;
sundry citizens praying appropriation of money to make a survey of a railroad route from Paint Rock to Knoxville. Signed by:

James P. H. Porter
Geo. McCown
J. H. Hill
Anthony Lawson
B. D. Brabson
Wm. McKinach
Felix Auly
Wm. Shamblin
Henry Jenkins
J. Love
Saml Pickird
Jeremiah Mathes
P. M. Wear
James Cerryman
George McMabon
George Snapp
Alexr. Preston
N. C. Porter
T. Reaneau
Wm. Henderson
William Davis
John Jenkins
John Hunter
Joseph Keeler

Wm. K. Love
H. M. Thomas
John Evans
John Clabaugh
John Nichols
John Houk
John Hufpt(?)
Benja. Mallaird
Jesse Matson
John M. Kinzie
John Wear
James Cannon, Jr.
John Walker
Samuel Agnew
Isaac Love
Joseph Snapp
Morris R. Lusk
A. E. Smith
Hugh Duggan
William Crouch
James Canon, Sign.
Christopher Cunningham
William Mathice
J. B. Gistoy

Box 32. Petiton pertaining to Rutherford and Bedford Co. Line, 1823. Signed by:

G. A. Owen
Lamford Dilliard
Lewis H. Dillard
Joel Dilliard
Thomas Keele
William Keele
John Rushing
Richard Keele
Thos. N. Gipson
Jas. Gipson

Eley Eaton
Wm. Jacobs
Lewis Herald
Thomas B. Brown
Nathan Eaton
Thomas Nations
Joseph Alison
Greenbury Jacobs
Alfred Jacobs
Washington Gipson

Another petition regarding the same subject asking that certain sections be attached to Bedford Co., 1823. Signed by

Jacob Hoover
John A. Stowell
Samuel Bean
Jonathan B. Gentry
John Green
Edward Tailor
Aaron Todd
Joseph Alison
Robert Rabourn
Elijah Gentry
Lewis Harrell
Holmes J. Baty
W. Allen B. Reeves(?)
John Steine
John Painter
Nicolas Wich (or Wilch)
Phillips Zinicon
James Stons
Williamather Sher(?)
Joseph Smith
Brady Mayfield
Iace Miller
Reuben Mayfield
C. Jackson
F. Oliver Ferguson

John Newman
Green Freeman
John Newman
Bingiman Ralion(?)
Philip Crowder
Thomas Hall
Nathaniel Crowder
William Bleakley
Bland S. Scott
Squire Crews
John Cates
Thomas Kule
Joshua Cates
Nathaniel Eaton
John McFarland
Willim Jacolz
Hugh B. Jamison
Greenbury Jacobs
Eli Eppes
Marshall Duncan
Hardy Miller
James Gibson
Francis P. Dewe(?)
Eli Eaton
James W. Devoe

J. A. Bleakley   Reazin Gaither
Joseph Newman   John H. Freeman
William S. Margin   John Rushing
Philip Prater   Stephen Vancleave
Edward Johnston   William Kele
William Fowler   Joel Dillard
Frances B. Thrasher   Washington Gibson
Lewis H. Dillard   Thomas B. Brown
William Duncan   Lunsford Dillard

Box 32. Judah Myers petitions for divorce from John Myers, 1 Oct. 1823, Williamson Co., Tenn. They were married 16 Jan. 1819. He was a foreigner by birth and deserted her, leaving her with an infant child. Signed by:

Nichol's Scales   N. Adams
Edward Elam   Wm. S. King

Norfleet Perry married Rachel Perry of Davidson Co., 1816, and they had issue. 1819. Subject of petition and box number not given.

James Kennedy of Warren Co., Tenn., petitions for divorce. He was a citizen of Rendletown District, S. C., for more than twenty years and was a lieutenant and captain for more than eight years in the Creek expedition. He lost his wife because she would not come with him to Tennessee. He has children. Hannah Cummins is his second wife. There is property involved with his children and first wife in North Carolina. Box not given.

Nancy Brachon petitions for divorce from her husband in 1819. Nancy married William Brachem of Warren Co., Tenn., with whom she lived a few months. Box not given.

Petition of citizens of Rutherford Co., asking legislature to favor certain children in 1819. Lettis Little left five children. Box not given.

Hardy Doyle petitions for divorce from his wife in Franklin Co., Tenn., in 1819. Capt. Hardy Doyle married Betsy S. Lumpkin in Georgia in Oct. 1817. Box not given.

Hugh Malony of Greene Co. petitions for divorce, 1819. He married Susannah Conway, daughter of Henry Conway of Greene Co., on 30 Sept. 1812. Box not given.

Isaac Matthews petitions for divorce in 1819. Deposition of Edward Baldwin and others. Tappenes Matthews divorce from Isaac Mathews. Robert Johnson Gulley is mentioned. Box not given.

Josea Jamison petitions for divorce from Nancy Jamison in 1819. They had issue. Maury Co., Tenn. Box not given.

James D. Bennett and Dorcus Irwine (Irvine) petition that their children be made legitimate; Knox Co., Tenn., 1819. Dorcas Irvine was formerly Dorcas Wright of Blount Co., Tenn. The children, Rufus Morgan Bennett and Salley Bennett are to bear the name of Bennett. Box not given.

Box 57. Divorce petition from Campbell Co., Tenn., 1831. Rhoda Dossett married Moses Dossett about 1827, and lived with him 1 year. Deposition of Nimrod Miller and William Heatherty pertaining to petition.

Box 57. Elizabeth Linn petitions for divorce, 1831, Campbell

Co., having married Jacob Linn about 7 years ago, and lived with him for about four months.

Box 57. Blount Co., 1832. Divorce petition of William Hamilton. He married Nancy Morrison in Blount Co. in Oct. 1828, and they lived together about three months.

Box 57. Carroll Co., 1831. Robert Baker petitions for divorce. On 30 June 1829 he married Charlotte Linn of Madison Co. Her child Zinnie was born 17 Nov. 1829, and was not his. Zinnie was the daughter of her uncle Marham Easley. Robert Baker was a minister. The petition is signed by a number of citizens of Carroll Co. on 2 Nov. 1831.

Box 57. Thomas Ross petitions for divorce, Carroll Co., 1831. In 1810 he married Catherine Yost, with whom he lived until 1825.

Box 57. 29 Sept. 1831. Petition of James Baker and Fanny Standley. In 1819 Fanny Maddin had a son called James Maddin. James Baker took the child and reared him until he was twelve years old. He now wants to adopt him. Fanny Maddin married William Standley. Campbell Co., Tenn.

Box 57. Sally Misingo petitions for divorce from Charles Misingo in Campbell Co., Tenn., 1831. They were married Jan. 1828 and lived together for five or six weeks. He left and went to Virginia.

Box 57. Blount Co., 1831. James R. Sexton petitions for divorce. In 1827 he married Elizabeth. A statement as to his good character is signed by: William Penn, Noah Lane, Leroy Bowman, R. P. Bowman, W. H. Stephenson, Geo. Bowman, James Senter, and Jackson Smith. The file contains a number of depositions:
David Hamintree, age 35, Blount Co., on 24 Aug. 1831.
Thomas Cartwright, age 23, 24 Aug. 1831.
Mark Sexton, age 60, 23 Aug. 1831.
Joseph Duncan, age about 40, 23 Aug. 1831.
Mary Carson, age about 25, 23 Aug. 1831.
James Alexander, age about 26, date of deposition not given.

Box 57. Carroll Co., 1831. Rhoda Murfree petitions for divorce from Nimrod Murphree. They were married in 1812, and have four children.

Box 57. William Blalock petitions for divorce from Sary Blalock, Bledsoe Co., Tenn. Sary Blalock left him on 8 Jan. 1828 and went to Rhone (Roane?) Co., Tenn, leaving him with six small children. The affidavit was made before John Billingsley on 7 Sept. 1832. A petition of William Blalock's character was signed by:

Samuel McClellan	Charles Clark
Robert Porter	Elijah Tucker
Mose Roberts	Michael Agee
Philip Sigler	W. Brown
Isaac McPherson	Jon McDowell
Reuben Brown	John Billingsley
John Swafford	

Box 85. Petition asking that Iron Masters keep their places enclosed with fence.
To the Honorable the Legislature of the State of Tennessee now in session in the Town of Nashville, The undersigned petitioners would respectfully solicit your Honorable Body to take into consideration the property of passing a law to compel all

Iron Masters to keep their stables and feeding places inclosed
with a good and sufficient fence so as to keep the stock of other
persons from gathering around such work as the neighbors living
adjacentto some of the Iron works suffer Great damage from their
stock being killed and crippled for the want of such Inclosure;
dated 8 October 1843.   (Signed by):

1	Robert McNeilly	32	M. S. Coleman
2	Tho. J. Kelly	33	L. J. Reynolds
3	Thos. Palmer	34	S. T. Page
4	Tho. McNeilly	35	Edward N. G. Walker
5	Thos Overton	36	Simeon C. D. Walker
6	A. Roberts	37	George Choate
7	Willie Roberts	38	John Matlock
8	J. J. Roberts	39	D. L. Matlock
9	Wm. W. Roberts	40	John Benton
10	J. A. (I. A.) Kams	41	Eli Ashworth
11	John W. Hutton	42	Benjamine Gray
12	Wilkins Corban	43	Wm. Matlock
13	A. H. McCallam	44	Jas. A. Edmund
14	R. J. McCollom	45	T. Carnes
15	W. T. Reynolds	46	Simon Durard
16	Thomas Murrell	47	James Hicks
17	Bathol Smith	48	Joseph Durard
18	John Hall	49	Wm. M. Norman
19	Charles Hedges	50	R. L. Dundway (Dunnaway)
20	Robt. Livingston	51	James B. Reynolds
21	Peter R. Light	52	Dennis H. Tilley
22	John H. Ladd	53	Thomas M. Wheeler
23	Richar Cock	54	Wm. A. Willey
24	W. C. Glenn	55	Samuel W. Sanders
25	D. D. Pritchard	56	John C. Light
26	M. A. Reynolds	57	W. T. McClelland
27	Robert Oakley	58	John W. Fussell
28	R. Larkins	59	Thos. M. Reynolds
29	D. L. Matlock	60	P. T. Bledsoe
30	John L. Martin	61	Tillman Edwards
31	G. W. Larkins		

(Note: No. 50's name is badly obliterated, and Dunnaway
is the editor's interpretation - E. R. W.)

Box 85. Maury Co., Tenn. 14 June 1820. To the Honorable
Representatives of this State, Greetings: We your memorials do
present you this petition mendicating that the aggrievances of
many of us your constituents and our citizens may be (alleviated?).
     The first thing that we excite your attention to and lay
the same before your equitable consideration for redress, is
the important suit which freed this state from the detrimental
detrusions and devastations of the State of North Carolina our
depracations are that those gentlemen who were defendants in
behalf of this state be redressed. We abjure all temporal authority except that of our sovereign we acknowledge no preemi-
nence save our constitution and for their lavish and voluntary
expenditure we with them only mendicate a reciprocity of bene-
fits.
     The next excitement is that those acting or those that have
acted under their regularities of North Carolina have been redressed undeservedly by this state. Col. R. Burton who was the
active instrument of North Carolina endeavoring to deprive this
State of her inevitable right to have been permitted to survey
seven miles from the beginning of his entry, which survey encludes
many of the settlers on public lands who by this last cession
were given an occupancy we your petitioners depricate that you
may duly take in consideration the grievances of those settlers
and alleviate them by placing Burton in an equal footing with
other land claimants or by giving them a redress by which their

detriment may be equal with other settlers in public lands in
the name of that Justice which breathes charity to man we seek
equity for all the inhabitants of their state. May it therefore
please this house to abolish every penal and disabling laws,
which in any manner infringes equal liberty and Justice.
And we your petitioners do ever pray... (Signed by):

Andrew Caradine	Simeon Perry
Michael Robinson	Wyatt Harris
Waller McConnell	Smal Fairies
Henry Harris	E. P. Abernathy
Nathan Coffey	Andrew M. Lackey
Thomas Canadine	Joel Coffey
Alexander Osburn	R. G. Abernathy
Wallis Hays	Wm. Lackey
David Abernathy	Landon Coffey
Enoch Needham	George Johnston
James Osburne	Wm. H. Lee
Wm. J. Johnston	John Curry
John G. Abernathey	Thomas Bell
Evender Kennedy	James Smith
James Collings	James Howard
John Williams	Joe T. Curry (?)
John H. Bills	James M. Lea
Samuel Davis	Saml Gadden
Dan Williams	Elisha Estes
Jacob Williams	William Finley
Geo. M. Johnston	Will A. Johnson
Lemuel L. Bowers	Taswell S. Alderson
George White	William Knott
Lewis Needham	Sylvanus W. Smithson
Bailey Needham	Armstead Blankenship
Isaac Needham	J. J. Alderson
James Merryman	James Turney
Isaiah Tidwell	Adam Cline(?)
James O. Alexander	James Garret
M. P. Abernathy	Julius Woodwald
William Smitherman	Charles Murphey
John Tidwell	Michael Lancaster
John Eddleman	William L. Hays
A. B. Alexander	John McKissick
Robert Pearce	James Sourrell
Lewis Watts	James Tidwell
Josiah Murphey	Abner Osburn
Wm. Pearce	Mathias Georgas
James T. Crofford	Agrippa Nicholas
Spencer Clack	Robert McKissick
Thomas B. Henry	James McGilley
Archibald McKissack	Nathaniel Osburne

Box 85. Perry Co. To the Honourable the General Assembly of the
State of Tennessee now setting. Your petitioner William Tucker
prays your Honourable Body to grant him a preference right to
twenty five acres of land in Perry Co. on Buffaloe River including a place known by John Smith's old Fish Trap Shoal for the
purpose of building a Mill. Your petitioner would further shew
that the land is vacant and entirely unappropriated and that he
has no other views only for the purpose aforesaid which he believes would be of considerable benefit to the neighborhood and
Publick Generally which will shew by their unanimous petition in
accordance with your Humble Petitioner who in duty bound prays
etc.   (Signed by) William Tucker.
We the undersigned would shew to your Honorable Body that
we are citizens of Perry County and in the vicinity of the plan
spoken of in the above petition. (We) unanimously agree with
Mr. Tucker and Hope that his petition may be granted.

We in duty bound will ever pray, etc.:

1	West Wood	55	John Epperson
2	R. C. Patterson	56	Lewis W. Horner
3	Allen G. Tucker	57	Asa Epperson
4	B. Brown	58	(?) Horner
5	Wm. Culleh	59	Gard Bird
6	Jeremiah Wood	60	Wm. Daniel
7	Wilkerson Parish	61	John Daniel
8	John Winns	62	John Young
9	Jas. Doherty	63	Hardy Oquin
10	James Kenney	64	James Scott (?)
11	C. Moore	65	Daniel Oquin
12	William G. Patton	66	Jacob Coplin
13	Jesse Childress	67	Benjamine Stenitte
14	Giles Copeland	68	John Copeland
15	Richard Scroggans	69	Benjamine Hensley
16	Ely A. Griffin	70	James Copeland
17	Jessee Dobbs	71	Wm. Kelley
18	Robt. Johnston	72	Thomas Smith
19	John Easley	73	Thos. Sunnan (Sunman)
20	Lemuel Glass	74	William James
21	Eleaner Parrish	75	Evan Smith
22	John Hunt	76	Jessee Parkes
23	Amos Randel	77	John Horner
24	Wm. Holmey	78	Thomas Medlock
25	David Walker	79	Horner Cude
26	William Thomas	80	Ruben Griffin
27	John Davis	81	David Hufstedler
28	David Bunch	82	Moses Copland
29	William Wilburn	83	Smith Medlock
30	John Scragins	84	Richard Delebs
31	Oliver French	85	Jessee Simons
32	Ambros Hill	86	Ezekil Crowder
33	Simeon Campbell	87	Richard Cates
34	Josiah Brown	88	Leonard Barnitt
35	David W. Evans	89	George W. Shelton
36	Edmon Stabaugh	90	Selather Campbell
37	Josiah Glass	91	James Thu(?)
38	Joseph Tucker	92	John Sisco
39	Lewis Horner	93	James Win
40	Jesse Curry	94	Josiah Hill
41	John Meaders	95	John Brown
42	Dickson Hooper	96	Abraham Davidson
43	Standley Johnson	97	Hartwell Barhane
44	Williamson Maosney(?)	98	William Ragsdale
45	David Hustdler (sic)	99	William Young
46	John Bunch	100	William Mose
47	Jacob Childers	101	Thomas Bird
48	John T. Talley	102	William Bird
49	Abraham Davidson	103	Mical french (sic)
50	Isaac Bacon	104	John Middleton
51	James Penyhouse	105	John Campbell
52	name deleted	106	Elbert Mathew
53	Abraham Bouckhan	107	Nathaniel Renfrew
54	Aaron Bouldwin	108	Elijah Welch

Box 32. 1823. William Little, by birth a Scotchman but for the last 25 years a citizen of the U. S. of America and for 5 years a citizen of White Co., Tenn., owns landed property with the State of Tennessee. On 25 July 1823(?) he was accidentally drowned, and he left no will. 28 May 1823. He brought his brother Thomas Little and family with him from Scotland with the expressed determination of his inheriting the estate of the said William Little, dec. Thomas Little now lives in White Co., Tenn., and is the only known blood relation to William Little on the

continent of America, etc. The petition is signed by:

Joseph P. Dibrell
Philip Mallory
Alexander Reed
Peter Howard
Wm. Parks
Peter Foster
Saml. Gassaway
Thos. B. Eastland
John H. Anderson
John W. Hoffman
C. Dibrell
Anthony Dibrell
G. W. Anderson
Edmond Carrell
Martin Waddell
John Herbert
Mark Lowery
Vinson Woods
Robert H. Davis
W. C. Butan
A. Lowery
Thomas Long
George Reesce
Richard Nelson
C. Fen. Gardeniar(?)

Jerre Lincoln
Charles S. Barthe
Levi Olliver
John W. Ford
W. F. Bennet
Chas. Mannird
W. Leftwich
John Smith
C. Hoffman
Alex B. Lane
Lewis Fletcher
Sevier Evans, Capt.
Sam Thatober(?)
W. M. Hunter
Joseph Atwater
George Waddell
Jas. H. Jenkins
John Jett
Nath. Evans
William Glenn
George Price
Wm. Gist
Thomas Lyons
David Davis
William Mathews

Box 10. 1812. David Rowland of Humphreys Co. petitions to be pensioned by the state. He was wounded by the hostilities of our savage for the Indians (sic). Signed by a large number of citizens of Humphrey County.

The following record is taken from Legislative Petitions of 1813 pertaining to the removal of the county seat from Jefferson to Murfreesboro in Rutherford Co. It is in State Archives Legislative Papers Box 11. This is an old news item. "Report of the improved Lots in the town of Jefferson." The file contains a number of papers, on which are found the following names:

B. Shipley from Maryland
T. Sappington from Maryland
B. Coleman from Virginia
J. Bradley from Virginia
George Simpson from Virginia
Claresse Bushoug, woman of color from one of the
    French islands
A. Harris from Kentucky
T. Mitchell from East Tennessee
N. B. Rose from North Carolina
D. Patton from West Tennessee
Joel Dyer from East Tennessee
J. L.Armstrong from Kentucky
A. Porter from East Tennessee
J. Allen from Virginia
J. Hill from North Carolina
G. R. Nash from Virginia

List of Entry Takers and Surveyors from each county, Nov. 1823. This paper was found in the land office of the State Archives.

COUNTY	ENTRY TAKER	SURVEYOR
Carter	Alford W. Taylor	Leonard Taylor
Washington	John Neilson	Spencer E. Gibson
Sullivan	Jacob Sturm	John Anderson
Campbell	Moses P. Swan	Joseph Hart
Claiborne	Thomas L. Walker	Walter Evans

COUNTY	ENTRY TAKER	SURVEYOR
Jefferson	Caswell Lee	Wm. Taylor
Knox	Robert Lindsay	Robert Armstrong
Anderson	John Gibbs	Robert M. Carny
Cocke	Thomas Gray	Jonathan Woods
Roane	Addison Currick	John Farris (or Furris)
Morgan	John Ridington	Benjamine White
Rhea	Robert Locke	James Wilson
Hamilton	Cornelias Mullican	John Patterson
Franklin	John C. Pryor	George Gray
Smith	Thomas M. Nutt	Robert J. Chester
Davidson	Jos. L. Ewing	Saml. Weakley
Giles	Charles C. Abernathy	James Patterson
Maury	John C. Brook	Alex. Jackson
Dickson	Sterlin Brewer	Thomas Williams
Montgomery	Isaac A. Dennison	John Caldwell
Stewart	James D. Russell	Wm. Bayless
Humphreys	Wm. W. Mallory	Nimrod Murphey
Perry	James Dickson	Wm. Patterson
Marion	David Rankin	Daniel C. Pryor
Sevier	John W. Footes	Daniel Carr
Hawkins	Richard Mitchell	James McCarty
Graves	Geo. T. Gillespie	James Patterson
Grainger	Benjamine Craighead	Martin Cleveland
Blount	Andrew Cowan, Jr.	Robert Wear
Warren	Wm. Lusk	Aaron Higginbotham
Jackson	John Wilson	Wm. W. Woodfolk
Bledsoe	Robert Fister	Peter Hoodanpyle
Sumner	Ashley Stanfield	James Blakemore
Wilson	James Allcorn	Thomas Edwards
Rutherford	James D. Martin	Hugh Robinson
Robertson	James Sawyers	Andrew Stewart
Lincoln	Vance Greer	Joel Pinson
Williamson	Hinchey Pettway	Gen. L. Nolen
Bedford	Abram Martin	Joel H. Webster
Hickman	Robert Shegog	James Witherspoon

Miscellaneous Papers

These documents are not filed or arranged but were found stored in a box at the State Archives.

Cocke Co. Deed from Wm. Small to Alexander Outlaw for 218 acres. On 6 Aug. 1800 William Small of Cocke Co., Tenn., conveyed land to Alexander Outlaw of Jefferson Co., Tenn; the land is that whereon said Small now lives and William Thornton formerly did live, on Big Peagon River, adjoining (land of) said Thornton, John Nave, and Wm. Bells. The deed was witnessed by Paul McDermott, Chas. T. Porter, and Thomas Mitchell. Proved in Cocke Co., Tenn., Aug. Term, 1804.

Cocke Co., Tenn.; 5 Feb. 1799. John Nave, Sr., of Cocke Co., for 100 lbs of Virginia money conveys to John Nave, Jr., of the same county, land on Pigeon River, adjoining Henry Nave's part of the original grant no. 1067.

Jefferson Co., 14 May 1796. John Nave of Jefferson Co., Tenn., conveys to Jacob Nave of said county a tract of land on Pegeon (Pigeon?) River in Jefferson Co., adjoining Henry Nave's line.

Jefferson Co., 12 Oct. 1792. William Bell conveys to John Nave land in Jefferson Co.

(Miscellaneous unsorted papers)

Deposition of Dave Smith concerning land from grants 1068 and
1082 made in 1809, Carter Co., Tenn. David Smith of Bertie Co.,
N. C., the only surviving heir of David Smith, dec., made oath
before Nathan Hendrise, J. P. for Carter Co., that he is informed
and he believes that his father David Smith, formerly of Washington Co., Tenn., did make two entries in Carter County's office
of no. 1068 and no. 1082 for 200 acres each, and that a grant
was never issued on same.

Deposition concerning land made in 1807, Carter Co., Tenn., on
10 July 1807. Titer Crowel of Culpeper Co., Va., made oath before Nathan Hendrix, J. P. of Carter Co., that he made entry of
150 acres of land of no. 2459, to the best of his recollection
and belief, in Carter County's office and that no grant was ever
issued on the same.

Carter Co., 10 Feb. 1808. James Woods and Henry Woods, heirs of
John Woods, dec., both of Currituck Co., N. C., made oath that
they are informed that their father John Woods made entry in the
Carter County office for 200 acres of land on no. 2214, which
said entry has never been granted, nor has any warrant ever been
issued on that.

Deposition of John Hutcheon made 1814 about land of no. 1992,
granted 1779 to Thomas Hutchen. Maury Co., Tenn. John Hutchins,
heir at law of Thomas Hutchens, dec., made oath before James
Love, J. P. of Maury Co., Tenn., that said Thomas Hutchens in his
life time made an entry in Carter County for no. 1992, dated 19
Oct. 1779, for 300 acres on Christie's Road, near the Long Island,
and that all legal fees were paid and that there never was a
warrant issued for the same.

Beaufort Co., N. C. George Warkard of the said county made oath
that in 1785, at the request of Francis Williams who had been a
soldier in the N. C. Cont. Line, he (Warkard) sold John Gray
Blount a land warrant which was for the said Williams. The grant
was assigned by John Gray Blount to Gen. James Robertson on 15
May 1807. (The document is in poor condition and has partly
disintegrated).

No. 148. Robert Young, marked "Invalid." (Only a small piece
of the record).

No. 1253. Grant to Robert Young, Jr., for 400 acres in Green Co.,
Tenn., registered in Green Co., Book D, page 73, on 23 Oct. 1795.
This appears to be a fifty shilling grant. It is also recorded
in Washington Co. Book E, page 63, dated 23 Nov. 1793. (The
document is partly missing).

No. 408. William White; 4995 acres located on Duck River below
Gen. Green's land on the north side of said river running down
including the mouth of a creek where the commissioners and
guards crossed when they returned from running out Gen. Green's
land, and extending up the said creek and down the said river
for Complement. Rutherford Co., Tenn.: Joseph Dickson made oath
on 29 Oct. 1806 that he was commissioned by William White of
Burke Co., N. C. Thomas Simpson made oath in Burke Co., N. C.,
that about 1794 he received a warrant for 4995 acres on Duck
River adjoining or opposite Gen. Greene's land, and that William
White sent the warrant to Sipson's house. 17 Nov. 1806.

No. 90. The heirs of James Hodges, 640 acres, based on service
as private in the N. C. Cont. Line; issued 22 March 1804. James

Hodges of Edgecombe Co., N. C., as heir at law of James Hodges, dec., a private in the N. C. Line, relinquishes all rights to the said grant to Thomas Macnair and Dr. Henry Haywood, 28 Aug. 1805. These men in turn assign the same to John Armstrong.

No. 89. To the heirs of Benjamine Bell, a private in the N. C. Line; issued 17 Feb. 1804. John Bell on 11 Dec. 1804 as a resident of Camden Co., N. C., transferred the same to Jacob Mercer in the presence of Malachi Sawyers. Jacob Mercer of Smith Co., Tenn., assigned it to Armstead Stubblefield and James Davison on 21 June 1806, with Wm. Stephenson and Hugh Stephenson as witnesses.

No. 51. David Dawley, corporal; 428 acres; issued 19 Dec. 1801. F. Garvey note to Howell Tatum, Esq., of Camden Co., N. C., on 25 Nov. 1804. Having taken the liberty of sending a land warrant granted to David Dawley for 428 acres, having deposed of to Capt. Wells Sawyer, you will please deliver to him or order and oblige. J. Hall of Currituck Co., N. C., witnessed the same. David Dawley, late a corporal in the N. C. Line, in the Regt. of State Troops in the service of the U. S., sold the grant to Patrick Garvey on 24 Feb. 1801.

No. 78. The heirs of John Jordon; 640 acres. John Jordon was a private in the N. C. Line. The grant was issued 18 Dec. 1802. Samuel Jordon and John Jordon on 17 Jan. 1803 assigned this. In 1805 Hugh Williams assigned it to Henry Goodloe. On 17 Aug. 1805, M. D. Williams assigned it to M. Duke Williams. On 28 June 1806 Henry Goodloe transferred it to Thompson Wright.

No. 77. Joseph Harrison, private; 640 acres; issued 18 Dec. 1802. Joseph Harrison assigned the same to George W. Donnell on 14 Feb. 1806, with Wm. Falkner a witness. Darnell (sic) assigned the same to John Hillis and Robert McLaughlin on 21 June 1806.

No. 110. Richard Harper, marked "Invalid." This was a ten pound warrant.

No. 23. Jno. McDonald had warrant delivered on 28 May 1818. (Rest of document missing).

No. 76. The heirs of Samuel Brient; 640 acres. Samuel Brient or Brunt was a private in the N. C. Cont. Line. The grant was issued in Dec. 1802. Caleb Perkins, J. P. of Camden Co., N. C., made oath on 24 April 1807 before Henry Forles that Samuel Brunt, dec., a soldier in the last war, left as his legal heir one John Powell. Powell assigned the grant to David Durking who in turn assigned it to Benjamine Harvey in 1807.

No. 450. Charles Partee; 5000 acres; 25 Oct. 1784. The land was on the north side of Green Lick Creek. Daniel Leatherman, living on the road leading from Salisbury to Salem on Ready Creek, was son-in-law to the within named Charles Partee, who has been engaged to survey the within warrant.

No. 462. Thomas Winston; 5000 acres lying on the Mississippi River, including the White Bluff, 12 Jan. 1785. Joseph Winston of Stokes Co., N. C., received the land in October 1803.

No. 511. Pleasant Henderson, no. 20; 5000 acres in Greene Co. on Little Tom Bigby Creek; issued 10 July 1784. The same entry was transferred to Robert Burton on 19 Nov. 1783. Pleasant Henderson of Orange Co., N. C., assigned it to Robert Burton in Jan. 1801.

Nos. 429 and 427. Joseph Bullard, dec. Grant no. 76 dated Nov.
1790 for 80 acres. Ditto no. 70. Another to the same for 200
acres, and grant no. 819 dated 19 Nov. 1790 for 200 acres, and
no. 71 dated 4 July 1810. No. 76 a fifty shilling grant to
Joseph Bullard in Hawkins Co., 80 acres on the south side of
Holstein River, on Beaver Creek. This grant was registered on
2 Aug. 1792 in Ledger A, p. 79, Jefferson Co. No. 819, Joseph
Bullard, 200 acres, Green Co.; a fifty shilling grant on south
side of Holston River adjoining another place of the said Bullard's. This was registered in Jefferson Co., 2 Aug. 1792 in
Ledger A, p. 76. David Stuart of Jefferson Co., made a sworn
statement on 11 May 1810 before William Mills, J. P. for that
county. Affidavit of John Bullard, Grant no.76 and 819. John
Bullard one of the heirs of Joseph Bullard, dec., made oath
that he searched for the grant to Joseph Bullard, dec. The
deponent said he was a chain carrier in surveying the 200 acre
tract on 2 Oct. 1809.

No. 166. William-Shield, a certificate for 5000 acres, 2 March
1812. No. 1359 a ten pound grant by N. C. to Stockley Donelson
on the waters of the Nolychicky River on 20 Aug. 179-(?). Green
Co. Has plat. (The land is) adjoining that of Thos. Rees. William Shields in an affidavit on 2 March 1812, claimed the title
of the said grant to Donelson dated 28 Aug. 1795 before Luke
Lea, commissioner of East Tennessee.
    Deed dated 28 Oct. 1801 from John Newman, sheriff of Green
Co., to Saymore Catching for 5000 acres. This was a sheriff's
sale and was witnessed by James Hays and Jas. Brown.
    Affidavit of William Shields in Green Co., before John Rus-
sell, J. P., and Samuel Y(?). Balch, on 25 Jan. 1812. John
Shield, Jr., (and) Henry Messimer carried the chain for the survey of William Shields' 5000 acre grant.
    Deed dated 4 Jan. 1812, Saymore Catching to William Shield,
both of Green Co., witnessed by Abm. Born, James Hays, and James
Shields.
    Conveyance of Stockley Donelson to John Love, Josiah Watson,
and Samuel Love for 5000 acres, witnessed by George Gordon, Jr.,
D. Squire, Samuel A. W. A. Love, Charles J. Love, Washington J.
Washington, and George Gordon. George Gordon appeared before
John Gregg, J. P. for Green Co., and deposed that in the spring
of 1795 he made a survey for S. Donelson in the said county for
5000 acres, and that same time, month of July following, John
Love of the State of Virginia purchased a considerable quantity
of land from S. Donelson, etc.

No. 25. Geirge Wilson; a N. C, grant no. 905, a fifty shilling
grant. Grant to Andrew Greer for 640 acres in Green Co. on the
west side of Four Mile Creek at the ford where the Indian path
crosses the said creek, and running down the said creek for
compliment.

No. 56. Samuel George; a copy of grant to Edward George for 200
acres. No. 832. Jefferson Co., 28 May 1807; granted 12 May 1789
(C. B.) Edward George and Edward George, Jr. Registered in Jefferson Co. on 12 Nov. 1814. Thomas McCuiston(?) Deputy Surveyor
in land.

No. 394. Deposition of John Garkins concerning land in No. 2366
made 1811. Carter Co., Tenn. John Garkins, heir of Francis Garkins, dec., made oath that his father Francis Garkins regarding
entry in Carter County's office, no. 2366, for 200 acres on 15
March 1811.

No. 341. Deposition of John and Dave Smith, made in 1814 as to
the lands from no. 944. Carter Co., Tenn.: John and David, sons

of William Smith, made oath regarding land due the orphans of said Smith. The land was on the north fork of the Holston River.

Henry Spar deposed in 1807 that he made an entry of land in 1780.

No. 393. Deposition of William Young, made in 1814 concerning the land of no. 1838, Hawkins Co., Tenn. William Young as one of the heirs of Robert Young, dec., deposed regarding the entry of land on 7 Oct. 1779. Deposition dated 30 Nov. 1814.

Deposition of Jacob Carpenter made in 1809 concerning the land from no. 2585 and 2756 in Carter Co., dated 25 July 1809. Jacob Carpenter of Fauquier Co., Va., made oath regarding the entry.

Hugh Parks of Greenville Co., S. C., appointed William Roark of Sumner Co., Tenn., his attorney to sell 274 acres of land to John Harper. The land was on the Cumberland River beginning at the first bluff below House Shells pond and recovered by said Parks for his service in the N. C. Line. Edward Gwin and John Harper were witnesses. Sworn to in Pendleton Dist., S. C., on 5 Nov. 1802. Registered in Sumner Co., Book B, page 271.

No. 379. Deposition of Joseph Tipton made 2 Dec. 1814 concerning the land of no. 777, Warren Co., Tenn.; 500 acres on Sink Creek adjoining Christopher Cunningham, Wm. McNabb, Thomas Farrow, Samuel Denton, including the plantation whereon the said Tipton now lives.

No. 454 and 455. Deposition claiming land in no. 15 and no. 16 by entries but no grant issued Deposition made 1809. Carter Co., Tenn., 6 March 1809. Cornelius Barker, entry in Sullivan County.

No. 342. Richard Moon, deposition as to land in no. 21. Carter Co., Tenn. Richard Moon of Hyde Co., N. C.; 640 acres of land on Long Creek on south side of Nolichucky River, on 1 Jan. 1814.

Deposition of Richard White concerning land of no. 46, granted 1778. The deposition was made in 1814 in Carter Co., Tenn. Richard White, son of Richard White, dec.

Grant no. 205. General Assembly Resolution regarding grant for 1000 acres by N. C. to Robert King.

Richard Jones agreement. Craven Co., N. C. Andrew Richardson certificate states: "I have let Mr. William Phillips have one land warrant of 640 acres granted to William Cole and endorsed to me." A quit claim deed by said Richardson dated 23 Feb. 1798. Fred Fonville and Wm. B. Fonville were witnesses.

Bazell Kornegay. Letter of attorney. Land warrant for 1000 acres, no. 3610. Duplin Co., N. C., 23 March 1803, and Mr. Isaac Bezzel, etc.

No. 392. Heirs of Emanuel Carter. Deposition of Alfred M. Carter concerning land in no. 1950 and made in 1814, Carter Co., Tenn. Alfred M. Carter was one of the heirs of Emanuel Carter, dec. and appeared before Charles Reno, acting J. P., and stated that Emanuel Carter made an entry in Carter County's office of no. 1950 for 350 acres adjoining Abraham Rice, and running down both sides of the creek. Deposition dated 13 Dec. 1814.

Perquiman Co., N. C., Samuel Smith and Hannah Smith of said

Co., heirs at law of Thomas Eduless, late a musician in Capt.
Stedman's Co. in the 5th Regt. of the N. C. Line in the Revolution, do hereby appoint Joseph H. Bryan their attorney, 24 July
1821.

Sumner Co., July 1797. Ordered that John Fisher be appointed
administrator of Joshua Fisher, dec. John Fisher enters bond
for $500.00 with William Hall and James McKain as securities.

Grant no. 544. Roane Co. Affidavit of John Trimble, Sr., before Nathaniel Cox, J. P., that he had 100 acres of land
in Carter's office, no. 2075 in Washington Co., adjoining Isaac
Taylor's line upon Holly Creek. 7 Dec. 1800.

Grant no. 321. Alexander McKee and Reuben Whithite, Carter Co.,
Tenn John Carter, entry taker of Washington Co., warrant no.
1370 dated 15 May 1799. Also appeared Samuel Williams and made
oath that he was the original enterer. John Ireland is not an
inhabitant of the state aforesaid. 14 Aug. 1799. Washington
Co., Tenn.; William Bayles assigned it to George Nail on 1 May
1800. A. Aeston (sic) Coppock a witness. On 17 Dec. 1802 George
Neal assigned the same to Reuben Willhight, with James Ballinger
a witness. Nathaniel Taylor, sheriff of Carter Co., on 13
Aug. 1798...to Landon Carter who sold it by public sale to Aaron
Cunningham who vested the title in Joseph Ford and to William
Bayles.

Grant no. 490. David Reece to Thos. Johnston, certificate for
122 acres. 9 Aug. 1783. David Reece of McLinburgh Co., N. C.,
and Thos. Johnston of Washington Co., N. C. Knox Co., Tenn.:
Cornelius Newman made an affidavit before Josiah Nichol, J. P.,
that Nathaniel Jones claims title by birtue of a patent issued
to Davis (sic) Reese of N. C. dated 5 Dec. 1778 for 400 acres.
March 1795. John Tye (Comt.) vs. David Rees (Deft.); bill and
injunction. David Rees of Cabarrus Co., N. C., made a quit
claim to Nathaniel Jones of Green Co. for 400 acres in Washington Co. now claimed by John Tye, Jan. 1808. Green Co.: James
Petterson, Deputy Surveyor of the 6th Surveyor Dist., appeared
before Cornelius Newman, J. P., and deposed in regard to survey
of said grant, on 23 Dec. 1808. No. 6, a fifty shilling grant
tp David Reese for 400 acres of land in Washington Co. on the
head of a branch above Great Falls of Waters Lick Creek. (Signed)
Richard Caswell, 9 June 1780.

MISCELLANEOUS STATE RECORDS

NORTH CAROLINA CERTIFICATES
OF SURVEY

Military Warrants issued by the Secretary of State from 3 June
1800 to 19 December 1800. These records are in the Tennessee
Land Office, Nashville.

Soldier's Name	page	Soldier's Name	page
Alexander, William	14	Alexander, Charles	14
Adams, Howell	20		
Barton, Samuel, Jr.	3	Baker, Norris	4
Bradley, Thomas	4	Bailey, Joseph	5
Barton, Elizabeth	9	Barton, Joseph	9
Bailey, William	10	Barin, John	11
Barry, Richmond D.	13	Berry, Solomon	16
Blackledge, William	24	Blackbourne, James	29
Boyd, John, Jr.	29	Brooks, Stephen	33
Chambless, Joel	1	Cheek, William, heirs	5
Coppage, James, heirs	8	Cherry, Willie	11,16
Christmas, William	14,41	Creacy, Thos. and	
Cook, Richard	23,24	and Wm. Murray	30
Coonrod, Nicholas	34	Coart, John	39
Davis, Samuel	2	Dabney, John	6
Dixon, Benjamine	8	Danley, Samuel	12
Deal, Isaac	13	Darnell, George	19,20
Dange, Enoch	25	Davis, James,	30
Ellis, Robert	4		
Freeman, Samuel	15	Foster, Wm.	28
Foster, John	41		
Green, William	2	Gibson, Colm	9
Givin, James	12	Gilston, David	15
Givin, Edward	23		
Harris, Edward	22,28,32,33	Hardin, Moses	24
Johnson, Benjamin	1	Jones, Evan	32
McLemore, Robert	3	McGee & Tooley	7
Murry & Parrish	7	Murrey, Thomas, heirs	10
Moreen, Stephen	12	Moore, William	16
McCauley, Mathew	17	Mahan, Archibald	21

Soldier's Name	Page	Soldier's Name	Page
Mouldin, Ambrus	25	McKnight, James	34
Molloy, Thomas, 35,37,38,39			
Noble, Mark	6		
Pendergrass, Raleigh, heirs	8	Polk, William	41
Roper, John	5	Russell, Buchnell	17
Roe, Samuel	18	Russell, James	28,36
Robertson, James	40		
Sherrod, William, heirs	12	Stump, Fred	28
Stubblefield, Thomas	31		
Tatum, Howell	18	Tooley, Henry and James	34
Urell, William	2		
Williams, Joseph	2	Wood, John	6,13
Weakley, Samuel	10	White, William	15
Willis, Hayden	21	Weakley, Robert	31
Wheaton, Tisdale and Molloy	35	Wheaton and Tisdale	36,40
		Williams, Nehemiah	41
Yarbrough, Reuben	1	Young, Thomas	3
Young, John	26,27,28	Young, Robert	27

Petition of Johnson Farris, an old soldier of the Revolution, found in the State Archives and Land Office. This petition is dated Washington Co., Tenn., 1826. The papers are in regard to Johnson Farris and John Donelson in the year 1779.

SURVEYORS' CERTIFICATES

These certificates, numbered 1432 to 2095 inclusive were issued between 1 Nov. 1814 to May 1816 in the Sixth District. They are in the Tennessee State Archives at Nashville.

Adams, Samuel, heirs,	1466	Armstrong, William	1475
Armstrong, William	1476 and 1477	Arnold, Harat	1590, 1594
		Allison, John	1639
Alway, Isaac B.	1625 and 1626	Anderson, Thomas	1814
		Asher, John	1753, 1754
Arginbright, George	1870	Allen, James	1962
Acton, James	1975	Anderson, James	2002
Armstrong, William	2052	Acuff, Spencer	2080, 2081
Blevins, Abraham	1474	Bean, Mordecai	1484
Boyer, Jacob	1507	Bainard, Reuben	1524, 1525
Barnard, Jonathan	1526	Bryan, Benj.	1552-1559 inc.
Bowers, Leonard	1584	Bitner, Samuel L.	1595
Baker, Mindy	1613	Broadhunt, Joseph	1653
Barnes, James, 1682, 1683 and 1684		Bassinger, Jacob	1695
		Babb, Thomas	1729
Bassett, Spencer	1723,1724	Byles, David	1776
Brown, Jesse	1764	Brown, Henry	1802, 1803

Bacon, John	1784	Baker, Isaac	1830,1831
Baker, Samuel	1818	Brumtrutter, Daniel	1848
Boulton, Noah	1844	Boyer, Jacob	1863
Bair, Peter	1860	Buck, Moses	1887
Broyles, David	1869	Bricker, William	1924
Brown, George	1898,1899	Beno, Moses	1940
Brown, George	1931	Broyles, Saml	1983
Bowman, George	1956	Bassendine, Charles	1988
Buck, Ephraim	1986	Bucke, Abraham	1993
Bradley, James	1989	Barger, George	2012
Brown, Joseph	1998	Boothe, Joseph	2023
Burge, Michael	2016,2017	Biggs, John	2091
and 2018		Buckner, James	2086

Conway, Thomas	1456	Cowper, Thomas	1464
Carter, Ellis	1505	Cain, Hugh 1725,1535,1536	
Casey, Daniel	1572	Carriger, John	1578
Carton, Peter	1581	Carriger, G and C.	1582
Carriger, Godfrey	1583	Campbell, Hugh	1594
Cox, William (S.C.)	1627	Cox, Jeremiah	1628
Crockett, Andrew	1650	Crouch, Jesse	1679
Carter, Hiram	1708	Cox, Eliakin	1710
Cox, William (G.C.)	1711	Carter, Benjamin	1713
Clarke, Davie	1721	Carter, Elijah	1737
Carter, John	1738	Carter, Ezekiel	1741
Carter, David	1742	Carter, Hugh	1743
Connor, Julius	1763	Curton, Richard	1776,1777
Campbell, Hugh 1785,1791		Conkin, John	1786
Casey, John	1820	Cox, James (S.C.)	1853,1854
Cox, James (G.C.)	1859	Cowan, John	1876
Cook, John	1928	Cobb, Jessee	1939
Connor, John W.	1952	Cross, Henry	1960
Carringer, Godfrey	1987	Conway, William	2004
Campbell, Andrew	2006	Cain, Hugh	2021
and 2007		Conway, Edward	2035,2036
Colpole, John	2043	Childress, John	2045
Cowan, William	2046	Carter, Caleb	2050
Collins, James	2055	Cunningham, James	2085
Clark, Henderson	2087	Clark, William	2088

Darter, Michael	1481	Doak, John W.	1569
Delany, William	1642	Durkill, Richard	1661
Durkill, Daniel	1662	Donelly, Hezekiah	1696
Dabzell, Francis	1729	Davis, James	1750
and 1728		Drane, Benjamin	1787
Darter, Michael	1798	Deantone, Michael	1828
Daleny, Elmanah R	1839	Dobson, George B.	1862
Dugger, William	1883	Dyche, Andrew	1905
and 1884		Davis, Milley	1917
Dotson, Charles	1921	Durkill, Joshua	1950,1951
Davis, James	1994	Davis, Benjamin	2029,2030
Dickard, John	2068	Dyche, Henry	2092
Dyche, Henry, Jr.	2093		

Early, Nicholas	1458	Eddleman, Leonard	1550
Etherton, Samuel	1551	Elkins, George	1566
Embree, Elihu	1596	Etter, Mary	1660
Elkins, Ralph	1722	Everett, Joseph	1840
Ennis, William 1872,1873		Elkins, Ralph	1918
and 1874		Evans, William	1960
Easterly, Moses	1977	Easterly, Jacob	1981,1978
Eslinger, Jacob	1980	Edwards, John	2078

Fowler, Isaac	1471	Fry, John	1483
Fowler, Thomas	1530	Fudge, Solomon	1547,1548
		and 1549	

Fincher, John	1597	
Faubion, William	1657,1658	
Forgey, James	1732	
Farrens, Jacob	1829	
Farnsworth, George	1834	
Farner, Isaac	2014	
Finley, Samuel	2055,2056	

Fowler, Thomas	1655,1656
Furhour, John	1696
Farnsworth, John	1825,1826
and 1897	
Far, John	1967
Farner, Conrad	2015
Francisco, James	2064

Gillenwaters, Robert	1453
Gann, Adam	1460
Gillenwaters, Joel	1482
and 1492	
Galgarth, Aneas S.	1417
Gibbons, William	1541
Garlan, Ezekiel	1586
Gaines, J. T. and Kin-	
kade	1619
Grubb, Abraham	1647
Guimley, Loftin	1674
Galbrath, James	1897,1688
and 1714	
Gulley, Meedy	1768
Gillenwaters, Thomas	1797
Gragg, William	1864
Gouch, William	1912
Gladdin and Hopper	1914
and 1915	
Gladdin, Joseph	1947
Guin, Daniel	1949
Galbreath, James	1982
Gullick, John	2003
Greenway, George	2040
Gannon, David	2059
Gordon, Robert C.	2090

Guin, Daniel	1459
Gilliam, Hynch	1480
Gladden, William	1485
Gaines, James T.	1513
Gibbins, Epps	1537
Gragg, Thomas	1570
Greer, John	1589
Guister, Adam	1643,1644
and 1645	
Garner, Brice M.	1669
Gray, Asa	1685
Gibson, Henry	1755
Gragg, Henry	1757,1758
Goad, William	1782
Goad, Jacob	1843
Grant, William	1902
Gladdin, William	1913
Guin, Daniel	1932
Green, Arnold	1945
Gladdin, William	1948
Gillespie, Thomas	1963
Gilliland, James	1992
Gregory, George	2019,2020
Gamble, Saml.	2044
Grant, Richard	2079
Glass, John	2094

Hopkins, Thomas 1432 through	
1452, incl.	
Hird, John	1489
Hire, Jacob	1501
Hale, Frederick	1515,1516
Hoff I. and Irons, W.	1560
Heaton, John	1576
Hughes, James	1640,1641
Hughes, David	1651
Hillsley, Christian	1668
Hankins, William A.	1706
and 1707	
Hale, Hugh D.	1734
Hale, Thomas	1765
Hopkins, Jabish	1812
Hull, Frederick	1845
Hampton, Johnson	1882
Howell, James	1890
Hackney, Jacob	1896
Hutspiller, Jacob	1972
Humphreys, Moses	1985
Howry, Daniel	2011
Haines, William	2022
Harrison, Jermiah	2031
Harle, Hazle	2054
Hord, William	2069

Hartsell, Abraham	1461
Hendry, William	1468
Hilton, Adam	1500
Hamilton, Robert	1512
Harle, Hazle	1546
Hale, Hugh D.	1561,1562
Hinkel, Philip	1615
Hyringer, Henry	1648
Harmon, Moses	1665
Howell, Jesse	1693,1694
Humbert, Adin	1712
Hays, Joseph	1715
Henry, Abraham	1751
Hendley, Robert	1811
Houston, William	1835
Harris, John	1865
Hedrick, Wm. (C.C.)	1888
Howell, Jesse	1893
Hollars, Zachariah	1906
Harned, Samuel	1979
Haworth, Abraham	2005
Headrick, William	2013
Harbearson, George W.	2025
Holt, David	2049
Hickman, Micajah	2067
Hodges, Willis	2095

Ingram, Thomas	1499,1538
Iron Factory Co.	1508
Ingran, Thomas	1756

Ingram, Thomas	2061
Ingram, T., and L. Wilson	
	1529

Johnson, James	1531	Justin, Sarah	1575	
Jones, John	1601	Johnston, James	1603	
Johnston, Walter	1629	Jones, William	1666,1667	
Johnson, Joseph	1691	Johnson, John F.	1813	
Johnston, James	1819	Johnston, John	1821	
Justin, Jonathan	1837	Jones, Thomas	1846	
Johnson, Thomas	1886	Jack, John F.	1895	
Jones, George	1961			

Kyle, Absalom	1490,1565	Kipper, Peter	1418	
Kinner, Eskridge C.	1544	Kearns, John	1568	
and 1545		Kincade, David	1621	
Kibler, Jacob	1673	Kearns, George	1627	
Killen, Henry	1740	Klipper, Jacob	1794	
Kinnedy, John	1822,1823	King, William	1841	
and 1824		Kinner, Winder	1891,1892	
King, Andrew	1908,1909	Kilbrey, Matthias	1936	
Kinner, Winder	2026,2027	Kelly, John	2033	
and 2028		Kittering, John	2041	
Keen, Matthias	2042			

Lott, Casper	1467	Lamm, John	1487	
Laughmiller, Jonas	1519	Laughmiller, John	1520	
Long, David	1521	Larkin, William	1522	
Lyons, William	1573	Love, Samuel B.	1608	
Looney, Joseph W.	1630	Lane, Idina	1675,1670	
Lauderdale, John	1698	Looney, Absalom	1705	
Lofty, William	1735	Long, David and James	1766	
Laughmiller, Henry	1795	Leiper, Francis	1799	
Looney, Absalom	1805	Long, Joseph	1806	
Long, James Y.	1808	Looney, David R.	1810	
Laughmiller, Frederick		Lon., Jacob	1885	
1815		Long, Nicholas	1894	
Luntz, Martin	1935	Laughmiller, Jonas	1920	
Lynn, John	2048	Looney, Absalom	2063	

Mitchell, Richard	1494	McMinn, J., and Hamilton R.		
1495, and	1496	1509 and	1510	
McMinn, Joseph	1498,1511	McHenry, Robert	1587,1588	
(and 1597?)		McCollum, John	1606,1607	
Murray, Ephraum	1610,1611	Murray, J. and W.	1612	
Mitchell, William	1614	Miller, Jacob (G.C.)	1620	
Mooneyham, James	1622	Motton, George	1631	
Miller, Jacob (S.C.)	1646	Massengill, Henry	1652	
Moore, Robert	1659,1660	Moorelock, Thomas	1681	
McCurry, Joseph	1689	McCraw, Gabriel	1720	
Milbank, Joseph	1730	McMean, Joab	1760	
Miller, James	1762	Massengill, Henry	1772,1773	
Miller, Thomas	1681	McKee, Alexander	1783	
Myers, George	1792,1793	McCullough, Thomas	1796	
Molton, William	1851,1852	McMurtry, James	1866	
Mitchell, William	1868	Mitchell, Thomas	1889	
McNeese, Evan	1919	Maloney, Hugh	1929	
More, Daniel	1944	Moon, William	1960	
Miller, Peter	1974	Moreland, Charles	1990	
McGee, John	1984	McHenry, Robert	1991	
Maloney, Robert	1991	Mitchell, William G. C.		
Montieth, George	2070	2001		
and 2071				

Nelson, John, Sr.	1462	Nelson, Berryman	1463	
Nicholas, James	1486	Nall, Robert	1999,2000	
Nail, Adam	2062			

Ottinger, Jacob	1616	Odell, Abraham	1867	

Patterson, James   1465
Petrenburger, Peter   1473
Pogue, John   1506
Pope, Simon   1532,1533,1534
Phipps, William   1571
Palmer, Thomas   1663,1664
Pope, Simon   1716
Patterson, James   1736
Phillips, Charles   1847
Painter, Adam   1926
Philin, Thomas   1938
Parsons, James   2010

Parker, Caleb J.   1469
Pilant, Joseph   1491
Parrott, George   1527,1528
  and 1529
Patterson, J. and D. Guin
  1598, and 1599
Pearce, James   1733
Pogue, John   1739
Painter, David   1925
Patterson, James   1933
Perkins, Simon   1976
Pogue, Farmer   2051

Reavis, Moses   1503
Rhea, John   1652,1653,1654
Rankin, David   1686
Richards, John   1809
Rhea, John   1855,1856
Russell, Elijah   1916
Ritchie, Eli   1946
Rinker, Philip   1966
Rogers, William   1995
Reynolds, David   2032
Rockhold, Francis   2047

Russell, Isaac   1574
Rhea, Mathew   1649
Rush, Jacob   1770
Reynolds, William 1832,1833
Reynolds, John   1907
Robertson, (?)   1937
Ramsey, Francisco A.   1957
Russell, David   1968
Rudder, Robert   2008
Rhea, John   2037,2038,2039
Rogers, Benjamin   2084

Simmons, James   1455
Sproul, Thomas   1478,1479
Starns, Geo. and Leonard
  1502
Smith, Anthony G.   1563
Smith, Jacob   1577
Sharp, John   1635,1636
Spurgen, William   1676,1677
Sitton, Samuel   1687
Stoncypher, Absalom   1709
Scott, John   1748
Stockley, John   1764
Shipley, Nathan   1789,1790
Starns, Leonard   1836
Shipley, Eli   1857,1858
Stuart, David   1903,1904
Smith, Charles, heirs of
  1934
Smith, Coleman   1954,1955
Stuart, Hamilton   1970,1971
Sailor, Jacob   1996
Shields, David   2034
Sullivan, Burwell   2065
Smith, Stephen   2075

Scruggs, William   1470,1472
Stubblefield, Witt   1495
Snider, William   1504
Shropshire, William   1563
Shanks, Michael   1567
Shipley, Nathan   1609
Scott, John   1637,1638
Shurfey, John   1680
Shannon, Joseph   1692
Stuart, Thomas   1719
Shields, David   1759
Smith, Robert   1778,1779
  1780, and 1781
Sturdivant, Anthony   1849
  and 1850
Sheckless, Abraham   1922
Snodgrass, James   1941,1942
Smith, Stephen   1953
Stanfield, Samuel   1964
Smith, Nathaniel   1973
Sanders, Arden   2024
Shough, John   2060
Shannon, William   2072
Shields, James   2089

Taylor, James P.   1454,1592
  and 1593
Tucker, Archibald   1523
Thompson, James   1605
Taylor, Nathaniel   1672
  and 1881
Taylor, Andrew   1744,1745
  1746,1747, and 1838
Temple, James   1927
Tibbs, John   2082,2083

Tompkins, William and Ben-
  jamin   1579
Thompson, Alexander   1604
Tiery, Nathan   1623,1624
Thompson, John   1717,1718
Tucker, William   1731
Taylor, John   1842
Taylor, James P.   1875,1876
  1878,1879,1880, and 1901

Wendell, David   1457
Walker, Edwards   1514
Wilson, Samuel   1540,1703
  1704,1807

Waddekk, Seth Q.   1485
  (Waddell?)
Wingar, A. and P.   1542
Winegar, Frederick   1543

Wills, Lewis	1580	White, Lawson	1585
Wilson, John	1602	Willer, John	1617,1618
Waddell, John	1654	Whitlock, Alexander	1671
Waggoner, David	1749,1752	White, William	1767
White, Samuel	1769	Weston, William	1775
Wood, Elijah	1788	Winegar, Frederick	1800
Winegar, John	1804	and 1801	
Woods, Joseph	1816,1817	Woolaver, John and Philip	
White, William	1910,1911	1827	
White, George	1923	Welty, John	1930
Wier, Joseph	1943	Williamson, Clement	2009
Wilson, Samuel	2057,2058	Walden, James	2066
Young, William	1699	Young, John	1700
Young, Robert	1701	Young, Arthur	1702
Young, Jonathan	1900		

The original certificates are on file in the Tennessee State Archives, Nashville, Tennessee.

NORTH CAROLINA LAND GRANTS, 1793-1794

These grants are in the State Land Office of the Tennessee State Archives, and show the grant no., to whom issued, the date of the grant, service and other remarks. The book has no index.

No. 1614. Issued to Benjamin Coleman, 27 April 1793. Coleman was a captain in the North Carolina Line. The grant was registered in Davidson County.

No. 219. Issued to Benjamin Smith, 7 March 1785. Smith was a sergeant in the North Carolina Line.

No. 2499. Issued to Lardner Carter, 18 Nov. 1795. Granted for the services of Job Jackson, as a private soldier.

No. 453. Oliver Williams, issued 5 Nov. 1795. Granted to David Hay, heir at law to Joseph Hay, a ten pound for every 100 acres grant. No service shown.

No. 486. Martin Armstrong, issued 15 Sept. 1787. Grant was based on the service of David Bothwell, private in the North Carolina Line.

No. 429. Wm. McClure, issued 15 Sept. 1787. William McClure was a surgeon in the North Carolina Line. The land was located in Davidson County.

No. 451. Ezekiel Douglas, issued 27 Nov. 1793,"a ten pound for every 100 acre grant." No service mentioned. The land was in Davidson County.

No. 71. Benjamin Carter, issued 14 March 1786. Carter served as a captain in the North Carolina Line. The land was in Davidson County.

No. 346. Heirs of Jacob Castlemen, issued 27 Nov. 1792. Benjamin, Jacob and Joseph Castlemen were heirs of Jacob. No service shown. A "ten pound for every 100 acre grant." The land was in Davidson County.

No. 376. John Provine, issued 26 June 1793. A "ten pound for every 100 acres grant." No service shown.

No. 2493. Willoughby Williams, issued 1 April 1794. Granted to John Bates, a private in the North Carolina Line. The land was in Davidson County.

No. 2494. Willoughby Williams, issued 1 April 1794 for the service of James Cousin, a private in the North Carolina Line. The land was in Davidson County.

No. 1101. Willoughby Williams, issued June 1790. Based upon the services of William Fryer as a private in the North Carolina Line.

No. 127. Anthony Newman, issued 10 July 1788. A "ten pound for every 100 acres" grant. No service shown.

No. 180. Moses Shelby, issued 26 March 1795, for the services of Martin Armstrong, surveyor. The land was in Davidson County.

No. 2591. Thomas Molloy, issued 7 March 1796, for the services of Marmaduke Moore as a private in the North Carolina Continental Line. The land was in Davidson County.

No. 179. Thomas Molloy, issued 26 March 1795 for the grant to Martin Armstrong. The land was in Davidson County.

No. 129. Edward Cox, issued 27 April 1793 for his services as a pack horse master in the Commissioners Guard. The land was in Davidson County.

No. 404. William Stuart, issued 26 June 1793. A "ten pound for every 100 acres" grant. The land was in Davidson County.

No. 2512. Thomas Cotton, issued 27 August 1795 for the services of James Smith, private in the North Carolina Line. The land was in Davidson County.

No. 2528. Thomas Henry, issued 8 Dec. 1795. Granted to John Seagrove, private in the North Carolina Line. The land was in Davidson County.

No. 1648. John Lockharts, issued 27 April 1793 for services as a private in the North Carolina Line. The land was in Davidson County.

No. 1606. Howell Tatum, issued 23 Feb. 1793, for services of John Cheason, private in the North Carolina Line. The land was in Davidson County.

No. 2441. James Glasgow, issued 20 Jan. 1794 for the services of Jesse Willard, private in the North Carolina Line. The land was in Davidson County.

No. 104. John Allen, issued 7 March 1786 for the services of Wm. Smith, a private in the North Carolina Line. The land was in Davidson County.

No. 990. Geo. A. Sugg, issued 18 May 1789 for the services of Wm. Shevers or Shivers, private in the North Carolina Line. The land was in Davidson County.

No. 893. George A. Sugg, issued 7 Jan. 1789 for the services of John Stinson, private in the North Carolina Line. The land was in Davidson County.

No. 2472. George Walker, issued 13 Dec. 1792; 640 acres located in Davidson County, on the south side of the Cumberland River. The grant was based on the services of William Gipson, a private.

No. 2139. George Walker; issued 17 May 1793; 640 acres located in Davidson County, on a small creek on the south side of the Cumberland River. The grant was based on the services of William Diggins, a private.

No. 617. John Eburn, issued 15 Sept. 1787; 1645 acres on Stones River, Davidson County. John Eburn was a captain in the North Carolina Line.

No. 1741. James White; issued 20 May 1793; 640 acres on the north side of Cumberland River, in Davidson County. The grant was based on the services of Saml. Guin, a private in the North Carolina Line.

No. 157. Jethro Sumner, issued 29 April 1793 for his services as a brigade general in the Revolution from North Carolina. The grant was for 12,000 acres of land on Big Harpeth River, Arrington Creek, Stuart and Mill Creeks in Davidson County.

No. 11. Jethro Sumner, issued 10 July 1788 for 1740 acres in Middle District on Richland Creek, Elk River. This was a purchased grant at the rate of ten pounds for every 100 acres.

No. 1508. William Vann, issued 4 Jan. 1791; 640 acres in Sumner County on the north side of Cumberland River on the Middle Fork of Jennings Creek. The grant was based on the services of Daniel Mathea(?) a private in the North Carolina Line.

No. 1363. Thomas Massey, heir of Ruben Massey, issued 16 Nov. 1790 for the services of said Reuben Massey as a private in the military; 640 acres in Davidson County on a small fork of Stewarts Creek.

No. 2697. Sampson Williams, issued 6 June 1796, for 274 acres in Davidson County between Duck River and Harpeth River, for the services of Isaac Dawson, a private in the N. C. Line.

No. 66. Saml Ashe, issued 10 March 1786; 2500 acres in Davidson County om Wolf Creek, for the services of Samuel Ashe in the North Carolina Line.

No. 27. Saml Ashe, issued 10 March 1786 for services as a captain in the North Carolina Line; 1508 acres in Davidson County, on both sides of the west fork of Thompsons Creek.

No. 374. Geo. Birdwell, issued 26 June 1793; 640 acres in Davidson County, one mile above Heaton's Station. This was a purchase grant of ten pounds for every 100 acres.

No. 2760. Daniel Joslin, issued 20 July 1796, for the services of Rowlin Cramelle, private in the North Carolina Line. The land was 274 acres in Davidson County, on Leeper's Fork.

No. 187. James White, issued 19 Nov. 1785 for services rendered by Martin Armstrong. The 363 acres were in Davidson County on the south side of Cumberland River.

No. 180. Thomas Taylor, issued 20 July 1796 for the services of John Frazier, soldier in the Commissioner's Guard. The 252 acres were in Davidson County on Whites Creek.

No. 349. Martin Armstrong, issued 25 Sept. 1787 for the service of Thos. Padgett, private in the North Carolina Line. The 640 acres were in Davidson County, on Sturgeons Creek, on the north side of Sulphur Fork of Red River.

No. 2756. John Buchanan, issued 20 July 1796 for the service of Francis Corbin, private in the North Carolina Line. The 640 acres were in Davidson County on Hurricane Creek adjoining the land of Daniel Frazier and Elizabeth Rardons(?).

No. 1771. John Medearies, issued 20 May 1793 for his service as a captain in the North Carolina Line. The 3840 acres were in Davidson County on the west fork of Stones River, adjoining the land of William Gill.

No. 1846. Jeremiah Sexton, issued 20 May 1793 for his services as a private in the North Carolina Line. The 640 acres were in Davidson County, three fourths of a mile below the first bluff on the south side of Cumberland River below the mouth of Harpeth River.

No. 1524. Peter Pyette, issued 10 April 1792 for the services of Peter Haddock, a private in the North Carolina Line. The 640 acres were in Tennessee County, on the south side of Cumberland River.

No. 2768. James Robertson, issued 20 July 1796 for the services of Ephraim Daniel, a private in the North Carolina Line. The 320 acres were in Davidson County on both sides of the Big Harpeth River.

No. 149. Peter Dunnick, private soldier in the North Carolina Line; issued 14 March 1786; 280 acres in Davidson County, on the south side of Cumberland River, the east fork of Yellow Creek.

No. 311. William Terrell and Jno. Buchanan, issued 20 July 1796 for the services of Martin Armstrong, a surveyor. The 180 acres were in Davidson County on Mill Creek.

No. 301. George Walker, issued 20 July 1796 for the services of Martin Armstrong, a surveyor. The 247 acres were in Davidson County, on Harpeth River, adjoining the land of Jno. Craig.

No. 295. Andrew Castleman, issued 20 July 1796 for the services of Martin Armstrong, surveyor and who is called colonel. The 150 acres were in Davidson County on Mill Creek, adjoining the land of Jno. Williamson.

No. 299. Andrew Castleman, issued 20 July 1796 for the services of Martin Armstrong as surveyor. The 249 acres were in Davidson County on Cedar Lick Creek.

No. 2770. James Robertson, issued 10 Sept. 1796 for the services of James Marrald, a private in the North Carolina Line. The 640 acres were in Davidson County on the south side of Cumberland River, on both sides of Richland Creek.

No. 2758. Jno. Buchanan, issued 20 July 1796 for the services of John Ross, private in the North Carolina Line. The 640 acres were in Davidson County on Hurricane Creek.

No. 2759. Jno. Buchanan, issued 20 July 1796 for the services of John Manson, private in the North Carolina Line. The 640 acres were in Davidson County on Hurricane Creek.

No. 2757. Jno. Buchanan, issued 20 July 1796 for the services of Lewis Sowell, private in the North Carolina Line. The 640 acres were in Davidson County on Hurricane Creek.

No. 143. Alex'r Greer, issued 27 April 1793 for services as an ensign in the Commissioner's Guard. The 720 acres were in Davidson County, on South Harpeth Creek.

No. 2769. Wm. Terrell, issued 12 Aug. 1796 for the services of John McNees, a captain in the North Carolina Line. The 3840 acres were in Davidson County at the mouth of Bull Run.

No. 128. James White, issued 8 April 1794 for the services of Col. John Armstrong, surveyor. The 25 acres were in Davidson County on the north side of Cumberland River.

No. 1572. James White, issued 23 Feb. 1793 for the services of Jones Morton, a private in the North Carolina Line. The 274 acres were on the north side of Cumberland River.

No. 1624. James White, issued 23 Feb. 1793 for the services of Michael Hendrick, private in the North Carolina Line. The 228 ac-es were in Davidson County on Cumberland River in White's Bend, opposite the lower end of Robertson's Island.

No. 369. Geo. Maxwell, issued 26 June 1793. The 640 acres were in Davidson County on the south side of Harpeth River. No service shown. This was a ten pound for every 100 acres grant.

No. 475. Thomas Moncrief, issued 15 Sept. 1787 for services as a private in the North Carolina service. The 274 acres were in Davidson County on the south side of Cumberland River, adjoining the land of Thomas Davis.

No. 384. Anderson Hunt, issued 17 Dec. 1794 for 5000 acres in Middle District, south side of Duck River on both sides of Big Tom Bigby Creek, four miles south from General Greene's. (This was General Nathaniel Greene of the Revolution - E. R. W.) This was a purchase grant at a rate of ten pounds for every hundred acres.

No. 1906. Solomon Parks, issued 20 May 1793 for his services as an ensign in the North Carolina service. The 793 acres were in Davidson County on the east fork of Lick Creek, north waters of Duck River.

No. 205. Robert Thompson, issued 27 Nov. 1792, for 5000 acres in Middle Dtistrict on the north side of Duck River opposite the mouth of Cedar Creek. This was a purchase grant on the basis of ten pounds for every one hundred acres.

No. 320. Wm. Moore, issued 11 Dec. 1796 for the services of Martin Armstrong as surveyor. The 274 acres were in Davidson County on the north side of Cumberland River, adjoining Hogan's preemption, on the waters of Whites Creek.

No. 1981. John Womble, issued 20 May 1793 for the services of said Womble as a private in the North Carolina Line. The 640 acres were in Davidson County, adjoining Anthony Newman and A. Tatum.

No. 2143. Wm. Lewis, issued 20 May 1793 for the services of Joel Morrison, private in the North Carolina Line. The 640 acres were in Davidson County, on Stones River, based on Warrant no. 3132.

No. 242.   James Menees (Meness?), issued 27 Nov. 1793, for 250 acres on Cumberland River between the Virginia Line and Obid's River. This was a purchase grant, at the rate of ten pounds for every one hundred acres.

No. 1761.   Thomas Allen, issued 20 May 1793 for services as a lieutenant. The 2500 acres were in Davidson County on Duck Creek, based on warrant no. 1827.

No. 185.   John Overton, issued 20 July 1796; 480 acres in the Middle District. Frederick Morgan was a corporal in the Battalion of Troops for the Protection of Davidson County, as assigned to Patrick Kelley, for the second half of years pay.

No. 183.   John Overton, issued 20 July 1796 for raising troops for protection of inhabitants of Davidson County, and for the services of Patrick Kelley, a sergeant in the battalion of troops for that service. The land was in Davidson County, on Stones River.

No. 182.   John Overton, issued 20 July 1796 for the service of raising troops of soldiers for the protection of Davidson County and for the services of Frederick Morgan or Marians, a corporal in the said battalion, for the first half years pay. The 480 acres were in Middle District, west of the Cumberland Mountains.

No. 181.   John Overton, issued 20 July 1796 for raising troops for the protection of Davidson County, and for the services of Bazzle Fry, private in the said troops. The 400 acres were on the west bank of the main west fork of Stones River.

No. 186.   Jno. Overton, issued 20 July 1796 for the services of James McCain, a private in the battalion of troops raised for the protection of Davidson County. The 400 acres were on the main west fork of Stones River.

No. not given.   Jno. Overton, issued 20 July 1796 for the services of Patrick Kelley, a sergeant major in the battalion of troops raised for the protection of Davidson County. The 640 acres were on the main west fork of Stones River, adjoining the 3840 acre tract of Joseph Rhodes.

No. 187.   Jno. Overton, issued 20 July 1796 for the services of John Talley, private in the battalion of troops raised for the protection of Davidson County. The land was on the main west fork of Stones River, and on the east fork of the west fork of the same.

(These appear to be all that were abstracted by the author. R. W. B.)

COPY OF WARRANT no. 1816 to the heirs of Capt. George Gray, a Revolutionary Soldier. Copies of Phillips and Campbells Claim of 2840 acres on Yellow Creek. Found in the Tennessee State Archives, Nashville.
     Phillips and Campbell of the heirs of George Gray 3840 acres of land on Brush Creek of Yellow Creek to include the spring, etc. 6 Jan. 1786. The paper mentions "Heirs of Captain George Gray deceased in the line of this State." Another paper reads "I surveyed for Phillips and Campbell the eight following preemptions to wit: Christopher Guice, Sr., Christopher Guice, Jr. Jonathan Guice, Isaac Mayfield, Isaac Rounewal, Mark Noble, Joshua Thomas and Emas Thomas, which business was done in the

year 1790 by myself, Edwin Hickman and Josiah Payne," etc. etc.
(Signed) James Mulherrin and before William Hall, Esq., 15 July
1807.

LIST OF SOLDIERS, filed under label "1785-1790." "Martin Arm-
strong's office." A list of military land warrants claimed by
Phillips Phillips and Michael Campbell. Tennessee State Archives,
Nashville. All warrants were claimed by Phillips and Campbell.

Soldier's name	Number of warrant	Number of acres
Oneal and c.	965	640
Capt. Gray	1816	3840
Geo. Cook	2995	1000
Jno. Cook	3020	1000
Jno. Ganler	2420	640
Abraham Peters	2221	640
Wm. Spoolman	1663	1000
David Rose	1675	1000
Warburton Hubbard	2530	1000
Henry Stonner	2623	1000
Philip Marlin	2384	640
Andrew Ramsey	2541	640
Lazrous Hart	2424	640
Bushnell and Allen & co.	1664	640
Lanier and co.	2362	640
Lanier and co.	2449	640
Lanier	3461	640
Lanier	519	640
Lanier and Mitchell	3473	640
Thompson Robertson & co.	3373	640
Thompson and Co.	2366	640
Bushnell and Co.	3563	1000
Jas. Harrell	2188	640
Rich'd Knowles	3436	640
Bryan Trulock of Geo. Trulock	3474	640
Dav'd Cockburn	3451	640
Dav'd Cockburn	1738	640
Wm. Osten's heirs	3688	640
Henry Bunnet	3837	640
Lide OBryan	2618	1000
Jas. Grace	2124	640

LEGAL NOTICE in the Nashville Tennessee Gazette, 16 April 1807.

A page in the newspaper gives the following items in land
transfers subjoined reported to be in arrears for the tax col-
lected and charges due thereon for the year 1804 or so much
thereof as will satisfy the said Tax collector and charges.

Miller Sawyer	120 acres	mouth of Saline Creek
William Polk	400 acres	adjoining James Gatlin
Charles Baker	640 acres	adjoining Polk's tract
John Rice	1000 acres	opposite James Gatlin
Martin Armstrong	640 acres	adjoining Rice
David Davis	640 acres	on Bull Pasture
David Davis	274 acres	on Bull Pasture
Lewis Cannon	383 acres	on Dyer's Creek
Doctor Hennen	1000 acres	on Cub Creek

William Tyrrell	640 acres	on Saline Creek
Abner Lamb	2048 acres	below North Cross Creek
Joseph McDowel	1000 acres	on Dyer's Creek
Elisha Clark	640 acres	on Hay's Fork of Saline Creek
Wykoff and Clark	1000 acres	adjoining B. Shepherd
Kit Dudley	640 acres	on Wells Creek
Lardner Clark	1000 acres	adjoining T. Smith
Lardner Clark	640 acres	on Elk Creek
Solomon Hill	640 acres	adjoining James Stewart
William Belford	640 acres	on Well's Creek
Jacob Matthews	640 acres	on Well's Creek
Marmaduke Scott	388 acres	South Side Cumberland River
Alexander McCall	640 acres	branch of Cross Creek
James C. Mountflorence	640 acres	six or eight miles below first timbered island below Cross Creek
Willoughby Williams	274 acres	third creek below Cross Creek
David Kinder	640 acres	on Saline Creek
Thomas Molloy	96 acres	between Well's and Elk's Creek
William Tyrrell	640 acres	between Elk and Cross Creek
John Coats	1176 acres	on Borth Cross Creek

The same begins at ten o'clock.   (Signed) William Curl, S. C.

NOTES ON OLD BURIAL GROUNDS AND TOMBSTONE INSCRIPTIONS

Darr, Daniel, died 1833, age about 42 years.
Darr, Elizabeth, wife of Daniel, died 1833, age about 42 years.
    Both are buried in the Hogan Graveyard near Henrietta,
Montgomery Co., Tennessee.

Dusenberry, John, born 1776 in North Carolina, moved to Lincoln
    Co., Tenn., early, died there 8 Jan. 1851, and is buried
    in the county.

The Everett Graveyard is in Rutherford Co., Tennessee, about
    four miles west of Christiana on the McCord Farm, original-
    ly called the Everett Farm.

Farris, John, born 25 March 1768, died 6 April 1853 in the 86th
    year of his age.
Farris, Mary, wife of John, died 17 April 1846 in her 81st year
    of age.
Farris, Lealelah, daughter of J. S. and L. J. Farris, born 8
    October 1855, died 25 June 1890.
Farris, James S., born 24 May 1832, died 29 December 1889.
Farris, Lucy J., wife of J. S. Farris, born 10 Jan. 1828, died
    23 June 1883.
Farris, Lucy Jane, born 13 Feb. 1865, died 1 Sept. 1895, aged
    30 years, 6 months, and 13 days.
    These are all buried in the Farris graveyard, about four
miles from Winchester, Franklin Co., Tennessee, on the Belvedere
Road.

Fitzpatrick, Lucy, wife of John, born 25 March 1787, died 1 Nov.
    1867, aged 80 years, 7 months, and 25 days.
Fitzpatrick, John, born 22 Jan. 1770, died 22 Nov. 1872, age 92
    years and 10 months.

Flanikin, Robert, born 15 May 1791, died 8 May 1875.
    These are all buried in the cemetery at Culleoka in Maury
Co., Tennessee.

Note: The Frazor Graveyard is located on the Long Hollow Pike
from Gallatin to Nashville just a short way from Shackle Island,
near Drakes Creek, where it crosses the pike. Some of the prominent settlers buried in this graveyard bear the names of Clendenning, Maurry, and Shaw.

Gower, Rev. William, born 6 Nov. 1776, died 11 Oct. 1853.
Gower, Charlotte, born 1 July 1782, died 16 April 1860.
Gower, Nancy L., born 27 March 1808, died 11 July 1802.
Gatlin, Nathan, born 30 Jan. 1782, died 8 March 1855 (Marriage
    records show that he married Obedience Gower).
Gatlin, Obediance, born 16 Dec. 1787, died 18 June 1860.
    These are buried at Gower's graveyard at Gower's Chapel in
Davidson County, near River Road leading to the Cheatham County
line from Charlotte Pike.

Note: The Gordon Graveyard is located just off the Midland Road
in Rutherford County, about four miles from Christiana on the
farm known as the Alf Gordon farm.

Note: The John's graveyard is located in Rutherford County
about three and one-half miles from Christiana just off the
road leading from Walnut Grove Methodist Church to the Midland
Road. This is very near Panther Creek and about one-half mile
from where old Johnson's Mill (later called John's Mill) and
where the said creek empties into the west fork of Stones River.
There are no stones in this cemetery and it has long since been
plowed over so that the graves are not visible. Living persons
have identified some of those known to be buried in there: Paul
Vaughan Johns, America Smith Johns, Robert Cooper, Mary Eliza-
beth Johns Cooper, Lee Cooper, and an infant child of Robert
Cooper and wife Mary Johns. Also Grundy Miller, Matilda Johns
Miller, and som infant children of John Palmer and Susan Allen
Johns.

"Here lies William Goode who Departed this Life June 10, 1784,
    aged about 50 years." Tombstone located on Gallatin Road
    near Hendersonville on the highway, in a lot just back of
    a Church on the right hand side going from Nashville. The
    church was known as Christ Church and there was only one
    stone in the lot.

Note: The Huff graveyard is located in Rutherford County, about
four and one-half miles from Christiana on the road from Walnut
Grove Methodist Church to the Midland Road, at the old Huff Place.

LETTERS AND CERTIFICATES ON FILE IN THE TENNESSEE STATE ARCHIVES

                                        Raleigh, Sept. 1824

Hon. Daniel Graham, Sec. of State
Murfreesboro, Tennessee

Dear Sir

        At the request of the land committee of the University of
North Carolina, I send you the enclosed certificates; the object
of which is to satisfy the Legislature of your State that the
issuing of Warrants for Military Services performed by Officers

and Soldiers of the Continental line of this State in the revolutionary war is at an end; and that after making provisions for
such as have been issued, they will not again be troubled with
applications of this sort.
     Since forwarding the abstract of Warrants issued to and in-
cluding the 21st of February 1822 and no. 1074, I have issued
underresolutions of Assembly, one hundred and forty-three warrants
(143) ending with no. 1217, a part of which I have understood
have been adjudicated and satisfied.
     I am very respectfully

Your most Obt. servt.

Wm. Hill

(The following was enclosed in the letter)

State of North Carolina
Secretary's Office

     I, William Hill, Secretary of State in and for the State
aforesaid, do certify that I have, under a Resolution of the
last General Assembly of this State, passed the 8th, and ratified
on the 10th of December 1823, issued from the muster rolls of the
Continental line of this State in the revolutionary war, Warrants for the services of such Officers and soldiers of the said
line as appeared from the said rolls to be entitled, and had not
been previously issued; and that it is believed there are none
remaining to be issued, and that the issuing of Warrants for
lands on account of military services performed by officers and
soldiers of the Continental line of this State in the revolutionary war, is at an end and forever closed.

     Given under my hand at office in office at Raleigh this 3rd
September 1824.

W. Hill

* * *

State of North Carolina
No. 1173.

To the Surveyor of Military Lands, Greetings:
     Pursuant to a resolution of the General Assembly of this
State, ratified 10 Dec. 1823, you are hereby required, as soon
as may be, to lay off and survey six hundred and forty acres of
land for the trustees of the University of North Carolina, within
the limits of the lands reserved by law for the Officers and Soldiers of the Continental line of said state, it being for the
services of David McDonel a private of the line aforesaid in the
revolutionary war, observing the directions of the Acts of the
Assembly in such case made and provided for running out lands.
Two just and fair plans thereof, with a certificate to each annexed, you are to transmit to the proper office within the time
limited by law.

     Given under my hand at Raleigh, the 17th day of February,
1824.

Wm. Hill

* * *

To the Honourable the General Assembly of the State of Tennessee
in their present session in --- Knoxville for the year 1799.

The remonstrance of Martin Armstrong, entry taker of the
lands reserved for the officers, and soldiers of the continental line of the said state of North Carolina, showeth:
That being perfectly acquainted with the decayed state of
the old books, in the Military land office at Nashville, thinks
it duly incumbent on him to make the same known To your Honourable body, so that in your wisdom, such ways and means may be
put in practice For the preservation of such valuable records;
being the chief evidence of landed property of the citizens of
Mero District, & c.
The State of North Carolina/ by their Agents/ have lately
taken a Transcript of said books, by which, they are very much
impared, together with such constant searching, will soon render them (useless?), and in many places, not fit to appear as
evidence in any court record.
With due respect I have the Honour to be, Gentlemen

                              Your
                              Most Obedient and
                              Most Humble SERVANT

                              Martin Armstrong

(Note: the original is on file in Legislative Petitions, Box
No. 2, Tennessee State Archives.)

                        * * *

Marriage Record from Maury County, Tennessee:

    Eli Love and Sela Skipper, 3 Jan. 1821

                        * * *

No. 2, Certificate, Capt. Looney, Wm. Reasons, 19th, Valid 9
April 1807, benefit to William Reasons, 250 acres (Found in
Box R, Revolutionary soldiers).

    I hereby certify that William Reasons was a soldier in my
company when in the service of the State of North Carolina as a
guard, to Griffith Rutherford, Absolom Tatum, James Robertson,
Archibald Lytle, and Anthony Bledsoe, Commissioners for ascertaining the bounds of the Military reservation in the year 1784
and that the said William Reasons served his tour of duty and
faithfully, and is entitled to all the pay and bounty as aforesaid agreeable to an Act of the State in such case made and provided.
    Given under my hand the 2nd day of October, A. D. 1805.

                              Moses Looney
                              Capt. of said guard.

    We being appointed commissioners by the State of North
Carolina in the year 1783 to lay off the lands for the Officers
and Soldiers of the Continental line of said State, do hereby
certify that William Reasons did serve as a private in the
guard of said commissioners in Capt. Moses Luney's company and
is entitled to two hundred and fifty acres of land.
    Given under our hands the 12th of April 1804.

                              Jas. Robertson, Com.
                              Griffith Rutherford, do.

* * *

Raleigh
4 September 1824

Dear Sir

Your friendly and much esteemed favours of the 6th July
and 18th Ultimo, have been received and shown to the Trustees
of the University of this State. In consequence of the first
I forwarded to you some weeks past an abstract from the Warrant
Book of my office, at the expense of the Trustees which it is
hoped that you have received. At the time of enclosing the abstract I was much too hurried to write you. Your letter of the
18th Ultimo is the cause of your being troubled with the enclosed
certificate etc. The abstract sent does not include all the
Warrants issued since no. 1074. I believe I left out from no.
1075 to no. 1104 inclusive, believing they had been adjudicated
but should it be necessary that an abstract of those omitted
should be had at your office, please let me know it, and it shall
be sent.
Grateful for many favours

I am much and truly yours

W. Hill

Addressed: Hon. Daniel Graham; Murfreesboro, Tennessee.

* * *

Respecting my Service right and how I have missed obtaining land
for it.

General Robertson was to locate and survey my land allowed me for
myService as a chain acrrier when he went down the River on the
Mississippi Surveying and when he and his Surveyor Henry Rutherford, Esq., both returned, General Robertson told me that he had
done it and likewise he had Surveyed Six hundred Acres by virtue of a Treasury Warrant of that quantity I had purchased of a
Mr. Kughindall he told me he himself had run off one of the
tracts and Henry Rutherford the other. Sometime after Mr. Rutherford (saw?) me in Nashville and told me that money was wanting
to clear the expenses and likewise the Certificate I had from the
Commissioners. I gave hom my certificate, but I told him that if
Gen'l. Robertson would furnish him with money sufficient I would
Settle with him for the same as the General owed me for Schooling
his children being at School with me at Nashville then. I heard
no more but before Esq. Rutherford returned from the Settlement I
received a patent for my six hundred Treasury Warrant but no account of my service right - when Esq. Rutherford came here I asked
him about my Service Right he told me Several times he did not
know nor remember anything of it altho I expected Surely the
grant for my Service right would come the same time the grant for
the Treasury Warrant because Henry Rutherford's name is to the
Plat that is with the patten of the Treasury Warrant which I now
have in my possession and recorded in this county likewise I have
not sold, gave away, or exposed s'd Service Right to any person
whatsoever.

Alexander Reed

Sworn and subscribed before me this 19th day of July 1806.
Thos. A. Claiborne

This will certify that Major John Buchanan came before me this day and made oath that Alexander Reid served a Tour of duty as a chain carrier the Second time the Continental Officers and Soldiers Boundary line was run under the direction of Genl. Rutherford, Gen'l. Robertson and Major Tatum com'rs.

John Buchanan

Sworn to and subscribed before me the 19th day of Feb. 1806.
Thos. A. Claiborne

This will certify that James Mulherrin, Esq., came before me, Thos. A. Claiborne, Esq., this day, and made oath that Alexander Reid served a Tour of duty as a chain carrier the Second time the continental officers and Soldiers boundary line was run under the direction of Genl. Rutherford, General Robertson and Major Tatum Commissioners.

James Mulherrin

Sworn to and subscribed before me this 19th day of July 1806.
Thos. A. Claiborne

* * *

Scribner, John, born 3 Feb. 1798, died 15 Dec. 1877. Buried at Scribner's Mill, Maury Co., Tennessee.

* * *

TENNESSEE COMPANY

Much of the land included in the following record is in the Tennessee Valley and Muscle Shoals sections. This record is from original papers in the Tennessee State Archives in Nashville and is among a collection of 1799 and 1801 papers.
E. R. W.

No. 9. This indenture made 13 March 1797 between John Johnson of Greene Co., Tenn., attorney for Zachariah Cox of Montgomery Co., Georgia of the one part, and John Rhea of Sullivan Co., Tenn., of the other part.
Witnesseth that whereas the State of Georgia in and by a certain grant from under the hand of his Excellency George Mathews, Captain General, Governor, and commander in chief in and over the said State, bearing date 24 January 1795, did give and grant unto Zachariah Cox and Mathias Maher, and their associates called the Tennessee Company, their heirs and assigns for ever in fee simple, as tenants in common and not as joint tenants, all that tract or parcel of land, including Islands, situate, lying and being within the following boundaries, that is to say, Beginning at the mouth of Bear Creek on the fourth side of the Tennessee River, Thence up the said creek to the most Southern source thereof, Thence due south to the latitude of 34 degrees 10 minutes north of the Equator, Thence a due east course 120 miles, Thence a due north course to the Great Tennessee River, Thence up the middle of the said river to the northern boundary line of this State, Thence a due west course along the said line to where it intersects the Great Tennessee River below the Muscle Shoals, Thence up the said river to the place of beginning, Together with all and singular the rights, members and appurtenances whatsoever, to the said parcel of land being belonging or in anywise appertaining. To hold to them the said Zachariah Cox and Matthias Maher and their associates called the Tennessee Company, their heirs and assigns forever in fee simple as tenants

in common and not as joint tenants, as in and by the said recited
grant made of record in office of the Secretary of State in Book
MMMM, folio 713, 714, 715, 716, and 717.

And whereas the said Zachariah, by a Letter of Attorney
bearing date 27 June 1796 has fully and legally authorized John
Johnston of Greene Co. as aforesaid as his lawful attorney to
dispose of townships nos. 5, 6, and 7, or any part thereof, the
whole estimated to contain 86,973 and 3/4 acres; Scituate and
lying and being in the great Bend of the Tennessee River, in the
tract of land granted as aforesaid to Zachariah Cox and Matthias
Maher, Esq., and their associates called the Tennessee Company,
and bounded as follows, viz: Benjamine on the South side of the
Great Tennessee River at the South West corner of Township no.
4, running thence a due north course by the West boundary of
Township no. 4,3, and 2, 2052 chains and 52 links to the Northern boundary line of the State of Georgia, thence a due west
course along the said northern boundary line 400 chains, thence
a due south course to the Great Tennessee River, thence up the
said river Tennessee to the place of beginning which area is
estimated to contain 86,973 and 3/4 acres and lying in the Great
Bend of the Tennessee in the Tennessee Company purchase as aforesaid, to make, do, and execute in the name of him the said Zachariah Cox sufficient deed or deeds of Conveyance for the last described 86,973 and 3/4 acres of land or any part thereof, and to
receive the payment for the sales thereof, all which acts or
deeds relative thereto, or touching the same, by him the said
John Johnston, attorney for the said Zachariah Cox as aforesaid
and by virtue of the said power of attorneys, shall be binding
on him the said Zachariah Cox as fully and as effectually as
though done by himself.

Now this indenture witnesseth that the said John Johnston
as attorney for and in consideration of the sum of $4000.00 law-
ful money unto him in hand paid by the said John Rhea at or before the sealing and delivery of these presents, the receipt of
which is hereby acknowledged, Hath granted, bargained, sold,
aliened, released, and confirmed, and by these presents doth
grant, bargain, sell, alien, release and confirm unto the said
John Rhea and unto his heirs all that tract or parcel of land
situate lying and being within the following boundaries: That is
to say--Beginning at the North east corner of lot number 3 of
Range no. 7 of Township no. 5, thence due north running by lots
nos. 4 and 5 in range no. 6 and range no. 5, 200 chains to a
stake, thence due west by lots nos. 3 and 2 in range no. 4 running 200 chains to a stake, thence due north running by lots
no. 1 and 1 in ranges no. 5 and 6, 200 chains, thence due east
by lots no. 2 and 3 in range no. 7, 200 chains to the beginning,
including lots no. 2 and 3 in range no. 6, and lots no. 2 and 3
in range no. 5, containing in the said four lots, 4000 acres of
land lying on the north side of Tennessee River in township no.
5 in the Great Bend of said river in the Tennessee Company purchase, together with all and singular the rights members and appurtenances whatsoever thereunto belonging or in anywise appur-
taining, and the remainders, reversions, rents, issues and prof-
its thereof, and every part thereof. To have and to hold the
said tract or parcel of land unto him the said John Rhea and his
heirs and assigns to the only use, benefit, and behoof of him
the said John Rhea and his heirs and assigns forever. The said
tract or parcel of land against them the said Zachariah Cox and
Matthias Maher and their Associates, their heirs, and assigns
and all and every other person or persons by these presents shall
and will warrant and forever defend.

In witness whereof the said John Johnston, attorney for
Zachariah Cox hath hereunto set his hand and seal the day and
date first above written, and the hand and seal of the said
Zachariah.

Signed, sealed and delivered in the presence of:
                                    James Penney
                                    Alex'r Nelson.

                    (Signed) John Johnston (SEAL)
                             atty for
                        Zachariah Cox (SEAL)

(There are 13 deeds, etc., pertaining to this transaction and
to the holdings of the Tennessee Company in the Tennessee Valley
and the Muscle Shoals sections. All are in their original and
are on file in the State Archives. I have copies of each of
them. The above is just one of the number. - E. R. W.)

                            * * *

                        PENSION REPORTS

These pension reports refer to persons who served in Tennessee
or lived in Tennessee at some time. They are taken from the U.
S. Pension Reports, 1832, Washington, D. C.

Missouri Pension List

    JOHN LEIPER, private, Cape Girardeau, Mo. Served in Tenn.
Militia. Placed on roll 21 July 1830 for pension commenced 19
July 1830. Transferred from East Tennessee to Cape Girardeau,
Missouri.

    JOHN PICKETT, private, Franklin Co., Mo. Served in the 24th
Regt., U. S. Infantry. Pensioned 8 Jan. 1816, commenced 16 March
1825. Transferred from Tenn. to Mo.

    JOHN ESTES, private, Gasconade Co., Mo. Served in the Tenn.
Militia, and was pensioned 24 July 1816, commenced 22 May 1815.

    ANDREW S. McGIRK, private, LaFayette Co., Mo. Served in
East Tenn. Militia. Pensioned 17 Jan. 1818, commenced 9 Feb.
1814.

    THOMAS ROBERTS, private, Morgan Co., Mo. Served in the
Tennessee Rangers. Pensioned 27 Sept. 1826, commenced 8 Sept.
1826.

    THOMAS ROBERTS, private, Morgan Co., Mo. Served in the
Tenn. Rangers. Commenced pension 25 July 1834. (Note: This
appears to be a distinct record from the first Thomas Roberts,
but probably refers to the same Thomas Roberts - E. R. W.)

    FRANCIS HICKMAN, pensioned under Act of 1832. Transferred
pension from Tenn. to St. Louis Co., Mo. He served in the Penna.
Continental Line. Pensioned 23 June 1834, commenced 4 March
1831, aged 81 years.

Alabama Pension List

    NATHANIEL MILLARD, Invalid Pensioner, private, Dallas Co.,
Ala. Served in the Tenn. Militia. Pensioned 15 Jan. 1823, commenced pension 16 Sept. 1822, under Act of Military Establishment.

    ABNER DICKSON, Invalid Pensioner, private, Franklin Co.,
Ala. Served in the Tenn. Volunteers; pensioned 10 March 1818,
commenced 4 May 1815. 24 April 1816 was transferred from Montgomery Co., Tenn., as of 4 March 1827.

SAMUEL MILLER, private, Franklin Co., Ala. Served in the 39th Regt. of U. S. Infantry. Pension commenced 9 July 1814 under Act of 24 April 1816. Transferred from West Tennessee from 4 Sept. 1819.

PEYTON MADISON, private, Greene Co., Ala. Served in the 39th Regt. of U. S. Infantry. Pensioned 16 Sept. 1816; pension commenced 9 July 1814 under Act Military Establishment. Transferred from Bedford Co., West Tenn., from 4 March 1825.

JOHN MADISON, corporal, Greene Co., Ala. Served in the 39th Regt. of U. S. Infantry. Placed on pension 16 Sept. 1816; pension commenced 9 July 1814. Transferred from Lincoln Co., Tenn., from 4 March 1825.

EDMUND BORUM, corporal, Laurence Co., Ala. Served in Tenn. Regt. of Mounted Gunners. Pensioned 21 Aug. 1815; commenced pension on 21 Aug. 1815. Pensioned under Act, 30 April 1816.

SAMUEL DALE, captain, Laurence Co., Ala. Served in the Tenn. Militia. Pensioned 25 Jan. 1833; commenced 22 Jan. 1833, under Act, 24 April 1816.

MATHEW PAINE, private, Marion Co., Ala. Served in the Tennessee Volunteers. Pensioned 3 Feb. 1826; commenced 26 Oct. 1825 under Act of 24 April 1816.

BENJAMINE BLACKBURN, private, Tuscaloosa Co., Ala. Served in Lewis' Regt. Pensioned and begun 1 April 1810 under Act of 3 March 1811. Transferred from Tenn. from 4 Sept. 1819.

JESSE MEREDITH, private, Dallas Co., Ala. Pensioned under Act of 1818. Served in Va. Cont. Line. Pensioned 10 Nov. 1819; commenced 27 Sept. 1819 aged 79 years. Suspended under Act of 1 May 1820. Cont'd from 4 March 1823 and transferred from Smith Co., Tenn.

JOHN JACKSON, private, Jackson Co., Ala. Served in South Carolina Cont. Line. Pensioned 19 Nov. 1819. Pension commenced 21 Sept. 1818, aged 82 years. Transferred from Lincoln Co., Tenn., from 4 March 1816.

SAMUEL BOYDSTON, private, Perry Co., Ala. Served in Tennessee Militia. Pensioned 17 Sept. 1833. Pension began 4 March 1831, aged 72 years.

Georgia Pension List

DANIEL CLOWER, private, Gwinnett Co., Ga. Served in the N. C. Cont. Line. Pensioned 8 Nov. 1819. Pension began 6 Sept. 1819, aged 71 years. Transferred from Giles Co., West Tenn.

Kentucky Pension List

PRESTLEY SHEPHERD, private, Clarke Co., Ky. Served 44th Regt. of U. S. Infantry. Transferred from West Tenn., 4 March 1831.

JOHN BEATTY, private. Served in Tenn. Volunteers. Pensioned 12 April 1820 in Fayette Co., Ky.

BENJ. COONS, lieutenant, Oldham Co., Ky. Served in Tenn. Militia. Pensioned 1 June 1830.

SAMUEL NEWELL, lieutenant. Served in Campbell's Regt., in the Rev. War. Pensioned 6 Jan. 1817. Transferred from West

Tennessee on 4 Sept. 1816. His pension commenced on 2 March 1811.

BUCKNER HAYWOOD, private, Todd Co., Ky. Served in Tenn. Cavalry. Pensioned 14 Jan. 1819. Transferred from West Tenn.

HENRY THOMAS, private, Caldwell Co., Ky. Served in the Virginia Line. He was pensioned 24 Nov. 1818, aged 77 years. He was transferred from West Tenn., commencing 4 Sept. 1827.

LUKE METHEANY, private, Monroe Co., Ky. Served in the Va. Line. Pensioned 6 May 1819, aged 81 years. Transferred from Tenn. 22 Feb. 1826, from 4 March 1826.

Mississippi Pension List

JOHN BARGER, private, Adams Co., Miss. Served in the Tenn. Militia. Pensioned 9 Nov. 1819. Transferred from West Tenn.

ALLEN PYRON, private, Monroe Co. Served in the Mounted Riflemen. Pensioned 21 Aug. 1815.

DAVID ADAMS, private, Monroe Co. Served in the N. C. Cont. Line. Obtained pension 21 July 1819, aged 70 years. Transferred from West Tennessee.

Indiana Pension List

DANIEL RUMINER, private, Daviess Co., Ind. Served in the Tenn. Militia. Pensioned 9 Nov. 1824. Transferred from West Tennessee.

STEPHEN COLLINS, private, U. S. Artillery, Marion Co., Ind. Pensioned 21 Feb. 1817. Transferred from New York and West Tenn.

SAMUEL SCOTT, private in the Mounted Volunteers, resided Posy Co., Ind. Pensioned 12 April 1823. Transferred from West Tenn.

THOMAS WYATT, private in U. S. Army, resided Wayne Co., Indiana. Pensioned 17 Oct. 1821. Transferred from West Tennessee.

JOHN GARRETTSON, private in the South Carolina Line, resided Fayette Co., Ind. Pensioned 11 March 1829 aged 77 years. Transferred from Jefferson Co., Tenn.

JOHN ANDREW SMITH, private in the Virginia Line, resided in Lawrence Co., Ind. Pensioned 3 May 1819, aged 80 years. Transferred from Blount Co., Tenn.

THOMAS TURNHAM, private in Virginia Line, resided in Spencer Co., Ind. Pensioned 5 April 1819, aged 84 years. Transferred from Wilson Co., Tenn.

CHARLES BOWEN, private in the Virginia Militia, resided in Putnam Co., Ind. Pensioned 15 Dec. 1832 aged 84 years. Transferred from East Tenn., 4 Sept. 1833.

ANDREW McPHESTER, private in Va. Militia, resided Putnam Co., Ind. Pensioned 17 June 1833 aged 70 years. Transferred from East Tenn., 4 March 1834.

WILLIAM GALBREATH, private and sergeant, Penna. Militia., resided in Scott Co., Ind. Pensioned 29 May 1833 aged 77 years. Transferred from East Tenn., 4 March 1831.

Illinois Pension List

WM. ABNEY, private 24th U. S. Infantry, resided Gallatin Co., Ill. Pensioned 21 Oct. 1816. Transferred from West Tenn.

JOHN BARGER, private in East Tenn. Militia, resided in Gallatin Co., Ill. Pensioned 17 Sept. 1816. Transferred from West Tenn.

HENRY J. WILLIAMS, private in 11th U. S. Infantry, resided in Hamilton Co., Ill. Pensioned 30 Dec. 1816. Transferred from Virginia and West Tenn.

THOMAS ROBERTS, private in U. S. Rangers, resided in Morgan Co., Ill. Pensioned 27 Sept. 1826. Transferred from West Tenn.

WILLIAM HENLEY, private in Dyer's Regt. of Militia, resided in Randolph Co., Ill. Pensioned 15 Feb. 1819. Transferred from West Tenn.

WILLIAM LANE, private in Tenn. Volunteers, resided in Randolph Co., Ill. Pensioned 21 June 1823.

JOB JENKINS, private in Va. Cont. Line, resided in Morgan Co., Ill. Pensioned 3 June 1819. Transferred from West Tenn. Died Jan. 1832.

DANIEL CHAPMAN, private in Tenn. Militia, resided in White Co., Ill. Pensioned 11 Oct. 1825.

JOHN TAYLOR, private in U. S. Army, resided in White Co., Ill. Pensioned under Act of 5 July 1812. Transferred from West Tenn.

JACOB SEAGRAVES, private in N. C. Line, resided in Clinton Co., Ill. Pensioned 18 June 1822. Transferred from West Tenn.

AARON SMITH, private in N. C. Line, resided in Green Co., Ill. Pensioned 13 Jan. 1819. Transferred from East Tenn. Formerly resided in Washington Co., Tenn.

GEORGE ROPER, private in N. C. Cont. Line, resided in Jefferson Co., Ill. Pensioned 11 March 1825. Transferred from West Tenn.

JOHN COLLINSWORTH, private in Va. Cont. Line, resided in St. Calir Co., Ill. Pensioned 20 March 1833. Transferred from East Tenn. in 1833, aged 70 years.

RANDLE McDANIEL, private in the South Carolina Cont. Line, resided in White Co., Ill. Pensioned 18 July 1833, aged 79 years. Transferred from Tenn.

Ohio Pension List

HEZEKIAH SEALS, private in 39th Regt. U. S. Infantry, resided in Butler Co., Ohio. Pensioned 10 Dec. 1820. Transferred from East Tenn.

Virginia Pension List

WILLIAM TONEY, private in 20th Regt. U. S. Infantry, resided in Campbell Co., Va. Pensioned April 1814. Transferred to East Tennessee.

JOHN MARTIN, sergeant, resided in Caroline Co., Va. Pensioned under Act, 24 April 1816. Transferred to Tennessee.

BENJAMINE SADLER, private in 9th Va. Regt., resided Goochland Co., Va. Pensioned under Act of 24 April 1816. Transferred to West Tenn.

JOSEPH LIGON, private in Rev. Army of Va. Line, resided in Halifax Co., Va. Pensioned under Act of 24 April 1816. Transferred to West Tenn.

HENRY J. WILLIAMS, private, in 10th Regt., U. S. Infantry, resided in Mongalia Co., Va. Pensioned 30 Dec. 1816. Transferred to West Tenn.

JAMES TAYLOR, private, resided in Patrick Co., Va. Pensioned under Act of 24 April 1816. Transferred to West Tenn.

ALEXANDER M. GRAY, private in 2nd Regt. of Tennessee Volunteers, resided in Scott Co., Va. Pensioned 15 March 1821. Transferred from West Tennessee.

WILLIAM TIPTON, private in Parker's Regt., resided in Shenandoah Co., Va. Pensioned under law of 24 April 1816. Transferred to Tenn.

JOHN CALDWELL, private, Invalid; no county given. Pensioned. Transferred to Tenn.

SOME TENNESSEE SOLDIERS IN WAR OF 1812

There is a card index to these soldiers on file in the Tennessee State Library. This list is not complete but contains names found in scattered documents, etc. Numbers in parentheses after a name indicate the number of times that name appears in the card index. E. R. W.

Aaron, Alexander
Aaron, Jacob
Aaron, John
Aaron, Thomas
Abanatha, Laban
Abanatha, Robert
Abathany, Robert
Abernathy, Allen
Abernathy, Chas.
Abernathy, David
Abernathy, Jno.
Abernathy, Littleton
Abar, John (2)
Abbets, David
Abbot, Jonathan
Abbot, Sam'l
Abbot, William
Abbott, David (3)
Abbott, Geo.
Abbott, Jas.
Abbott, Lewis
Abbott, Wm.
Abel, Michael
Abels, John (2)
Able, Anthony
Able, Chas.

Able, Philip (2)
Ables, Wm.
Abner, John
Abney, Elias
Abney, Isaac
Abney, Wm.
Abraham, ---, servant
Abram, ---, servant to Capt.
Abram, ---, waiter
Acard, Jno.
Achley, Isaac
Achley. Jesse
Ackley, Joshua
Achor, Jas.
Acker, Jos. (2)
Ackerson, Henry (2)
Ackland, Alexander S.
Acord, Jonas
Acridge, John (2)
Acres, Uriah
Acton, Jas.
Acuff, Carter (3)
Acuff, Chas.
Acuff, Hamilton
Acuff, Isaac (3)
Acuff, Spencer

Acuff, William (2)
Adair, Alexander
Adair, James (3)
Adam, Eli
Adam, Henry
Adam (negro)
Adair, Jas. (2)
Adams, Aaron L. (3)
Adams, Abraham (6)
Adams, Amos
Adams, Bailey
Adams, Bucknor
Adams, Dan'l
Adams, David (4)
Adams, Edwin
Adams, Enos
Adams, Geo.
Adams, Hardin S.
Adams, Howell
Adams, Isaac
Adams, James (5)
Adams, John (19)
Adams, Joshua (2)
Adams, Martin (2)
Adams, Peter
Adams, Reeves
Adams, Robert I or J (3)
Adams, Robert L.
Adams, Robert S.
Adams, Simon (3)
Adams, Thos. (4)
Adams, Toliver (2)
Adams, William (12)
Adams, Wm. G.
Adamson, David (2)
Adamson, Jos.
Adcock, Barney
Adcock, David
Adcock, Henderson
Adcock, Jas.
Adcock, John
Adcock, Jos.
Adcock, Mark
Adcock, Tyree
Adcock, Wm. (2)
Addir, Jas.
Addington, Vardy
Adear, John
Adeylotte, Arthur
Adkerson, Absolom
Adkerson, David
Adkerson, Jas.
Adkerson, Jesse
Adkerson, Walker
Adkins, Anderson
Adkins, Andrew
Adkins, Drury
Adkins, Elijah
Adkins, Ephraim
Adkins, Gabriel
Adkins, Jackson
Adkins, Jacob (2)
Adkins, James

Adkins, Jos.
Adkins, Levi
Adkins, Owen (2)
Adkins, Read
Adkins, Sherod
Adkins, Thos.
Adkins, William
Adkins, Zedikiah
Adkinson, Arthur
Adkinson, Ephraim
Adkinson, Jordan
Adkison, Jos. (2)
Adkinson, Wm.
Adwell, John
Adyelette, Arthur
Aeburthrott, Jno. (2)
Affill, Jesse
Age, Moses
Agree, Edmund
Agee, Jas. (2)
Aiken, Benjamin
Aiken, John, sergeant
Aiken, Samuel
Aikins, Wm.
Aikmen, Wm. E.
Ainsworth, Josiah
Akard, John
Akens, Sam'l
Aken or Aker, Jos.
Aker, Adam
Akin, Abraham
Akins, Davis
Akins, Geo.
Akin, Harrison
Akins, Jesse
Akins, John
Akin, John
Akin, John H.
Akins, Joseph (2)
Akins, Thos.
Akins, Wm.
Akuff, Jesse B.
Alberson, Solomon, drummer
Albert (negro)
Albertson, Wm., 4th sergeant
Albion, John
Albright, Lewis
Albutt, Jas.
Alcorn, John (2)
Allcorn, John, Lt.-Col.
Aldens, Thos.
Alder, Barnabas
Alderson, Curtis
Alderson, John
Alderson, John D.
Aldridge, Enoch
Aldridge, Enoche
Aldridge, James., sergt.
Aldridge, Jas., sergt.
Aldridge, John (3)
Aldridge, Nathaniel
Alexander, Aaron (4)

These were all that were published - R. W. B.

FORMATION OF EARLY COUNTIES

WASHINGTON COUNTY, 1777

Beginning at the most northwesterly part of Wilkes County on the Virginia line; thence running with the line of Wilkes County to a point 36 miles south of the Virginia Line; thence due west to the ridge of the Great Iron Mountains, which heretofore divided the hunting grounds of the overhill Cherokees from those of the middle settlements and valley; thence running a southwesterly course along the said ridge to the Unacoy Mountains where the leading path crosses the same from the valley to the overhills; thence South with the line of the State adjoining the State of South Carolina; thence due west to the great river Mississippi; thence up the said river the course thereof to a part due west from the beginning; thence due east with the line of the State to the beginning.

SULLIVAN COUNTY, 1779

Dividing Washington by a line beginning at the steep rock thence running along the dividing ridge that divided the waters of great Canawa and Tennessee to the head of Indian Creek; thence along the ridge that divides the waters of Holston and Watauga to the mouth of Watauga; thence a direct line to the highest part of the chimney top mountain at the Indian Boundary all the part of Washington lying northwardly of said line to be Sullivan; all southwardly of the said dividing line shall contain Washington County.

GREENE COUNTY, 1783

By a direct line beginning at William Williams in the fork of Horne Creek at the foot of Iron Mountain, thence a direct course toGeorge Gillespie's house at or near the mouth of Big Limestone, thence a north course to the line which divides the Counties of Washington and Sullivan, thence with the said line to the Chimney Top Mountains, thence a direct course to the mouth of Cloud's Creek in Holston River, and all the part of Washington Westward of said line from the passing to be Greene County.

DAVIDSON COUNTY, 1783.

All that part of this State lying west of Cumberland Mountains and South of the Virginia Line beginning at the top of Cumberland Mountains where the Virginia Line crosses extending westward along said line to Tennessee River, thence up the said

River to the mouth of Duck River thence up Duck River to where
the line of marks and cows run by the Commissioners for laying
offland granted to the Continental Line of tjis State, intersects
said River, which said line is supposed to be in 35 degrees 50
minutes N. L., thence east along said line to the top of Cumberland Mountain, thence northwesterly along said mountains to the
beginning.
        Entry takers for preemption rights.

SUMNER COUNTY, 1786

        The said County of Davidson by a line beginning where the
county line crosses the west fork of Stones River down the same
to the Junction with the main Stones River thence...direct line
to the mouth of Drakes Lick Creek, thence down Cumberland River
to the mouth of Kaspus Creek thence up the said creek to the
head to the wartrace from thence a northwardly course to the
Virginia line at a point that will have Red Riverold Stations
one mile to the east; all west David(son County); east (will
be) Sumner County.

HAWKINS COUNTY, 1786

        Beginning where the boundary line between the commonwealth
of Virginia and the State of North Carolina crosses the North
fork of Holston River, thence down said fork to its junction
with the main Holston River, thence across said river due South
to the top of Boyce Mountains, thence along the top of said
mountains and the top of the Jarding (?) ridge between Holston
River and the French Broad River to its punches with Holston
River, thence down the said River to its junction with the Tennessee River, thence down the same to the creek where said River
runs through Cumberland Mountains thence along the top of said
mountains to the aforesaid boundary line and thence along the
said line to the beginning; east of N. F. of Hol.; to extreme
Sal. West of do. Hawkins.

TENNESSEE COUNTY, 1788

        Beginning on the Virginia Line, running along Sumner Co.
to the dividing ridge between Cumberland River and Red River,
then westwardlyalong the said ridge to the main South branch of
Sycamore Creek, thence from the said branch to the mouth thereof,
then due south across Cumberland River to the Davidson County
Line; East Dav.; West Tenn.

GREENE AND HAWKINS COUNTIES, 1792

        By a line beginning on Nolichucky River at the place where
the ridge which divides the waters of Bent and Lick Creek strikes
at, thence with that ridge to Bulls Gap of Bays Mountain, thence
a direct line to the place where the road that leads from Dodsons
Ford to Perkins Iron Works crosses the waters fork of Bent Creek,
thence down that road to the head of Panther Creek, down the
meanders of that creek to the River Holston, thence a northwest
course the River Clinch again from Nolichucky River where the
ridge that divides the waters of Bent and Lick Creek strikes it
a direct course to Peter Fines Ferry on French Broad, then south
to the Ridge that divides the waters of French Broad and Big
Pigeon and south...Ridge to the Eastern boundary of the Territory.

JEFFERSON COUNTY, 1792

        To be butted and bounded by the above described line (the
Line circumscribing Greene and Hawkins) from the Eastern boundary

of the Territory to the River Holston and down the river Holston
to the mouth of Crosswells Mill Creek thence a direct line to
the mouth of Dumpliss Creek on French Broad, thence up the meanders of French Broad to the mouth of Boyds Creek thence No. 25
East to the ridge which divides the waters of Little Pigeon and
Boyds Creek and with the said Ridge to the Indian Boundary or
the Eastern bounds of the Ter.: as the case may be & by the
Eastern boundary.

KNOX COUNTY, 1792

By the line of Jefferson County from the mouth of Overalls
Mill Creek to the Indian Boundary or Eastern Boundary of the
Territory as the case may be again from the mouth of said creek
up the meanders of the River Holston to the mouth of Panther
Creek thence northwest to the River Clinch to the place where
the line shall cross Holston at the ridge that divides the waters of Tennessee and Lick River according to the Treaty of Holston, shall strike it and by that line...

Note: The original of the above boundaries will be found in the
Tennessee State Archives, Nashville. This is taken from an original paper and not from the work of any present day surveyors
knowledge.   E. R. W.

PETITION OF BEDFORD COUNTY, 1822

Box 34 of Legislative Papers filed in the Tennessee State Archives. Petition of William Galbreath, 1822. He purchased in
Shelbyville a lot together with a wood(?) carding machine for
which he paid the sum of $2500.00 The said machineis on the
north side of Duck River in the Town of Shelbyville, etc. etc.
He seeks a permit to build a dam across Duck River. Dated 22
Sept. 1825.   (signed by)

Wm. Galbreath	James A. Walker
Henry Marc	Edw'd Waile
James Alexander	Runnex Daley
Jesse Evans	Wm. Adcock
Thephan Loyed	James R. White
John Strickles	John Burrow
Muhl Green	Jesse Allen
James Killingworth	L. C. Derieaux(?)
Moses M. Robinson	Geo. M. Bradshaw
John Lanier	Micajah Bullock
James More	John Mak-(?)
Saml K. Nelson	Samuel Walker
Jo Galbreath	Samuel Nelson
Henry Morgan	James Stoney
Greene Holland	Thos. Dryain
William T. Sells	A. H. White
Samuel A. White	Edmund Greer
Nathan Springer	O. W. Bradshaw
Thomas Tyrrell	Alex'd E. Morrison
John Nicholas	John Poole
Pelter Crowel	Man(?) Cowrd(?)
Thomas R. Kinwar(?)	Martin Fisher
Benjamine Walden	Wm. McGee
Saml Fowler	Wm. Hasting
George Davidson	John Trolinger
John Olsmell	Richard Davis
Wm. Gambell	Wm. Ward
Saml Suddath	John Stephens
James Ward	Wm. F. Daugherty

Griffin Randle
Martin T. Ward
John Blagg
Isaiah Bledsoe
Joseph Patton
Thos. G. Sills
Enic Doty
Pitts Chilutt
Isaac Moulton
John Srie(?)
Birkett D. Jett
James Jones
Thomas Cawlell(?)
Giles Burartt
Kintchen Tipper
Andrew Neill
Elijah Seay (Lacy)
Isaah Hartfield
Isaac Doty
Jno. Eakin
Amrza Anderson
Curdes Clamans
William Herbert
Thomas Gambill
Jos. Thompson
Thomas Davis
Robert Cooper
James Holland
Henry Conway
Fordyce Wilson
Ezekl Dickson
William Johnson
Sterling Brown
John Walden
Morton Jones
John T. Harris
Jonathan Harrison
Wm. Young
David Telford
James Tant
John Pierson
John Lince(?)
Thomas Norsworthy
Benjamine Lince
John H. Hubbard
Wm. (X) his mark Field
William Tucar
John Young
Wm. Harman
John Lantz
John Hooker
James Treavis
George W. Parsone
Amos Balch
Jonathan F. Claxton
Jesse Phillips
Thomas McCustron
J. Haygog(?)
James Holms
Carthon Garrison
John Maccadam
William Phillips
Andrew Hartfield
Johnson B. Clardy
Thos. Foster

Musel Ward
Willie Stephens
James Gammill
Jno. Daugale
William McIntosh
N. E. Coldwell
Martin Ferrell
Ezarie Doty
J. or I. Wardlow
John Hartsfield
Richard Owens
J. Thompson
Nathaniel King
Benj. Oneal
Weightstile A. Coffey
David Driden
Gilbert Clifft
Alex'd Eakin
James Spain
Joeeph Trice
Abraham Shook
Jacob Hartfield
William Nelson
Geo. W. Ruth
D. D. Temple
Robert Nelson
James McKeine
H. S. Wilson
Robert J. or I. Green
Danl McKeseck
Zadoc Springer
John Moore
Jesse Muse
Joseph Burnett
Thos. Willingham
William Gore(?)
Allen Philpott
Charles Taliaferro
R. G. Wynne
Joel Freeman
Wm. Gamble
Joseph Nance
Benjamine Harrinhart(?)
John Knott
John McClintock
William Yeats
Reuben Nance
George Freeman
Robert Huddlestone
James Graham
John Leffler
Wm. Bozwell
D. Dawdy(?)
John Hickison
William Carrigon
Nathan Fields
Saml. A. Holmes
John Fisher
James Fields
James D. Holmes
William McClure
John Buckelew
Benj. (Beym) Lintz
Wm. Armstrong
Samuel Sutton

Thos. Wallace
Richard Omohundro
Willie Rogers
Henry King
Abraham Sriver
John F. Doherty
A. Gill
Jacob Whitworth
Moses Nelson
John Brand
Edward Holland
John Robinson
Kenneth Anderson
Jon Bussey
Elex Freeman
Edward Freeman
W. W. Patterson
Willy Arnal
H. L. Sugg
Jesse Conbut
John B. Cummings
Isaac McAddams
Le-(?)
M. A. Cunningham
James Garrett
Michal Fisher
William Dixon
James Claxton
George Osburn
Frances McCrnay(?)
Thomas McFarling
William McGeoyer
Samuel Minter
Joseph McElwrath
Henry Moore, Sr.
Jordan C. Holt
John Bachuldew
Wm. M. Gilson
Michael Fisher
Thos. P. Burns
Wm. McLarzhlin
T. F. Thompson
George Pressgrove
Henry Wise
D. Thompson
Rabise Allin
Alfred Balch
Francis McGuire
Thomas Burris
Robert Parks
Thos. Wheeler
William M. Shaw
Ziza Morrison
Martin Wheeler
Jas. Harris
Joseph Alexander
John M. Presgrove(?)
B. S. William
Sam'l McLaughlin
John B. Younger
John W. Ashbrook
H. C. Hastings
Wm. Barnett
John McPer(?)
Henry F. Graham

James Ivey
Anderson Hensey
John Loyd
Jacob Gingrey (Kingrey)
Thomas Caldwell
James Knott
Wm. Davis
Jesse Cheek
Elijah N. Marshall
Thos. Holland, Sr.
James R. Terry
Nicholas Hanney (?)
Benjamine Phillips
Amos McAdams
Wm. H. Freeman
Jas. Holland
John Slade
Henry Tucker
Jas. Cunningham
Casley Ray
Nathan Morgan
D. D. Hix
William Wilkinson
Wm. Reed
Saml Neally
Stephen Murphree
Charles Morgan
Joel Albright
Augustine Rowland
Charles W. Coats
Aaron Ashbrooke
Wilson Steel
Jesse Arnold
James M. Harvey(?)
Th(?) S. (?)-dw
James Price
Wm. (?)
Weathes Lee Haynes
Jacob Albright
John Thompson
James Pressgrove
Isaac Bennett
R. Thompson
Andrew Pressgrove
James R. Carother
A. W. Thompson
Green B. Green
Andrew Gamill
James Y. Omohundue
Thomas Foster
James P. Parks
Wm. Willis
Joseph Williams
Robert Weir
Absolom Reaves
David McKissick
James C. Morrison
John H. Anderson
Sam'l Patton
Robert M. McJenny(?)
Jeremiah Cloanch
Jehu Long
Russell Freeman
James Canady
William W. Wilson

John Harrison
Lancaster Lovetts
Jas. Younger
Jas. Gamble
Joshua Townsend
James Boswell
Henry Blagg
Jeremiah Feabus
Richard Anderson
A. M. Daugharty
Hugh Davis
Henry Tidwell
Wm. M. Newlason
Joseph A. Greer
Robert G. Morgan
Dru Gilehrist
John Robertson
Jesse Peck
James Dixon
F. Killingworth
Alex Newton
Robert Maukin
John Williams
Charles Ward
Wm. M. Evens
Alex Green
Samuel B. Truce
John Fuzon
Isac Crumb
Benj. Gambill
Jesse Williams
John B. Robertson
Jacob Lentz
John Lawrence
R. E. Bradshaw
Isaiah Lintz
Wm. Newton
Wm. Dryden
Milik Brawnes
Isaac Anderson
Nelson Holland
Nathin Whealon
Willis Moore
W. (?) F. Morrison
Joseph Williams
H. C. Bradford
Aaron Gambeler
Daniel Busser
J. D. Anderson
J. Adams
John Robertson
John Barrett
Asa Head
James F. Hamilton
Jno. T. Shanks
James Clifft
Hartwell Freeman
John Tindale
John Harrison
Isaac Collier (Collins?)
Thomas Davison
Jas. Gamble
Richard H. Sims
Robert McLintock(?)
Henry Blagg

Wilson H. McKisick
Thos. Cunningham
Robert Greear
James McCullough
Wiley Saloman
Alex. S. Tureline
John Byrace
Robert Logan
Charles Ward
S. T. White
Jacob Morton
Joseph Patton
Thomas Holland, Jr.
John Sutton
Jonathan Dwyden
Moses A. Morgan
G. C. Temple
Archard Wallers
M. M. Marshall
John Armstrong
Long Davis
M. D. Mitchell
Samuel Crowell
Jacob Long
Turner Sharin
William Shook
Elijah Beard
James Gregory
John Hineman
W. D. Williams
Henry Earnhart
George Landers (?) Sandle
Joseph Dyer
Alex Morgan
Mat. Turpin
S. B. Morrison
Mathew Phillips
Richard Mure (Muse)
Milton Morison
Thos. Wheaton
James H. Mosley
J. M. Robinson
Thomas Ponders
John Willhite
Jacob Tipper
Reuben Thompson
William Adams
William Corloe(?)
Jacob Crowell
Joseph Morton
Wm. Solomon
John Robertson
Jonathan Markham
Andrew Dukes
David Davenport
R. R. O(?) Dennison
James Canady
Lewis Green
William Green
Thos. Cunningham
Harberd Smith
Zachariah Davis
Wiley Saloman
L. P. Sims
James Smith

Thomas Allred
Robert Logan
Wm. Sonvill
Warren Hale
Jacob Morton
George W. Cunningham
R. H. Bell
John Sutton
James Barnes
J. S. Laird
Nicl Norsworthy
Labon Pry (Fry)
G. C. Temple
John Armstrong
Samuel Crowell
Andrew R. Martin
John Williams
John Gant
Jonas Martin
Wm. B. Sutton
Benjamine P. Jett
Henry B. Coffee
Thomas Phillips

Robert Dougherty
D. Patton
A. M. Daugherty
Bedeah Browning
Ire G. Meginny
Wm. M. Newlason
John Nance
N. K. Blagg
Dru Gilehrist
David Rozar
James Fauber
John Clift (Clifft)
James Dixon
Robert Maukin
J.(I?) D. Pammell (Pannell)
Geo. W. Justice
John Justice
Solomon Davie (Dowe)
Jas. R. Newton
G. W. Epilman
Lewis T. Greer
John Jenkins (Ginkins)

Note: Bedford County was formed from Rutherford County in 1807.
The court house burned about 1865 and all wills and marriages
prior to that date were lost, but the deed books were saved.
Another fire in 1934 destroyed the court house at which time most
of the books were saved, but many loose papers were lost. The
above petition appears to have a few duplications of names, but
it is the best list of the county for the early period that I
have been able to locate. It will almost suffice as a census of
the taxables of the county, escpecially those in the vicinity of
Shelbyville in 1822.

BLEDSOE COUNTY

Note: Bledsoe County was created by an Act of the Legislature
of Tennessee on 30 Nov. 1807. The first county seat was Old
Madison, six miles from Dunlap, and fifteen miles from Pikeville.
After the erection of Sequatchie County in 1857, the county seat
was moved to its present location at Pikeville. The territory
included in the original Bledsoe County was cut from Roane
County, whose county seat was then and still is Kingston. The
area of Bledsoe County is about 300 square miles. It is noted
for its beautiful scenery, and is valuable for fine timber, coal
and limestone. Corn, oats, and wheat are the most successfully
grown products.

The mountain lands attracted many prospectors in the early years
of the county. For the first twenty years of history, large tracts
of land were purchased by eastern fortune seekers, who speculated
in various ways with their purchases. It was a thinly settled
section with many of the settlers gaining title to their lands
as "Occupant titles." They were often termed squatters, gaining
title to lands by the length of their residence thereon.

Many of the older records of Bledsoe County were lost, burned,
and for this reason much of the early history is lacking in de-
tail. The following extractions are from the oldest record
books prevailing at this date and are on file in the court house
at Pikeville. Except for the deed books, the oldest record book
available in this county is the Minute Docket, 1841-1846. The

first group of records extracted herein have been taken from the old Minute Book and are most valuable. (The marriages and wills to 1908 have been lost.)

Minute Docket, 1841-1846

Among the family names which appear prominent are: Page 1 - William Brown, John M. Beaty, Aron Schoolfield, Esqrs., 6 Sept. 1841.

James Sparks, Constable, 6th Dist.

James A. Tulloss, clerk

James A. Tulloss produced in court a settlement made with Mary Massey, guardian of the minor heirs of Richard Massey, deceased.

James A. Tulloss, clerk, settlement made with William Foster, guardian of minor heirs of David Poiner, deceased.

James Allen, guardian of the minor heirs of Thomas Ingram, deceased, tendered his resignation as such. James Allen was a guardian to Hester A. Ingram and James E. Ingram, minor heirs of said Thomas Ingram.

Page 2: Ephraim Nelson, constable, 9th dist.

Certificate from Bird Thomas, with A. H. Coulter and Joseph Hixon as bondsmen, Sept. 1841, session.

George Real, guardian to the minor heirs of Wm. Green, deceased, resigned as such.

Page 3: James A. Tulloss, clerk, settlement with Joseph Hixson, guardian to the minor heirs of John Hixson, deceased.

The court appropriated $12.50 for the support of Sarah Keener, an old and infirm woman. The money was to be placed in the hands of John M. Beaty.

Page 4: Isaac Robertson appointed guardian to the minor heirs of William Green, deceased. (Signed by) Charles Schoolfield, W. Brown, and John M. Beatty.

At a court held 4 Oct. 1841, the following were present on the bench: John M. Beatty, Ason Schoolfield, William Stephen, Burrell Lee, William Brown, William Foster, Isaac Roberson, Thomas J. Rogers, Joseph Hickson, and Peter D. Willcox.

Page 5: Session, Oct. 1841. James A. Tulloss, clerk. Miller Francis, Treasurer. William Walker, Trustee.

Page 6: Burdle Lee, John M. Beatty, Ruben Brown, Martin A. Smith and Isaac Anderson are to view the road passing Samuel Billingsby's to Pikeville near Billingsley's house and to unite near the top of the hill toward Pikeville.

A. H. Coulter, county coroner, regarding the body of a deceased child found in the Sequatchie River.

Page 7: Jesse Brownlee appointed overseer in the room and stead of James Stephens with the following hands, beginning at Old John Parham's, thence to John Prestley's on the Mountain, to include Point Barger's and Wm. Prestley's to James Houston's, then to Obediah Wright's, etc., to the Sequatchie River, to Tolletts Mill, to include the hands to Tolletts Store, thence to Joseph Patton's.

James Swoffard appointed Road overseer in the stead of Real H. Millard.

John Smith, present overseer on the Stage Road from Standifer's Still House branch to the county line include. James Thompson, John Leatons, A. B. Evtan (Ewtan), Philip Hoots, Elijah Austan, James Clemans, George Jones, Thos. Matthews, Jacob Newman, Thos. A. Pope, James J. Pope, Linsey (Linzy) Hoots,

Frederick Hopkins, Ezekial McVay, Edward Sparkman, and Young Eperson.

Page 8: Robert Driggin, services as constable, 1840.
William Worthington, jury service in July 1841.
Matthew Pendergrass and James Cantrell were allowed pay for burying a child found in the River.

Page 9: October 1841 Term. James P. Spring appointed the guardian to Philander D. Moore, a minor orphan boy.

Page 10: Jurors in October 1841 were Henry Duger, Wm. P. Cook, William Hale, Jeremiah Cloud, Abel Harrison, George H. Billingsley, Eli Turner, Wm. Jones, Nicholas Nany or Many, Enoe Green, Thos. Moonyhan and Barribus Thomas, in trial of Wm. Goff accused of passing counterfeit money.
William L. Dalton, jailor, allowed (pay) for following cases: Solomon Godsey, David Reed, Hiram Godsey, and Julius Edwards.
J. N. Love allowed the use of one of the jury rooms as a tailor.

Page 11: Thomas Foster, Deputy Sheriff: Be released from Poll tax in 1841: Isaac M. Leage, Richard M. Catchum, Joseph Pew, Saml Worley, Henry Kizy, William Dupee, Nathan Howard, Andrew Holder, Harry H. Holland, Joseph B. Leathers, James Pickett, William B. Snatgrass, Young Eperson, Daniel Horn, Isaac Miller, George W. Coleman, William Dotson, Joel Dotson, Tilman Hany, JohnT. Flemen, J. A. James (?), Benj. Looney, Jasper McClue, Thos. Mansfield, Fielding Turner, Wm. Wilch, Manjdith Wilch, Bird Smith, Lewy Smith, and Joseph Smith.

Page 12: Thomas Crutchfield, Tax Collector.

Page 13: William Stephen, Esq., tenders his resignation as J. P.
Nov. 1841 Session: On bench: Isaac Robeson, Wm. Brown, and Thos. J. Rogers, Esq.
Robert Owens, admr., settles the estate of Wm. Green, dec.

Page 14: Settlement: Wm. Kearly appointed guardian of the minor heirs of Daniel Kerly.

Page 16: Dec. 1841: On bench were John M. Beatty, Burrell Lea, and Aaron Schoolfield, and Isaac Roberson, Esq.
The following were appointed tax listers for 1841: Dist. 1, Peter D. Wilcox; Dist. 2, Wiley Redwine; Dist. 3, Burnell Lea; Dist. 4, Wm. Brown; Dist. 5, John Billingsley; Dist. 6, Saml W. Roberson; Dist. 7, Aron Schoolfield; Dist. 8, Isaac Robeson; Dist. 9, Alexander Lamb; Dist. 10, Joel Wheeler.

Page 17: Dec. 1841 Session. James A. Tulloss admin. of Wm. Hinson, dec.
Application of Susan Smith, widow and relict of David Smith, dec. Byram Heard appointed admin. of David Smith, dec.

Page 18: March Term Court ordered.

Page 19: Dec. 1841 Session. Ordered that Nancy Newby, an insane woman, be brought to court and be let out to the lowest bidder.
Application of the widow Ingram. Robert Owens is appointed guardian of the minor heirs of Thomas Ingram, dec.

Page 20: Jan. 1842 Session.

Page 21: Settlement with court, James L. Killem and A. M.

Anderson, admins. of the estate of John Henninger, dec.
Settlement with Isaac Robeson, guardian of the minor heirs
of Wm. Lee, dec.

Page 24: Road overseers were Hugh Pike, Chas. Loving, and
James L. Killem.

Page 25: Commissioners appointed.

Page 26: Regarding the commissioners appointed.

Page 28: Regarding the commissioners appointed.

Page 29: Inventory of David Smith, dec., filed by Byram
Heard.

Page 34: Jan. 1842. A. M.Anderson appointed guardian of the
minor heirs of John Hemminger, dec.
James Tulloss, admin. of Wm. Henson, dec.; settlement.
Feb. 1842 Session.

Page 35: James A. Tulloss, admin. of estate of Wm. Henson,
dec.
Settlement of Isaac Robeson, guardian of the minor heirs
of William Green, dec.

Page 36: Settlement with Robert Owens, admin. of estate of
Wm. Green, dec.
Settlement with Robert Lowden, admin. of estate of James
Lowden, dec.
John Tollett appointed admin. of estate of B. W. Tollett.

Page 37: Application of Pheaby Tollet, widow and relict
of G. W. Tollett, dec., and it appearing to the satisfaction
of the court that her husband the said G. W. Tollett died intes-
tate... she asks for support for herself and family.

Page 38: Application of Lucy Davis, widow and relict of
Wm. Davis, dec., for James Hixson to be appointed admin. of the
estate of William H. Davis, dec.

Page 40: Francis Hughes was a pensioner of the United States
at the rate of $51.66 per annum, that he was a resident citizen
of Bledsoe County, Tenn.; that he died in the county and state
aforesaid on 25 Jan. 1841, that he left no widow, but did leave
four children, his heirs, whose names are John Hughs, Margaret
Hughs, Ingabow Hixson, and Rebecca Hixon and they were the only
heirs at law known to be living, etc. certified.

Page 41: March 1842. Inventory of G. W. Tollett, dec.,
filed by John Tollett, admin.
Settlement with James Robers (Rogers?), guardian of the
minor heirs of Frederick I. or J. Rogers, dec.

Page 42: Settlement with James Allen, guardian of the minor
heirs of Thomas Ingram, dec.
Settlement with John Hutcherson, guardian of the minor heirs
of Joseph Peters, dec.

Page 43: Regarding Phoebe Tollett; to have support from the
estate of her husband, dec.

Page 45: Regarding the death of Henry Grason.

(Book not paged from hereon.)

Elijah Hale appointed Road Overseer.

April 1842: Settlement with Jesse H. Standifer, admin. of
James Standifer.
Settlement with Isaac B. Vernon, admin. of John Clark, dec.
Eli Thurman, late of Bledsoe Co., died leaving a will, nam-
ing Wm. R. Thurman exec.; proved April 1842.

May 1842: Adam Lamb appointed guardian of Jane Read, minor
heir of Joel Read, dec.
2 May 1842: Latan Smith was a pensioner of the United States
at the rate of $80.00 per annum, and was a resident of Marion
Co., Tenn., where he died on 12 Dec. 1840. He left no widow
at his death, but he did leave four children, his heirs, whose
names are: Patsy Rogers, formerly Patsy Smith, Moses Smith,
Aron Smith, and Elizabeth Step, formerly Elizabeth Smith. The
said Laton Smith known to be living at Moses Smith is a citizen
of Hamilton County. Aaron Smith and Patsy Rogers are citizens
of Marion Co., and Elizabeth Step is a citizen of Bledsoe Co.
Nathan Coulston to be bound to Allen Green until he is 21.
Inventory of William Davis, dec., returned by James Hixson.
Nathan Coulston, orphan of the age of 18 years next Dec.
to be bound to Allen Green.
Inventory of Eli Thurman, dec., returned by Wm. R. Thurman.

June 1842: Thomas Smith and James Smith, orphans, to be
brought into court.
Anderson Oneil, orphan, to be taken by John M. Beatty.
Court allows Mistress Payne $5.00 for keeping Sarah Macall
a pauper now dec. at her house.
William Foster guardian of the minor heirs of David Poiner,
dec.
Joseph Hixson guardian of the minor heirs of John Hixson,
dec.
Isaac Roberson, guardian for the minor heirs of Wm. Green,
dec.

July 1842: Isaac Roberson guardian for the minor heirs of
Wm. Lee, dec.
Nathan Coulston, orphan boy bound to Allen Green in 1842,
May, has run away.
Settlement by Jane Rogers, admnx. of Frederick J. Rogers.

Aug. 1842: Aaron Schoolfield, admin. of (name of dec. not
given), to pay all minor heirs or orphans the money due g.
children.
James Cox to be bound to Aron Swafford by consent of his
mother until he is 21. He will be 18 on 25 Sept. 1842.
Ordered that Thomas Swofford, Jr., son of Thomas, be appointed road overseer.
Settlement of Mary Mapen, admin. and guardian of the minor
heirs of Richard Mapen, dec.

Oct. 1842: Settlement of J. R. Wheeler, admin. of Elisha
Thomas, dec.
Settlement of Joseph Hixson, guardian of the minor heirs
of John Hixson, dec.
Settlement of estate of Moses Owens, dec., by James Owens
and George F. Jons. (sic), admins.
Samuel Rankins settlement with J. R. Wheeler, admin. of
estate of Elisha Thomas, dec.
Elizabeth Phillips appointed admin. of John Phelps, dec.
Robert Barger and Lotott Barger were securities.
Settlement of estate of John Clark, dec., by Isaac B. Ver-
non, admin.

Dec. 1842: Application of Mary Clark, widow of John Clark, dec., appointed guardian to his minor heirs, namely: Daniel Clark, Nancy Clark, Carolina Jane and Mary, orphan children of John Clark.

Nancy Newbern, a pauper now at the Poor House, to be brought into court.

Bond for administration of estate of John Beaty, dec., by Edwin Beaty.

Isaac Roberson and Saml H. Hunt to lay off a year's support for the widow of Henry Busy, dec.

Application of Sarah Rusy, widow of Henry Rusy (or Busy), dec.; appointed admin.

Isaac Roberson and Saml H. Hunt commissioners to lay off allowance for Sarah Reasy, widow.

Jan. 1843: Eliza Phelps, widow, to have a year's support.

Administrator report of Edmund Beaty, admin. of John M. Beaty.

Settlement by Samuel W. Roberson, Treasurer, Board of Trustees for Lafayette Academy.

James Lloyd Kease allowance at Poor House. Isaac L. Anderson, Supt. of Poor House.

John Thomas settles the estate of Jonathan Hinson, dec.

Settlement of the minor heirs of William Lee, dec.

John Thomas settlement with Isaac Roberson, guardian of the minor heirs of William Green, dec.

Gilberth Keely bound to Wm. L. Kellerm(?) until he is 21. Keely is now 11 years old.

Susannah Maner, orphan, to be brought to court.

March 1843: Three orphans of Matild Manning, Daniel and the next two, are to be produced in court.

Application of Elizabeth Kimon (or Kimmer?), widow and relict of Jehu (or John) Kimon, dec. Wortherston L. Green is appointed admin. of said John (or Jehu) Kimon, dec.

April 1843: Estate of John Hale, dec., admin. by Isham Hale.

Saml. W. Roberson, guardian of the minor heirs of Nancy Hay (or Hany), dec.; namely, Nancy Hany, dec., Jefferson Hany, aged 12 years, and Polly, aged 8 years.

Orphan children of John Kimmer, dec., were: Eliza Mayan, Christopher Andrew and Sarah.

Two orphan children of Julianna Foster ordered to be brought into court to be disposed of as may think best.

Court orders Peter Hoodenpyl to pay support of bastard child of Anna Rogers.

Inventory of John Hale, dec., returned.

June 1843: James Own appointed guardian to the minor heirs of Amy Laner (?), David and James Laner.

James A. Whiteside, admin. of estate of Plunkett Y. Glntworth, dec., late a citizen of New Jersey who was a non-resident of this state, and owned personal property in the county, files an inventory.

Anderson O'Neil, orphan boy, to be bound to John Thurman until 21 years of age.

Widow of John Hale, dec., to have support.

Estate of Robert Farr, dec., by Thomas Maupin, admin.; inventory; filed bond as exec.

Settlement of estate of Wilson Tollett by John Tollett.

July 1843: Settlement of William Foster as guardian of minor heirs of David Poiner.

Settlement with Mary Maupin regarding the orphans of Richard Maupin, dec.

Aug. 1843: Anna Cook, admin. of estate of Wm. R. Cook, dec.
Thomas Maupin, admin., returns inventory of estate of Robert
Farr.
    Anna Cook, admin. of Wm. R. Cook, returns inventory of the
estate.
    James Cowan ordered to be released from paying Poll Tax
for 1843.

Sept. 1843: Catherine Thomas declared in court for pension
as widow of John Thomas, dec. John Thomas was a soldier in the
Revolution. Court approved the pension.
    Keziah Thurman, widow of Philip Thurman, applied for his
pension as a revolutionary soldier; the court approved the pension.

Nov. 1843. Settlement of Mary Clark for the minor heirs
of John Clark, dec.
    Kesiah Thurman, widow of Philip Thurman, proved she was
the wife of the said Philip.
    Settlement of Joseph Hixson as guardian of the minor heirs
of John Hixson, dec.
    Settlement by Jane Rogers as guardian of the minor heirs of
Frederick J. Rogers, dec.
    Settlement of Wm. L. Brown as guardian of the minor heirs
of Josiah Crawford, dec.

Dec. 1843: Settlement of the estate of David Smith, dec.

Jan. 1844: Patsy Smith an Edict heir (sic) of age, of
David Smith, dec.

NOTES FROM BLEDSOE COUNTY DEED BOOK "A"

    Page 1: 15 Jan. 1808, Christian Rhodes of Knox Co., Tenn.,
for $1000.00, sells to Thomas Menefee of Anderson Co. and James
Daver (Davers or Deavers) of Bledsoe Co., 1000 acres; Sequatchie
commonly called Crow Creek it being part of a 5000 acres granted
Stokley Donelson by North Carolina. Test: Stephen Heard, Israel
Standefer.

    Page 5: John Brown, Esq., High Sheriff of Roane Co., Tenn.
Court Decree. 24 July 1806. Judgement. James Charter, exec.
of James Allison, dec., on the last Mon. of Oct. 1795 to command the goods and chattells of Abraham Swaggerty. Breach of
covenant. Land was in Roane Co. 5000 acres to Geo. Williams,
Allest (sic), Wm. Brown, James Brown, and James Rogers.

    Page 104: 20 Jan. 1799. Thomas Swann of the Town of Alex-
andria, Va., and John Love of Buckland, Prince William Co., Va.
(This might be page 10 - R. W. B.)

    Page 14: 10 Oct. 1795, Stokley Donelson to John Love of
Prince William Co., Va. Josiah Watson of Alexandria and Samuel
Love of Loudon Co., Va. 5000 acres on Crow Creek (Sequatchie
Creek).

    Page 16: 29 Jan. 1798, John Love and his wife Elizabeth,
of Prince William Co., Va.,and Charles Jones Love of Loudon Co.,
Va. $3000.00, land on Crow's Creek, being the same conveyed
to Love on 10 Oct. 1795 by Donelson. Witnesses: Chas. Thompson
Samuel Love, Jr., Samuel Love, etc. Proved in Knox Co., 1798.

    Page 17: Another deed names the same parties that appeared
in the previous deed.

Page 22: Another deed pertaining to the same land. Material on this same land is found on pp. 26 and 30-35 inclusive.

Page 48: 28 Aug. 1795, indenture between Hugh Dunlap of Knox County, Territory south of Ohio, and Josiah Danforth of Washington Co., Va.; deed.

Page 60: 14 April 1808. Deed naming Robert Love, Robert Carter of Fairfax Co., Va., Charles J. Love of same county, and George McCampbell of Knoxville, Tenn.

Page 70: 3 Nov. 1805. Charles J. Love deeds to Richard H. Love of Alexandria County, District of Columbia.

Page 75: no date. Richard Handley Love, now in Tennessee, is given power of attorney by Charles Jones Love.

Page 77: 8 Aug. 1808. Josiah Danforth of Blount Co., Tenn., and Samuel Terry of Bledsoe Co., and Aquila Johnston of latter county; deed.

Page 141: 3 Oct. 1801. Property of John Rummy late of Whitehouse in Kingdom of Great Britain. Judgement proves possession of property. Power of attorney in Fairfax Co., Va., granted (by?) Thomas and Wm. Hogson (Hodgson?) to John McIver.

Page 167: Wm. James Hall of Alexandria Co., District of Columbia deeds to John McIver of same place and Joseph Park of Nashville, Davidson Co., Tenn.; in 1807. Deed also names James and William Park of Knoxville.

Page 172: Robert Patton to John McIver, deed; 1808; of Fairfax Co., Va.

Page 178: 28 Dec. 1807. John McClellan of Knox Co., Tenn., deeds to Bledsoe Co., Tenn.

Page 275: 10 Oct. 1809. John McIver deeds to Benjamine Greyson Orr of Montgomery Co., Md., 5000 acres on Crow Creek.

Page 284: 3 July 1804. John Davidson and wife Fanny of Norfolk, Va., deed 1500 acres of land to Robert Mateland of the same place.

Page 305: 8 Feb. 1809. John C. Scott and wife Ann of Fairfax Co., Va., deed 2000 acres of land to Charles J. Love and George McCampbell of Knox Co., Tenn.

Page 310: 26 Dec. 1796. John Love and wife Elizabeth of Prince William Co., Va., deed 1000 acres of land to Robert Carter of Loudon Co., Va.

Page 395: 23 Jan. 1798. John B. Armstead of Loudon Co., Va., deeds land to John Love of Prince William Co., Va.

Page 380: 16 March 1811. John Kelly of Bledsoe Co., buys negroes from James Standefer. Registered 10 Aug. 1811.

Page 413: date not given. Alexander Kelly has a grant of land located in Bledsoe County and duly registered.

Page 127. The will of Samuel Love of Salisbury, Fairfax Co., Va., is recorded in full. He names his wife Sarah Love; daughter Nancy Love; daughter Harriot Love; son John Courts Love, who are to have 5000 acres in Tenn. bought from John Love. His two sons Richard Hendley Love and Henry Jones Love were to have 5000 acres in Tenn. He also mentioned negroes bought from Anthony Thourton and Benjamine Berryman Thornton as will appear by a deed recorded in Stafford Co., the said negore being held by Dr. Robert Wellford and Nathaniel Fox who married the two widows Thornton. When the negroes become the property of Love's heirs (after the deaths of Mrs. Wellford and Mrs. Fox), they are to be divided among the testator's children: Charles Jones Love, Richard Hendley Love, Henry Jones Love, Nancy Love, and Harriott Love. Also named was Peter Huffman who had lived with the testator for many years. Charles Jones Love was made exec. The will was signed 22 July 1800 and proved 15 Dec. 1800. Samuel Love signed, and the will was proven in Fairfax Co., Va., Court by Edmund J. Lee, James Nisbett, and Charles Binns, Jr.

NOTES FROM BLEDSOE COUNTY DEED BOOK "B"

Page 1: Dated Madison, 25 May 1812.

Page 46: 5 Aug. 1812. Robert Bumpass of Wilson Co., Tenn., gives bill of sale to Amos Griffith.

Page 63: 7 Oct. 1812, William C. Tucker of Nottoway Co., Va., sells a negro boy to William Rippetee.

Page 76: 4 May 1813. Jacob Meyers for natural love and affection conveys a horse etc. to his son John Meyers.

Page 77: 5 May 1813. Jacob Meyers for natural love and affection conveys household furniture to his daughters Elizabeth and Anna Meyers.

Page 95: 18 Dec. 1813. Thomas Sim of Washington Co., married Harriett late Harriet Love who was willed property by Samuel Love, late of Salisbury, dec. Charles J. Jones of Fairfax Co., Va., also named.

Page 125: 9 Jan. 1814. Will of John Anderson names his wife Betsy as extx.; debt owed to Cosson James Skillian; children (not named).

Page 209: 1 April 1816. Signers of one of the numerous deeds of Love land were: Thomas Sim and wife Harriett, Henry Fonest and wife Jane (Forrest?), James Watson and wife Elizabeth, all of Washington, D. C., and Richard H. Love of Fairfax Co., Va., as heirs of John C. Love late of Washington, D. C., which Harriet, Jane, and Elizabeth were females, and Charles J. Love of Fairfax Co., Va., was party of second part.

NOTES FROM BLEDSOE COUNTY DEED BOOK "C"

Page 1: 7 May 1817. Isaac Runyan for natural love and affection conveys cattle etc. to his grandson William Runyan.

Page 11: date not given. Joseph Williams mortgages to John Tollett 50 acres where Williams now lives. The place Williams bought from Kinza Coats being in White Co.

Page 66: 11 Jan. 1817. Richard Moore, Jr., of Bledsoe Co., deeds land in said county to Pleasant Dawson of Albemarle Co., Va.

Page 89: 1816. John W. Salmons of Franklin Co., Tenn., gives bill of sale to Alexander Coulter of Bledsoe Co.

Page 154: 1 Nov. 1818. Aaron Higinbotham of Warren Co., Tenn., deeds to Jamy Standifer.

Page 311: 20 Oct. 1819. Jeremiah Benton and Martha C. Benton, daughter of John F. Benton. Jeremiah Benton for natural love and affection deeds property to Martha C. Benton, (now going for two years old), daughter of John F. Benton who was a son of Jeremiah Benton.

Page 314: April 1819. William Beazley for love and affection deeds a negro boy to his grandson David Shiley or Davis Skeley.

Page 317: 6 Oct. 1819. Anne Wakefield of Marion Co., Tenn., deeds 21 acres of land to John Haile of Bledsoe.

Page 325. Plunkett F. Glendworth and Hugh Thompson give power of attorney to John McIver. Glendworth was of Trenton, New Jersey. Thompson was of Baltimore Co., Md. McIver was of Alexandria District of Columbia. Mentions land in Bledsoe Co., Tenn.

INDEX TO CARTER COUNTY WILLS TO 1850.

Not all wills in Carter County are in the will books. The following list includes only those contained in Will Book no. 1. Following the list are notes on some of the wills.

Page 86: Will of Sarah Blevens, made 28 Oct. 1818, and filed Nov. 1818. Son-in-law Permans Lovelace; dau. Agnes his wife.

Page 87: Will of Elizabeth Carter made 22 March 1841, names daughter Sally S. Brewer a part from her husband Berryman (Benj.) Brewer; ; George S. Duffield in trust for support of his mother Sally S. Brewer during her life; grandchildren George Duffield, Wm. P. Brewer, and Eveline H. Brewer, children of Sally S. Brewer; daughter Mary C. Taylor; granddaughter Elizabeth Rhea, formerly Elizabeth Carter, daughter of A. M. Carter; granddaughter Mary C. P. Taylor, daughter of my daughter Mary C. Taylor; daughter Eliza Gillespie; son Alfred M. Carter; Alfred W. Taylor, husband of my granddaughter Elizabeth Taylor, daughter of Sally S. Brewer

Page 90: Will of James H. Crawford, made 17 Dec. 1845, names brother John H. Crawford to have an interest in father's estate; brother Jehu H. Crawford. At the death of my father property to my brothers.

Page 83: Will of Samuel Bogart, made 22 Oct. 1833, filed 13 Feb. 1843; names son Jeremiah to have land in Washington Co.; daughter Lydia to have land and home place; daughter Margaret McNabb to have part of home place/ Son Jeremiah to be exec.

Page 84: Will of William Dugger, Sr., made 10 April 1839 and filed 1839, names daughter Anna Wilson, son Mark Dugger, son James Dugger, son Julius Dugger, daughter Elizabeth, daughter Lavinia Vanhouse, son Thomas Dugger, daughter Pody Pierce, and daughter Martha, daughter Rosanna Morton. Land in Carter Co. where Mathias Vanhouse and Anderson Pierce now live. Daughter Nancy and daughter Sabra Morgan to have an equal part where son Thomas lives. Wife Ann to have land she now lives on and at her death to my sons William, David, and Tarlton.

Page 78: Will of John Hyder, made 23 March 1833, and proved May 1833, names son Michael E. Hyder, wife Ann, daughters Jane Haun, Nancy Haun, Lucinda Young, Lavinia Edens, Margaret Emmert and heirs of my daughter Betsy Parkison. John Haun and Nathiel T. Eden to be execs.

Page 80: Will of Joseph Powell, made 22 Nov. 1839, and filed Nov. 1839, names wife Elenor, son Joseph, son Robert H. to be exec.

Page 81: Will of Thomas D. Love, made 13 Nov. 1832, proved May 1833, names: wife Anna; children under age; Jas. P. T. Love; Mary T. Love; Robert Love; Louisa Elizabeth and Sarryferra Love; Thos. D. Love; Eveline Love; infant son John.

Page 76: Will of Jeremiah Miller, made 14 Oct. 1825, names: Malinda Dearman an illegitimate daughter of Lydia Dearman who charges me with being the father, and I have no right to dispute it; Mary Ann Emmert to have 100 acres; David Sweddinborough a son of Elizabeth Emmert; Louisa Blevins daughter of Sarah Blevins; cousin Betsy Killey to have $30.00; Rachel Wilson to have $10.00; balance to my mother. At mother's death to my children as they come of age. David Wagner, Sr., and William Bleaster execs. Will proved 1825. Codicil to Reuben Miller and Abraham Miller, my brother's clothes.

Page 27: Will of Mathias Wagner, made 13 Feb. 1835 and filed 9 Nov. 1835, names wife Susanna; son Jacob and his wife Silea; son Frederick; son Joseph; son Mathias; six daughters Elizabeth Reece, Susanna Wagner, Catherine Wagner, Nancy Tuff, Sarah Carriger, and Margaret Carriger.

Page 75: Will of John Carrell, made 23 Nov. 1833, filed

1833, names wife Rebecca; son Isaac Carrell; son Wm. Carrell;
daughter Ellener Buckner; daughter Elizabeth Smith; son John;
son Elexander; daughter Sintha Carrell. Wife to be extx.

RECORDS OF DAVIDSON COUNTY

The following records from Davidson County Will Book no. 1
show where many of the settlers came from.

Page 1. Philip Alston of Freelands Station, Davidson Co.,
being about to move appoints Thomas Mosely of the same place
his lawful attorney. 6 Jan. 1784.

Page 2. Elizabeth Marney, wife of Thomas Marney, admx. of
John Turner, dec., on behalf of said Turner's children. 6 Jan.
1784.

Page 3. Dan'l Oglesby; record of sale of lands to Jas.
Hoggett by Dan'l Oglesby son of Elisha Oglesby of 96th Dist.,
S. C. 6 Jan. 1784.

Page 4. Bill of sale, Oglesby to Hoggett.

Page 5. Stephen Holston; record pertains to his heirs and
to Elisha Oglesby. 1783.

Page 6. Jasper Butler of Davidson Co., N. C.; Jacob Shive-
ly of Washington Co., Tenn., appointed attorney. 6 April 1784.

Page 6. Inventory of Edward Larimore, dec. 6 Jan. 1784.

Page 7. Inventory of Nicholas Gentry, Isaac Mayfield,
admin. 6 Jan. 1784.

Page 8. William Ellis of Cumberland District gives bill
of sale to Jno. McFarland. 7 Dec. 1781.

Page 9. Evan Shelby of Sullivan Co., N. C., bill of sale
to Jonathan Drake of Cumberland District. 6 July 1784.

Page 9. John Cockrell of Davidson Co., N. C., appoints
James Robertson of same place his attorney to sell lands in
Green Co. Date not given.

Page 10. Will of James Leeper, made 16 April 1781, and
filed 6 July 1784. Names wife Susanna; "if she now be pregnant
with child." Mentions his father. James Robertson and Hugh
Leeper to be admins.

Page 10. Inventory of Nicholas Tramel. 25 June 1784.

Page 11. Will of Jonathan Jennings, filed 6 July 1784.
He mentions land he received from the Indians, and named son
William, son Edmund, daughter Elizabeth Harnner, Mary, Aggey,
Anne, Susanna, son Jonathan who was scalped by the Indians.
Wife is mentioned but not named.

Page 11. Inventory of David Gowen, filed 1781.

Page 13. Philip Allston of Davidson Co., N. C., sells land
to John Turnbull. 14 Aug. 1784.

Page 16. Inventory of James Freeland, Margaret Freeland
the admnx. 6 July 1784.

Page 15: Power of attorney between Micajah Mayfield of Jefferson Co., Va., and his brother Isaac Mayfield of N. C., Davidson Co., who is appointed by Micajah to settle the estate of their father James Mayfield, and to divide between their younger brothers Elisha and Elijah. 5 Oct. 1784.

Page 17: Jno. Childress gives bill of sale to orphan named Jno. Green Childress of Davidson Co., N. C. 6 June 1784.

Page 17: Inventory of Patrick Quigley returned by William Overall, admin. 6 July 1784.

Page 18: Jno. Childress gives bill of sale to Jesse Hughs for "my making to him so soon as deeds can be issued from the Secretaries Office to the Continental Line Officers in the State of Virginia good sufficient deeds in fee simple to 350 acres of first rate land lying on the west fork of Red River." 13 July 1784.

Page 19: Christopher Guise of Davidson Co., and Margaret his wife, to Jonathan Guise of the same place. 1 Sept. 1784.

Page 22: William Leaton of Lincoln Co., Virginia, for divers good reasons...appoints George Neville of the same place his attorney to sell property in the area of Cumberland in Davidson Co. 7 Aug. 1784.

Page 23: Rebecca Woods of 96th Dist., S. C., gives letter of attorney to Geo. Neville of the Dist. to settle the estate of John Woods, dec. 25 Aug. 1785.

Page 24: Nicholas Long of Halifax Co., N. C., gives letter of attorney to Anthony Bledsoe of Sullivan Co. 29 May 1784.

Page 25: James Gerald gives bill of sale for a negro to William More. 5 Jan. 1785.

Page 25: Daniel Ross, dec.; Thomas Molloy his admin. 5 Jan. 1785.

Page 26: Deposition of Sarah Payne, daughter of Josiah Payne, being of full age, states that her father Lewis Green (sic) made his abode in Washington Co. on the Clinch River. Her father wanted his money divided among his children. In the month of October afterwards her father and her husband's family moved to the settlement on the Cumberland before her father left the Clinch (about eighteen months before) and that he left the written will with Benjamine Nichols. Among the children were Zachariah Green; Mary Payne her mother-in-law; George Payne her brother-in-law; and Jno. Payne. Mary Payne, wife of Matthew Payne, of full age, also made a deposition at the same time regarding the same matter. 1 April 1785.

Page 27: James Rentfro of Fayette Co., Va., for divers reasons, moving, etc., appoints George Neville of Davidson Co., N. C., his attorney. 5 July 1785.

Page 28: William Joiner of North Carolina appoints Stephen Jett his attorney. 4 Oct. 1785.

Page 29: Bond between James Robertson and others. 1785.

Page 30: Bond between James Robertson and others. 1785.

Page 31. Bond between James Robertson and others. 1786.

Page 33: Thomas Spencer gives a bill of sale to Ephraium Payton for land. 4 March 1783.

Page 34: Solomon Kitts of Baltimore Co., Md., merchant; John Rice of Hillsborough, Orange Co., N. C., Gentleman, agreement pertaining to lands in Davidson Co. 23 Aug. 1785.

Page 36: James Bosley of Davidson Co. gives bond to William Macklin, Sr., that he will marry Macklin's daughter Rebecca. 3 Jan. 1786.

Page 38: Thomas Barker of Davidson Co., N. C., gives a power of attorney to Luke Shelby to sell lands in Green Co., N. C. 4 Jan. 1786.

Page 38: Thomas Martin of Davidson Co., N. C., gives bill of sale to Benjamine Drake of same county, for a negro. 30 July 1786.

Page 39: Will of John Kennedy, Sr., of Davidson Co., N. C., leaves sons John and Abraham 640 acres of land each. Daughters Margaret and Mary are to have 320 acres each. George Kennedy's heirs mentioned. James Mulherrin and John Buchanan are named executors. Will made 9 Oct. 1785 and proved 3 Jan. 1786.

Page 40: Thomas Gist, Jr., appoints James Winchester his attorney to sue and recover from Capt. James Bosley on the Cumberland River of N. C. He mentions litigation with John Gwinn, Jr., of Frederick Co., Md. 1785.

Page 41: Inventory of Catherine Lefever appraised by James Shass and George Neville. 6 Oct. 1785.

Page 42: John Rice of Davidson Co., N. C., appoints Marham Roston and Elisha Rice his attorneys to sell 10,000 acres of land on either the Duck or Tennessee or Mississippi Rivers lying in Davidson Co. 7 April 1786.

Page 43: Robert Gooseberry of Burke Co., N. C., gives bill of sale to Francis Hodge for land on Cumberland River. Dated 28 April 1780, and proved (sic) 4 April 1786.

Page 43: Inventory of estate of John Clendenning; contains one military warrant for 2360 acres and another for 420 acres, neither of which have been located. 6 April 1786.

Page 43: Catherine Lefever; estate admin. by Francis Armstrong. April 1786.

Page 44: James Robertson given letter of attorney by John Turnbull of Davidson Co. 22 July 1786.

Page 45: John Porter, dec.; inventory of his estate, which is admin. by Hannah Porter. 3 Jan. 1786.

Page 46: David Lucas, dec.; inventory of his estate. Leah Lucas, admnx. July 1786.

Page 46: Samuel Vernon, dec.; inventory of estate. Elizabeth Vernon, admnx. July 1786.

Page 47: James Moore, dec.; inventory of his estate. John Rice, admin. July 1786.

Page 48: Charles Robertson gives power of attorney to Jonathan Drake to collect for him in Davidson Co., N. C. 20 Nov. 1786.

Page 49: Nicholas Coonard(?) appoints Jno. Mastin his attorney in Davidson Co., N. C. 2 Jan. 1787.

Page 49: Moses Bush gives bill of sale to Timothy Demumbre and John Hodge, merchants, for a negro. 11 May 1786.

Page 50: Hugh Gilliland appoints John McDaniel of Amherst Co., Va., his attorney (because of Gilliland's moving) to sell land in Amherst Co., Va. 6 April 1787.

Page (?): Wm. Stuart of Davidson Co., N. C., appoints David Vance of Burke Co., N. C., his attorney to sell lands in Burke Co., N. C. 3 April 1787.

Page 51: Will of Rebecca Bosley, dated 15 May 1786, and proved by Thos. Smith in Jan. 1786. In it she mentioned the property comprising one-third of the estate of Capt. James Bosley, which she left to her four brothers: William Macklin, James Macklin, Shackfield Macklin, and John Macklin. She mentions a possible unborn child she is carrying. William Cocke, Elijah Robertson, and Thomas Molloy to be execs.

Page 52: William Polk of Davidson Co., N. C., is bound unto James Bosley regarding debt. May 1787.

Page 53: Matthew and Mary Payne give power of attorney to their son Josiah to sell land on Clinch River in Russell Co., Va. July 1787.

Page 53: Will of Mark Robertson, dated 12 Aug. 1784 and proved 2 July 1787. Sister Ann Cockrell's three daughters, Mary, Elizabeth, and Charity Johnson, to have 5000 acres of land on the Duck River. Brother Charles Robertson to have 640 acres of a military warrant lying one and a quarter miles above the mouth of Wells Creek, and entered in James Robertson's name. Sister Clash to have 320 acres on Little Harpeth. Also named was brother James Robertson. Wife Mary Robertson to be extx.

Page 54: Inventory of Cornelius Ruddle, dec. Jas. Mulherrin and Jane Ruddle, admins. Jan. 1787.

Page 59: William Gubbins or Cubbins, dec. Inventory and admin. by Larkin Clark. 4 July 1786.

Page 61: James Allen of Davidson Co., gives power of attorney to Daniel Rowan in 1787.

Page 61: Margaret Allen of Davidson Co., N. C., appoints Daniel Rowan of same place her attorney to sell John Scott of Penna., land in Sulphur Fork of Red River. 1787.

Page 62: Alexander Moore of Davidson Co., N. C., gives bond to Thomas Edmiston of same county, as agent and attorney for Matthew Buchanan of Washington Co., Va., to discharge matters. 1788.

Page 63: James Lenear of Davidson Co., N. C., gives bill of sale to Henry Lenear for a mare. 1788. .

Page 64: Records pertaining to sales etc. of property of James Lenear. 1788.

Page 65: Julius Sanders sells to James Hogatt 990 acres on the Big Harpeth, 24 miles from French Lick. 3 July 1787.

Page 65: Benjamine Drake, Sr., of Davidson Co., N. C., sells a negro to Benjamine Drake, Jr. 1788.

Page 66: Dabiel Dunam of Cumberland, N. C., gives power of attorney to Isaac Johnston of the same place. 1788.

Page 66: Jonathan Drake of Davidson Co. sells property to John Drake. 1788.

Page 67: James Bosley sells property to Elijah Robertson. 1788.

Page 67: Ralph Fleming and John Thomas make oath that they saw James Hollis and Samuel (sic) agree on a Continental Line. 1788.

Page 67: John Turner gives bill of sale to Jno. Boyd. 9 April 1788.

Page 67: William Hays, dec. Inventory returned by Daniel Frazier, admin. 1 Oct. 1787.

Page 68: Thomas Nowland, dec. Inventory returned by Ann Nowland. April 1788.

Page 68: William Mabane of Orange Co., N. C., for divers reasons, moving, etc., appoints Col. Anthony Bledsoe of Davidson Co., N. C., his attorney to attend to land sold to Lewis Robert of Kentucky in Virginia. 20 Jan. 1787.

Page 69: John Buchanan, dec. Estate inventories and admin. by James Mulherrin. 4 Oct. 1787.

Page 69: James Juson(?), dec. Inventory of estate returned by William Crutcher. July 1788.

Page 70: Headon Wells of Davidson Co., N. C., assigns his right and title to certain lands in the District of Kentucky and neighborhood of Lincoln to Alexander Parker, surveyor of Lexington, for locating. 1788.

Page 70: Landon Carter of Davidson Co. appoints William Wicoff of Monmouth Co., N. J., his attorney to sell lands he possessed in Davidson and Sumner Counties. 1788.

Page 71: Henry Lenier of Davidson Co., N. C., sells property to Isham Lenier. 1788.

Page 71. Hy. Lenier of Davidson Co. sells property to John Phillips, in 1788.

Page 72: William Lewis of Surry Co., N. C., sells property to Jonathan Drake of Davidson Co., N. C. 1788.

Page 72: Thomas Taylor of Davidson Co., N. C. sells to Jonathan Drake property. 1788.

Page 72: James and Geo. Winchester of Sumner Co. pay for property. 3 July 1788.

Page 72: William Hays, dec. Sales of property by admins. 7 July 1788.

Page 73: Anthony Harmond, commonly called Sansansion, has appointed James Cole Mountflorence his attorney. 1788.

Page 74: John Vernon of Nashborough Co., N. C., gives bond to Hugh Bradshaw of same county. 1788.

Page 75: James Maxwell of Davidson Co. gives bill of sale to Timothy Demumbre. 1788.

Page 77: Will of Margaret Mitchell, proved 8 July 1788. She names land in Guilford Co., N. C.; her granddaughter Margaret Ross; and friend James Ross, who is to be exec.

Page 77: Samuel Vernon gives bond to Absom Hooper. 1788.

Page 78: James Wood gives bill of sale to James Maxwell. 1788.

Page 78: James Bosley gives bill of sale to Daniel Rowan. 1788.

Page 78: Sinclair Pruit, with the consent of his guardian David Hay, is bound out as an apprentice to Christopher Owens, hatter in Davidson Co., N. C., for a term of seven years. 1788.

Page 79: Elizabeth Cripps of Nelson Co., Va., appoints her brother Thomas Brashears as her attorney to transact business in N. C. for her. 29 Sept. 1788.

Page 80: John Marney sells a negro to Thomas and George Blakemore. 1788.

Page 80: James Bosley sells a negro to Joseph Love. 1788.

Page 81: John Fry of Pitt Co., N. C., transfers to James and Margaret Leniear (Lenier), both the children of James and Sarah Lenier, for love and affection, a negro; same lent to James Lenier, Sr., of Davidson Co. 1788.

Page 81: Articles of Agreement between Wm. Terrell Lewis of Surrey Co. and James Cole Mountflorence of Sumner Co. 1788.

Page 82: John Sappington of Davidson County gives a bill of sale to James McGavock of Montgomery Co., Va. 1788.

Page 83: Lavinia Simpson gives deposition concerning the nuncupative will made by her husband William Simpson. She and the child she was pregnant with and his two sons Gabriel and William Simpson should have the whole of the land whereon they then lived. He desired that the lands on Harpeth be equally divided among his three daughters, Sarah, Mary, and Elizabeth. Sworn to before Saml Barton on 7 Oct. 1788.

Page 83: Abraham Riston of Davidson Co. in regard to collecting debts owed by Capt. James Bosley of said county. 1788.

Page 84: Malchiah Fry sells a steer to Frederick Stump. 1788.

Page 84: James Bosley sells negroes to his son John Bosley. Jan. 1789.

Page 84: Joshua Hadley sells a negro to Landon Clark. 1789.

Page 85: John Gibson of Davidson Co., N. C., sells negroes to Landon Clark of the same place. 1789.

Page 85: James Forde of Davidson Co., N. C., sells a negro girl to John Drake of same county. 16 May 1788.

Page 86: Col. Robert Hays buys from John Rice, through Joel Rice, his attorney. 6 Jan. 1789.

Page 86: Samuel Loggins of Davidson Co., N. C., sells 150 acres of land on Sycamore Creek, adj. John Rylee's, and some livestock, to James Mills. 25 July 1789.

Page 87: Thomas Smith sells to Elijah Robertson. 16 March 1789.

Page 87: Elijah Robertson of Davidson Co., N. C., gives bond to Laurence Pourtozman (Portzman) of Washington Co., Md., for $2900.50, for merchantable beaver fur. 8 July 1788.

Page 88: Thomas Smith sells a horse to Isaac Thomas. April 1789.

Page 88: Thomas Smith gives a bill of sale to Andrew Jackson of Davidson Co. for a horse. 9 April 1789.

Page 88: Articles of Agreement between Henry Turney of Cumberland, Settlement of North Carolina, and Daniel Chambers of Lincoln Co., Va. Government. Turney sells one-half of his right as a settler in the above said county and settlement of Cumberland, etc. 2 Sept. 1782.

Page 89. William Collinsworth gives letter of attorney to Wm. Gallaspy. 27 Oct. 1791.

Page 89: John and Elisha Rice of Davidson Co., N. C., sell a negro girl to Edgar and Traitt of the same place. March 1789.

Page 90: Thomas Smith sells a still set up at Capt. James Hoggatts to Jas. Bosley. 13 Dec. 1789.

Page 91: Stockley Donelson of Hawkins Co., N. C., for 300 pounds and for real affection gives to Rachel Donelson all his right, title, and interest to the personal estate of his father, John Donelson, dec. 21 Jan. 1789.

Page 91: Stockley Donelson of Hawkins Co. sells a negro girl to Edward Douglass of Sumner Co. 26 Jan. 1789.

Page 92: Adam Hampton of Davidson Co., N. C., sells a negro girl to William Taitts of same place. 7 April 1789.

Page 92: Will of John McCutchens, made 30 Jan. 1789, and proved in court in April 1789. He names his wife Elizabeth McCutchens, and Hugh his son; his children younger than Hugh; two eldest sons James and Hugh McCutchens. Friend and brother Patrick and James McCutchens.

Page 93: Will of William McCutchens, proved April 1789. Wife Elizabeth to have land on Mill Creek adjoining Southerlin Mayfield. Daughters Grizzle (Grizzel) and Jane. Execs. to be wife and James and Saml McCutchens.

Page 94: John Sappington sells a negro girl to John Rice. 25 March 1787.

Page 94: Joseph Brook of Davidson Co., N. C., makes Anthony Foster his attorney. 20 Dec. 1788.

Page 95: Inventory of estate of Thomas McQuains, by Benjamine Cassellman.

Page 95: Inventory of estate of Jacob Mills; Jesse Evans admin. April 1789.

Page 95: Will of John Hunter made 27 March 1788, proved April 1789, names wife Mary Hunter, and appoints her and Hugh Bell to be execs.

Page 96: Will of Christopher Leightholder, made 8 May 1788 and proved April 1789; also in court Jan. 1790. He leaves all his worldly estate to the Methodist Church as the conference or members shall think most proper. Headen Wells to be exec.

Page 96: John Sappington sells Thomas Molloy a negro. 20 Jan. 1789.

Page 97: Thomas Blackmore sells John Manney a negro. 24 March 1789.

Page 97: Will of Acquila Sugg, made 13 Feb. 1785, filed July 1789, describes himself of Tarr River, Edgecombe Co., N. C., and names wife Abigail, sons William and Noah, and refers to his children.

Page 97: Jumpier Lieri(?), alias Peter, being a free man of age, binds himself of his own accord to Isaac Thomas for 10 years as a servant. 26 Dec. 1788.

Page 97: Jonathan Drake sells a red cow to James Campbell. 8 July 1789.

Page 99: Received of Major Mountflorence the following warrants with the locations therein; to wit;

No. 293.	Major Thomas Hogg	4800 acres
No. 294.	Capt. John Ingler	3840 acres
No. 295.	Capt. John Davis	3840 acres
No. 296.	Capt. Jesse Read	3840 acres
No. 297.	Capt. Wm. Goodman	3840 acres
No. 288.	Lieut. John Fordd	2560 acres
No. 299.	Lieut. Thos. Parteur	2560 acres
No. 300.	Pvt. Jacob Matthews	640 acres
No. 304.	Pvt. Theophilus Hays	455 acres
No. 321.	Pvt. John Jeffery	274 acres
No. 322.	Pvt. William Sweat	228 acres
No. 324.	Brigad.-Gen. Hogan	12000 acres
No. 325.	Pvt. Saml Garner	640 acres
No. 326.	Pvt. Moore Walker	228 acres
No. 327.	Pvt. Joseph Hartly	383 acres
No. 328.	Fifer Thomas Bryant	595 acres
No. 329.	Capt. Jno. Vance	3840 acres
No. 330.	Lieut. Jno. Vance	2560 acres
No. 332.	Maj. William Fenner (or Tunner)	2057 acres
No. 333.	Capt. Robert Fenner(?)	3840 acres
No. 334.	Lieut. James Campden	2560 acres
No. 336.	Capt. Jno. McNees	3840 acres
No. 337.	Capt. And'w Armstrong	1286 acres
No. 339.	Surgeon David Love	2057 acres
No. 340.	Capt. Jos. Montfort	3840 acres
No. 341.	Capt. Howel Tatum	3840 acres
No. 342.	Lieut. Blount Whitwell	824 acres
No. 345.	Lieut. Anthony Crutcher	2560 acres

The within mentioned warrants were rec'd and came to hand about 20 Dec. 1783, with locations inclosed.
(Signed) Martin Armstrong, Sur.

        Capt. Anthony Crutcher and Maj. Mountflorence inform me
that the within warrants and their locations are entered in the
office which must have been long after I received them as no office was established in the year eighty-three, but it's my opinion that every one of the returns made on such locations should
in Justice bear date from the date mentioned in the above receipt. To wit, 20 Dec. 1783.
                    (Signed) Martin Armstrong

        The last above mentioned was proven to be the Act and
Deed of the said Armstrong by the oath of Charles Garrard in
Court held for the County of Davidson, July Term, 1798.
            Test: Andrew Ewing, C. D. C.

        Page 100: Phillip Phillips and Michael Campbell, both of
State of Virginia, District of Kentucky, appoint James Cole
Mountflorence of Davidson Co., N. C., their attorney regarding
the sale of land in Mero District. 21 May 1789.

        Page 100: Squire Grant of Davidson Co., N. C., appoints
William Crutcher of same place his attorney. 18 July 1788.

        Page 101: Hugh Gibbs of Mercer Co., Va., appoints William
Crutcher of Davidson Co. his attorney. 14 Jan. 1789.

        Page 101: James Lenear of Bourbon Co., Dist. of Ky., appoints
Wm. Crutcher his attorney. 18 April 1789.

        Page 101: Edgar and Taitt of Davidson Co., N. C., appoint
James Maxwell their attorney. 17 March 1789.

        Page 102: Jonathan Skinner of Davidson Co. sells two copper
stills etc. to George Neville of Tennessee Co., N. C. 27 June
1789.

        Page 102: Thomas Hickman of Nash'll, Davidson Co., on Cum-
berland River, sells Timothy Demumbreum negroes for behoof of
Simon de Hubardcan(?). 2 May 1789.

        Page 103: John Sappington sells Wm. Galaspy a negro. 16
June 1789.

        Page 103: Wm. Crutcher of Davidson Co. sells lot # 19 in
Nashville to Robert C. Foster of Nelson Co., Dist. of Ky. 3
July 1789.

        Page 104: Stokley Donelson of Hawkins Co., N. C., sells
David Shelby of Sumner Co., N. C., a negro boy. 16 April 1789.

        Page 105: Joseph Ross and Co. of Edgecombe Co., N. C.,
appoint James Cole Mountflorence their attorney. 13 Feb. 1789.

        Page 105: John Elliott of Tennessee Co., N. C., appoints
Thomas Johnston of aforesaid his attorney. 6 May 1789.

        Page 106: Agreement between Ann Harkin late from Ireland,
now of Baltimore Co., Md., and John Rice of Davidson Co., N. C.
Ann Harkins sells herself to Rice as a servant. Signed Nancy
Harkins (her mark) and John Rice. July 1789. (Since the record
gives her name as Ann and she signs herself as Nancy, her name
must have been Nancy Ann - E. R. W.)

        Page 107: Inventory of Thomas McClain's estate returned by
Benj. Cassellman, admin. July 1789.

Page 108: William Lemmons of Davidson Co. sells a horse to John Lane of the same place. 11 April 1789.

Page 108: Sarah Lucas and William Stuart, both of Davidson Co., sell a negro girl to Jonathan Drake of N. C. 18 Sept. 1789.

Page 109: Inventory of estate of John Donelson returned by Wm. Donelson, admin. July 1789.

Page 110: John Forde of Davidson Co., N. C., appoints Jas. Cole Mountflorence his attorney to collect from John Baker, Esq., of Gates Co., N. C., and from Col. Archibald Lytle of Orange Co., N. C. 25 Sept. 1789.

Page 111: Thos. Green of Davidson Co. sells a negro to Eustins Bushnell. Aug. 1789.

Page 111: James Robertson of Davidson Co., N. C., gives a bill of sale to Abner Green of Natchez Dist., N. C. 29 Aug. 1789.

Pages 112-113: Moses Shelby and Adam Hampton give bond to Michael Campbell and Philip Phillips of Nelson Co., Ky. 6 Oct. 1789.

Page 114: Edin Hickman and James Martin Lewis of Davidson Co., N. C., gives bond to Philip Phillips of Nelson Co., Va., in the sum of 1000 pounds Va. currency to convey land on Duck River. Dated 18 Oct. 1786, proved 6 Oct. 1789.

Page 116: Mauldin Sanders and Shelby (give bond to?) Campbell and Phillips. 1789.

Page 117: Bond. Hampton, Shelby, Phillips, and Campbell. 1789.

Page 118: John Marney gives bill of sale to Jonathan Marney. 21 Sept. 1789.

Page 118: David Deadrick of Frederick Co., Va., sells a negro girl to Nancy Wood(s), daughter of John James Wood(s) of Davidson Co., N. C. 21 Sept. 1789.

Page 119: John Minor of Davidson Co., N. C., sells a negro to Samuel Martin of the same place. 12 Aug. 1789.

Page 119: Thos. Green gives a letter of attorney to Sampson Williams and Andrew Jackson. 26 Aug. 1789.

Page 120: James Cole Mountflorence gives bill of sale to George Walker. 10 Oct. 1789.

Page 120: Eustins Bushnell of Davidson Co. gives bill of sale to Griswold Latimore. 2 Oct. 1789.

Page 121: Jas. Foster gives bill of sale to John Hay. 1789.

Page 121: Inventory of sale of the estate of Aquilla Sugg, returned by Abigail Sugg, extx. Oct. 1789.

Page 122: Nicholas Concord of Tennessee Co., N. C., appoints Sampson Williams his attorney. 17 Sept. 1789.

Page 122: Will of William Berry made 16 July 1789 and proved Oct. 1789. He names his infant dau. Mary Berry and his wife Keziah Berry.

Page 123: Inventory of Curtis Williams returned by Nancy Seward. Oct. 1789.

Page 123: Bryant Soverants (servants) to Samuel Martin. Oct. 1789.

Page 124: Philips and Camobell give instructions to James Cole Mountflorence. 1789.

Page 125: Eustius Bushnell gives bill of sale to Frederick Stump. Jan. 1790.

Page 127: Eustius Bushnell of Davidson Co., N. C., gives bill of sale to Frederick Stump. 1790.

Page 127: Turner Williams of Davidson Co., N. C., gives power of attorney to Sampson Williams of same place. 1790.

Page 128: Amos Heaton and Isaac Drake are appointed to appraise the estate of Wm. McGough, dec. 1790.

Page 129: Inventory of estate of Curtis Williams returned. Jan. 1790.

Page 129: Headon Wells of Davidson Co., exec. of Christopher Leightholder, dec., appoints Gen. Winchester of Sumner Co. 9 Jan. 1790.

Page 130: Release by Jonathan Drake. Hardy Murfree, a Continental Soldier. 17 April 1790.

Page 130: Philip Trimm sells to William Loggins, etc. 13 April 1790.

Page 131: Samuel Martin sells stock and cattle to Henry Lane. 19 March 1790.

Page 131: John Smith of Davidson Co. sells a negro girl to James Cooper of Va. 10 April 1790.

Page 131: James Atwood of Laurence Co., S. C., sells a negro to Daniel Frazer of Davidson Co., N. C. 22 Feb. 1790.

Page 132: Thomas Green of Natchez Dist. gives power of attorney to Daniel James of Davidson Co. 13 March 1790.

Pages 133-134: John Dodge appoints James Bosley of Davidson Co., N. C., his attorney in suits in Equity in Mero Dist. agst. Landon Clark. 30 Jan. 1790.

Page 135: Samuel Moore of Lincoln Co., Va., appoints Samuel Wilson of Davidson Co., N. C., his attorney to deliver a deed to Joseph Martin of Tennessee County. 20 Oct. 1789.

Page 136: Inventory of estate of John Dunam, dec. April 1790.

Page 136: Inventory of estate of Southerlin Mayfield, dec., returned by Margaret Mayfield, admnx. April 1790.

Page 136: Inventory of estate of Abedngs(?) Llewellen returned by Nancy Llewelllen. 1790.

Page 138: David Allison of Davidson Co. appoints James Cole Mountflorence his attorney to handle deed for land sold to James Robertson. 1790.

Page 145: James Bosley and wife Mary sell a begro to Beal Bosley. 1790.

Page 145: Murfree gives release to Drake. 1790.

Page 149: Adam Hampton gives bond to William Nash of Davidson Co. 1790.

Page 151: Sampson Williams; bond. 1790.

Page 152: George Walker of Davidson Co.; bond. 1790.

Page 154; John Duffle of Davidson Co., N. C., sells horses, etc., to William Brown. 1790.

Page 155: Peter Rentfrow sells land on Cumberland River to George Pirtle. 9 Sept. 1780; proved July 1790.

Page 155: Jessee Read of Davidson Co., Mero Dist., gives power of attorney to J. C. Mountflorence. 1790.

Page 156: William Erwind, of Davidson Co., Mero Dist., agrees to work for Gen. Augustus Sugg of same place. July 1790.

Page 160: Edwin Hickman gives power of attorney jointly with Anthony Crutcher a bond to Philip Phillips and Michael Campbell. Aug. 1790.

Page 161: Wm. Gowen sells a negro girl to Frederick Stump. 13 Aug. 1790.

Page 161: Samuel Shannon of Davidson Co., Mero Dist., gives bond to John Forde to make good a deed for land on Mill Creek. 1790.

Page 163: John Boyd of Davidson Co., N. C., gives bill of sale to Frederick Stump.

Page 163: George Augustus Suggs of Davidson Co., N. C., sells a negro to Frederick Stump. 13 Aug. 1790.

Page 163: Robert Nelson of Tennessee Co., N. C., sells to Wm. Wicoff a slave formerly owned by John Edmondson. 24 April 1790.

Page 166: Inventory of estate of William Neely. July 1790.

Page 166: Sale of estate of John Donelson. July 1790.

Page 168: Account of sale of estate of John Donelson, dec. 1790.

Page 169: Inventory of estate of Wm. Ramsey, dec., returned by Hannah Ramsey and Isaac Rounswell. July 1790.

Page 170: John Sappington gives power of attorney to Sampson Williams. 1790.

Page 171: Trustees of Nashville Town. Assembly of Hillsborough, April 1784, established the town of Cumberland River near French Lick. Samuel Baxter, Thomas Molloy, and James Shaw, the remaining trustees of said Town, appoint and nominate Joel Rice and David Hay, directors and trustees of town of Nashville in room of Daniel Smith and Isaac Linsey, Esq. 8 July 1790.

Page 171: Edwin Hickman of Davidson Co. sells a negro boy to John Drake of the same. 11 Oct. 1790.

Page 171: Joseph Margue, factor to Andrew Fage, gives power of attorney to Thomas Molloy on 2 Sept. 1786. Registered Oct. 1790.

Page 172: John Hinds sells a negro to Frederick Stump. 1790.

Page 172: Deposition. Martha Cassellman against Mr. Mulherrin.

Page 172: Inventory of estate of Christian Distow, dec. 1790.

Page 173: William Brown of Tennessee Co., N. C., sells negroes to John Duff of same place. 12 May 1790.

Page 173: William Rowan of Somerset Co., Md., sells to Thomas Molloy of Davidson Co., N. C. (Date not given)

Page 174: Patrick Morgan and James Mathew, late merchants and carpenters of West Florida, at present in the town of New Orleans in the province of Luisiana, for certain good causes and hereto moving, give power of attorney to James Robertson and James Hoggett to transact business for them with Philip Alston and James Thomas, late inhabitants of Natchez, but now of Cumberland Co., N. C. 26 April 1790; registered 15 Nov. 1790.

Page 174: Justinian Cartwright of Davidson Co., N. C., sells a horse to Robert Cartwright of the same place. 17 Nov. 1790.

Page 175: Inventory of estate of Wm. Gowen, dec., returned to court by Sarah Gowen, admnx. Oct. 1790.

Page 176: Inventory and sale of estate of Wm. Ramsey, dec., delivered in court by Isaac Roundswell, admin. Oct. 1790.

Page 176: Estate of John Donelson, dec. Inventory of a subsequent sale of chattels returned to court by Wm. Donelson, admin. 1790.

Page 177: Bond between Anthony Crutcher of Davidson Co., N. C., and Stockley Donelson of Spencer Co. Jan. 1791.

Page 177: William Rowan of the State of Maryland gives power of attorney to Daniel Rowan of Davidson Co., N. C., to settle debts for him. 3 Aug. 1790.

Page 178: Jordan Roach sells horse etc. to John Dobbins. 8 Nov. 1790.

Page 178: James Bosley of Davidson Co., and Territory South of the Ohio River, sells a negro woman to John Phillips of Tennessee Co. 11 Jan. 1791.

Page 179: Evan Shelby sells negroes to Jaques Clamorgan of Illinois Co. in April. Acknowledged in court Jan. 1791.

Page 179: Daniel Young of Davidson Co., Terr. south of the Ohio River, sells negroes to Frederick Stump of the same place. 13 Jan. 1790. Proved 1791.

Page 180: Laurence Thompson of Sumner Co., N. C., sells

to Grisesold Latimore of Davidson Co., N. C., a horse, etc. Proved in court Jan. 1791.

Page 181: Will of Andrew Simpson, made 8 April 1789, filed 7 Jan. 1791. To Levice Simpson formerly the wife of William Simpson, dec., and to her daughter Mary Simpson, my plantation, etc. "all land lying in Chesterfield Co. Va., about fifteen miles from Richmond on the waters of Falling Creek on the Buckingham Road." To my four children, Elizabeth, Jeane, Mary, and Andrew Simpson.

Page 182: George Meldrum and Park, merchants of Detroit, did on 24 Oct. 1785 nominate John Dodge, merchant of Kaskaskias I-linois Co., their true and lawful attorney for lawful recovery, etc. etc. due said Meldrum and Park, said letter registered in Davidson Co., Territory south of the Ohio River on 31 May 1790. James Bosley appointed attorney, etc., 1791.

Page 185: Articles of agreement between Wm. Terrell Lewis and James C. Mountflorence of Surry Co., N. C., and Davidson Co., N. C., respectively. 1791.

Page 188: William Gallaspie of Davidson Co., Territory south of the Ohio, appoints Capt. Simon Spring his attorney regarding debt concerning an Indian or negro girl. 11 April 1791.

Page 189: John Blakemore of Davidson Co., appoints Charles Carter of Sumner Co. his attorney pertaining to negroes once the property of Lucy Carter of Amherst Co., Va. 11 April 1791.

Page 189: David Walker of Fayette Co., Va., appoints George Walker of Davidson Co., N. C., his attorney. 21 Sept. 1790.

Page 190: Articles of Agreement between Southerlin Mayfield and John Campbell, showing that Campbell has moved his family to Mayfield's fort on Mill Creek in November, and there continued for one year. 31 July 1786. Acknowledged in court, April 1791.

Page 191: Letters from John Marshall to Moses Shelby regarding the sale of certain warrants. 29 April 1786; registered 14 May 1791.

Page 192: William Thompson of Mercer Co., Dist. of Ky., appoints James Cole Mountflorence of Davidson Co. his attorney. 1791.

Page 195: Articles of agreement between Robert Hays, Thomas Overton, John Overton, and James Cole Mountflorence regarding the manufacture of salt at French Lick. 1791.

Page 194: Inventory of Jacob Cassellman(?), dec., returned to court by Eve Cassellman (Castleman). April 1791.

Page 194: James Bosley in behalf of John Dodge gives power of attorney to Beal Bosley. 25 Jan. 1791. Acknowledged April 1791.

Page 195: Anthony Crutcher gives power of attorney to J. C. Mountflorence of Davidson Co. Crutcher is of Tennessee Co., N. C. 1791.

Page 195: John Forde gives bill of sale to Samuel Budd. 1791.

Page 196: John Donelson's inventory; regarding negroes.

Page 199: Division of estate of John Donelson. Estate divided among Alexander Donelson, Samuel Donelson, Stockley Donelson. Notes on other heirs; to wit: John Donelson, Jane Hays, Catherine Hutchings, Rachel Jackson, William Donelson, Samuel Donelson, Mary Caffrey, Severn Donelson (mentions eleven children and widow).

Page 202: Joseph Doherty of Fayette Co., Dist. of Ky., gives power of attorney to Samuel Barton of Davidson Co., N. C., regarding sale of land in Davidson Co. 8 June 1790; acknowledged in court, 1791.

Page 203: David Hay of Davidson Co., N. C., appoints Major John Hays, John Caruthers and James Caruthers of Rockbridge Co., Va., his attorneys regarding sale of lots in Lexington and Rockbridge Co., Va. 16 April 1791. Proved in Davidson Co., 1791.

Page 203: Landon Clark appoints Elisha Clark of Gloucester Co., N. J., his attorney in that state. 18 May 1791.

Page 205: Anthony Sharp gives receipt to James Cole Mountflorence.

Page 207: Sheriff's bond. Daniel Williams. 6 Oct. 1783.

Page 208: Sheriff's bond. John Mulherrin. 8 July 1784.

Page 209: Sheriff's bind. Thomas Mastin. 5 July 1785.

Page 211: Sheriff's bond. David Hays. 3 July 1787.

Page 212: Sheriff's bond. Thomas Hickman. 1788.

Pages 213-215: Sheriff's bond. Sampson Williams. 28 Nov. 1788. 1789. 1790.

Page 216: Arthur Macadoo of Davidson Co. gives power of attorney to Hayden Wells. 5 Aug. 1791.

Page 216: Elijah Robertson sells a negro girl to David Shelby. 5 Aug. 1791.

Page 216: James Bosley of Davidson Co. sells a slave to John Erwin. 5 Aug. 1791.

Page 217: Agreement between James Bosley and David Allison. 23 May 1791.

Page 218: James Forde of Tennessee Co., N. C., sells a slave to John Erwin. 5 Aug. 1791.

Page 218: William Harrison of Lincoln Co., Dist. of Ky., on account of moving, gives power of attorney to Robert Cartwright of Davidson Co., N. C. 5 Aug. 1791.

Page 219: Turner Williams of Davidson Co., N. C., sells a negro man to Andrew Jackson. 5 Aug. 1791.

Page 219: Jonathan Skinner of Davidson Co. sells a copper still to James Shaw. 5 Aug. 1791.

Page 220: Estate of Christian Crips, dec., admin. by Landon Clark; returned to court, April 1791.

Page 221: Hayden Wells of Davidson Co. buys a copper still from Jonathan Skinner of same place. 5 Aug. 1791.

Page 223: Inventory of estate of Edwin Hickman, dec., returned by Thomas Hickman. 1791.

Page 229: Account of estate of Christian Cripps returned to court. 1791.

Page 229: Estate of Christopher Lightholder, dec., admin. by Hayden Wells, exec. July 1791.

Page 230: Estate of William Neely, dec., appraised and returned to court, July 1791 by William Neely. Division of estate among: Samuel Neely, William Neely, Margaret Neely, dau. Jane Caldwell, son Isaac Neely, Elizabeth Spears, Mary Spears.

Page 232: Division of estate of William Neely: dec. left issue: Jane Caldwell, Elizabeth Spears, Isaac Neely, Mary Spears, Samuel Neely, Peggy Neely, John Neely, Jenny Neely, and William Neely.

Page 233: William Lucas of Berkeley Co., Va., appoints his brother John Lucas of Davidson Co., N. C., his attorney regarding conveyance of land on Richland Creek to Andrew Lucas and Jacob Casselman, etc. 1789; acknowledged in court, 16 June 1789.

Page 234: Richard Hightower of Davidson Co., Territory south of the Ohio River, appoints his brother John Hightower of Rutherford Co., N. C., his attorney. 21 Sept. 1791.

Page 234: James Cooper of Davidson Co., N. C., sells a slave to William Leggins of same place. 13 July 1791. Registered 21 Nov. 1791.

Page 235: Elijah Robertson of Davidson Co., N. C., sells negroes to Phillips and Campbell of the Dist. of Ky. 1791.

Page 235: Phillips Cattering of Montgomery Co., Va., gives power of attorney to his brother Francis Cattering. Sept. 1785. Acknowledged in Davidson Co., Oct. 1791.

Page 236: Alexander Ewing of Davidson Co. gives bill of sale to Wm. Loggins. 13 March 1791.

Page 237: Rice Curtis of Davidson Co. sells a negro man to George Curtis of same place. 12 Sept. 1791.

Page 237: Lewis Ruling of Davidson Co. sells a horse to William Stuart of same place. 12 Oct. 1791.

Page 237: William Fort, sheriff of Edgecomb Co., has by virtue of attachments and executions Andrew Greer and Greer and Ford against Grisham Coffield (Colfield) have sold at public auction, slaves. 1 June 1791.

Page 238: Inventory of George Clark, dec., returned by Robert Clark, admin. Oct. 1791.

Page 239: John Boyd, Sr., of Davidson Co., sells to Levecia Simpson of said county a negro girl. 24 May 1791.

Page 240: Ephraium Hubbard of Davidson Co., N. C., sells a negro boy to George Blakemore of same place. 17 June 1791.

Page 240: George Augustus Sugg of Davidson Co. sells a slave to Andrew Jackson of same place. 21 Dec. 1791.

Page 240: Inventory of estate of Joseph French, dec., by

appraisers Joseph Dillander, Michael Glaves, and Zachariah Stull, 17 Dec. 1791.

Page 241: Joseph Howard of Natchez Dist., for divers good causes and moving appoints Andrew Ewing of Davidson Co., N. C., attorney. 3 Oct. 1791.

Page 242: Robert Weakley of Davidson Co., N. C., gives bond to Rev. Thomas Williamson, his heirs, etc., regarding the making of a deed for a piece of land sold to Williamson. Dec. 1791.

Page 243: John Bell of Davidson Co., N. C., in consideration of a judgement on James Bosley assigned to Bell by Andrew Fagot by order of George Bell, etc., for land lying in Henry Co., Va., sells to George Bell of Tennessee Co., a piece of land. 2 Sept. 1791.

Page 244: James Hoggatt gives a release to Elijah Robertson. 9 April 1792.

Page 245: Reace Porter of Davidson Co., N. C., sells to John Bell of the same place a negro. 10 Oct. 1791. Acknowledged in court April 1792.

Page 245: James White gives bill of sale to James Hoggatt. 1792.

Page 246: James Bosley gives a bill of sale to James Hoggatt. 1792.

Page 246: Inventory of Nicholas Baker, dec., delivered into court by Mrs. Baker, admnx. April 1792.

Page 247: Settlement of estate of Wm. Neely, dec.

Page 247: Estate of Joseph A. Silgreaves delivered into court by Josiah Love, Esq., admin. April 1792.

Page 248: Sheriff's sale of a slave of John Rice to Frederick Stump. 1792.

Page 248: Michael Shaver sells a slave to Frederick Stump. 1792.

Page 249: Will of John Rice, made 14 June 1784, probated May 1792, and recorded 11 Aug. 1792. Tract of land called Chickasas Bluff, belonging to Elisha Rice because he is willing to go to Western Country. My brothers to have their choice of land surveyed by Col. Polk, Capt. Lewis, or their deputies; my sisters to have 5000 acres of land. Jessee Benton to have next choice. For schooling the poor at the Cumberland, 5000 acres of land in the hands of the General Assembly. Execs. to be Col. Anthony Bledsoe, Jessee Benton, Wm. H. Rice, and Elisha Rice.

Page 250: Hardy Murfree of Hertford Co., N. C., promises Thomas Molloy of Davidson Co. he will make him the assignee of a legal title to 428 acres on the Middle Fork of Red River. 26 Aug. 1791. Registered 11 Aug. 1792.

Page 250: George Augustus Sugg sells a negro to Simon Sugg. 5 Dec. 1791. Proved 1792.

Page 251: John Angle of Davidson Co., N. C., sells to Matthew Talbot of the same place stock, etc. 28 April 1792.

Page 252: Frederick Stump gives bill of sale to John Overton. 1792.

Page 252: Estate of Samuel Deleach administered by Noah Sugg. July 1792.

Page 252: Inventory of Argolas Geter, dec., returned to court by Samuel Deason, admin. July 1792.

Page 253: Pleasant Lockett of Davidson Co. sells to John Barrow of the same place, a negro. Registered 13 Aug. 1792.

Page 253: Inventory of Richard Ashcraft, dec., delivered into court by Thomas Davie, admin. July 1792.

Page 254: Covenant between Samuel Barton and Jonathan Drake. Registered 13 Aug. 1792.

Page 254: William Maclin of Davidson Co., Tenn., receives power of attorney from Jordan Roach of Green Co., Territory of U. S., south of the Ohio. Registered 13 Aug. 1792.

Pages 255-258. Inventory of John Rice, dec., delivered by Joel and Elisha Rice. 1792.

Page 259: John Dodge of the Village of St. Geneive in La., merchant, for divers causes and because he is moving, appoints Seth Lewis of Davidson Co. his attorney. 10 June 1791. Recorded 1792.

Page 260: Inventory of James Thompson, dec., returned by Robert Thompson. Oct. 1792.

Page 261: Inventory of William Coon, dec., returned to court. July 1792.

Page 261: Estate of Richard Ashcraft, dec.

Page 261: Inventory of William Clack, dec., delivered in court by James Maclin, admin., Jan. 1793.

Page 262: Estate of Argolas Getor, dec., admin. by Samuel Deason. Returned to court, Jan. 1793.

Page 262: Thomas Perry of Sumner Co. sells a negro girl to Elizabeth Powell. 14 Jan. 1793.

Page 263: Judgement. Sampson Williams, sheriff, and Thomas Lightfoot of Davidson Co.; whereas a certain Benjamine Williams recovered a judgement against Willis Gunn, etc.

Page 264: William Fort of Davidson Co. sells a negro to Josiah Fort of the same. 5 Nov. 1792. Registered Jan. 1793.

Page 264: Joseph Metheral of Davidson Co. sells Frederick Stump a slave. 7 Nov. 1791. Registered 1793.

Page 265: William Terrell Lewis of Davidson Co., N. C., sells a negro boy to John Mays or Hays. 15 Jan. 1793.

Page 266: Sampson Williams, sheriff of Davidson Co., serves writ of venditions expenas, at the instance of James Bosley, (on) property of William Gunn, which was sold to Greenbury Cox, etc. 29 Dec. 1792. Registered Jan. 1793.

Pages 267-268: Inventory of estate of James Thompson, dec., returned by Robert Thompson. Jan. 1793.

Page 269: Robert Carrothers sells a negro to James Espey. 1793.

Page 270: Sheriff's sale. John and G. M. Deadrick, in suit of Sarah Gowen. Registered 6 May 1793.

Page 271: Thomas Lovel sells slaves to Absolom Hooper. Registered 6 May 1793.

Page 273: Richard Cross of Davidson Co. sells a negro woman to Jonas Miniffee. 6 May 1793.

Page 273: Isaac Pierce sells a negro to James Espey. 1793.

Page 274: Inventory of Jonathan Gee, dec., returned, and estate admin. By John Hauge. April 1793.

Page 274: Inventory of Anthony Harmond, dec., returned by Timothy Demumbreum, admin. July 1793.

Page 275: Alexander Moore of Davidson Co. sells property to Matthew Buchanan by Thomas Edmondson. Registered 8 Aug. 1793.

Page 281: John Cummins of Sumner Co. gives bill of sale to Michael Gleaves.

Page 281: Sutherlin (Sutherland) Mayfield of Davidson Co., N. C., gives bond to his brother Isaac Mayfield he will make good his title to land on Mill Creek. 3 Nov. 1785. Registered 13 Aug. 1793.

Page 281: Inventory of estate of George Ridley, Jr., dec., returned by George Ridley, Sr. July 1793.

Page 282: Inventory of estate of Eleazer Hamilton, dec., returned to court by James Hamilton, admin. July 1793.

Page 282: Inventory of estate of Thomas Brown, dec., returned and estate admin. by Mary Brown. July 1793.

Page 283: Inventory of William Overall, dec., returned and estate delivered into court by Susannah Overall, admnx. July 1793.

Page 283: Inventory of John Haggard, dec., returned and estate admin. Wm. Haggard. July 1793.

Page 284: Inventory of William Steward, dec., returned and estate admin. by Peter Brank Stuart. July 1793.

Page 285: Laurence Letter, dec.; inventory returned by James Bosley, admin. July 1793.

Page 286: Thomas Grayson of Davidson Co. appoints Daniel Young his attorney. 20 Aug. 1793.

Page 286: Inventory of Samuel Hays, dec., returned and estate admin. by Elizabeth Hays, admnx. Oct. 1793.

Pages 287-288: Supplementary inventory of Edwin Hickman, dec., returned by Thomas Hickman. Oct. 1793.

Page 290: Inventory of John Thompson, dec., returned and estate admin. by John Lancaster, admin. Oct. 1793.

Page 291: Inventory of John Low, dec., returned and estate admin. by Eleanor Low. Oct. 1793.

Page 292: Inventory of John Pillow, dec., admin. by William Pillow, admin., who also admin. the estate. Oct. 1793.

Page 292: Inventory of Samuel Martin, dec., and estate returned by James McCutcheon (McCutchen), admin. Oct. 1793.

Page 292: Samuel Lewis, dec.; estate admin. Thomas Blair, admin. Oct. 1793.

Page 293: Will of John Logue, made 13 Feb. 1793, and proved 1793, names daughters Mary, Margaret, and Ruth Logue, a son Manassah, and wife Eleanor.

Page 293: Inventory of Samuel Buchanan. Oct. 1793.

SOME OLD TOMBSTONES IN DAVIDSON COUNTY

Millip Austin, wife of Edwin Austin, born 5 Nov. 1785, died 22 Sept. 1840. Buried in Cane Ridge Graveyard near Antioch. Thomas Austin gave the land for the graveyard and Presbyterian Church, and the land is still used for its original purposes.

Edwin Austin. (Stone covered with dirt and inscription obliterated).

William Adams, born 21 April 1768, died 15 Jan. 1851. Buried in old City Cemetery, Nashville, Tennessee.

S. P. Bell, Jr., born 1 July 1831, died 18 Dec. 1838. Buried in Cane Ridge Graveyard near Antioch.

Depilah Brealey (Brialey), 1836-1876. Buried at Cane Ridge Graveyard.

Catherine Bell, wife of Thomas Bell, born 22 Feb. 1795, died 15 Sept. 1850. Buried at Cane Ridge Graveyard.

Jessee Benton, born 1783, died 1813. Buried at Old City Cemetery, Nashville.

Dorcus Becton, died 22 March 1813, aged 99 years. Buried in Belle Meade in what is newly called "The Highlands of Belle Meade," just back of Belle Meade Golf and County Club.

George Washington Campbell, son of Dr. Archibald Campbell and Elizabeth Mackay his wife, Immigrated to North Carolina in 1792. Born in the Parrish of Tongue, Sunderlandshire, Scotland on 9 Feb. 1769, and died in Nashville, 1848. Buried in Old City Cemetery, Nashville.

Harriett Campbell, daughter of Benjamin Stoddert, Secretary of the Navy under John Adams, and wife of G. W. Campbell, born 12 April 1789, and died 1849. Buried in Old City Cemetery, Nashville.

Edmund Cooper, died 1822, aged 62 years. Buried in Old City Cemetery, Nashville.

Thomas Crutcher, for 25 Years Treasurer of the State of
Tennessee, born 18 Feb. 1760, died 8 March 1844, aged 84. Buried
in Old City Cemetery, Nashville.

Nancy Jane, wife of J. W. Creech, and daughter of Thomas
and Catherine Bell, born 30 June 1825, died 19 Dec. 1850. Buried
at Cane Ridge Graveyard, near Antioch,

E. W. Chappell, died 8 July 1845. Buried at Cane Ridge
Graveyard, near Antioch.

Robert Bell Castleman, died 29 July 1886 in his 77th year.
Buried at Old City Cemetery, Nahville, Tennessee.

Little Maggie Castleman, daughter of Robert and Annie, born
1 May 1852, died 29 April 1855. Buried Old City Cemetery, Nashville.

Annie W. Castleman, wife of R. B. Castleman, and daughter
of James and Elizabeth Woods, born 8 Jan. 1825, died 19 March
1854. Buried Old City Cemetery, Nashville.

Mrs. Jemima Douglass, consort of the late William Douglass.
of Kentucky, born 30 Aug. 1779, died 3 Dec. 1844. Buried in the
Old City Cemetery, Mashville.

Rev. John Dillahaunty, born 8 Dec. 1728, died 9 Feb. 1816.
Baptist minister and Pioneer. Buried in Belle Meade, in "Highlands of Belle Meade," near Nashville.

Hannah Dillahaunty, born 1732, died 1801. Buried in Belle
Meade, in "Highlands of Belle Meade," near Nashville.

EVAN'S BATTALION

Note: In an old grant book on file in the Land Office at
Nashville, the pay roll of Evans Battalion was found in the
back. This company was established for the protection of the
Cumberland Settlement and gives the names of some of the earliest
settlers. It will probably give the location of some pioneers
who have been lost or who are not mentioned in any other record
of such early date. - E. R. W.

A statement of the men who served in Evan's Battalion as
Officers and Soldiers under the authority of an act of the As-
sembly of North Carolina passed in the year 1786, and entitled
"An Act for raising Troops for the Protection of the Inhabitants
of Davidson County," taken from the Pay Roll (there being no
Muster Rolls) deposited in the office of the Comptroller of
North Carolina together with an account of the names of Grantors
of land upon warranty aforesaid to be paid officers and soldiers.

(In the original book the information is arranged in
columns, but space requirements require the information be set
forth differently. Each column is coded, and the information
after any man's name is preceded by the code designation of that
column. - R. W. B.)

    Column A: names of men in service at the 1st Return, viz.:
       in Aug. 1787, and connections and the names of men who
       came in afterwards or are discharged.
    Column B: Deficiencies in men by death, desertion, and
       discharges.

Column C: Additions by enactments.
Column D: Substitutions.
Column E: Promotions.
Column F: Pay in land, to whom granted.

Captain Martin's Company

A: Capt. William Martin. F: 1st half year to Wm. Martin and 2nd half to same.

A: Sergt. Benjamine Darrow. F. 1st half year to An. McCoy and 2nd half to same.

A: Sergt. William Ridley. B: 18 April 1787. F.1st half year and 2nd half.

A: Corporal Abner Chappe. B: deserted 6 Jan. 1788. F. 1st half year and 2nd half.

A: Corporal Henry Robertson. F: 1st half year to An. McCoy and 2nd half to Anniuas McCoy.

A; Drummer Thomas Kenney. F. 1st half year to Esq. Payton and 2nd half to same.

A: Pvt. David Beaty. F. 1st half year and 2nd half year to David Beaty.

A: Pvt. Samuel Cooper. B: 1 Oct. 1788.

A: Pvt. John Fisher. B: deserted 1 Jan. 1788.

A: Pvt. Peter Fisher. F: 1st half year and 2nd half to Peter Fisher.

A: Pvt. Josua (sic) Fisher. B: 12 June 1788. F. 1st half year and 2nd half year to Joshua Fisher.

A: Pvt. Henry Hicks. F: 1st half year to Anninas McCoy and 2nd half to Anniasa McCoy.

A: Pvt. Neil McGloughlin. F: 1st half year to Charles Carter and 2nd half to Wm. Montgomery.

A: Pvt. Willoubey Lewis.

A: Pvt. Stephen Mark. D: Jas. Crabtree for March, June, 1788. E: to sergeant, 1 Aug. 1788. F. 1st half to E. Douglass and Wm. Montgomery, and 2nd half to James Crabtree himself.

A: Pvt. Jno. Byrch.

A: Pvt. Dempsey Ward. B: deserted 1 Feb. 1788.

A: Pvt. Samuel Birkley.

A: Pvt. Levi Ellis. C: Sept. 1787. F: 1st half year to Levi Ellis and board warrant, A. F.

A: Pvt. Thomas Price. C: Sept. 1787.

A: Pvt. John Bolie. C: Oct. 1787. E: to sergeant 1 Aug. 1788. F: 1st half year to Annias McCoy and 2nd half to same.

A: Pvt. John Wirow(?). F: 1st half year to William Dillard and
2nd half to Stephen Winchester.

A: Pvt. Brazil (Bazil?) Fry. C: Jan. 1788. F: 1st half year
to David Shelby and 2nd year (sic) to Jno.
Overton.

A: Pvt. Gallant Lamar. C: Jan. 1788. F. 1st half and 2nd half
to Wm. Coper.

A: Pvt. John Hendrick. C: Feb. 1788. F: 1st half to Annanius
McCoy. 2nd half to Jas. McCoin.

A: Pvt. Reuben Smith. C: Feb. 1788.

A: Pvt. Jonniah Guilford. C: April 1788.

Captain Joshua Hadley's Company

A: Major Com'l Thos. Evans.

A: Capt. Joshua Hadley. F: 1st half and 2nd half to Joshua Had-
lay.

A: Lieut. Jas. Nelson. B: Sept. 1787.

A: Thos. Smith. B: Sept. 1787.

A: Capt. James Nelson. 1st half and 2nd half year to Robert
Nelson.

A: Lieut. Thos. Smith. F: 1st half year to Saml Barton and 2nd
half to Jno. Hinds.

A: Sergt. Major Patrick Kelly. F: 1st half to John Overton and 2nd
2nd half to same.

A:Q-M. Sergt. Jno. Edward.

A:Sergt. Hardy Eskew. B: absent March 1788.

A: Drummer Thomas Davis. D: William Page, Oct. 1788.

A: Fifer, John Childress.

A: Corporal John Elliott. F: 1st half year to Stephen Bosen and
2nd half to Jacob McCarty.

A: Corporal Fred'k Morgan. F: 1st half and 2nd half year to Jno.
Overton.

A: Pvt. Dennis Carney. B: discharged Feb. 1788.

A: Pvt. Ichabod Radley.

A: Pvt. James Singleton. B: discharged May 1788. F: 1st half
and 2nd half to Wm. Henry.

A: Pvt. John Covington. B: deserted Nov. 1787. F: 1st half and
2nd half to Joshua Hadley.

A: Pvt. Edw'd. Covington. B: deserted Nov. 1787.

A. Pvt. Richard Covington, Sr. B: deserted Nov. 1787

A: Pvt. Richard Covington, Jr. B: deserted Nov. 1787.

A: Pvt. William Covington. B: deserted Nov. 1787.

A: Pvt. Joshua Harlen. F. 1st half and 2nd half year to John
        Payton.

A: Pvt. John Harlon. F. 1st half and 2nd half year to John
        Harlin.

A: Pvt. Peter Andrews.

A: Pvt. John Rowland. B: deserted Oct. 1787.

A: Pvt. Jacob Fitze. B: absent Nov. 1788.

A: Pvt. Matthew McCue. D: Dunham Clark, Oct. 1787.

A: Pvt. Thomas Laremie. F: 1st half to Robert Wood and 2nd
        half to John Sanders.

A: Pvt. John Tilly. F: 1st half and 2nd half year to John Over-
        ton.

A: Pvt. Samuel Wells. F: 1st half and 2nd half year to Wm. Mc-
        Neely.

A: Pvt. Robert McBride. B: deserted Oct. 1787.

A: Pvt. Ephraim Gordon.

A: Pvt. Daniel Watkins.

A: Pvt. Jas. McEyea. F; 1st and 2nd half year to Jas. McEyea.
        Bond warrant A. F. sergt.? that no grant was
        issued.

A: Pvt. William Baker. B: discharged Oct. 1787.

A: Pvt. John Parmer(?) F: 1st and 2nd half year to Samuel Barton.

A: Pvt. John Edwards.

A: Pvt. William Kirby.

A: Pvt. Andrew Justice. B: discharged April 1788. C: C. Camp-
        bell absent, Nov. 1788. D: by Chas. Camp-
        bell, April 1788. F: 1st half to Samuel
        Barton, and 2nd half year to afsd. C. Camp-
        bell.

A: Pvt. Solomon Wright. B: discharged Aug. 1788.

A: Pvt. Chas. Yates. B: deserted Oct. 1787.

A: Pvt. Joel Yates. B: deserted Oct. 1787.

A: Pvt. John Thompson. B: died Nov. 1788.

A: Pvt. John Martin. B: killed March 1788. F: 1st and 2nd
        half year to Robert Ewing.

A: Pvt. Edward Rogers. F: 1st and 2nd half year pay to Isaac
        McCallum.

A: Pvt. Lemuel Clayton. F: 1st and 2nd half year to Isaac Mc-
        Callum.

A: Pvt. Underhill Ellis. C: Oct. 1787. F: 1st half to Edward
        Douglas and 2nd half year to U. Ellis.

A: Pvt. Benj. Joslin. C: Oct. 1787. F: 1st half to Jas. R.
        Robertson and 2nd half to Jonathan F. Robert-
        son.

A: Pvt. Jacob Mills. B: killed March 1789. C: Oct. 1787. F.
        1st and 2nd half year to Edwd. Douglas.

A: Pvt. Jas. McCoun. C: March 1788. F: 1st half to Jno. Over-
        ton and 2nd half to Jas. McCoun.

A: Pvt. Jas. Campbell. C: Nov. 1788. F. 1st half and 2nd half
        to Samuel Barton.

A: Pvt. Rives Jardon. C. Nov. 1788.

A: Pvt. Jas. Riley. C: Nov. 1788.

A: Pvt. Jacob Fitzer. C: Dec. 1788. This supposed same Jacob
        Fitzer that in F. (sic)

              Captain Hunter's Company of Cavalry

A: Capt. James Hunter. B: killed 20 Jan. 1789. F. 1st half
        Mr. McNairy and 2nd half to ditto.

A. Sergt. John Dobbins. F: 2nd half to Jno. Dobbins.

A: William Dalton, Jr.

A: Pvt. Joseph Hendricks. F: 1st and 2nd half year to Joseph
        Hendricks.

A: Pvt. Same (sic) Griffis. D: Chas. Gardson for Griffis in Oct.
        1787, says a note from the Comptroller. F:
        1st and 2nd half year to Lewis Barker.

A: Pvt. Arch Martin.

A: Pvt. Azwell Phillips. F: 1st and 2nd half year to Hugh Ste-
        phenson and John Payton.

A: Pvt. Elijah Walker.

A: Pvt. Samuel Blair. F: 1st and 2nd half year to Samuel Blair.

A: Pvt. Hugh Kirkpatrick.

A: Pvt. Robert White. F: 1st half year to R. Nelson, and 2nd
        half year to Jno. Winton.

A: Pvt. Joel Echols. C: Sept. 1787.

A: Pvt. Joseph Hopkins. F: 1st and 2nd half year to Chas.
        Wheaton.

A: Pvt. James Donalson. C: March 1788.

A: Pvt. Hezekiah Wright.

A: Pvt. Wm. Durham. C: March 1788.

A: Pvt. Joseph Durham. B: absent Nov. and Dec. 1788. C: March
    1788.

A: Pvt. John Long. B: Aug. 1788. C: March 1788.

A: Pvt. Hardy Askew. B: Nov. and Dec. 1788, 10 days, Sury White.
    C: March 1788.

A: Pvt. Chas. Little. B: Year 1789, Lieut., 1st Regt., absent.
    C. Nov. 1787.

A: Pvt. James Morrison. B: absent Nov. and Dec. 1788. C: Nov.
    1787.

A: Pvt. Jas. Hunter. B: killed 1 Jan. 1789.

A: Bonnerd C. Brackett. B: absent Feb. 1788. F. a grant to
    Watron Reed on plat signed by A. McBain.

The payroll for this battalion commenced with the month of
August 1787 and ended with the month of December 1788 except
Capt. Hadley's return which is continued until August 1789. The
office here made monthly returns containing the number but not
the (names?) of the men in the battalion commencing with December
1787 and ending with the year 1788. There is also a general con-
solidated return of a like nature commencing with January and
ending with August 1789 completing the period of two years; viz.:
July 1787 to Sept. 1789.   (Signed) Jno. Overton.
                                Raleigh, 12 March 1804.

This record is found in the back of North Carolina Military
warrants, Land Office, State Archives, Nashville, Tenn.

Captain Hadley's Company

Revolutionary War; list of soldiers entitled to land grants.
Major Evan's Regiment, Capt. Hadley's Company. The papers are
on file in the Tennessee State Archives, Nashville.

List of Capt. Hadley's Company,   Battalion entitled to land
agreeable to an Act of Assembly for their half pay as soldiers
in said service.

1. Thomas Evans, Major.
2. Joshua Hadley, Capt.
3. James Nelson, Capt.
4. Thomas Smith, Lieut.
5. George Doherdy, Paymaster
6. Patrick Kelley, S. Major.
7. John Edwards, Q. M. S.
8. Benjamin Joslin, Sergt.
9. John Elliott, Corp.
10. Frederick Merriam, Corp.
11. Joshua Harlin, Pvt.
12. John Harlin, Pvt.
13. Lenard Clayton, Pvt.
14. James Medlay, Pvt.
15. Thomas Laramore, Pvt.
16. Peter Andrews, Pvt.
17. James Kerbee, Pvt.
18. Ephraim Gordon, Pvt.
19. Daniel Waters, Pvt.
20. John Joram, Pvt.
21. John Childers, Pvt.
22. Wm. Page, Pvt.
23. Edw't. Rogers, Pvt.
24. John Covington, Pvt.
25. John Tilley, Pvt.
26. Samuel Wells, Pvt.
27. Archibird Radley, Pvt.
28. Dawson Clark, Pvt.
29. James Campbell, Pvt.
30. John Edwards, Pvt.
31. Wm. Kerbee, Pvt.
32. River Jordan, Pvt.
33. James M'Kewan, Pvt.
34. Underhill Ellire, Pvt.
35. Jacob Fitzer, Pvt.
36. Jacob Mills, Pvt., killed.
37. John Martin, Pvt., killed.
38. John Thompson, Pvt., killed
39. James Riley, Pvt.

DAVIDSON COUNTY RECORD

I, Martin Armstrong, Surveyor and Entry Taker of the lands granted to the officers and soldiers of the North Carolina ContinentalLine, do hereby certify that the foregoing entries from Location Number 7491 to Number 8200 are true and perfect copies of entries the residue made in book C., being carefully and accurately compared with the original entries and that due faith and credit ought to be given them as such. Given under my hand at office this twelfth day of July 1799.

(Signed) Martin Armstrong, E. T., Sur.

Wake County   )   This day personally appears before me one of
State of North)   the acting Justices of the Peace for the Coun-
Carolina   )   ty aforesaid, John -(?)-, who being duly sworn
                    aaith that the several Cappiers (?) entries
in this book from Location no. 7491 to no. 8200 are true coppies of the entries of said numbers contained in the original book in the office of Martin Armstrong, Surveyor of the Lands granted to the officers and soldiers of Continental Line of North Carolina kept on the -(?)- of Nashville, Davidson Co. in the State of Tennessee, without alternation or addition except such notes and remarks as he has made in the margin for the purpose of giving information and explaining such information as he acquired in making the examination and that they were by him carefully compared and that the several Erasures, obliterations, and interlineations in said copies are as perfect and exact representation of those contained in the Original Books, as was in the power of the Transcribing clerks to make. Sworn to and signed this 3 Aug. 1799, before me   Jno. Marshall, J. P.

INDEX TO ENTRIES

Elisha Uzzle
Samuel McMurry
Duncan Stewart of Samuel
  Russell
Duncan Stewart of Wm.Hawthorn
Duncan Stewart of Maririan Paul
Duncan Stewart of Aron Pris-
  cote
Duncan Stewart of James Barker
James Taylor of William Pruele
Duncan Stewart of Henry Rhodes
Duncan Stewart of Daniel Ridge
Thomas Hickman of Robert
  Williams
Thomas Hickman of Simon Lumb-
  liss
Thos. Hickman of Thos. Alexan-
  der
Thos. Hickman of Andrew Hat-
  field
Duncan Stewart of -- Pitman
Duncan Stewart of Wm. Jacobs
Duncan Stewart of Thos. Jerrat
Joseph Irwin of Solomon Benton
  heirs
Jas. Irwin of Isaiah Brinkley
  heirs
Daniel Williams of Andrew Del-
  libs heirs

Robert McConnell of James Parks
William Nash of John Bumberder
James Mulherrin of Thomas Wood
Howell Tatum and H. Wiggins of
  Jacob Daughtry
James Taylor of Daniel Potter
Martin Armstrong of Jno. Hen-
  ton's heirs
Martin Armstrong of Joel Jef-
  ferson's heirs.
Martin Armstrong of George
  Truelock's heirs
Joseph T. Rhodes of Wm. Rhodes'
  heirs
Duncan Stewart of Joseph Newton
Duncan Stewart of Charles Pres-
  cot
Duncan Stewart of Andrew Hen-
  derson heirs
Duncan Stewart of Capt. Jno.
  Williams
Charles Stewart of Jones Brad-
  ley's heirs.
Heirs of Jeremiah Fletcher
Heirs of Jacob Whitaker
Martin Armstrong of heirs of
  Jno. Winn.
Heirs of William Welton

DYER COUNTY, TENNESSEE

INDEX TO DEED BOOK NO. ONE

Goodall, Wm., & Jonathan   Deed Trust from Robert I. Chester 159
  Pockett
Goodman, George   Deed from   John J. Thurmond   172

Hiter, Thomas, et al.,   Deed to   John Swinnet   28
Haywood, Sherod, et al.,   Deed Trust
                               from   Thomas Persons   119
Hughlett, William   Grant from   N. C.   153
Huling, F. W.   Deed of   John Hightower   155
                               Partition
Hightower, John   Deed to   Mark R. Cockrell   162
Hewlett, William   Deed to   Thomas Hedspeth   165
Hedspeth, Thomas   Deed from   William Hewlett   165
Hedden, Moses   Deed from   Samuel Dougan   211
Humphreys, P. W., et al.,   Deed from   Thos. & W. A. Turner 213
Herndon, Jas. W.   Deed from   Weakley & Rutherford 220
Herndon, Jas. W.   Deed from   Robert Weakley   223
Hill, Ransom   Deed from   G. & H. Rutherford 229

Knight, Thomas   Deed from   John Rutherford   4,5,6
Kennelly, John   Deed from   Hugh Dunlap   169

Murray, Robert   Release from   Wm. C. Chambers(?)   7
Murphey, Archibald   Grant from   North Carolina   8
Murphey, Archibald   Power of At-   James W. Smith   11
                               torney to
Murphey, Archibald   Deed to   Wm. Gaston   15
McCrory, Charles and
  William   Deed to   Michael S. McCrory 23
McCrory, James   Deed to   James McCutchin   25
McCutchin, James   Deed from   James McCrory   25
McGaw, Eli, et al.,   Deed to   John Swinney   28
McCrory, James   Deed to   Charles S. McCrory 31
McCrory, Charles S.   Deed from   James McCrory   31
McCrory, Michael S.   Deed to   William Martin   32
Martin, William   Deed from   Michael S. McCrory 32
McCorkle, Robert and
  Samuel   Deed to   Joseph P. Porter   34
McCulloch, Benjamine   Deed from   John Stokes   130
McNairy, John   Deed from   Henry M. Rutledge 138
McCrory, Chas. S., sheriff   Bill of
                               Sale to   Wm. Stoddert   171
Murphey, Alex & Arch. D.   Deed to   E. J. Ash & Sophia
                                                Steadwick   180
McCrory, Michael S.   Deed to   Joseph Wyatt   185
McCrory, James   Deed to   Wm. Edmonston and
                                                Thos. Berry   187
Murphey, Arch D.   Deed to   Montford Stokes   189
McCulloch, Benjamine
  et al.,   Bond to   Moses Woodfin   193
McIver, John   Power of At-   Evander McIver   210
                               torney to
McCrory, Michael S.   Deed to   Joseph Wyatt   234
McCrory, Charles S.   Deed to   William McCrory   239
McCrory, William   Deed from   Charles S. McCrory 239
McIver, John   Deed to   Town Commissioners 241

North Carolina, State of   Grant to   Archibald Murphy   8
North Carolina, State of   Grant to   William Hughlett   153
Nash, Redmond B.   Power of At-
                               torney to   Wm. Nash, Jr.   164
Noe, Peter   Deed from   James Dougan   176
Nash, Redmond B.   Bond to   William Nash, Sr. 178

Porter, Joseph B.   Deed from   Robert & Samuel
                                                McCorkle   34

* * *

BURK MARRIAGES IN FRANKLIN COUNTY

Note: Franklin County, Tennessee, was erected on 3 December 1807 from Warren and Bedford Counties, and was named in honor of Benjamin Franklin. The county seat of Winchester was named in memory of General James Winchester. The site for the county seat was purchased from Christopher (sic) for the price of one dollar. The first county court was held at the home of Major William Russell in 1808, and the county courts were held in Winchester beginning in 1814.

W. H. Burke and Sallie Birch; 1 March 1893; W. H. Burks and B. M. Rice, securities.
Elmore Burk to Betsy Vaughn, issued 29 Sept. 1870; solemnized 29 Sept. 1870 by G. S. Wedington, J. P.
James Burks to Mary Duncan, issued 23 Dec. 1871; solemnized 23 Dec. 1871, by J. L. Payne, M. G.
Martin C. Burkes to Sally Osbourn, issued 21 Sept. 1838.
Richard Burkes to Charlotte Burkes, issued 27 Sept. 1838.
John Burks to Martin (sic) Lucas, issued 28 June 1839.
Thomas M. Burk to Mary C. Lucas, issued 15 Oct. 1847.
John W. Burks to Harriett Denson, issued 21 Sept. 1858.
D. B. Burks to Clara Landus, 24 Dec. 1898.
Rily Burks to Emma Hinchie, 13 May 1899.
Adie Burks to Ethel Watson, 19 Oct. 1923.

MISCELLANEOUS NOTES ON HAWKINS COUNTY

This county took its name from Benjamine Hawkins, who as United States Senator, conjointly with Senator Samuel Johnston, who on 25 Feb. 1790, executed the deed which transferred what is now Tennessee to the United States.

The early settlers of this county were largely from North Carolina and Virginia. A few Pennsylvania and New England natives came here. Among those first settlers were some families which are still among the leading families of the county. Some of these families were: Amis, Mulkey, Carter, Parker, Love,, Kinkeads, Longs, Gillenwaters, Lucas, Parsons, Bradley, McKinney, Miller, Powell, McMinn, Cocke, Rogers, and Armstrong.

In the early days of the state, no county contributed more to the education of its population than did Hawkins County. Some of the early notable teachers were: John Long, 1783; William Evans, 1784; James King, 1786; Samuel B. Hawkins, 1796.

Rogersville, the county seat, was named in honor of Joseph Rogers, one of the early settlers.

The first will recorded in Hawkins County was that of Thomas Amis, 6 Nov. 1797. This will is on the first page of the first will book. There may be other wills but they were not recorded in the probate books, and if existing may be among the rapidly detereorating old papers scattered in the four corners of the ancient courthouse.

The will of Thomas Amis, dated 6 Nov. 1797, names his wife

wife Lucy, children John, Willis, Thomas Gale, Haynes, Tabitha, and Mary. John Ray, Esq., Col. James Armstrong, Wm. Armstrong, Esq., Joseph McMinn, Esq., and Wm. Howard, Surveyor, were requested to divide the estate.

The next will recorded in the county is that of William Amis, dated Dec. 1809, on p. 3.

William Armstrong's will, dated 17 Feb. 1810, but probated in 1809 (sic) is also on p. 3. He names his wife Abinah Armstrong.

The will of John Armstrong, dated 17 April 1813, and proved in 1813, on p. 4, names wife Jane, "plantation in Carter's Valley," daughter Jane Armtrong, son Thomas, daughter Amos Baker, daughter Mary Armstrong, and son Baker. Thomas Armstrong and John Young were to be executors.

Other early wills included those of of:

William Armstrong, dated 10 May 1817, p. 6.

Lucy Amis, dated 17 Dec. 1818, p. 6.

David Anderson, 1822, p. 7.

Deborah Alexander, 1827, p. 8.

William Armstrong, Sr., 1835, p. 8.

Haynes Amis, 1847, p. 13.

NOTES ON HENRY COUNTY

Henry County was erected on 7 Nov. 1821, and named in honor of Patrick Henry. It was taken from the Western District.

John B. House was the first settler in 1819. Among the other early settlers were: Joel and Willis Hagler, Alex Harmon, John Young, James and David D. Greer, Samuel McCorkle, Johannon Smith, William Walters, Rev. Benjamine Reoples, Rev. John Mauly, Abraham Walters, William Porter, Thomas Grey, Adam Rome, and others.

The first court was held on Monday, December, 1821, at the home of Peter Wall.

The county seat of Paris was laid out by commissioners in 1823. Joseph Blythe and Peter Ruff were the commissioners selected by the Legislature.

Henry County is not an old county, but it is a progressive one. Paris is a thriving town as well as the county seat. The records of the county are preserved but are not classified or arranged in any degree of system, many being original papers tied in packages.

The county is bounded on the north by Kentucky, on the west by Weakley County, Tennessee; on the south by Carroll County, Tennessee; on the southeast and east by Benton County and Stewart County. The Tennessee River divides this county from Stewart on the east, and is spanned by a handsome new bridge erected by the State in 1932.

SOME EARLY WILLS FROM HENRY COUNTY

Henry Allen, will dated 27 Nov. 1869, proved April 1873; names wife Alley Allen, sons William R., James W., and John F. Allen, daughter Amandy wife of James Whitworth, and granddaughter Alley, wife of Flem. Allen.

Susan Jane Atkins, will dated 2 Nov. 1911; names son Elonzo T. Atkins, children Zadok Franklin, Matie, Catherine, Samuella, and Anne Bell.

James Allen, will dated 21 Aug. 1830; names wife Jane, children William, Isabella, Margaret, Samuel B., Benjamine, and Becky Allen, and grandson William Allen.

Joseph Alexander, will dated 19 July 1847; names wife Flora, daughter Margaret, and "rest of my children." Margaret to receive her share of the estate of Asa Adkins. Josiah Owens and Erasmus Harris to be executors.

Edmund Almond, will dated 11 Oct. 1871; names granddaughter Elizabeth Jackson, daughter Mary Harris, grandson Tommy Woods, son John Almond. Also names Kizziah Rumbley, Jane Morphis, Nehemiah Almond, Sarah Jackson, Peralian Ralls. John Almond and Wm. A. Morphose to be executors.

John Atkins, will dated 1845; names daughter Martha M. Jones, wife of Dennis Jones; daughter Eveline Harris, wife of William R. Harris; son Eldridge G. Atkins; son John Dement Clinton Atkins; two youngest sons William Edmond Travis Atkins, and James Knox Polk Atkins; wife Mary Atkins.

Mary Atkins, widow of R. S. Atkins, will dated 3 April 1850; names sons Green T. Atkins, George E., Daniel L., Joseph T., Richard L., and four youngest, Milly, Baldwin S., John, and Rebecca L. Atkins.

Asa Atkins, will dated 1830; names wife Winiford; land in Stewart Co.; daughter Nancy; daughter Polly; son Alfred; son Hampton; daughter Martha; daughter Lucy; daughter Betsy; son James.

Matthew Anderson, nuncupative will dated 23 Oct. 1829; leaves to Solomon Denny "for his wife in case of his death."

Samuel Anderson, will dated 1850; children, William C. Anderson, Andrew W. Anderson, Harmione C. Miller, Robert S. Anderson, Temperance Y. Anderson, Samuel G. Anderson, Francis L. Anderson, and Alfred F. Anderson.

Daniel Arya (Ary), will dated 21 June 1846; names wife Rebecca, sons Daniel Jefferson and Thomas Holland.

Isaac Akers, will dated 18 Oct. 1839; names wife Lucinda Akers, sons William and Thomas; also names Benjamine, Isaac, Lucinda, Uriah, and Abner Akers,

Jessee Alexander, will dated 1871; names son J. E. S. Alexander, J. L. Alexander, son A. L. Anderson, and daughters Henrietta, Isabella, and Pauline. (J. L. Alexander was also a son.)

Martha M. Burnett, will dated Oct. 1866; Edward Burnett (relationship to testatrix not stated) of Henry Co. to have all my property.

Crawford Bradford, will dated Aug. 1868; names David Bradford, Ann Kay, Polly Ann Williams, Sally K. Gray, William Crawford Bradford. Grandchildren, heirs of William C. Bradford. James H. Williams to be one of the administrators.

Dorren Bell, will dated 26 May 1856; names wife Nancy Bell; mentions but does not name his children.

James S. Brown, will dated 1870; names wife Elizabeth T. Brown; daughter Mary; mentions but does not name other children.

Mary J. Brown, will dated Feb. 1869; names daughter Mary T. Mattherson, son John L. Brown, daughter Elizabeth wife of son James S. Brown (probably means daughter-in-law: R. W. B.), son James S. Brown, granddaughters Emma, Anna, and Ella Dawson, and daughter Mary T. Their father (sic) was J. S. Dawson.

Nicholas Byars, will dated 10 July 1839; names son William Byars, sons George, David, Henry, and John. Heirs of Elizabeth Byars, dec. A sgare to Sarah Barton and then to her heirs. Wife is mentioned. W. Byars mother-in-law.

Thomas T. Browning, will dated 1867; names daughter Elizabeth Hughes, and Ann Terdue; grandchildren Mollie Fleming and Mollie Bradley; son-in-law Robert D. Hughes.

Allen Bowles, will dated Oct. 1857; names wife Arvarilla, daughter Julia Ann Jackson, daughter Mary H. Rasburrey, daughters Frances J. Sullivan and Avarilla H. Bishop; sons William J., James B., and Alexander A. Boles; grandson Charles A. Bowles and his mother Sarah Bowles.

Samuel Arnett, will dated 12 May 1844; names son Andrew J. Arnett.

William Brooks, will dated March 1835; names wife Elizabeth; children are under age; James H. F. Atkins, my wife's brother.

Elizabeth G. Beasley, will dated 6 July 1840; leaves all possessions to cousin William Duke.

Augustine Berry, will dated 13 Aug. 1842; names wife Piety, sons William and Harris, daughters Elizabeth Jane, Martha Juldean, Piety, and Emily Caroline.

Henry T. Baldwin, will dated 30 June 1859; names children Francis J. Miller, Sarah A. Kimber, Mary C. Groom, William R. Baldwin, Eliza A. Groom, Carolina M. Baldwin, and Henry C. Baldwin. Wife mentioned but not named.

Henry T. Baldwin, will dated 1864; mentions beloved wife; youngest daughter Caroline M. Baldwin; Francis J. Miller; Sarah A. Kimbro; Mary C. Groom; William R. Baldwin; Eliza A. Groom; Henry A. Baldwin; Caroline M. Baldwin.

Harod Bomar, will dated 12 Aug. 1848; mentions wife; daughters Ann, Nancy, Martha, Cynthia, Prudence, and Elizabeth; sons Hosea, John, William, Herod, and James.

Wiley Brake, will dated 14 April 1857; names daughter Elizabeth Brake; sons Jesse, William D., John M., Wiley Brake; daughters Malina J. Brake, Parthenia Robertson, and Carolina Miller.

George Byers, will dated 1850; names daughters Anna Daniel Jackson (the eldest) and Emily Jane Lampkins; sons John Henderson Byars and William Henry Byars; youngest daughters Mariah Frances and Sarah Hawkins Byars.

W. G. Blount, of Henry Co., now on a visit to his brother R. B. Blount of Montgomery Co., will dated 11 Nov. 1826; names brother R. B. Blount, sister Eliza J. B. Wiatt and her late husband, Edwin Wiatt.

Charles Burton, will dated 7 Sept. 1826; names wife Prudence and sons John and Drury Burton.

Jehu (Jahue) Ballard, will dated 30 Sept. 1863; names wife Lucy B. Ballard, son-in-law John W. McFarland; mentions his own children but does not name them.

Henderson Baucum, will dated 16 Dec. 1853; names wife Mary L. Baucum, and children: David, Clark. George, Ransom, William, Henderson, Sarah, Elizabeth, Martha, and Maria Lee.

Joseph Barton, will dated 4 July 1843; names wife Sophia W. Barton, son D. W. Barton (under age), daughter Martha McNab (widow of John McNab), my gandchildren. Also named are John Gore who married my deceased daughter Sophia; Sophia's children; the children of my deceased son Benjamine.

Jacob Bushart, will dated March 1843; names wife Nancy; sons, John, Henry, Jacob, Caleb, and Daniel; daughters Elizabeth Riden, Sally, Anna Deets, and Polly Coldwell.

William Burks, will dated 1844; mentions wife and children.

John Babb, will dated April 1827; names wife Media Babb; sons John P., Henry B., Thomas, and William Babb; daughters Ann Watters, Media Davis, and Martha Coldwell.

(These are all that were abstracted).

* * *

PETITION FROM JACKSON COUNTY

The petitions prays for an amendment to the Constitution so as to create a new county; Jackson County; 1837. (Found in the State Archives, Nahville; Box 75 of Legislative Papers).

Line Creek or Lime Creek, 28 Nov. 1837. The signatures to this petition are all in the western part of Jackson and Smith Counties, asking for a part of both counties to be cut off and a new county formed for convenience. Those in favor of a division of the county:

Levy Gist, Esq.	Thomas B. Wood
Christon Eakle	Pleasant Boyd
Wm. Hibbetts	Henry Eakle, Jr.
Louis B. Purcell	William York
James Hibbitts	Alexander Kieath
Daniel Kieath	John Boyd
James Crawford	Stephen Miller

James Pursell
Isaac Crawford
Watson Bennett
Watson Gist
Curtice W. York
John Miles
Jonathan Eakle
John R. Welch
William Willis
Jesse Gass
James Davidson
William Stith
Samuel Comer
Meredith York
Nathan Price
Luke Hail
Jacob Goodner
B. H. Baity
Benjamine Gist
Robert Davice

A. M. Haston, Esq.
Samuel Lane
Benjamine Gist, Sr.
James Kieath
Henry Eakle
Benjamine Taulman
George Condra
Louis Crawford
William Comer
Benjamine Eakle
Henry Ritter
Harvey Woods
Philip Condra
Wilson Cherry
John Hall
L. B. Moor
Elzy C. Stith
David Taylor
Abram Hughes

The petition is signed: Samuel Martin

* * *

INDEX TO EARLY JEFFERSON COUNTY WILLS

Year	Name	Book	Page	Year	Name	Book	Page
1810	Hugh Kirkpatrick	1	319	1800	Matthew Roulston	1	61
1798	Jno. King	1	54	1794	Jones Randolph	1	80
	David Kerr	?	?	1816	Franky Ralston	2	159
				1815	Thos. Rodgers	2	236
1805	Tidance Lane, Sr.	1	90				
1792	Marshall Loveday	1	3	1793	Robert Stephenson	1	8
1807	Geo. Lewis	1	283	1792	Jno. Sanders	1	79
1810	David Layman	2	182	1801	Wm. Summers	1	38
1816	Aquilla Lane	2	215	1797	Jeremiah Shelly	1	39
1816	Major Lea	2	350	1813	Samuel Swann	2	40
1806	William Malsby	1	92	1814	Jno. Sterling	2	90
1794	Aaron Mills	1	78	1819	Jno. Smith	2	227
1801	Jno. Mahler	1	64	1819	Jno. Shields	2	286
1804	Jno. Moore	1	29				
1801	Jno. Maxwell	1	269	1792	Lew Todd	1	13
1807	Geo. Malcom	1	345	1796	Wm. Thornburgh	1	53
1813	Christopher Mayers	2	97	1804	Henry Thornburgh	1	28
1809	Jno. Mills	2	101	?	Frederick Taylor	?	?
1819	Thos. Morgan	2	218				
1818	Wm. Maze	2	228	1804	Joseph Williams	1	35
				1793	Alexander Ward	1	4
1813	John Nance	2	56	1793	James Wright	1	75
				?	Jno. Ward	1	6
1819	Benjamine Beal	2	416	1799	Geo. Willcockson	1	82
				1801	James Walker	1	41
1788	Saml Odel	1	45	1812	Wm. Woodward	2	36
				1814	Abraham Woodward	2	184
1812	Robert Pierce	2	30	1818	Jonathan Wilson	2	203
1814	Adam Peck	2	176	1816	Wm. Williams	2	239
				1814	Jno. Watkins	2	373
1805	Daniel Russell	1	261	1818	Isaac Williams	2	427

* * *

FIRST DEED BOOK, MAURY COUNTY

1807 - 1818

(The book is in poor condition; many of the front and back pages are gone - E. R. W. Page numbers are given in parentheses after the entry - R. W. B.)

14 July 1812. John Kennedy granted 1435 acres, Grant no. 3 located on Big Tom Bigby Creek. (1)

Abner Pillow granted 400 acres, N. C. Grant no. 26, for protection of the inhabitants of Davidson Co., N. C. (2)

1814. Jno. and Benjamine McCuston(?), 200 acres from Josiah Reece. (Record nearly gone)

10 Oct. 1793. James Houston of Iredell Co., N. C., 5000 acres on Little Tom Bigby; James Reece of Sumner Co., Territory south of River Ohio. (?)

17 Sept. 1812. Gerrard T. Grunfield, 450 acres, from Tyree Rodes. (?)

24 Sept. 1812. Zilmon Spencer, 200 acres on Green Lick Creek, conveyed by Henry Walker; 1 Oct. 1812.

13 Aug. 1811. Charles Polk of Clemont, S. C., conveys to Samuel Polk of Maury Co., Tenn., 153½ acres of land. (?)

26 May 1812. Sam'l H. Williams of Maury Co. conveys 311 acres on Rutherford Creek to Duncan Brown of Maury Co. (?)

13 Aug. 1811. Charles Polk of Clemont Co., S. C., conveys 311 acres on Rutherford Creek to James Lockrick of Maury Co. (?)

10 Dec. 1811. James Holland of Maury Co. is conveyed 5000 acres on Fountain Creek by Samuel H. Williams of same county. (35)

William Page granted on land on Big Tom Bigby Creek; Grant no. 25, for services in protecting inhabitants of Davidson Co. (?)

12 Nov. 1811. Wm. Bradshaw conveys 300 acres on Snow Creek to McLean and Carothers. William Martin, for the use of Joseph Martin, Judgement, against Spencer Griffin and Ephraim McLean in Circuit Court. Sheriff's sale. (37)

22 Sept. 1812. Michael Campbell of Davidson Co. for himself and as executor of Philip Phillips, dec., conveys 240 acres on Silver Creek to John Record. (39)

16 Dec. 1811. Henry Rutherford conveys 130 acres on Rock Creek to John Farris. (40).

28 July 1812. David Moore of Madison Co., Mississippi, and James McCuiston of Bedford Co., Tenn.; 369 acres on Duck River. (The grantor and grantee are not designated - R. W. B.) (41)

30 Jan. 1812. James M. Lewis conveys deed of trust of some negroes to Henry G. Kearney in trust for his wife Lucy Davis Kearney and their children. (42)

24 Jan. 1812. Michael Campbell, exec. of Philip Phillips, dec., conveys Sion Record 200 acres on Silver Creek. (44)

21 March 1812. John Welch of Haywood Co., N. C., conveys Kinchen Holcombe of Lincoln Co., Tenn., 280 acres on Knob Creek. (45)

21 Sept. 1812. James and John Owen of Bladen Co., N. C., convey 134 acres on Globe Creek to Wm. Pickens of Maury Co. (47)

29 July 1812. Joseph Brown conveys one acre for a meeting house to Joseph B. Porter, Benjamine Thomas, and Joseph Brown, commissioners of Lytle Creek Meeting House in Maury Co. (48)

9 Nov. 1811. Joshua Nichols of Giles Co., Tenn., conveys 900 acres to Daniel Woods of Maury Co., Tenn. (49)

27 Nov. 1812. John Welch of Haywood Co., N. C., conveys William Ragsdales of Lincoln Co., Tenn., 400 acres on Nob Creek or Snow Creek. (50)

William Bradshaw conveys John M. Taylor 600 acres on Duck River. Suit in Circuit Court. Caveat Claim.

1 Dec. 1812. William Donelson registered a grant of 300 acres; grant no. 1938, cert. no. 137 dated 27 July 1807, from

the Board of Commissioners of West Tennessee, by William Donelson, Wm. Nash, Michael Gleaves, John Overton, and Thos. Gleaves. The land was located on Rock Creek of Duck River, and was in Bedford Co., Second District, First Range, 5th Section, adjoining land of John Record. (54)

1 Dec. 1812. John M. Taylor of Maury Co. conveys 600 acres on Ruck River to John Brown of Knox Co., Tenn. (55)

4 Dec. 1812. Henry E. Turner, physician in East Greenwich, Rhode Island, conveys 3333 1/3 acres in Maury Co. to James V. Turner also of East Greenwich, R. I. Martha Turner also signs the deed. The land was on the south side of Duck River, and was the land formerly granted by North Carolina to General Nathaniel Green. (57)

30 Nov. 1812. William Polk of Wake Co., N. C., claiming and holding certain lands granted to George Dohorty of Tennessee in 1806, on Walleys Creek, to John Butler of Maury Co., 100 acres. (60)

4 Dec. 1809. Perry Coper (Roper, or Cooper) of Maury Co., Tenn., conveys 200 acres on Flat Creek to William Roper of Davidson Co., Tenn. (62)

24 Aug. 1812. Isaac L. Henderson and wife Lucinda of Mecklenburg Co., N. C., convey 400 acres to Jam Creiser and David Wilson McRee of Iredell Co., N. C. The land came by descent from David McRee, dec., to Lucinda, being one-fifth of a 5000 acre tract in Giles, Lincoln, Bedford, Maury Counties conveyed by John Nelson to said David McRee on 11 Nov. 1796. The land was registered in Davidson Co. on 16 Nov., Book D, page 84. (63)

26 Sept. 1812. Allen C. Yates conveys lot # 20 in Columbia, Maury Co., to Isaac B. Hardin. (65)

Jabus Nowlin of Maury Co., Tenn.; lot # 94 in Columbia; William and Peter S. Voorhies of Maury Co. (66)

22 Dec. 1812. James Reese, Sr., of Maury Co., conveys 2 acres to Silas Alexander, Samuel B. McKnight, and Samuel Ashmore, trustees, for the purpose of building a Presbyterian Society Meeting House. Ebenezer. (67)

11 Feb. 1811. Charles Smith; 10 acres; Joseph Morehead. (69)

22 June 1812. Jacob McKee; 130 acres, Grant no. 206 on Lytles Creek; Isaac Acuff Looney. (70)

11 Feb. 1811. Isa Pall conveys 35 acres on Little Flat Creek to Joseph Morehead. (71)

25 Feb. 1813. Date of registration. Thomas Ingram, assignee of the heirs of David Hatfield; 80 acres in consideration of military service performed by David Hatfield of North Carolina. Warrant no. 4399, dated 22 Dec. 1796. Grant no. 2978, Leepers Lick Creek of Duck River, first district, Maury Co. (72)

25 Feb. 1813. Date of registration. Thomas Ingram, assignee of heirs of D. Hatfield; 80 acres in consideration of military service by David Hatfield of North Carolina. Warrant no. 4399, dated 22 Dec. 1796. Grant no. 2979. (73)

13 Aug. 1812.   Richard Faussett of Maury Co.; 180 acres on Silver Creek; Newtom Cannon of Williamson Co., Tenn.   (74)

9 May 1812.   George Hanks conveys 100 acres on Knobb Creek and Snow Creek to John Fitzgerald.   (76)

23 Feb. 1809.   James Scott conveys 250 acres the land Spencer Griffin lived on to Spencer Griffin and Robert Hill.   (77)

27 Nov. 1812.   John J. Zollicoffer; 2 acres on Little Tom Bigby; Ephraium Davidson.   (78)

Zelmon Spencer conveys lot # 34 in Columbia to James Walker.   (79)

21 June 1812.   Howell Tatum and Robert Searcey of Davidson Co. convey 640 acres on Duck River to Joseph Hopkins.   (80)

8 Aug. 1812.   John Lyons; 100 acres on Wallays Creek; Nathaniel Simmons.   (81)

21 Dec. 1812.   Alexander Breckenridge, Sr., of Bourbon Co., Ky., conveys 1223½ acres on Duck River, adjoining Looney Line, to John Rowland, Geo. David and Benjamine Rowland, heir of George Rowland, deceased, of Gilford Co., N. C., and the aforesaid heirs of Smith Co., Tenn.   (82)

6 June 1812.   Thomas Dillon of Maury Co., Tenn., conveys land to Edwin Jay Osborn of Salisbury, Rowan Co., N. C.   The land was on Duck River previously deposited in the hands of said Dillon for location.   Also mentioned is a power of attorney, executor of Adler Osborn, Iredell Co., N. C. of Belmont, in Iredell Co., N. C.   (83)

22 Jan. 1813.   Joel Burrow conveys 50 acres on Duck River adjoining land of Richard Harris to Gilbert G. Washington and Samuel Craig.   (87)

9 Nov. 1812.   John Hardgrove conveys 200 acres on Duck River to William M. Berryhill.   (88)

22 Jan. 1813.   Lard B. Boyd conveys 14 acres adjoining land of Wm. Bradshaw to John Spencer.   (89)

8 Oct. 1812.   Thomas Bartlett of Columbia conveys lot no. 46 in Columbia to John Spencer of Maury Co., Tenn.   (90)

23 Jan. 1813.   John Spencer conveys 38 acres on Lytles Creek to Lard B. Boyd.   (91)

17 March 1813.   John Strain conveys lot no. 89 in Columbia to Hinchey Pettway and Thomas J. Maury of Williamson Co., Tenn.   (93)

16 March 1813.   Zilman (Tilman) Spencer conveys 100 acres on Green Licks Creek to Geo. M. Dickie.   (94)

24 Dec. 1812.   Hugh Leeper conveys 168 acres on Leepers Creek to Samuel Polk.   (95)

10 March 1813.   James and John Owen of Bladen Co., N. C., sonvey 512 acres on Globe Creek to James Houston.   (97)

6 March 1813.   David Shannon, Esq., of Williamson Co., Tenn., 50 acres on Brush Creek to Joseph Haynes, Sr., of Beadford Co., Tenn.   (98)

1 Jan. 1812.   Joseph Braden of Williamson Co., Tenn.; 75
acres on Fountain Creek; Samuel Gregg of Maury Co., Tenn.   (99)

7 April 1813.   James Night conveys 150 acres on Fountain
Creek to Natus Kirk.   (101)

15 March 1813.   Alexander Breckenridge, Sr., of Bourbon
Co., Ky., conveys 40 acres on Hurricane Branch, the same land
owned by heirs of George Rowland, to Alexander Gillespie of Maury Co., Tenn.   (102)

15 March 1813.   Alexander Breckenridge, Sr., of Bourbon Co.,
Ky., conveys 63 acres on Hurricane Branch, the same land owned
by said Breckenridge and David Looney, dec., to John Gillespie.
Deed calls for Warrant no. 498 and Grant no. 206.   (103)

13 March 1813.   James Paisley; 130 acres on Fountain Creek;
conveyed William Daniel (not clear of land was conveyed to or by
Daniel - R. W. B.).   (104)

No date.   Joseph Kilpatrick conveys 200 acres on Duck River
to Elibugh Kilpatrick.   (105)

2 March 1813.   James Rankin of Maury Co., Tenn., conveys
122½ acres on Bear Creek to William Polk of Wake Co., N. C.
(106)

28 Jan. 1813.   John Craig of Orange Co., N. C., by his attorney Samuel Craig, conveys 585 acres on Bighby Creek to David,
Richard, and Samuel Jennings.   (108)

28 Jan. 1813.   Samuel Craig conveys 500 acres on Bigton
Bigby (Big Tom Bigby?) Creek, being part of the tract granted
to David Craig of N. C., including Spencer Springs, to William
and Alexander Glass.   (109)

March 1813.   Johnson Craig of Maury Co., Tenn., conveys 150
acres on Big Tom Bigby Creek (being part of a 3200 acre tract
granted by North Carolina to David Craig, 1812, Grant no. 40)
to William Stockard of Maury Co.   (110)

8 July 1812.   Joseph B. Porter for love and affection conveys to his single daughter Elizabeth Brown Porter 140 acres on
Lytle Creek, surveyed in the name of James Brown, adjoining the
land of Lynn Brown.   (111)

14 Dec. 1811.   Ebenezer Kilpatrick; 312 acres on Duck River;
Joseph Kilpatrick.   (112).

17 Dec. 1811.   William D. Ewing of Bedford Co., Tenn.; 140
acres on Sinking Branch of Rock Creek; Michael Campbell, Sec. of
Philip Phillips, of Davidson Co., dec.   (114)

29 Sept. 1812.   John White of Davidson Co., Tenn., and Jam
White and Joseph McDowel of Maury Co., Tenn., convey 125 acres of
land adjoining that of Nicholas Long near the town of Columbia
to Robert Weakley of Davidson Co., Tenn., and John Crawford of
Williamson Co.   (115)

3 Dec. 1812.   William Daniel; 445 acres out of Grant no.
153 from North Carolina for 5000 acres on Fountain Creek and Duck
River; Richard Dallam of Logan Co., Ky.   (119)

19 Feb. 1787.   State of Tennessee grants 600 acres on Duck
River, opposite mouth of Lytle Creek (an Armstrong Grant), out of
Grant no. 4438, Warrant no. 1709, to David Ross.   (120)

26 Feb. 1797. Martin Armstrong of Stokes Co., N. C., conveys 35170 acres to Josiah Watson of Fairfax Co., Va. The land was located on Sturgeon Creek, N. Sulphur Fork of Red River, and North side of Cumberland River adjoining the land of Wm. Caswell (?) and tract on Middle District, south side of Duck River on Sinking Creek, etc., etc. (121)

9 July 1803. John McIver of Alexandria, District of Columbia; 35170 acres; bankrupt sale of Josiah Watson; George Gilpin, JOnah Thompson, and Francis Payton. (130)

15 March 1813. George Breckenridge of Maury Co., Tenn., conveys 35 acres on Hurricane Branch (part of a grant to David Looney and Breckenridge, out of warrant no. 495 (3), and by Breckenridge to George Rowland, Sr., and by heirs of said Rowland to Breckenridge) to Alexander Gillespie. (143)

15 March 1813. George Breckenridge conveys 125½ acres on Hurricane Creek to John Gillespie. (Same as above). (145)

19 June 1813. Thomas Hardeman and Thos. Hardin Perkins, all of Williamson Co., Tenn., convey 1360 acres on Globe Creek to Nicholas Perkins, Jr. (147)

22 June 1813. John Keeman conveys a lot in Columbia to Tyree Dollins (Dallams, or Dollars). (149)

12 Jan. 1813. William Donelson; 124 acres on Knob Creek; Thomas Ramsey. (152)

7 Sept. 1812. Littleberry Hamley; 200 acres on Knob Creek; Charles Partee. (154)

17 Oct. 1812. William Polk of Wake Co., N. C., conveys 449 acres on the headwaters of Walleys Creek lands of George Doherty to William Polk. (156)

1 May 1812. James Keer of Maury Co., Tenn.; 40 acres on Rutherford Creek adjoining land of Nicholas Perkins; Leroy Pope of Madison Co., Mississippi. (158)

25 March 1813. Samuel Carter; 318 acres on Snow Creek; Samuel Polk. (160)

6 March 1813. William Pickens; 100 acres on Globe Creek; David Shannon of Williamson Co., Tenn. (162)

4 June 1813. Seth Barns of Caswell Co., N. C.; 320 acres on Big Tom Bigby Creek; Nathan Williams of Caswell Co., N. C. (164)

Nov. 1792. North Carolina Grant no. 305; Warrant 1627; to Reese Porter, 640 acres on south side of Duck River, Middle District above mouth of Lytle Creek. Registered in Davidson Co., Book F, p. 317. (165)

21 April 1813. Wm. Nash of Rutherford Co. and Richard C. Harris of Maury Co., Tenn., convey 150 acres on Silver Creek (part of tract granted to said Nash by Nos. 3541, 3542, and 3543) to Edward Puckett. (166)

21 April 1813. William Nash of Rutherford Co., Tenn., and Richard C. Harris of Maury Co., Tenn., convey land on Silver Creek, Creek, part of the grants mentioned in previous record, to William Stone. (168)

19 June 1813. Thomas Hardeman and Thos. Hardin Perkins of

Williamson Co., Tenn., convey 640 acres on Globe Creek to Black-stone Hardeman of Maury Co., Tenn. (170)

2 Feb. 1813. James Stockard; 240 acres on Big Tom Bigby Creek; David Craig of Maury Co., Tenn. (172)

16 Aug. 1808. William Frierson, Joseph Brown, John Lindsey, and Isaac Roberts, Commissioners of the Town of Columbia, convey a lot in that town to Thomas Deadrick. (174)

No date. Samuel Polk, attorney for William Polk of Wake Co., N. C., conveys 190 acres on Rutherford Creek formerly George Doherty's land, to Ezekial Akin of Maury Co., Tenn. (176)

26 April 1813. Abraham Looney of Sullivan Co., Tenn., conveys 257½ acres in Lytles Creek, part of North Carolina Grant no. 206 to David Looney and Alexander Breckenridge, to Adam R. Alexander of Maury Co., Tenn. (178)

26 April 1813. Abraham Looney of Sullivan Co., Tenn., conveys 57 acres on Lytle Creek to William Maxwell of Maury Co., Tenn. (180)

5 Feb. 1813, Washington L. Hammun and wife Patsy, Sterling C. Robertson, John Childress and wife Betsy, and Eldridge B. Robertson, by W. L. Hammun their attorney, convey 320 acres on Little Tom Bigby Creek, granted by North Carolina, Grant no. 1045, to Elijah Robertson, to John Goff. (181)

5 Feb. 1813. Same grantors as above, by Washington L. Hammun, convey 200 acres on Little Tom Bigby Creek to Nathaniel Thompson. (183)

23 March 1813. James McMabon; 151 acres on Rutherford Creek; A. J. Turner, Anthony J. Turner. (185)

22 June 1813. Samuel Polk conveys 500 acres on Flat Creek to Hezekiah Almond. (186)

3 June 1809. Dividend of the Frierson Settlement. Samuel Frierson, Benoni Dickey, Thos. Stephenson, Samuel Weatherford, Moses G. Frierson, James Blakely, Wm. J. Frierson, Nath'l Stephenson, Elias Frierson, John White Stephenson, Geo. Frierson, James Armstrong, David Frierson, Paul Fulton, Alexander Dobbins, and William Frierson, all of Maury Co., Tenn. The land was purchased from Gen. Nathaniel Green, 5120 acres on Duck River; to Rev. James W. Stephenson and Robert Frierson of South Carolina. (188)

23 June 1813. Josiah Carthell and wife Sarah, formerly Sarah Morehead, one of the legatees of Charles Morehead, dec., convey land to Daniel Thomas of Richmond Co., N. C. The land is that where Thomas now lives on in Richmond Co. (191)

8 June 1813. Anthony J. Turner of Maury Co., Tenn., conveys 202 acres on Rutherford Creek to Cambridge Green, Franky Green, Susannah Green, Philip Washington Green, Polly Caterne Green, the heirs of William Green, dec. (192)

21 June 1813. Samuel Polk, attorney for William Polk of Wake Co., N. C., conveys 160 acres on Rutherford Creek, part of land owned by George Doherty, to Goldman Kimbrough. (195)

24 Aug. 1812. Isaac L. Henderson and wife Lucinda of Mecklenberg Co., N. C., convey 400 acres to James Creeser McRee and David Wilson McRee of Iredell Co., N. C. (197)

No date. Isaac Acuff Looney(?) of Maury Co., Tenn., conveys 50 acres on the east fork of Little Tom Bigby to William Henderson of Maury Co. The land was part of Grant no. 206, Warrant no. 498 by North Carolina to Breckenridge and David Looney. (202)

3 Jan. 1812. Richard Garrett of Davidson Co., Tenn., conveys lot no. 12 in Columbia to Mathew Simons of Maury Co., Tenn. (204)

25 Oct. 1802. Grant no. 391 by Tennessee of 2000 acres on Duck River to David Justice. This was a 10 pounds for every 100 acre grant. (206)

Aug. 1813. James Kendrick, Alinus Kendrick, John Brantley and John Kirk, complainants; 5000 acres on Fountain Creek; decree of Court of Errors and Appeals; Richard Dallam, defendant. (208)

10 July 1784. North Carolina Grant no. 4437, Warrant no. 535, 500 acres on Fountain Creek, to James Kindrick. (211)

5 Dec. 1812. James Gambling, Nancy Pitt, Polly Strother, Phebe Hollis, Stephen Pitt, Robert Strother, Jessie Hollis, and Eli Stalcup all of Sumner Co., Tenn., heirs of John Gambling of Maury Co., Tenn., dec.; 320 acres on Duck River; (to?) Oliver B. Hays and David Moore. (213)

23 April 1813. Alfred Blach of Davidson Co., Tenn., conveys lot no. 27 in the town of Columbia to John Shelton of Maury Co., Tenn. (215)

20 July 1808. John Thompson of Davidson Co., Tenn., conveys 400 acres on Duck River to James Russell also of Davidson Co. (216)

19 Aug. 1813. John Joseph Long conveys 140 acres on Big Tom Bigby Creek to John Frierson. (219)

10 Aug. 1812. John Davidson conveys 100 acres on Green Lick Creek to Henry Payton. (221)

21 Sept. 1813. Adam R. Alexander conveys 76 acres on Lytles Creek to Joseph Kinkade. (Land contains 76 acres and 55 poles). (223)

19 Oct. 1813. Henry Rutherford and Elizabeth Crawford, administrators of the estate of John Crawford, dec., all of Williamson Co., Tenn.; 100 acres on Leepers Lick Creek; (to?) Samuel Nesbet. (224)

19 Oct. 1813. Same grantors as in previous deed; 28 acres on Leepers Lick Creek; (to?) Hance Hamilton (Hambleton). (226)

7 December 1811.. Michael Campbell of Davidson Co., Tenn.; 50 acres on Glove Creek; (to?) William Cowden of Maury Co., Tenn. (228)

8 March 1812. Andrew Mitchell conveys 60 acres on Leepers Lick Creek to Moses Holmes. (230)

10 July 1788. North Carolina Grant no. 113; land on Duck River to William Cocke. (232)

12 Oct. 1812. Burwell Kennon conveys 100 acres adjoining that of Nicholas Long, Sr., to John Joseph Long. (233)

25 Nov. 1812.   Alfred Balch, Isaac B. Harden, and Peter R. Booker, all of Maury Co., West Tenn., convey a lot in Columbia to John Montgomery of East Tenn.   (235)

3 Oct. 1812.   James Trimble and George W. Campbell convey 300 acres to Osburne P. Nicholson.   (237)

5 Sept. 1811.   Due to an attachment against Robert and John Blair, the sheriff of Maury Co., Tenn., conveys 380 acres on Fountain Creek, part of the land granted to Elijah Robertson, to William W. Craig.   North Carolina Grant no. 1043.   (239)

12 Dec. 1813.   Samuel Polk conveys to his daughter Jane Maria Walker 260 acres on Knob Creek.   (242)

1814.   Tennessee Grant no. 241, 10 pounds for every 100 acres; 1000 acres on Duck River to Joseph Hart.   (243)

19 Dec. 1813.   Daniel Pain; 113 acres on Rutherford Creek; Robert Sellers of Maury Co., Tenn.   (244)

20 Dec. 1813.   George Breckenridge, attorney for James and John Owens of Bladen Co., N. C., conveys 353 acres on Globe Creek to John Wilkes, Sr., of Maury Co., Tenn.   The land was part of a grant to John Porterfield, no. 163, and willed by said Porterfield to James and John Owen.   (246)

23 Oct. 1813.   John L. Hickman of Bourbon Co., Ky., conveys 407 acres on Globe Creek to Samuel McConnell of Maury Co., Tenn. (248)

26 Oct. 1813.   Same grantor as above conveys 2310 acres on Globe Creek to George Breckenridge.   (249)

28 June 1813.   Samuel Davis conveys 125 acres on Little Tom Bigby Creek to Ephraim E. Davidson.   (252)

1 Sept. 1813.   John Davidson conveys 105 acres adjoining Whiteside's land to A. B. Mayfield.

21 Aug. 1811.   James Davis of Williamson Co., Tenn., conveys 206 2/3 acres on Plunkets Creek to William and Gideon Pillow.   (255)

23 Oct. 1813.   Robert Hill conveys 300 acres on the north side of Duck River at the mouth of Churchwells Spring Branch to John Spencer.   (256)

1 June 1809.   Winslow J. McKee, heir of D. McKee, conveys land to James C. McKee and David W. McKee, two legatees of the deceased (D. McKee).   David McKee, Sr., of said county was seized of certain property at his death.   (260)

18 Feb. 1810.   Catherine Miller of Camden Co., Ga., widow of Nathaniel R. Green of East Greenwich, R. I.; Martha W. Nightengale of East Greenwich, widow; Louisa C. Green of Camden Co., Ga., spinster; Edward B. Littlefield of Camden Co., Ga., heirs of Nathaniel Green, convey land to Ray Land or Sands of Camden Co., Ga.   (262)

8 Oct. 1804.   Ephraium McClean, Sr., of Christian Co., Ky., conveys 1272 acres on Knob Creek to John McGinsey of Burke Co., N. C.   (265)

5 July 1813.   Alfred Balch of Davidson Co., Tenn., conveys lot in Columbia to Isaac B. Hardin, and William and Geo. Morgan. (268)

23 Oct. 1813. John L. Hickman of Bourbon Co., Ky., conveys 242 acres on Globe Creek to James Houston of Maury Co., Tenn. (269)

17 Dec. 1813. Thomas Hardeman and Thos. H. Perkins of Williamson Co., Tenn., convey 1000 acres on Globe Creek to Nicholas Perkins of Williamson Co., Tenn. (271)

3 Sept. 1813. Lydia B. Estates of Columbia conveys lots 39 and 40 in Columbia to Nathaniel Willis; mortgage. (273)

8 May 1813. Samuel Cannon of Wilson Co., Tenn., conveys lot no. 102 in Columbia to Eliphes Smith. (279)

21 June 1813. William Polk of Wake Co., N. C.,conveys 77 acres on Rutherford Creek, being part of the George Doherty land to Bryant Bangus of Bedford Co. (280)

28 Oct. 1813. Thomas Shute of Rutherford Co., Tenn., conveys 50 acres on Duck River to Jonathan Brown of Maury Co., Tenn. (282)

11 Oct. 1813. Joel Burrow conveys 50 acres on Globe Creek to Elijah Jones. (283)

8 Dec. 1813. William Henderson of Maury Co. for love and affection conveys 178 acres on Little Tom Bigby Creek to William Land Henderson and Richard Henderson. (285)

15 April 1813. Washington S. Hammun and wife Patsey, John Childress and wife Elizabeth, Sterling C. Robertson and Elbridge B. Robertson, by their attorney W. S. Hammun, convey 100 acres on Little Tom Bigby Creek, originally granted to Elijah Robertson by North Carolina Grant no. 1045, to William L. Henderson and Richard Henderson. (287)

No date. Same grantors as above convey 100 acres on Fountain Creek convey to Lander Veach of Maury Co., Tenn. (290)

19 April 1813. Elizabeth Williams, Daniel Williams, and William Rice, executors of the will of Henry Williams, dec., of Caswell Co., N. C., convey 1000 acres on Big Tom Bigby and Indian Creeks to Nathan Williams of Caswell Co., N. C. (293)

13 April 1813. Salomon, Alexander, Murphey, and Hundon Harrelson all of Caswell Co., N. C., convey 500 acres on Big Tom Bigby and Indian Creeks to Nathan Williams of Caswell Co., N. C. (296)

21 April 1813. David Jennings conveys 1175(?) acres on Big Tom Bigby Creek to Stephen Jarman. (299)

22 Feb. 1813. Thomas H. Hardin of Bedford Co., Tenn., conveys a lot in Columbia to Peter B. Voorhies of Maury Co., Tenn. (301)

2 April 1814. William Cocke; 5000 acres; plat of land for proceedings on Duck River. (302)

24 Dec. 1813. Abraham Shiteside and wife Ruth of Maury Co., Tenn., convey 150 acres on Plum Branch to John J. Zolicoffer. (304)

5 Feb. 1813. Constantine, James H., and John Mack, Jr.; 95 acres of Grant no. 1045 to Elijah Robertson; (evidently) same grantors as on p. 287 above. (307)

26 Jan. 1814. John and Ephraim E. Davidson convey 290 acres on Green Lick Creek to Adam Klyce. (370)

1 Jan. 1814. Benjamine Thomas conveys 260 acres on Globe Creek to James Dysert. (312)

14 Jan. 1814. John Smith of Williamson Co., Tenn., conveys 100 acres on Tom Bigby Creek to Samuel Griffith. (314)

14 Jan. 1814. John Smith of Williamson Co., Tenn., conveys 161 acres on Tom Bigby Creek to his daughter Mary Griffith, wife of Samuel Griffith. (316)

20 July 1814. Alexander Martin of Dickson Co., Tenn., conveys 100 acres on Big Tom Bigby Creek to James Johnston. (318)

28 Oct. 1814. Thomas Shelby conveys 240 acres on Duck River to Thomas Shute of Rutherford Co., Tenn. (320)

20 June 1810. David Looney of Smith Co., Tenn., conveys 100 acres on Lytles Creek to Francis Findley of Lincoln Co., Tenn. The land was part of a tract granted to Alexander Breckenridge and David Looney, Sr.; Grant no. 206, North Carolina. (321)

20 Sept. 1813. Joseph Hopkins conveys 39 acres on Duck River to John Hoge. (323)

20 Sept. 1813. Nathaniel Willis conveys 203 acres on Big Tom Bigby Creek to Edward English. (325)

6 July 1810. James Welsh conveys land, 66 degrees and 22 poles (sic) to Thomas H. Perkins and Nicholas Perkins of Williamson Co., Tenn. (327)

19 April 1814. James Davis; 40 acres on Leepers Lick Creek, on Duck River adjoining land of Nancy Shepard; Tenn. Grant no. 4996; 1810. (329)

No date. James David; 140 acres on Leepers Lick Creek; Tenn. Grant no. 4995; 1809. (330)

12 Feb. 1814. William Polk of Wake Co., N. C., conveys 51 acres on Rutherford Creek to Elizabeth McKain. (331)

15 April 1814. John Childress of Davidson Co., Tenn., conveys 65½ acres on Fountain Creek to Washington S. Hammun of the same county. This is a deed of confirmation. (332)

15 April 1814. John Childress of Davidson Co. conveys 284 acres on Fountain Creek to Eldridge B. Robertson of the same county. (333)

13 Jan. 1814. A. H. Goforth conveys negroes to Lucy D. Kearney. (336)

July 1813. William Bradshaw conveys by a sheriff's sale a lot in Town of Columbia to Washington Shaw. (338)

21 Sept. 1813. Nathaniel Taylor of Carter Co., Tenn., attorney for John Keith of same place, conveys land on Catheys Creek to Jacob Beffitt, John Burns, and Miles Burns. (340)

1 Jan. 1814. Benjamine Thomas conveys 200 acres on Globe Creek to William Cowan. (343)

April 1814. Attachment against B. Turner for Lot no. 27 in Columbia being the lot of Nicholas Tate Perkins. William Bradshaw, sheriff, conveys the lot to Isaac B. Hardin, partner in firm of Hardin and Morgan. (344)

1813. Washington L. Hammun and others convey 200 acres of the land of Elijah Robertson on Fountain Creek to Thomas Richardson. (347)

17 April 1812. William Henderson of Rutherford Co., Tenn., conveys 1049 acres on Silver Creek to Robert McCord, James Hill, and David McCord. (350)

No date. John Lyon of Carthage, Smith Co., Tenn., conveys a lot in Columbia to Capt. Gilbert C. Russell of the U. S. Army. (352)

21 Sept. 1813. Richard C. Harris conveys 100 acres on Silver Creek to Michael Steel. (353)

13 Dec. 1812. James Henderson, Sr., of Lincoln Co., N. C., (now dec.) conveyed 200 acres on Duck River to James Henderson Petterson. (354)

24 Dec. 1813. Sion Record conveys 100 acres entered in names of Philips and Campbell to William D. Ewing. (356)

7 Jan. 1814. George Breckenridge conveys 43 acres on Fountain Creek to Benjamine Wilkes. (357)

15 March 1813. James Reese conveys 31 acres on Little Bigby Creek to Silas Alexander. (359)

21 Sept. 1814. Richard C. Harris conveys 80 acres in the 2nd District on both sides of Silver Creek and south side of Duck River to Samuel Park. (362)

19 Feb. 1810. John Starkey of Overton Co., and Jesse Starkey of White Co., Tenn., convey 150 acres on Duck River to Joseph Scott. (363)

9 June 1813. Nathaniel Williams of Caswell Co., N. C., conveys 675 3/4 acres on Big Tom Bigby Creek or Indian Creek to Hezekiah Puryear. (366)

Oct. 1810. William Leintz of Davidson Co., Tenn., conveys one-third part of Lot no. 31 in Columbia to Hermson Hardy of Davidson Co., Tenn. (367)

19 Aug. 1812. Andrew Boyd, attorney for John Hacket of Ray Co., Tenn., conveys 400 acres on east fork of Little Bigby Creek and Fountain Creek, to William Henderson. Boyd was a resident of Maury Co., Tenn. (369)

2 Feb. 1814. George Breckenridge, attorney for James and Jno. Owen of Bladen Co., N. C., conveys 118 acres on the waters of Globe Creek to Robert Edmond of Maury Co., Tenn. (371)

18 Oct. 1813. Thomas Shute of Rutherford Co., Tenn., conveys 100 acres on north side of Duck River, to Stephen Hawkins. (372)

18 Oct. 1813. Thomas Shute of Rutherford Co., Tenn., conveys 150 acres on north side of Duck River to William Hawkins. (374)

1814.   Return of the division of Gen. Nathaniel Green's land. A very long court record which explains the division in details. (376)

12 Oct. 1810. Thomas Hunt, executor of Muncan Hunt of Granville Co., N. C., conveys 1500 acres on the north side of Duck River to David Graves of Granville Co., N. C. (381)

11 Oct. 1810. David Graves of Granville Co., N. C., conveys 1500 acres on Duck River to Nathaniel Gunt of Granville Co., N. C. (382)

Aug. 1814. Return of division of land of Robert Weakley and other heirs of John Crawford, dec., as received by Robert Weakley. (384)

14 Dec. 1811. Ebenezer Kilpatrick conveys to Eleazer Kilpatrick 200 acres on Duck River. (386)

30 July 1813. Philip Anthony; 200 acres on east bank of Globe Creek; John Childress of Davidson Co. (387)

15 May 1812. Richard Churchill, Sr., of Maury Co., and Richard Churchill, Jr., of Bedford Co., Tenn., convey 70 acres on Snow Creek to Thomas Brooks. (389)

20 Sept. 1813. Ephraium E. Davidson conveys 125 acres on Little Tom Bigby Creek to Samuel Davis. (390)

20 May 1814. Gideon Pillow conveys 70 acres on Silver Creek to William Gifford. (392)

7 Feb. 1814. Alexander Henderson conveys a mortgage to James Hardison for 100 acres. (394)

No date. James Morehead of Richmond Co., N. C., conveys 1400 acres on the north side of Duck River to Benjamine Smith. (395)

30 Dec. 1812. Samuel Polk; 393 3/4 acres on Knob Creek; Nathaniel Benton or Burton of Williamson Co., Tenn. (397)

3 March 1815. John Grimes conveys 50 acres on Fountain Creek (the same land that was granted to Richard Dallam by North Carolina) to James Grimes. (398)

13 June 1814. Mathew Gleaves of Davidson Co., conveys 73 acres and 38 poles on Rock Creek to John Record. (400)

12 Jan. 1813. Harman Miller conveys 50 acres on Rutherford Creek to Ezekiel Polk. (401)

29 June 1813. Joel Reese conveys 100 acres on Littleberry Creek to Burwell Cannon. (402)

13 Nov. 1812. James Robertson of Davidson Co., Tenn., conveys 168 acres on Leepers Lick Creek to Hugh Leeper. (405)

16 Jan. 1813. William T. Lewis of Davidson Co., conveys 200 acres on Globe Creek, to James Kennedy. (406)

20 Aug. 1813. John Hunter conveys 50 acres and 25 poles to Sterling Tinsley. The land was located on Big Tom Bigby Creek. (407)

18 Sept. 1813. Thomas H. Benton of Williamson Co., Tenn., conveys 296 3/4 acres on north side of Duck River to William Yancey. (409)

20 Sept. 1813. Joseph Hopkins conveys 80 acres on north side of Duck River to Thomas Craig. (410)

16 Sept. 1813. Alex. Martin of Dixon Co., Tenn., conveys 150 acres on Big Tom Bigby Creek to Perminas Williams. (411)

22 Sept. 1813. Aaron R. Alexander conveys 100 acres on Lytle Creek to James Irwon. (413)

28 Sept. 1813. James Johnson conveys 50 acres on Knob Creek to Isham Johnson. (414)

24 Jan. 1814. Wm. Cowen, Esq., conveys 28 acres adjoining the land of Wm. T. Lewis to James Dysart. (415)

15 April 1814. John Childers (or Childress) of Davidson Co., Tenn., conveys land on Fountain and Globe Creeks to Sterling C. Robertson. (416)

11 July 1812. William Alexander conveys 75 acres in Maury Co. to John Campbell and Charles Nelley. (417)

21 April 1813. Stephen German (Jarman) conveys 35 acres on Big Tom Bigby Creek to James Beaty. (418)

1813. Jno. Childress of Davidson Co., Tenn., conveys 50 acres on Fountain Creek to William Rentfro. (420)

1814. Jones Kendrick conveys 415 acres on Fountain Creek to Wm. Weems. (421)

5 Jan. 1814. Jones Kendrick conveys 300 acres on Fountain Creek to Obumus Kendricks. (422)

Aug. 1813. Alexander M. Rogers of Williamson Co. conveys 250 acres on Big Tom Bigby Creek to Permenas Williams of Maury Co., Tenn. (424)

Feb. 1814. Jonas Kendrick conveys 200 acres on Fountain Creek to Samuel Jameson. (425)

Feb. 1814. John Dearing conveys 200 acres on Globe Creek to Minor Wilkes. (426)

18 Jan. (year not given). James Houston of Iredell Co., N. C., by his attorney James H. Houston, conveys 101 3/4 acres on Tombigby Creek to Thomas Jones. (428)

Dec. 1812. Samuel Benton of Williamson Co., Tenn., conveys 337 3/4 acres to Robert Sellars. (429)

15 May 1814. James Houston conveys 51 acres and 80 poles in Maury Co., Tenn., to Jonathan D. Bills. (430)

28 Dec. 1813. Perry Cohea conveys lot in Columbia to John Strain. (432)

1813. John Bitteman conveys lot in Columbia to Bird S. Hunt; lot no. 33. (433)

* * *

MARRIAGES FROM MONTGOMERY COUNTY

Due to a fire in the early history of Montgomery County, Tennessee, formerly "Old Tennessee County," many of the early marriage records have been destroyed. The following are a few of the marriage records that have been preserved. The marriages are on file at the court house in Clarksville, the county seat of Montgomery County. E. R. W.

28 Aug. 1799	Henry Gibson	Hariott French
3 Aug. 1799	Thomas Hamilton	Rachel McGrace
24 Dec. 1799	Charles Rose	Polly Ross
6 Aug. 1799	John Karr	Timby Gardner
28 Aug. 1799	John Scott	Polly Dobbs
7 Nov. 1799	Thomas Tinnin	Nancy Allen
30 Nov. 1799	William Dunbar	Elizabeth Hall
30 May 1799	Thomas Jones	Rebecca Hurt
27 Feb. 1799	John Clerk	Lucy Elliott
25 Feb. 1799	Richard Cook	Elizabeth Coff
23 Jan. 1799	Alexander Trousdale	Jean Nelson
Jan. 1799	Joseph Woodfork	Zeburch Penning
3 Aug. 1799	James Cockran	Mary Philips
13 June 1799	Henry Bryant	Milly Taylor
7 May 1799	James Tyard	Susanath McCarty
Aug. 1799	Cornelius McGraw	Betsy Allen
6 March 1799	Samuel Watson	Catherine Edmonston
4 Jan. 1799	Jonah Hibbs	Lucy Miller
30 Jan. 1799	Gideon Walker	Betsey Johnson
20 Dec. 1799	Cordel Norfleet	Polly Pennington
4 Oct. 1802	Alexander Patterson	Rebecca Bird
3 July 1802	Robert Ragh	Nancy Varnes
4 Feb. 1802	James Edwards	Elizabeth Sparks
19 Dec. 1802	Yancy Thornton	Amdia Thornton
3 Nov. 1802	Lawrence Tennen	Elizabeth Allen
3 Aug. 1802	Nathaniel Hews	Isbel McGarrity
6 Sept. 1802	William Grayson	Susannah Tennen
3 April 1802	George Ellis	Joniah Helton
11 May 1802	William Bogard	Ador Chism
11 Feb. 1802	John M. Langford	Peggy Oneal (ONeal)
26 June 1802	John Williams	Elizabeth Smith
15 June 1802	James Hened	Elizabeth McCarty
3 Jan. 1802	Ebenezer Piatt	Abigail Lindzy
4 Oct. 1802	Alexander Patterson	Rebecca Bird
23 June 1802	John Kizer	Polly Cook
25 May 1802	John Ellis	Masson Thompson
25 May 1802	Robert Duke	Charlotte Duke
14 Sept. 1802	James Whitehead Cocke	Lucy Hargrove
13 July 1802	Benjamine Ray	Anne Henry
9 Sept. 1802	Benjamine Mason	Mary Reeves
10 Aug. 1802	Jonathan Aldridge	Sarah Harvey
9 Nov. 1802	Charles Seal	Christianna Miller
15 Nov. 1802	Robert Drake	Polly Ross
5 Oct. 1802	Joseph B. Neville	Elizabeth (?)
23 Nov. 1802	William Montgomery	Fenny Miller
25 Oct. 1802	Matthew Rybourn	Polly Drake
25 April 1802	Davil McIntoch	Franky Beard
4 Nov. 1802	Benjamine Gainis	Rebecca Raborom
22 Dec. 1802	John Neeley	Peggy Patten
14 Sept. 1802	Vincent Ennis	Mary Awinge

25 April 1808	James Williams	Patsey Marshall Sims
17 May 1808	Joseph Hardikinon	Mrs. Jennett Watt
14 May 1808	Hugh Stanford	Rachel Clerk
12 Sept. 1808	Hartwell Cocke	Elizabeth Saunderson
15 Feb. 1808	Owein Perdue	Agnis Young
27 Jan. 1808	Henry Green	Luendy Reasons
29 Nov. 1808	John Jacob	Nancy Bridges
4 Oct. 1808	Mosses Ingram	Nancy Darnell
30 Aug. 1808	James Reade	Martha Epps
27 March 1808	John Seats	Polly Tyler
15 Nov. 1808	James Taylor	Silvy Marten
3 March 1808	John Lee (?)	Sarah Morgan
9 Nov. 1808	Conrad Hawkersmith	Rachel Groves
13 Feb. 1808	William Samasters	Phebee Bunling
12 Jan. 1808	Goodman Frawick	Nancy Trebble
13 Oct. 1808	Robert Revel	Peggy Cuny
20 Sept. 1808	William Roach	Alcey Man
12 March 1808	John H. Poston	Nancy L. Nelson
25 July 1808	John Andrews	Levina Stallings
15 Sept. 1808	William Carter	Nancy Knight
12 Sept. 1808	Herbert Wheeles	Penelopy Morris
25 April 1808	James Williams	Patsy Marshall Sims
1 Dec. 1808	Micasah Baggote	Ally Parker
2 Dec. 1808	Henry Weaks	Anny Smith
25 Aug. 1808	Oswell Potts	Rachel Cannon
12 Dec. 1808	Thomas H. McEbrath	Rebecca Tomkins
9 Aug. 1808	Elisha McGehe	Rachel Saterfield
1 Aug. 1808	Archebauld Howell	Rebecca Williams
3 Nov. 1808	William Parker	Winny Powers
14 Jan. 1808	William Hubbard	Sarah Sims
24 Aug. 1808	Robert Kilbuck	Patience Norman
22 Nov. 1808	David Laid	Ferbey Norman
25 Dec. 1808	George Criffe	Sarah Riscoe
21 Feb. 1808	Martwell Weaver	Betsy Dickson
15 June 1808	William Hubbard	Sally Blanton
11 March 1808	Richard Heckerdson	Jinny Mallory
20 Jan. 1808	Joseph Black	Tindey Watt
3 May 1808	Zebidee Dennis	Patsey Oneal
11 July 1808	John Hunt	Dixey Emmerson
5 Sept. 1808	John Martin	Mary Neblett
8 March 1808	Annias Boatwright	Rebeccah Baker
10 Sept. 1808	Joseph Reaves	Redah Miller
23 Jan. 1808	Sterling Ingram	Betsey Gordon
17 Jan. 1808	James Stewart	Saona Stewart
29 Jan. 1808	William Good	Nancy Rook
29 Jan. 1808	Jonathan Anderson	Joselliah Taylor
4 June 1808	Simon Holt	Mary Miller
13 Aug. 1808	John H. Hyde	Polly Gray
2 Aug. 1808	Jesse Mitchell	Judith Pearce
20 Jan. 1808	David Daves	Betsy Allen
1 March 1808	Nedum Taylor	Patsey Killebrew
15 March 1808	James Tubs	Peggy Standford
20 June 1808	Isaac Saterfield	Susannah Wetherford
26 Sept. 1817	Joseph Perry	Drusilla Martin
19 Nov. 1817	John Duke	Catherine B. Duff
18 Dec. 1817	Eaton Coley	Betsey Funk
19 Sept. 1817	Berry H. Hambleton	Sally Potts
No date	William Moble	Lorath Baker

* * *

PETITION FROM OVERTON COUNTY

To the Honourable the General Assembly of the State of Tennessee Now in Session, the Petition of the Subscribers, Inhabitants of the County of Overton, Humbly Sheweth That They Feel Disposed to Have a Part in the Present War With His Britannic Majesty's Savage Allies, Viz., the Creek Nation of Indians and Conceiving They Can Render Greater Services to the United States As Mounted Men Than They Could Possibly Do on Foot, Do Humbly Request That Your Honourable Body Would Pass a Law Authorizing Collonel Stephen Copeland of Said County To Raise by Voluntary Inlistment a Force of 500 Mounted Men out of the 3rd Judicial Circuit in Said State to March Against the Said Nation of Indians or Other Tribes of the Savage For and Fight Them in Their Own Savage Way and Act as Rangers, etc., So Long as it May Appear Necessary and That the Said Voluntary Forces When so Raised May be Paid and Allowed the Same Pay for Their Services as Other Mounted Men are Allowed in the Service of the United States on Similar Occasions - And That the Senators and Representatives in the Congress of the United States Be Instructed to Cause the Said Act when Passed by Your Honourable Body to be Sanctioned by the National Legislator, etc.

And Your Petitioners Shall Ever Pray etc.

1. B. Tatton
2. Jas. McCampbell
3. Moore Matlock
4. James Fenley
5. Wilie Hudleston
6. Thos. Sevington
7. John Stockton
8. Robt. Adkinson
9. John Miller
10. Phillip W. Bever
11. Arthur Urchel
12. Isaac Smith
13. Benjm. Parrott
14. Samuel Miller
15. Thomas Burford
16. Joseph Campbell
17. Arthur Babb
18. John Hughes
19. Wm. Fleming
20. Benj. Brown
21. Jos. Harris
22. Jno. Kennedy
23. Eliga Rogers
24. John Cisco
25. Hershel Speck
26. John R. Nelson
27. James Boswell
28. James Smith
29. Stephen Horn
30. Sam Brown
31. Jacob Swallows
32. Zachiah Eldridge
33. John Hamoc
34. William Copeland
35. James Copeland
36. Stephen (?)
37. Henry Dillion
38. Land Dillion
39. Wm. Allen
40. James McBotts
41. Simon Sims
42. James Bradsaw
43. Sampson Eldridge
44. John Eldridge
45. Thompson Gardenshire
46. Richard Postton
47. W. Harrison
48. Wm. Upton
49. Peter Arnet
50. Jessee Arnet
51. William Upton
52. William McConnay
53. John Horn
54. John Walker
55. Carnilous Cannady
56. Thomas McDaniel
57. Seven Alley
58. Joseph Raney
59. William Boswell
60. James Lee
61. James Officer
62. Filep Upton
63. John Thomas Young
64. Quillow Lamb
65. Jacob Davie
66. William Sims
67. Hollel Herran
68. Corneles Cannady
69. Isaac Hooser
70. Edmon Crafford
71. William Stark
72. Hennery Gore

73. Isa Roe
74. John Lee
75. Robert (?)
76. Andrew Swallows
77. Stephen Mayfield
78. James Mayfield
79. Jaec Hurst
80. Isaac Taylor
81. Richard (?)
82. Nelson Ray
83. Henry Gillmore
84. Wm. Taylor
85. Hall Dilling
86. Emstort Walker
87. Merel Littel
88. Wm. Harlow
89. Joel Paris
90. David Stuart
91. Jos. H. Windle
92. Wm. Evens
93. Isaiah Ruckman
94. Wm. Alred
95. Solomon Alred
96. Isaac W. Hooser
97. Britton Smith

98. James Parks
99. Joshua Morrison
100. Saml. Calliham
101. Francis Chany
102. Alexr. Fenslery
103. Chas. Natney
104. Larkin Cox
105. James Key
106. Wm. Cooksey
107. Patk. Roof
108. Ephraim Wykoff
109. John Workman
110. Benjm. Workman
111. Robt. Dale
112. Peter Bilyew
113. John Maxwell
114. Hardy Honeycutt
115. James Maxwell
116. Isaac Cunningham
117. Jessy Gentry
118. Thos. Gallion
119. Wm. Dale
120. Mathew Dale
121. Thos. Chamberlan

The above names were written by me, Jos. H. Windle, at a
Genl. Muster by their request.

W. Harrison
Jeremiah Holman
John Patrick
William Officer
Stephen Sewel
Walter Fisk
John Grayham
Tiry Harp
Charles Staples
Eli Harrison
Greenwood Harrison
Hiram Allen
Carter Dalton
Achillis Stephens
Joseph Garrett
Elijah Davis
John Flat
Joel Cain
Joseph Harris
Thos. R. Harris
Jessee Hull
John Rolls
Jon Huddleston
Thos. Masters
George Moore
John Cannon
John Goodpasture
Madison Fisk
Solomon Eaves
Randal Murray
John Smart
James McRoberts
David Liles
James Woods
Daniel Liles
Stephen Row

John Harris
John Savage
John Goode
Reubin Witt
Benjamine Flowers
Arthur Goodpasture
Benjamine Harrison
John McCord
Fras. McConnell
William Willard
Arthur Mitchell
Samuel Harris
Arthur Babb
Isam Johnson
James Willard
James Murray
Robert Boyd
James McConnell
Abraham Goodpasture
Isaac Holiman
Joseph Grammer
Jessee Masters
Sterling Collier
Allen Brock
John W. Moore
Wm. Holeman
John Cargile
James Zachery
John Grimsley
Joel Brook
Gideon Thomas
James Mabry
Daniel Camon
Isaac Shell
Wm. Gunnells
John Erwin

Henry Wood
Isaiah Row
Jacob Rook
John Davice
William Bobbs
Henry Baily

Martin Grimsley
Vardiman Lee
Wm. Part
Arthur Flowers
George Gilpatrick

Copied from original legislative petitions on file in Book 12, for year 1813, Tennessee State Archives, Memorial Building, Nashville, Tenn.

PETITION FROM SMITH COUNTY

Petition of Smith County inhabitants regarding county line between Smith and Cannon Counties; 1837.
    Signed by:

Logan D. Key
Samuel Brown
S. P. Hughes
John R. Redman
Jeremiah Belk
David Phillips
Silas Pope
Tmes(?) Adams
Seabourn J. Hart
David Linch
Josiah Rice
Wm. B. Whitley
James Long (Tony)
Robert McMinn
Nepthah Fulks
Mathew L. Mann
G. W. Reasonover
John Ward
L. H. Cardwell
Robert Warren
Charles Paty
Robt. Nickson
Preston Hewett
Joel J. James
Horace Oliver
James Rasis, Jr.
Wilson Boulton
Jordan McKinney
John C. Lonony
David Tyry
Z. F. Hodges
John Shoemake
Joseph Moses
Ramsey Nance
Isaac Kitrell
Mathew Harper
Thomas Kitrell
James Saunders
M. W. Sloan
Robert Allen
William Ashley
Thos. A. Fooherb(?)
Jordan Beasley
Luke Skelton
Daviel Ritenbury

Solomon Smalling
Woodson Knight
Wm. F. Allen
John Hallum
Thomas Jackson
D. A. Cornshard
Richard Jones
John Payne
Nathan Ruch(?)
Exum Whitley
Henry Mann
Gabriel Dinney
Calvin Harris
Clem McKinney
James T. Cortello
Josiah Whitley
Asa Beaslley
Peter Webster
Diggs W. Thomas
Charles Hallum
Wm. Smalling
Alexander James
Obadiah Paris
James Razizer
Fleming Gillespie
Richard Hodge
C. Mede
Armstrong Allen
J. J. Burnett
Henry W. Brazall
John Winston
David L. Douglas
W. W. D. Lee
Claiborne Eulegan(?)
George Baker, Sr.
Stephen H. Douglas
Robert L. Hodges
L. C. Beasley
John Nollenen
William Overstreet
Jos. W. Allen
Allen Wood
Michael Shumake
James Rawlings
Judd Strother

G. L. Lynch
Tyree Adcock
Theodorick Ferrill
John Boze
William Allen
Peater Craget
C. Crutchfield
Moses Evitte
Thos. Hale
John Palman
Y. Orange
Woodson Fitts
Wm. Carter
Peter Hackett
Michael Ughees
Wootson Palmon
James Alexander
Dawson B. Harris
Jas. H. Vaden
John Pattey
Drury Denton
Jones Pattey
John Pope
Jacob Roberts
John Slate
Wm. Harper
Rufus Perry
John Bates
Harvey Mills
John High
Wm. C. Owens
John D. Owen
John Goodall
Timothy Walton, Sr,
Jacob Waggoner
John Johnson
Isaac Lynch
Joseph Gaies(?)
Cyrus W. Hazard
Samuel Surberry
Dempsey Maurice
Lint Botton
Charles Boulton
A. Hallum
James Boulton

Isaac Bradley
Henry Strother
Erin Bateman
N. W. Parrott
Joseph Vandepool
G. W. McGee
John W. McNutt
George W. Harris
Jas. P. McKee
John Harper
Jas. Rawland
Benj. Parrott
David Boyd
David Whitley
Wm. Pendarvis
Richd T. Whitley
James Ranoris
John Gordan
Richard Rison
John A. Farmer
Jas. Gripson
Edmund P. Hobson
Davy Hatland
Matthew Harper
J. W. Allen
Jack Farmer
David Davis
James High
Stephen Sampson
Camil Wright
Wihlton High
Henry Beasley
Samuel Robertson
Joseph Payne
W. O. Riley
David Robertson
Harrison Fergans
Jack Lynch
George Waggoner
B. J. Jones
Saml Jenkins
Nicholas Waggoner
Wm. Black
Clabron Hall
Joseph Lynch

A few of these names have been difficult to transcribe and therefore are subject to error in spelling in a few places. E. R. W.

* * *

Petition for an alteration in the Constitution from sundry Citizens of Smith County, 27 Nov. 1837, asking for a new county. Signed by a number of citizens of Dist. 11 of said Smith County. This petition is filed in Box 75, Legislative Papers, Tennessee State Archives, Nashville.

Hezekiah Blankinship
Isaac Hatckett
William Matox
Joel Blankenship
Lewis Cooper
Patrick Ramsey

Lewis Law
Lewis Bandy
Ira Meador
Samuel Martin
Bennet Meador
Epsor Epperson

Isham Blankenship
Benj. Talley
Francis Cooper
Calvin Cook
Rice Snider
John Howel
Edward Glover
Henry Snider
Samuel Woodcock
King Silovin(?)
Joel Turkey
Samuel R. Tucker
John Woodcock, Sr.
Lewis Lin
Wiley Woodcock
Charley Woodcock
Peter Epperson
Smith Woodcock
Jehu Meador
Henry Woodcock
John Stowers
Robert Bratton
Wesley Meador
Joel Hire
William Dunn
James Jenkins
Cyrus Hanes
William Robinson
Stephenson Holland
G. B. Parker
Wm. C. Chamberlain
Nedam Holland
Joel M. Woodcock

Thomas Haney
John Blankenship
Jam. C. Gammon
John Martin
John Wood Cock
J. H. Snider
Joseph Meador
John Butler
Jonah Wilderman
Alfred Simmons
Joseph Woodcock
Jobe Meador
Mark Woodcock
Nathan Woodcock
John Clebon
William C. Simpson
William Ferguson
Eli Hire
Andrew Simmons
John O. Cosby
James M. Chamberlain
George Lamb
William Ragland
Edward Bradley
Daniel Clebon
Christopher Meador
Austin L. Hanes
Smith Epperson
Banister Meador
David F. Gilbert
Anderson Meador
Joel Simmons
Joel Meador

The following petition pertaining to the same subject was taken on 9 Dec. 1837 and signed by a number of citizens. Although the exact section or district was not stated, all the signers were from Smith County, and the petition pertained to the formation of a new county.

Rich'd McConnell
A. Sloan
John O. Wilkerson
Jno. Stevens
Nelson Hamilton
Wm. R. Hodges
L. E. Mitcher
Robert Hughes
W. C. Jones
Harvey Hogg
W. C. Hamilton
John Hallum
George Stevens
Prichy Askins
Jno. Morris
Jefferson Rowland
Ira B. Cown
John Cochran
O. B. Hubbard
James Bradley
A. J. Chapman
Geo. W. B. Duncan
Andr. Allison
B. B. Uhls

A. Fergn Stone
William C. Hubbard
Harvey H. Holland
W. V. Hallum
Geole Seven(?)
John McNairy
Don C. Dixon
Allen S. Watkins
James R. Loney
John G. Park
Timos Walton
George L. Lynch
Swan Thompson
Samuel Oldham
H. A. Nichols
W. Robinson
Leml Tilestone
A. B. Roleyt
Daniel Wrelenberg(?)
H. B. McDonald
Allen Martin
Johnson Samson
Benjamine Rucker
R. S. McKinney

L. B. Hughes
S. J. or I. Hart
James Alexander
Vincent Thompson
Charles Powell
Lot Hayard
Benja. Parrott
Thomas Durham
Benj, R. Owen
B. S. Cardwell
Hardy Boze
Mitchell High
Joseph W. Allen
Arch G. Goodloe

Leonard J. Carden
Wm. Hodges
John Hudson
William Pendervas
Richard Glover
John Carpenter
John Paty
Charles Thompson
Joseph Guess
And. G. Pickett
Thos. J. Black
Orville Green
M. W. Sloan

SMITH COUNTY WILLS AND OTHER RECORDS

Many of the early records of this county were lost in 1865
when the courthouse was used as the home of troops. There are
some valuable documents, mostly in record books on file in the
county, but only a few original papers. Recently, some interest
has been taken by the County Court Clerk and the earliest books
have been rebound. The earliest will book is marked B, and begins in 1805. The book contains other records besides wills.

Will Book December 1805 to March 1809

John Douglass; will made 9 Nov. 1805, proved 25 Dec. 1805.
Names wife Hannah; Thomas Armstrong; two children of Martin
Douglass; dau. Jean McMurry; dau. Mary Day; dau. Sarah Hargis;
heirs of Martha Douglass, dec.; land whereon Joseph Leek lives
to be sold; John Armstrong; Wolf Muddy; granddau. Hannah Hargis;
Jacob Stone. Execs.: wife Hannah Douglass, Jacob Lake, and
Charles McMurry. Witnesses: B. Douglass, John Stafford (Jurat),
and John Reed (Jurat). (Pages 1, 2, 3)

John Douglass; agreement 10 Dec. 1805.

Hannah Douglass; children of John Douglass as legal heirs;
grandchildren of said John Douglass not considered. Signed and
acknowledged in presence of John Reed (Jurat), John Sarratt
(Jurat). Signed by Hannah Douglass, Charles McMurry, Philip
Day, and Sally Hargis on behalf of her husband John Hargis.
(Pages 4,5)

Abraham Thompson; will made 29 Sept. 1805, proved Dec. 1805.
Names wife Sarah; dau. Anne Lorance; dau. Ellen; oldest son Archibald; youngest sons Thomas and Laurence; youngest dau. Elizabeth. Execs.: wife Sarah, Jessee Lorance, and John Douglas.
(Pages 6,7)

Abraham Karr; inventory filed by H. Karr, admin. (Page 9)

Robert Bowman; inventory filed 29 Nov. 1805 by Rachel Bowman, Joseph Bowman, admin. (Page 10)

John Conger; will made 19 Nov. 1808 (sic). Names sons
Joshua Conger, Eli Conger, as execs; wife Judith; son Jonathan
Conger; dau. Elizabeth Cole; dau. Jean Moores; son Isaac Conger;
son Josiah Conger; dau. Maray Elston; son John Conger; dau. Ross
Railback. (Pages 14, 15)

Josiah Gale of Chesterfield Co., Va.; will made 1 Aug. 1791 filed April 1795. Names wife Sally Gale; son James Gale; brother-in-law Thomas Laxon; friend Philip Turpin of Swift Creek; latter two to be execs. (Page 18)

Josiah Gale; inventory filed Feb. 1796. (Page 22)

James Bradley; deed of gift, Jan. 1806; three cousins: Pleasance H. Burton, Lewis H. Burton, and Willie Burton, minors, sons of Edmond and Betsy Burton. (Page 33)

John Roberts; deed of gift dated Sept. 1805, to two sons Silas and Caleb; registered 20 Feb. 1805. (Page 37)

Joseph Williams; sale, 1805. (Page 39)

David Caruthers; memo of his property, 10 March 1806 (Page 45)

Saml. Bathell; will made 10 Feb. 1806, proved June 1806. Lark Bethell and Canthel Bethell, execs.; wife Molly; children, Edy, Sampson, Saml, James; son Carter Bathell; dau. Lettice Pistole. (Page 47)

Henry W. Lawson of Livingston Co., Ky.; deed of sale dated 13 June 1805, to James Wallce; registered June 1806. (Page 49)

Daniel Jackson and Jesse Smith, deed for love and affection to children of William Taylor, Sara Wilmer Taylor, Polly Scott Taylor, Easter Carriaton Taylor, Vincy Lopton Taylor, Charles Sullivan Taylor; 1806. (Page 50)

Cannon Taylor; will made 19 March 1806, proved 1806. Names wife Maray; son Eppes; brother John Taylor; Charles Sullivan. Exec. dau. Temty. Lands in North Carolina. (Page 61)

Jessie Nicholas (Nichols), Sr.; will made 29 Nov. 1805, proved 1806. Names son Robert Nichols; dau. Febby Parker; son John Wilson Nichols to have land in Halifax Co., Va.; son Bird Nichols; dau. Polly Wade; dau. Sally Nichols; wife Lucy Nichols; children Jessie Matthew; Lucy; Joel; Nancy; Bettsy James; Henry Nichols. (Page 64)

Elisha Weatherford; will made 2 July 1806, proved 1806. Names wife Nancy; mentions but does not name children. (Page 74)

John Anderson; will made 8 Oct. 1805, proved 1806. Names wife Rebecca; mentions but does not name children. (Page 75)

James Dyer; will made 23 Nov. 1805; proved 1805. Names brother Joel Dyer; land in Christian Co., Ky.; my share of father's estate divided between Elizabeth Dyer and Hazer Dyer and Micajah Dyer, Joseph Dyer; brother John Dyer. (Page 76)

Borrman Turner; will made 26 Aug. 1806, proved 1806. Names daughter Polly Hamelton; son Berreman; dau. Nancy; dau. Eliz.; dau. Susanna; son Robert; son John; wife Susannah. John C. Hamelton, Thomas Banks, and wife execs. (Page 79)

Robert Harper; will made Sept. 1807; proved (?). Names wife Feeby Harper; dau. Mary McDonald; dau. Martha Burd, Catsy Harper; son Johnson Harper; Isaac Harper; William B. Harper; Mathew Harper; dau. Sarah. (Page 120)

Thomas Lacey; will made May 1805, proved 1807. Names wife

Jean Lacey; dau. Jean; son Samuel; son John; son James (who has been absent from home for two years. (Page 137)

Benjamine Cooper; will made 16 Sept. 1807, proved 1807. Names wife Polly; William Wilmon; Sidney Wilmon. (Page 138)

Temperance Smith; will made 5 Oct. 1807, proved 1807. Names sister Dellia Stallians; Thomas Stallians; Willie Stallians; William Laine, exec. (Page 140)

Francis Parkers; will made 28 Sept. 1807, proved 1807. Names wife Lucy; children under age; son Abraham; son Francis; son Archibald; John D. Warmack and Lucy under age; dau. Polly wife of Thomas Nash; Francis Nash son of my dau. Tiatha; wife Lucy Miles West and William Martin, execs. (Could Miles West be the name of a second exec.?) (Page 140)

John Rhoads, Sr.; will made 3 April 1807, proved 1808. Names wife Abraella; son Henry; Abner; dau. Polly; John Baker Rhodes; Millie Brown; Moses Rhodes. Execs.: Abraell Rhodes, Abner Rhodes, and Josiah Howell. (Page 176)

Isaac King; will made 6 Feb. 1808, proved 1808. Names wife Lydia; children under age; three sons, Joseph, Abram, and Josiah King; Sally Griffen, an orphan girl living with the testator. (Page 190)

William Owens; will made 15 Feb. 1808, proved 1808. Names wife Mary; grandson Thomas Swan; son Alexander Owens; Thomas; Sam Swan Owens; dau. Martha Bond Hill; Mary Freeman; Sarah Paul; Margaret Prattle; Mary Owen; Sam. Swan Owens exec. (Page 194)

Gabrial Shaw; will proved 1807. Mentions land in North Carolina; wife Mavil; children mentioned but not named. Daniel Shaw of Mercer Co., Ky., and Thomas Jones of Smith Co., Tenn., to be execs. (Page 223)

William King; will. Deposition, 1808, relating to will in Washington Co., Tenn.

Will Book 1812-1814

Morgan William (Williams);. will made 15 June 1812; probated 1812. Names brother Silas Mercer Williams; sister Elizabeth; John Baker. (Page 1)

Delila Stalling; will made 1812, proved 1812. Names dau. Delia Stalling; son John Stalling. (Page 4)

John Ricks; sale of property proved 1812. (Page 5)

Richard Britten; inventory proved 1812. (Page 9)

John Buchanan; estate settled, 1812. (Page 10)

William Saunders; division of estate proved 1812. Heirs were Raumulus M. Saunders; Franklin Saunders; Gordian Saunders; Laffayette Saunders; Ethelbert Saunders. (Page 20)

Effy Johnson; administration of estate granted 1812. (Page 23)

Amos Ellison; articles appraised, proved 1812. (Page 24)

Rhoda Powell; inventory by James Powell, admin., proved 1812. (Page 26)

Peter Turney; division of estate made 12 Sept. 1812. Heirs were James, Samuel, Hopkins, Elizabeth, Polly, and Charlotte. (Page 27)

James Brass; list of property made 22 Sept. 1812; proved 1812. (Page 33)

James Brown; will made 22 Dec. 1812, proved 1813. Names sons Josiah, William Brown; wife Sally Brown; dau. not named; some children not of age. (Page 44)

John Chappell; account of sale made 18 Dec. 1811, proved 1813. (Page 51)

Joseph W. Allen; inventory of property made 6 Dec. 1812; proved 1813. (Page 53)

John Chappell; division of estate, proved 1813. (Page 58)

John Lancaster; inventory proved 1813. (Page 62)

James Bradley; inventory proved 1813. (Page 63)

Penelope Breese; widow of James Breese; dower; proved 1813. (Page 64)

Angus McDugald; inventory of perishables made 25 June 1813; proved 1813. (Page 70)

Angus McDugald; inventory and administration by Obediah Woodson proved 1813. (Page 71)

John Davis; inventory and sale, proved 1813. (Page 74)

Matthias Bates; will made 4 Jan. 1813, proved 1813. Names wife Jane Bates; son Benjamine; dau. Nancy. Hannah; Rachel; son Joel. (Page 75)

Wm. Jones; inventory and administration proved 1813. (Page 77)

Francis Childs; division of estate proved 1813. Heirs were Sam'l Childs, Wilson Childs, and Francis Childs. (Page 77)

William Goodalls; division of estate proved 1813. Heirs were John, William, Elizabeth, Nellie, Zachary, Isaac, Lucy, and the widow. (Page 81)

Duncan Ferguson; administration proved 1813. (Page 85)

John E. Barkers; estate sales made 9 Oct. 1813, proved 1813. (Page 86)

Charles Laurance; will proved 1813. Names wife Charity; Moses Allen; John Philips, exec. Children mentioned but not named. (Page 86)

James Bradford; inventory proved 1813. (Page 88)

Abraham Brittans; inventory proved 1813. (Page 89)

Mathew Bates; inventory proved 1813. (Page 90)

Angus McDugald; estate sale proved 1813. (Page 91)

William Jones; sale of property proved 1813. (Page 93)

Morgan Williams; inventory proved 1814. (Page 95)

Abram Brittan; account of sale made 29 Oct. 1813, 5 Feb. 1814, 20 Oct. 1813; proved in court 1813 (sic). (Page 96)

Thomas Dale; division of estate proved 1814. (Page 107)

Samuel Caruthers; sale of estate proved 1814. (Page 109)

John Chappell; settlement proved 1814. (Page 115)

Richard Banks of Wake Co., N. C.; will made 3 May 1796, proved 1814. Names wife Kerrenhappuck Banks; son Thomas Banks; dau. Ruth Jane (Jones); granddau. Polly Jones a debt due to Ralph Banks in the State of Georgia. Friends Saml Parker, George Brassfield, and Willis Jones, execs. (Page 120)

James Hodges; will made 4 Oct. 1813, proved 1814. Names dau. Sary Hale; Mary Strickling; son David Hodges; Richard Hodges; grandson James, son of my son dec.; dau. Liddy Basuch?: sons Willis,; Robert; dau. Elizabeth Howard; Caty Wormack; grandson James Hodges, son of Richard Hodges; son David. (Page 124)

John Hubbard; will made 22 Jan. 1813, proved 1814. Names wife Sally; sons Peter, John, Jacob. (Page 127)

Robert Furlong; will made 3 July 1814, proved 1814. Names brother and sisters, Hubbard, John, James, Samuel, Meredith, Hudson, Anthony Wheeler; heirs of sister Elizabeth Emmerson, to wit: Amy, Henry, Eliza, Mahala, and Jesse Emmerson; brothers Martin and Samuel Furlong, execs. (Page 128)

George Cox; will made 23 Aug. 1812, proved 1814. Names sons James, Dreury, Absolum Cox; daus. Mary Johnston and Pattsy Daneron; four children of dau. Elizabeth Moss, John, Patsy, Rebecca, and Hugh; children of my son John Cox by his wife Polly Cox who was Polly Murry. Friend Samuel Allen to act as guardian of children of son John. Friends Mathew Duke and John Harvey, execs. (Page 129)

Benjamine Barton; administration by Leonard Belew proved 1814. (Page 131)

Henrod Morris; list of property proved 1814. (Page 133)

Davis Foster; inventory by Wm. Foster proved 1814. (Page 135)

Charles F. Mabias; division of estate proved 1814. (Page 136)

Louis Pipkin; will made (?), proved 1814. Names wife Clemicy; Sally Taylor widow and Sam'l Taylor; son Jessie Pipkin; Louis Pipkin; dau. Charlotte. (Page 147)

John Hayes; will proved 1814. Names dau. Margaret Davis; wife Mary; son Charles; dau. Hannah Horne; Jennie Shannon; son John; dau. Nancy; Moses Fountain Garrison; Saml Hayes, son of Charles. John Horn, exec. (Page 154)

Randolph Casey; will made 3 Aug. 1814; proved 1814. Names
sons Abram P. Casey; Saml. Casey; Isaac; Randolph; Hiram; dau.
Rebecca; wife Charity; son Ladock. (Page 161)

Will Book 1814-1816

Peter Webster; inventory dated 18 Nov. 1814, proved Nov.
Court, 1814. Cash received for tour to Indian country under
command of Major Gen. Jackson, $60.00. Mary Webster, admnx.
(Page 1)

Morgan Williams; 16 May 1814, proved 1814. John Baker and
Silas M. Williams, execs. (Page 1)

Richard Brittan; division of estate dated Oct. 1814, proved
1814. Heirs: Sally Brittan; William Brittan; Nancy Brittan;
Amy Brittan; Abram Brittan; John Brittan; Polly Brittan; Mrs.
Presley. (Page 3)

Richard Banks; dowry of his widow Ravenhappuck Banks dated
Sept. 1814, proved Nov. 1814. (Page 6)

Daniel Witcher; will made 5 Jan. 1815, proved Feb. 1815.
Names Susannah Witcher; wife; Tandy K. Witcher; Cary Witcher;
son Daniel H. Witcher; dau. Nancy Young; dau. Martha Good; dau.
Tabitha Young; dau. Sally Ramsey; dau. Sabra Jenkins; son Tandy
K. and grandson Alphons; Lacy Witcher; dau. Bowker Witcher;
Elizabeth Maraign(?); Susannah Wakefield. (Page 7)

George Bradley, Sr.; will made 15 Jan. 1815, proved Feb.
1815. Names wife Elizabeth; dau. Judith not yet of lawful age;
son Richard and dau. Elizabeth both not yet of lawful age.
(Page 12)

John Corder; will made 28 Sept. 1815, proved Feb. 1815.
Names wife Gracy; son Joel, dec., his heirs; dau. Elizabeth Cartwright; Lewis Corder and Jannett Cowell execs.; mentions "my
children," not named. (Page 16)

James Bobett; inventory, Feb. 1815. (Page 18)

Thomas Graham; inventory dated 10 Feb. 1815; proved Feb.
1815. (Page 18)

John Davis; estate settled 1815. (Page 19)

John Hays; inventory, 1815. (Page 20)

Lewis Pipkins; amount of property sale, 5 Dec. 1814; proved
1815. (Page 23)

Wm. Wooten; sale proved 1815. (Page 25)

Benj. Barton; settlement of estate by Leonard Ballew,
exec.; proved 1815. (Page 26)

Olive Randolph; Joel Randolph exec.; proved 1815. (Document dated 8 Feb. 1815.) (Page 27)

Charles Jones; list of property dated Dec. 1814; proved
1815. (Page 28)

Briton Moss; inventory filed 13 Feb. 1815 by Hopkins Richardson, proved Feb. 1815. (Page 33)

Levi Laurence; inventory taken by Wm. Laurence 2 Feb. 1815, proved Feb. 1815. (Page 34)

James Ewen; Wm. Lancaster house to settle with Robert Lancaster, admin. of Jno. Lancaster, dec., exec., Nov. 1815. (Page 35)

Saml Caruthers; inventory proved 1814. (Page 39)

James Bradford; inventory proved 1814. (Page 40)

Pat. H. Martin; will made 21 April 1814, filed May 1815. Names bro. William. (Page 41)

James Paschall; will made 28 Sept. 1814, proved May 1815. Names Samuel Paschall, son of Silus Paschals; Anderson and Ire Paschals, sons of Silus; Betsy, Jenny, and Patsy Paschal. James Burchett, Jr., and Benj. Denny, execs. (Page 43)

Jesse Sampson; will made 8 Nov. 1814, proved May 1815. Names wife Betsey; children not named. (Page 45)

John Carter; will made 18 March 1814; proved May 1815. Names wife Charlotte; mentions but does not name children. (Page 47)

William Estis; will made 2 March 1815, proved May 1815. Names wife Elizabeth; mentions sons; children under age. (Page 48)

Edwin Williams; estate settled 8 May 1815 by James Williams, admin.; proved May 1815. (Page 52)

James Meador; inventory of his estate and inventory of the estate of Jonas Meador, made 10 May 1815, proved May 1815. (Page 54)

Jessee Samsons; inventory filed by John Crews; proved May 1815. (Page 55)

Daniel Witcher; inventory filed by Tandy K. Witcher and Lacy Witcher, execs., made 28 Feb. 1815. (Page 56)

Jacob Wright; inventory proved May 1815. (Page 58)

Joseph Jenkins; inventory made 7 May 1815; proved 1815. (Page 59)

George Bradley; inventory proved May 1815. (Page 62)

Randolph Casey; inventory filed by Saml Casey, exec. (Page 63)

Levi Lawrence; sale of property made 3 March 1815; proved May 1815. (Page 64)

Richard Banks; will made in Wake Co., N. C.; statement regarding the witnesses of the will; 1815. (Page 67)

James Kavander; will made 29 Sept. 1814, proved 1815. Names wife Elizabeth; eldest dau. Elizabeth Kavander not yet eighteen years of age; Mary Commins Kavander; child my wife is now(?) pregnant with. Friends Daniel Alexander and Stewart Doss to be execs. (Page 69)

William Massey; will made 6 Nov. 1814, proved 1815. Names wife Sarah; son William; dau. Mary. Friends James Wright and Judd Strother. (Page 71)

Thomas McAult; deposition of Henry Vandike and Bazil Shaw made 23 May 1815, proved 1815. Statement that McAult was a private in Capt. Jones' Company of the 39th Regt. Infantry in the service of the United States, and died at Fort Montgomery, and in Vandike's presence, stated that he wished Jane Murphey, wife of John Murphey of Carthage, to have all his pay due him at his death, the said Jane being his youngest sister. (Page 72)

Robert Ward; will made 7 Oct. 1813, proved 1815. Names wife Mary; dau. Susana Ward; son Dicken Ward; dau. Nancy Hodges; dau. Frances Barkley; dau. Emily Wooten; Elizabeth Lane; Sally Lawson; Pattsy Wooten; son John; dau. Mary Wooten; son-in-law William Leane. (Page 73)

William Orange; will made 30 April 1815; proved 1815. Names wife Elizabeth Orange; dau. Polly Belcher; son John; Byrd; Zephaniah Orange; dau. Chizziah Bailey; son Yearby Orange; dau. Eliza; dau. Nancy. (Page 78)

Anderson Williams; inventory returned by Susana Williams the admnx.; proved 1815. (Page 80)

Joel Mading; inventory returned by William Alexander, the admin.; proved 1815. (Page 81)

Lemuel Parker; return of sale of estate by David Lynch, admin., made 12 Aug. 1815; proved 1815. (Page 83)

Minord Morris; Elizabeth Morris draws pay for Mimrod (sic) Morris, dec.; 7 June 1815; proved 1815. (Page 84)

Archibald White; inventory made 14 Aug. 1815; proved 1815. (Page 85)

George Cocks; supplementary inventory proved 1815. (Page 85)

Jessie Sampson; sale of estate by John Crews, admin., made 23 May 1815; proved 1815. (Page 86)

Jessie Paty; inventory made May 1815. Certain amount set aside for widow and children of dec.; Elizabeth Paty, admnx. (Page 87)

James Brown; sale of estate by John Allen, exec.; proved 1815. (Page 89)

William Pruitt; inventory and sale of estate by Josiah Duncan and Thomas Whaly; proved 1815. (Page 90)

William Estis; estate admin. by John Estis; 1815. (Page 91)

Daniel Morrow; inventory of estate made 12 July 1815; proved 1815. (Page 92)

Nehemiah Garrison; inventory of estate made by Moses Allen, admin. Names Jane, Saml., Moses, Ephraim, and Jessie Garrison, but relationship not given; 1815. (Page 93)

James Bratton; inventory made 3 Aug. 1815; proved 1815.
(Page 95)

Saml. Paschal; list of property by James Burcket and Benjamine Denny, execs., made 19 May 1815; proved 1815. (Page 96)

John Allen; estate admin. by Sarah and Louis Allen, admins., proved 1815. (Page 98)

Joseph Jenkins; list of property filed 25 May 1815 by Eliza Jenkins, widow and admnx.; proved 1815. (Page 99)

Thomas Stocks; court procedure pertaining to his heirs, 1815. (Page 101)

John Lancaster, Sr.; Robert Lancaster, admin., 1815. (Page 105)

James Burnett; will made 28 Aug. 1815; proved 1815. Names wife Sabre; Polly Carter; son William Burnet; dau. Agness Southwarth; son Thomas R. Burnett; Joel W. J. Carter. (Page 110)

Adkins Pope; will made 2 Sept. 1815; proved 1815. Names wife Martha Pope; dau. Polly Barret; rest of my children, unnamed. (Page 112)

Saml. Beard; inventory made 12 Aug. 1815; proved 1815. (Page 113)

Stephen Farmer; inventory filed by Nancy Farmer, admnx., 1815. (Page 114)

John Reckets; inventory filed by Elizabeth Reckets, admnx., 18 Nov. 1815. (Page 116)

James P. Kavanaugh; inventory made by Charles and Eliza Kavanaugh, 1 Nov. 1815; proved 1815. (Page 117)

John Hayes; inventory made by admnx. Elizabeth Hayes, 1815. (Page 118)

Michael Helmantoller; inventory made by Jacob Helmantoller, admin., 1815. (Page 119)

George Gregory; inventory made by Jerry Gregory, admin., 1815. (Page 120)

William Caldwell; list of property made 18 Nov. 1815 by Daniel Caldwell, admin.; proved 1815. (Page 121)

John Holme; list of property by John F. Cockey, admin., 1815. (Page 121)

James Bratton; list of property by William Bratton, admin., 1815. (Page 121)

Hector McNeal; list of property made 22 Sept. 1815; proved 1815. (Page 122)

Charles Forrester; account of sale by Robert Forrester, admin., 13 Nov. 1815; proved 1815. (Page 127)

Philip Rayn; account of sale made 13 Nov. 1815, by Damaris Payn and George Forrester, admins.; proved 1815. (Page 133)

William Hogan; account of sale by A. S. Hogan, made 7 Nov. 1815. Estate divided among widow Nancy Hogan and heirs James Hogan and Elizabeth Hogan, and William Hogan. (Page 136)

Daniel Mungle; last settlement of estate made 1 Nov. 1815; proved 1815. (Page 140)

George Given; estate settled by William Given, admin. The heirs were: widow Nancy Given, and two sons, William and Joel. Settlement made 8 Nov. 1815, proved 1815. (Page 142)

James Burnet; inventory of personal property made 12 Dec. 1815; proved 1815. (Page 155)

Benjamine Holladday; list of sale of property made 15 May 1815; proved 1815. (Page 160)

William Wooten; pertaining to heirs (not named), 14 Feb. 1816; proved 1816. (Page 164)

Stephen Farmer; widow's allowance to Nancy Farmer, 5 Dec. 1815; proved 1816. (Page 168)

Willis Jones; will 8 Feb. 1816. Names dau. Polly Turner; son-in-law James O. S. Jeffreys; son Banks Jones; James Jones; Auston Jones; Jefferson; Willis; Franklin; Thomas Allen; dau. Brunetta; Ruth. Wife and Banks Jones to be execs. (Page 176)

William Wilson; amount of property, made 8 May 1815; proved 1816. (Page 182)

Jonas Meadow, Jr.; amount of sale; 25 May 1815; proved 1816. (Page 183)

William Woodcock; amount of sale, 25 May 1815; proved 1816. (Page 184)

William King of Washington Co., Va.; pertaining to estate and will, 1816. (Page 186)

William Walton (Wallon); inventory made 1816. (Page 188)

Phillemon Burford (Burfard); inventory of estate made by John H. Burford, admin., 1816. (Page 189)

Saml. Baird; amount of sale; Andrew and William Beard, admins.; 1816. (Page 191)

Hezika Blankenship; list of property filed by Rhody Blankenship, 1816. (Page 193)

Joseph W. Armstrong; supplementary inventory, 1816. (Page 194)

John Carder; exhibit of the sale of the estate on 23 and 24 Feb. 1815; proved 1816. (Page 195)

Daniel Burford; inventory of personal estate; Berriman Turner; 1816. (Page 196)

Daniel N. Featherston; inventory, 1816. (Page 198)

John Betty; account of sale, 1816. (Page 199)

Yeardy Partee; support of widow Sally Partee, 1816. (Page 206)

Collison Payne; administration granted to David Wallace. (Page 206)

Tillman Dixon; will 26 Oct. 1816. Names son Americus Dixon; land in Jackson Co.; son Don Carolus Dixon; dau. Polly Greenway Overton; Elizabeth Henry Dixon, land in Davidson Co.; Robert Corum; Elizabeth H. went to school at Lexington, Ky. Execs. were: George Matlock, Robert Allen, Archibald W. Overton, and Don Carolus Dixon. (Page 208)

William Marrow or Morrow; will made 6 Nov. 1816, proved 1816. Names wife Mary and mentions children. (Page 213)

Archibald Wright; will made 3 May 1816, proved 1816. Names wife Nancy and mentions children. (Page 214)

Thomas Darnell; will made 30 March 1816, proved 1816. Names wife Mary; the child wife is now pregnant with. (Page 215)

Cordie N. Rogers; will made 17 Feb. 1816; proved 1816. Names wife Elizabeth; son Warren Rogers. George Aliston exec. (Page 218)

John Stevenson; list of property made 23 Nov. 1815; proved 1816. (Page 251)

Josiah Martin; inventory made 28 May 1816; proved 1816. (Page 253)

John Ricketts; sale of property, 1816. (Page 259)

Miles Broom; inventory filed by Elizabeth Broom, admnx., 1816. (Page 262)

Will Book   1816-1820

Louis Pipkin; account of property proved 1816. (Page 10)

William Pritchett; nuncupative will, proved 1816. Names wife Mary and mentions children. (Page 12)

Saml Leak; will made 22 Aug. 1816, proved 1816. Mentions but does not name wife and children. (Page 13)

Richard Brittan; dower right ot Susanna Presley, formerly the widow of Richard Pritchett (sic), 29 Aug. 1816, proved 1816. (Page 19)

Archibald White; list of property and sale, 6 Dec. 1816. (Page 28)

Sam'l White; account of sale, 19 Sept. 1816. (Page 38)

Thomas Darnell; inventory filed by Isaac A. Dale and Mary Darnell, exec., 1816. (Page 39)

John Anderson; dower right of widow Nancy Wright, 1816. (Page 59)

Robert Bowman; dower right of widow Rachel Bowman, 1816. (Page 60)

George Dobbs; amount of sale, 1816. (Page 67)

James Haynes; Adam Dale, exec., 1816. (Page 67)

James Ragland of Albemarle Co., Va.; will made 15 Sept. 1810, proved 1817. Names brother Saml Ragland; niece Nedvida Ragland, dau. of Rebecca Ragland. (Page 71)

John Parker; inventory of property, 1817. (Page 73)

Michael Burris; deed of gift to his children, 24 Feb. 1817, proved 1817. To Susanna Ashberry and Carolin M. Burris, land in possession of Anthony Walk , their grandfather, who may have control of said land. (Page 87)

Anthony Walke; deed of gift to grandchildren, Susanna Asbery and Caroline M. Burris, 2 Feb. 1817. (Page 89)

Justice Ruleman (Reedman); will made 9 June 1816, filed 1817. Names wife Ruth; dau. Elizabeth Reedman; child my wife is now pregnant with. Friends William Standefer and Thomas Banks, execs. (Page 90)

Thomas Sanderson; will made 14 Dec. 1816, proved 1817. Names dau. Amie Sanderson; Hannarella Sanderson; Bashba; son Thomas; wife Susana; son Hardy; son Joseph; dau. Elizabeth Hall; grandson Robert Stevenson. (Page 93)

Andrew Green; estate admin. by Sarah Greer; inventory proved 1817. (Page 97)

Thomas Dale; list of property by Isaac Dale, exec., proved 1817. (Page 109)

Silby Harney of Camden Co., N. C., appoints Clement Stubblefield of Sumner Co. his attorney in matters pertaining to land granted by North Carolina to his father Silby Harne(y) and Anthony Bledsoe, 20 May 1817. (Page 112)

Louis Wimberly; will made 3 March 1817; proved 1817. Names wife Polly Wimberly; dau. Polly Yates; Sally Bird; Betsy Yates; son Isaac; Noah; dau. Wimmie Wimfrey; son Hardy Wimberly; dau. Eddy Baren; Ready Miller; son Enoch; dau. Patsy Barker; son Louis; dau. Dicca; son Elijah; sons Thomas and Washington not yet of age; daus. Susannah, Betsy, and Milly Wimberly not yet of age. James Montgomery and Josiah Howell. (Page 118)

Jacob Fite; settlement with the field officers of the 41st Regt., 1816; proved 1817. (Page 122)

Josiah Martin; supplementary inventory, 1817. (Page 125)

William Sheperdson; bond; sold and delivered to John Sheperdson the land located by John Payton for Peter Fisher, now under the claim of Jessie and James Clayton left them by their father who is deceased, 1817. (Page 147)

William High; will made 19 June 1817, proved 1817. Names Rebecca High; daughter Barthena; Carolina High; son Robert not of age; dau. Mary; son William; son-in-law Isaac Walter; son Samuel; Mitchell High; John High; Bowling High. (Page 149)

Luke T. Eddington; inventory of estate returned by Anne Eddington, admnx., proved 1817. (Page 156)

Thomas Martin, Sr.; inventory, 1817. (Page 162)

Barbara Capahon; inventory, 1817. (Page 163)

Daniel Ford, Jr.; inventory of property, 1817. (Page 166)

Daniel Jackson; inventory, 1817. (Page 167)

Margaret McClellan; will made 8 Jan. 1818, proved 1818.
Names dau. Mary; dau. Ruth; Sidney Story; Susanna Wright; son
Jourdan; James; John; William; Saml. Jonathan Key. (Page 189)

James Kitchen; will made 30 March 1806, proved 1818. Names
wife Marning (Morning); son James; Thomas; dau. Sarah Odam. Wife
and son James execs. (Page 191)

William Ealstan; will made 31 Aug. 1817; probated 7 March
1818. Names wife Hannah; dau. Sarah; son Jonathan; Josiah;
dau. Mary; son Elias; Jessie; grandchild Rheby McAmmack; Marit
Conger; Levina Campbell; and Jessie Elstan; grandson William
Campbell; William Barry; Ezekiel Elisan. (Page 198)

William Hogan; inventory of estate, 1818. (Page 205)

S. Stocks; inventory of personal estate, 1818. (Page 207)

John Glover; inventory of personal property, 1818. (Page
208)

Thomas Gregory; will made 13 July 1811; proved 1818. Names
his seven children; namely, Harden, Bry, William; the children
of Thomas Gregory, dec.; Thomas Douglas the only son and representative of Sime?, dec., who married John Douglass; Elizabeth Gearge
wife of Isaac Gearge and Abraham Gregory. (Page 231)

Jacob Lake; will made 14 July 1817; proved 1818. Names eldest dau. Lucy; Nancy; eldest son Daniel T. Lake; dau. Anna; son
Allen I. Lake; two youngest daus. Jenny and Polly; three youngest daus. Ann, Jenny, and Polly. (Page 249)

Francis Coulter, Sr.; will 19 Aug. 1818. Names wife Sarah;
children, Charles, Sarah, Francis, Richard. (Page 255)

Allen Powell; will 27 June 1818. Names wife Mourning Powell. (Page 256)

Randolph Thompson; will 22 June 1818. Names wife Elizabeth; dau. Matilda; Sally; sons William, David; Richard; and Jacob. (Page 258)

William Parker; will, 19 May 1817. Names children, Wm.;
Richard; Edward; Joseph; Luce West; Marian (Will designates five
children). (Page 269) (Page 259? - R. W. B.)

William Granade (Grant); will made 15 Sept. 1818; son Silas;
grandson William Wilson; son-in-law Ephraim Wilson; dau. Nancy;
son Fosque Granade. (Page 261)

Hester Ballews; will made 1 March 1811, proved 1818. Names
dau. Tansey Barton; son Lenard; James; friend William Martin.
(Page 293)

Mill Stalling; will made 5 Nov. 1818, proved 1819. Names
wife Charity; son James; mentions other children. (Page 294)

William Stalcup; will made 15 Nov. 1815, proved 1819. Names
granddau. Margaret Stalcup and wife Margaret Stalcup; children
Peter; Isaac; John; William Stalcup. Kittie Martin; Peggy Aus-
din; Elie and Samuel Stalcup. (Page 296)

Henry Woodcock; will made 29 July 1818, proved 1819. Names wife Eleaneanor; John and Bettsy Woodcock; dau. Polly Dillan. (Page 297)

John Burks; will made 27 Dec. 1818, proved 1819. Names son Samuel.

PETITION FROM STEWART COUNTY

Legislative Petition of 1823; to General Assembly. George Green married Rachel Gely in Stewart County in 1813. She left him in September 1818 and married Briant Guise and went to Nachey, and has not been seen or heard of since. The petitioner is now a resident of Henry Co., Tenn. This petition signed by:

John Atches
James W. Jones
James Greer
James Mormps(?)
William Atchison
David Cole
Thomas Dun
Jesa Sider
James Laton

Handy Rushing
William Hales
Peter Atchison
David Watson
David Bomar
Lemuel Brittain
John Birchett
Levin Cotingham

ENTRIES OF SULLIVAN COUNTY FROM 1780

These entries are on file at the Tennessee State Land Office in Nashville. They are loose papers in one file with just notations regarding grants, etc. E. R. W.

23 Feb. 1780. William Anderson enters 400 acres of land on head of Spring of Fall Creek, joining William McMullin's conditional line, Wm. Rogers' land, including my improvements where I now live.

26 Feb. 1780. William Armstrong enters 200 acres in Carter's Vallie adjoining the claim of land where Jonathan Muhly located and Robert Young. No. 234.

26 Feb. 1780. William Armstrong enters 50 acres at the mouth of Little Brushia Valley adjoining Carter's Vallie. No. 235.

No date. John Adams enters 100 acres on the north side of Holston River on Linsey Creek, adjoining my former entry and Nob Bottom. No. 256.

9 March 1780. Robert Allison enters 400 acres on Sinking Creek on the new road comprehending all the improvement and the plantation where he now lives. No. 279.

22 Feb. 1780. George Burdwell enters 100 acres joining Wm. Blythe's land on the north side of Holston Fall creek.

2 March 1780. Kore (Kear) Bealley enters 640 acres on the north fork of Beach Creek, beginning near the mouth of said fork. No. 246.

3 March 1780. Robert Burch enters 100 acres on the head
waters of Robert Snodgrass Creek, being the head branches of
the said fork of Reedy Creek, extending up the (valley?) and
Walker's Ridge. Another entry lying between Robert Snodgrass
Line and Margaret Elliott and between the Kentucky Road and
Walker's Mountain. nos. 250, 251.

3 March 1780. George Burdwell enters 100 acres on the south
side of Holston River on Kindrecks Creek where the Watagua Road
crosses said creek. He also enters land on the south side of
Holston, opposite the mouth of Fall Creek. Nos. 253, 254, 255.

6 March 1780. Abraham Bledsoe enters 640 acres on the north
side of Clinch River on Buffalow Creek at the mouth of a small
fork on the upper side of the creek, including improvements, also
an entry for 640 acres on Bige Walnut Bottom below said entry on
said creek beginning. Nos. 257, 258, 259.

No date. George Brooks entrs 200 acres on the river adjoining James Williams and Kenors Line. No. 197.

No date. George Brooks enters 640 acres on north fork of
Clinch River. No. 199.

10 March 1780. William Coy enters 100 acres between the
stake of Bays Mountain and the River Holston opposite to the
plantation whereon he now lives. No. 286.

No date. John Carmack enters land on north side of Big
Creek. No. 290.

No. date. Elijah Chisum enters 100 acres on the left side
of Dalton's Creek. No. 291.

10 March 1780. John Snodgrass enters 200 acres adjoining
the plantation of Moses Looney and including the improvements the
said Snodgrass had made, and running to an old agreement of Moses Looney and Robert Gray. No. 293.

No date. William Calvert enters 400 acres on Perrenen's
Creek near the fork. No. 300.

9 March 1780. Edward Coy enters 380 acres on the north
side of Holston River, joining Job Coy and Henry Cross including
my improvements. No. 281.

2 March 1780. Hugh Crawford, for James Crawford, soldier,
enters 640 acres on the north side of Clinch Mountain, joining
Hugh Crawford's former entry contending up to Big War Gap. No.
249.

7 March 1780. John Driver enters 200 acres on the north
side of Holston River on the waters of Fall Creek joining Thomas
Ramsey and William Blythe. No. 263.

No date. Stockley Donelson enters 300 acres joining Malone's line on the Waters of Beaver Creek. No. 213.

No date. Stockley Donelson enters 640 acres on the north
fork of Clinch River. No. 198.

No date. Jno. Donelson enters 640 acres on Little Warrsors
Creek. No. 200.

No date. Jno. Donelson enters 640 acres on Brooks Creek.
No. 202.

9 March 1780. Nicholas Edwards enters 250 acres on Big Creek, adjoining the land of John McMurray (or John W. Murray) on the west and David Gamble on the east, including the plantation where said Edwards now lives. No. 278.

9 March 1780. Timothy Ecuff enters 400 acres on Sinking Creek on the new road comprehending the improvements and plantations where he now lives. No. 90.

25 Feb. 1780. David Erwin enters 640 acres on the waters of Fall Creek joining Martin Holler and James Patterson and toward Samuel Kear and David Grahams. No. 230.

9 March 1780. David Gamble enters 240 acres on the Big Creek adjoining where Nicholas Edwards lives on the west and John Rice on the east including where the said Gamble now lives. No. 277.

29 Feb. 1780. William Hughes enters 225 acres on White Top Creek joining lands with James Hughes.

26 Feb. 1780. James Hollos enters 200 acres adjoining Heaten's place on the north, adjoining Walker's and Catteral's conditional line beginning at Robert Gilliland's line extending down the ridge, including a spring below Heaton's barn. No. 33.

7 March 1780. Alexander Hamilton enters 250 acres on a branch of Fall Creek joining lines with Robert Gilliland and Cotteral, extending to David Erwin, Wm. Mitchell, and David Grahame. No. 260.

8 March 1780. Joseph Kinhead enters 400 acres on the south side of Holston River on Bryce Russell's branch lying between David Hunter's, Joseph Rogger's, and Stephen Coplain, including Sinking Spring. No. 261.

No date. Thomas King enters 200 acres on both sides of the Main Road. John King mentioned. No. 212.

No date. James King enters 600 acres on Lick Branch on both sides of the North Fork. No. 216.

No date. Barklelot Kenson enters 100 acres on Holston River. No. 205.

March 1780. John King enters 50 acres on a branch of Stanley's (?), a mile northwest of Mr. Cooper's, including the (?) Cave. No. 271.

No date. James Lard enters 640 acres in Powells Valley, including Thompson's Improvements. No. 287.

No date. Edmund Lyne enters 640 acres near Powels River including the place called Role Camp and George Elliott's improvements. No. 289.

10 March 1780. John Laughlen, Sr., enters 400 acres on the north side of Holston River joining Alexander Laughlin including the plantation where William King now lives. No. 292.

10 March 1780. John Laughlin, Jr., enters 400 acres adjoining Jno. Scott, Jno. Sharp, and Abraham Grub, including the improvements where he now lives. No. 295.

10 March 1780. Alexr. Laughlin enters 400 acres adjoining

the place where Wm. King and John Gifford or Gillford lives;
also an entry for 400 acres adjoining John Carmack. Nos. 296
and 297.

7 March 1780. Daniel Miller enters 300 acres on the north
side of Holston River on the waters of Sinking Creek, joining
John Laughlen, John Gilbert, and Col. Shelby, joining my former
entry. No. 264.

No date. Joseph Martin enters 640 acres. No. 214. Also
200 acres. No. 215.

25 Feb. 1780. William Melone (Nelson) enters 100 acres
lying between John Melone, Sr., and James Dertion's, at the east
end of the nob. No. 229.

No date. Peter Morrison enters 100 acres on Oissem Creek,
joining my former entry. No. 299.

No date. James McNair enters 150 acres on the south side
of Reedy Creek on Heaton's shugar Camp Branch and the Ratling
Branch, bounded on the north by the place I live. No. 267.

8 March 1780. Michael Morrison enters 600 acres on the
north side of Holston River beginning at a conditional line
formerly made between John Gilliland and said Morrison on the
bank of the river above the mouth of (?). No. 272.

March 1780. Nathan Page enters 200 acres on the head spring
of the Oald Bullock-pen-Branch, north of Mr. Colage's place.
No. 268.

9 March 1780. Charles Parker enters 50 acres on the
(illegible) side of Holston River, on the (illegible) of Jer-
rick's Creek, including my improvements. No. 283.

25 Feb. 1780. James Patterson enters 300 acres on the
north side of Holston River on the waters of Fall Creek beginning
where the old wayside crossed the said creek on the north side of
the creek. No. 231 and 232.

7 March 1780. Joab Runnals enters 200 acres on the north
side of Holston River on Byce Russell's branch lying between
David Hunter's, Joseph Rogger's, and Stephen Coplain's including
Sinking Spring. No. 269.

9 March 1780. John Rentfrow enters 640 acres on Cloud's
Branch on the main fork of said creek adjoining John Cremer who
enters 640 acres on Cloud's Creek. Nos. 265 and 266.

9 March 1780. Josiah Ramsey enters 200 acres on Renfrows
Creek in the fork of said creek joining my former entry. No.
282.

No date. John Scott enters 250 acres joining land of John
Laughlin and John Sharp. No. 294.

22 Feb. 1780. Thomas Sharp enters 400 acres lying on Clouds
Creek, including the improvements formerly made by William Walker.

22 Feb. 1780. John Shelby enters 400 acres adjoining where
I now live and the east and northeast of my old survey. No. 226.

29 Feb. 1780. William Tathum enters 40 acres on the branch

above Benjamin Looney's and Joseph Kinkaid including the said
Looney's sugar camp and the mill seat above Hollis' cabin; transferred to John Johnson. No. 239.

No date. Wm. Thomas enters 40 acres on the south side of
Sinking Creek joining James Coffer's line and William Pemberton's
line. No. 285.

No date. Jno. Vinyam enters 640 acres. No. 201.

10 March 1780. William Wallace enters 150 acres on the
north side of Holston River joining George Littel and Andrew
Greer joining my former improvements. No. 298.

9 March 1780. William Wallace enters 200 acres on the
north side of Holston River joining William Hicks, Rogers Tops
and William Rutlesge's land. No. 278.

9 March 1780. Manen? Waldrop enters 90 acres on Jerreck's
Creek on the south side of Holston River adjoining Waldrop's
entry. No. 284.

27 Feb. 1780. Joseph Wallace enters 640 acres on Holston
River adjoining George Webb's conditional line.

1 March 178(?). James Williams enters land beginning at
the river, on the south side of Holston River, adjoining Joab
Milihel's upper line.

No date. Elizabeth Young enters 200 acres on Riddle Creek
known by the name of Mine Spring or Halbert's Cabbin; 640 acres.
No. 248. Elizabeth Young, widow and administratrix of the estate of James Young, enters 640 acres on behalf of the orphans
James and Joseph Young, it being the place on which she now
lives, the said improvement that John Long and William Young
bought of Thomas Sharp bounded at the lower end by agreement.

No date. John Young enters 150 acres between Margaret
Elliott's line and Wm. Cook's place extending up the Valley. No.
252.

24 Feb. 1780. William Young enters 200 acres on Reedy Creek
on the north side of the Big Ridge including a spring between
Gentry's pace and Henry Robert's mill.

9 March 1780. Henry Turney enters 400 acres on Big Creek
including my own improvements on the north side of Holston River joining Col. Evan Shelby's claim. Also an entry that joined
Andrew Cowan, Abraham Grub and John Scott's survey. Also another
entry on Clinch River at the mouth of the second creek below the
little war gap; also one at the mouth of the first creek that
empties in Clinch River below the little war gap, also an entry
on the north side of Holston River, joining Col. Shelby's claim.
Nos. 273, 274, 275, and 276.

PETITION FROM SUMNER COUNTY

The petition, from the Tramell Creek section of the county
is signed by a number of persons living in that area in 1837.

Ananias Epperson   Jeremiah Alsop
James Fagg   John Gilliam

B. P. Wilson
Elijah Butler
Daniel Marcum
Jeremiah Able
Josiah Dalton
George Ramsey
Robert Holmes
Zachariah Fagg
Albert G. Holmes
John Doss
William Fagg
Edward Duffer
James Butler
Samuel Butler
Bartlett Y. Turner
Martain Turner
Rylie Teel

James Gilliam
Samuel Davis
Isaiah Davis
John W. Davis
Stephen R. Gilliam
George Morris
Harris Carter
Asa Duffer
Flimen Duffer
Hardy Colwell
Chas. Simmons
Alfred Simmons
David Alsop
William Colwell
Yancey Turner
Simeon Saunders
Seaton Duffer

SUMNER COUNTY MARRIAGE RECORDS

John Roberts	Nancy Ferguson	19 Oct. 1791
Martin Parpoll (Harpool)	Betsy Rule	16 Aug. 1791
Charles Myars	Betsy Biter	23 May 1791
William Cage	Nancy Morgan	19 June 1791
Cornelius Herndon	Polly Harrison	27 Sept. 1791
John Benton	G. Winchester	filed with 1791
William Fisher	Faithey Hese(?)	17 May 1791
Jno. Gatlin	Eleanor Burt	26 March 1791
Amos West	Frances Herndon	3 April 1791
John Neilly	Masy Harrison	6 April 1791
Thomas Christian	Agnes Christian	22 Jan. 1791
Bazel Fry	Jane Mansker	8 March 1791
John Laurence	Betsy Hynis	4 Feb. 1791
William Smith	Elsy McDonald	25 March 1791
John Cotton	Fanny Hamilton	4 Jan. 1791
Richard Douglas	Betsy Cowards	23 Jan. 1791
William Anderson	Betsy Jones	23 Nov. 1791
Nathaniel Parker	Jane Willis	4 Dec. 1791
James Carson	Nancy Sheart	19 Dec. 1791
Edward Williams	Darkuss Edwards	12 Dec. 1791
John Purveince	Martha King	26 Dec. 1791
William Reed	Peggy Rule	16 Aug. 1791
Nathaniel Parker	Jane Willis	29 Nov. 1791
David Hainey	Sarah Camp	19 Oct. 1791
Thomas Payton	Alice Gethert	16 Nov. 1791
Jacob Landers (Sanders?) Sarah Hardin		31 May 1791
John Carr	Sally Cage	22 Nov. 1791

Joseph Steel	Darcus Wilson	19 Nov. 1792
John Rule	Peggy Bord (Boyd?)	20 March 1792
John Laurence	Lydia Malone	29 Aug. 1792
Elijah Burk	Mary Robinson	25 Aug. 1792
This bond was returned with notation that no ceremony was performed.		
Thomas Edwards	Elizabeth Turner	7 Feb. 1792
John Nancarro(?)	Celia Slade	24 Jan. 1792
Josiah Hunter	Rachel Hannah	20 Aug. 1792
William Gipson	Polley Brigance	27 June 1792
Isaac Towel	Sarah McAdams	20 June 1792
Frances Glazer	Molley Barnes	29 Aug. 1792
William Haynes	Polly Laurence	7 Jan. 1792

Joshua Harlin	Susannah Bone	2 Jan. 1792
Thomas Perry	Catherine McAdams	24 July 1792

Robert Patton	Betsy Farrier	16 Dec. 1793
Joseph Griggs	Sally Cowan	28 Feb. 1793
Richard Freeman	Salley Haynes	6 June 1793
James Farr	Polley King	13 March 1793
Elijah (Elijha) Clary	Polley Barnes	20 Feb. 1793
Joseph Morgan	Peggy Maxwell	22 Sept. 1793
Jacob Houarshele(?)	Elizabeth Wilson	27 June 1793
William Maxey	Mary (?) Allen	11 Feb. 1793
Ezekiel Lindsay	Nancy Greer (Green)	21 Sept. 1793
John Benton	Jane Kendrick	18 March 1793
Robert Campbell	Martha Hamilton	29 March 1793
William Wilson	Salley Brevard	13 Nov. 1793
Robert McKinley	Sally Cowan	18 Dec. 1793
Flower McGreggor	Polly Payne	5 Oct. 1793

Isaac Handley	Betsy Pankey	16 Nov. 1795
John Pankey signed.		

John Ragan	Nancy Neill	22 Jan. 1800
James Ball	Biddy Keizeal(?)	4 Sept. 1800
John Reason	Sally Simpson	13 Sept. 1800
Matthew Cowan	Katey Trousdale	8 March 1800
Edward Sanders	Sokey Trigg	26 April
Signed by Edward Sanders and William Trigg		
William Thompson	Polly Parker	3 May 1800
William Jenkins	Savary Witcher	25 April 1800
Luke Dugger	Isbel Gibs	26 April 1800
Robert Wynne	Cyntha Hamion	6 Jan. 1800
Isaac Philips	Charlotte House	6 Jan. 1800
Joseph Sebarton	Polly Summers	1 March 1800
Signed by Wm. Brazil		
Dave Harper	Rachel Riley	24 April 1800
Signed by John Railey		
Stephen Brown	Milley Rhodes	21 Oct. 1800
Charnel Corbin	Celia Barnes	30 Oct. 1800
James Stuart	Jane Anderson	22 July 1800
Peter Billew	Mary Casselbury	22 July 1800
John Hail	Peggy Carr	7 July 1800
Signed by John Carr		
William Bradshaw	Betsy Espey	11 Nov. 1800
Leonard Dugger	Elizabeth Taylor	27 Nov. 1800
James Caruthers	Jane Irwin	29 Jan. 1800
Isaac Hooks	Sally Douglas	21 May 1800
George Johnson	Molly Berry	15 Aug. 1800
Jos. Weatherly	Bizisy Anderson	6 Aug. 1800
Jeremiah Hale	Sarah Carr	30 July 1800
Signed by James Carr		
James Hodges	Hannah Wilson	16 Sept. 1800
Manoah Taylor	Elizabeth Taylor	6 Dec. 1800
John Orr	Telitha Cotten	20 March 1800
Edwin S. Moore	Polly Walton	21 Oct. 1800
Reuben Cage	Polley Morgan	7 Jan. 1800
David Orr	Jenny McElarath	21 Feb. 1800
Signed by Joseph McElarath		
Lazarus Brown	Peggy McCarty	5 Aug. 1800
George Logan	Peggy Alexander	27 May 1800
William McCorkle	Jenny Graham	9 June 1800
James Edwards	Betsy Cartwright	19 June 1800

Joseph Sloan	Polly Hamilton	22 Sept. 1800
James Clark	Leah Gilleland	24 Sept. 1800
Benj. Smith	Keziah Dixon	10 June 1800
John Cotton	Jennet Crafford	22 Nov. 1800
Clendenaning Greenshaw	(?) (?)	15 Aug. 1800
John Harrison	Ann Story	13 Aug. 1800
Isaac Donohoo	Critia Totevine(?)	6 Aug. 1800
William Morrison	Eleanor Wilson	27 Aug. 1800
David Beard	Jenney Wallace	24 March 1800
David Brown	Betsy Patton	24 Jan. 1800
William Lambuth	Elizabeth Greenshaw	13 Sept. 1800

Signed by Cloudsberry Greenshaw

George Stout	Jenny Cooper	25 Nov. 1800
Joseph Bishop	Sally Harris (Norris)	16 Sept. 1800
William Temple Cole	Mary Brown	19 Sept. 1800
Richard Hankins	Sally Cartwright	7 Feb. 1800
Moses Adam	Harty Bass	23 July 1800
Thomas Clark	Salley Diggins	27 March 1800
Abraham Ellis	Prudence Lindsey	24 April 1800

Signed by Ezekiel Lindsey

Montgomery McConnell	Judah Bond	31 March 1800
Jonathan Campbell	Priscilla Rogers	17 Sept. 1800
William Sheppard	Elizabeth Enox(?)	3 Oct. 1800
Edmund Caruthers	Jimmy Allewn(?)	23 Sept. 1800
Richard Waller, Jr.	Sally Harrison	18 Oct. 1800
John Reed	Sarah Dixon	7 May 1796

Filed with the 1800 records

William Thompson	Polly Parker	3 May 1800

Nathaniel McBride	Elizabeth Davidson	19 March 1803
John McBride	Fanny Clark	19 March 1803
Griffith Cathey	Susannah Cathey	15 March 1803
Thomas Reed	Susannah Shaw	8 April 1803

Signed by Robert Shaw

Richard Hassell	Nancy Reasons	24 Feb. 1803
James Latimer	Jenney Hamilton	16 July 1803
William Ogols	Peggy Orr	15 July 1803

Signed by John Orr

William Robinson	Patty Melton	10 Dec. 1803

Signed by William Melton

Enos Hannah	Sally Harris	10 Dec. 1803

Signed by Drury Milan

William Espey	Susanna Suiter	26 Dec. 1803

Signed by Benjamin Suiter

Robert Strother	Polly Gambling	18 June 1803
John Parks	Hannah Latimer	15 June 1803

Signed by James Latimer

Stephen Stone	Polly Seving(?)	24 Dec. 1803

Signed by Stephen Euselius Stone

James Franklin, Jr.	Prudy McKain	19 Feb. 1803

Signed by Jas. McKain

William Reed	Polly Turner	11 Feb. 1803

Signed by John Turner

James Wallace	Lydia Gillespie	11 Feb. 1803

Signed by Jacob Gillespie

James Turner	Nancy Goodrum	11 Feb. 1803

Signed by John Goodrum

Joseph Biggs	Patsy Kelly	29 Jan. 1803

Signed by Elijah Biggs

Nathan Stiner	Hatey Warnock	31 Dec. 1803

Signed by Barnabas Stiner

Armstead Rogers	Bridia Whitsett	27 Sept. 180(?)

Signed by Laurence Whitsett

John Hoover	Lydia Waller	12 Feb. 1803

Signed by Samuel Donelson

Jacob Null   Elizabeth Graham   30 Aug. 1803
    Signed by Jas. Alililson
David Bradley   Nancy Taylor   29 Aug. 1803
    Signed by John Taylor
James Sullinger   Levinia Cracatt   5 Aug. 1803
    Signed by Thos. Farmer and Edwd. Gwin
John Garrett   Jenny McMurtry   4 Aug. 1803
    Signed by Henry McMurtry
Archibald Davis   Elizabeth McBride   26 Aug. 1803
    Signed by David Stuart
Jeremiah Murphey   Sally Gwin   14 June 1803
    Signed by Earnest Watson
William Bradshaw   Betsy Stubblefield   19 Aug. 1803
    Signed by Daniel Trigg
Were Dickerson   Polly Etherly   24 Aug. 1803
    Signed by Zacheras Wilson
Moses Hardin   Orpy Hassell   16 June 1803
    Signed by Jesse Hassell
Jacob McKee   Elizabeth Hamilton   4 Aug. 1803
    Signed by James Latimer
Lewis West   Margaret Cowan   29 June 1803
    Signed by Lewis West and William Bell
William Trigg, Jr.   Mary Ann Burton   10 Dec. 1803
    Signed by Daniel Trigg
Goldberry Sanders   Susannah Grasser(?)   2 July 1803
    Signed by Goldberry Sanders and Henry Parmer
William Stuart   Dililah Vinson   no date
    Signed by John Stuart
William Palmer   Sally Rankins   5 July 1803
    Signed by Samuel Gibson
Blair Harris   Rachel Gardner   1 Aug. 1803
    Signed by Joshua Bradley
James Locke   Peggy Cathey   19 May 1803
    Signed by Jas. McCreevan
Thomas Silliman   Sally Wilkins   18 July 1803
    Signed by Thomas Anderson
George Dempsey   Polly Brigance   26 Oct. 1803
    Signed by James Brigance
Thomas Barrett   Charlotte Reason   18 July 1803
    Signed by John Reason
Thomas Willis   Milly Edwards   11 June 1803
    Signed by William Phipps, Jr.
Robert Moffitt   Patsy Simpson   1803
    Signed by Robert Moffitt and Elijah Simpson
John Sidgley   Mary Willis   24 Feb. 1803
    Signed by Thomas Barret and Nathaniel Wilcomb
Josiah Hammond   Polly Jones   2 May 1803
    Signed by Richard Jones
James Elder   Polly Watwood   21 Sept. 1803
    Signed by Benjamine Suiter
Samuel Simpson Kennedy Rebeccah Simpson   12 April 1803
    Signed by William Kennedy
W. Wire Dickerson   (?)   23 Aug. 1803
    Signed by Elijah Prewett
Bartlet Rinfro (Rinpho) Chloe Parker   14 Nov. 1803
    Chloe was dau. of Thomas Parker. Signed by Jno.
    Parker and Zini Parker
William Ring   Polly Cunningham   27 April 1803
    Signed by William Ring and Isaac Bledoe
James A. Wilson   Peggy Graham   5 July 1803
    Signed by John Shelby
Daniel Woods   Flavia Reese   4 Nov. 1803
    Flavia was dau. of James Reese
George Johnson   Penny Seat   3 Feb. 1803
    Signed by William Crauford

William Wright	Nancy Cochran	8 Sept. 1803
Signed by Francis Locke and Wm. Hubbard		
Benette Vinson	Jane Patton	14 Nov. 1803
Signed by William McCall		

Isaac M. Bledsoe	Nancy Lockett	23 April 1804
Joseph Waller	Elizabeth Railey	21 Nov. 1804
John McDaniel	Bathsheila Suiter	16 June 1804
Thomas Shackleford	Agnes Clopton	21 July 1804
Lewis Boethe	Winna Richardson	23 July 1804
John Powell	Courtney Brasil	24 July 1804
James Dyer	Kesiah Smith	28 July 1804
Henry Parmer	Patsey Angel	22 May 1804
James Harder	Elizabeth Pitt	12 May 1804
John Reasons	Anny Hereford	1 May 1804
John Dailwood	Nancy Reed	13 July 1804
Obediah Martin	Sarah Abbott	7 (?) 1804
Job Williams	Nancy Campbell	10 Oct. 1804
Merrill Willis	Peggy Cherry	8 Dec. 1804
Isaac Hust	Sally Boothe	28 Dec. 1804
Web Bloodworth	Mary Benthall	8 Dec. 1804
Henry Allen	Polly Barns	18 Dec. 1804
John Billens	Rebeckah Barns	2 Feb. 1804
Abraham King	Penelope Todd	8 Feb. 1804
Robert Trousdale	Linsey Wynham	28 Jan. 1804
Richard Jones	Elizabeth Cavatte	26 Jan. 1804
Stephen White	Jenney Bell	24 Jan. 1804
Elisha Looney	Polly Eenix	2 Jan. 1804
Cornelius Tinsley	Fanny Stone	16 Jan. 1804
William T. Henderson	Eliza J. Smith	6 Aug. 1804
Walter Danoho	Caty Hames	22 Nov. 1804
Thomas Summers	Celia Summers	3 Dec. 1804
Caleb Willis	Sarah Cantrell	19 Nov. 1804
James Ward	Sally Henson	9 June 1804
James L. Armstrong	Sophia W. Smith	27 Sept. 1804
John Simpson	Celia King	18 Sept. 1804
Mathew Dixon	Polly Hill	18 Sept. 1804
Michael Looney	Caroline Latimer	14 April 1804
Samuel McAdams	Margaret Robinson	2 June 1804
Asa Todd	Polly Jones	17 July 1804
John Johns	Juliet Trigg	19 June 1804
Francis McDonald	Rebecca Suiter	16 July 1804
Nathan Atchison	Nelly Beamord	24 May 1804
James Clark	Edy Loury	18 Aug. 1804
Frederick Turner	Catherine Grimes	28 Aug. 1804
Richard Willis	Batsy Brigance	13 Dec. 1804
William Hale	Polly Alexander	25 Sept. 1804
Walker Brair	Polly Smith	10 Oct. 1804
James Walwood	Jenny Williams	3 Oct. 1804
Anthony Sivit(?)	Hannah Groom	2 Oct. 1804
James Kirkham	Elizabeth Kirkham	4 Oct. 1804
Joseph Norman	Hannah Jones	25 Sept. 1804
John Giles	Eliza Morrison	17 Oct. 1804
Ephraium Wells	Nancy Hoage	5 Oct. 1804
Aaron Butler	Rosanna Braken	11 Feb. 1804
William Cloar	Polly Hubbard	27 March 1804
Edmund Turpin	Charity McBride	26 May 1804
Daniel Webster	Elizabeth Lloyd	30 April 1804
John Brachshaw	Amey Cherry	4 Sept. 1804
Wm. Dill	Eve Houch	18 Sept. 1804
John Lemmons	Priscella Abbitt	3 Sept. 1804
John Hutson	Elizabeth Dorris	15 Sept. 1804
Richard Sanders	Sally Storey	7 Jan. 1804
Nathan Stiner	Harty Womack	12 Jan. 1804

Daniel Ogilsby	Mary White	3 Sept. 1804
Shadrack Olvis (Alvis)	Nancy Hall	21 Oct. 1804
George Crossner	Catey Couch	26 Nov. 1804
James Looney	Polly Smith	7 Aug. 1804
John Eliott	Nancy Briton	11 Aug. 1804
Peter Looney	Polly Barnes	7 Nov. 1804
Adam Atachin	Maryan Jones	13 Aug. 1804
Francis Eury (Bury)	Peggy Espy	14 Aug. 1804
Sterlin Owensbrooks	Polly Barber	11 Aug. 1804
Vatihel Stevens	Jenny Jones	27 Oct. 1804
Samuel Sulivan	Bettsy James	12 Nov. 1804
Kinchin Carter	Mary Benthall	25 Feb. 1804
Hesiki Gardner	Elizabeth Lauderdale	16 Jan. 1804
James Reason	Charlotte Bryant	11 April 1804
Shadrack Nye	Elizabeth Latimer	20 March 1804
Thos. Granger	Margaret Lilley	10 March 1804
Wm. Lilly	Elizabeth Martin	10 March 1804
John Marlow	Aney Faulk	7 March 1804
Thos. Camell	Fanny McHenry	6 March 1804
Bural J. Thompson	Celia Powell	28 Dec. 1804
David Hobbs	Cloe Hunt	31 Dec. 1804
Francis Garnick	Elenor Blair	16 Oct. 1804
Wm. Thomas	Patsy Hashlock	22 Oct. 1804
Thomas Carothers	Sally Holland	23 Oct. 1804
Zachriah Hogan	Catherine Bunckley	25 April 1804

Daniel Looney Minor   Elizabeth Briley   24 Oct. 1805
  Signed by James Brigance, Jr.
Randel Owens   Hannah Ogelsby   11 June 1805
  Signed by Jonathan Wilson
James Reed   Elander Crawford   2 Nov. 1805
  Signed by Greenberry Orr and Elijah Simpson
Robert Marshall   Sally Dobbins   26 Feb. 1805
  Signed by Carson Dobbins; attached note signed by
  Alexander Dobbins
John Brisley   Rosey Clendenin   10 June 1805
  Signed by Robert Campbell
Barnet Rock   Story Heaspeth   10 June 1805
  Signed by Robert Allen
David Demant   Elizabeth Kirkpatrick 5 Nov. 1805
  Signed by Thomas Demant
Samuel McReynolds   Millery (Milbery) Dement
  Signed by John Pendergast   8 Oct. 1804
Wm. Sholars   Clasissa Dement   10 Aug. 1805
  Signed by Abner Sholars
Abner Reeves   Polly Nipper   27 June 1805
  Signed by Wm. McAdams
Joshua Smith   Nancy Panky   4 July 1805
Jacob Robertson   Elizabeth Cherry   6 July 1805
  Signed by William White
Nathaniel Irwin   Polly Irwin   10 July 1805
  Signed by Wm. McWhiter
Robert Williams   Polly Barnes   13 July 1805
  Signed by John Billings
William Pitman   Mary Ragsdale   28 Dec. 1805
  Signed by Abraham Rutledge and Jas. Cryer
William Robertson   Fanny Harris   16 Sept. 1805
  Signed by Robert Harris
Charles Simpson   Salley C. Harris   2 Aug. 1805
  Signed by Robert Harris
Loptain Cage   Naomi Gillaspie   19 Sept. 1805
  Signed by Jesse Cage
Daniel Shaver   Josa Chaddock   18 Sept. 1805
  Signed by Wm. Provine

William Stuart   Sally Cougher   20 Sept. 1805
  Signed by Wm. Sample
Elijah Adams   Elizabeth Miller   23 Sept. 1805
  Signed by James Oglesby
Adam Milan   Jonny Short   15 Oct. 1805
  Signed by Drury Milan
Isaac Jones   Polly Oglesby   14 Oct. 1805
  Signed by Purvatt Cuffman and Isaac Jones
Abraham Rutledge   Nancy Wells   16 Oct. 1805
  Signed by Wyat Wells, att'y in fact
John Cloar   Sally Turner   19 Oct. 1805
  Signed by John Hubert
Shadrack Dunn   Polly Pankey   30 May 1805
  Signed by John Pankey
Daniel Trigg   Nancy Hodge   3 June 1805
  Signed by James Cage
Samuel Moore   Betsy Pearce   15 March 1805
  Signed by Thos. Kirkham
Henry Derr(?)   Eve Grimes   6 Aug. 1805
  Signed by Frederick Miller
Samuel Kerr   Cynthia Wynne   31 July 1805
  Signed by Richard Taylor
John Moss   Polly Stevenson   31 Aug. 1805
  Signed by Josiah Stevenson
William Pittman   Tabitha Burton   7 Jan. 1805
  Signed by Abraham Trigg
Arthur Ervin   Sarah Davidson   Sept. 1805
  Signed by Robert Bell
James Gamblin   Nelly Noel   12 Feb. 1805
  Signed by Reuben Noel
Joel Reese   Sarah Ramsey   14 Aug. 1805
  Signed by Joshua Ramsey
Henry Bledsoe   Nancy Gillespie   22 May 1805
  Signed by Thos. Gillespie
James Roberts   Patsy Evans   8 May 1805
  Signed by Jas. Harten
Stephen Evans   Rebecca Claxton   7 May 1805
  Signed by Thos. Higgombottom
James Burnes   Amy White   24 Dec. 1805
  Signed by Stephen Cantrell
John Lathon   Elizabeth White   2 Aug. 1805
  Signed by Page Rank(?)
John Thompson   Mary Young   30 Aug. 1805
  Signed by Wm. Caldwell
Henry Williams   Elsy Ridley   26 Aug. 1805
  Signed by Isaac Iewell
Wm. Pitman   Mary Ragsdale   3 Dec. 1805
  Signed by Abraham Ragsdale and James Cryer
John Bridges   Dicy Hunt   8 Feb. 1805
  Signed by Edward Bridges
William Cathey   Elizabeth Cathey   5 Feb. 1805
  Signed by Wm. Cathey
James Trousdale   Milindy May   16 Feb. 1805
  Signed by Robert Trousdale
William Crutcherfield   Hannah Mabry   4 March 1805
  Signed by Jno. Jarrett
Marmaduke Ingram   Peggy McConnell   24 July 1805
  Signed by Montg. McConnell
John McCartney   Polly Thomas   7 March 1805
  Signed by Saml. Killough
James Bratton   Betsy Wilson   14 Dec. 1805
  Signed by Jas. Wilson
Wm. Brackin   Penelope Searcy   20 Nov. 1805
  Signed by W. H. Douglass
John Hatfield   Sally Thompson   26 Jan. 1805
  Signed by Wm. Shoulders

John Brown   Elizabeth Ball   29 July 1805
  Signed by Abner Ball
Summers Harper   Keturah Pearis (Peairs)
  She was a dau. of Jonathan Peairs.   8 Jan. 1805
  Signed by Jas. Charlton
Robert Nuley   Margaret Young   18 Jan. 1805
  Signed by James Richardson
Allen Josey   Nancy McKinsey   22 Jan. 1805
  Signed by Jas. McKinsey
Joseph Stevenson   Polley Pittman   22 Jan. 1805
  Signed by John Donohoe
John Gambill   Hanner Suiergrass   11 Nov. 1805
  Signed by Henry Gambill
T. Porter   Rebeah Snoddy   9 March 1805
  Rebeah is dau. of Wm. Snoddy. Signed by
  Thos. Marginet(?)
John Cowan   Peggy McCarty   18 March 1805
  Signed by Elijah Prewett
Francis Boren   Edy Wimberly   30 March 1805
  Signed by John Boren
Thos. Whitford   Polly Henderson   27 March 1805
  Signed by Abraham Hollingworth
James Brown   Sylvia Break   1 April 1805
  Signed by James McKain
Francis Tinsley   Polly Cary   7 May 1805
  Signed by Jas. Cary
Abraham Bledsoe   Milly Wethersed   4 May 1805
  Signed by Jas. S. Rawlings
Bartheleman Osburn   Betsy Abbott   30 April 1805
  Signed by Saml Roaney
Duncan Patton   Polly Givin   29 April 1805
  Signed by Saml. Watson
Andrew Parkes (Parker) Elizabeth Noble   22 April 1805
  Signed by Robinson Ross
William Wyles   Nancy McKee   18 April 1805
  Signed by John Wyles
Joseph Seawell   Prudence Bledsoe   1 April 1805
  Signed by Jno. Lyon
James Burns   Amy White   23 Dec. 1805
  Amy was widow of Reuben White. Signed by
  Stephen Cantrell
William White   Jinney Burton   24 Oct. 1805
  Signed by Jesse McClendon

Jesse Hereford   Polly Turner   1 Jan. 1806
  Signed by John Hereford and Adam Turner
Alexander McElroy   Polley Elliott   6 Jan. 1806
  Signed by William Davis and Alex McElroy
James Love   Sally Watwood   4 Jan. 1806
  Signed by Samuel Roney
Jesse Coker   Polley Chance   21 Jan. 1806
  Signed by Edward Maxey and William Maxey
William Lyon   Rebeccah Steel   8 Jan. 1806
  Signed by Robert Steel, Jr.
Adam Wallace   Sally Stuart   7 Jan. 1805
  Signed by Saml Stuart
William Payton   Barbara Rogers   26 Nov. 1806
  Signed by William Norvell
George Bush   Elizabeth Marlin   27 Nov. 1806
  Signed by Archibald Marlin
Benjamine Grainger   L(?)illey Groves   8 Nov. 1806
  Signed by William Grainger
Charles Hafford   Polly Herring   3 Nov. 1806
  Signed by Jesse Hereford

Joseph Christopher   Rebeccka Coleman   1 Nov. 1806
  Signed by Thomas Groves
Mashak William   Nancy Pritchett   25 Oct. 1806
  Signed by Joseph Clark
William West   Polly Taylor   8 Oct. 1806
  Signed by John Taylor and David Bradley
David Bradley   Rebecca Granger   8 Oct. 1806
  Signed by John Taylor
Vardimun Smith   Polly Gains   6 Oct. 1806
  Signed by Jas. McKain
John Mitchell   Sally Gardner   3 Oct. 1806
  Signed by Benj. Rawlings
Edmund Green   Rhoda Harris   4 Oct. 1806
  Signed by Thomas Edwards
Thomas Marlin   Polly Rice   1 Oct. 1806
  Signed by Archibald Marlin
Jesse Hollis   Pheobe Gambling   3 Dec. 1806
  Signed by William Marlin
Thomas Gordon   Rebeccah Wornock   13 Dec. 1806
  Signed by Hiram Wornock
Allen Purvis   Peggy Franklin   27 Dec. 1806
  Signed by Henry Vinson
John McGee   Elizabeth Rogers   22 Dec. 1806
  Signed by James Rogers
Jesse Cartwright   Patsy P. Rawlings   24 Dec. 1806
  Signed by James Rutherford
John Lindsey   Nancy Smothers   20 Dec. 1806
  Signed by James Carr
Moses Rhodes   Polly Noris   22 Dec. 1806
  James Raper signed.
Marcus Dodd   Polly Wilson   22 Dec. 1806
  Laurence Owen signed.
Herrod Seat (Seet)   Jenny Murrell   15 Dec. 1806
  Thomas Barrot signed.
William Cavennough   Polly Bruce   16 Dec. 1806
  John Chapman signed.
Levi Fox   Nancy White   29 Dec. 1806
  Signed by Littlebury (Little B.) White
James McCallaster   Elizabeth Asque   26 March 1806
  Signed by John Fillingham
Abner Shoulders   Elizabeth Comlis   26 March 1806
  Signed by Isaac Baker
Robert Parks   Nancy Given   18 March 1806
  Signed by Jacob Parks
William Newton   Polly Tire   17 April 1806
  Signed by Henry Allen.
George Farrier   Sally Mooney   19 April 1806
  Signed by George Farrier and John Mooney
David Campbell   Catherine Bowen   10 April 1806
  Jas. Desha signed.
James Hamilton   Susannah Vinson   8 April 1806
  Signed by John Hamilton, Jr.
William Cathey   Betsy Gale   9 April 1806
  Signed by Alex'r Cathey
Jeremiah Smith   Fanny Ashlock   1 April 1806
  Signed by Peter Fisher
John Lyon   Agnes Kusie(?)   21 April 1806
  Signed by William Hungs(?)
John Jones   Hannah Oglisby   31 March 1806
  Signed by Daniel Ogilsby
Josiah Dixson   Dusty Williams   29 April 1806
  Signed by David Stafford
Walter Loving   Dolly Stone   23 April 1806
  Signed by Eulitis Stone
Joseph Bowman   Peggy Hamilton   14 May 1806
  Signed by Jno. W. Hamilton

James Sanders   Molly Donelson   26 Feb. 1806
  Signed by Edward Sanders
Lewis Martin   Anny Clendening   13 Feb. 1806
  John Brisby signed.
Hardy Warren   Sally King   11 Feb. 1806
  William King signed.
Isrial Ambrose   Gilly Wright   11 Feb. 1806
  John Wright signed.
Joseph Spradlin   Nancy Bradley   19 Feb. 1806
  John Bradley signed.
John Freeland   Catherine McKee   18 Feb. 1806
  Wm. McKee signed.
Henry Hunt   Darcus Giles   31 Jan. 1806
  Josiah Giles signed.
Wm. Weathers   Dicey Trible   18 Feb. 1806
  Jesse Skenn (Sheen) signed.
Thos. Malone   Hannah Cathey   1 March 1806
  John Lyon signed.
William Coventon   Priscilla Bloodworth   28 Feb. 1806
  Webb Bloodworth signed.
John Willis   Jinney Kirkpatrick   26 Feb. 1806
  Waller Kirkpatrick signed.
Kincher Barnes   Elizabeth Braswell   22 July 1806
  Ruffin Delock signed.
Robert Moore   Nancy Green   30 March 1806
  John Trice signed.
William Cage   Fanny Street   12 March 1806
  James Winchester signed.
Thomas Ferrell   Betsy Shaw   Jan. 1806
  Joshua Smith signed.
Thomas Barrnett   Henney Noble   27 Jan. 1806
  Jeremiah Claxton signed.
Thos. Kirkham   Betsy Prewett   23 May 1806
  Wm. Grady signed.
Jonathan Trousdale   Sally Josey   21 May 1806
  Wm. Murrell signed.
John Dobbins   Elizabeth Shaw   May 1806
  Jonathan Trousdale signed.
William Buckett   Sally Doyal   28 May 1806
  John Doyal signed.
John Taylor   Barbary Bason   26 May 1806
  David Bradley signed.
Henry Bloodworth   Dolly Griffin   28 May 1806
  Metes Anderson signed.
Green Berry Orr   Aramintha Juliett Harris
  Wm. Alderson signed.   28 May 1806
Richard Cocke   Elenor Desha   1 July 1806
  Eleanor was dau. of Robert Desha who gave consent.
  Thomas Cocke signed the bond.
David Foster   Anny Beard   26 June 1806
  Signed by David Beard, Sr.
Robert Fleming   Nancy Mitchell   16 June 1806
  John Mitchell signed.
Samuel Roulston   Elizabeth Shaw   28 Jan. 1806
  Elizabeth was dau. of Hugh Shaw who gave consent.
  Hugh McBride signed the bond.
Samuel McAdow   Hannah Coop   24 July 1806
  Wm. Hodge signed.
Joseph Underwood   Betsy Young   25 July 1806
  Amos Gowen signed.
Burwell Fulks   Patsy Locke   Feb. 1806
  Thos. White signed.
John Maclin   Rebecca Anderson   3 Feb. 1806
  Robert ANderson signed.
John Bentley   Rachel Brown   5 Feb. 1806
  John S. Swaney signed.

John L. Swaney   Anny Belote   5 Feb. 1806
    John Bentley signed.
Robert Sanders   Jane Keesee   16 July 1806
    Wm. Henry signed.
Allen Graves   Polly Uzzell   10 Feb. 1806
    Thomas Graves, Jr., signed.
William Simmons   Patsy Gipson   17 Feb. 1806
    Peter Simmons signed.
Benjamine Tarver   Sally Odam   18 Aug. 1806
    George Elliott signed.
William Hammond   Jane McMurtry   4 Aug. 1806
    John McMurtry, bro. of Jane, signed.
William Hamilton   Fanny Latimer   15 Aug. 1806
    Danl Latimer signed.
James Summers   Polly Hood   31 July 1806
    Saml Watson signed.
William Barret   Cassander Barret   25 Sept. 1806
    Nathan Alihisen signed.
Richard Moore   Elizabeth Johnson   6 March 1806
    James Johnson signed.
Littleberry White   Nancy Dillard   25 Sept. 1806
    Bernard Ferrell signed.
Goolsby Thurman   Patsy Stovall   14 July 1806
    Thomas Stovall and Frances Wethered signed.
Moses Gaines   Elizabeth Marshall 20 Nov. 1806
    William Capps signed.
John Dinnind   Elizabeth Whitworth 11(21) Aug. 1806
    Thomas Graves, Jr., Cader Hunder, and Joseph
    McGloughlin signed.
Elsworth Baynes   Peggy White   28 Aug. 1806
    Jacob Leave(?) signed.
Robert Williamson   Kiniah Whitsett   10 Sept. 1806
    Laurence Whitsett signed.
John Weaver   Elizabeth Crop   4 Sept. 1806
    John Bailey signed.
Millenton Wall   Sally Ellis   13 Sept. 1806
    Simon Ellis signed.
William Edward, Jr.   Peggy Hassel   13 Sept. 1806
    Richard Edwards signed.
William Rainey   Sibella Elliss   16 Sept. 1806
    Everard Ellis signed.
Abraham Tribble   Polly Nelson   18 Sept. 1806
    William Moody signed.
Isaac Dillon   Polly Kitbroth   19 Sept. 1806
    Tarlton Bonen signed.
Everett Ellis   Polly Carlson   17 Sept. 1806
    William Rainey signed.
Daniel Latimer   Elizabeth Given   23 Sept. 1806
    John Pendergast signed.
Edwin Smith   Susannah Thomas   20 Sept. 1806
    Jacob Smith signed.
George Browning   Sally McIntosh   27 Jan. 1806
    Reuben Nowell (Noel) signed.
John Hutchings   Susannah Yource   13 Jan. 1806
    Patrick Yourse signed.
John Spadling   Susannah Bradley   16 Jan. 1806
    George Stalcup signed.
William Moody   Rebecah Trible   Feb. 1806
    Abraham Trimble signed.
Andrew Denning   Polly Groves (Graves) 15 Sept. 1806
    Thomas Graves signed.
Alexander Cathey   Mary Malone   8 April 1806
    Thos. Malone signed.
James Allen   Peggy Franklin   3 March 1806
    Jas. Franklin signed.

William Davis   Nancy Collom   15 Nov. 1806
    Signed by Robert Redding and James Cryer

William McCarty   Polly Chappell   31 Dec. 1808
    Polly was dau. of John Chappell.
Nathaniel Boon   Betsy Thorn   29 Dec. 1808
David Mitchell   Elizabeth Clary   1 Jan. 1808
Nicholas Stone   Betsy Loving   24 Feb. 1808
    Signed by Euseleuis Stone
Daniel Frailey   Milley Miller   22 Feb. 1808
Nathan Neil   Sally Trousdale   1 March 1808
Simon Edwards   Elizabeth Hail   6 March 1808
    Signed by Adonjah Edwards
John Gaines   Charlotte Prewitt   9 May 1808
John Hubert   Sally Bougles (Boughs) 25 Apr. 1808
Samuel Hollaway   Theedy Hassell   20 April 1808
Joseph Easley   Betsy Withers   19 April 1808
Alexander Frazer   Elizabeth Harper   8 April 1808
    Signed by Wm. Harper
Henry W. Newlin   Polly N. Sims   16 April 1808
James Ewin   Billey Bates   30 March 1808
John Turner   Anny Bouldright   27 Jan. 1808
Philip Reyman   Susannah White   30 Jan. 1808
William Taylor   Nancy Edwards   5 Jan. 1808
Thomas Bloodworth   Aly White   13 Oct. 1808
William Paradice   Elizabeth Stuart   17 Nov. 1808
James Rayen   Betty Simpson   7 Sept. 1808
    John Simpson signed.
Richard Moore   Eustaute Cowin   21 March 1808
Pleasants Cuws   Eusstuth Laurence   21 March 1808
Garrard Ethridge   Polly M. Wisman   25 Dec. 1808
Noah Parker   Roda Parker   30 Jan. 1808
    She was dau. of Thos. Parker. James Fisher
    signed.
Samuel Kennedy   Lucinda Prewitt   31 Dec. 1808
William M. King   Preckilla Hassell   8 Dec. 1808
    Signed by Jno. Pendergast
David King   Sarah Pike   10 Sept. 1808
Davies King   Sally Jones   27 Jan. 1808
    Signed by Jno. Pendergast
Samuel Roaney   Patsey Norman   19 Jan. 1808
    Signed by Reuben Norman
Henry Boyer   Mary Gambell   2 Jan. 1808
    Signed by Jno. Gambell
William Stones   Sally Gaires   11 Jan. 1808
    Signed by Moses Gaines
William Davis   Polly Sebastian   6 Jan. 1808
    Signed by John Davis
Abraham Young   Peggy Cavett   9 Jan. 1808
    Signed by James Reney
Richard Smith   Peggy Senning   6 Feb. 1808
    Signed by Groge Steel.
Sterling Tinsley   Kesiah Wynn   16 June 1808
    Signed by John Pendergast and James Edwards
(?) Raines   Hannah Cooper   28 Sept. 1808
    Signed by John Cooper
Martin Gambill   Susannah Shaddin   21 Sept. 1808
Thomas Graves   Susannah Roney   19 Dec. 1808
    Signed by Reuben Searcy
John Payton   Sally Rogers   24 Dec. 1808
    Signed by Joseph Campbell
John Yourly   Prudince Wilson   15 Dec. 1808
    Signed by William Kirkpatrick and John B. Pendergast
John Mitchell   Fanny Bushy   23 July 1808
    Signed by Hugh Findley

Reuben Norman	Vina Brackin	16 Sept. 1808
Signed by Wm. Brackin		
Green Wellixford	Lucy Alley	12 Sept. 1808
Signed by John Pendergast and Wm. Smith		
James Job	Catherine Pitt	10 Sept. 1808
Signed by Robert Pitt		
Greenwold Latimer	Celia Gardner	17 Sept. 1808
Signed by Peter Looney		
John Hall	Patsy Douglass	4 Oct. 1808
Signed by Wm. H. Douglass		
John Finere	Polley Hoane	15 March 1808
Signed by David Clark and Richard Ball		
William Mitchner	Elizabeth Cordle	14 March 1808
Samuel Watson signed.		
Binpm (sic) Terrell	Sally Cloe	15 March 1808
Jas. Douglas signed.		
Jarrett Loyd	Rebechah Stuart	16 Feb. 1808
John Pitt	Susanna Strather	12 March 1808
James Strother signed.		
Pavott Cuffman	Jinney Gunsaw(?)	15 Feb. 1808
Geo. C. Chapman signed.		
William Jones	Polly Haw	25 July 1808
Joseph Clark signed.		
Eli Stalcup	Rebeccah Osburn	3 Aug. 1808
David Graves and Wm. Roney signed.		
Mason Garrison	Betsy Hasten (Harten)	19 Aug. 1808
Signed by James Huston		
James Mabry	Susannah Bernard	15 Aug. 1808
Wm. Atchison signed.		
Thomas Bloodworth	Aly White	13 Oct. 1808
Signed by Henry Bloodworth and Serrel White		
Hugh Patterson	Synthia Murray	17 Oct. 1808
Signed by James Grayham		
Shadrack Finn	Rebecca Henderson	31 Oct. 1808
John Parson	Sally Wilson	31 Oct. 1808
James Storry	Nancy Watson	29 Sept. 1808
Joshua Short	Rebecca Abbott	1 Sept. 1808
Abraham Trigg	Martha Saunders	29 Aug. 1808
Signed by Will Trigg, Jr.		
Robert Johnson	Patsy Goodrum	31 Aug. 1808
William Durham	Francis Marshall	15 July 1808
Andrew Buckner	Charlotte Taylor	15 July 1808
Needham Hunter	Polly Parnell	15 Dec. 1808
James Kirkham	Milley Anderson	19 May 1808
Signed by William Payton		
George Harpole	Gelly Chapman	23 May 1808
James Bell	Betsey Easley	9 June 1808
Robert Parker	Patsy Martin	27 May 1808
Signed by Thomas Parker		
Synde Latimer	Polly Hamilton	26 May 1808
Henry Miller	Nancy Garrison	27 May 1808
Archibald Johnson	Elizabeth Gilmore	12 July 1808
Signed by Abner Gilmore		
James Whitworth	Anne Hardine	13 Aug. 1808
Rhodam Rawling	Aley Seawell	3 Nov. 1808
Garrad Ethridge	Polly Nurnan(?)	25 Dec. 1808
Benj. Dickison signed.		
John Scott	Betsy Bradshaw	1 Nov. 1808
Signed by John Bradshaw		
William Roney	Leah Graves	3 Aug. 1808
Signed by David Graves		
Eleanor Wilson (sic)	Rebeccakah Pearson	30 June 1808
David Bruce (Brice)	Lucy Bruce (Brice)	24 Dec. 1808
Thomas Davis	Clounda Eckels	4 Aug. 1808
Signed by Jno. Pendergast		

John Hicks	Philpeny Holt	10 Nov. 1808
Daniel Liggett	Sally Garrison	18 Nov. 1808
Start Lines(?)	Phanny Paradise	17 Nov. 1808

Signed by Wm. Paradise

John Allen	Laettitia Sanders	21 Dec. 1808
William Paradice	Elizabeth Stuart	17 Nov. 1808
Jones Lina	Glisby May	16 Aug. 1808

Signed by Hezekiah Jones and Isaac Simpson

Simon Ellis	Delilah Smith	25 Nov. 1808

Signed by Abraham Ellis

John Mabrey	Peggy Trayo	9 Dec. 1808
Jacob Hicks	Polly Lewis	6 Dec. 1808

Signed by John Hicks

Richard Center	Betsy Hunt	9 July 1808
John McElworth	Oliver (sic) Deloach	23 Nov. 1808

Joseph Sloss	Ann Hooper	25 Nov. 1813

Signed by John Turner

William Gampson	Kesiah Smith	26 June 1813

Signed by William Delap and James Blakemore

Samuel Young	Betsy George	24 Aug. 1813
Joseph Campbell	Nelley Norris	13 Jan. 1813
Thomas Hunt	Mary Davis	11 July 1813

Signed by Jonathan Davis

Joseph Carter	Betsy Mallard	30 June 1813

Signed by Gideon Carter

William Young	Nancy Patterson	24 April 1813

Signed by Lemuel (or Samuel) Young

Elijah Russell	Sarah Drewny	5 April 1813

Signed by Daniel Williams

William (?)	Eliza B. Smith	12 Jan. 1813

Signed by William L. Rurner, Benjamine Brown, and
James Blakemore

William Pitt	Jane Robertson	9 Jan. 1813

Signed by William Pitt and Isaac Baker

Miles Miers	Lucy Duker	26 June 1813

Signed by Solomon Shoulders

James Barnard	Jemima SHort	25 Aug. 1813

Signed by James Banard and Zadock Barnard

James M. Cary	Mania Saunders	1 Sept. 1813

Bond signed by Matthias Bellurner(?)

Jonathan Mencum	Betsy May	7 Aug. 1813

Signed by Michael Green

David Parrish	Lucinda Hunt	3 July 1813

Signed by Elijah Boddie

Charles Wood	Elizabeth Reeves	26 July 1813

Signed by Wm. H. Douglass and H. Shelby

Barry R. Starks	Betsy Lindsey	16 July 1813

Signed by James Mills

Thomas M. Dement	Elizabeth Bowler	3 March 1813

Signed by David Dement

James Elliss	Susannah Cottron	4 Sept. 1813

Signed by Everet Ellis

William Carroll	Cecilia M. Bradford	1(?) Sept. 1813

Signed by Henry Bradford

William Owen	Martha Edwards	5 Feb. 1813

Signed by William Crenshaw

Nicholas B. Prior	Sally M. Thomas	16 Sept. 1813

She was dau. of Cornelius Thomas who gave his
consent and stated she was of age. John Johnson
signed.

James Nowell	Betsy Proctor	27 Nov. 1813

Signed by Edmond Boaz

Meredith Walton	Nancy Stubblefield	10 Dec. 1813

Mabry Walton signed.

Joseph Lister   Rebecca Dorris   4 Dec. 1813
  William Capps signed.
John Easley   Anny Wonldrum (sic)   25 Nov. 1813
  Isaac Tracy(?) signed.
James Landers   Lucinda Bowen✓   19 March 1813
  William Glover signed.
John Wallace   Matilda Wilson   1 Sept. 1813
  Ezekial Cherry signed.
Leanner Blackman   Elizabeth Elliott   22 June 1813
  James Odhum signed.
Hugh Morrison   Sarah Williamson   27 Feb. 1813
  John Morrison signed.
Edmund Hogen   Polly Walton   13 May 1813
  Hugh Turner signed.
William Snyder   Fanny Weadkins   20 May 1813
  Signed by Paul Turly
William McKinnie   Lynthia Melisa Wilson 14 Dec. 1813
  Signed by James T. Wilson
Thomas Knife   Polly Evans   2 Feb. 1813
  Signed by Thomas Knife and Will Trigg, Jr.
Little B. Green   Fanny Tyres   12 Jan. 1813
  Signed by Michael Green
Jonathan Anderson   Elizabeth Goudon   14 April 1813
  Signed by David White
Adam Clines   Sarah Black   29 Nov. 1813
  John Cline signed
Hugh Barr   Katy Hoope (Hooper)   23 Nov. 1813
  Robert Hoope signed.
Beverly Fleming   Polly Aspy   15 Nov. 1813
Robert Neely   Fanny Boswell   11 Aug. 1813
  George Blakemore signed.
John Gibson   Polly Treble   5 Aug. 1813
  Abraham Treble signed.
Samuel Young   Betsy George   24 Aug. 1813
  John Douglas signed.
Jessee Douglass   Patsy Cunning   8 Sept. 1813
  William Ring and Robert Payne signed.
David Barrett   Patsy Ingram (Ing)   11 Dec. 1813
  George Barnett signed.
William Henderson   Martha Hinson   14 March 1813
  James (?) signed.
James Fleming   Polly Ross   20 Sept. 1813
  Signed by Josiah Lauderdale
Daniel Miers   Mary Wilson   18 Oct. 1813
  Thomas Shoals signed.
Edmond Wagoner   Charloty Wilson   17 Oct. 1813
  Signed by Joseph T. Wilson
Thomas W. Johnston   Marthew Carson   23 Oct. 1813
  Signed by Benjamine Johnston
James Gouly   Violet Wilson   18 May 1813
  Signed by Jacob Howdeshalt
King Luton   Caroline Walton   8 Oct. 1813
  Signed by John Perry
Edward Choat   Sally Ascum (Akum)   4 June 1813
  Signed by Charistopher Woodall and Allen Graves
Thomas Miles   Esther Summers   30 April 1813
  Signed by William Summers and Henry Hamilton
William Glover   Betsy Motherall   15 July 1813
  Signed by Samuel K. Blythe
William Murphey   (?)   (?)   6 Nov. 1813
  Signed by Jacob Gregory
Jacob Striter   Bundy Dean   6 June 1813
  Signed by Nicholas Cockleness and John Warron
Francis Berry   Sarah Frost   4 July 1813
  Signed by Jonathan Hoedy

Silas Alexander   Nancy Anderson   19 April 1813
   Signed by Raven C. Follis
John Alsupt   Prudence Henderson   6 Oct. 1813
   Signed by David Alsupt
John Dobbs   Sarah Anderson   6 May 1813
   Signed by William Wygal
David Dowel   Elizabeth Shook   12 Aug. 1813
   Signed by Charles B. Stubbins
Vinson Lee   Lily Jenkins   24 Dec. 1813
   Signed by Thomas Jenkins
Asa Hassell   Sally Edwards   3 Feb. 1813
   Signed by Nathan Edwards
James McGee   Matilda Wallace   19 Jan. 1813
   Signed by Joseph Wallace
William Trail   Sally Hammon   29 Jan. 1813
   Signed by Willis Alckison and Andrew Blythe
John Woldrum   Rody Hide   20 May 1813
   Signed by William Henderson
Daniel Williams   Mary Mayhue   18 May 1813
   Signed by Edmon Waggoner
Isaac Short   Polly Overby   22 July 1813
   Signed by Jacob Bunard
Stephen Lewis(?)   Oma Laurence   4 Jan. 1813
   Signed by David Dement
Isaac Atkins   Mahala Allen   10 Sept. 1813
   Signed by Webb Bloodworth
Gideon Carter   Betsy Swainey   15 May 1813
   Signed by Joseph Carter and Joseph Mallard
Waid Davis   Patsy Dnweney (sic)   23 May 1813
   Signed by Fielden Hankins
William Hubard   Sally Dalton   31 July 1813
   Signed by Joseph Motheral
Jesse Graham   Peggy Alexander   11 July 1813
   Signed by Zadack Ingram
Thornton Clayton   Fanny Beardon(?)   6 March 1813
   Signed by John Bentley
Clem Jennings   Richard B. Estes   26 May 1813
   Signed by Clen Jennings and Elizabeth Bennett
Joseph Campbell   Milley Norris   13 Jan. 1813
   Signed by David Green
Samuel Hendricks   Rebeccah Davis   4 Oct. 1813
   Signed by Samuel F. Davis and William Summers
Greenbury Greenshaw   Sally Bridges   19 June 1813
   Signed by Jonathan Spooner and Hugh Cowin
Abraham Smith   Ludia Pearce   13 Jan. 1813
   Signed by Benjamine H. Stubblefield and George
   Pearce
Isaac Pavott   Thomlind Elliss   3 May 1813
   Signed by Pavott Cuffman

The above records do not include all the records up to
1814 but are those given for the years included. The records
are in bad condition and are not filed in any order except by
years in packagaes and tied with strings. E. R. W.

INDEX TO SUMNER COUNTY DEEDS

Except for records lost by carelessness, the records of
this county are fairly complete. although those records not in
book form have been damaged. The deeds are in unindexed record
books at Gallatin, the county seat of Sumner County.

Deed Book A (contains records prior to 1797)

Name	Page	Remarks
Allen, Theophilas	55	
Allen, Walter	216	Craven Co., N. C.; Sumner Co., 1791
Alexander, William	145	in Sumner Co., Tenn., 1798
Alexander, Daniel	203	in Sumner Co., Tenn., 1798
Alexander, Ebenezer	28	in Logan Co., Ky., 1797
Anderson, Daniel		in Petersburg, Va., 1798
Barbour, Richard	136	of Orange Co., Va.
Barrow, Sherred		of Glasgow, N. C., 1796
Black, Michael	11	of Sumner Co., Tenn.
Barnes, Jordan	25	
Baker, John	195-97	Montgomery Co., Tenn., 1798
Barrow, William	204	
Barthal, Luben, heirs of	159	
Barton, Samuel	47	of Davidson Co., Tenn., 1797
Benthal, Laban	142	
Bervard, Frederick	101	of Jefferson Co., Ky., 1797 (wife Mary)
Bell, William	202	
Bloythe, James	122	
Baartney (Bratney), Robert	157	
Briton, Richard	107	Sullivan Co., Tenn., 1797
Briggance, (?)	229	
Cage, Wilson	218	
Cage, Reuben	146	
Caffery, John & Deadrick	161,104	D. G. Michael
Cathey, Wetham	156	
Campbell, William	103	Montgomery Co., Tenn., 1797
Carruth, Adam	230	Lincoln Co., N. C.
Cathey, John	111	
Cherry, William	201	
Clary, Elijah	15	
Clarke, Joseph & William	106,114	Rockingham Co., N. C.
Crabtree, William	147	
Colwell, David	30	
Cryer, James	66	
Cross, Samuel	116	
Curtice, Thomas	214	Craven Co., N. C.
Deeks, James	174	Knox Co., Tenn., 1798
Deouglass, James	88	
Dillard, John	10	
Donnald, William	69	Guilford Co., N. C., 1790
Donoho, Patrick	129	of Sumner Co., from Caswell Co., N. C.
Donoho, Charles	130	Caswell Co., N. C.
Donoho, Edward	171	
Donoho, Thomas	14, 24	Caswell Co., N. C., 1797
Donelson, Stockley	138	
Douglas, Elmore	151	
Douglass, James	227	

Name	Page	Remarks
Easton, James		Wake Co., N. C., 1796
Echols (Echoles), Moses	206	
Edward, Benjamine	134	Northampton Co., N. C.
Ellis, Robert	57	
Ellis, Benjamine	85	
Elliott, Hugh	109	
Estetill, Wallace and Trewett	119	Madison Co., Ky., 1797
Eststill, Henry & Elisha	119	
Espy, John & Alexander	132,133	sons of Robert Espy, 1798
Exum, Arthur	155	
Fleming, Henry	164	Bertie Co., N. C.
Fleming, Samuel	63	Iredell Co., N. C., 1797
Fleming, John	75	Rockingham Co., N. C.
Fonville, Francis	1, 2	Sumner Co., Tenn., 1797
Fork, William	194	Madison Co., Ky., 1797
Foster, Alexander	75	Guilford Co., N. C., 1797
Foster, John	74	Guilford Co., N. C., 1797
Foster, William & Wm. McClain	76	Guilford Co., N. C., 1797
Gambill, Bradley	8	Davidson Co., Tenn., 1797
Gambill, Henry	64	
Garrett, Edward	4	
Garrison, John	50	
Gordon, Richard & Susannah	194	Madison Co., Ky., 1797; she is his wife.
Goff, Andrew	162	
Gilson, Patrick	166	
Gilmore, Nathaniel	141	
Godfrey, James	190	Orange Co., N. C., 1797
Gray, William	221	
Gray, Samuel	105	
Greham, Alexander	93	
Harris, Thomas		Mecklenburg Co., N. C., 1797
Harpole, John	4	1797
Harpole, John	15	
Harpole, Paul	112	
Harris, Edward	224	
Hall, William	225	
Hall, Francis & Edward	125	Edgecombe Co., N. C.
Hart, James	110,152	
Hasler, Thomas	195	Gates Co., N. C., 1798
Hasser, George	205	Stokes Co., N. C., 1797
Hays, John	75	Davidson Co., Tenn., 1798
Hays, Charles	154	
Hendricks, Joseph	42,53	
Hicks, Joab	52	
Hinds, John	103,140	Bourbon Co., Ky., 1797
Holinshead, Frances	113	
Hodges, C. James	172	
Holmes, Albert	46	
Howell, Josiah	13	
Holland, Joel	13	
Houdeshalt, Jacob	59	
Isabella, Thomas	170	Stokes Co., N. C.

Name	Page	Remarks
Shurgen, John		Sullivan Co., Tenn., 1797
Shipherd, Benjamine	179	Glasgow, N. C., 1798
Sloan, John, Jr.	230	Spartansburg Co., N. C., 1797
Sloss, John	176	Logan Co., Ky., 1798
Spain, AUstin	208	private in N. C. Cont. Line
Smith, Benjamine	5	Botetourt Co., Va., 1797
Smith, Oliver	211	Greenville, N. C., 1798
Smith, Thomas	205	
Stalcup, William	120	
Taylor, Pergin	123	
Taylor, Robert	179	Robertson Co., Tenn., 1798
Taunt, Jessee	213	drummer in N. C. Line (S. C., 1795)
Tauler, Benjamine	163	
Thacker, Jeremiah	49	
Thomas, Jacob	155	
Tise, Jacob	33	
Tompson, Robert	48	Nelson Co., Ky., 1797
Waller, Thomas	6	
Wallace, Joseph	25	
Walton, Isaac	92	
Walker, Thomas	21,23	
Watwood, George	125	
Watson, James	136,139	Alexander, Va., 1798
Watson, Josiah	137	Alexandria, Va., 1797
White, Samuel	144	
Wherry, William	31	
Weathers, John	124	
Winchester, James	61	Gen. James Winchester
Witheral, Latimer	192	
Wilson, Aaron	219	Mecklenburg Co., N. C., 1799
Wilson, James	1	Sumner Co., Tenn., 1797
Wilson, Jessee	2	
Wynne, Deacond	223	
Wynne, John King	189	

Note: Some of the pages here are unnumbered because they were unnumbered in the original book. The remarks given above are lagely the place of origin of the party. Where spellings of names have been corrupted, I have corrected them as far as possible. E. R. W.

Deed Book # 1, 1793-1797 (the second book of deeds, at the court house at Gallatin, Tenn. Due to the length, only names and pages are given).

Allison, David, to John Dawson	45
Allin, Rody, from John Williams	52
Alexander, Mathew, from David Wilson	126
Allen, Theophilus, from John Delock	145
Anderson, Mathew, to Charles Carter	173
Alexander, George, to James Doroty	179
Armstrong, Martin, to George Aust	187
Aust, George, from Martin Armstrong	187
Anderson, Mathew, to Jeremiah Doxey	212

Armstrong, Martin, to Andrew Stul   219
Alexander, Stephen, from George D. Blakemore   257
Aspey, Robert, to Edward Jones   294
Archer, Thomas, from Howel Tatum   301
Anderson, Alex'd, from William McGee   310
Armstrong, John, from John Knox   349
Armstrong, Martin, to David Shelby   396
Archer, Thomas, to William Moore   399
Anderson, Wm., from Abraham Sanders   462
Anderson, Jno., from Jas. Winchester   475
Armstrong, Andrew, to Jno. Gilmore   500
Allen, Nathan, from Edward Gwin   505
Allen, Theophilus, to Melvin Bloodworth   514

Barton, Samuel, to William Hays   1
Barton, Samuel, to William Hays   2
Barton, Samuel, to Wm. Hays   3
Brown, Lewis, to Abraham Rodgers   5
Brown, James, from Abraham Sanders   6
Blackmore, George D., from Peter Tuney   7
Same, from same   8
Bledsoe, Anthony, exec., to David Shelby   11
Board, William, from David Shelby   39
Barton, Samuel, from William Ewing   40
Barkley, John, from Peter Tuney   49
Barton, Samuel, to Zachara Green   64
Barton, Samuel, to James Green   74
Bell, Robert, from Joseph Hendricks   80
Bowie, Reason, to Wm. Edwards   81
Bowie, Reason, to Thomas Edwards   82
Brigance, David, to William McAdams   98
Britton, Thomas, from J. and M. Johnson   98
Brown, George, from Joseph McElrath   105
Brigance, David, to Hugh Carphart   114
Bowen, William, to Jno. Camaus   118
Bowie, Reason, to James Odom   125
Bowie, Reason, to James Harrison   128
Blythe, Andrew, from Abram Sanders   136
Byrum, Lawrence, to Robert Goodloe   139
Bowie, Reason, to Jno. Neeley   160
Bledsoe, Catherine, from Winn Dixon   162
Bloodworth, Henry, from Jno. Delock   164
Bledsoe, Catherine, to James Sanders   177
Botts, William, from Theadus Mallor   180
Boyd, Andrew, to Isaac Patton   199
Buckhannon, James, from Robert Espey   204
Brown, George, and Joel Eckels, to Joseph McElrath   208
Bledsoe, Catherine, from Tilmon Dixon   211
Brigance, David, to William Gilson   221
Barrow, Micajah, from Howell Tatum   224
Brown, George, from Ephreum Peyton   227
Blunt, William, from Elisha Price et al   233
Batts, Frederick, from Phillip Piphin   235
Brigance, James, from John Gordon   238
Blunt, William, from Elisha Rice   241
Board, David, to William Boyd   242
Boyd, William, from David Board   242
Board, David, to Thomas Board, Sr.   250
Board, Thomas, Sr., from David Board   250
Brigance, James, to Robert Patterson   254
Blackmore, George D., to Stephen Alexander   257
Black, William, from Ezekel Norris   290
Boyd, John, to Richard Jones   296
Blunt, William, from Jessee Read   299

```
Dixon, Tilmon, to Catherine Bledsoe                          211
Doxey, Jeremiah, to Mathew Anderson                          212
Donnell, Thos., to William Morrison                          216
Donnell, Geo., from David Shannon                            228
Donnell, Thos., from Wm. and Elizabeth Spencer               231
Devis (Davis), Jno., to Jas. Sharp                           245
Donoho, Wm., from Jas. Sanders                               247
Deshae, Robert, from Jno. Young                              259
Dawson, Jno., from Jas. McCain                               266
Delock, Jno., to Thos. Leach                                 304
Delock, Jno., from Ephraim Peyton                            342
Dixon, Winn, to Thos. Bradley                                359
Davis, Arthur, from George D. Blackmore                      367
Drummond, William, and others, to Jas. (Jos.)  Ennever      376
     also pp. 377, 378
Douglass, Reubin, to Hugh Elliott                            395
Dillard, William, from William Parmer                        421
Dixon, Chas., and Wynn Dixon, to Tilmon Dixon                443
Donnell, Thos., to Jno. Morgan                               449
Donohoe, Thos., from Jno. Ore                                480
Deadrick, J. and G. M., to Henry Bun (Boon)                  482
Delock, Jno., from Ephraim Peyton                            397


Ewing, William, from Saml Barton                              40
Edwards, William, from Reason Bowie                           81
Edwards, Thos., from Reason Bowie                             82
Espy, Robert, to Edward Jones                                 85
Espy, Robert, to Thomas Cribbins                             150
Edwards, William, from Elmore Douglass                       175
Ellis, Robert, from Edward Williams                          178
Enock, Robert, from William Cage, Sheriff                    190
Espey, Robert, to Jas. Buchannon                             204
Elliott, Falkner, to Sampson Williams                        300
Egnew, Thos., from Zach. Green                               327
Erwin, Jas. (Jos.), from Annamas McCoy                       372
     also p. 373
Ennever, Jos., and others, from Wm. Tyrrell                  374
Ennever, Jos., from William Drummond and others             376
     also pp. 377, 378
Estill, Wallace, from Micoll (Miceil) Kimbering              380
Edwards, Thos., to George Womeldorf                          392
Elliott, Hugh, from Reuben Douglass                          395
Edwards, William, to Wm. Beackley                            441
Eaton, Chas. R., to Jas. Winchester                          442
Espy, Robert, to Armsted Rogers                             453
     also p. 353
Echols, Elkanah, from Jas. Montgomery                        456
Edwards, Thos., to Cornelius Forsley                         473
Edwards, Thomas, to Nathan Edwards                           516
Edwards, Nathan, from Thomas Edwards                         516


Fisher, Archibald, from Robert Steel                          25
Funkhouser, Christopher, from Jethro Sumner                   60
Funkhouser, Crilly, from Thos. Clark                          61
Fuller, Burton, to Daniel Hunter                             123
Fuller, Burton, from Barnard Tatum                           124
Fleming, Peter, from David Purvance                          133
Fort, Wm., and H. Tatum, to Wm. Pryor                        185
Fort, Wm., and H. Tatum, to Jno. Hannah                      185
Frazer, Jas., to Elisha Oglesby                              205
Funkhouser, C., to Jno. Williamson                           206
Fisher, Peter, to James Winchester                           252
Fisher, Archbld., to Henry Malone                            291
```

Fisher, William, from Samuel Gray   324
Fenner, Richard, to Thos. Stokes   361
Fleming, Sam'l, from Isaac Patton   415
Fenner, Jno., to Dan'l Rogers   487
Farr, Ephraim, to James Wilson   495

Good, Adam, from Robert Hays   4
Glaves, Michael, to Richard Waller   9
Gambling, Jas., from Just. Cartwright   13
Grant, S., to Thos. Donnell   24
Green, Zach., from Samuel Barton   64
Green, Jas., from Samuel Barton   74
Calting, Jno., to Moore Stevenson   78
Grant, Jno., to Jno. Sterns   134
Goodloe, Robert, from Laurence Byrum   139
Goodloe, Robert, from Thos. White   140
Glaves, Michael, from William Cage, Sheriff   176
Gilmore, Mary, to Henry Hayde (Hyde)   182
Gray, Samuel, from David Looney   188
Gardner, Jno., from Ephraim Peyton   230
Gordon, Jno., to Jas. Brigance   238
Gwin, Edwd., to Peter Lemons   244
Goodloe, William, to Adam Lawrence   264
Green, Zach., from Jas. McCain   265
Gillespie, William, from Jno. Knox   297
Gardner, Jno., from Epham (Ephraim) Peyton   313
Glasgow, Cornelius, from Robert Hays   320
Gray, Samuel, to William Fisher   324
Green, Zach., to Thos. Egnew   327
Good, Wm., from Abraham Rodgers   332
Green, Zach., to David Board   357
Gwin, Edwd., to Francis Catron   423
Garner, Bryan, from Isaac Walton   448
Gwin, Edwd., to Jno. McMurtry   460
Gillispie, Wm., to Jnob. Bass   490
Gilmore, Jno., from Andrew Armstrong   500
Gwin, Edward, to Nathan Allen   505

Hays, Wm., from Samuel Barton   1
Hays, William, from Samuel Barton   2
    also p. 3
Hays, Robert, to Adam Good   4
Hamelton, Thos., to Rowland Hughes   32
Hughes, Rowland, from Thos. Hamelton   32
Howell, Jno., to Sampson Williams   38
Hamelton, Jno., to Peter Looney   79
Hendricks, Jas., to Robert Bell   80
Hendricks, Jas., from Jas. Sanders   84
Hamelton, Thos., Sr., to Robert Hamilton   110
Hamilton, Robert, from Thos. Hamilton, Sr.,   110
Holman, Daniel, from Robert Campbell   113
Hendricks, Obid, from William Spencer   119
Harrison, Jas., from Reason Bowie   128
Heaton, Amos, from Wm. Cage, Sheriff   130
Harrison, Jas., from Jno. Withers   131
Harris, Samuel, from Chas. Campbell   137
Hamelton, Jno., to Moore Johnston   148
Hays, Jas., from Simon Kuykendall   163
Hutson, Chamberland, from Alexd. Montgomery   170
Hyde, Henry, from Mary Gilmore   182
Hannah, Jno., from Fort and Tatum   186
Heaton, Robert, and others, to Sampson Williams   191
Hogin, Richard, to Anthony Mitcelpt(?)   192

Hankena, William, from Daniel Smith   203
Higgs, Jacob, from Jas., Sanders   210
Hansborough, Peter, from Thos. Matson   214
Harpole, Jno., from Andrew Stell   220
Hannah, Jno., to Jas. Hayes   234
Hayes, Jas., from Jno. Hannah   234
Hamilton, Jno., to Isaac Walton   239
Hays, Robert, to Jno. Perry   240
Hays, Robert, to William Ore   249
Hamilton, Jas,, from Reubin Cage, Sheriff   268
Hansborough, Smith, from Daniel Smith   292
Hamilton, Hance, to Jno. Sloss   303
Howell, Thos., from Anthony Sharp   308
Hendrichs, Jos., from Sampson Williams   318
Hays, Robert, to Cornelius Glasgow   320
Harpole, Solomon, from Ephraim Peyton   344
Hays, Jno., to Jno. Young   347
Hamilton, Thos., to Jas. Summers   353
Hall, Edmond, from Thos. Walker   364
Haney, Jesse, from George Blackmore   368
Hardy, Chas., to Benj. Bashaw   401
Howell, Josiah, from Medy White   412
Harpole, Jno., from Thos. Simpson   422
Hendricks (Hendricks), Jas., from Andrew Jackson   439
Harderson, Nicholas, to Harry Smith   192
Hobdy, Robert, from Jno. Peyton   447
Hart, Susannah, to Thos. Love   498
Harmon, Thos., Sr., from Chas. Moore   511
Hays, Robert, to Robert Moore   518

Ingle, Jno., to Jas. Winchester   253
Ingles, John, to Wm. Bowden   385
Irby, Joseph, to John Taylor   145
Inman, John, to Edmond Turpin   393

Jameson, Thomas, to Wm. Crawford   28
Jones, Robert, to David Shelley   77
Jones, Edward, from Robert Espey   85
Johnson, J. and M., to Thos. Brooth   98
Jones, Ambrose, to Wm. Roper   116
Johnston, John, from Robert Hayes   148
Johnston, John, to Valentine Choat   151
Jameson, Thos., to James Stell   161
Johnston, Robert, from John Young   184
Jett, James, from Bennet Searcy   255
Jones, Benjamine, to John White   262
Jones, Edward, from Robert Aspey   294
Josey, John, from David Looney   295
Jones, Richard, from John Boyd   296
Jenkins, Rodrick, to Thos. Willis   333
Juland, David, from John Knox   350
Julin, Chas., from Tyrell & Donelson   375
Jenkins, Roderick, from Pearce Wall   402
Jackson, Andrew, to John Hayes   412
Jenkins, Roderick, from Wm. Snoddy   413
Jackson, Andrew, to Wm. Martin   417,425
Jackson, Samuel, from Wm. Blount   427,431
Jackson, Andrew, to Jas., Hendricks   439
Jameson, Thos., to John Wilson   451
Jackson, Andrew, from Elijah Rice   472

Kerkendall, Matthew, to Archibald Martin   41

Moore, Israel, from Jas. Winchester   504
McGee, Wm., to Alexd. Anderson   310
McCann, Nathaniel, to Thos. Overton   370
McCoy, Annanias, to Jos. Ewin and others   372,373
McNary, Francis, from Geo. Parkes   397
McGee, Jno., to Jas. McCrory   400
McCrory, Jas., from Jno. McGee   400
McConnell, from Wm. Sanders   408
McMurtrey, from Edwd. Gwin   460
McKinsey, Jas., to Jno. Reasone   465
McCasland, Andrew, from Saml Barton   484
McKookle (McKorkle), Wm., from Jas. Wilson   485

Neely, Wm., from Mary Parker, extx.   34
Newton, Wm., from Jno. Williams   51
Nelson, Robt., to Jno. Overton   62
Nevill, Geo., to Jas. McCarrell   111
Nevill, Geo., Guardian, to Robert Nelson   121
Nelson, Robert, from Geo. Nevill, Guardian   121
Nelson, Robt., to Jno. Overton   122
Neely, Jno., from Reason Bowie   160
Nihous, Thomas, to Hardy Murfee   261
Norris, Ezekiel, to Wm. Black   290
Newton, Wm., from Jas. Winchester   510

Odam, Jas., to Robert McKorkle   17
Overton, Jno., from Robert Nelson   62,122
Odam, Jas., from Reason Bowie   125
Oglesby, Elisha, from Jas. Frazer   205
Oglesby, Dan'l, from Andrew Steel   222
Overton, Jno., to Sampson Williams   243
O'Neill, Thos., to Alex'd McKee   246
Ore, Wm., from Robert Hays   249
Odam, Jas., to Wm. White   325
Overton, Thos., from Wm. Slade   334
Overton, Thos., from Nathn'l McCann   370
Oglesby, Elisha, to Wm. Montgomery   419
Ore, Robert, to Thomas Donoho   480

Phillips, Phillip, and others, to Elijah Robertson   10
Parker, Mary, extx., to Jas. Clendenning   33
Parker, Mary, extx., to Wm. Neely   34
Patterson, Jno., from Mathew Kuykendall   46
Perry, Sion, to Henry Vinson   63
Peyton, Ephraim, to Adam Noser (Moser?)   67
Peyton, Ephraim, to Jno. Dawson   75
Peyton, Thos., to Jno. Peyton   88
Peyton, Jno., from Thos. Peyton   88
Payne, Jos., from Robert Campbell   89
Patton, Thos., from Henry Vinson   96
Penny, Wm., and wife, to Nath'l Parks   120
Parker, Nathaniel, from Wm. Penny and wife   120
Purvence, David, to Peter Fleming   133
Pennington, Jacob, from Jno. Donelson   159
Pryor, Wm., from Fort and Tatum   185
Patton, Isaac, from Andrew Boyd   199
Pryor, Wm., to Thos. Travis   217
Peyton, Ephraim, to Geo. Brown   227
Pryor, Jas. (Jos.), to Rich'd Pryor   229
Pryor, Rich'd, from Jos. Pryoy   229
Peyton, Ephraim, to Jno. Gardner   230
Pepkin, Phillip, to Frederick Batts   235

WASHINGTON COUNTY

OFFICERS IN THE WAR OF 1812

This list of officers for the years 1812 and 1813 is in the Tennessee State Library

Robert Baker	Ensign	28 July 1812	1st Regt.
John Capas	Capt.	24 April 1812	1st Regt.
John Cosson	Ensign	8 Oct. 1812	1st Regt.
John Doke (Duke)	Lieut.	29 April 1812	1st Regt.
Robert Gray	Lieut.	8 Oct. 1812	1st Regt.
Lesley Humphreys	Lieut.	5 March 1812	1st Regt.
Samuel Lain	Ensign	5 March 1812	1st Regt.
Elisha McCeacy	Ensign	5 March 1812	1st Regt.
John Patton	Lieut.	28 July 1812	1st Regt.
James Yeager	Ensign	8 Oct. 1812	1st Regt.
Joseph Bacon	Capt.	8 Nov. 1813	1st Regt.
Joseph Britton	Lieut.	8 Nov. 1813	1st Regt.
John Bean	Capt.	27 April 1813	1st Regt.
William Cruckshanks	Capt.	8 Nov. 1813	not given

WASHINGTON COUNTY

PETITION TO THE GENERAL ASSEMBLY

This petition from inhabitants of Washington Co., 1799, request-ing that the legislature pass an act "confirming certain marri-ages made during the years 1785 and 1786, by authority of the State of Franklin." The petition is in Box 3, Tennessee State Archives.

To the Honourable The General Assembly of the State of Ten-nessee: The Petition of Sundry of the Inhabitants of the County of Washington Humbly Sheweth That in the Years 1785 and 1786 a Number of Marriage Contracts Were Entered into by Inhabitants of sd County the Licenses for which Marriages were Issued by the Clerk of sd County Court & Under Sanction of the State of Frank-lin: Upon reverting back to the State of North Carolina, the As-sembly thereof discontinued all the proceedings done during that period and refused to confirm those marriages under an appre-hension that the refusal thereof in cases of persons dieing in-testate may occasion many law suits and be a means of hindering many children from possessing their father's property, your peti-tioners request that your honourable body will take the same un-der consideration and pass an Act to confirm those marriages, and they as in duty bound will pray etc.:

Henry Nelson	John Fain
Colvin Finch	Wm. Boyles
David Brown	James Gillespie

John Yancey	Samuel Wood
George Nolen	Jesse Payne
John Boyles	Darling Young
Adam Lowry	James Gray
Alex Stuart	Joseph Crowch
John McAlister, Jr.	Charles McAlister
Brice Clair	George Hau--
Richard Jones	Jos. Young

WHITE COUNTY

SURVEYS, 27 APRIL 1824 TO 28 MARCH 1828

These Surveys, from Book A, are at the Tennessee State Land Office

Surveyed for	Page	Surveyed for	Page
Anderson, James	1,390	Bryant, William M.	273
Adair, Wm.	34,381	Beshears, Isaac	275
Anderson, G. W.	62	Bryant, John	275
Austin, Nathaniel	68,480	Bryant, William	286
Austin, John	70	Blain, James H.	302
Ames, David	80,87,88,182	Baker, Wm.	305
Allen, Jesse,	118	Bradshaw, Charles	322
Anderson, Wm.	145	Brown, William	351
Allen, George	266	Beadwell, Isaac	353
Anderson, Edward	358	Bryan, Andrew	358
Anderson, Wm. P.	360	Buck, Isaac	361
Austin, John	365,408	Byers, Moses	370
Ames and Elrod	371	Burdin, Wm., Jr.	377
Arnold, Francis	379	Baker and Ames	385
Anderson, Jacob	395	Blain, H. James	390
Anderson, Robert	430,433,439	Bramblett, Nathaniel	428
Allred, Jonathan	442,443	Brown, John	429
Allred, B.	443	Broiles, George	435
Anderson, William	445,446	Braylor, George	436
Allison, John	452,457	Brown, William	437
Allen, G. and S. H.	455	Barr, John	450,454,455,462
Allison, Joseph	460	Burton, Henry	452
		Brown, Isaac	469
		Bradshaw, Charles	471
Baker, David	29	Bohannon, Wm.	489
Balch, William	37,299,369	Bartlett, Wm.	491
Bouldin, Noble	77	Bohannon, Lewis	510
Brown, Samuel	91	Bartlett, Joseph	515
Byers, Moses	96	Bounds, B. John	516
Bartlett, Nathan	110	Brown, John	530
Baker, Wm.	103,216,225	Brumbelough, Jno.	533
Beshears, W. Jeremiah	117	Bullock, John	534
Beshears, Bazzell	120	Bartlett, Joseph	537
Berry, Ephrim	123	Bohannon, Wm.	538
Brown, Rebecah	124	Bartlett, Wm. 540	540
Bounds, Thomas	154,515	Buram, Peter	547,548
Bohannon, John	156,197,199	Buram, and Vaughan	549
Burden, Wm., Sr.	172	Brown, Richard	562
Brown, Wm. L.	173		
Burden and Lane	193,194,195		
Bohannon, James	196	Cary, Milford	4
Burden and Lane	207	Campbell, Robt.	9.478
Bradshaw, George	217,220	Copeland, Singleton	31
Brown, William	222	Certain, Charles	36
Bozorth, Levi	256	Crowder, Richard, Jr.	57

A FEW MARRIAGE RECORDS FROM WILLIAMSON COUNTY

These marriage records are on file at the county seat of Franklin. E. R. W.

Aaron Dodd	Lovey White	16 May 1825
Aaron Dodd and Lewis Johnson, securities		
Samuel Eastep	Sarah Loyd	27 May 1825
Absolom Weaver, sec.		
Absolom C. Tennison	Mary Ham	15 June 1825
Elijah Ham, sec.		
Benjamine German (Jerman)	Jane Alexander	11 Jan. 1825
Thos. Hulm, sec.		
James Shannon	Mary Gray	9 June 1825
Thos. Holt, sec.		
John Walker	Nancy McKinney	5 June 1825
Randall McKinney, sec.		
James M. Smith	Martha Page	18 June 1825
Thomas Hardman, sec.		
Joshua Collins	Rebecca Tucker	24 June 1825
Thomas Gillespie, sec.		
William Davis	Lucy Walls	6 Jan. 1825
Samuel Merritt, sec.		
Sylvester Jones	Anna Frazier	1 Feb. 1825
Thomas P. Cassey, sec.		
Samuel Forehand	Sally McPherson	8 Jan. 1825
John Forehand, sec.		
George Andrews, Jr.	Winifred E. Matthews	3 Jan. 1825
Marks Andrews, sec.		
Robert Howard	Sally Crouse	3 Jan. 1825
John Crouse, sec.		
Randolph McKinney	Parthenia Dungan	26 Sept. 1825
Nathan Dungan, sec.		

MARRIAGE RECORDS OF WILSON COUNTY

John Stockard	Polly Thomas Flood	2 May 1806
Consent of Thomas Flood, sec.		
Samuel Gibson	Sally Browning	3 Nov. 1806
Jacob Boung	Ann Ray	4 Jan. 1806
James Johnson	Elizabeth Nelson	18 Feb. 1806
John Powel	Sally Boothe	23 June 1806
Benjamine Munford	Elizabeth Badd	19 Nov. 1806
John Ferguson	Patsey Harris	18 Jn. 1806
Robert Boyd	Elizabeth Gardner	11 Aug. 1806
John B. Belford	Ruth Broan	7 July 1806
John Givin	Jenny Berry	26 May 1806
John Paukey	Peggy Smith	15 June 1806
Thomas Wooldridge	Jenny Bradley	7 July 1806
Elisha Brown	Polly Allen	1806
John Phillips	Elizabeth Scott	6 Jan. 1806
Jules Alford	Ann Hays	18 Feb. 1806
Daniel Walls	Rebecca Buff	11 Jan. 1806
Benjamine Alexander	Sarah Cloyd	21 July 1806
Peter Walker	Drucilla Hendrick	2 Sept. 1806
Peter Cotton	Lebenah Tucker	20 May 1806
Samuel Dickins	Polly Clampet	11 April 1806

James Newby	Sally Butley	22 Dec. 1806
Isaac Johnson (Johnston)	Priscilla Avnton	1806
(Record is torn)		
Jessee Cunningham	Rosey Beasley	30 June 1806
James Smith	Christian Devault	4 Dec. 1806
(Bride's name might be Devautt)		
Zachariah Tact	Rebeccah Williamson	22 Dec. 1806
Alexander Steele	Lucy Compton	28 Aug. 1806
Hugh McCoy	Caty Wilson	27 Aug. 1806
Amos Winset	Polly Philips	3 May 1806
George Brown	Polly Thompson	10 April 1806

Alexander Boyd	Rosannah Boyd	2 June 1807
John Boyd signs		
Wyett Bottes	Milly Powers	7 Aug. 1806
Edward Brown	Sally Bandys	12 Sept. 1806
Joseph Jadwin	Mary Vanhoosen	26 July 1806
Garland Tidwell	Susannah Magness	18 July 1806
George Allen	Sally Johnson	28 Aug. 1806
John Alford	Nancy Taylor	27 Aug. 1806
Thomas Clifton	Letty Rogers	22 Dec. 1806
Avery Brown	Sarah Marlow	22 Sept. 1806
Leven McNatt	Nancy Smith	24 Feb. 1806
Patrick Yourse	Posey Chapman	6 Aug. 1806
Kennedy Bay	Fanny Barnett	9 Oct. 1806
William Holland	Fanny Stile	14 Nov. 1806/7
(The date is written in that manner in the Whitely transcription - R. W. B.)		
George Allen Brough	Mirah Bone	18 Nov. 1806
Hugh McElyea	Polly McElyea	2 Sept. 1806

John Fake (Faks)	Mary Edwards	7 Nov. 1808
Richard Hancock	Mary Hancock	10 Oct. 1809
Hardy Pennuel	Lucy Patterson	21 Jan. 1806
Samuel Thomas, Sr.	Barbary Petner	21 Dec. 1806
Anthony Winston	Sally Ann Watson	27 Aug. 1806
William Smith(?)	Alsey Munday	15 Dec. 1806
(The record is partially obliterated)		
Stephen Lankford	Lear Herrod	5 July 1806
George Ross	Lydia Dickins	25 Jan. 1806
John Scoby	Ann Speers	21 Jan. 1806
Phillips Hinston	Elizabeth Tucker	28 May 1806
Donald McNicleds	Betsey Bradley	23 Sept. 1806
Christopher Cooner	bride not given	1806
Thomas Dell (Dill)	Agnes Hopson	3 July 1806
Elijah Jones	Patsey Browning	15 March 1806
Andrew Morrison	Jane Robertson	6 Sept. 1806
Amos Small	Polly Cooner	27 Jan. 1806
Charles B. Smith	Elly Hutson	26 Dec. 1806

John Woodall	Polly Collings	30 June 1809
Levi Lannon (Lannom)	Rachael Gibson	30 Aug. 1806
Alexander Mars	Marthew Donnell	20 Sept. 1809
John Baker	Jenny Boarding	13 Feb. 1809
Noah Kelley	Hannah Hicks	8 July 1806
Joseph Dixon	Polly Clack	23 July 1806
Rowland W. Gressam	Betsey Rather	6 Dec. 1809
Vachel Blalack	Patsey Chapple	19 Jan. 1806
Edward Jones	Margaret Thomas	6 June 1808
Phillip Anderson	Polly McNatt	24 Feb. 1806
Isham Wynn	Sally Eckels	5 April 1806
George Lockmiller	Polly Porter	30 April 1806

William Holebrooks	Sarah Davis	9 Feb. 1806
Andrew Hays	Susannah Enochs	4 Aug. 1806
John Echols	Judith Compton	3 July 1806
Levi Holland	Nancy Saddle	25 Aug. 1806
Stephen Hopkins	Polly Adamson	21 Oct. 1809
Elisha Gwyn	Sarah Odlett	5 Jan. 1806/7
Anthony Copeland	Nancy Craig	24 March 1806
Martin Frankling	Nelly Watson	21 March 1812
Alexander Rutledge	Nancy Cox	30 March 1812
Thomas Robertson	Betsy Wooten	17 Oct. 1812
John Compton	Lucinda Travillon(?)	9 June 1812
John Regan (Rogan)	Caty Hunnibill(?)	2 June 1812
John O'Neal	Darcas Midget	24 Feb. 1812
Robert King	Lydia Keeton	2 March 1812
Overton Harlow	Betsey Hunt	1 Aug. 1812
James McAdams	Judith Smith	4 July 1812
Elijah Armstrong	Peggy Higgins	18 Jan. 1812
John Caplinger	Catherine Harpole	24 July 1812
Byrd Smith	Martha McAdams (McAdow)	5 Dec. 1812
Joseph Gray	Agnes Denton	4 Jan. 1812
James Cawthorn	Sally Peak	29 Sept. 1812
Thomas Knight	Rebeccah Jones	20 May 1812
Robert Bonds	Polly Benton	31 March 1812
John Eagon	Margaret Wray	16 May 1812
Joseph Humphries	Nancy Broune	4 Jan. 1812
Thomas Patterson	Mary Harpole	3 Dec. 1812
Richard Carmack	Agnes Smith	12 Sept. 1812
Michael Robertson	Mary Hawk	3 Jan. 1812
John Hays	Betsey Estes	26 July 1812
Eli T. Hunt	Sarah Webb	11 July 1812
Levi Howell	Polly Jennings	7 Jan. 1812
Pleasant Irby	Kezia Lambert	5 Oct. 1812
James and Caty Shaw		1812

This is how the bond reads.

James McDaniel	Amy B. Vaughan	10 Feb. 1812
George Smith	Ally Martin	21 March 1812
Adam Harpole	Polly Bettes	15 April 1812
John Blackburn	Caty Carver	3 Feb. 1812
Henry Black	Patsey Brown	14 June 1812
Dickson Williams	Patsey Allen	20 April 1812
Lewis Dickings	Hannah Ashford	26 Aug. 1812
Arden Summers	Nancy Tucker	16 Feb. 1812
William Benson	Fanny Dodd	22 Feb. (1812?)
Jesse Brinson	Susanna Moss	29 Jan. 1812
Dudley Brown	Edness Henderson	30 May 1812
Robert Mitchell	Agey Moore	28 July 1812
James Calhoon	Winney Woodward	7 Nov. 1812
Norman McDaniel	Widow Perryman	21 Oct. 1812
David Williams	Betsey Hoozer	23 June 1812
Theodore Ross	Peggy Carnary(?)	23 June 1812
Carter Marlow	Gerlater Bryant	1 Aug. 1812
William Jennings	Elizabeth Gibson	10 April 1812
Brunt Blurton	Nancy Bass	1 Oct. 1812
William Terry	Betsey Marlow	29 Jan. 1812
Patrick Anderson	Fanny Chandler	13 May 1812
James McDaniel	Peggy Greer	31 Jan. 1812
Dempsey Lambuth	Huckney Bettes	17 March 1812
Joseph Hays	Susannah Adams	25 April 1812
David Smith	Priscilla Bennett	4 May 1812
William Kelley	Mornan (Norman) Keeton	March 1812
William Woods	Elizabeth B. Harris	29 April 1812

William Cooper	Mary Slaylock	17 Jan. 1812
Joseph Young	Peggy Stuart	24 March 1812
Aaron Ramrine	Polly Wells	21 Jan. 1812
Lewis Riding	Elizabeth Johnson	5 Feb. 1812
Hugh Bradley	Patsey Hunter	13 Aug. 1812
William Potter	Winney Lambuth	17 March 1812
Smith Belote	Nancy Gill	2 Nov. 1812
John C. Tippet	Caty Kail (Hail)	14 March 1812
Henry Shelby	Hannah Brown	10 March 1812
James Drew	Rebecca Brown	22 Feb. 1812
Isaiah Triblett	Patience Pemberton	26 May 1812
Robert Wilson	Junny Donall	29 Aug. 1812
Samuel Raily	Cinthia Waller	29 Sept. 1812
George Hamilton	Daluthen Hamilton	5 Feb. 1812
Luke Kent	Polly Mann	2 April 1812
Wiley Whitley	Polly Soddy	3 Dec. 1812
William McHaney	Sally Word (Ward)	23 March 1812
Thomas Knight	Alley Martin	24 Dec. 1812
Lawrence Sypert	Polly Lambuth (Lamberth)	
		3 March 1812
Harris Smith	Nancy Flood	27 Nov. 1812
William Parrish	Martha Davis	11 Feb. 1812
John Kimbro	Nancy Bearden	13 March 1812
Lewis Johnson	Edy Wright	10 Sept. 1812
Nicholas Edwards	Milly Powers	24 Oct. 1812
William Mount	Mary Jones	25 March 1812
William Marshall	Catherine Marshall	23 July 1812
Shadrack (Shadrick) Smith	Nancy Howard	15 Oct. 1812
Lemuel Brichan	Polly Logan	28 Feb. 1812
William Jewell	Amy Thomas	2 Oct. 1812
McKinsey Marlow	Nancy McMillin	5 Aug. 1812

(These are all that were published - R. W. B.)

FAMILY RECORDS

The following records were taken from the files and correspondence of the compiler.

Anderson

John F. Anderson was born 27 Feb. 1808 in Sullivan Co., Tennessee, son of Thomas and Mary (Davis) Anderson. Thomas was born in Abington, Va., and when small he moved to Sullivan Co., Tennessee. In 1812 he moved with his family to Bedford Co., Tennessee. Mary Davis was born in Philadelphia, the daughter of a Revolutionary Soldier who was killed during the War. She moved to Sullivan Co., Tennessee with her step-father. She died in West Tennessee in 1825.

Armstrong

John Armstrong, born 1768, had a brother Joseph, born 29 Jan. 1787 and his was Sarah Gober, born 15 March 1789.

Tabitha Ellen Armstrong, born 3 Jan. 1849, was the daughter of Robert Armstrong, born 28 Sept. 1806. Robert was the son of John Armstrong, born 10 March 1768 and Mary Ann Dudley, born 10 August 1777 (The Bible and tombstone records call her Polly), married 1791. Robert and his wife were married 10 October 1836.

The Rev. John Armstrong did not settle in Tennessee, but his widow moved there with her son and Mary Ann (Polly) (Dudley), his wife, and family. This was when Robert was about six weeks old. John and Mary Ann had two sons named John. The first died young, and before moving to Tennessee they had another one which they named John. John and Polly Armstrong are buried in Bond Co., Illinois. John's mother is thought to have died and been buried in Maury Co., Tennessee before the family moved to Illinois. Those buried in Illinois will be found in the Bethel Cemetery in Bond County, and have markings at their graves. John Armstrong was born in Georgia. They moved to Maury Co., Tennessee in 1806. John II had a brother Joseph who moved to Bond County with him in 1829.

Barksdale

(These nites are taken from Wilson County records at Lebanon, the county seat.)

Indenture made 26 Dec. 1807 between William Crabtree and William Crutcherfield of Wilson Co., Tenn., of the one part, and Daniel Barksdale of the same county of the other part. Crabtree and Crutcherfield, executors of William Thomas, dec., for consideration of $1813.50, sell to Barksdale 220 acres on Cedar Lick Creek. Signed by William Crutcherfield and William Crabtree. Witnessed by George Smith, William McClain, and Samuel Deakins.

Indenture made 1 August 1812. Daniel Barksdale sells the land purchased from Crutcherfield and Crabtree to Edward Blurton of Wilson County, Tenn.; tract contains 152 acres. Proved June Term, 1813. (Deed Book E)

The Barksdale family of Wilson County intermarried with the Lowe family. Green B. Lowe was from Lincoln Co., N. C., and came to Wilson Co., Tenn. See Wilson Co. Deed Book F, page 412.

Bell

Robert Bell came from Guilford Co., N. C., in 1783, and settled near Bledsoe's Lick in Sumner Co. Later he moved to Mill Creek, ten miles southeast of Nashville. He died in Feb. 1816 of smallpox, aged about 85 years. He was twice married, and had a total of nineteen children, six by his first wife and thirteen by his second wife, Mary. His first wife's name is not known.

Cannimore-Custer-Mitchell

Jacob Cannimore (spelled Kennamore, Kennemer) served in the Indian Wars of 1812-1815 under General Andrew Jackson. He moved from Alabama to Giles Co., Tenn., where he acquired land. The oldest son of Hans Cannimore, he was born about 1776 and died about 1 Oct. 1856. (from letter)

Michael Custer (Custard) and Rebecca Jones, daughter of Morton Jones, stated in pension application that he moved from Orange Co., Va., to Wilkes Co., N. C., where he resided until 1818, then moved to Tennessee and resided in Bedford Co. of that state for seven years. He then moved to Franklin Co., Tenn., and died in Coffee Co., Tenn., on 8 Nov. 1841. (from letter)

Mary Jane Custer Mitchell, daughter of Michael Custer and Rebecca Jones, was born 8 Feb. 1818 or 1819. (from same letter)

The editor has searched the land records of Bedford, Franklin, and Coffee Counties, but has not found the names of Jacob or Hans Cannimore, or Michael Custer or Custard.

Charlton

John Charlton, Revolutionary Soldier, resided in Davidson County when he received a pension.

Elizabeth Charlton, born 21 Feb. 1811, married John Barkley on 26 March 1827. He was born 16 Dec. 1802 at Leesburg, Tenn., near Jonesboro. Elizabeth died 13 Aug. 1897.

Cleere

Richard Cleere was born in Va., in 1799. In October 1829 he signed the charter of the F. and A. M. Lodge No. 73, and was its first master. He was a tailor and learned his trade in the shop of Andrew Johnson, who later became President of the United States. He lived at Summerville, Tenn. Richard Cleere died in Fayette Co., Tenn., in 1846.

Douglass

Mrs. Jemima Douglass, consort of the late William Douglass of Kentucky, is buried in Old City Cemetery, Nashville. She was born 20 Aug. 1780, and died 3 Dec. 1844.

Edmundson of Davidson Co., Tennessee

John Edmundson's inventory, recorded in Will Book 7, page 5, was recorded 11 June 1816, made 16 April 1816; returned into court by John and Robert Edmiston, April Session, 1816.

David Edmiston's inventory, recorded in Will Book 7, page 12, was taken 15 April 1816, and recorded 13 June 1816. William Harris, Mary Edmondson, and John Edmondson were administrators.

Robert Edmiston's inventory in Will Book 7, pages 51,64, 171. Recorded 16 Aug. 1816, by Peter Wright, administrator.

Mary Edmiston support laid off. She was widow of David Edmiston and received a year's support. Children are mentioned but not named. Signed R. Edmiston and L. Keeling (Kuling). Recorded in Will Book 7, page 66.

John Edmundson and Mary Buchanan married 6 Sept. 1796 in Davidson Co.

Samuel Edmiston married Nellie Dean, 23 May 1791, in Davidson Co.

William Edmondson married Polly Edmondson, 24 Sept. 1804.
Wm. Edmondson married Betsy Burge on 14 Feb. 1810.
Wm. Edmondson married Martha Buchanan on 7 June 1808.
Robert Edmonson married Anna Meek on 6 Jan. 1816.

Will of Thomas Edmondson recorded 27 Nov. 1824 in Will Book 8, page 365, names: son Samuel; son John Black; wife Martha; daughter Elizabeth; daughter Martha; daughter Esther; daughter Esther; daughter Louisa; mentiones suit in Circuit Court of Bedford Co. over land in Lincoln Co.; mentions grandchildren Hugh McClung and Obediah, sons of William Edmondson. Son Samuel and friend William Black executors. 17 Sept. 1821.

Ellis

        Moses Ellis lived in Wilson Co., Tenn., in 1820, and had a
family.
        Robert Ellis and family were in Wilson Co. in 1820.
        Thomas Ellis and family were in Wilson Co. in 1820.
        John Ellis and family were in Wilson Co. in 1820.
        James Ellis and family were in Wilson Co. in 1820.
        Benjamine Ellis, Presley Ellis, and Isaac Ellis resided in
the lower end of Sumner Co., in 1799. Benjamine Ellis, Willis
Ellis, and Abraham Ellis lived in the upper part of the county
in the same year.
        In 1820, James G. Elliff (sic), Similion Ellis, Ransom El-
lis, James Ellis, Everd Elliff (sic) all lived with families.
        Sims Ellis, Aaron Hudson, and Stephen Ellis all lived
with families in Robertson Co. in 1820.
        Miles Elliss and family were in Montgomery Co. in 1820.
        Underhill Ellis was in Capt. Joshua Hadley's Company of
Evans Battalion, for the protection of settlers in Davidson Co.
in 1787.
        George Ellis married Jeniah Holton on 3 April 1802 in Mont-
gomery Co.
        John Ellis married Masson Thompson on 25 May 1802.
        A number of Ellises were mentioned in deeds in Sumner Co.
on 28 Nov. 1805.
        Everett Ellis married Polly Carlson, 17 Sept. 1806, Sumner
Co.
        James Elliss married Susannah Cottron on 4 Sept. 1813.
        Simon Ellis married Delilah Smith on 25 Nov. 1808, with
Abraham Ellis a surety.
        Abraham Ellis married Prudence Lindsey on 24 April 1800.
        William Ellis of Cumberland Dist. and Jno. McFarland,
Bill of Sale, 7 Dec. 1781, in Davidson Co. Will Book no. 1,
page 8.
        North Carolina Certificates of Survey Military Warrants:
Robert Ellis; John Ellis a private in the N. C. Line (his grant
was transferred to Thos. Henderson, 1820).
        Tennessee Grants also show Charles Ellis a private.
        Edward Ellis will made 20 May 1800, proved 1800 (Davidson
Co. Wills, Book 2, page 175) named Edward Ellis of Davidson Co.,
wife Sarah Ellis to have all estate real and personal, daughter
Abbee Ellis. Thos. Hickman a witness.
        There is an Ellis graveyard on Stewart Ferry Road in David-
son Co., but no old stones with markers.
        Wm. E. Ellis married Mary Ann Ellis on 12 Feb. 1838 in Dick-
son Co.
        William Ellis was in War of 1812, from Davidson Co.
        Simeon Ellism orphan, age 9, bound to William Crockett to
learn art of tanning and curing. (Sumner Co. Minute Book, 1818,
page 60).
        Margaret Ellis appointed guardian for her five minor child-
ren: Robert, Samuel, John, Thomas, and Joshua. Isaac Ellis and
Joseph Spradlin were her securities. (Sumner Co. Minute Book,
1832-1834, p. 11).
        Inventory of Robert Ellis, dec., taken 17 Aug. 1820, and
returned Aug. Term, 1820, signed by Somelling and Abram Ellis.
(Sumner Co., 1808-1821, page 446).
        Samuel Ellis, private in the Revolutionary War in the N. C.
Militia, was pensioned in Adair Co., Ky. He was born 9 April
1762 in Montgomery Co., Md.; entered service in Rowan Co., N. C.
and lived there for three years after the war. He moved to
Surry Co., N. C., then back to Rowan Co., and in a few years to
Burke Co., then to Jefferson Co., Tenn., until 1826 when he
moved to Cumberland Co., Ky., where he lived until 1832, when

he settled in Russell County, Kentucky, where his wife died. He
had a son and two daughters. His pension began 4 March 1831.

Etheridge

Emerson Etheridge was born in Currituck Co., N. C., in Oct.
1819. His farmer was a farmer and migrated to Weakley Co., Tenn.,
from N. C., about 1821.

Ezell

Margaret Ezell died 1874, about 86 years old. She is buried
in the Ezell graveyard near Buchanan's Creek in Giles Co., Tenn.
She died at Milton Buchanan's in Lincoln. Her husband was W. M.
Ezell. The graveyard is on the edge of Pulaski, Giles Co.
Tenn. Other graves are there also.

Gilliland

James Gilliland of East Tennessee married first a Miss Rainbow and second a Miss Cable. James had a brother Hamilton Gilliland who lived and died in White Rock, Tenn. Another brother,
David Gilliland, went to Alabama.

John Gilliland was on the first grand jury of Jefferson
Co., Tenn., in 1792.

John Gilliland was a member of the Convention held at
Greenville, Tenn., with Jno. Sevier and Jno. Tipton.

Abel Gilliland settled on Wolf Creek about five miles from
Pell City, Alabama. He had two sons, Patrick and Wesley Gilliland. A Methodist Church was erected on the land occupied by
Gilland or Gilliland. The church has been discarded and the
membership moved to Eden, some three miles away. There was an
old graveyard at the church, which has not been used for some
fifty years, and is badly neglected. Wesley Gilliland is said
to have moved to Texas. Abel Gilliland was from East Tennessee.

James Gilliland lived on what is known as the fork of
Pegeon River and was prominent in the early history of Cocke
Co., Tenn. His family intermarried with the Axley family. They
also intermarried with the family of Peter Huff who lived on the
French Broad River.

In the Davidson Co., Tenn., records, Will Books 1 and 2,
pages 188, 200, 201, 345, and 346, are mentions of James Gilliland. 23 Aug. 1800, James Gilliland names his family, Robert,
Daniel, James, and wife Nancy. James was the youngest son, and
a daughter Sarah would be 21 years old in 1800.

One James Gilliland was a leader in the Zion Church. His
wife was a sister of Jas. Axley and an excellent woman. This
is the Cocke Co., Tenn., Gilliland family. Abel Gilliland, a
brother of James, was a remarkable man. In 1821 he moved to
Wolfe Creek, St. Clair Co., Alabama, and founded a church at
that place. Before he left Cocke Co., he gave land between
French Broad and Pigeon Rivers one mile west of Newport for the
erection of a church.

John Gilliland was granted land in Greene Co., on French
Broad, an island in Warford.

Silas Jasper Gilliland was in the early history of Tenn.

Alexander Gilliland had sons: John, Robert, Thomas, and William. They were from Tyron Co., N. C. In 1783 John lived at the mouth of Pigeon Creek and was a friend of John Sevier.

James E. Gilliland died in 1810.

Sheppard Gilliland was a son of Susannah Gilliland, wife of James E. Gilliland. She came from Lancaster Co., Penn., and settled in Rockingham Co., Va. Susannah died in 1842 at age 92. She and her husband had Jessie; Benjamine; William, born 1771; Samuel, born 1775; Henry, born 1777; Nancy; Susannah; James E., Jr., born 1783; Sheppard, born 1786; Sarah, born 1790; Elizabeth and Tolly.

Silas Jasper Gilliland was a grandson of Jno. Gilliland who was with Jno. Sevier. Silas Jasper moved to Missouri where he was with the soldiers of the country.

James Gillialand had a grandson W. H. Huff who lived at Newport, Tenn. His mother was Sarah Gilliland, and her mother was a Miss Axley.

Abel Gilliland was from East Tennessee. One James Gilliland lived on the French Broad River near Newport, Tenn. He owned what was known as the "Fork of Pegeon River," the finest farm in Cocke Co., containing about 400 acres. When he sold it to Mr. Coleman he moved to Missouri where he died. J. B. Gilliland, son of James, lived in Knoxville in 1928. This James married first Miss Rainbow, and second, Miss Cable, who was the mother of J. B. Gilliland. James had a brother named Hamelton who lived and died at White Rock, Tenn., and another brother, David, who went to Alabama.

John Gilliland was granted land in Greene Co., Tenn., as early as 1796. (State Archives, Land Grants Book C.)

John Gilliland was granted an island in Warford on French Broad. (State Archives, Land Grants, Book C.)

Graham

George Graham, born Cumberland Co., Eng., in 1774, died 3 Jan. 1844. Buried in Old City Cemetery, Nashville.

Gray

Isaac Gray, son of George and Lucy (Benning) Gray, was born 1815, and except for three years, lived in Franklin Co. George Gray was born 1777 in N. C., his father being a Revolutionary Soldier at the time. George went to Kentucky as a boy, and in 1809 moved to Franklin Co.

Greer

Alexander Greer, the progenitor, emigrated from Ireland and settled in Virginia about 1755 with his first wife, Ruth Kincaid and an only child, Joseph. Alexander moved to North Carolina. His second wife was Mary Vance of N. C., and had five children. Joseph was in the Revolutionary War and his descendants settled in Middle Tennessee. He lived in Lincoln Co., Tenn.

Groomes

Mrs. Elizabeth Groomes, born in Virginia, 23 Dec. 1793, died 25 July 1860. Buried in Old City Cemetery, Nashville.

Grundy

Felix Grundy, born 11 Sept. 1777 in Berkeley Co., Va., and moved to Ky.; later to Tennessee in 1806, aged 29 years.

Jones

John Jones, born 8 May 1750 in Albemarle Co., Va.; enlisted and served three months in the militia, 1777-1778, then he enlisted and served three years as a private in Capt. Leander Jones' Company, John Cole's Va. Regt. Shortly after the expiration of his service he again enlisted and served seven months as a private in Capt. Benj. Harris' Company, Cole's Va. Regt., and was at the taking of Cornwallis. In 1790 he moved to Franklin Co., Va., and in 1796 to Smith Co., Tenn., and in 1832 to Maury Co., Tenn While living in Maury Co., he was allowed a pension, beginning 12 Nov. 1832. At that time he had a wife but her name is not given. (Record from War Department, Washington, D. C.)

This John Jones left a long line of descendants in both Tennessee and Illinois. Records of Mrs. J. H. Travis of Greenville, Illinois, a copy of which is in the hands of the editor, show the following family relationships:

John Jones, born 8 May 1750. He married Barshaba (last name not shown), born 25 Dec. 1758. They were the parents of:
1. Judah, born 5 July 1776.
2. Hezikiah, born 24 Nov. 1778.
3. John M., born 17 Oct. 1780.
4. Pleasant, born 20 Sept. 1782 - see below.
5. David, born 23 April 1784.
6. Sarah, born 7 March 1786.
7. James, born 5 March 1788.
8. Rhoda, born 8 Jan. 1790.
9. Barshaba, born 30 Nov. 1792.
10. Polley, born 7 Dec. 1793.
11. Lewis, born 25 Dec. 1795.
12. Nancy, born 6 Feb. 1798.
13. Stephen, born 6 June 1800.

4. Pleasant Jones, son of John and Barshaba, was born 20 September 1782. He married Sarah (last name not shown), by whom he was the father of:
13. John Lewis, born 14 July 1814.
14. Patsy Eleanor, born 24 Aug. 1815.
15. Mary Minerva, born 7 December 1816, died 24 March 1909 at Reno. Bond Co., Illinois. She married James McCracken on 23 July 1834 at Greenville, Illinois. He was born 28 Nov. 1814 in Clinton Co., Illinois, and died 31 Oct. 1897 at Reno. Bond Co., Illinois.
15. James Madison, born 16 Feb. 1820.
16. Alex Osborn, born 8 Sept. 1818.
17. Rebecca Louise, born 1 Oct. 1821.
18. Sarah Lovina, born 1 Sept. 1823.

19. Ruth Naomi, born 2 Dec. 1825.
20. Daniel Douglas, twin, born 28 Dec. 1827.
21. Nathaniel Calbert, twin, born 28 Dec. 1827.
22. Elizabeth Jane, born 14 August 1831.

List of transactions of John and Pleasant Jones in deed
books at court house in Columbia, Maury Co., Tenn.:
John Jones, Deed Books D, p. 319; F, p. 504; G, p. 322;
H, p. 450; J., pp. 212,643,718; K, pp. 216-219;
L, p. 414; V, p. 295; and X, p. 14.
Pleasant Jones, Deed Books L, p. 12; N, p. 31.

James Jones married Nancy N. Jones on 4 Dec. 1816 in Maury
Co., Tenn.
Bryan Jones married Margaret Thomison on 17 Oct. 1823 in
Maury Co., Tenn. Signed by Bryan Jones and Major C. Howell.
Theophalus Jones married Epissa Powell on 2 Feb. 1829 in
Maury Co., Tenn.

Pleasant Jones married Sarah Osburn in June 1813 in Giles
County. The Giles County records are partly lost and those
remaining are in poor condition.

John Jones and Sam Jones settled in the Brick Church neigh-
borhood of Giles County between 1808 and 1810. John Jones was
probably there as early as 1807.
Samuel Jones died in 1815. He was probably a brother of
John Jones, Sr. About the time that John Jones arrived in this
section, David and Alexander Jones were settled there also.
Rebecca, widow of David Jones, was age 90 in 1876. Hezekiah and
David Jones settled on or near Shore's Mill about 1817-1818.
John Jones, Revolutionary Soldier, age 90 in 1840, was liv-
ing with Hizar Jones in Giles County. (United States Census of
Revolutionary Pensioners).
Pleasant Jones and wife moved from Maury Co., Tenn., to
Bond Co., Illinois in 1830. He had a large grant issued to him
there in 1834.

Mayberry

These heretofore unpublished notes are from the files of
the editor.

John Mayberry came from Peaks of Otter, Virginia, to Hick-
man County, Tennessee, about 1806. He is buried at Centerville,
Hickman County, in the Mayberry family graveyard.
George and Gabriel Mayberry were brothers of John Henry.
There were other brothers also. George had two sons.
John Walker and Frances Cicily Mayberry had a first cousin
named Sim Mayberry, whose son lived at Gatesville, Texas.

The 1850 Census of Hickman County Tennessee, lists the
following Mayberrys.

Henry Mayberry,	age 60, farmer,	b. in Va.
Hannah Mayberry	age 65, farmer	b. in N. C.
John Mayberry	age 34, farmer	b. in Tenn.
He had real estate worth $4000.00		
Mahilda Mayberry	age 30, farmeress	b. in Miss.
Frances Mayberry	age 11	b. in Tenn.
Atlantic Mayberry	age 8	b. in Texas
Amelia Mayberry	age 4	b. in Texas
Lucy Mayberry	age 1	b. in Texas

Amily Mayberry Rogers.

George Mayberry, born in Tenn., lived in Bibb Co., Alabama, near Centerville, died in Marion Co., Ark., 15 Feb. 1854.

Margaret Henry Mayberry, born in Lincoln Co., Tenn, died in Marion Co., Ark., on 22 Feb. 1854. She is said to have been a second cousin of Patrick Henry.

Henry Mayberry served in the Revolution, as shown in the Auditor's Account Books, Vol. 32, (M.S) in Virginia State Library, Richmond, Va.

Record Book, Hamelton District, on file in Tennessee State Library.

To the Honorable the Judges of the Territory South of the River of Ohio: the bill of James Turman complainant, vs. Frederick Mayberry, respondent: Humbly sheweth to your Honors, that your Orator in the month of September in the year of Our Lord one thousand seven hundred and ninety-two, purchased a steer from Frederick Mayberry for the sum of fifty-five shillings, Virginia money, which sum your orator agreed to pay in goods out of store, except the sume of threee shillings, six pence, or thereabouts which the said Frederick told your orator he must receive in cash. Your orator directly afterwards, vz.: on the same day the purchase was made went into the store with the said Frederick Mayberry and delivered his goods to the amount of fifty-five shillings, Virginia money, except the three shillings and six pence, which your orator paid to the said Frederick in cash, your orator well remembers the delivery of five yards or upwards of broad cloth and several yards of fine linen in payment for the aforesaid steer, and that those goods were delivered to the said Frederick on the same day in which the purchase was made. Sometime afterwards the said Frederick Mayberry purchased other goods of your orator to the amount of three pounds Virginia Money or thereabouts for which he agreed to give your orator beef cattle at fifteen shillings per hundred to be paid the fall following or when your orator should call on him for that purpose. Your orator saith that after the time of payment expired he procured a Summons to be issued against the said Frederick, etc., etc. Signed: James Turman. Court in Hamelton District, 2nd Monday of October; 29 Sept. 1794.

Frederick Mayberry made a will in Oct. 1801 in Bedford Co., Virginia.

Henry Mayberry who settled in Hickman Co., Tennessee, married Mary Carnes, daughter of Gabriel and Dorcus Carnes, all born in Germany. The exact date of Henry's death has not been established, but Dr. H. H. Mayberry, a descendant living in Nahville, Tenn., says he died shortly after the election of Andrew Jackson for President the last time, and this is known to be a fact for it is family knowledge that he made the statement he was happy he was spared to cast that vote. He never cast another.

Frederick Mayberry is thought ot have been the eldest child of Henry. He was a giant in size. It is said he was a rather bad man and kept the people in the surrounding territory in terror and after so long he moved to Arkansas where he was killed about 1835-40.

Other children of Henry included: Peter, one of the oldest children; George Washington, the youngest child; Mike; Gabriel; John; Dosia, married a Mr. Russell; Durbon, married Mr. Fly; Hannah, married Mr. Kinzer; and Clara, married Mr. Walker. There may have been other children as well.

Moore

Burials in Lockridge Graveyard, near Carter's Creek, Maury Co., Tenn.
Sarah Moore, born 20 Oct. 1794, died 24 July 1853.
Alexander Moore, born 10 Oct. 1789, died 29 June 1851.
John Moore, born 7 Nov. 1780, died 12 Feb. 1837.
Nancy Moore, born 15 Nov. 1790, died 28 April 1846.

Osbourne

Among the noted physicians of Maury County in 1807 was a William Armstrong who was associated with the Jones and Osbourne families.

Indenture made 15 Oct. 1827 between Robert Osborne of Maury Co. of the one part and Alexander Osborne of the same county of the other part. Robert deeds to Alexander a tract of land on the south side of Duck River on the east waters of Globe Creek, a fork of Fountain Creek, being a part of a tract of 5000 acres granted to William T. Lewis, and conveyed to Alexander Osborne by Robert Osborne, and by Robert Osborne to Alexander Osborne, containing by estimation 79 acres. Witnessed by William Shannon and Henry Thompson. Maury Co. Deed Book N, page 60, registered 15 Aug. 1828.

Indenture made 19 June 1815 between Thomas H. McGaugh of Williamson Co., Tenn., and Robert Ozburn of Lincoln Co., Tenn. For $875.00 McGaugh sold to said Osburn a parcel of land in Williamson Co. on the north side of Arrington Creek of Big Harpeth River, adjoining William McKmight's northwest corner, etc. etc. Williamson Co. Deed Book # 2-D, page 287. 125 acres. Registered 21 Dec. 1815.

Will of Richie Ozburne, 1848, names wife Nancy D., and mentions small children. Williamson Co. Will Book 1847-1851, page 149.

Robert Ozburne was born 4 March 1755 and died 8 June 1834, and is buried in the Ozburne Graveyard in the 19th District, Williamson Co. He was from Mecklenburg Co., N. C. He was born in 1755 and served under Capt. James Osborne, his brother. (Report from the Pension Bureau)

In 1816 Anthony M. Copeland and Wm. W. Craig of Maury Co., Tenn., sold land on Fountain Creek to John Osburn of Giles Co. The land contained 100 acres. Wm. Craig, Daniel Douglas, and William Gifford witnessed. Maury Co. Deeds, Book F # 1, page 343, entry 350.

29 April 1834: William Davidson executed a deed for 492 acres on the waters of Rock Creek to James Osburn. Maury Co. Deed Book R, page 310.

Maury Co., Tenn., Book O, page 319. Richard Bentley, dec'd (sic), 100 acres conveyed by Jno. Armstrong, registered 26 Oct. 1830. 24 Aug. 1830 sold his property on Fountain Creek, signed Jno. Armstrong. Witnessed by Andrew M. Kerr and A. A. Freeman. (This is how the deed was transcribed. R. W. B.)

Feb. 1835. Alexander Osburne to Nathan Glenn. Maury Co. Book S, page 159.

5 May 1834. James Osburne conveys land on west fork of Rock Creek to Absolom Alexander. Maury Co. Book R, page 323.

24 March 1836 (date of registration). Alexander Osburn conveys land on Globe Creek to James Davis. Maury County Book T, page 410.

Letter from Mrs. Lum Osborne, 11 Aug. 1929, Franklin, Tenn.: My grandfather was named Jno. Robert Osborne and married Mary Turner. They are both buried near Arrington. He was buried in 1875. His brothers were Noble, Lom, and Jack Osborne, and I suppose they are buried in the same place.
My father was Robert Ewing Osborne and was buried on the home place near here, but I don't know his inscription. My grandfather was a Revolutionary Soldier. My father had relatives in Maury and Marshall Counties and in Kentucky.

25 Sept. 1833: William Davidson of Mecklenburg Co., N. C., of the one part, and Alexander Osburne of Maury Co., Tenn., of the other part. For $381.00 Davidson conveys to Osburne land in Maury Co. on the headwaters of Globe Creek, being part of a 5000 acre tract granted to John Nelson by the State of North Carolina and by him conveyed to Thomas Davidson and by descent to said William Davidson. The land adjoins Elenzer Elliot's northwest corner. The land conveyed 170½ acres, and was recorded on 8 Nov. 1833. Maury Co. Book Q, page 469, entry no. 443.

29 Nov. 1832 (date of registration). Alexander and Robert Osburne deed 8 acres to Thomas Wilson. Maury County Book Q, page 98.

Sept. 1832. Alexander and Robert Osburne sold land on Globe Creek, Maury Co., to Thomas Wilson. Proved in court, Sept. 1832.

23 July 1833, recorded a power of attorney executed by Henry Gill to James Osburne. Maury County Book Q, page 411, entry no. 331.

Alexander Osburne deed. Maury County Book Q, page 469, entry no. 443.

22 June 1812. Know all that I, Adlici Osburn of Belmont County, North Carolina, have nominated and appointed and hereby do nominate and appoint Thomas McNeill of Maury County, Tenn., my true and lawful attorney in fact for me, in my name to make and execute a sufficient transfer and conveyance of the following land warrants:
No. 1969, 500 acres, on Buffalo River, to John Tate.
No. 1970, 500 acres, on Buffalo River, to   Jno. Campbell
No. 2003, 2500 acres, on Tennessee River, to Ezekiel and Samuel Polk.
No. 1971, 500 acres, on Cane Creek a fork of Buffalo River, to Samuel and Ezekiel Polk.
No. 1972.
Signed at Belmont, 23 Aug. 1812, in presence of Edwin J. Osburn and Franklin W. Osburn.
Maury Co., Tenn., Book B, Vol. 1, page 88, entry 97.

James Osburn and others were appointed commissioners to lay off and sell town lots in Lewisburg. Marshall Co., Tenn., 7 Nov. 1836.

Robert Osburn, born 4 March 1755, died 8 June 1834, buried in Ozburn Graveyard in 19th District of Williamson Co., Tenn. He was born in York Co., Penna., and moved from Mecklenburg Co.,

N. C., to Tennessee.
    He served from October to 25 December 1775, and then re-
enlisted in Jan. 1776 for three months. He enlisted in July
1776 for three months, and again in Sept. 1781 for three months.
    He was a private, and served under the Captains Jas. Hous-
ton, James Ausborne, Morrison, Lowney, and James Ausburn. He
served under Colonels Thomas Polk, Adam Alexander, and Erwin.
He served in North Carolina.
    He was engaged in skirmishes with Indians and Tories.
    At the time of his enlistment he lived in Mecklenburg Co.,
North Carolina.
    He applied for pension on 9 October 1832, while a resident
of Williamson Co., Tenn. His claim was allowed.
    He was born in 1755 in York Co., Penna., and died 8 July
(sic) 1834 in Williamson Co., Tenn. He married Jane (last name
not shown), on 16 Aug. 1785 in Mecklenburg Co., N. C.
    His name appears as Osburne, Ausburn, etc.
    (From pension application of Robert Osburne).

    Alexander Osburn married Eleanor Ewing. Their daughter
Sarah, born 1792, married Pleasant Jones. They are buried in
Bond County, Illinois.

Overton

    John Overton came from North Carolina to Davidson Co., Tenn.,
by 1805; was in Williamson Co., 1808, in Maury Co., in 1818, and
removed to Louisiana where he died about 1832. He had a daughter
who married Tristram Patton of Williamson Co.; another daughter
who married James Byers of Williamson County. He had a son,
Thomas Jefferson Overton, of Maury Co., born 1805. He only had
one child by his last wife, Susannah (maiden name unknown). His
descendants are known to be living in Maury Co., Tenn., and Texas,
and probably in Louisiana.

Pointer

    Burials in Pointer Graveyard near Spring Hill, Williamson
County, Tennessee:
    Henry Pointer, born 19 Dec. 1785 in Halifax Co., Va.,
        died 24 June 1864 age 79 years, 6 months, and 5 days.
    Wilmouth, wife of Henry Pointer, born 8 Feb. 1788, died
        1 Oct. 1855, aged 67 years, 7 months, and 22 days.

Porter

    Dr. Samuel Shaw Porter, born 3 Feb. 1793, died 25 Jan.
1873. He is buried at Williamsport, Tenn., (in) Maury Co.,
near Duck River and the Hickman Co. line. Catherine Todd, wife
of Dr. Samuel S. Porter, born 17 Sept. 1817, died 28 July 1895,
and is buried in the same place.

Potter

Tillman Potter was born in South Carolina, and married there; moved to White and Warren Counties, Tennessee. He settled at Seven Springs with the Cantrell Family. He married Elizabeth Cantrell before leaving South Carolina. Among their children was a son Watson Potter.

INDEX

The reader is advised that a name may appear more than once on a page. Where several different spellings of a name have been indicated by the author, the names have been indicated under each spelling, and variations in spelling have been cross-referenced.